CRIMINOLOGY

Connections among theory, research, and practice are the heart and soul of criminology. This book offers a comprehensive and balanced introduction to criminology, demonstrating the value of understanding the relationships between criminological theory, research, and practice in the study of crime and criminal behavior. Utilising a range of case studies and thought-provoking features, it encourages students to think critically and provides a foundation for understanding criminology as a systematic, theoretically grounded science. It includes:

- A comprehensive overview of crime in American society, including the nature and meaning of crime and American criminal law, as well as the scientific study of crime.
- A concise, straightforward, and practical approach to the study of the American criminal justice system and its various components, including individual chapters on police, courts, and corrections.
- An overview of criminological theory, including classical, biological, psychological, and sociological approaches.
- A survey of typologies of criminological behavior including interpersonal violent crimes, property crime, public order crime, organized and white collar crime, state crime, environmental harm, and cybercrime.
- Concluding thoughts exploring challenges facing criminal justice policy and the future of criminological theory.

This new edition has been thoroughly revised and updated and includes brand new chapters on corrections, courts, criminal law, law enforcement, and technology and cybercrime. It is packed with useful and instructive features such as themed case study boxes in every chapter, critical thinking questions, lists of further reading, and links to e-resources. A companion website includes PowerPoint slides for lecturers, links to useful resources, and lists of further reading.

Aida Y. Hass is an Associate Professor of Criminology and Criminal Justice at Missouri State University.

Chris Moloney is the Criminal Justice Study Abroad Program Director and an Instructor of Criminal Justice at the American Center for Study Abroad at Sichuan University in Chengdu, China.

William J. Chambliss (1933–2014) was Professor of Sociology at George Washington University.

"Hass, Moloney and Chambliss's *Criminology*, second edition, connects theory, research and real-world application in a way that no other book does. It is written in a style that is perfect for undergraduates in criminology or criminal justice courses, or for any practitioners in criminal justice generally. This is a book most students would be wise to keep on their shelves long after graduation."

Todd M. Krohn, Program/Intern Coordinator, Department of Sociology, The University of Georgia

"With so many criminology texts to choose from, this book provides a unique perspective that emphasizes criminal law, critical thinking, and the relevance of theory for criminal justice policy and practice. Its integration of concrete legal vignettes and real life case studies provide provocative examples that will help students better understand how crime is socially constructed, and to see how crime and policy impact society, as well as their own lives."

Karen G. Weiss, Associate Professor, Department of Anthropology and Sociology, West Virginia University

"Bringing together theories and typologies of offending with research and practical implications, *Criminology: Connecting Theory, Research and Practice* illuminates for our students the 'how' and 'why' of crime and justice. Hass, Moloney, and Chambliss use lively case studies to engage readers with real-world illustrations of the criminal justice system and explanations for criminal behavior. Their 'working in' feature allows students a rare glimpse into the daily activities of practitioners in the system and the 'crime in global perspective' feature provides an important international context. With attention to emerging forms of offending, such as terrorism and cybercrime, as well as contemporary issues facing practitioners of courts, policing, and corrections, this is one of the most comprehensive texts in the field."

Jamie J. Fader, Assistant Professor, Department of Criminal Justice, Temple University

"In this new edition of *Criminology: Connecting Theory, Research and Practice*, Hass, Moloney and Chambliss once again offer a phenomenal instructional resource helping students to truly grasp criminology. Connecting theory to the importance of research and its practical implications illuminates the excitement of the field, making theory relevant to future practitioners and scholars. This is a must-have text for criminology courses."

Jennifer C. Gibbs, Assistant Professor, School of Public Affairs, Penn State Harrisburg

CRIMINOLOGY

CONNECTING THEORY, RESEARCH AND PRACTICE

—SECOND EDITION—

AIDA Y. HASS, CHRIS MOLONEY
AND WILLIAM J. CHAMBLISS

Routledge
Taylor & Francis Group

LONDON AND NEW YORK

Second edition published 2017
by Routledge
2 Park Square, Milton Park, Abingdon, Oxon OX14 4RN

and by Routledge
711 Third Avenue, New York, NY 10017

Routledge is an imprint of the Taylor & Francis Group, an informa business

First edition published by McGraw-Hill 2012

British Library Cataloguing-in-Publication Data
A catalogue record for this book is available from the British Library

Library of Congress Cataloging in Publication Data
Names: Hass, Aida, author. | Moloney, Chris, author. | Chambliss,
William J., author. | Chambliss, William J. Criminology.
Title: Criminology : connecting theory, research and practice /
Aida Y. Hass, Chris Moloney and William J. Chambliss.
Description: Second Edition. | New York : Routledge, 2016. |
Revised edition of Criminology, 2012. |
Includes bibliographical references and index.
Identifiers: LCCN 2016020640| ISBN 9781138888685 (hardback) |
ISBN 9781138888692 (pbk.) | ISBN 9781315713267 (ebook)
Subjects: LCSH: Criminology.
Classification: LCC HV6025 .H337 2016 | DDC 364—dc23
LC record available at https://lccn.loc.gov/2016020640

ISBN: 978-1-138-88868-5 (hbk)
ISBN: 978-1-138-88869-2 (pbk)
ISBN: 978-1-315-71326-7 (ebk)

Typeset in Minion Pro and Trade Gothic
by Florence Production Ltd, Stoodleigh, Devon, UK
Printed by Bell & Bain Ltd, Glasgow

Visit the companion website: www.routledge.com/cw/Hass

MIX
Paper from
responsible sources
FSC® C007785

To my mom and dad: Your endless love and support taught me to make dreams come into reality through determination and hard work.
– Aida

To my grandparents: Ed, Ruth, Walt, and Lorraine. Your strength and love inspire me every day.
– Chris

In loving memory of our dear friend and mentor, William J. Chambliss

Brief contents

Detailed contents

Images

Figures

Maps

Tables

Boxes

About the authors

Aida Hass is an Associate Professor of Criminology and Criminal Justice at Missouri State University. She has over 20 years of experience teaching courses at the graduate and undergraduate level, as well as prior experience working for the federal government in research and evaluation. She continues to pursue her research interests in crime causation, victimology studies, and re-entry programming.

Chris Moloney is the Criminal Justice Study Abroad Program Director and an Instructor of Criminal Justice at the American Center for Study Abroad at Sichuan University in Chengdu, China. He previously worked as an Instructor of Criminology, Sociology, and Criminal Justice at Colorado State University, where he remains affiliated with the Center for the Study of Crime and Justice.

Preface

MAKING CONNECTIONS

Connections among theory, research, and practice are the heart and soul of criminology. This book offers a comprehensive and balanced introduction to criminology and demonstrates the value of understanding the relationship among criminological theory, research, and practice in the study of crime and criminal behavior. Encompassing a range of case studies and features designed to encourage critical thinking, it emphasizes the key role of criminological theory and research in the development of criminal justice policies and practices.

PART I: CRIME, CRIMINAL LAW, AND CRIMINOLOGY

Part I provides a comprehensive overview of crime in American society, with specific attention given to the varieties of crime and the victims of crime, the principles of criminal law, the sources of data on crime, and the tools for evaluating the scientific utility of criminological theories and research. This builds a foundation for students to understand criminology as a systematic, theoretically grounded science, whose goal it is to define crime, understand criminal behavior, and offer scientific solutions to lawmakers and politicians to form the basis of policies to alleviate the problem of crime in society. Students are introduced to the nature and meaning of crime and American criminal law, as well as the scientific study of crime.

PART II: THE CRIMINAL JUSTICE SYSTEM IN ACTION

Part II provides a concise, straightforward, and practical approach to the study of the American criminal justice system and its various components. We distinguish between criminology and criminal justice as distinct areas of study united by a common interest in better understanding crime. Individual chapters are dedicated to a critical examination of the primary components of the criminal justice system: police, courts, and corrections. Within the chapter on corrections, we also devote special attention to the topic of juvenile justice and juvenile corrections.

PART III: AN OVERVIEW OF CRIMINOLOGICAL THEORY

Part III provides an overview of criminological theory. It begins by briefly examining the roots of criminological theory in Classical and Neoclassical paradigms and then turns to a focus on contemporary theories. We move from biological and psychological theories of crime causation to sociological theories. Sociological theories are further divided into social structural, normative, and social conflict theories. We then examine the underlying policy implications of the theoretical perspective in light of specific case studies.

PART IV: TYPOLOGIES OF CRIMINAL BEHAVIOR

Part IV gives students the opportunity to better understand the various categories of criminal behavior, by focusing specific chapters to criminal typologies. We introduce discussions on a variety of violent crimes that go beyond the typically studied forms of interpersonal violence, to include terrorism, organized crime, military rape, and police brutality. We further carry this discussion into the individual chapters on property, public order crimes, and white collar crimes, as well as exploring cyber- and green crimes in their own chapter.

PART V: A LOOK AHEAD

Finally, Part V provides the student with a glimpse into the future of crime, criminological theory, and research. It proposes a practical synthesis of the various definitional elements of crime, the theoretical integration of crime causation, and a pragmatic discussion of effective crime control strategies. We highlight the trans-national aspects of many crimes today, especially crimes like terrorism, organized, state, green, and cybercrimes.

How to use this book

We packed this book with useful and instructive features that will facilitate classroom learning and encourage critical thinking and further discussion. These features include:

CONSIDER THIS

This feature attracts student interest with a surprising, ambiguous, or inequitable real-world situation and asks the student *"What do you think?"*

CRIME IN GLOBAL PERSPECTIVE

This feature highlights the importance of exploring criminology from the perspective of diverse cultures, criminal justice systems, and crime problems in different parts of the world.

CONNECTING THEORY TO PRACTICE

This feature allows students to understand and appreciate how certain theories drive crime control strategies in the real world of criminal justice policy.

CONNECTING RESEARCH TO PRACTICE

This feature brings to life the aspects of criminal justice research that have a direct impact on implementing and evaluating crime control strategies.

WORKING IN . . .

This feature provides a realistic and vivid portrayal of the field of criminal justice practitioners.

IN THIS CHAPTER . . . QUESTIONS

This feature gives students a glimpse of what is to be covered in each chapter.

KEY TERMS

This feature highlights important concepts, ideas, and terminology that are essential components of each chapter.

LISTS OF FURTHER READING

This feature lists various materials to reinforce, expand upon, and explore in greater detail certain topics covered in the chapter.

CRITICAL THINKING QUESTIONS

This feature is designed to enhance student learning by allowing instructors to assign interactive activities and discussion points that engage students in further inquiry and illustration of the reading material.

E-RESOURCES

This feature provides students with further material via links to various resources that supplement reading material in the chapters as well as give additional foundation to policies, programs, and practices that are discussed.

CHAPTER SUMMARIES

This feature provides a brief overview of the main themes and ideas contained in each chapter.

Crime, criminal law, and criminology

PART I

CHAPTER OUTLINE

Crime, deviance, and criminology: a brief overview

In this chapter we will explore the following questions

- How do we define crime?
- What is deviance?
- When is crime deviant, and deviant behavior criminal?
- What is criminology?
- Does the popular image of crime measure up to reality?
- How does criminology guide our study of crime?
- How does criminology influence social policy?
- How do criminology and criminal justice relate to one another?

KEY TERMS

legalist perspective

political perspective

sociological perspective

psychological perspective

deviance

social norms

folkways

mores

taboos

laws

crime

criminology

criminologist

criminal justice

law enforcement agencies

courts

correctional system

criminal law

theory

consensus model

conflict model

In 2015, America was shocked to witness the man who once stood second in line to the presidency appear in federal court on charges of improperly withdrawing large amounts of cash from his bank account, violating federal laws, and lying to federal agents about the reason for the withdrawals. What's even more dismaying are emerging reports that the former U.S. Speaker of the House, Dennis Hastert, had allegedly withdrawn the amounts, totaling over $3 million, in order to compensate and keep quiet a man who, as a high school student, was sexually abused by Hastert.[1] The allegations of sexual misconduct and abuse have expanded to include several other victims as well.

The plethora of stories and events we hear about through various media sources, whether newspaper, radio, internet or television, are many and diverse. Whether in Los Angeles or Little Rock, Harlem or Beverly Hills, they draw our attention and pique our interest. They are stories of thrill-seeking youth and defiant adults entangled in drugs, sex scandals, acts of violence, abuse of power, and corruption motivated by personal gain or as an expression of discontent. While the stories are different, they all have one thing in common: the behaviors they describe are generally condemned by society and prohibited by the law.

The study of crime has two main dimensions: a behavioral dimension that seeks to describe and explain the origins and causes of criminality, and a definitional dimension that explains why certain behaviors come to be defined

Image 1.1 *In 2015, Dennis Hastert was indicted on charges relating to nearly $3 million of bank withdrawals from four different bank accounts. The transactions were never disclosed, a violation of federal law. Hastert was accused of using those funds for payment as "hush money" to an individual who threatened to report past sexual misconduct by the politician. When a public official like Hastert violates the public's trust by committing criminal acts, we want to know why.*

Charles Rex Arbogast/AP/Press Association Images

as crime. When we hear about a crime story or criminal event, we want immediate answers that tell us why: why a mother kills her three children, why a priest molests a child, why a sports hero commits rape, and why a respected public servant engages in fraud. However, in order to study and account for the diversity in crime causation, we must first come to an understanding of why certain behaviors are legally prohibited.

The reaction to the activities of former House Speaker Dennis Hastert is a testimony to society's disapproval of his conduct, which constituted a violation of the trust given to a public servant. While acts such as child abuse and political corruption are met with immediate social disapproval, there are far more behaviors that we cannot so easily or arbitrarily define as crime. In a study of the organization and growth of police bureaucracies in U.S. cities, researcher Eric Monkkonen notes that "real crime leaves an injured or dead victim, an outraged community, or inflicts some kind of human suffering."

Moreover, we can categorize social behavior as either conforming to the established order or contributing to social disorder. Crime control is often a means of maintaining social order. Meanwhile, the need to balance the rights of individuals against the overall protection of society is critical to the way we define certain behaviors as crime and others as non-crimes.[2]

Individual rights are at the heart of the constitutional protections and civil liberties guaranteed to each and every U.S. citizen. We look upon the government

Where Do You Draw the Line?

Individual Rights	versus	Public Order
←		→
Gay Marriages	**Sexuality**	*Anti Abortion: Right to Life*
Legalizing Marijuana	**Drugs**	*Treatment and Addiction*
Opening a Strip Club	**Pornography**	*Exploiting Women*
Political Dissent	**National Security**	*Ethnic Profiling*
DNA Evidence	**Capital Punishment**	*Incapacitating Dangerous Criminals*
Freedom of Expression	**Hate Speech**	*Bias Inspired Violence*
The Right to Die	**Euthanasia**	*Lawful Killing*

Figure 1.1
Individual rights or public order . . . You decide

as a sovereign protector of those rights and guarantees. The fact is, however, that we also look to the law and government to protect us from individual behaviors that threaten our sense of security. We desire order, safety, conformity, and enforcement of society's interests. We feel we have a right to be protected from acts that may threaten the integrity of our society, and we may even, in the face of threat, be willing to give up some of our personal rights in the interest of public safety or order.[3] As a society, we do not always agree on where to draw the line between individuality and conformity. We can clearly see such disagreement in the various debates on issues such as abortion, gun control, and freedom of speech (see Figure 1.1). The question this chapter will seek to answer is: where and how do we draw the line of definition in deeming the acts of individuals as criminal?

Scholars, writers, politicians, the media, and the general public have long been fascinated with crime and punishment. This chapter introduces criminology as a systematic science, grounded in theory, whose goal is defining crime, understanding criminal behavior, and offering scientific solutions to help policymakers alleviate the problem of crime in our society. Are there elements common to all crimes? Are all crimes wrong? Are all crimes immoral? Can a mere thought or plan be a crime? Where do we draw the line in defining and limiting peoples' behavior? We turn now to the science of criminology to answer these questions.

HOW DO WE DEFINE CRIME?

The subject of crime has become an integral part of U.S. popular culture. Think of prime-time television shows such as *The Detective, Orange is the New Black, Law & Order, Criminal Minds, The District, The Shield, The Wire,* and various spin-offs that reflect the public's fascination with criminal motive, criminal intent, the apprehension of suspects, detective work, and forensics. Media coverage continues to draw our attention to the criminal acts of celebrities, athletes, and other well-known individuals. Unofficial experts try to explain through the eyes of popular culture why pop star Chris Brown was arrested

Image 1.2 *Crime stories often receive an inordinate amount of coverage in the media when they involve the rich and famous, as in the 2001 murder of Bonny Lee Bakley, wife of actor Robert Blake, shot to death while sitting in their car in an alley behind a restaurant in affluent Los Angeles. Blake was charged with one count of murder and two counts of solicitation for murder. The excessive media coverage of such trials often misleads us into thinking that these are the most common types of crimes being committed.*
Mona Shafer Edwards/AP/Press Association Images

for physically abusing intimate partner Rihanna, Lindsay Lohan's probation was revoked due to a failed drug test, Winona Ryder was convicted of shoplifting, and Mike Tyson served time for rape. Gossip, headlines, and media commentary become the shaky foundations upon which the meaning of crime and understanding of criminal behavior are built.

Considering the real complexity of criminal behavior, it makes sense for us to study it with a more scholarly approach. To arrive at a comprehensive understanding, we turn to four perspectives—legalist, political, psychological, and sociological—that each offers a distinct approach to the meaning of crime (see Table 1.1). We will first examine the nature and meaning of crime from the legalist point of view.

Table 1.1 What is crime? Four perspectives

The legalist perspective	Crime is behavior that violates criminal codes and statutes
The political perspective	Crime is socially constructed behavior
The psychological perspective	Crime is maladaptive behavior
The sociological perspective	Crime is behavior that threatens the social order

Image 1.3
Whose definition of right and wrong is imposed in the controversial issue of war and the fight for freedom in other lands?

John Giles/PA Archive/
Press Association
Images

The definition of crime from a "legalist perspective"

Within the legalist perspective, criminologists view crime as conduct that violates criminal laws of local, state, or federal government. For example, federal law makes it a crime to lie under oath in a court of law; this offense is called perjury. The legalist perspective assumes that without a legal definition, there would be no criminal act, no matter how deviant or offensive to society a behavior may be.[4]

The legalist definition is good as far as it goes, but it makes some unsupported assumptions. First, it assumes everyone agrees with the laws that forbid certain behaviors, such as jaywalking or euthanasia. That, in turn, implies that everyone shares the same definition of moral right and wrong. We can clearly see the error in this assumption by merely considering all the various issues we disagree about in our society, such as gun control, the death penalty, abortion rights, and the legalization of certain drugs such as marijuana.

Moreover, the legalist definition assumes that the power to define certain behaviors as violations of the law is fair and legitimate. This implies that everyone's views of right and wrong are equally reflected in the law, without the interest of any particular group outweighing another. This is also an incorrect assumption, as those with the power to define are capable of imposing criminal definitions that reflect their own interest. Clearly, we need a definition of crime that doesn't make this assumption. Let us examine what the political perspective has to offer.

The definition of crime from a "political perspective"

The political perspective assumes individuals with political power use their position to define illegal behavior and establish laws governing crime. Their goal is to protect their own interests and gain control over those with less power, who may represent direct or indirect threats to their interests.[5] Laws thus reflect not what society agrees is right and wrong, but rather who has the power to define certain behaviors.

Critics of the political perspective say many laws do protect the relatively powerless against such crimes as murder, rape, and assault. However, the point of the political perspective is not that there are no such laws, but rather that the primary motive behind creating laws is to serve the interests of those in power.[6] While it gives us a better understanding of the creation of legal definitions, the political perspective does not assess the role of individual behavior in determining whether certain acts are criminal. We turn to a discussion of the psychological perspective to shed some light.

The definition of crime from a "psychological perspective"

Criminologists relying on the psychological perspective view crime as maladaptive behavior, or an individual's inability to be in harmony with his or her environment.[7] The environment poses stressful stimuli every day— someone cuts us off while we're driving, we get laid off from our jobs, we find our spouse in bed with our best friend—and the way we react and adapt to these pressures determines whether a crime will be committed. For example, if someone cuts you off on the road, you can either drive on (no crime) or chase and ram the other car (crime).

The psychological perspective, while insightful, provides us with a very broad definition of crime that includes overeating, alcohol abuse, and compulsive gambling. If we adhered to this definition alone, criminologists would need to understand, combat, and control a wider variety of human behavior than we normally consider criminal.

The definition of crime from a "sociological perspective"

A final viewpoint on crime is the sociological perspective. This defines crime as any anti-social act that threatens the existing social structure or the fundamental well-being of humans.[8] Laws serve to protect human relationships, preserve individuals' well-being, and provide for their security and safety. The focus of criminological inquiry in this view is to examine *all* actions that cause harm, misfortune, and distress to others. The sociological perspective forces us to examine crime as behavior anyone can commit—first-degree murder, rape, robbery, and arson are crimes, but so are job discrimination, unsafe dumping of manufacturing waste, creating hazardous working conditions, misleading consumers, and insider trading. This broader understanding allows us to define as criminal those actions by individuals in power that may slip through the cracks of a narrower perspective on crime[9] (see Box 1.1).

Our discussion of perspectives on crime may leave you thinking a definition of crime must be somewhat elusive. For example, why and how do we come

BOX 1.1: CRIME IN GLOBAL PERSPECTIVE

Protecting a country from its protectors

Public turmoil and dissent against the Egyptian government spawned a plethora of demonstrations, civil disobedience, and peaceful protests in communities throughout the country. Protests began in January of 2011, with activists leading an uprising to protest against rampant government corruption and police brutality that lead to unprecedented poverty and unemployment throughout Egypt. For nearly three weeks, men and women of all ages, backgrounds, and interests united together and called for freedom, democracy, and social justice, demanding the removal of President Mubarak and an end to his thirty year "reign" of exploitation and abuse.

The revolution in Egypt continued for almost three years, and consisted of citizens from a wide range of socioeconomic and religious backgrounds demonstrating, striking, marching, occupying public plazas, and engaging in non-violent civil acts of resistance and disobedience. Their actions were loud and clear, and their voices were united on various legal and political issues, calling for freedom of speech, democracy, and justice, and an end to government corruption, police brutality, low wages, inflation, high unemployment, and repression. Their voices were heard throughout the world, but silenced by officials in power. During this time period, and in the years to follow, peaceful demonstrations throughout the streets of Cairo, Alexandria, Suez, and other cities, turned into the bloody mass killings of unarmed protestors by government forces that took the lives of well over 2,000 people.

In the aftermath of protests, political unrest, and civil turmoil, a *Human Rights Watch* (HRW) taskforce investigating the killings of at least 1,000 protestors at a Rabaa al-Adawiya Square sit-in in Cairo in 2013, where Egyptian security forces gunned down unarmed protestors, concluded that this can be considered a "crime against humanity." Their report (2014) calls the massacre one of the world's largest killings of demonstrators in recent history. According to HRW Executive Director Kenneth Roth, this was part of a government policy to use lethal force against largely unarmed protesters on political grounds, and not "merely a case of excessive force or poor training; it was a violent crackdown planned at the highest levels of the Egyptian government … Many of the same officials are still in power in Egypt, and have a lot to answer for." Egyptian laws, statutes, and ordinances provide guidelines for which acts of crime, abuse, and violence are defined and prosecuted accordingly, in order to protect human rights and preserve the social order. It seems that in the case of the revolution in Egypt, it was this law and its creators, upholders, and enforcers, that fell short of a true assessment of defining criminal behavior.

Sources

Kingsley, Patrick. 2014. How Did 37 Prisoners Come to Die at Cairo Prison Abu Zaabal? *The Guardian.* Retrieved from www.theguardian.com/world/2014/feb/22/cairo-prison-abu-zabaal-deaths-37-prisoners.

All According to Plan: The Rab'a Massacre and Mass Killings of Protesters in Egypt. 2014. *Human Rights Watch.*

Egypt's Rabaa Deaths "Crime Against Humanity": Human Rights Watch Says Killings Were Planned at Highest Levels of Government and Calls for Senior Leaders to be Probed. 2014. *Al Jazeera.* Retrieved from www. aljazeera.com/news/middleeast/2014/08/rabaa-deaths-crime-against-humanity-hrw-20148884531513947.html.

to impose meanings and labels upon certain acts and not others? Do these meanings and labels change over time? Why do some acts elicit a stronger negative reaction, draw more attention, and require a stronger social response than others? Why does that social response vary across time, place, and individuals instead of being limited to the act itself? We can, in fact, answer these questions by looking at the relationship between crime, deviance, and social norms.

WHAT DOES DEVIANCE MEAN?

Image 1.4 *What influences our impression of the way people look? Under what circumstances would tattoos and body piercings be considered a form of deviance?*

iStock/Slavaleks

When we think of criminal acts such as serial murder, rape, and child molestation, the word "deviant" seems an appropriate label. We cannot agree so easily on other acts. Drinking under age, driving above the speed limit, and betting on a football game are all illegal, yet few people would consider them deviant. By the same token, many acts that some consider deviant are not violations of criminal law; body piercing, excessive tattooing, and poor hygiene are a few examples. So, if all crime is not deviant and all deviant acts are not criminal, what then is deviant behavior, and where do the two concepts intersect? (See Table 1.2.)

Deviance is behavior that elicits a social reaction by violating the standards of conduct defined by society.[10] Social reactions to deviance range along a continuum from mild disapproval to arrest, based on a hierarchy of **social norms** or rules of behavior that guide our everyday interactions with one another.[11]

Social norms fall into four categories (see Table 1.3): folkways, mores, taboos, and laws. **Folkways** are non-binding social conventions and include guidelines on appropriate dress, manners, and hygiene. Western folkways suggest we shake hands with someone when first introduced. **Mores** are strong convictions about certain behaviors— rules of etiquette, matters of respect, or shared understandings of "the way things are done" in our society. We know we should stand in line at the grocery store, wait our turn to be served at a restaurant, eat with a fork at dinner, and be respectful during religious services. **Taboos** informally forbid socially offensive acts. They regulate sexual conduct, race relations, and other ethical matters. For example, in U.S. society, it is taboo for blood relatives to get married, a

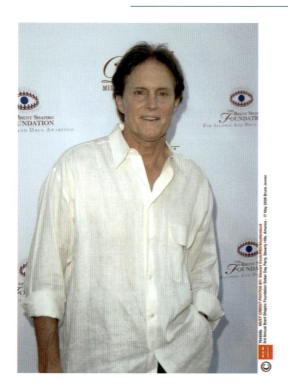

Images 1.5a and 1.5b *The public transformation of Bruce Jenner into Caitlyn created much debate and discussion, with some calling it an act of courage and others questioning motives surrounding publicity. Is this considered a form of deviant behavior? How does society react to what has become known as gender dysphoria? What changes in society have influenced the public's support or lack of support of this type of behavior?*

Stewart Cook/REX/Shutterstock; David Buchan/Variety/REX/Shutterstock

Table 1.2 Criminal, deviant, neither, or both?

When do the following acts become deviant? When are they criminal? When are they both? What about neither?	
Taking a human life	In the service of vigilante justice, in self-defense, as euthanasia, during wartime, in the heat of passion
Getting married	To someone of the same sex, to someone 20 years older, to a blood relative
Drinking alcohol	At 6 a.m., while driving, in church, at a party
Disciplining a child	At home, in public, by a school teacher, causing bruises
Watching an X-rated movie	While children are present, alone at home, in the theater
Engaging in sexual intercourse	In private, in public, with a same-sex partner, with an under-age partner, without consent, with another person's spouse
Practicing a religion	By wearing certain clothes, by eating and avoiding certain foods, by engaging in certain ceremonies, by teaching followers to hate
Driving a car	Without a valid license, above the speed limit, into a tree
Being naked	At home, at home with guests present, at the beach, in class
Not paying taxes	By taking allowed deductions, by hiring a good accountant, by making charitable donations, by manipulating numbers

Table 1.3 Are all rules created equally?

Social norm	Definition	Example of violation	Social reaction	Continuum of deviance
Folkway	Non-binding social convention	Wearing cut-off shorts to a formal wedding ceremony	Stares of disapproval or a verbal reprimand	Less deviant
More	Strong conviction about right/wrong	Talking on your cell phone during a movie at the movie theater	Verbal altercation and demand to stop or be removed from the premise	
Taboo	Prohibition on socially offensive acts	Engaging in sexually explicit conduct at a public park	Verbal and/or physical confrontation; may resort to formal authority such as calling the police	
Law	Written formal decree	Walking away from a restaurant without paying	Being arrested and charged with theft	More deviant (criminal)

common practice in various other cultures such as in the Middle East. **Laws** are formal written sanctions designed to regulate behaviors society considers to require the greatest level of response and control. It is in this last category of social norms—laws—that we find the overlap between crime and deviance.

The legal status of certain behaviors—and the negative societal reaction they elicit—renders them both criminal and deviant.[12] What complicates matters is that we don't all always agree on the social and legal status of some behaviors. Even when we do, consensus can change from time to time and place to place. When and how does behavior become a crime?

Let's get straight to the point. The definitions of both deviance and crime are subject to culturally influenced interpretation by a specific individual or group in a specific time and place. For example, commercial gambling is socially acceptable and legal in Las Vegas, Atlantic City, and on some Native American reservations but outlawed in most other parts of the United States. Likewise, prostitution is morally unacceptable and illegal in nearly all states but a legally regulated and acceptable behavior in parts of Nevada.

To understand the role of subjective interpretation in the way we assign definitions to behavior, consider how school officials, police, and the community responded to the actions of two different groups of delinquent boys. Although the "Saints" were more delinquent by sheer number of illegal acts than the "Roughnecks," these upper-middle class boys were perceived as good, upstanding, non-delinquent youths with bright futures. A Saint who got drunk in a nightclub or tavern, even if he drove around afterwards in a car, was perceived as someone who had simply made a mistake. Because a lower-class boy who drinks in an alley and stands intoxicated on the street corner, steals a wallet from a store, or associates with someone who has committed a burglary is considered a delinquent, the Roughnecks were seen as tough young criminals headed for trouble.[13]

Essentially, then, crime and deviance are socially constructed—they are what society says they are. With this understanding, we can finally develop a comprehensive understanding of crime by integrating components from the various perspectives on crime that we have discussed. **Crime** is human behavior that we interpret as violating society's norms for a specific time and place and that must be controlled and prevented by legal decree. Now let's turn to a discussion of criminology and its role in understanding crime as human behavior.

WHAT IS CRIMINOLOGY?

For thousands of years humans have attempted to understand, define, prevent, and punish crime and deviance. In Europe, early beliefs about criminals and social deviants were influenced by religion and explained them as possession by spirits, to be extracted through surgical means or physical torture.

In 1885, Italian law professor Raffaele Garofalo coined the term "criminology" to describe the study of crime as an individual act in a social context. Around the same time, French anthropologist Paul Topinard defined the field as the study of criminal body types, separate from the field of anthropology.[14] In the 1920s sociologist Edwin Sutherland described criminology as "the body of knowledge regarding delinquency and crime as social phenomena. It includes within its scope the process of making laws, of breaking laws, and of reacting towards the breaking of laws."[15]

Today we define **criminology** as the scientific study of the incidence and forms of crime and criminal behavior, their causes and consequences, and social reaction to, control of, and prevention of crime. Criminology emphasizes research, theory testing and theory building. It has become an interdisciplinary study that seeks to explain why some people engage in crime and others do not, and why some criminals are arrested and sentenced to prison while others are not.

Criminologists are academics, researchers, and policy analysts who focus on understanding the nature and meaning of crime, patterns of criminal behavior, various causes of criminality, and society's reaction to crime. They examine and evaluate the origins, nature, and interpretation of criminal laws, and try to find ways to alleviate crime as a social problem. Criminologists also rely on scientifically grounded theories and explanations of criminal behavior—and society's responses to it—to help us understand the experiences of victims throughout the criminal justice process. Table 1.4 summarizes the various tasks criminologists undertake. Regardless of which task they engage in, criminologists are dedicated to the study of crime and criminal behavior.

Table 1.4 How do we do criminology?

Field in criminology	Specific tasks
Statistics and research	We focus on analyzing crime data, developing methods for gathering crime information, measuring crime trends, and developing and evaluating crime prevention programs and strategies
Criminal profiling	We study specific categories of offenses to determine the anatomy of criminals; understand the specific nature, cause, and motive of certain types of criminal behavior.
Theory development	We conduct scientific research about the causes of criminality, its beginnings, and its continuation.
Law, policy, and social control	We examine the evolution of law within the context of social reaction and change, and its impact on criminal sanctions and crime control policies.
Victimology	We highlight victims issues, advance theories of victimization, and promote programs to support crime victims.

What is criminal justice?

Criminal justice is a newer field of academic study than criminology, arising in the early part of the 20th century with the creation of the first criminal justice program at the University of California Berkeley in 1916.[16,17] Like criminology, the study of criminal justice emphasizes the use of research and theory, but it differs in that its focus is not on describing different types of crime or understanding the causes of criminal behavior. Instead, it is concerned with advancing our understanding of the how the American criminal justice system functions and can be improved.

The American criminal justice system has three primary components: (1) the police (law enforcement agencies), who enforce criminal laws, investigate crimes, and arrest criminal offenders, (2) the courts that ensure law breakers are held responsible for their conduct, and (3) the correctional system, where convicted criminal offenders are punished for their unlawful behavior. The American criminal law is another area that has a significant impact on the American criminal justice system, so it too receives significant attention from criminal justice scholars as well. Thus, the study of criminal justice is, ultimately, the study of police, courts, corrections, and the criminal law. The study of criminal justice, unsurprisingly, is often attributed a more practical or applied focus than criminology, given the impact that criminal justice system research can, and does, have on public policy.

To illustrate how the criminal justice system's three main components—law enforcement, courts, and corrections—work with each other (Figure 1.2), let's imagine a young man named Jack has just committed an armed robbery at a local pharmacy. Clearly, Jack has violated at least one criminal law—that which prohibits people from committing robbery. Jack's violation of the criminal law activates the first phase of the criminal justice system: law enforcement.

Law enforcement, discussed in detail in chapter 5, is primarily carried out by local and state police agencies, though there are many federal law enforcement

What is the sequence of events in the criminal justice system?

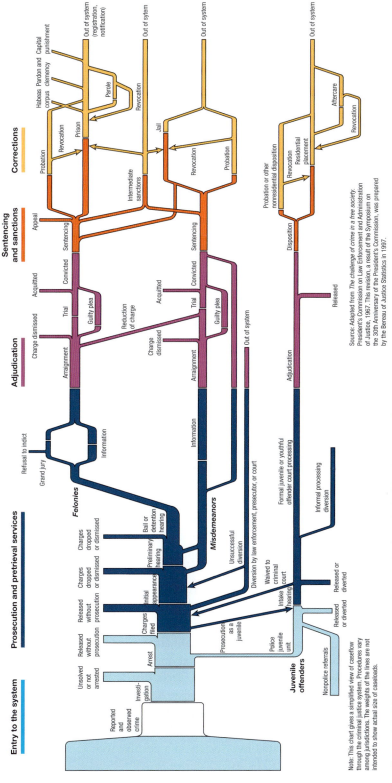

Figure 1.2 What is the sequence of events in the criminal justice system?

Source: Adapted from Bureau of Justice Statistics, 1997.

agencies as well. Law enforcement is the first phase of the criminal justice system because law enforcement agencies are tasked with, among many things, investigating crimes and arresting people who violate criminal laws (i.e., criminals). Think of law enforcement agencies and officers as translators of the criminal law in the real world. They are at the front lines of the criminal justice system. In order to end up in a criminal court and, possibly, incarcerated, one must first come into contact with law enforcement.

Now, let's assume Jack got arrested two days after the armed robbery and that the local district attorney decides to charge him with that crime. Jack's arrest and subsequent charging by the D.A. activates the second phase of the criminal justice system: the courts.

The court phase is a dynamic, complicated one. While we discuss courts in more detail in chapter 6, for now it is worth pointing out that just ending up in a criminal court does not mean you will end up serving a sentence in a jail or a prison. Indeed, the vast majority of criminal cases do not lead to sentences of incarceration, but instead receive other dispositions. All kinds of social, economic, and political factors influence how criminal court proceedings play out, from the wealth of the defendant (i.e., the person charged), to their race/ethnicity, to the number of cases on the court docket. However, let's assume that Jack's case proceeds in a very straightforward manner. He is charged with armed robbery and put on trial for the crime. His trial ends swiftly and a jury of his peers finds him guilty. The judge in Jack's case then determines a sentence. Jack is sentenced to 6 years in prison for armed robbery.

In banging her gavel after reading Jack's sentence, the judge activates the third and final phase of the criminal justice system: corrections. Once a person is found guilty of committing a crime and is given a sentence of incarceration, they are immediately remanded into the custody of the state and are transported to whatever jail or prison they will serve their sentence in corrections is the topic of chapter 7, but for now we wish to point out that sentences of incarceration for more than 1 year are almost always served in a state or federal prison facility, while sentences of less than 1 year are served in a local or county jail. Ostensibly, the crimes that get people a prison sentence are more serious than the crimes that get people a jail sentence.

What happens to Jack after arriving at prison? Many things are possible. Depending on various factors, Jack may become eligible for parole (early release) before his complete prison sentence is served. However, if Jack commits another crime in prison, like assault, he might serve a longer sentence. As we discuss in the corrections chapter of this text, for many people, getting arrested, convicted, and incarcerated initiates a cycle that is tough to break. A criminal record and time behind bars block many opportunities to becoming a successful member of society. Jack, like many real-life people who have moved through the criminal justice system, undoubtedly will face an uphill battle in his efforts to become reintegrated into society in a positive way.

THE "POPULAR IMAGE" OF CRIME V. THE REALITY OF CRIMINAL BEHAVIOR

In the mid-1980s, high-level government officials and military personnel within the Reagan-Bush Administration, during the course of their jobs, hid behind political rhetoric to sell arms to terrorist groups in Iran, divert profits from the sales to themselves, and cover up their acts. The result was one of the nation's most embarrassing political scandals, the Iran-Contra Affair.

On January 6, 1994, at a practice session during the 1994 U.S. Figure Skating Championships, competitor Nancy Kerrigan was attacked and injured in a conspiracy allegedly instigated by co-competitor Tonya Harding, whose ex-husband Jeff Gillooly hired Shane Stant to strike Kerrigan on the knee. On February 1, Gillooly accepted a plea bargain in exchange for his testimony against Harding. Harding avoided further prosecution and a possible jail sentence by pleading guilty to hindering the investigation. After conducting its own investigation, the United States Figure Skating Association concluded Harding knew of the attack before it happened, stripped her of her 1994 title, and banned her for life from participating in sanctioned events and from becoming a coach.[18]

There was nothing extraordinary about Mary Kay Letourneau. She was a bright, energetic, well-dressed teacher who always showed interest in and enthusiasm for her students. She also went to prison for over seven years for the rape of 13-year-old Vili Fualaau, a former student who was 21 years her junior. After serving her time in prison, Letourneau married Fualaau, and they had two children together.[19]

Crime is committed by ordinary people—politicians, doctors, lawyers, opera singers, school teachers, nurses, business men and women, car mechanics, movie stars, media figures, students, and athletes. Regardless of the crime, however, we want to know *why*. Why do politicians abuse their power, doctors and nurses kill, teachers engage in sex with children, business men and women cheat, and professional athletes commit rape? As a society we want immediate answers that help us understand the extraordinary behavior of apparently ordinary individuals. We want solutions to crime that satisfy our demand for justice, but that also address the apparently inexplicable acts of individuals, acts with consequences that often hit close to home.

Crime continually challenges law enforcement officials, criminal justice agents, and politicians to whom we look for protection. Close your eyes for a moment and picture the word "crime." What do you see happening? Who are the actors? Is someone being shot or stabbed? Do you hear screams or imagine a struggle? Is it late at night? Where is the crime taking place? Are you angry or afraid? Does your response have anything to do with the image of crime we have as a society, and if so, where does that image come from?

We derive our popular image of crime from media portrayals that convince us to be afraid and to barricade ourselves behind locked doors, barred windows, and security systems. Is this fear justified? Should we be concerned about an

Images 1.6a and 1.6b *Who fits our perception of a criminal? When you think of crime, do you see an image of this gang banger, or do you see Leona Helmsley, the successful businesswoman and owner of a real estate empire who was convicted on several counts of tax evasion and sentenced to 16 years in federal prison? From where do we get these images about crime and criminals?*

iStock/Yuri; RICHARD DREW/AP/Press Association Images

alleged soaring rise in violence that leaves us afraid to be free in our own homes, streets, and society? We'll address these questions in more detail in chapter 3 when we discuss patterns and trends in criminal behavior. For now, we recognize the faces of crime and crime victims are many. Yet, we tend to hear far more about peculiar or especially offensive acts of violence because they are so sensationalized by the media and public portrayal (see Box 1.2).

We must go beyond this perception to a more comprehensive understanding of the many different types of crimes. Our interpretation of and reaction to crime is built upon a false representation of crime-related facts and incidents, a problem largely perpetrated by the media, as we stated above. The truth is that crimes reported by the media, such as murder and rape, are often crimes that take place the least.[20] Studies show that violent crimes represent 60 to 90 percent of crime news stories while making up only 12 percent of all crimes. Newsworthy stories emphasize the dramatic, the unusual, and the shocking, while placing less emphasis on the everyday criminal behavior of regular people who assault family members, cheat on their taxes, steal from retail stores, and abuse drugs.[21]

Trying to capture the varieties of crime is like trying to draw a map of the world. If the map has all the details in it, it is as large as the world and worthless as a map. If it leaves out all the rivers and mountains, roads and alleys, it is

BOX 1.2: CONSIDER THIS . . .

Surviving a house of terror

Box 1.2 Image 1 *For more than a decade, Ariel Castro imprisoned Michelle Knight, Gina De Jesus, and Amanda Berry just minutes away from their homes. Castro tormented and tortured the women for years, shackling them in chains for 24 hours a day and abusing them both mentally and physically. Their stories unfolded through various media outlets, including the Dr. Phil show, ABC News, The Washington Post, and various other sources.*

Tony Dejak/AP/Press Association Images

There was nothing remarkable about the dilapidated home in the Tremont neighborhood of Cleveland, Ohio. Inside however, was a completely different story. Inside, for over a decade, Ariel Castro imprisoned three women, subjecting them to horrible acts of violence, rape, physical and psychological abuse, and torture. Between 2002 and 2004, three young women, Michelle Knight, Amanda Berry, and Gina DeJesus, were kidnapped by Ariel Castro and kept locked in his "house of horrors" for ten years. On May 6, 2013, Amanda Berry escaped with her 6-year-old daughter, fathered by Castro during her imprisonment, and called 911. That day, the other two women held in captivity were rescued by officers responding to the call; Castro was arrested within hours of the rescue. He was charged with multiple counts of kidnapping and rape, pleading guilty to 937 criminal offenses and sentenced to life in prison without the chance of parole plus 1,000 years. Nearly one month later, Castro, age 52, was found dead in his prison cell, hanging himself using bedsheets.

Michelle Knight was 21 years old when she was kidnapped after visiting a relative that day. Amanda Berry, just one day shy of turning 17, was offered a ride home from work by Castro, who was a friend of her father. Gina DeJesus was only 14 went she went missing after walking home from her middle school. In the months and years after their rescue, the gruesome tales of the three victims unfolded and their stories of unspeakable acts of abuse at the hands of Castro emerged. The public learned of how Castro chained them like dogs in the basement of his home, raping them several times a day, starving them, keeping them in darkness, and forcing them to go to the bathroom in trashcans. Their horror was compounded by Castro's psychological abuse and taunting as he showed them news stories of how agonized their families were about their disappearance and claimed that they now "belonged to him."

Newspaper and television media all over the world flooded the stories of these three brave women, telling the tales of their hope and survival in their fight against despair and imminent harm. Their stories are documented in a Lifetime movie production "Cleveland Kidnapping," and two written memoirs, *Finding Me: A Decade of Darkness, a Life Reclaimed: A Memoir of the Cleveland Kidnappings* and *Hope: A Memoir of Survival in Cleveland*.

What brought this case such wide public attention? Was it the length of time that the victims were held captive? Was it the heinous nature of the acts committed against them by Castro? Or perhaps the fact that it was more than one victim? What about a desire to make the public more aware of the dangers that are out there? *What do you think?*

Sources

Caniglia, John and Blackwell, Brandon. 2013. Cleveland City Prosecutors Charge Ariel Castro With Kidnapping, Rape In Case Of Missing Women. *Cleveland.Com*. Retrieved from http://www.cleveland.com/metro/index.ssf/2013/05/cleveland_city_prosecutors_cha.html#incart_river#incart_maj-story-1.

McClam, Erin. 2013. Cleveland Man Charged With Kidnapping, Rape; No Charges For 2 Brothers. *NBC News*. Retrieved from http://usnews.nbcnews.com/_news/2013/05/08/18123601-cleveland-man-charged-with-kidnapping-rape-no-charges-for-2-brothers?lite.

Perez, Alex, Portnoy, Steven and Newcomb, Alyssa. 2013. Cleveland Kidnapping Suspect Ariel Castro Hid a Dark Side, His Uncle Says. *Good Morning America*. Retrieved from http://abcnews.go.com/US/cleveland-kidnapping-suspect-ariel-castro-hid-dark-side/story?id=19122845.

compact but does not tell us enough to give us a sense of where we are or where we are going.[22] However, reality forces us to settle on maps in our descriptions of crime, in an effort to capture its endless varieties without being overwhelmed. In chapter 2, we'll elaborate further on the nature and extent of crime, crime trends, and patterns of criminality. To get started, however, Table 1.5 lists the various official categories of criminal behavior, with a brief description of each. Only by understanding the variety of criminal behavior can we move forward with social control measures that intervene on behalf of *all* criminals to address *all* criminal behavior. Only then can we properly draw the link between crime and theory.

CRIMINOLOGY AND THEORY

Crime affects the lives of many people, even those who are not direct participants in a criminal event. The perpetrator, victim, police, witnesses, family members, judge, jury, and lawyers are all touched by crime. While we may not all agree on why individuals engage in criminal activities, crime generally makes us angry and afraid.[23] Our response to crime is often embedded in these emotions, without a true understanding of the social context of criminal behavior. Unfortunately, without this understanding, we can develop crime prevention strategies and solutions that compound the problem and do little to address its origins.[24]

Table 1.5 Major categories of crime

Interpersonal violence (chapter 14)	Crimes against property (chapter 15)	Public order crimes (chapter 16)	Crimes of the powerful (chapter 17)	The new face of crime (chapter 19)
Murder The willful (non-negligent) killing of one human being by another human being. **Rape** Penetration of the vagina or anus with any body part or object, or oral penetration by a sex organ of another person, without the consent of the victim. **Assault** The attempted commission of bodily injury to another human being. Assault can also mean putting an individual in fear of imminent bodily harm, injury, danger, or threat. An assault can therefore include threats, taunting, intimidation, and harassment; it requires no physical contact. **Robbery** The taking or attempting to take anything of value from the care, custody, or control of a person or persons by force or threat of force or violence and/or by putting the victim in fear. **Hate crime** Crimes directed at certain individuals because of their race, sexual orientation, religion, national origin, political orientation or physical condition.	**Larceny** The unlawful taking away of someone's property without using force, violence, or by fraud. **Burglary** The unlawful entry into a building or structure to commit a theft or felony. **Arson** The willful and malicious burning of a home, vehicle, building, or other structure or property. **Motor vehicle theft** The theft or attempted theft of a motor vehicle.	**Prostitution** The unlawful engaging in sexual activities for profit. **Pornography** The portrayal or depiction of sexually explicit material. **Drug abuse** The violation of laws pertaining to the possession, use, manufacture, or sale of controlled substances.	**White collar crime** Non-violent acts involving deception, concealment and guile committed by individuals, businesses, and corporations, for the purposes of obtaining money, avoiding loss, or gaining personal advantage. **State crime** Illegal activities by government officials to advance their political agendas or promote their own interests. **Organized crime** The illegal activities of groups of individuals in the course of some type of illegal business or enterprise set up for monetary gain.	**International crime** Systematic practices involving the infringement of human rights, peace agreements or other violations of international laws. **Political crime** Crimes committed to threaten, oppose, or challenge the government in power. **Technology crimes** Criminal offenses that are perpetrated using some type of network communication device such as the internet.

Source: *Crime in the United States.* 2015. Uniform Crime Report, Federal Bureau of Investigation. U.S. Department of Justice, Washington, D.C. www.fbi.gov/about-us/cjis/ucr/ucr.

BOX 1.3: CONNECTING THEORY TO PRACTICE

Does white collar crime "make sense"?

How do individuals who often appear to be respected members of society—who take leadership roles in the community and perform charitable deeds—participate in illegal activities? According to the Association of Certified Fraud Examiners, over 90 percent of white-collar crime felons have no prior criminal history. In an interview with *Wall Street Journal* columnist Herb Greenberg, Sam E. Antar, former chief financial officer of Crazy Eddie, a New York electronics retailer that cheated investors out of millions of dollars, describes how he put on a front to protect his image:

> As criminals we built false walls of integrity around us; we walked old ladies across the street. We built wings to hospitals. We gave huge amounts of money to charity. We wanted you to trust us.

Criminologist Edwin Sutherland defined white-collar crime as "crime committed by a person of respectability and high social status in the course of his occupation." His definition put regulatory and public welfare violations by businesspeople on the same footing as other criminal acts and attached to them the same stigma earned by criminals of lower social and economic standing. Sutherland's theories set the stage for decades of fruitful research on the nature and extent of white-collar crime and how the structure of modern organizations makes such acts possible. Criminology has since brought to light the acts of apparently upstanding members of the community and redefined their behavior as crime. We can now attribute white-collar offenses to larger forces like organizational structure and competition and personal factors like greed.

Sutherland and his followers laid the foundation for the passage of laws targeting white-collar offenses. In fact, the Racketeer Influenced Corrupt Organizations Act (RICO), one of the most important such pieces of legislation, was largely influenced by the work of Donald Cressey, a student of Sutherland, and the U.S. Sentencing Commission cited Sutherland and other social science researchers as evidence of the need for standards to avoid the preferential treatment of white-collar offenders.

Sources

Baker, John S. 2004. The Sociological Origins of White Collar Crime. *Legal Memorandum*. The Heritage Foundation. Retrieved from www.heritage.org/research/reports/2004/10/the-sociological-origins-of-white-collar-crime.

Greenberg, Herb. 2009. What 2 Crooks Told Me Over Lunch. *DeepCapture*. Retrieved from www.deepcapture.com/tag/herb-greenberg/.

Hayes, Jack L. 2011. *Business Fraud: From Trust to Betrayal*. Minneapolis, MN: Hillcrest Publishing Group.

Vaughan, D. 1992. The Macro-micro Connection in White-collar Crime Theory. In Kip Schegel and David Weisburd (eds.), *White-collar Crime Reconsidered*. York, PA: Maple Press Company, 124–45.

Criminology helps us think theoretically, without anger, about crime, criminal justice, and social control.[25] It guides our understanding by developing theories that elaborate on the nature, occurrence, and distribution of crime in various segments of society. In chapter 4, we will discuss how theories are constructed in greater detail. For now, we define a **theory** simply as a set of propositions that put forward a relationship between the categories of events or phenomena we are studying. For example, heredity theory is used to explain how certain traits—eye color, hair texture, height, intelligence—are passed down from biological parents to their children.

Criminological theory must account for the great diversity of crime, from petty theft to corporate fraud, simple assault to first-degree murder, campaign bribes to political assassination. It must incorporate a variety of perspectives that take into account individual, psychological, social-psychological, and social-structural variables that influence the commission of crime.[26] Only then can it guide criminal investigation toward the solution of difficult cases and help us understand why some individuals break the law (see Box 1.3).

In the chapters to come, we will present criminological theories on the nature and origin of criminal behavior that go beyond the representation of crime in the mass media, to help us gain insight into criminal events in an analytical and reflective manner. It is in this context that we recognize the significance of criminological theory in shaping the course of criminal justice policy and practice.

CRIMINOLOGICAL RESEARCH AND PUBLIC POLICY

Criminology provides the research and other tools policy makers like Congress need to make informed decisions in responding to crime.[27] Policies shaping the response to crime and crime-control strategies must be grounded in evidence-based criminological research. Developing a knowledge base from which politicians can derive an understanding of criminal behavior is essential to creating programs that effectively respond to the problem of crime. Political debates on crime control policy are often driven by public opinion and media persuasion on issues surrounding crime and punishment. This can lead to a misguided discourse on the state of crime and the real policy choices available.

Criminologists provide a more accurate representation of the nature and extent of crime, describe and explain the variables associated with criminal behavior, and evaluate the effectiveness

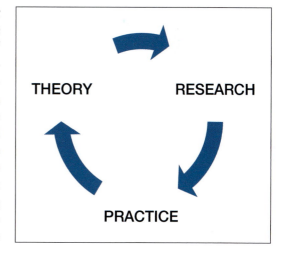

Figure 1.3
Criminology: linking theory, research, and practice

BOX 1.4: CONNECTING RESEARCH TO PRACTICE

Does increased surveillance reduce crime?

We've seen them at stop lights, ATM machines, and department stores, sometimes hidden and sometimes out in the open. They are designed for our protection, keeping us safe from the reckless driver and secure from the predatory thief. They are video surveillance cameras, and since September 11, 2001, they have been sparking debate about the expanded use of domestic surveillance by the Department of Defense, the FBI, and the National Security Agency.

Some fear the danger to individual rights and civil liberties from increased government surveillance and the use of sophisticated technology that allows facial scanning and computer-readable identification tags. They see such monitoring as damaging to the fundamental civil rights guaranteed to citizens and a threat to freedom, privacy, and anonymity. A legal debate over the right to privacy was sparked by the finding of an FBI global positioning system tracking device attached to Yasir Afifi's car. The device was discovered by a mechanic during an oil change. Puzzled, Afifi took pictures of the device and posted the photos online. A couple of days later, FBI agents showed up at his home and demanded the return of their device.[28]

Others, however, see such types of surveillance as necessary, considering the challenges faced by law enforcement in high-crime areas where gangs, violence, terrorism, and drug trafficking are prevalent. Some local politicians and police officials have turned to the federal government to sponsor video surveillance as another way to monitor and apprehend crime suspects.

There is very little evidence to show that video surveillance deters criminal activity, curbs violent behavior, or reduces fear of crime. Studies in Great Britain, where such monitoring is more widespread than in the United States, reported little change in crime statistics before and after the installation of video surveillance equipment. The University of Cincinnati found the installation of video cameras was an ineffective deterrent to crime that simply shifted criminal activity away from the view of the camera. Other research has shown that young male minorities are disproportionately targeted by video monitoring programs.

If video surveillance is a costly alternative that has not yielded the anticipated results, why do you think its use continues to expand?

Sources

"The Effect of Closed Circuit Television on Recorded Crime Rates and Public Concern About Crime in Glasgow." 1999. *Crime and Criminal Justice Research Findings,* 30. The Scottish Office Central Research Unit.

Nestel, Thomas J. 2012. *Using Surveillance Camera Systems to Monitor Public Domains: Can Abuse Be Prevented?* Post-Graduate Thesis, Naval Postgraduate School, Monterey, CA.

Scholsberg, Mark and Ozer, Nicole A. 2009. *Under the Watchful Eye.* The California ACLU Affiliates. Retrieved from www.aclunc.org/docs/criminal_justice/police_practices/under_the_watchful_eye_the_proliferation_of_video_surveillance_systems_in_california.pdf.

Walsh, Brandon, Farrington, David P., and Taheri, Sema A. 2015. "Effectiveness and Social Costs of Public Area Surveillance for Crime Prevention." *Annual Review of Law and Social Science* 11: 111–130.

of crime control intervention strategies. Is violent crime increasing? Does punishment deter criminal behavior? Do individuals brought up in a deprived social environment turn to crime? Criminologists answer by conducting research guided by principles of the scientific approach, which includes defining the problem, reviewing the literature, formulating a hypothesis, collecting and analyzing the data, developing a conclusion, and sharing the results. We will discuss criminological research methods in detail in chapter 4. For now, it is important to recognize the important role criminology plays in developing research studies that provide policy makers and politicians with evidence-based criminal justice strategies and interventions.[29]

Herein lies the connection between criminological research and public policy. In the 1990s, for example, a surge in school shootings prompted public concern over growing violence among youth.[30] The effects of television violence on children's behavior became the focus of deliberation in public, academic, and political arenas.[31] Studies concluded that extensive viewing of violence on television leads to an increase in aggressive and violent behavior among children, making them gradually accept violence as a means to solving problems, imitate violent behavior they observe, and become insensitive to the pain and suffering caused by violence in the real world.

Relying on expert testimony and research findings, in 1999 the Senate Judiciary Committee issued a report on media portrayals of violence, outlining national reforms aimed at reducing their effects on children.[32] The Committee's policy recommendations focused on practical results, such as ensuring media companies comply with existing industry ratings systems; developing guidelines for measuring media violence and industry efforts to reduce it; allowing parents access to filtering technology to block certain types of entertainment on their TVs; criminalizing the posting of violent hate material on the Internet; and conducting further research on the effects of media violence on children and youth. Legislators relied on scientific evidence, gathered through criminological research, to create policies for controlling the impact of media violence on children and adolescents.

As technology continues to advance, debates on the effects of media violence will widen, with policy makers turning to experts to find effective solutions.[33] Criminology continues to be the source on which we rely to guide our unbiased understanding of criminal justice issues today (see Box 1.4). While it may not have all the policy answers we need at any given time, only criminology can help us understand the criminal acts of ordinary individuals and what to do about their not-so-ordinary behavior.

Before we leave this chapter, we must revisit the question we began it with, regarding the definition of behavior as criminal. What defines the behavior of individuals as *not so ordinary*? We turn now to a brief description of the development of criminal law.

CRIMINOLOGY AND THE LAW

We noted earlier in this chapter that what constitutes crime changes over time and from society to society. What remains consistent is that most people accept criminal law as a given. Like the chemical composition of water, the pressure of the atmosphere, and the physics of gravity, it is just there. Criminologists, however, approach the study of criminal law by raising two very important questions: how do certain behaviors come to be defined as criminal acts, and who benefits from legally defining these behaviors as criminal acts? Two perspectives offer viewpoints on the origins and development of criminal law: the consensus view and the conflict view (see Figure 1.4). Each operates from a unique understanding of the relationship between deviant behavior, crime, law, and society. Let us turn now to a discussion of these two perspectives, beginning with the consensus view.

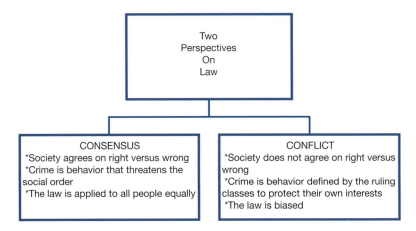

Figure 1.4 Two perspectives on law: which is more convincing?

The consensus view

French sociologist Émile Durkheim noted that social conformity is achieved through sanctions that society imposes on those who choose to deviate.[34] Whether these sanctions are strict such as the formal sanction of imprisonment, or less formal like social isolation, as signs of disapproval they are sufficient to coerce individuals to conform to the prevailing norms of society. Crime as a social phenomenon therefore is behavior that society has generally agreed is harmful, undesirable, and disruptive to the smooth functioning of society. Thus, according to this **consensus model**, criminal law defines as criminal all behavior believed to be repulsive to all individuals in society. The law reflects the beliefs, morals, and values of mainstream society that views certain behaviors as needing to be managed, controlled, and eliminated for the good of society as a whole, and it is therefore applied uniformly and equitably to all members.

Individuals adhering to the consensus model of understanding crime and crime control note that we would all agree behaviors such as murder, rape, and robbery are clearly wrong and certainly morally repugnant to society. How, though, do we justify the control of certain types of behavior that elicit a little more disagreement and controversy, such as gambling, prostitution, and drug use?[35] While society is obligated to protect its members from danger and harm, how can it do so when there is not always agreement on what we need protection from? Moreover, if society does criminalize these behaviors, how do they find their way into the criminal codes and statutes given there is no consensus? Whose view of right and wrong wins in the end? The conflict perspective offers an alternative understanding of crime.

The conflict view

The **conflict model** views crime and deviance as products of unequal power relationships in society.[36] Society is made up of diverse groups of individuals—business owners, students, factory workers, engineers, clergymen, teachers, and politicians—each with its own set of unique values, norms, and interests. Individuals themselves come from different classes, races, religions, and cultures. With this breadth of diversity, it is very difficult for everyone to agree about right and wrong, so conflict arises between competing groups to impose their own views on the rest of society. Groups with the greatest financial resources and political power control legislation and define as criminal the behaviors that threaten their own interests.

Crime control therefore becomes a tool of the rich and powerful to control the behavior of the less powerful, in an effort to advance their own interests and maintain their privileged position in society.[37] Conflict criminologists note that even laws forbidding crimes such as robbery and murder, which on the surface appear to be in the interests of protecting society as a whole, nevertheless are designed to maintain the overall social order by ensuring that the anger and hostility of the poor and powerless does not become directed at the wealthy and privileged.[38] Crime control efforts are therefore primarily directed at the lower classes, who are under constant surveillance by criminal justice authorities for committing "street" types of crime such as theft and assault. On the other hand, the equally detrimental and sometimes more harmful acts of the upper classes such as discrimination, environmental pollution, and political assassinations go relatively undetected and unpunished.

Criminology cannot simply accept the law as a given. It must investigate how the law came to be the way it is, why some acts are defined as criminal and others are not, what the goals of criminal law are and what the legal definition of a criminal act is. We turn to a further exploration of these questions in chapter 2.

A period of change in criminology and the criminal justice system: 1970s–1990s

The 1970s, 1980s, and 1990s were critical decades in the history of the American criminal justice system and for the field of criminology. Events taking place in those decades continue to effect the functioning of the American criminal justice system as well as the type of research criminologists conduct.

History textbooks often depict the decades of the 1960s and 1970s as a period of tremendous social upheaval in America, that, despite causing many conflicts, generally led to positive social change in American society. For example, during that brief period, progressive social movements developed around civil rights and race, women's rights, prisoner's rights, gay rights, and the environment. Moreover, there was dynamic growth in art, literature, music, and film. Politically, the presidential administrations of John F. Kennedy and, later, Lyndon B. Johnson, sought to implement far-reaching, liberal reforms via their New Frontier and Great Society programs. Finally, many critical perspectives and voices emerged within social science disciplines like sociology and criminology. Those perspectives challenged both the academic and societal status quo as it existed at the time and helped push research on important topics like crime in new directions.

As so often happens, however, periods of social progress are often followed by periods of social conservatism and retraction. Even as many aspects of American society were changing for the better during the 1960s and 1970s, some things, like our approach to crime and criminals, were experiencing changes that, in hindsight, were anything but positive.

The election of Richard Nixon as president of the United States in 1968 was an important moment for our criminal justice system and the field of criminology. By 1971, Nixon had declared drugs "public enemy number one" and pledged to fight a "war on drugs." Nixon's pledge reflected his personal views toward drugs and drug users and was designed to appeal to Americans who were unhappy and frightened by rising drug use among young people and increasingly liberal attitudes toward drugs and sex.

Nixon convened a special commission[39] to examine federal marijuana policy and provide guidance on what to do about marijuana. Despite that commission recommending widespread decriminalization of marijuana, Nixon placed marijuana into the most dangerous category of illicit drugs—Schedule I—alongside heroin and cocaine. Nixon also got "tough on crime" by enhancing mandatory minimum sentences and passing legislation allowing police to conduct "no-knock" searches of homes and businesses.

Despite these changes, the progressive idea of rehabilitation remained the dominant punishment philosophy in America through much of the 1970s. However, rehabilitation was not universally supported. Some detractors considered it expensive, ineffective and too "soft" an approach for dealing with criminal behavior. Publication of the Martinson study in 1974, which reviewed rehabilitative programs across the U.S., led some to conclude "nothing works" with respect to rehabilitative programming and criminal offending. This conclusion, which vastly oversimplified the Martinson report's findings, helped erode support for rehabilitation in the U.S. and contributed to the redefinition of both crime and punishment in the 1980s as an individual level problem whose solution lay in "tough" crime control policies.

Ronald Reagan's ascendance to the White House in the early 1980s solidified the power and influence of the "New Right"—an extremely conservative branch of the Republican party that helped get Reagan elected. Sociologists Craig Reinarman and Harry G. Levine describe the moral stance and political impact of the New Right:

> [they] set about to impose what they called "traditional family values" on public policy and philosophy. This . . . New Right felt increasingly threatened by . . . modernist values, behaviors, and cultural practices—particularly . . . forms of 1960s hedonism . . . sex outside marriage and . . . illicit drugs . . . Once in office, Reagan . . . attempted to restructure public policy according to radically conservative ideology. Through the lens of this ideology, most social problems appeared to be simply the consequences of individual moral choices.[40]

In the 1980s, crimes, including illegal drug use, were politicized by both Republicans and Democrats.[41,42] The outcome of the politicization of crime and rise of ultra-conservative crime ideology was: (1) a redefinition of problems like crime and drug use as individual, rather than social, problems, and (2) the development of new, harsh criminal justice policies to deal with those problems.

Thus, in the context of the 1980s, the causes of crime were increasingly divorced from larger structural factors like unemployment and poverty. In the discourse that emerged, criminal behavior became the exclusive product of bad personal decisions or moral failings. The solution pitched to deal with crime, public disorder, and drug issues was thus to get tougher, not softer, on criminals, with the idea being that harsher punishments and "tough love" would show criminals the error of their ways, cause them to reform, and also deter other people from committing similar acts. Politicians on both sides of the political aisle embraced this rationale and supported policies that aligned with it. The mass media further supported the view of crime as an individual-level problem and the American public was swayed toward that line of thinking as well.[43]

Every phase of the criminal justice system was impacted by this logic. Even the election of democratic president Bill Clinton in 1992 did little to alter the course of criminal justice policy in America. Under Clinton's reign, the multi-billion dollar wars on drugs and crime escalated further. Clinton's Violent Crime Control and Law Enforcement Act garrisoned the nation while three-strikes laws underlined the ideology of locking people up and throwing away the key.

As a result of the many ideological and policy changes accruing since the 1970s, the American criminal justice system has gotten tougher on crime and criminals. Below we preview just a few of the impacts policy reforms and tough-on-crime laws have had on the various phases of the criminal justice system.

Impacts on law enforcement

In terms of law enforcement, getting tough on crime and waging a war on drugs necessitated a massive increase in the number of law enforcement officers in America. For example, in the mid-1980s[44] there were approximately 344,000 state and local law enforcement officers and an additional 54,000 federal agents. In 2013,[45] there were more than 1.2 million law enforcement officers at the local, state, and federal levels. President Clinton's **Violent Crime Control and Law Enforcement Act** alone led to the hiring of 100,000 new officers.

How law enforcement agencies operated changed, with zero tolerance and public order policing strategies rising to prominence, backed by arguments of sociologists and criminologists and ideas like Broken Windows Theory[46] (see chapter 5). The result: more arrests, especially for minor crimes like drug possession and public intoxication.[47]

For many law enforcement agencies the emphasis on cracking down on low-level crimes served as a mandate to more intensely police particular communities, and particular groups of people—often communities and people of color—where issues of disorder, crime, and drugs were often most pronounced. Thus, one effect of 1980s policies on law enforcement was to concentrate the police focus on urban, low-income minority communities, thus exacerbating racial tensions between the public and police. Another effect of having to rapidly increase the number of law enforcement officers to meet the new mission of law enforcement was that hiring standards and personnel quality declined. Also, in harshly cracking down on drugs and crime, new opportunities opened up for police officers to engage in drug-related misconduct and corruption.

Impacts on courts and corrections

Prior to the 1980s, judges presiding over criminal court cases were able to exercise their discretion when handing out sentences to convicted criminals thanks to indeterminate sentencing policies, which allowed judges to tailor punishments to fit both the specific crime and the particular criminal.[48] Judicial discretion exercised through indeterminate sentencing structures generally allowed for flexible sentences that could meet the dual goals of punishment and rehabilitation. Discretionary parole, where inmates could be released early from prison even for violent crimes like assault and murder, was frequently utilized.[49]

The dominant punishment philosophy in America prior to the 1980s was rehabilitation.[50] In the 1960s and 1970s, correctional officials, politicians, researchers, and the public embraced the notion that the primary goal of incarceration should be to rehabilitate the criminal offender and ensure their successful reintegration back into society. Rehabilitation entailed attending closely to the individual needs of each offender by providing therapy, medication, and other forms of medical or mental health treatment (including for drug addiction), as well as helping the offender build work-related skills, and improve their literacy and education. Unsurprisingly, rehabilitation aligned well with indeterminate sentencing structures and the use of discretionary parole. Throughout the 1970s, researchers argued that America was moving ever further away from extensive incarceration.[51] Indeed, the National Advisory Commission on Criminal Justice Standards and Goals argued in a 1973 report[52] that America should not build adult jails or prisons and should close as many existing ones as was feasible because "incarceration had achieved nothing but a shocking record of failure."

As the political and social climate shifted in the 1980s, extant court and correctional practices—like indeterminate sentencing, discretionary parole, and rehabilitation—came under attack for being too "soft" on crime and criminals. Proponents of those methods were accused of coddling criminals and ignoring the plight of victims, the community, and research which allegedly showed that those programs were ineffective.[53] Politicians, the media, and the public clamored for harsher court and correctional policies that would solve America's crime problems.

The Comprehensive Crime Control Act passed by Congress in 1984,[54] went a long way toward meeting these demands by instituting a host of criminal justice system reforms. Among many things, the 1984 CCA included the Sentencing Reform Act, which abolished parole for federal prisoners sentenced after 1987 for violating any federal criminal statute, including drug possession or trafficking. Across America, states also began abolishing or significantly curtailing the use of discretionary parole, including Iowa, Maine, Louisiana, Pennsylvania, and South Dakota.[55] Also, many states and the federal government replaced indeterminate sentencing structures with fixed, determinate ones that took away even more judicial discretion. Alongside the rise of determinate sentences were mandatory minimum sentences, which set a minimum amount of time to be served for a particular offense and truth-in-sentencing policies, which required that "offenders serve a substantial portion of their prison sentence"[56] before being released.

The impact of all of these policy changes—from those impacting law enforcement, to courts and correctional systems—can be visualized by picturing a fishing net used for trawling. Those nets typically have a large opening at one end and a small opening at the other, and are pulled through the water to capture fish or shrimp or whatever might be swimming along. The 1980s criminal justice policy reforms functioned much like a trawler's fishing net. Reforms intended to get tougher on crime and criminals increasingly widened one end of the net, thus drawing more and more people into the criminal justice system. At the same time, many of those policy changes, especially those targeting the courts and corrections, continuously narrowed the opening at the other end, ensuring that while more people were being drawn into the criminal justice system, fewer and fewer would be getting out.

Even today, the American criminal justice system and American society are grappling with the consequences of tough on crime and War on Drugs policies; the War on Drugs continues to cost taxpayers $26 billion per year.[57] Policy changes led directly to America's current standing as the nation with the highest incarceration rate in the world. The vast majority of prisoners are incarcerated for relatively minor offenses, especially drug possession.[58] In our nation's effort to solve the crime problem through tougher law enforcement and sentencing, some individuals have received 25-year-to-life sentences for such innocuous acts like stealing VHS tapes or spare tires thanks to three-strikes laws. Current controversies over police misconduct, corruption, and excessive use of force can also be linked to the legacy of the 1980s, when law enforcement agencies across the nation lowered or relaxed their hiring and training standards. Thus, it is imperative that every student of criminology and criminal justice recognizes the importance of historical events taking place over the last five decades. Those events have shaped the study of crime and the practice of criminal justice in our present society.

SUMMARY

How do we define crime?

Four perspectives offer us different ideas on the nature of crime: the legalist perspective defines crime as behavior that violates criminal codes and statutes; the political perspective views crime as socially constructed behavior; the psychological perspective sees crime as maladaptive behavior; and finally, the sociological perspective defines crime as any behavior that threatens the social order. A comprehensive definition sees crime as human behavior that we interpret as violating society's norms for a specific time and place, and that must be controlled and prevented by legal decree.

What is deviance?

Deviance is behavior that violates society's standards of conduct or social norms, which range from folkways, non-binding social conventions; to mores, strong convictions about certain behaviors; taboos, which define socially offensive acts that are informally forbidden; and laws, written decrees with formal sanctions. It is in this last category of social norms—laws—that crime and deviance overlap.

When is crime deviant and deviant behavior criminal?

All crime is not deviant, and all deviant acts are not criminal. Because crime and deviance are both products of social interpretation, what is criminal can vary according to time, place, and individual or group. Certain types of behavior that society deems important to regulate and control through formal intervention are subject to law, the extreme form of social approval.

What is criminology?

We define criminology as the scientific study of the incidence and forms of crime and criminal behavior, its causes and consequences, as well as social reaction, control, and prevention. Academics, researchers, and policy analysts who study crime, criminals, and criminal behavior, are called criminologists.

Does the popular image of crime measure up to reality?

The popular image of crime is derived from media portrayals of violent criminal acts that suggest these are the most urgent and pressing social problems facing our society today. In reality, anyone can commit a crime, and crimes such as shoplifting and burglary are far more common than murder, rape, and other crimes sensationalized in the media.

How does criminology guide our study of crime?

Criminology helps us think critically about crime, criminal justice, and social control by offering various theories that expand our understanding of the nature and extent of criminal behavior.

How does criminology influence social policy?

Criminology shapes the course of crime control policies and procedures through scientific research findings that address the complex issues related to crime and crime causation.

CRITICAL THINKING QUESTIONS

1. How far can the government go to ensure domestic peace and tranquility? What individual rights would you give up in exchange for the goal of public order and social conformity? Which would you retain under any circumstances?

2. Assuming we don't all agree on major social issues such as the legalization of marijuana, government surveillance of social media, and the right to bear arms, how does society come up with rules and regulations that define these controversial subjects? What if your instructor allowed the class to come up with the rules defining classroom attendance, course requirements, and grading procedures? How would you reach a decision? Whose interests would become the standard of conduct?

3. If you asked your family, friends, neighbors, or co-workers, "what is crime?" what definition would they give? What examples of criminal activities would they use? How is their description shaped by the popular image of crime? How does it measure up to the reality we know about crime?

4. Policy makers want to know whether fear of punishment will deter crime. You are the expert whose opinion will serve as the foundation for a shift in crime control strategies for repeat offenders. Where do you begin your

efforts toward gaining a scientific understanding of this subject that would effectively guide policy makers toward creating the proper legislation? What questions do you ask, and how do you go about answering them?

E-RESOURCES

More information on the effects of media violence on children and youth can be accessed at National Youth Violence Prevention Resource Center website at http://www.aacap.org/Default.aspx.

Visit the American Civil Liberties Union (ACLU) website at http://www.aclu.org/ for further information and debates on individual rights and personal freedoms.

For a discussion of both sides of the argument on criminalizing euthanasia, visit http://www.religioustolerance.org/euthanas.htm.

Further information on the various segments of the criminological enterprise, can be found on the National Criminal Justice Reference Service website at http://www.ncjrs.gov/.

Details about criminology academic organizations and professional associations can be accessed at http://www.cybrary.info/.

NOTES

1   Jaffe, Alexandra, LoBianco, Tom and Brown, Pamela. 1 June 2015. Hastert's Hush Money Was to Cover Up Sexual Misconduct with Former Student. *CNN Online*. Retrieved from http://www.cnn.com/2015/05/29/politics/dennis-hastert-indictment-questions/.
2   Schuilenberg, Marc. 2015. *The Securitization of Society: Law, Risk, and Social Order*. New York: New York University Press.
3   Newsmax. 19 January 2015. Poll: By 2–1 Margin, Americans Favor Security Over Privacy. Retrieved from http://www.newsmax.com/Newsfront/security-terrorism-threat-privacy/2015/01/19/id/619346/.
4   O'Connor, T. 2004. Crime Theories. In *Crime Theories, Mega Links in Criminal Justice*. Retrieved from http://www.newlearner.com/courses/hts/cln4u/pdf/crime_theories.pdf.
5   McCaghy, Charles H., Capron, Timothy A., Jamieson, J.D., and Carey, Sandra H. 2016. *Deviant Behavior: Crime, Conflict and Interests Groups*, 5th ed. London and New York: Routledge.
6   Chambliss, William J. 2001. *Power, Politics and Crime*. Boulder, CO: Westview Press.
7   Farrington, D. 2011. Crime Causation: Psychological Theories—Family Influences, Individual Influences, More Comprehensive Theories, Conclusions, Bibliography. Retrieved from http://law.jrank.org/pages/813/Crime-Causation-Psychological-Theories.html.
8   Adler, Patricia, and Adler, Peter. 2015. *Construction of Deviance: Social Power, Context and Interaction*, 8th ed. Boston, MA: Cengage/Wadsworth.
9   Reiman, Jeffrey and Leighton, Paul. 2016. *The Rich Get Richer and the Poor Get Prison*, 10th ed. London and New York: Routledge.

10   Hammond, R., Cheney, P., and Pearsey, R. 2015. Deviance and Crime. In *Introduction to Sociology*. Retrieved from http://freesociologybooks.com/Introduction_To_Sociology/08_Deviance_and_Crime.php.

11   Schultz, W. and Tabanico, J. 2009. *A Social Norms Approach to Community-Based Crime Prevention: Implicit and Explicit Messages on Neighborhood Watch Signs*. Final report submitted to the National Institute of Justice. Washington, D.C.: U.S. Department of Justice. DOJ No. 226821.

12   Hammond, R., Cheney, P., and Pearsey, R. 2015. Deviance and Crime. In *Introduction to Sociology*. Retrieved from http://freesociologybooks.com/Introduction_To_Sociology/08_Deviance_and_Crime.php.

13   Chambliss, William J. 1973. The Roughnecks and the Saints. *Society* 11: 24–31.

14   Miller, J. Mitchell. 2009. *21st Century Criminology: A Reference Handbook*. Thousand Oaks, CA: SAGE.

15   Sutherland, Edwin. 1924. *Principles of Criminology*. Philadelphia, PA: Lippincott.

16   Finest of the Finest. 1966. *Time*, February 18.

17   Savelsberg, J.J., Cleveland, L.L. and King, R.D. 2004. Institutional Environments and Scholarly Work: American Criminology, 1951–1993. *Social Forces* 82(4): 1275–1302.

18   Brennan, C. 2014. Tonya, Nancy Reflect on The Whack Heard 'Round the World. *USA Today*. Retrieved from http://www.usatoday.com/story/sports/olympics/2014/01/02/christine-brennan-tonya-harding-nancy-kerrigan/4294753/.

19   Joseph, J., Stangeland, B., Putrino, L., and Effron, L. 2015. How Mary Kay Letourneau Went From Having Sex With a 6th Grader to Becoming His Wife. *ABCNews*. Retrieved from http://abcnews.go.com/US/mary-kay-letourneau-sex-6th-grader-wife/story?id=30144806.

20   Surette, R. 2015. *Media, Crime, and Criminal Justice*, 6th ed. Stamford, CT: Cengage.

21   Ibid.

22   Chambliss, William J. 1988. *Exploring Criminology*. New York: Macmillan Publishing.

23   Wilson, James Q. and Kelling, George L. The Police and Neighborhood Safety: Broken Windows. Retrieved from http://www.cptedsecurity.com/broken_windows_theory.pdf.

24   Surette, Ray. 2015. *Media, Crime and Criminal Justice: Images, Realities, and Policies*. Stamford, CT: Cengage.

25   Small-Jordan, D. 2014. The Science of Criminology: Understanding Crime from the Inside Out. *DecodedScience.org*. Retrieved from http://www.decodedscience.org/science-criminology-understanding-crime-inside/41408.

26   Frame, Rapella. 2009. The Development of Integrated Theories in Criminal Justice. Retrieved from http://www.cj-resources.com/My_Writings/The%20Development%20of%20Integrated%20Theories%20in%20Criminal%20Justice%20-%20Rapalla%20Frame.pdf.

27   Bueermann, J. 2012. *Being Smart on Crime with Evidence-based Policing*. Washington, D.C.: National Institute of Justice.

28   Thigpen, M., Beauclair, T., Keiser, G., and Banks, C. 2011. *Evidence-based Policy, Practice, and Decision-making*. Retrieved from http://static.nicic.gov/Library/024198.pdf.

29   Blumstein, A. 2002. Youth, Guns, and Violent Crime. *The Future of Children* 12(2): 39–53. http://doi.org/10.2307/1602737.

30   American Psychological Association. 2013. Psychologists Study Media Violence for Harmful Effects. *Psychology: Science in Action*. Retrieved from www.apa.org/action/resources/research-in-action/protect.aspx.

31   American Academy of Pediatrics. 2000. Joint Statement on the Impact of Entertainment Violence on Children. Congressional Public Health Summit, July 26. Retrieved from http://www2.aap.org/advocacy/releases/jstmtevc.htm.

32 Youth Violence: A Report of the Surgeon General. 2001. NCBI Resources. Rockville, MD: Office of the Surgeon General. Retrieved from http://www.ncbi.nlm.nih.gov/books/NBK44294/.

33 Elias, Paul. 2010. "Discovery of GPS Tracker Becomes Privacy Issue." *Associated Press*. Retrieved from http://phys.org/news/2010–10-discovery-gps-tracker-privacy-issue.html.

34 Cotterrell, Roger. 1999. *Emile Durkheim: Law in a Moral Domain*. Edinburgh, UK: Edinburgh University Press.

35 Mannheim, H. 2013. *Group Problems in Crime and Punishment*. New York: Routledge.

36 Chambliss, William J. 2001. *Power, Politics and Crime*. Boulder, CO: Westview Press.

37 Ibid, see 9.

38 Bernard, T. J. 1981. Distinction Between Conflict and Radical Criminology. *Journal of Criminal Law and Criminology* 72(1): 362–379. Retrieved from http://scholarly commons.law.northwestern.edu/cgi/viewcontent.cgi?article=6223&context=jclc.

39 The National Commission on Marijuana and Drug Abuse, 22 March, 1972.

40 Reinarman, C. and Levine, H.G. 1989. Crack in Context: Politics and Media in the Making of a Drug Scare. *Contemporary Drug Problems* (Winter): 560–561.

41 Ibid.

42 Several key cases and events highlight how crime and criminals were utilized extensively by politicians in the 1980s to achieve political ends. If interested, read about Willie Horton and Len Bias.

43 For an in-depth analysis that examines the interplay between politics, media, public opinion and crime, read Reinarman and Levine, Crack in Context: Politics and Media in the Making of a Drug Scare, *Contemporary Drug Problems* (Winter), 1989.

44 Bureau of Justice Statistics. 2015. Personnel, Policies and Practices. U.S. Department of Justice, Office of Justice Programs. NCJ248677.

45 Ibid.

46 Seiver, S. 2015. A Millennial's Guide to Broken Windows. *The Marshall Project*, May 20. Retrieved from https://www.themarshallproject.org/2015/05/20/a-millennial-s-guide-to-broken-windows#.iDuVcMSzT.

47 FBI. 2014. Crime in the United States—Persons Arrested. U.S. Department of Justice. Retrieved from https://www.fbi.gov/about-us/cjis/ucr/crime-in-the-u.s/2014/crime-in-the-u.s.-2014/persons-arrested/main.

48 Bureau of Justice Statistics. 1999. Truth in Sentencing in State Prisons. U.S. Department of Justice, Office of Justice Programs.

49 Stohr, M.K. Walsh, A. Hemmens, C. 2013. *Corrections: A Text/Reader*. Thousand Oaks, CA: SAGE.

50 Ibid.

51 Rothman, D. 1971. *The Discovery of the Asylum*. Boston, MA: Little, Brown and Company, p. 295.

52 National Advisory Commission on Criminal Justice Standards and Goals. 1973. A National Strategy to Reduce Crime. U.S. Department of Justice, Law Enforcement Assistance Administration, pp. 358, 597.

53 Martinson, R. 1974. What Works? Questions and Answers about Prison Reform. *The Public Interest* 35: 22–54.

54 S. 1762, 98th Congress, 1983–1984.

55 Bureau of Justice Statistics. 2016. Reentry Trends in the United States. U.S. Department of Justice, Office of Justice Programs. Retrieved from http://www.bjs.gov/content/reentry/releases.cfm.

56 Bureau of Justice Statistics. 1999. *Truth in Sentencing in State Prisons*. U.S. Department of Justice, Office of Justice Programs.

57   Office of National Drug Control Policy. 2016. National Drug Control Budget Funding Highlights. Press release from the Office of the White House. Retrieved from https://www.whitehouse.gov/ondcp/the-national-drug-control-budget-fy-2013-funding-highlights.

58   Johnson, C. and Penaloza, M. 2014. Judge Regrets Harsh Human Toll of Mandatory Minimum Sentences. *National Public Radio*, Dec. 16. Retrieved from www.npr.org/2014/12/16/370991710/judge-regrets-harsh-human-toll-of-mandatory-minimum-sentences.

CHAPTER OUTLINE

Criminal law

KEY TERMS

blue laws
common law
case law
stare decisis
statutes
statutory law
legality
actus reus
harm
causation
mens rea
concurrence
punishment
corpus delicti
ex post facto
void for vagueness
fair warning
general intent
specific intent
punishment
criminal law
substantive criminal law
procedural criminal law
due process
civil law
plaintiffs
statute of limitations

Imagine you're living in New Orleans, Louisiana. Having just finished work for the day, you get in your car and begin driving home. Nearing your neighborhood, you see a column of thick black smoke rising into the air and you begin to worry—something is burning near where you live. As you turn the final corner onto your street your worst fear is confirmed: your apartment building is on fire! Thankfully, fire fighters are already on the scene.

"Hey!" You shout toward a group of firefighters after parking your car. They look in your direction, but then go back to consulting with each other. "Please," you say, "I have a dog and cat in my apartment!" Again, there is no response from the firefighters. In dismay, you glance around and notice a firefighter climbing out of another truck that has just arrived. You run over to her. "You've got to help! My pets are on the third floor, apartment C—please rescue them!" The firefighter assures you that others are already clearing the building and that they will get to your apartment very quickly, but that's not enough for you. You need more than assurances—you need action right now!

Overwhelmed by fear and anxiety, and frustrated by what you take as a lack of serious concern, you hurl some not-so-pleasant curse words at the firefighter

Model Penal Code

consensus theory

societal needs theory

ruling class theory

pluralistic theory

patriarchy

status offenses

and her co-workers. The firefighter attempts to reassure you that everything will be all right and then walks toward a police cruiser parked nearby. You feel much better having vented. A moment later, a police officer approaches. "Sir," she says, "I need you to step over here." The police officer asks you if you just cursed at the firefighter and you sheepishly reply that you did. What happens next shocks you: the police officer tells you that you're under arrest. "For what?" you stammer. "Because it's a crime in New Orleans to use obscene language when addressing a firefighter while they're working." You are stunned and begin to protest, thinking that swearing at someone—firefighter or not—can't actually be a crime. But it is. Soon enough you are cuffed and loaded into the rear seat of a patrol car.

This example might seem outlandish and it certainly has the feel of bordering on the melodramatic. But it is neither fantasy nor fiction. In New Orleans, Louisiana, according to Section 74–2 of the New Orleans municipal code: "It shall be unlawful and a breach of the peace for any person wantonly to curse or revile or to use obscene or opprobrious language toward or with reference to any member of the city fire department while in the actual performance of his duty."[1] The New Orleans obscene language law is not the only law that may leave you scratching your head. In at least 13 U.S. states "blue laws" make certain acts illegal on Sundays—such as selling cars in Pennsylvania,[2] selling alcohol in Indiana,[3] or playing cards in Alabama.[4]

In practice, these laws may not be enforced often, yet taking note of them provides a useful jumping-off point for exploring America's system of criminal law in greater detail. Collectively, laws banning obscene language or playing cards on Sunday highlight several crucial points. First, laws governing social behavior do not exist independent of human efforts to create them. What this means is that laws that make some acts illegal are constructed or created by people. Let's take a minute to consider this in more detail by drawing upon the concept of gravity.

Gravity is a physical force, which we can define mathematically, that keeps people firmly planted on Earth's surface. More importantly, gravity exists whether we understand it scientifically or have a specific word to describe it. Even if we knew absolutely nothing about gravity, how it worked or why it worked, gravity would still keep us from floating off into space. Thus, gravity is a physical law—it exists whether we perceive it, think about, or comprehend it.

This is not true for social laws, including those that define what conduct is criminal. For example, using obscene language toward firefighters while they're working is only a criminal act if we say it is criminal. Otherwise, it would just be another act of speech. Thus, the process of creating laws and identifying crimes and criminals is a process of consciously setting certain acts, and the people who commit them, apart from others. This process of setting apart, of making laws and crimes, would not occur if we (people) didn't actively make it happen. The important point for you to remember is that people actively determine what is or is not socially acceptable, legal or illegal, deviant or criminal—these things are not determined by nature. Therefore, laws and crimes are not immutable and unchanging; rather, they are flexible and always capable of change.

This fact highlights a second very important point about the law, and criminal law in particular: the process of making certain acts crimes is often contested and ripe with conflicts, disagreements, and a good deal of confusion. That being so, laws structure nearly every aspect of our social world and our lives. Indeed, the primary functions of laws, especially criminal laws, are to protect people from harm, establish boundaries and order within a society. This is accomplished by formally defining which behaviors are acceptable and which are not, and then establishing procedures for controlling and punishing people who engage in those behaviors. Because criminal laws are surrounded by conflict, but also influence nearly every aspect of social life, we as criminologists, criminal justice practitioners, and students must take a serious interest in understanding the law, its key attributes, its impacts as well as how it changes.

THE CRIMINAL LAW, CRIME, AND CRIMINAL JUSTICE

Developing knowledge about the law, and the criminal law in particular, is important for any criminology or criminal justice student.

Why?

First, the key subjects of criminology—crime and criminals—are often (though not always) defined in reference to what a society's legal system deems criminal. Thus, knowing what makes a particular act a "crime," and how a society determines what is criminal and what is not, is very important.

Second, many criminologists focus their research and teaching around well-defined subject areas: juvenile offending, environmental crime, etc. In order to be both effective and successful, a good criminologist will understand how specific laws relate to their area of study, including the history and evolution of those laws, and how they produce social impacts. From an academic and professional standpoint, becoming a good criminologist, or good student of criminology, means understanding the criminal law and its importance for social life.

Likewise, becoming a "good" criminal justice system practitioner (and by good we mean skilled, knowledgeable, and effective) requires knowledge of the criminal law, how it is enforced, and how it structures the actions of citizens, law enforcement, courts, and corrections. If you have any desire to work within the criminal justice system, for example as a police officer, special agent, or attorney, knowledge of the criminal law will be both required and vital to your success. Thus, honing one's knowledge and critical appreciation for the criminal law and how it works is as key to achieving success within the criminal justice field as it is within criminology.

The sections that follow provide a concise overview of some of the major topics surrounding the criminal law that are covered during the first year of law school. This chapter is an important one for developing foundational knowledge about the criminal law, which is critical for successfully studying criminology and criminal justice.

ORIGINS OF U.S. LAW

The origins of the American legal system reside in England. There, from the 11th century onward, formal rules for conduct and behavior were developed, which were far better at controlling people's conduct than the informal systems utilized prior. Because these laws were uniformly defined, applied, and enforced throughout England, the legal system was referred to as the "common law" system. When English settlers began colonizing America, they brought the common law system with them.

Two elements of the English common law tradition remain especially important to America's legal system today. First, the English believed the common law should evolve and improve primarily through judicial decisions occurring within the courts. This is known as judge-made law or, more commonly, case law. The emphasis on case law led to a second key development in English common law. Legal scholars and practitioners in England argued that prior legal decisions made by judges should influence future interpretations and/or applications of the law—thus was born the important idea of the legal precedent, or stare decisis.

When the American colonies gained their independence from England in 1776, the United States of America formally adopted many features and laws from the English common law system. However, there were some key differences.

Under America's common law system, the state and federal legislatures had the primary responsibility for creating laws, called statutes. Legislative law is thus referred to as statutory law. Also, while laws might be derived separately from the legislature, Constitution (constitutional law), and the executive branch (administrative law), their *interpretation* is almost always left to the courts. And, crucial to the process of interpreting the laws are past precedents.

For example, under the common law a person who is "insane" is not responsible for his or her actions and therefore cannot commit a crime. This principle was adopted within the American legal system from England. But what constitutes "insanity"? That decision was ultimately left to

Image 2.1 *Historically punishments for rule breaking have been swift and harsh. Corporal punishments and death sentences were common for "crimes" like witchcraft, theft, and more.*

Mary Evans Picture Library/Interfoto Agentur

Image 2.2
When Thomas Jefferson, John Adams, and others signed the declaration of independence in 1787, the newly formed United States of America adopted many custom from England, including the use of the common law system.

Mary Evans/Interfoto

the courts, which decided that a person is insane if, at the time of the act, he or she "did not know right from wrong" (for more on this see chapter 6). Thus, the legislature decided insanity was a defense against guilt, but the courts interpreted what insanity actually meant. Today in the United States, courts, especially the Supreme Court, play a critical role by interpreting how laws are enforced and applied (see chapter 6).

PRINCIPLES OF CRIMINAL LAW

The United States also adopted many broad legal principles from England. In most law textbooks today we refer to these principles as the *seven principles of criminal law*. It may help you to think of these principles as ingredients necessary to create valid criminal laws. You can also think of these principles as elements that a prosecutor must demonstrated existed beyond a reasonable doubt when a crime was committed in order to establish a defendant's criminal liability and obtain a conviction.

The seven principles of American criminal law are: (1) legality, (2) actus reus, (3) harm, (4) causation, (5) mens rea, (6) concurrence, and (7) punishment. Actus reus, harm, causation, mens rea, and concurrence—the five elements of criminal liability—are often termed the corpus delicti, or body of the crime. Let's now look briefly at each principle.

The principle of legality

In the former Soviet Union—and in some other countries today—lawmakers could pass laws that are retroactive. The following is a hypothetical example of a retroactive law: in December the State government made it a criminal offense to write or publish any report or story critical of the government. Amelia wrote an anti-government story four months before the law was created. However, the state has written the law so that people like Amelia can be arrested and prosecuted now even though their conduct was not criminal when it originally occurred.

This type of behavior is not allowed within English and U.S. law, both of which specifically prohibit **ex post facto** (i.e. retroactive) laws from being created. The primary reason the United States does not allow these types of laws, as you may have intuitively surmised, is because they are highly unfair and create an opportunity for lawmakers with bad motivations to exploit them.

More specifically, ex post facto laws are not allowed because they violate the principle of legality. The principle of legality says there must be a law written down (or "codified") that specifically prohibits a certain act at the time the act was committed for there to be a crime. If there is no law against the act when it occurs, there cannot be a crime (see Box 2.1).

An Oklahoma man was convicted of transporting a stolen airplane under a state statute that prohibited the transportation of stolen motor vehicles in 1931. By our standards today, his guilt seems clear because we know that we can't take someone else's plane and move it wherever we want. However, in 1931, things were different. The man appealed his conviction citing the principle of legality. In other words, he argued that the existing law prohibited transporting stolen motor vehicles, but said nothing about airplanes and, therefore, he could not be guilty of a crime. The U.S. Supreme Court ruled that the man was correct. Airplanes were not motor vehicles as defined in the state statute. Thus, while the man may have clearly done something morally wrong (i.e., stealing the airplane), there was no criminal statute explicitly prohibiting the transportation of a stolen airplane and his conviction was overturned.[5] Needless to say, the Oklahoma legislature quickly added "airplanes" to their law to fix this loophole. However, since criminal laws cannot be applied retroactively, the man was set free.

Actus reus (the criminal act), harm, causation, mens rea (criminal intent), and concurrence

The principle of actus reus indicates that criminal laws must prohibit wrongful "acts"; more importantly, a defendant must be shown to have committed that wrongful act in order to be guilty of a crime. In other words, a person cannot be guilty of a crime simply for thinking about doing something criminal.

The principles of harm and causation also factor in here insofar as the illegal, or wrongful, act must cause harm. In addition to the wrongful act that causes harm there must also be a guilty state of mind. This is the principle of mens rea, which translates from Latin into "guilty mind." A more familiar term for mens rea is criminal intent. In other words, the mens rea principle says that the wrongful act must have been committed intentionally.

BOX 2.1: CONNECTING THEORY TO PRACTICE

Ambiguity and the principle of legality

The issue of ambiguity, or vagueness, has been addressed in many cases throughout the history of U.S. criminal law.

Papachristou et al. v. City of Jacksonville, decided by the Supreme Court in 1972, is considered a landmark case on this topic and has had far-reaching implications for how homeless people in America are treated. The case centered around five homeless people who were convicted in Jacksonville, Florida for violating a city ordinance prohibiting vagrancy. The guilty verdict was appealed. The defense for the accused argued that the convictions should be overturned.

Specifically, the defense argued that the city vagrancy statute should be deemed **void for vagueness** because it did not provide adequate **fair warning** about exactly what type of behavior constituted "vagrancy." In other words, the concept of vagrancy was so broadly defined that it was impossible to know what, exactly, would constitute vagrant, and illegal, behavior v. lawful and acceptable behavior.

The appellate court agreed with the defense counsel. The convictions of the five defendants were reversed on the basis that the city ordinance was, in fact, too vague. The court cited an earlier case (*United States v. Reese*, 1875) in which it was said, "It would certainly be dangerous if the legislature could set a net large enough to catch all possible offenders, and leave it to the courts to step inside and say who could be rightfully detained, and who should be set at large."

Since the 1972 *Papachristou* case ruling, the interrelated ideas of vagueness, ambiguity, fair-warning, and the explicitness of the criminal law have continued to attract the attention of the nation's courts, including the United States Supreme Court.

For example, in the case *State v. Foglio* (1981) the defendant was charged with disorderly conduct resulting from the sale of tickets to view a pornographic film. The trial judge dismissed the complaint because he felt that the criminal statute, while it prohibited the sale of obscene materials, did not specifically mention the sale of tickets to *live* pornographic performances, and was therefore ambiguous and could not be applied. The prosecutor appealed, but the appellate court upheld the judge's dismissal of the case on the grounds that the statute was too vague, reiterating the principle that "before a man can be punished, his case must be plainly and unmistakably within the statute."

Even more recently, two cases went before the U.S. Supreme Court due to issues of vagueness and ambiguity. One involved the conviction of a neo-Nazi charged under the Federal Armed Career Criminal Act, which has long raised constitutional concerns due to issues of vagueness. Another case involves an individual facing a lengthy prison sentence for distributing "bath salts" in violation of the Controlled Substances Analogue Enforcement Act of 1986.

Both recent cases highlight the fact that the principle of legality, and what it takes for a criminal law to be considered valid and enforceable, is vital to the American criminal law and remains a key way that criminal defendants and attorneys can challenge the constitutionality of vague and/or ambiguous statutes.

Sources

State v. Foglio 182 NJ Super 12, 440A.2d 16 (1981)

Papachristou v. City of Jacksonville 405 US 156, 92 s ct. 839, 31 L. Ed. 2d 110 (1972)

United States v. Reese 92 US 214, 23 L. ed. 563 (1875)

Johnson v. United States 13–7120 (2015)

McFadden v. United States 14–378 (2015)

Also see Epps, G. 2014. "Too Vague to be Constitutional." *The Atlantic,* April 17.

Finally, the act, harm, causation, and intent must be linked—this is the principle of concurrence. That is, the criminal act that resulted in the harm must follow naturally from the intent to commit that act. It might be useful to think of concurrence as the glue that binds all of those other important principles together. Generally, a prosecutor must prove beyond a reasonable doubt that the act, harm, causation, mens rea, and concurrence elements existed and are linked to an individual's conduct. Conversely, a good defense attorney will try to show one or more of these elements were lacking.

Both harm and causation are broad ideas. Often, when we think of crimes we think of physical harms—injuries and death. Yet financial, emotional, sexual, psychological, and ecological harms can also result from wrongful acts.

Causation, like harm, is also a broad idea. Causation can be demonstrated in a number of ways and need not be as overt as the proverbial "smoking gun." For example, if you are charged with engaging in a criminal conspiracy, the prosecution need only demonstrate that you planned or intended to commit some wrongful act with other people and took at least one step, no matter how small, toward committing that act.

Likewise, for very serious violent crimes like murder, causation has no expiration date. This was illustrated recently with the death of James Brady. In the early 1980s, Mr. Brady was working as President Ronald Reagan's press secretary. On March 30, 1981, as President Reagan exited the Hilton Hotel in Washington, D.C., a deranged man, John Hinckley, Jr., opened fire with a pistol. One ricocheting bullet struck President Reagan, who survived, and another struck James Brady. As a result, Mr. Brady was partially paralyzed for the rest of his life. On August 4, 2014, at age 73, James Brady died. The coroner for Alexandria, VA ruled that Brady's death resulted directly from complications caused by Hinckley's bullet and was, thus, a homicide. Although prosecutors have said they will not charge and prosecute Hinckley for Brady's death, since Hinckley is confined to a secure mental hospital, if they wanted to they could, thanks to the principle of causation: Hinckley's violent criminal act (shooting Brady) led directly to Brady's paralysis and eventual death.

Image 2.3 *The attempted assassination of Ronald Reagan by John Hinckley Jr. on March 31, 1981 outside the Hilton Hotel in Washington, D.C. gained worldwide attention and eventually led to major reform of the insanity defence.*
ZUMA/REX/Shuttestock

Image 2.4 *John W. Hinckley, Jr. is shown arriving in chains at the Quantico Marine Base in 1981 after attempting to kill President Ronald Reagan. Hinckley was later convicted of his crimes and confined to a mental hospital. In September 2016, Hinckley was finally released into the care of his mother in Virginia.*

Bob Daugherty/AP/Press Association Images

Finally, the principle of intent or mens rea, which holds that for an act to be a crime, the person committing the act must have *intended* to commit it, does not mean the person had to intend to commit a *crime*. People may believe they are behaving legally, but if their act is a crime and they intended to commit the act, then they can be held accountable for the crime.

For example, a husband may believe he has the right to have sex with his wife whether she consents or not. Indeed, in the not-too-distant past, statutes and court decisions gave a husband the right to rape his wife. Rape laws have changed, however, and it is now a crime if anyone (man or woman) physically forces sexual intercourse on another person, including a spouse. Therefore, whether or not someone believes he/she has the legal right to have sex with their spouse, it is nonetheless against the law to force anyone, including a spouse, into a sexual activity. A person who forces or coerces such behavior has committed a crime.

Thus, for most offenses prosecutors must only demonstrate that the accused possessed **general intent**—they intended to commit the wrongful act regardless of whether they intended the actual outcome or harm that resulted (i.e., death). For other offenses, however, prosecutors must show the defendant possessed **specific intent**, meaning they intentionally committed the wrongful act *and* intended to produce the harm that resulted. For example, a statute that defines burglary as the "unlawful entry of a structure with the intent to commit a crime therein" would be a specific intent crime—first, prosecutors would need to show you committed the wrongful act (unlawfully entering the structure) in order to commit a specific harm (committing a crime therein).

Over the years the courts have expanded and broadened the applicability of intent to cover a wide range of behaviors and to hold people responsible for the consequences of acts they intended to commit even if they did not intend the consequences. In fleeing a robbery, a robber may be chased by a policewoman who crashes her car into a light post and dies. The robber may be tried for murder (under the *felony-murder rule*) even though he did not intend to kill the policewoman, he only intended to flee the crime scene. Nevertheless, the act of fleeing the scene of the robbery put others at risk to such a degree that the perpetrator is considered to have intended the consequences.

BOX 2.2: CONSIDER THIS . . .

Interpreting mens rea or criminal intent

In 1946, two young men were playing a game of "Russian Roulette," where one bullet is placed into the cylinder of a revolver. Each player points the partially loaded gun at the other and pulls the trigger, hoping, of course, that the firing pin strikes an empty chamber. When Malone, 17 at the time, pointed the gun at his friend Long, the chamber with the bullet in it fired. Long was killed instantly, and Malone was eventually convicted of the crime of manslaughter.

Malone appealed his conviction on the grounds that he did not intend to kill his friend, and because he lacked "criminal intent," he could not be guilty of committing a crime. The appellate court disagreed, affirming his conviction on the grounds that although Malone may not have intended to kill his friend, his recklessness was so blatant that he could, and should, have anticipated the likelihood that his intended action (pulling the trigger on a partially loaded gun) could result in Long's death. There was, then, according to the court, the necessary intent to commit a reckless act that led to the death of another person.

A later case, *People* v. *Newton* (1973), illustrates the principle that there must be a combination of *mens rea* and *voluntary* action for a person's conduct to be considered criminal. In this particular case, the defendant, Newton, was convicted under a New York statute for possessing a pistol and ammunition. Newton did not dispute that he was clearly in possession of these items, but he argued, successfully, that his possession of these items in New York was neither intended nor voluntary, because the aircraft on which he was a passenger made an unscheduled landing in the State, whereupon the prohibited items were discovered.

How might the decision in the case of *People v. Newton* have been different if Newton's actions were believed to be part of a terrorist plot? Suppose the law enforcement agency that arrested him thought he was carrying the weapon to another destination in order to hijack the plane after it left New York. Would the court's decision have been different? *What do you think?*

Sources
Commonwealth v. Malone 354 Pa. 180, 47 A.2d 445 (1946)
People v. Newton 72 Misc.2d 646, 340 NYS 2d. 77 (Sup. Ct. 1973)

Notice that merely *intending* to commit a crime is not a crime. In criminal law, intention must be accompanied by an *act*. If someone simply intends to rob a bank but does not engage in any overt action toward accomplishing the robbery, there is no crime. Intent must be tied to an action. That action need not be the crime, however: *preparing* to commit the crime is also considered part of the necessary act. If a politician plans to accept a bribe, contacts a potential briber, and arranges to meet him or her, these actions are sufficient to constitute a coincidence of intent and act and could well be found to constitute a crime (see Box 2.2 for two other examples).

There is, however, an important qualification with respect to intent. Someone who suffers "diminished responsibility" cannot be assumed to have the element of intent in his or her actions. The most important example is a person who suffers a mental illness; other exceptions are those under the influence of alcohol or drugs, the mentally incompetent, and people whose mental condition impairs their judgment. All may be defended against criminal charges on the grounds they had "diminished responsibility" even though they clearly intended to commit the crime.

Punishment

Criminal law also requires that some punishment be specified in order for an act, or a failure to act, to be a crime. **Punishment** means a person found guilty of violating the law must be given a fine, imprisonment, or both. A criminal law is not valid and cannot be enforced if the crime does not have a defined punishment.

Thus, in reviewing municipal code violations, one might read: "violations of these codes may be punished by fines of no less than $50 and no more than $300, or imprisonment for no longer than 30 days." These general punishments are thus applicable to every single code. Other times, a crime might have a specific punishment noted after it is defined. A statute that simply says it is against the law to spit on the sidewalk, but does not specify the punishment for violations would be non-enforceable. Indeed, one of the key differences between criminal and civil law is that criminal laws must specify a punishment, whereas civil laws do not have to do so.

INTERNATIONAL COMMON V. INTERNATIONAL CIVIL LAW

The legal system of the United States is based on the idea of common law, where prior cases and decisions inform present cases and decisions. Common law is thus law that is built up over time. Because of this, common law is considered a complicated legal system and is not very popular. Only 19 percent of the world's nations—primarily former English and American colonies (i.e. India, Philippines, Australia)—utilize the common law system.

Within a common law system there can be multiple branches of law. In America, for example, there are separate systems of criminal and civil law. It is worth noting that in the common law system, judges play a significant role at the appellate (appeals) level, but during criminal and civil trials they act more as court room managers. Courts in a common law system are sites of competition; especially in criminal cases the defense and prosecution square off, arguing over evidence collected by police investigators.

The most prevalent legal system in the world differs significantly from the common law system we use in the United States and should not be confused with American civil law (discussed below). Civil law, also called continental law, is used by nearly half the world's nations, including nearly all the countries in Europe, Central and South America, and many countries in Africa and Asia. As a legal system, civil law is much older than common law, dating back at least as far as King Hammurabi of Babylonia (discussed in chapter 7) and the Roman Empire.

Unlike common law, the international civil law system is one where each country creates laws not through the building up of past cases and legal precedents (as in common law), but by debating and then writing down a "code" of laws that is then universally applied from the top (national legislature) down to the citizens. As such, laws are considered whole and complete the day they are codified (made official) and are not subject to as much interpretation or change over time as laws within the common law system.

One of the most glaring differences between the common and civil law systems is, however, the way things play out in the courtroom. Civil law systems utilize juries far less than in the common law and give a much bigger role to judges. Indeed, civil law systems are considered "inquisitorial" rather than "adversarial." What does this mean?

Well, first it means that prior to trial in the civil law system nearly every piece of evidence, every witness, all suspects, and so on, will be identified and analyzed in minute detail. By the time the trial occurs there is essentially no doubt about the guilt of the suspect being charged. The purpose of the intensive inquisitorial process pre-trial is to ensure only the truly guilty are subjected to a trial. By contrast, in the common law system, the trial itself serves as a "fact-finding" endeavor, with guilt or innocence determined after each side argues and presents evidence to support its case.

Throughout the inquisitorial process and trial, the civil system judge (or judges) plays a big role. They are allowed to call and interview witnesses, review evidence, and so on. And, when juries are used, they too are given significant power to question witnesses and the accused. Some argue, however, that much of what takes place in a civil system trial is for show, since the very act of having a trial presumes the guilty person has already been clearly identified and brought forward. Thus, for instance, some have written of the French legal system that "the French investigation takes place under the presumption of innocence, but a French trial takes place under the presumption of guilt."[6]

Take a moment and think about both systems of law. Which would you rather live within? Would your opinion change if you were in trouble for a crime? Why or why not?

AMERICAN CRIMINAL V. CIVIL LAW

Most law students eventually choose a legal specialty area to focus upon, such as environment, civil rights, family, or intellectual property law. However, prior to choosing a specialization, all law students are exposed to core courses that tackle the cornerstones of legal knowledge and practice: criminal and civil law.

The criminal law is where some types of conduct considered very harmful are outlawed by society. This conduct can be committed by individuals or organizations. Most criminal laws are created by legislatures of the States and the federal government. Because the operative principle that justifies the creation of criminal law is that of harm and its prevention on behalf of the greater good, when a crime is committed there are always at least two victims: the individual or organization who is directly harmed, and the State, whose law was broken. For that reason, the State always files charges and prosecutes people accused of committing crimes. As a result, this responsibility never falls on the shoulders of ordinary people.

Types of criminal law

America has two equally important areas of criminal law.

The substantive criminal law is where crimes and punishments are specified. In other words, this branch of law tells us what behavior is unacceptable and what the punishment will be if we engage in that behavior. Additionally, the substantive criminal law provides us with important information about the elements of crimes that must be proven by the State in order to obtain a conviction. Importantly, it is from the substantive criminal law that we also learn what sorts of defenses can be raised by people who are accused of committing crimes (see Figure 2.1).

The substantive criminal law contrasts with procedural criminal law, which deals exclusively with, as you may have guessed, issues of process and procedure. The procedural criminal law specifies how crimes can be investigated and prosecuted. This branch of law is where the balance between individual rights and autonomy and government oversight and control is negotiated. Among the topics covered within the procedural criminal law are those dealing with the processes police can use to investigate crimes and detain and question suspects, such as when and how they can conduct a search and seizure, an arrest, an interrogation, etc. Additionally, the procedural criminal law describes many of the processes used during criminal trials, including pre-trial motions, sentencing, and appeals. (To learn what it's like to work in criminal defense, see Box 2.3.)

Figure 2.1
Key foci of
substantive and
procedural criminal
law

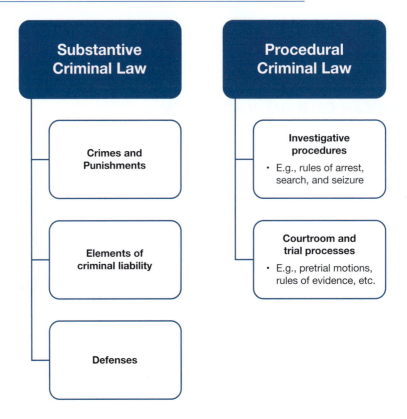

The concept of **due process,** which ensures our individual rights are protected against government overreach, is important to the procedural criminal law. Both the 5th and 14th Amendments to the U.S. Constitution invoke the concept of due process. Other key aspects of procedural law are derived from the 8th and 4th Amendments to the United States Constitution. These amendments and their key elements, including those related to "due process," are summarized in Table 2.1.

By contrast, **civil law** deals with private wrongs that occur between individuals and corporations (see Table 2.3 for a quick summary of the main differences between criminal and civil law). Civil law serves an important function in society by specifying an even broader range of unacceptable conduct and providing remedies when unacceptable, though not necessarily criminal, conduct occurs (see Table 2.2 for brief description of the major types of civil law).

Because civil law deals with private wrongs, individuals or organizations must advocate on their own behalf; this means they must file a civil lawsuit or otherwise seek redress against the party alleged to have harmed them, thus becoming the **plaintiffs.**

In some instances, a wrongful act can be prosecuted as both a crime and a civil wrong. One excellent example of this occurring involves the former NFL football player and Heisman Trophy winner Orenthal J. Simpson, better known as O.J. Simpson.

Table 2.1 The Constitution and criminal law

Amendment	Key elements
14th (due process)	• No person shall be deprived of life, liberty, or property without due process of law. • Everyone is entitled to due process and equal protection under the law.
8th	• Prohibits cruel and unusual punishments • Prohibits excessive fines and bail
6th	• Ensures right to speedy, public trial • Ensures right to an attorney • Ensures right to an impartial jury • Ensures right to know your accusers

5th (due process)	• Guarantees due process rights and protections, including:
	  – The right to a grand jury hearing in capital cases
	  – Protection against double jeopardy
	  – Protection against self-incrimination

4th	• Protects against unreasonable searches and seizures • Protects against arbitrary arrests • Declares that warrants for searches and arrests must be based upon probable cause

Table 2.2 Major types of civil law

Type of civil law	What it deals with
Torts	Injuries to people or property
Property	Property rights, ownership, acquisition, and inheritance
Contracts	Private agreements between people and organizations
Family	Marriage, divorces, child custody
Juvenile	Behavior and punishment of minors (under age 18)

In the early 1990s, O.J. Simpson was put on trial in California for killing his ex-wife, Nicole Brown Simpson, and a local waiter, Ron Goldman. If convicted, Simpson would certainly have earned a lengthy prison sentence and could have faced the death penalty. However, after a highly publicized and contentious trial, a jury acquitted Simpson of the two murders.

Believing him to be guilty, the family of Nicole Brown Simpson filed a wrongful death lawsuit against Simpson in California's civil court system. After a jury again heard the evidence against Simpson, they found him liable for Nicole's death. The jury was able to arrive at this verdict in part because the standard of proof necessary to find someone liable for commiting some act in civil court proceedings (by a preponderance of the evidence) is much easier to meet than in criminal trials. In other words, in a civil court all that needs to be demonstrated is that the accused "probably caused" the harm. Because he

Table 2.3 Major differences between civil and criminal law and procedure

Criminal law	Civil law
Victims are individuals and the state	Victims are individuals and organizations
State prosecutes on behalf of individuals	Individuals and organizations must file suit
Opposing parties are prosecutor and defendant	Opposing parties are plaintiff and defendant
Burden of proof is beyond a reasonable doubt and is borne by the prosecution	Burden of proof is by a preponderance of the evidence and is mostly borne by the Plaintiff
Hearsay evidence is inadmissible	Hearsay evidence is admissible
Spousal testimony may be admissible if given but court cannot be required	The court can require spousal testimony
Findings are of guilt or innocence	Findings are of liability
Conviction culminates fines, imprisonment, or both	If found liable, one may be fined or ordered to pay restitution; imprisonment is never an option.
Defendant rights are protected under various Amendments to U.S. Constitution	Rights provided by Amendments are not applicable in civil cases

was found liable for Nicole's death in civil court, Simpson was ordered to pay her family millions of dollars in restitution.

The outcome of Mr. Simpson's civil trial highlights several important points. First, there are times when a defendant may face criminal and civil charges and move through both the criminal and civil court systems. Violent crimes, in particular, can often result in a separate civil lawsuit. Second, because Mr. Simpson avoided a finding of guilt in his criminal trial, there was no chance he could be incarcerated for the deaths of Ron and Nicole because the double jeopardy clause of the Fifth Amendment prohibits anyone from being prosecuted twice for the same crime. Civil court penalties are distinct from criminal court ones. Thus, even if you are found liable in civil court for committing some violation of the civil law, as Mr. Simpson was for harming his ex-wife Nicole, a finding of civil liability cannot lead to incarceration.

STATE AND FEDERAL CRIMINAL LAW

State-level criminal law

Every state in the United States has a criminal code where criminal conduct is defined. These criminal codes are crafted by state legislatures. The reason for this is because the United States Constitution vests authority for determining criminal liability primarily with the states.[7]

There are 52 separate criminal codes in America (one for each state, one for Washington, D.C., and one for the federal government). Each state's criminal

BOX 2.3: WORKING IN . . . CRIMINAL LAW

Contributed by **Elise Logemann, Director of Client and Member Services and Supervising Attorney, Colorado Juvenile Defender Center**

Working as a "criminal lawyer" can mean many things: Some lawyers become prosecutors, some work in criminal defense, and others become civil attorneys whose work specializes in issues that relate to the criminal law—for example, they may file claims of false arrest, false imprisonment, or the excessive use of force by police officers.

Criminal defense attorneys are critical in the United States because our criminal courts utilize an adversarial system where two parties (the victim and the person accused of committing an offense) present their positions to a judge or jury. Because the prosecution has the power to decide what charges to file, investigate the crime through the police department, and pay attorneys with government dollars to prepare a case for trial, the accused party is often unable to fairly defend themselves without the aid of a trained defense attorney. In the United States, unlike in some other countries, people accused of committing crimes are entitled to a defense attorney to prepare and present a defense and to protect his or her rights under the Constitution, even if he or she cannot afford to pay one.

Defense attorneys may work in a variety of environments. Public defenders work for counties, states, or the federal government. They get paid by the government to represent people who have been accused of committing crimes but who cannot afford to hire their own attorney. In some states there are no "public defenders"; instead, lawyers are appointed by the court to represent indigent people who are accused of crimes and paid by the government as appointed counsel. Defense attorneys may also work for clients who can afford to pay them privately, either as solo practitioners or as part of both small and large law firms. Defense attorneys may specialize in a particular area of law; for example, DUIs, juvenile defense, or sexual offenses. Because there are so many types of defense work, it is important for defense attorneys to become experts in their specific areas of practice.

Many defense attorneys start out by working in a public defender's office. Because public defender offices experience extremely high caseloads (sometimes in excess of a thousand cases per defender per year[8]) young attorneys who go to work as public defenders are given many opportunities to learn how to defend people in court. Law school classes often fail to teach the "ins and outs" of being in court. To learn to do this well, young defense attorneys must pick the right office and seek adequate training and supervision. Because some public defense offices have very little funding, many public defenders are overloaded with too many cases. National standards suggest a case limit of 150 felony cases per year per attorney, but felony caseloads of 500, 600, or 800 can be common among public defenders.[9] Also, because funding for public defense is limited, public defender offices may not have the capacity to provide new hires with thorough training or supervision. These are all things to research and ask about if you seek a job as a public defender after graduating from law school.

Lawyers who do work for public defenders have a job that is sometimes thankless and less well compensated than other types of legal work. However, being a public defender provides a unique opportunity to help others and serve the public. Public defenders are often not initially trusted by the accused person, since they are "free" lawyers offered by the very government that is prosecuting the accused person. Public defenders therefore must spend time building strong relationships with their clients to earn the trust necessary to provide good representation.

Good public defenders can positively influence the lives of each and every client they serve. These clients are indigent individuals who are often incarcerated as they await trial. As a result, they may feel even more helpless to defend themselves or find a fair outcome. Defense attorneys can assist these people by providing thorough and zealous representation, fighting unfair charges, and fighting for the best outcome for every client in every case.

code specifies which acts are illegal and prohibited within that state and what the corresponding punishment for committing those acts will be. Criminal codes also detail which defenses are acceptable, other rules of criminal procedure, and the **statute of limitations** for each criminal offense—the window of time after the crime was committed that the state can file charges and pursue a prosecution. In addition to the state criminal code, municipalities (cities and towns) within states also create their own municipal codes which contain laws called "ordinances." Violating a municipal ordinance can often qualify as committing a misdemeanor crime.

There is room for variation among state criminal laws and punishments— so much so that Robinson and Dubber note it is "often difficult to state *the* American rule on *any* point of criminal law."[10] The approach to homosexuality, which was criminalized and prosecuted in states like Texas and Alabama, and the recent decriminalization and then legalization of marijuana in Colorado and Washington are illustrative of this point. However, all states tend to similarly criminalize and penalize acts like murder, rape, robbery, burglary, arson, and the other street crimes.

Today, there is much less variation among state criminal laws than there used to be, thanks to the American Law Institute's creation of the **Model Penal Code** (MPC) in 1962. The MPC was developed to address the inconsistencies and variations among criminal codes in America. It is a guideline of "best" practices that many states have now utilized to reform and revise their criminal codes,[11] thus helping reduce the variation in criminal laws throughout the United States.

Federal criminal law

The United States constitution purposely limits the power of the Federal government. The founders of the United States had several reasons for both limiting and ensuring a system of "checks and balances" of federal power, not least of which was their desire to avoid the pitfalls that accompany the centralization of absolute power, which happens in monarchies, dictator-ships, and totalitarian forms of government. The Founding Fathers observed firsthand the wickedness of power wielded without constraint in the monarchies of old Europe (including England, France, and Germany) and in other nations where totalitarianism and authoritarianism were the primary foundation of government.

As a result, the U.S. federal government's role in criminal law and procedure is far more limited than the states'. The vast majority of all criminal prosecutions and court cases, over 90 percent, occur at the state level.[12] Nevertheless, there are criminal laws at the national (i.e., federal) level—laws that have been enacted by the federal legislature (the United States Congress) and codified within the Federal Criminal Code. The first attempt to create a federal criminal code occurred in 1826, but it was not until June 1948, that Title 18, "Crimes and Criminal Procedure," of the United States Code (USC) was formally established. Title 18 lists a variety of federal criminal offenses and their corresponding punishments.

In keeping with the stipulations of the Constitution, Title 18 primarily deals with conduct that would be difficult for states alone to enforce and prosecute. For example, crimes that transgress multiple state boundaries, like drug trafficking, organized crime, cybercrime, wire fraud, etc., are difficult for states to prosecute, so they fall under the purview of the federal government and its law enforcement agencies (like the Federal Bureau of Investigation or Drug Enforcement Agency). The federal criminal code also focuses on conduct that directly impacts the operations or functions of the federal government, its agencies, or its agents. Thus, acts of terrorism, espionage, treason, assassination, and counterfeiting of U.S. currency all fall under the jurisdiction of the Federal Criminal Code, as do crimes like bank robbery, tax evasion, and a slew of other financial crimes. Breaking any of those laws is considered a federal offense and prosecutions are carried out by district and deputy district attorneys within the federal court system. In many instances, committing one of these crimes also violates state laws, but it is the federal government that has first choice about whether or not to pursue a prosecution.

THEORIES OF CRIMINAL LAW CREATION

At the beginning of this chapter we explained that the primary functions of laws, especially criminal laws, are to protect people from harm and establish boundaries and a sense of order within society. We also highlighted the fact that the processes of creating laws, and identifying crimes and criminals, is that of consciously setting certain acts and people apart from others. This process of setting apart, of making laws and crimes, would not occur if we (people) didn't actively make it happen. And, as we already know, laws are technically made through legislative, executive, and judicial actions.

Table 2.4 Overview of theories of law creation

Theory	Key person	Main idea
Consensus	Emile Durkheim	Laws reflect societal consensus about what is right, and legal, versus what is wrong, and therefore illegal.
Societal needs	Jerome Hall	Laws are created in response to society's needs.
Ruling class/pluralist	Karl Marx and Lawrence Friedman	Interest groups compete for laws in their favor. Law reflects the interests and ideology of the ruling class.
Structural contradictions	William Chambliss	Contradictions in the structure of capitalist societies lead to social and political conflicts. These conflicts create dilemmas that legislators and judges attempt to resolve by creating new laws. The underlying contradiction is not fixed, which ultimately leads to new conflicts and more legal remedies.

But it is important to look beyond the technical aspects of law creation and seek out explanations of where the origins of laws reside. In other words, how do we explain where the ideas and motivation to create laws come from? Do laws reflect societal consensus about what is wrong or unacceptable? Do laws arise primarily to benefit certain powerful groups over less powerful ones? These questions and more are explored below as we discuss three different theories of law creation (also see Table 2.4).

Consensus theory

Empirical and anecdotal research on the origins of American criminal law does not appear to support consensus theory. **Consensus theory** argues that all laws reflect societal consensus about what is right (and should be tolerated) and what is wrong (and should not be tolerated). This view is closely associated with French sociologist Émile Durkheim, who claimed that criminal law reflects customary beliefs, widely held values, and widespread societal consensus about what is right or wrong.

Victimless crimes, otherwise called moral or public order offenses, illustrate just how little consensus can exist regarding the law. Laws prohibiting criminal acts like drug use, prostitution, gambling, and vagrancy do not reflect unanimous consensus among all members of society that those acts or behaviors are wrong and should be criminalized. Indeed, even referring to those acts as "victimless" implies a lack of consensus about the harm they pose to society.

Certainly, some people support the continued criminalization of drug use, prostitution, and other acts—but many others do not, which is one reason these acts are so hotly debated in American society. Changes to marijuana laws in states like Colorado and Washington, where it is now legal to sell, purchase, and consume marijuana, further highlight the fact that there may actually be growing consensus *against* the criminalization of these events. Legal changes like this also underscore the ideas that social laws are flexible, capable of change, and socially constructed.

This does not mean there is never any consensus among a community of people about right and wrong. It means we can't say that consensus uniformly explains why some acts are defined as criminal while others are not. And, even when there is apparent consensus, agreement can be fragile. Most people in the United States would certainly agree there should be laws against "violence," yet violence is an "ambiguous term whose meaning is established through political processes."[13]

Consider the politicization of aggression. In a speech on May 10, 1984, President Ronald Reagan characterized the government of Nicaragua as supporting and arming "terrorists and guerrillas" and the contras—a group fighting against the Nicaraguan government—as "freedom fighters." However, as is often the case, one person's "freedom fighters" are another person's "terrorists and guerrillas."

Even the dictum "thou shalt not kill" is a telling example of how slippery consensus can be.[14] Killing is not always against the law and is in fact often praised as honorable. Soldiers kill in wartime; executioners pull the switch. Governments plot and carry out assassinations of government leaders in peace and in war.[15] In fact, *not* killing may itself be a crime. For example, a soldier who refuses to kill the enemy is often guilty of committing a crime: dereliction of duty.

Image 2.5

Sociologist Émile Durkheim (1858–1917) is best known for his contributions to the development of the sociological discipline, his research on suicide and social change, and his view that criminal law reflects customary beliefs held by the majority of society's members.

Bettmann/Contributor

Societal needs theory

Another theory to account for the origins of law is associated with legal scholar Jerome Hall.[16] The societal needs theory says that criminal laws reflect the needs of the entire society—not just a segment or group within that society. The first critical question we should ask about this theory is, "whose needs are being met?" Every modern society consists of many different groups and social classes. Can we assume they all share the same basic needs and that *all* laws reflect what is best for everyone? In complex modern societies like U.S. society, people and groups are divided by many things, including race, class, ethnicity, gender, politics, and geography. Those divisions and differences translate into vastly different needs and interests so we clearly cannot make this basic assumption.

If we examine different laws created throughout history, we find plenty of examples that undermine the view that laws always reflect societal needs.

For example, laws against theft arose when merchants transporting goods began to have those goods stolen (i.e., the Carrier case of 1473). Stealing the property of others thus became a crime. In modern society, we are all protected by laws against theft, but the origins of those laws clearly benefitted one group's needs—merchants—over another group's needs—the people taking the goods. Perhaps those people committing the thefts had no money, no food, and no chance of getting a job and needed to steal to get money, food, etc. Regardless, their needs were not the needs the law responded to.

Laws against vagrancy (essentially unemployed homelessness) reflect the British monarchy's concern to protect the interests of feudal landowners by providing an abundance of cheap labor even as the feudal system was breaking down and the pool of available labor to work the land was being depleted around the 1300s.[17] Vagrancy laws offered people who had been arrested an out—go to work for these landowners or remain incarcerated under horrible conditions.

In the United States, during the late 19th and early 20th centuries, vagrancy statutes were used much as they had been in early England. The end of the Civil War left southern plantation owners and northern industrialists wishing to industrialize the south without an adequate work force. One solution was to arrest "free Negroes" for vagrancy and force them to labor by leasing them to landowners, mining companies, or industrialists (convict-leasing).[18] As a practical matter, the long, disreputable history of vagrancy statutes in the United States ended with the 1972 Supreme Court decision declaring a Jacksonville, Florida, ordinance unconstitutional because it was being used to arrest people on suspicion of future criminality (as discussed in Box 2.1).

Laws criminalizing vagrancy clearly responded to the needs of one group at the expense of other groups. "Societal needs" were nonexistent; the needs of one class of people were in conflict with the needs of another. The state chose sides, and criminal laws against vagrancy reflected this choice. The idea that criminal law reflects societal needs appears at first brush like indisputable common sense, and it may be that some laws do reflect widespread societal needs. Closer scrutiny and practical research suggest, however, that this "common sense" theory is not an adequate explanation for the origins of *all* laws.

Ruling class and pluralistic theory (conflict theory)

Both consensus and societal needs theories are sociological, but they are also inadequate as "general" explanations for where laws come from. Faced with the failure of these approaches, social scientists have sought alternative explanations.

Ruling class and pluralistic theories, whose origins lie in the ideas of political theorists like Niccolo Machiavelli, Wilfredo Pareto, Karl Marx, and Max Weber say that laws reflect the interests and ideology of the most powerful "ruling classes," or interest groups, in society.

Image 2.6
*The ruling class/
pluralist theory of
law creation views
society as a place of
conflicts between
classes or interest
groups. From this
view, laws tend to
benefit those with
money and power,
and work against,
even oppress, those
without money and
power, like this
destitute,
unemployed man.*

Franklin D. Roosevelt
Library

Sociologist Max Weber put it this way:

> with government as an instrument or vehicle available to whomever can
> control or use it, opportunities for gain, whether pecuniary or political or
> other advantage, accrue to those who can use government.[19]

Who is most likely to use and control the government? According to Karl
Marx: "In every era the ruling ideas are the ideas of the ruling class."[20]

For both Marx and Weber the ruling class consists of those who control the
most economic resources and political power. Likewise, the most powerful
interest groups are also likely to possess more resources and more connections.
Thus, the idea that the ruling class or dominant interest group determines the
content and functioning of criminal (as well as other) law makes sense. As we
have seen, it is also more consistent with what we know about the historical
development of laws, including those against theft, vagrancy, and public order
offenses like drug use.

Ideas from the ruling class/pluralist camp find some support from research
into the lawmaking process. Legislation requiring meatpacking companies to
comply with federal health regulations, for instance, was widely publicized as
a moral campaign to protect consumers. In reality, the legislation was sought,

Image 2.7 *Karl Marx, German radical political thinker*

Mary Evans Picture Library

Image 2.8 *Max Weber (1864–1920), German political economist and sociologist, one of the fathers of modern sociology. His best known work is* The Protestant Ethic and the Spirit of Capitalism. *Ca. 1910.*

Mary Evans/Everett Collection

lobbied for, and largely written by the nation's largest meatpacking companies to give themselves a competitive advantage over smaller ones that would struggle to bear the added costs of complying with the regulations.[21] We find similar results in research on other industries.[22,23]

These explanations fail, however, when we try to apply them to the entire spectrum of law. For instance, in the 1800s and early 1900s it was a crime for workers to engage in strikes or boycotts or try to organize themselves into labor unions. Today, the opposite is true and it is actually a crime for employers to interfere or prevent their employees from organizing and forming unions.[24] Thus, employment law changed against the desires, ideals, and interests of the most powerful classes or groups in society.[25]

However, one could argue that even when laws appear to be against the short-term interests of the ruling class or powerful interest groups, they are essential for purposes of legitimacy. If people felt the State and the most powerful classes were always working together to oppress or control everyone else, there would likely be massive protests and conflicts. Thus, according to ruling class/pluralistic theories of law creation, the law must *appear* to be representing everyone, which sometimes means occasionally passing laws against the most powerful classes and interest groups in society.[26]

The arguments of ruling class theory have some cogency, but they are nonetheless limited. Clearly, some laws that appear to conflict with ruling-class interests are, in reality, designed to subtly serve their interests.[27] On the other hand, the ruling class is not one monolithic class with identical interests. Nor do all laws favor only those people and groups with power. The history of legislation is full of examples of powerful groups and factions struggling against each other.

That the ruling class and powerful interest groups influence law creation, and even vast areas of law, cannot be denied. But it is important to note, as we have with the other theories discussed, that explaining the origins of law in reference solely to the interests of the ruling classes or most powerful interest groups in society is not by itself adequate for understanding where all laws come from or how they get made.

GENDER, RACE, AGE, AND THE CRIMINAL LAW

Women and the criminal law

In 1867, the U.S. Supreme Court ruled that a woman who had successfully completed law school and passed the bar in Illinois had no right to practice law. In 1869, the University of Edinburgh in Scotland refused to award the University's chemistry prize to the student with the highest marks, as was the tradition, because the student with the highest marks in chemistry that year was a woman. The controversy at Edinburgh grew so heated that the University ultimately decided women could no longer attend the school. The seven women who had fought for admission went to court to sue for their right to attend the University. The court ruled the University had the right to discriminate against women even though it could not discriminate based on religion or race.[28]

These and countless other examples—like the fact that English women could not serve in Parliament or city councils in the 1800s or that women in the United States were denied the right to vote until the early 20th century—illustrate that the law is not always applied equally or fairly. Laws have, and do, discriminate against particular groups based on a variety of factors, including one's biological sex.

The history of laws in England and the United States is also a history of institutionalized sexual discrimination. Laws in both countries reflect the concept of **patriarchy**, or a system of social organization where men hold more power and rights than women. Changes to the laws of both countries to create more equality and fairness only occurred once women began consistently opposing the institutionalized oppression and exploitation that confronted them at every turn. It was not the case that the law gradually changed as customs and beliefs changed, or that male legislators, lawyers, and judges became fairer and more

Image 2.9 *Women march down 5th Avenue in New York City in support of women's rights during the 1970s.*

AP/Press Association Images

tolerant as the logic of a democratic and free society for all slowly worked its magic through legal reasoning. The laws changed as women were willing to collectively and individually violate the law and demand equal justice.

One hundred and fifty years of female struggle for equality in law have brought changes but not complete equality. In Wisconsin a wife can be disinherited by her husband; in most states women cannot co-sign for a loan even though the property is jointly owned; in some states a man can legally kill his wife if he finds her having sexual relations with another man; in rape cases a woman with prior sexual experience is less likely to be believed if she claims she was raped. Women continue to be seen in law and in practice as "property" to be owned and controlled by men even if, on the surface, it appears that women are no longer legally discriminated against.[29]

Women's rights movements and struggles effectively changed the law in America. Perhaps the most important change to take place in the law with respect to women occurred when the Supreme Court decided *Roe v. Wade*. That case asked the Supreme Court to rule on the constitutionality of state laws that made it a crime to obtain or perform an abortion "during the first trimester of pregnancy."[30] Abortion laws had for years restricted a woman's right to determine her own destiny. They also discriminated against poor women by making abortions illegal, unaffordable, and incredibly dangerous. The women's rights movement focused considerable attention on these laws, generating conflict between those who sought to maintain male dominance over women and those who sought to give women the right to choose. While the Supreme Court ultimately decided in *Roe v. Wade* that those existing state laws were unconstitutional, thus making abortion legal, the conflict over abortion has not abated. Over the last decade, states like Texas[31] and Kansas[32] have continuously attempted to erode the rights of women to make decisions about childbirth and their lives. We can anticipate continued conflicts to arise as women seek to attain true equality within the law and those who fear such equality push back.[33]

Race and the criminal law

The history of U.S. law is also a history of racial and ethnic discrimination. At various times Native Americans, Hispanic Americans, Irish, Italian, and African Americans have all been legally discriminated against. Indeed, if one looks at the origins of laws prohibiting and criminalizing substances, including alcohol and drugs, one finds that these laws all have racially or ethnically discriminatory origins.

For example, laws outlawing opium use in the 1870s characterized the drug as the "Mongolian vice" at a time when Asian, particularly Chinese, immigrants were challenging whites for jobs in the American West. Laws against cocaine, which was widely available and used by middle and upper class whites into the late 1800s, targeted African American men for social and political reasons.[34] The American Temperance Movement, which led to the Volstead Act's nationwide ban on alcohol in the 1920s, portrayed alcoholism and alcohol-related public order offenses and crimes as a direct by-product of Irish and Italian immigration to America. Not surprisingly, at the time the Volstead Act was created, the predominantly Catholic Irish and Italian immigrants were challenging Protestant Americans, who considered themselves "true Americans," for jobs. Even the criminalization of marijuana has racist origins as that drug was portrayed as the drug of choice for Mexicans and other Hispanic ethnicities, who, to build on a common theme, were arriving in America and competing with those already here for employment.

There are several key takeaway points from this discussion of racial discrimination in drug laws. First, the creation of these laws seems to support the ruling-class/pluralistic notion of how laws get created. Second, these laws have produced stereotypes about certain racial and ethnic groups that exist to this day.

For instance, being Irish became so synonymous with being a drunk and a troublemaker that a new phrase entered common usage: the paddy wagon. "Paddy" is a slang term for "Irish" and the "paddy wagon" was a vehicle used by police to transport criminals to court or jail/prison. Similarly, given the history of cocaine legislation, it is not surprising that sentencing disparities arose in the 1980s that punished people caught with crack cocaine 100 times more severely than those caught with powdered cocaine. Possessing just 5 grams (about a teaspoonful) of crack would earn a 5-year mandatory minimum sentence in prison. To get the same prison sentence, one would need to possess 500g of powdered cocaine (over 1 lb). At the time these sentencing laws were passed, crack cocaine was considered to be almost wholly a problem of African American urban communities, while powdered cocaine usage was often glorified as the drug of choice for white middle- and upper-class America.

Laws in America have been especially discriminatory toward African Americans. To legitimize slavery, whites defined blacks as non-human, while demanding that they perform human tasks: building shelters, forming communities, raising children, working. Thus slavery was:

> a system constructed on the contradiction between denying the humanity of Blacks but depending on their human qualities for the survival of the system . . .[35]

This contradiction led to the creation of laws trying to make logical sense of what was inherently illogical. Slaves could not testify against whites, for example, because slaves were not human and only human beings had the right to appear as witnesses in court. Thus, a white abolitionist was set free during trial because the only witnesses who could have testified that he had incited the slaves on a plantation to rebel were the slaves themselves.[36]

Throughout the southern states as recently as the 1960s, it was a crime for a black person *not* to step off the sidewalk if a white person was walking past. Blacks attempting to form labor unions were arrested and fired from their jobs. Blacks could not enter "white" restaurants, drink from "white" water fountains, or use "white only" toilets.

Prior to 1954, if a black child attempted to attend a white public school, the child and his or her parents were subject to arrest for violating state statutes prohibiting the integration of blacks and whites in school. In 1954, the U. S. Supreme Court decided in *Brown v. Board of Education* that segregated schooling was unconstitutional. Since 1954, the most measurable impact of that decision has been to give legitimacy to continued racial discrimination in schooling.[37] More recent court decisions also undermine the effect the *Brown* decision might

Image 2.10 *A cafe near the tobacco market, Durham, North Carolina. Signs: Separate doors for "White" and for "Colored."*

Library of Congress Prints and Photographs Division

Image 2.11
Despite the ending of the Civil War and creation of basic protections for African Americans, many discriminatory laws remained in place well into the 1960s. These Jim Crow laws made it legal to keep blacks and whites separated, even at school. When these laws were ruled unconstitutional, it sometimes required the presence of military force, like here at Little Rock High School, to ensure compliance and integration.
US Army/National Archives

have by upholding the right of different school districts to spend vastly different amounts of money on education.

Discriminatory laws restricting the freedom of blacks were in blatant contradiction of the Constitution and of the overtly expressed values of many in the United States, yet they persisted for a hundred years after the Civil War. The contradiction between these laws and generally held values inexorably led to conflicts that were often personal, culminating in lynchings, beatings, and forced imprisonment for blacks (known as convict-leasing) who violated pretty much any laws.

The laws themselves changed, however, when blacks finally organized under the leadership of people like Dr. Martin Luther King Jr. and Malcolm X to form what has since been termed the 1960s Civil Rights movement. Like those who fought for women's suffrage, participants in the Civil Rights movement were often the victims of police brutality and injustices in the courts; many were sentenced to prison for trivial offenses or crimes they did not commit. Despite a systematic attempt to suppress the Civil Rights movement, it eventually culminated in a major overhaul of American criminal laws. The practice of racial discrimination in laws, law enforcement, and incarceration has not, however, disappeared.[38]

Juveniles, the criminal justice system, and the criminal law

In the United States today there are two separate criminal justice systems: one for adults and one for juveniles (people under age 18). Much of the focus of our discussion is on the adult criminal justice system. However, it is worth saying a few things about the juvenile justice system and the differences between adults and juveniles in the eyes of the criminal law.

Historically, young people have been given more leeway when it comes to their bad behavior and criminal offending than adults. One common reason given for applying a lower standard of culpability to juveniles is that they cannot appreciate the significance, seriousness, or consequences of their actions. If someone is unable to appreciate the seriousness or the consequences stemming from their actions, how can they possess the "guilty mind" needed to be guilty of committing a crime?

In America, this question has been central to debates about how to best deal with juvenile delinquency, as well as how and when to apply criminal laws to juvenile behavior. Even before the 1800s, when a separate juvenile justice system began to emerge in America, English courts had adopted a doctrine known as *parens patriae*, which roughly translated means "state as parent." As you may have guessed, this doctrine gives the state the ultimate power and authority to intercede on behalf of juveniles and make decisions in their (and the state's) best interests, which may include removing the child from a difficult home or punishing them for wrongdoing. The development of this doctrine remains very important today, since it forms the backbone of the American juvenile court and juvenile justice systems.

Generally, the purpose of separating juveniles from adults is to allow for greater discretion when dealing with juvenile offenders and promote more opportunities for rehabilitating delinquent youth.

Studies show a spike in delinquent behavior and criminal offending corresponding to the age of the individual. Young men and women, especially teenagers, seem to engage in bad behavior much more than any other age group. Scientific research indicates that this spike in juvenile offending may be a byproduct of other biological and psychological processes. In other words, some delinquent behavior may be quite normal and, also, unavoidable. Because of this, it is thought that youthful offending should be handled differently than adult offending.

For example, many studies show that the human brain does not fully mature until the mid-20s; prior to that time, it is undergoing a long process of re-wiring and maturation. In other words, the brains of young people really are different from those of adults, which certainly might explain why young people are prone to making bad or impulsive decisions.

Moreover, during puberty, male testosterone levels have been shown to increase up to 20 times their previous levels. And, studies have shown that levels of dopamine increase while levels of serotonin decrease in both young men and women.

Dopamine and serotonin are both neurotransmitters that impact how we feel. Dopamine is often referred to as a "feel good" chemical. It can get turned on (or "excited") by things like sex, consumption of alcohol and drugs, or engaging in a wide range of activities, including risky ones like fighting. When our dopamine levels go up, we feel really, really good—and thus may continue seeking out those activities that made us feel good, regardless of whether they are bad or illegal.

By contrast, serotonin functions more like a "chill out" chemical in our brains. It is more inhibitory than excitatory. Inadequate levels of serotonin may lead us to feel depressed and make it more difficult for us to check our impulses. Balance between dopamine and serotonin levels is key to normal cognitive and emotional functioning. If this balance is thrown off, which happens to young

BOX 2.4: CONNECTING RESEARCH TO PRACTICE

Kids without counsel

Contributed by: **Elise Logemann, Director of Client and Member Services and Supervising Attorney, Colorado Juvenile Defender Center**

Generally, the best public policies and practices are based on systematic research, which produces reliable and valid data. This is true in the field of criminal law, where research can, should, and often does inform how we arrest, prosecute, and sentence people accused of committing crimes. Non-profit organizations play key roles in conducting research about the criminal justice system, including how and when the American system of criminal law works and when it does not. While these organizations do not always conduct research specifically to influence or change existing policies, much of their focus is, typically, on leveraging data to affect positive change.

The Colorado Juvenile Defender Center (CJDC), based in Denver, Colorado, is one example of a nonprofit organization that conducts research to change extant practices within the juvenile justice system for the better. In 2012, CJDC reviewed data collected by the Colorado judicial branch. This data provided information about the number of young people accused of committing a crime who were appointed a defense lawyer for their juvenile delinquency case. CJDC reviewed this data and then conducted a court watching program to learn more. As part of this program, trained volunteers visited courtrooms across 15 judicial districts in Colorado, collecting observational data from over 250 juvenile cases. Data collected from this effort showed that 45 percent of children accused of committing crimes in Colorado never benefitted from the services and guidance of a defense attorney during their court cases. CJDC was also able to identify four key factors contributing to the fact that children were unrepresented.

Because juveniles accused of committing crimes have a constitutional right to defense counsel, the data collected by CJDC was very troubling. CJDC compiled this information into a report titled *Kids Without Counsel* and advocated for legislative changes to ensure that children accused of committing crimes in the future would be properly represented in the courtroom. In 2014, this effort culminated in the passage of legislation in Colorado to change and improve upon existing practices. Colorado House Bill 14–1032 now requires that all youth who are arrested and held in custody be represented by a defense attorney starting at their very first court appearance. The bill was specifically designed to address the key factors identified in CJDC's report.

Table 2.5 Differences between the adult and juvenile justice systems

Adults	Juveniles
An adult is ...	**A juvenile is ...**
Arrested	Taken into Custody
And becomes ...	**And becomes ...**
A Defendant	A Respondent
They are ...	**They are ...**
Arraigned	Given an initial hearing
Given a jury trial (open to the public)	Given an adjudicatory hearing (closed to the public)
Found guilty or innocent using the burden of proof of "beyond a reasonable doubt"	Adjudicated as "delinquent" (or not) by a judge who uses a civil "by a preponderance of the evidence" burden of proof
If, guilty, sentenced to probation, prison, halfway house, etc.	If guilty, sentenced to probation, incarcerated in juvenile correctional facility, a youth home, or some other special correctional program

people, it is not surprising that different behavioral outcomes may result, including delinquent ones (see Box 2.4 for more on how legal practice can be changed by research).

In America most juveniles who get in trouble are processed through the juvenile justice system, which differs from the adult criminal justice system in many ways, including the language used to refer to the participants and processes involved. This language reflects the *parens patriae* doctrine, the greater discretion given to juvenile court judges, and the desire to protect and rehabilitate juvenile offenders (see Table 2.5).

At this point, you may be thinking that there are very real differences between the abilities of a six-year-old and a sixteen-year-old when it comes to appreciating the seriousness and/or consequences of their actions. While both may be juveniles, should both receive the benefit of reduced culpability? More importantly, you might be asking yourself if all juveniles, regardless of their offense, should be processed through a separate juvenile justice system?

The answer to this question, philosophically and practically, is no. In America today juveniles are held accountable for violating the same criminal laws as adults and, increasingly, are prosecuted as adults for committing heinous offenses like murder and rape (for more on this see the section on juvenile courts in chapter 6). However, juveniles can also be prosecuted for a wide range of non-criminal offenses, called **status offenses**, simply because of their status as juveniles. Skipping school, smoking, consuming or purchasing alcohol, and violating curfew are all examples of status offenses for which juveniles can be prosecuted. Indeed, a large majority of cases handled in juvenile and municipal courts in America are for status, not criminal, offenses.

SUMMARY

In this chapter we introduced a variety of key topics related to the study of criminal law that are typically covered in the first year of law school. It's important to remember the criminal law unites the field of criminology with that of criminal justice. Criminologists interact with the criminal law on a daily basis, as do criminal justice system practitioners like police officers and attorneys. Ultimately, developing your knowledge of what the criminal law is and how it functions is critical to success in the fields of criminology and criminal justice.

We discussed the origins of laws in the United States, noting that American law is linked historically to English common law. We also explored the key principles of criminal law—legality, mens rea, actus reus, harm, causation, concurrence, and punishment—and explored how these principles connect.

There are various types of law, including criminal and civil law, which differ in many ways, including the language they use, the types of punishment that one can receive, and so on. The substantive criminal law describes what is illegal, while the procedural criminal law explains what processes must be used in the investigation and prosecution of crimes.

Finally, we looked closely at explanations for how laws get created and why and how the law has impacted people differently based on their gender or skin color.

The most important theories that attempt to explain how criminal laws are created include consensus, societal needs, and ruling class/pluralist theories. We have argued that each of these theories may explain how some laws are created, but not all laws. A large portion of research, including research on the origins of drug laws, does seem to support the idea that power and the interests of those with power get reflected within the law more often than not. In particular, the ruling class/pluralist theory of law creation can help us understand why the law has not applied equally to women or people of color in the United States.

CRITICAL THINKING QUESTIONS

1. What do you think about the various principles of legality and how they work together? In your opinion, do those principles make the law more or less effective? What problems would arise if those principles were loosened or altered?

2. Which theory of law creation do you most agree with? Why?

3. In what ways do laws continue to reflect difference in power in the United States? Can you identify and provide concrete examples of laws, or laws as they are applied, that target, disadvantage, or discriminate against specific groups?

NOTES

1   New Orleans Code of Ordinances, Chapter 74—Fire Prevention and Protection. Retrieved from https://www.municode.com/library/la/new_orleans/codes/code_of_ordinances?nodeId=PTIICO_CH74FIPRPR.

2   Graves, Jada A. 22 November 2010. 7 Strange State Laws. *U.S. News & World Report Travel*. Retrieved from http://travel.usnews.com/features/7_Strange_State_Laws/.

3   Distilled Spirits Council of the United States. n.d. Current Blue Law States. *Prohibition repeal.com*. Retrieved from http://www.prohibitionrepeal.com/legacy/hall.asp

4   Berlinger, Yehuda. 28 July 2008. The Truth about Dominoes on Sunday in Alabama. *Purplepawn.com*. Retrieved from http://www.purplepawn.com/2008/07/the-truth-about-dominoes-on-sunday-in-alabama/.

5   *McBoyle v. United States.* 1931. 283 US 25. Cited in Jerome Hall, B. J. George and Robert Force, 1976, *Cases and Readings on Criminal Law and Procedure*. Indianapolis: Bobbs Merrill, p. 44.

6   Walsh, A. and Hemmens, C. 2013. *Law, Justice and Society: A Sociolegal Introduction*, 3rd ed. London: Oxford University Press.

7   Robinson, P.H. and Dubber, M.D. An Introduction to the Model Penal Code. University of Pennsylvania Law School. Retrieved from https://www.law.upenn.edu/fac/phrobins/intromodpencode.pdf.

8   Benner, L.A. 2011. "When Excessive Public Defender Workloads Violate the Sixth Amendment Right to Counsel without a Showing of Prejudice." American Constitution Society, March. Retrieved from https://www.acslaw.org/files/BennerIB_ExcessivePD_Workloads.pdf.

9   "Five Problems Facing Public Defense on the 40th Anniversary of Gideon v. Wainwright," National Legal Aid & Defender Association. Retrieved from http://www.nacdl.org/Champion.aspx?id=25020.

10   Ibid.

11   Ibid.

12   Judicial Learning Center. 2014. State Courts v. Federal Courts. Retrieved from http://judiciallearningcenter.org/state-courts-vs-federal-courts/.

13   Skolnick, Jerome. 1969. *The Politics of Protest*. New York, NY: Simon and Schuster, p. 4.

14   Shumann, Karl F. 1975. Approaching Crime and Deviance. Paper presented at European Group for the Study of Deviance, Amsterdam.

15   Chambliss, William J. 1986. State Organized Crime. Presidential address at the annual meeting of the American Society of Criminology, San Diego, CA, November 17.

16   Hall, Jerome. 1968. Theft, Law and Society. *American Bar Association Journal*, p. 960–967.

17   Chambliss, W.J. 1964. A Sociological Analysis of the Law of Vagrancy. *Social Problems* 12(1): 67–77.

18   Blackmon, D.A. 2008. *Slavery by Another Name: The Re-enslavement of Black Americans from the Civil War to World War II*. New York: Anchor Books.

19   Gerth, Hans H. and Wright Mills, C. 1946. *From Max Weber: Essays in Sociology*. Glencoe, IL: Free Press, p. 66.

20   Marx, Karl. 1867/1980. *Capital: The Process of Capitalist Production. Vol. 1* (3rd German ed.), edited by Frederick Engels. Translated by Samuel Moore and Edward Aveling. New York: Humbolt Publishing Co.; Marx, Karl. 1853. Capital Punishment. *New York Daily Tribune*, reprinted in T.B. Boltomure and M. Rubel (eds.), Karl Marx, *Selected Writings in Sociology, and Social Philosophy*. Harmondsworth, Penguin.

21   Kolko, Gabriel. 1963. *The Triumph of Conservatism*. New York: Free Press.

22   Braithwaite, John. 1984. *Corporate Crime in the Pharmaceutical Industry*. London: Routledge and Kegan Paul, p. 276.

23 Carson, W.G.O. 1974. Symbolic and Instrumental Dimensions of Early Factory Legislation. In R. Hood (ed.), *Crime, Criminology and Public Policy*. London: Heineman.

24 Boyer, Richard O. and Morais, Herbert M. 1955. *Labor's Untold Story*. New York: United Electrical, Radio and Machine Workers of America.

25 Harring, Sidney. 1977. Class Conflict and the Suppression of Tramps in Buffalo, 1982–1984. *Law and Society Review* 11: 873–911.

26 Hunt, Alan. 1976. Perspectives in the Sociology of Law. In P. Carlen (ed.), *The Sociology of Law*. Keele, Staffordshire, England: University of Keele Press, pp. 33–43.

27 Kolko, G., op. cit.

28 Sachs, Albie and Hoff Wilson, Joan. 1978. *Sexism and Law*. London: Martin Robertson.

29 Griffin, Susan. 1975. Rape: The All American Crime. In W. Chambliss (ed.), *Criminal Law in Action*. New York, NY: Macmillan, p. 187.

30 *Roe v. Wade*, 410 U.S. 113 (1973).

31 Texas Passes One of Toughest Anti-abortion Laws in US. 2013. *The Guardian,* July 13.

32 Kansas Opens a New Front in the State Battle over Abortion. 2015. *Washington Post*, April 8.

33 Carangella-Macdonald, Susan. 1984. Marxian Theory and Legal Change in Rape: Michigan's Model Rape Reform Legislation. Paper presented at the American Society of Criminology, Cincinatti, OH, November.

34 Reinarman, C. 1994. The Social Construction of Drug Scares. In Peter Adler and Patricia Adler (eds.), *Constructions of Deviance: Social Power, Power and Interaction*. New York: Wadsworth Publishing Company, pp. 92–104.

35 Genovese, Eugene D. 1974. *Roll Jordan Roll: The World the Slave Made*. New York: Pantheon.

36 Ibid., p. 17.

37 Teddlie, C. and Freeman, J. 1996. Segregation, Desegregation, and Resegregation. In K. Lomotey and C. Teddlie (eds.), *Forty Years after the Brown Decision: Implications of School Desegregation for U.S. Education*. New York: AMS Press.

38 Chambliss, William J. 2001. *Power, Politics and Crime*. Boulder, CO: Westview.

CHAPTER OUTLINE

How much crime is there?

3

In this chapter we will explore the following questions

- Where do we get our information about crime?
- What picture of crime do official data sources give us?
- Is there a typical criminal?
- Are there certain crime trends or patterns of offending?
- Who are crime victims and what do they have in common?

KEY TERMS

Uniform Crime Report (UCR)

Part I Offenses

cleared by arrest

National Incident-Based Reporting System (NIBRS)

National Crime Victimization Survey (NCVS)

self-report study

career criminals

cohort

life course criminology

incapacitation

three strikes

Criminologist Ray Surette found that crime and justice topics occupy about 25 percent of all newspaper news space. He also found that 13 percent of all national TV News and over 20 percent of local news was devoted to crime reporting. Surette maintains that crime and justice stories are mass marketed and form a substantial portion of material presented within the mass media.[1] Studies show that over 30 percent of television programs in the United States are about crime or law enforcement.[2] In addition, shows like 60 Minutes, Nightline, and 48 Hours frequently focus on crime. The History channel, MSNBC, and numerous other cable channels present lengthy documentaries about organized crime, drug smuggling, and life in U.S. prisons. Judging from the frequency of newspaper and television coverage of violent crime, an observer might think we live in a sea of violence from which there is no escape.

Media attention is especially concentrated when a particularly heinous crime has been committed or when someone is arrested who has committed a series of violent crimes. The media had a field day, for example, when on August 18, 2005, Dennis Rader was sentenced to ten consecutive life terms in prison after pleading guilty to ten murders from 1974 to 1991. Sixty years old, an active member of his church congregation, and a Boy Scout leader, Rader had led a double life for decades. Referring to himself as BTK for "bind, torture, and kill," he eluded police investigators during his horrendous reign of terror in Wichita, Kansas. Graphic details of Rader's murders revealed a serial killer fascinated with taking control of and torturing his victims.

Image 3.1 *Dennis Rader murdered 10 people in Sedgwick County, Kansas, between 1974 and 1991. For years, Rader taunted police and local news sources with letters describing his killings. Stories about his life and crimes flooded the media after his arrest in 2005.*

Jeff Tuttle/AP/Press Association Images

It is safe to say that most people obtain their knowledge about crime from the media. They may realize that the picture they get from novels, TV shows, and films is not an accurate one, but the news they hear on television reporting an apparently unending stream of violent crimes has an effect on the public's image of the prevalence and seriousness of crime.

Media coverage of crime and news stories like that of Dennis Rader highlight the importance of objectively gathering data about how much crime there is and what types of crime are typical. The reality is that crimes such as those depicted in the media (almost always violent and especially those of serial killers like Dennis Rader) are extremely rare. The three crimes that account for the vast bulk of arrests in the United States are theft, driving while under the influence, and the possession or sale of illegal drugs.[3] Homicide, the subject of so much media attention, is in fact one of the least often committed crimes. Not only is homicide rare, but fewer than six people in 100,000 are the victims of murder in any given year. In fact, the homicide rate in the United States has shown a steady decline since the 1980s. The homicide rate in the last few years is the lowest it has been in 40 years (see Table 3.1).

Declining homicide rates, however, do not make for interesting headlines, unless, of course, a politician or law enforcement official wants to claim responsibility for them, as did New York's Mayor Rudy Giuliani in the 1980s.

CRIMINOLOGY AND CRIME DATA

Criminology is built on two great pillars: *facts* (or data) and *theories*. The goal of criminology is to know what the facts are and to create theories that explain the facts. Unfortunately, neither facts nor theories come to us in a package— we must discover both. In the chapters to come, we will introduce various theoretical perspectives on crime and examine their relevance in light of important facts presented in this chapter. In discovering what the facts are, we also uncover some common misconceptions, some of which derive from data gathered by organizations with a vested interest in having the facts turn out a certain way.

Most people realize that novelists, journalists, and script writers for television and movies promote images of crime that are tantalizing, exciting, sometimes

Table 3.1 U.S. homicide rates per 100,000 people, 1950–2014

1950	4.6	1971	8.6	1992	9.3
1951	4.4	1972	9.0	1993	9.5
1952	4.6	1973	9.4	1994	9.0
1953	4.5	1974	9.8	1995	8.2
1954	4.2	1975	9.6	1996	7.4
1955	4.1	1976	8.8	1997	6.8
1956	4.1	1977	8.8	1998	6.3
1957	4.0	1978	9.0	1999	5.7
1958	4.8	1979	9.7	2000	5.5
1959	4.9	1980	10.2	2001	5.6
1960	5.1	1981	9.8	2002	5.6
1961	4.8	1982	9.1	2003	5.7
1962	4.6	1983	8.3	2004	5.5
1963	4.6	1984	7.9	2005	5.6
1964	4.9	1985	7.9	2006	5.8
1965	5.1	1986	8.6	2007	5.7
1966	5.6	1987	8.3	2008	5.6
1967	6.2	1988	8.4	2009	5.0
1968	6.9	1989	8.7	2010	4.8
1969	7.3	1990	9.4	2011	4.7
1970	7.9	1991	9.8	2012	4.7
				2013	4.5
				2014	4.5

Source: *Crime in the United States* 2014. Uniform Crime Report, Federal Bureau of Investigation. U.S. Department of Justice, Washington, D.C.

horrifying, but inevitably misleading. What is not so well recognized is that police departments, politicians, prosecutors, and judges sometimes do the same thing. If police can convince lawmakers and the general public that crime is a serious problem that threatens everyone's well-being, they are better able to prove the importance of their work, increase their budgets, and improve their working conditions. Thus, when the FBI approaches Congress in the spring to request an increase in its budget, we must view with caution the claims it makes about crime and crime rates.

Politicians, prosecutors, and judges also share a vested interest in creating certain images of crime. If politicians in office have promised to "do something about crime," it is in their interest to show a decrease in crime. Politicians running for office, on the other hand, may use the "crime problem" as a way of attacking their opponent in an effort to win an election. Judges wishing to make legal decisions to justify being lenient on a particular offender may

Figure 3.1
Comparative crime
rates in seventeen
industrialized
countries

Source: Criminal
Victimization in
Seventeen Industrialized
Countries: Key Findings
from the 2009
International Crime
Victims Survey

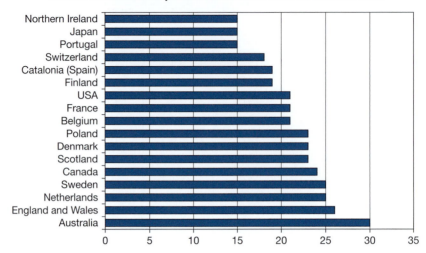

Overall victimization: percent victimized once or more in 1999

selectively report findings that show that this particular type of offender deserves leniency. One consequence of this is that the general public has a much distorted idea of what types of crime are most prevalent and *how much crime there is.* Law enforcement officials and politicians, for example, are fond of painting a picture of crime in the United States as being "out of control." They underscore this idea by claiming that crime is far more prevalent in the United States than in other industrialized (especially European) societies. The fact is, however, that with the exception of murder rates, past studies have shown that the U.S. crime rate is *lower* than in most other industrialized countries (see Figure 3.1).

Fortunately, we are not dependent on the media or politicians for the facts we need to have in order to scientifically study crime. To some extent we are dependent on law enforcement agencies (the FBI and the U.S. Attorney General's Office in particular), but because these agencies provide us with considerable information about how they collect their data, we are in a position to objectively assess the data's reliability.

The Uniform Crime Reports (UCR)

The Federal Bureau of Investigation systematically collects data on crime from about 17,000 local, state, and federal law enforcement agencies. These data are compiled and published annually by the FBI in the **Uniform Crime Reports (UCR)**. The UCR was created in 1929 on the recommendation of the International Association of Chiefs of Police, in recognition of the need to collect reliable, uniform crime data.[4] The FBI compiles data from over 17,000 police departments throughout the United States. On the basis of these reports, the FBI annually publishes the UCR which provides data on (1) crimes known to the police, (2) crimes cleared by arrest, (3) persons arrested, and (4) data on the number and employment of law enforcement personnel. While the UCR data are an important source of information about crime, it is also important to know how the data are collected and whether or not any bias is systematically built into the reporting.

Data collection for the UCR

The "crimes known to the police" concentrates on what the FBI defines as **Part I Offenses** also referred to as "index crimes." These are the crimes considered to be the "most serious crimes" by the FBI. Index Crimes include homicide, forcible rape, robbery, aggravated assault, burglary, larceny, arson, hate crimes, and motor vehicle theft. Arrest data for crimes considered by the FBI to be "less serious" such as public intoxication, drug offenses, simple assault, vagrancy, and gambling are also reported. The compilation of "crimes known to the police" is based on (1) telephone calls to the police station, and (2) crimes reported to or observed by police officers.

The UCR also reports the number of crime cases that are **cleared by arrest**. A crime is considered *cleared* when police have made an arrest, or when the perpetrator is known but has not been arrested for some reason (for instance, he or she has fled the country or died).

Problems with the UCR

The most glaring weakness of the UCR is its "mobilization of bias" towards certain types of crime while ignoring others. A few of the glaring omissions are corporate crime, corruption, political crimes, business violations of health and safety regulations, and terrorism (domestic and foreign). In recent years the UCR has begun reporting "hate crimes," which is a slight improvement, but the omission of crimes most often committed by businesses, politicians, law enforcement agencies, and governments reinforces the public's belief that the "really serious crimes" are those most often committed by the lower classes, when it is arguably upper-class crimes that cause the most harm and are the costliest to the general public.

Studies of how the FBI obtains crime statistics consistently show the process to be seriously biased, perhaps compromising its use for scientific purposes because the data gathering process yields some misleading information. Little attention is given to ensuring accuracy, for example. Since the data used for determining the extent and trend of criminality are "crimes known to the police," they may reflect an unknown number of "crank calls" where no crime has actually been committed. There is no requirement that the call be investigated to determine whether a crime was committed, and no suspect need be arrested. The categories used to classify acts as crime are arbitrary, inconsistent, and contradictory. "Homicide," which is usually interpreted by the media (and sometimes the FBI reports themselves) as "murder," includes "nonnegligent manslaughter." Nonnegligent manslaughter does not require that the perpetrator *intended to kill someone,* which is a legal requirement for murder. Nonnegligent manslaughter includes "any death due to injuries received in a fight, argument, quarrel, assault, or commission of a crime."[5] The instructions also tell police departments to report a death as a homicide regardless of whether objective evidence indicates otherwise: "the findings of coroner, court, jury or prosecutor do not unfound offenses or attempts which your [police] investigations establish to be legitimate."[6]

Other categories of crime are equally confusing for scientific purposes. Burglary requires the use of force for breaking and entering in many states, but the FBI tells local police departments to report the crime of burglary if there is simply unlawful entry.[7] With the exception of homicide, attempted crimes are counted as crimes. If several people get into a fight, each person involved is counted as a separate crime of aggravated assault: the instructions from the FBI to local police departments are consciously designed to show the highest incidence of crime possible: "If a number of persons are involved in a dispute or disturbance and police investigation cannot establish the aggressors from the victims, count the number of persons assaulted as the number of offenses."[8] In general, the UCR data are highly unreliable because of inconsistent definitions of crime and the FBI's systematic effort to inflate the incidence and severity of the crimes they report.

As early as 1931 the Wickensham Commission warned that the publication of the Uniform Crime Reports was problematic:

> Nothing can be more misleading than statistics not scientifically gathered and compiled. The uniform crime reports . . . make no suggestion as to any limitations or doubts with respect to the utility or authority of the figures presented. On the contrary they contain a graphic chart of 'monthly crime trends,' and along with them the bureau has released to the press statements quoting and interpreting them without qualification. It requires no great study of these reports to perceive a number of weaknesses.[9]

Equally problematic for using the Uniform Crime Report for scientific purposes is the degree to which crime rates are subject to political manipulation. Selke and Pepinsky report a longitudinal study of police reporting in Indianapolis demonstrating how crime rates fluctuate to suit those in political power.[10] Seidman and Couzens report a study of the crime rate in Washington, D.C., when President Richard Nixon was using the city to demonstrate that his "war on crime" was effective.[11] Under pressure to reduce the crime rate, the police consistently reported the dollar amounts of larcenies as $49.00, which kept them from being reported as felonies and thus kept the crime rate down.

Evidence suggests the police and FBI often manipulate and poorly report crime rates, thereby limiting their utility.[12] Police departments have the discretion to define certain crimes and may record an assault on a female as an attempted rape which the UCR then reports as a rape. This can lead to the false perception that crime rates are on the rise.[13]

BOX 3.1: CONSIDER THIS ...

The cost of corporate crime

The UCR does not include fraud as a crime, yet corporate and individual fraud are among the costliest and most harmful crimes prevalent in the modern world. Fraudulent reporting by corporations costs the taxpayers, employees, and individual retirees billions of dollars. The last thirty years have witnessed an almost continuous corporate crime wave.

In the 1970s and 1980s Michael Milliken perpetrated a gigantic fraud involving the sale of "penny stocks." Milliken spent several years in prison for his crimes which cost investors and taxpayers billions of dollars. Fraud and embezzlement in the savings and loan crisis of the 1980s cost investors over $500 million. Ten years later, fraudulent reporting of earnings by dozens of large corporations, including Enron, Rite Aid, Reliant Energy, Qwest Communications, and numerous other large corporations cost billions of dollars and led to the bankruptcy of dozens of corporations. Fraudulent practices in the mortgage lending industry in 2007–08 caused people to lose their jobs and their homes. Others were forced to declare bankruptcy. Billions of dollars in taxpayer money were spent by the government to bail out the banks and mortgage lenders that made loans through fraudulent practices such as overstating the value of homes.

In the aftermath of Hurricane Katrina, which in August 2005 devastated the city of New Orleans and much of the Gulf Coast region, fraud added to what was already widespread human misery. In March 2006, Henry Edwards and Dwight Thomas pleaded guilty to stealing federal funds from the Federal Emergency Management Agency (FEMA) designed to help victims recover from the devastation of Katrina. FEMA is a federal agency set up to respond to and assist with the relief efforts that follow the occurrence of a natural or man-made disaster. It is estimated that fraudulent activities perpetrated by individuals against the federal government cost tax payers billions of dollars each year in recovery. Despite the criminal nature of the FEMA fraud cases and countless other similar acts, they will go unrepresented in official crime statistics.

The need to provide a comprehensive understanding of crime patterns and trends must therefore rely on data gathered by sources that go beyond the reporting of the index crimes provided by the UCR. Society is not ready, however, to encounter the realities of such criminal activities—or is it? *What do you think?*

Sources

Former New Orleans Police Officer Sentenced in Theft of Louisiana Road Home Funds. 2015. *The Associated Press*, Nov. 13. Retrieved from https://www.justice.gov/usao-edla/pr/former-new-orleans-police-officer-sentenced-theft-government-funds.

Katrina News. U.S. Department of Justice. *Federal Bureau of Investigation*, Washington, D.C. Retrieved from https://www.fbi.gov/news/katrina.

Lipton, Eric. Study Finds Huge Fraud in the Wake of Hurricanes. *The New York Times*. Retrieved from http://www.nytimes.com/2006/06/14/us/nationalspecial/14katrina.html.

Another reason reported crime is an inadequate reflection of the crime problem is underreporting by victims. Studies show that victims often fail to report their victimization to police due to fear of retaliation by the offender.[14] Mistrust of police, ignorance that a crime has been committed,[15] and apathy about the criminal event also come into play.[16] A further reporting problem with the UCR is the fact that only a small sample of criminal offenses is included—those most likely to be committed by the working class. Completely absent are data on white-collar crimes, consumer fraud, child molestation, spousal abuse, and other offenses. Box 3.1 illustrates the variability in criminal behavior we must take into account when considering descriptions and explanations of crime.

The UCR also presents the data in misleading ways. Gimmicks like a "crime clock" distort the reality of crime, while making good newspaper copy and lending law enforcement agencies considerable political clout. This influence translates into ever-increasing budgets, pay raises, and more technologically sophisticated "crime fighting" equipment. It does not, however, provide policy makers or social scientists with reliable data about preventing crime or mitigating its effects. As Pepinsky and Selke conclude:

> the police cannot and should not be expected to be objective about the compilation of reported crime statistics. The field is one of the few where those who are evaluated are responsible themselves for gathering their own evaluation data . . . [17]

Official statistics, then, must be used with extreme caution. Organizational considerations dictate their content far more than reality does. For example, when police make an arrest they typically charge the suspect with a number of different offenses to increase the bargaining power of the prosecutor who confronts the suspect with the charges. The charges that appear in the arrest statistics, then, are a reflection of police activity but a very poor reflection of the offenses actually committed. Moreover, according to the *hierarchy rule*, in a multiple-offense situation, when more than one Part I offense is classified, the law enforcement agency must locate the offense that is highest on the hierarchy list and score that offense involved and not the other offenses.

This does not say that all official statistics are worthless. For example, the UCR reports the number of arrests made each year. These data will tell us with reasonable accuracy what charges the police use when they make arrests, though they cannot tell us how much crime there is or whether the rate of crime is increasing. Table 3.2 provides a summary of some of the built-in biases in the structure of the UCR.

National Incident-Based Reports (NIBRS)

In 1982, the Federal Bureau of Investigation and the Bureau of Justice Statistics sponsored a five-year redesign project that would revise the UCR program to better suit the needs of law enforcement agencies. The goal was to provide a

Table 3.2 Summary of methodological biases built into the UCR data collection

1.	Corporate and white collar crimes are not reported.
2.	Corruption is not reported.
3.	Political crimes are not reported.
4.	State crimes are not reported.
5.	Business crimes such as fraud and the violation of health and safety regulations are not reported.
6.	Reports are voluntary and vary in accuracy and completeness.
7.	Not all police departments submit reports.
8.	The FBI uses estimates in its total crime projections.
9.	Only one offense is counted per incident.
10.	Homicide includes intentional killing of another human being (which is murder) *and* the accidental killing of another human being through an assault, fight, argument, or quarrel.
11.	The decision of coroner, prosecutor, grand jury, or trial is not taken into account in counting homicides.
12.	Incomplete acts are lumped together with completed ones.
13.	Important differences exist between the FBI's definition of certain crimes and those used in different states.
14.	Victimless crimes are often undetected and unreported.
15.	Child abuse and family violence are often undetected and unreported.

more comprehensive measure of crime statistics that was driven by a reporting mechanism focusing on each reported criminal event. This effort culminated in the creation of the **National Incident-Based Reporting System (NIBRS)**, designed to collect data on each reported incident of crime. Under this new system, law enforcement agencies would provide the FBI an individual record for each reported crime in a single incident. The NIBRS records criminal incidents relating to 46 specific offenses, including the eight Part I crimes in the UCR. It also records arrest information about 11 lesser offenses (see Table 3.3).

Besides expanding the crime categories, the NIBRS reporting system requires the collection of a much more detailed description of each criminal incident:[18]

(1) **Information about the offense**—where it occurred, whether a weapon was involved, influence of drugs or alcohol on the perpetrator during the offense, and whether the offense had any gender, racial, or religious motivation behind it.
(2) **Information about the parties**—sex, age, and race of victim and offender; any possible relationship between them; and circumstances that may have motivated the criminal incident (such as breaking a relationship).
(3) **Information about the property (if any)**—the value of property stolen or damaged as a result of the criminal incident.

Table 3.3 Offence categories in the National Incident Based Reporting System

Group A Offences: Offenses and arrests are reported for the following crimes, for which a hierarchy does not apply	Group B Offences: Arrests only are reported for the following
Arson	Bad checks
Assault offenses	Curfew/loitering/vagrancy
Bribery	Disorderly conduct
Burglary/breaking and entering	Driving under the influence
Counterfeiting/forgery	Drunkenness
Destruction/damage/vandalism of property	Non-violent family offenses
Drug/narcotic offenses	Peeping Tom
Embezzlement	Runaways
Extortion/blackmail	Trespassing
Fraud offenses	All other offenses
Gambling offenses	
Homicide offenses	
Kidnapping/abduction	
Larceny/theft offenses	
Motor vehicle theft	
Pornography/obscene material	
Prostitution offenses	
Robbery	
Sex offenses, forcible	
Sex offenses, nonforcible	
Stolen property offenses	
Weapon law violations	

Incident-based data provides a wide array of complex and detailed information that has a significant advantage over summary-based crime reporting systems.[19] The data collected by the NIBRS should therefore provide a more adequate understanding of criminal behavior patterns and greater accuracy of official crime data than the UCR.[20] Table 3.4 provides a summary of the differences between the UCR and the NIBRS.

The NIBRS provides law enforcement agencies with a valuable tool in their crime fighting efforts by allowing for a more accurate description of when, where, and how crime takes place, as well as the characteristics of offenders and their victims. Moreover, criminologists are provided with data on crime that is more accurate, detailed, and meaningful than that provided by the traditional UCR. The FBI plans for all state law enforcement agencies to eventually submit incident-based crime data. As of 2012, a total of 6,115 law enforcement agencies had contributed NIBRS data. The data from those agencies

Image 3.2
*Both the UCR,
NIBRS, and other
crime data collection
systems gather
information about
crimes like murder,
theft, vandalism,
burglary, and more.
Data from these
reports are vital to
understanding the
scope of crime that
occurs in the U.S.*

iStock/Joseph C.
Justice Jr.

Table 3.4 Differences between summary UCR data and incident based NIBRS Data

UCR	NIBRS
Aggregates monthly crime counts for eight index crimes	Reports each individual incident for eight index crimes and 38 other crimes, including details on the offense, victim, offender and property
Counts one offense per incident according to the hierarchy rule	Counts each offense that is committed within a single incident
No distinction between attempted crimes and completed ones	Distinguishes between attempted crimes and completed ones
Records information about weapons use for murder, robbery and aggravated assault only	Records information about weapons use for all violent crimes
Arrest counts for 8 index crimes and 21 other crimes	Arrest details for 8 index crimes and 49 other crimes

represent 30 percent of the U.S. population and 28 percent of the crime statistics collected by the UCR Program.

National Crime Victimization Survey (NCVS)

One problem with the UCR is that many incidents of victimization go unreported to or unobserved by the police.[21] Because of this problem, the U.S. Department of Justice has sponsored the **National Crime Victimization Survey (NCVS)**, a comprehensive survey of crime victimization within the United States, in order to uncover the "dark figure of crime."[22] The first national victim survey was a pilot study conducted in 1967. The survey asked people whether they or any member of their household had been the victim of a crime. The questionnaires and sampling procedures were designed by sociologists and the interviews were conducted by the Census Bureau. The NCVS, in the words of a leading methodologist, is "the most important innovation in criminological research in several decades."[23] The pilot study was completed in 1971, and in 1972 the NCVS began collecting and publishing its findings.

The NCVS surveys a nationally representative sample of more than 90,000 households or approximately 160,000 people. Individuals interviewed must be over the age 12 and are asked to report their victimization experiences with certain targeted crimes, including rape, sexual assault, robbery, assault, theft, household burglary, and motor vehicle theft, during the past six months. Interview questions are designed to elicit information about:

(1) **The victim**—sex, age, race, ethnicity, marital status, income, and educational level; prior experience with the criminal justice system.
(2) **The offender**—sex, age, race, and relationship to the victim; possibility of substance abuse.
(3) **The offense**—time and place of incident, weapons involved, consequences of the crime including injury, and/or economic loss.

Respondents who are victims also answer questions about their perception of the handling of their case by law enforcement officials, if the criminal incident was reported to the police. The NCVS survey instrument is designed to draw adequate samples and to gather detailed data as objectively as possible. Interviewers are trained to ask questions so as to avoid "leading" the respondent in a certain direction. Thus, the NCVS provides a much better description of selected characteristics of criminality than do official statistics. While these surveys have their own shortcomings (which we discuss below), they are, nonetheless, quite useful for scientific purposes.

Victim survey data suggest that criminologists who questioned the reliability of official statistics generated by police departments were quite right to be skeptical. For decades, official crime data sources have reported a steady increase in the amount of crime.[24] Likewise, criminologists have questioned the official data and claims of ever-increasing crime rates, which periodically spark a public and media outcry over the crime problem, which in turn has an impact on the policy and legislation developed to address criminal justice issues and concerns.[25]

Victimization surveys provide a clearer understanding of the characteristics of crime and crime victimization, by (1) putting into proper perspective the actual level of crime and (2) directing attention toward the crime categories that actually lead to the most victimization, rather than focusing on popular images of stranger-precipitated and random acts of violence.[26] One of the most significant findings of the NCVS is that the rate of violent crime was steady for decades between 1973 and 1993. After 1993, a decline in violent crime rates occurred with it reaching the lowest level ever in 2014 (see Figure 3.2). Moreover, property crime rates have also declined in the past three decades, with there being a significant decline happening since 1993.

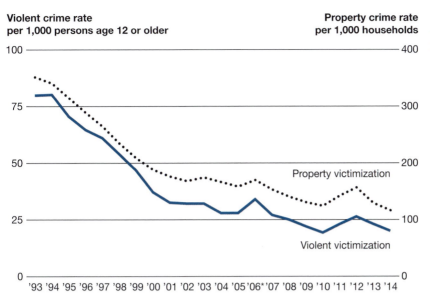

Violent crime rate
per 1,000 persons age 12 or older

Property crime rate
per 1,000 households

Figure 3.2 NCVS data on violent and property crime rates, 1993–2014

Source: Bureau of Justice Statistics, National Crime Victimization Survey, 1993–2014.

Another important finding of the NCVS is that the vast majority of crimes committed against persons are not very serious in terms of either personal or property damage. Of the 11.7 million completed thefts of property in 2008, over half were property thefts of less than $250.[27] Moreover, NCVS data indicate that 73.7 percent of crimes committed against individuals do not involve the use of any weapon, and that rape and sexual assault are twice as likely to be committed by a non-stranger (family, friend, relative, acquaintance) as by a stranger.[28]

The overwhelming findings of victimization surveys reveal that it is very unlikely anyone will be the victim of a crime in any given year. Over 85 percent of the respondents in the NCVS say neither they nor any member of their household was the victim of a criminal offense. Indeed, most people are unlikely to be the victim of a serious offense in their entire lifetime. The NCVS estimates the chance of an individual becoming the victim of a violent crime is about 2.3 percent (about 23 crime victimizations per 1000 persons age 12 and older).[29] Judging from the results of the victim surveys, the most likely crime of violence is a "simple assault," an "attack or attempted attack without a weapon resulting in either no injury or minor injury. Sexual assaults include attacks or attempted attacks generally involving unwanted sexual contact between the victim and offender that may or may not involve force."[30]

On the other hand, these findings do not include the risk of being victimized by drunk drivers, child abuse, and spouse abuse, which would likely not be reported on victim surveys. They also do not indicate the likelihood of being the victim of a crime in a lifetime. Still, the evidence is very persuasive that the risk of being victimized by crime in general, and by violent crime in particular, has been exaggerated by law enforcement officials, politicians, media, and the general public.

Image 3.3 *Data sources such as the NCVS help us better understand crimes such as domestic abuse that actually lead to the most victimization rather than the popularized random acts of violence perpetrated by strangers.*

iStock/KIVILCIM PINAR

Evaluating the NCVS

The NCVS clearly provides us with a more accurate depiction of crime in U.S. society.[31] The random sampling of households allows for a more reliable estimate of the number of crimes actually being committed and captures detailed data about the context of the victimization and characteristics of the victim and the offender. Criminological research can better analyze criminal behavior with this clearer understanding of issues surrounding race, gender, and victimization.

Despite the reporting advantages of victimization surveys, we must nevertheless approach their findings with caution. Inaccuracy is a major drawback of self-reporting that becomes more problematic when respondents are recalling a traumatic event. Over-reporting can also occur when victims mistakenly interpret certain acts as crime, such as sexual harassment as sexual assault or their losing an item as theft. Some victims may also report crimes that occurred before the six-month period of the NCVS.

On the other hand, the NCVS can also underestimate the amount of crime. Some victims may have forgotten about an incident or may not be aware that it was a crime. Underreporting can also be a result of the victims' unwillingness to disclose any information about their victimization, especially in the case of rape or sexual assault.[32]

Finally, the NCVS suffers the same design flaw as the UCR in that it excludes white collar crime, political crime, corruption, and state crime. By focusing on the categories more commonly associated with "street criminals the NCVS perpetuates the myth that these are the 'most important' crimes committed, a point of view that is arguable at the very least."[33]

Self-report surveys

One research technique developed by sociologists to reveal types of criminality ordinarily hidden from victim surveys or official statistics is the **self-report study**. This technique asks a sample of people to indicate whether they have committed certain criminal acts in a given time period. We use the results to measure the prevalence of both recent and lifetime criminal offending among respondents.[34] Respondents are assured anonymity and are informed of the usefulness of the survey's results in social science research. These techniques are used to increase the validity of self-report surveys by encouraging participation and increasing the likelihood of respondents answering questions truthfully.

In 1946, Austin Porterfield administered a questionnaire to Texas college students and discovered that over 90 percent of the respondents admitted to committing at least one felony.[35] A study conducted by Wallerstein and Wyle found similar results among 700 adults. Ninety percent reported committing at least one of 49 criminal acts punishable by at least one year in prison.[36] The men in the sample admitted committing an average of 18 offenses, the women an average of 11.

Since these pioneering studies, dozens of others have confirmed their findings. High school and college youth indicate frequent occurrences of being truant, fighting, stealing, running away from home, and drinking while underage.[37] The University of Colorado, under the auspices of Delbert Elliot and his colleagues, conducts the National Youth Survey (NYS), which began in 1976. Since then, the NYS has been an ongoing study spanning over three decades, which monitors respondents' changing attitudes, beliefs, and behaviors in delinquency, violence, drugs, and crime, amongst various other subjects. The NYS study also confirms earlier findings: over 90 percent of the respondents in the survey admit to having committed some type of serious criminal offenses over the course of their lives.[38] Table 3.5 provides a summary of data compiled by the Monitoring the Future survey, administered to high school seniors across the nation. Results once again indicate that many high school seniors have committed criminal acts.

Evaluating self-report studies

The data consistently confirm that virtually everyone sampled in self-report surveys admits to having committed criminal acts. What has proven controversial among criminologists is how to interpret the data.[39] On first brush there appears to be little difference by social class in the propensity to violate the law. Since the vast majority of people sentenced to prison or to juvenile institutions are from the lower classes, some interpreted the survey results to mean that the difference between lower-class and other youth was not in the frequency or severity of their criminality, but in the biased law enforcement practices of the police. Others pointed out, however, that lower-class youth committed more, and more serious, offenses than middle- or upper-class youth.[40] Michalowski comments:

Table 3.5 Percentage of high school seniors reporting criminal involvement in selected activities

Type of Delinquency	Percent Committed at Least Once	Percent Committed More than Once
Set fire on purpose	1.4	1.5
Damaged school property	5.9	5.2
Damaged work property	1.7	2.0
Auto theft	2.2	1.7
Auto part theft	1.5	1.9
Break and enter	11.0	13.0
Theft, less than $50	11.0	14.3
Theft, more than $50	4.0	5.0
Shoplift	10.4	13.4
Gang or group fight	8.5	7.7
Hurt someone badly enough to require medical care	6.8	6.0
Used force or a weapon to steal	1.3	1.7
Hit teacher or supervisor	1.0	1.8
Participated in serious fight	6.7	4.6

Source: Lloyd, D. J., Bachman, J. G., and O'Malley, M. P. 2013. *Monitoring the Future, 2011*, pp. 115–117. Institute for Social Research. Ann Arbor: MI. http://www.monitoringthefuture.org/data volumes/2011/2011dv.pdf.

Recent studies using national youth samples and more sophisticated questionnaires have tended to confirm both interpretations. That is, there appears to be no significant difference between lower class, working class, and middle class youth when it comes to self-reported involvement in property crimes (excluding robbery); drug offenses (either selling or using); status crimes such as truancy, runaway and underage drinking; or public disorder crimes such as carrying a concealed weapon, drunkenness, hitch-hiking, and so forth. However, lower class youth appear disproportionately among those reporting a high frequency of offenses. It should be noted, however, that high frequency offenders accounted for less than 5 percent of the juveniles surveyed in each of the three social classes.[41]

A common criticism of self-report studies is their failure to ask questions about the more serious forms of personal violence such as murder, rape, and aggravated assault.[42] Studies of college students reveal a high incidence of date rape.[43] Meyer reports that over 20 percent of college women are the victims of rape or attempted rape.[44]

Self-report studies also suffer some of the same shortcomings as victim surveys. Gauging the criminality of inner-city youth through self-reports is difficult. Most surveys are of local high schools, although recent data from national surveys reduces the shortcomings of earlier studies. In the end, of course, one of the most serious limitations is the perception of the respondent.[45] Respondents may not think their act was criminal and therefore may not report it.[46] Child abuse, sexual assault of a girlfriend or wife, rape on a date or at a party where both parties were drinking . . . all these incidents may go unreported because the respondent does not perceive them as criminal or does not want to admit to committing a crime.

If the questionnaire does not ask about certain offenses, they will not be recorded; for example, none of the questionnaires ask about driving under the influence of alcohol. Evidence from participant observation studies indicates, however, that this may be one of the most common and most serious criminal acts committed by middle- and upper-class youth.[47] Even with the promise of anonymity, respondents may be reluctant to admit they have committed very serious offenses.[48] It seems unlikely that many would place the accuracy of questionnaire results above their own safety from prosecution. Finally, the questionnaires do not tap white-collar, corporate, and governmental crimes. In short, although self-report studies provide yet another piece of valuable information about crime and delinquency, it is only a piece, which we must study in conjunction with many others before the picture is complete.

SOCIAL CORRELATES OF OFFENDING

Two of the most consistent findings of criminological research are (1) that women commit far fewer crimes than men and (2) that the frequency of committing crime is correlated very strongly with age.

Age and crime

The first thing to realize about the relationship between age and crime is that criminal behavior decreases with age.[49] Criminal activities tend to peak between the ages of 19 to 24 and then decline through adulthood and aging, regardless of differences in race, gender, economic status, and other social variables (see Figure 3.3).[50]

Several explanations help account for the relationship between age and crime.[51] A study conducted by criminologist Robert Agnew accounts for the peak of criminal activity during adolescence by linking criminality to features of adolescent life in U.S. society.[52] Agnew points to several factors that seem to be in play during adolescence:

- The desire of youth to be more accountable to peers and seek their approval
- An increase in economic demands on youth

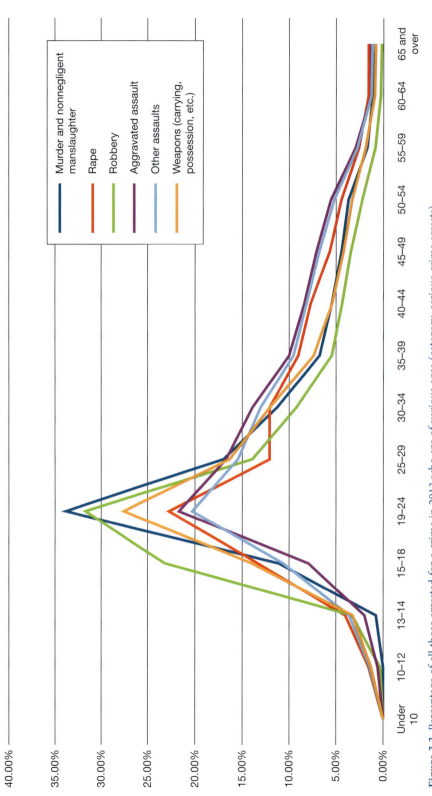

Figure 3.3 Percentage of all those arrested for a crime in 2013 who are of various ages (category: serious crime arrests)

Source: Crime in the United States. 2013. Federal Bureau of Investigation, U.S. Department of Justice, Washington, D.C. Retrieved from http://wpsites.maine.edu/criminology/lecture-4-general-characteristics-of-crime-and-criminals/

Image 3.4 *What social pressures of the teenage years make youth more susceptible to criminal activity?*

iStock/monkeybusinessimages

- A decrease in adult supervision
- A desire for independence and adult privileges
- The propensity to resolve problems in a criminal manner.

Other studies account for the decline in criminality with age by citing the natural human life cycle, whereby individuals begin to mature and become better integrated into society as they take on conventional roles.[53] The strengthened bond to society gives individuals an increased sense of responsibility to social values and norms, making it more difficult for them to take the risk of involvement in crime. This pull is especially strong when individuals begin to take on the tasks of acquiring a full-time job, getting married, and having children.

Race and crime

A common and persistent trend is the disproportionate arrest rate of young black males compared to young white males.[54] While African Americans make up about 13 percent of the U.S. population, they account for over 30 percent of the arrests for UCR index crimes (see Table 3.6). In the 2014 FBI publication *Crime in the United States*, blacks constituted 37.7 percent of arrests for violent crimes, and 28.4 percent of arrests for property crimes. A leading authority on the social correlates of criminal behavior, Roland Chilton, found that in Boston, Massachusetts, although the 15–19 year old age group constituted 7.4 percent of the population, it accounted for 32 percent of the arrests for robbery, assault, burglary, theft, and rape (Part I offenses).[55] The age group of 15–29 year olds accounted for 59 percent of all Part I arrests in 1960 and 76 percent in 1980. Non-white males in Boston constituted less than 1 percent of the Boston

Table 3.6 Comparing rates of arrest for whites and blacks

Offense charged	Total	Number of arrests		Percent distribution	
		White	Black	White	Black
Murder and nonnegligent manslaughter	6,370,830	4,272,421	1,909,281	67.1	30.0
Forcible rape	11,832	2,414	3,379	40.7	56.9
Robbery	62,897	25,996	35,745	41.3	56.8
Aggravated assault	221,048	133,856	79,670	60.6	36.0
Burglary	136,531	87,423	45,931	64.0	33.6
Larceny-theft	815,706	559,329	231,223	68.6	28.3
Motor vehicle theft	39,759	24,903	13,749	62.6	34.6
Arson	5,467	3,825	1,433	70.0	26.2
Aggregate violent crime data	301,714	169,693	122,830	56.2	40.7
Aggregate property crime data	997,463	675,480	292,336	67.7	29.3

Source: *Crime In The United States*, 2014. Federal Bureau of Investigation, U.S. Department of Justice, Washington, D.C.

population in 1960, but made up approximately 15 percent of those arrested for Part I offenses. In 1980 non-white males were 4.5 percent of the population and accounted for 33.6 percent of the arrests.

The finding that young minority males are most often arrested for crimes such as theft, burglary, assault, and robbery is consistently reported by studies relying on arrest data supplied by police and other law enforcement agencies. Moreover, data obtained by the NCVS seem to support the findings of the UCR: the proportion of offenders identified by NCVS respondents as African American is similar to the proportion of black offenders identified in UCR statistics.[56] These findings lead many to conclude that African Americans are responsible for the majority of violent criminal offenses.

Again, however, we must approach these conclusions with caution. The most obvious flaw in these researches is that the underlying statistics reflect only a tiny fraction of the criminality at any point in time. Completely absent from the data are white-collar and corporate crimes, police corruption, organized crime, crimes of the state, prostitution, child pornography, and assault, rape, and battery by family members against one another. Moreover, studies suggest that differences in rates of arrest between African Americans and whites can be a by-product of police bias within the criminal justice system.[57] Police departments make decisions about where to look for crime and whether to make an arrest and generally devote a disproportionate amount of their surveillance energies to areas where non-whites live. The finding that blacks are more likely to be arrested than whites thus becomes a self-fulfilling prophecy.

Recent studies examining self-report data from the National Youth Survey suggest that racial disparities between black and white youth are smaller than actually reported in the UCR.[58] Thus, we must analyze arrest data in the context

BOX 3.2: CONNECTING RESEARCH TO PRACTICE

Demonstrating the effects of police bias in New York City

The Fourth Amendment of the United States Constitution protects the right of individuals against unreasonable searches and seizures by police officers. The practices of law enforcement officers must strike a careful balance between that right and their duty to control crime and apprehend criminals. Achieving this balance can be a challenging task for any metropolitan police department.

In the mid-2000s, the New York City Police Department (NYPD) came under scrutiny for engaging in practices that border on the violation of civil liberty. These practices are often the result of the discretion granted to police officers to stop and question individuals whom they suspect to be involved in criminal activity. According to the New York City Civil Liberties Union (NYCLU), the NYPD arrested nearly 400,000 individuals for marijuana possession between 1997 and 2007. These arrests were marked by significant racial disparities between blacks and whites, with blacks accounting for over 50 percent of the arrests, while only comprising 26 percent of New York City residents during that period.

In 2006, the NYPD stopped and frisked nearly 500,000 individuals suspected of being involved in criminal activity. Data on these encounters indicated that almost 90 percent of the stops were of minority individuals, with blacks comprising over 50 percent. Researchers at RAND Corporation analyzed data on more than 500,000 street encounters between law enforcement officers and pedestrians to assess the degree to which the overrepresentation of minorities was due to racial bias in police practices. The research produced illuminating findings, with significant implications for policy changes in police practices and procedures. RAND's report suggests that statistics on the disparity between black and white suspects exaggerates the existence of racially biased police practices, since it does not preclude external factors such as the proportion of stops made relative to the representation of the racial group in descriptions of crime suspects, or internal factors such as time, place, and circumstances of the stop.

These findings suggest the importance of research guided policies and practices that adequately address the issue of racial bias in police procedures. An accurate measure of the scale of the problem can effectively direct law enforcement agencies, public officials, and policy makers to make small-scale changes in policy to improve reporting and administration, as opposed to a large scale organizational restructuring. As a result of their findings, RAND researchers recommended policies to improve communication between police officers and potential suspects during a stop, revise police reports to capture data on the use of force, initiate the internal review of areas with the largest racial disparity in stop outcomes, familiarize all officers with training pertinent to stop and frisk documentation policy, and monitor the behavior of police officers with recurrent patterns of racial disparity in their policing practices.

Sources

New York Civil Liberties Union. 2008. NYC Marijuana Possession Arrests Skyrocket Illustrate NYPD Racial Bias, New Report Shows. Retrieved from http://www.nyclu.org/node/1736

Ridgeway, Greg. 2007. *Analysis of Racial Disparities in the New York Police Department's Stop, Question, and Frisk Practices.* Santa Monica, CA: RAND Corp.

of police practices that routinely profile African Americans as suspects in certain crimes and stop them disproportionately often for routine searches, citations, and arrests without probable cause (see Box 3.2).[59]

Gender and crime

The UCR reports that men are five times as likely to be arrested for a violent crime as women, with the ratio of male to female arrests for homicide being 8 to 1. Figure 3.4 indicates that, according to UCR arrest data, men are responsible for about 80 percent of arrests for violent crimes, and 62 percent of arrests for property offenses.

Moreover, victimization surveys and self-report studies also support the finding that men are disproportionately responsible for the majority of serious violent crimes. In the NCVS, respondents identify the perpetrator as a male in about 86 percent of violent offenses,[60] and in a study of self-reported involvement in various criminal activities, male high school seniors report more criminality than their female counterparts (see Table 3.7).

While most criminologists agree with the obvious conclusion that females are less criminal than males, there is less agreement on the reasons.[61] Early theories focused on trait differences. That is, they regarded women as weaker, more emotional, and less aggressive than men, and therefore less likely to engage in criminal activities.[62] Criminologist Cesare Lombroso argued that women who did occasionally commit acts of crime were essentially exhibiting masculine characteristics not typical of most females.[63] Later studies saw hormonal differences between the two genders, linking aggressive and anti-social behavior to male sex hormones.[64]

Image 3.5 *How has the changing role of women contributed to an increase in their crime rate?*

iStock/PeopleImages

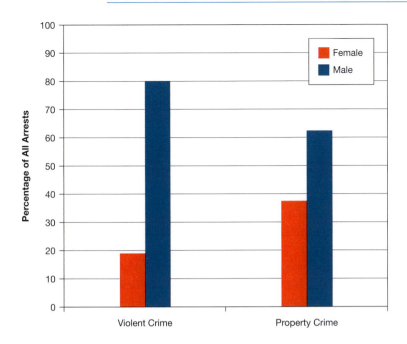

Figure 3.4
Gender and arrest rates (percentage of all arrests) for violent and property crimes

Source: Data from Federal Bureau of Investigation. 2011. Crime in the United States, 2010. Washington, D.C. Retrieved from http://2012books.lard bucket.org/books/ a-primer-on-social-problems/s11-03-who-commits-crime.html.

Table 3.7 Percentage of high school seniors admitting to at least one offense during the past 12 months, by gender

Delinquent behavior	Male students	Female students
Serious fight	14	9
Gang fight	19	13
Hurt someone badly	17	6
Used a weapon to steal	5	2
Stole less than $50	29	20
Stole more than $50	12	6
Shoplifting	28	23
Breaking and entering	27	17
Arson	4	1
Damaged school property	15	6

Source: Adapted from *Monitoring The Future*, 2012. Institute for Social Research, Ann Arbor, MI.

Other studies of gender differences in crime rates look at the way socialization affects the behavior of women. A study conducted by Bottcher examines gender socialization and delinquency.[65] Male behavior is a product of males' socialization into an assertive, aggressive, and powerful gender role, accounting for their higher rate of involvement in delinquency and crime. In contrast, females are socialized into passive and submissive gender roles and are more likely to consider their attachment to peers and seek social approval, thereby reducing their risk of becoming involved in criminal behavior.

With the emergence of feminist criminology in the early 1970s (see chapter 10), researchers began to explore the connection between lower rates of criminality among females and their relatively lower economic and social position. As the lifestyles and roles of women have changed, factors contributing to criminality seem to be affecting them as much as men.[66] Trends in crime statistics seem to support the feminist view of crime rate differences between men and women. Data show that female criminality is increasing considerably, while male rates tend to be steady and in some instances are actually declining.[67]

Criminal careers

The study of crime and criminal behavior reveals that the majority of offenders engage in a single act of criminality and then stop. Most criminal behavior is thus accounted for by a small group of persistent offenders who are chronic or career criminals. This concept was first studied in 1972 by Wolfgang, Figlio and Sellin, who followed a cohort or group of individuals with similar characteristics, of 9,945 boys from birth to age 18.[68] The study, which used police records to identify delinquents and track their criminal careers, found that about 54 percent of those identified as delinquent were repeat offenders, while 46 percent committed a single offense. Among repeat offenders, a small percentage (about 6 percent of the total cohort) were chronic offenders who

BOX 3.3: CONNECTING THEORY TO PRACTICE

Three strikes and you're out! Life course theories in action

In October 1993, 12-year-old Polly Klaas was abducted at knifepoint during a slumber party at her home in Petaluma, California, and later found raped and strangled. Her assailant, Richard Allen Davis, was convicted of her murder in 1996 and received the death penalty for his crime. The case drew nationwide attention due to the fact that Edwards was a paroled felon with an extensive history of violence and brutality, including arrests, charges, and convictions for crimes such as burglary, robbery, kidnapping, extortion, and sexual assault.

The focus shifted to a get-tough political ideology which called for the incapacitation of repeat, chronic offenders. The outcome of these debates culminated into the passage of California's "three-strikes laws" in 1994, which mandated prison terms of 25 years to life without the possibility of parole, for defendants convicted of a third felony. Several states followed with similar laws, and in 1994, Congress passed federal laws enacting the same type of policy. The stated rationale behind these laws was to enact the automatic and long-term imprisonment of chronically incorrigible criminal offenders in order to ensure public safety from their repeated acts of crime. However, the practical outcome of such policy initiatives does not take into consideration the variable effects they may have on criminal justice dynamics.

An offender convicted under this type of legislation can theoretically and practically be sentenced to life in prison for committing a relatively minor offense such as shoplifting, which can, in some states, be the theft of property valued at $200. Studies have also shown that three-strikes legislation disproportionately affects minority offenders, especially African Americans. The original goal of three-strikes laws was to protect the public from repeat violent criminals. The reality, though, is that these policy initiatives have resulted in the long-term imprisonment of criminals with a history of petty infractions involving theft or drugs and an explosion in prison populations across the nation, placing an even heavier toll on correctional management and staff.

Nor does a lengthy prison sentence for this category of chronic offenders decrease crime or reduce violence. Over the years, numerous research studies on the impact of three-strikes laws on crime have collectively found that the incapacitation of offenders at the end of their careers is not likely to have an impact on the overall crime rate. Moreover, the crime rate is more likely to be a reflection of national trends in crime rather than specifically related to the application of three-strikes laws. The practical application of theory to crime control policy and practice must be balanced against research evidence suggesting the success of such theoretical application. A more careful assessment of three-strikes laws may suggest a re-examination of their goal as an effective crime control strategy.

Sources

Auerhahn, K. 2004. California's Incarcerated Drug Offender Population, Yesterday, Today, and Tomorrow: Evaluating the War on Drugs and Proposition 36. *Journal of Drug Issues* 34(1): 95–120.

Chen, E. Y. 2008. Impacts of 'Three Strikes and You're Out' on Crime Trends in California and throughout the United States. *Journal of Contemporary Criminal Justice* 24(4): 345–370.

Dickey, W. J. & Hollenhorst, P. 1999. Three-Strikes Laws: Five Years Later. *Corrections Management Quarterly* 3(3): 1–18.

Jones, J. 2012. Assessing the Impact of 'Three Strikes' Laws on Crime Rates and Prison Populations in California and Washington. *Student Pulse* 4(9).

were arrested more than five times and responsible for about 52 percent of all acts of delinquency committed by the group.

The discovery that there are persistent patterns of criminal behavior has had a significant impact on criminological theory and practice. Longitudinal studies that track the behavior patterns of chronic offenders over a period of time have sparked debates about why people stop offending. A 1986 National Academy of Sciences (NAS) panel report emphasized the need to study criminal behavior over the life course of the offender.[69] **Life course criminology** emerged, drawing upon the concept of life course, "pathways through the life span involving a sequence of culturally defined, age-graded roles and social transitions enacted over time."[70] Life course theorists examine patterns of continuity, frequency in life events, and sequences of behavior to establish a causal link between the early development of delinquency and later adult deviant behavior. The sequential continuity of anti-social behavior in different life domains throughout various stages of life, from childhood to adulthood, is regarded as

Image 3.6 and 3.7
*Three-strikes laws
are designed to
incapacitate repeat
violent offenders
such as Richard
Allen Davis, who
kidnapped, assaulted,
and killed 12-year-
old Polly Klaas.*

AP/Press Association
Images; Ben Margot/
AP/Press Association
Images

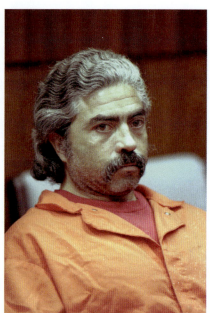

a variable in the persistence of adult criminality. On the other hand, informal social bonds and attachment to primary group members such as family, peers, and co-workers during adulthood can explain the desistence in patterns of adult criminality over the life span, despite early childhood tendencies to delinquent behavior.

The study of chronic offending has also affected criminal justice policy. The goal of rehabilitating offenders has become secondary to **incapacitation** or the removal of offenders from society so that they are no longer a threat to public safety. The logic behind these policies is that chronic life course offenders are not likely to be deterred by apprehension, punishment, and treatment. Thus, laws targeting these habitual offenders have become more focused on longer prison sentences, mandatory minimum sentences, and **three strikes** policies advocating mandatory life imprisonment for offenders convicted of a third felony offense (see Box 3.3).

CRIME TRENDS IN THE UNITED STATES

Crime rates that are officially reported tend to focus on street crimes: what the UCR classifies as "Type I" or "Index Crimes." As we have pointed out consistently in this chapter, such depictions of crime are misleading. Corporate crimes, white-collar crimes, corruption, and political crimes are rarely reported unless there is a major scandal. Recent years bear witness to a host of enormous losses to tax payers and employees resulting from fraud, corruption, embezzlement, and other offenses engaged in by corporate executives and government officials.

Beginning in the late 1980s the United States has witnessed an uninterrupted series of corporate criminal activities that has cost taxpayers, employees, retirees, and average citizens hundreds of billions of dollars:

> The savings and loan crisis of the 1980s was one of the worst financial disasters of the 20th century. The estimated cost to taxpayers, not counting the interest payments on government bonds sold to finance the industry's bailout, is $150 to $175 billion. If interest over the next thirty years is added to this tab, the cost approaches $500 billion.[71]

Between 1988 and 1992 over 646 criminal cases involving more than 1,000 defendants were brought against former savings and loan officers and employees (see Table 3.8). As sociologists Calavita, Pontell and Tillman, who investigated the collapse, point out, these defendants had engaged in the systematic plundering of the companies they worked for at the expense of the stockholders and ultimately the taxpayers. These crimes were made possible by collusion between company officers from different institutions and government regulators who failed to oversee the business operations.[72]

The criminality of officers and employees in the hundreds of savings and loan corporations was followed in the 1990s by massive fraud in myriad industries from drug stores to telephone companies and energy providers. The most thoroughly researched corporate criminal enterprise in this period took place at Enron Corporation, which at the time of its collapse was the largest bankruptcy in U.S. history.[73]

The officers of Enron committed a multitude of crimes during its brief history as one of the most profitable and successful energy companies in the world. The crime that ultimately brought the company to its heels was *fraud*, intentionally lying for economic gain. For years Enron executives lied to stockholders, accountants, the government, and the general public in order to increase the firm's stock share value. Even when they knew that Enron had lost billions of dollars and that there was no possible way to avoid bankruptcy, the officers lied about the income of the company and its future profits, all the while taking millions of dollars in salary and bonuses for themselves. Thousands of people working for the company who had purchased the company stock in good faith were encouraged to continue buying it, although ultimately it was practically worthless and its drop in value wiped out the retirement savings they had counted on. Enron was not alone in fraudulently reporting profits and earnings during the 1990s and early 2000s:

Table 3.8 Major savings and loans criminal cases, 1988–1992

Number of cases	646
Defendants charged	1,098
Defendants convicted and sentenced	580
Defendants sentenced to prison	451
Median prison term (months)	22
Median loss per case	500,000
Total losses	8,222,398,550
Total restitution paid	335,620,349
Total fines	11,917,061

Source: Calavita, Kitty, Pontell, Henry N., and Tillman, Robert H. 1997. *Big Money Crime: Fraud and Politics in the Savings and Loan Crisis*. University of California Press.

- The giant telecommunications firm WorldCom was found guilty of committing the largest accounting fraud in U.S. history. In 2000–01 the company was telling stockholders it was profitable when its officers knew that in fact it had lost $64.5 billion. In all the company made over $74.5 billion in accounting errors.

- Reliant Energy Services and four current or former employees are accused by the state of California of conspiracy, fraud, and manipulating the price of electricity in California that led to a severe energy crisis in 2000 and 2001.

- Rite Aid CEO Martin Grass plead guilty to conspiracy to inflate company earnings in a plea bargain that included a five-year prison sentence, forfeiture of $3 million, and a $500,000 fine.

- Two former executives and a former trader from Duke Energy were accused of fraudulently using bogus trades to make the company appear more profitable and raise its stock prices. The phony trades resulted in more than $50 million in fraudulent profits.

- Microsoft was found guilty of systematically violating anti-trust regulations. The firm settled by paying billions of dollars in fines and settling suits with companies ($1.3 billion with PeopleSoft) and with the EU.

While the list could go on for pages, these examples are sufficient to make the point that corporate crime has been rampant for at least the past 30 years.

The exposure of corruption by government officials also has been on the rise. Because of the paucity of data, we do not know whether the recent revelations of corruption represent an increase in these crimes or merely an increase in public awareness. The U.S. Attorney's office reports that in a 10-year period between 1994 and 2003 it successfully prosecuted over 5,000 cases of corruption brought against public officials. One of the most infamous cases of public corruption in recent years involved Representative Randy "Duke" Cunningham, a congressman from California. In November 2005 Cunningham plead guilty to taking more than $2 million in bribes. Cunningham's crimes consisted of selling his influence as a member of Congress to obtain Defense Department contracts for contractors who paid him in cash, houses, luxury yachts, and expensive vacations. Cunningham was sentenced to 10 years in prison and forced to pay $350,000 in fines.[74]

Despite their seriousness, the criminal activities of businessmen, corporate executives, and political officials remain relatively unnoticed by public scrutiny and are generally absent from official crime data gathered by police departments. We turn now to an examination of those types of crimes that are more visible to the public, beginning first with the category generating the most amount of attention, violent crime.

Trends in violent crime

As we noted earlier, the violent crime rate has been steadily decreasing since 1994, reaching the lowest level ever recorded in 2014.[75] Moreover, crime data indicate that, as a whole, violent crime rates dropped over 16 percent from 2005 to 2014, and property crime rates dropped over 18 percent for the 10-year trend.[76] Some criminologists believe homicide statistics are among the more accurate data provided by law enforcement agencies; since their consequences are difficult to hide, homicides are more likely to be reported. While this may be true, the way the UCR instructs police to report a death as a homicide even if the coroner, the prosecutor, a jury, and a judge do not confirm a murder took place makes the data suspect. Victim surveys offer another indication that police may over-estimate the number of homicides. Only in 1967 did the victim survey ask respondents whether any member of their household had been the victim of a homicide. The answer was 3.1 people per 100,000 in the population. The UCR for that year reported a homicide rate of 5.1; almost twice the rate indicated by the victim survey. It is quite possible the discrepancy is the result of consistent overreporting by the police, much of which would be accounted for by the reporting methods we pointed out earlier.

Despite flaws in the data collection methods of the UCR, criminologists rely on official crime reports to examine trends in rates of criminality over the years. Crime data provided by the UCR indicate that between the mid-1960s and the late 1970s, the homicide rate in the United States nearly doubled, peaking in 1980 at 10.2 per 100,000 people, and falling to 7.9 per 100,000 in 1984. It rose again in the early 1990s, reaching 9.8 per 100,000 in 1991. Between 1992 and 2000, the rate declined significantly and has been stable since then. Figure 3.5 provides a summary of homicide rate trends.

The highest percentage of homicides, (almost 50 percent), occurs between relatives and close acquaintances. About 18 percent of the homicide victims in 2005 were strangers to the perpetrator. The relationship between victim and offender could not be determined in over one-third of the homicides. Individuals between 18 and 24 have historically had the highest rate of offending across

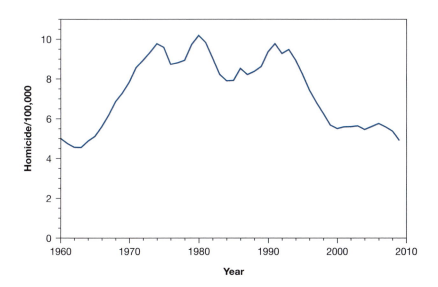

Figure 3.5
1960–2009 homicide rate trends in the United States

Source: Federal Bureau of Investigation. Crime in the United States. 2010. Washington, D.C.

all race and gender categories. While males commit about 90 percent of all homicides, black males between the ages of 18 and 24 have the highest rate of homicide offending. White females in all age groups have the lowest rate.

A study conducted by Riedel and Zahn combines data from the police department reports, interviews with police officials filing the reports, and data from other sources.[77] They analyzed data for the period 1968–1978 and compared homicides by sex, age, race, city, region, and a host of other variables. Some of the most important findings are that (1) homicide rates show minor fluctuations from year to year and (2) between 1968 and 1978 the homicide rate rose slightly. Other data of interest from this report show that:[78]

- Males are almost three times as likely to be victims of homicide as females.
- Blacks are twice as likely to be victims as whites.
- The age group 20–49 has the highest homicide victimization rate, while the elderly and the very young have the lowest. The greatest proportion of all homicides takes place between acquaintances; the lowest proportion between strangers. Surprisingly, 56 percent of homicide victims within the family are men and 43 percent are women. In cities this ratio increases to 70 percent of male victims and 30 percent of female.
- Among victims of acquaintance homicide 84 percent are men and 16 percent women. This pattern is the same for stranger homicides: 88 percent of victims are men, 12 percent are women.
- Over 80 percent of offenders are male.
- The age of the majority of offenders is 15–29.
- Blacks and whites commit about an equal number of homicides but, since blacks constitute only 15 percent of the population, they are overrepresented in the category of offenders.

The research conducted by Riedel and Zahn paved the way for the study of homicide as patterned according to certain socio-demographic characteristics. In the theory chapters to come, we will examine these studies in light of their development of violent crime causation models based on variables such as neighborhood characteristics, cultural norms and values, geographic region, and victim-offender relationship.

Trends in property crime

Property crime rates have declined in recent years, although not as significantly as violent crime rates. According to the UCR, a little over 8 million property crimes were reported to the police in 2014, representing a rate of almost 2,600 per 100,000. Property crimes include burglary, larceny, motor vehicle theft, and arson. Larceny theft represents the largest category of property crimes committed, accounting for about 71 percent of all property crimes.[79] Property crime makes up slightly more than three-quarters of all crimes committed in the United States. Data provided by the Bureau of Justice Statistics report a number of trends with regard to property crimes:[80]

- In over 80 percent of all burglaries, the offender gained entry to the victim's residence or other building on the property.
- In about 79 percent of all motor vehicle theft attempts, the vehicle was stolen.
- Of all larceny thefts committed in 2014, 1.6 million netted less than $50, 1.2 million between $50 and $200, and 2.4 million $200 or more.
- Larceny theft accounted for 70.8 percent of all property crimes in 2014. Burglary accounted for 20.9 percent, and motor vehicle theft for 8.3 percent.
- Property crimes in 2014 resulted in losses estimated at $14.3 billion.
- Households in rented property had more than twice the rate of motor vehicle theft than those in owned property.
- Urban households experienced higher overall property crime rates than suburban or rural households.
- Black males have the highest rate of victimization of property crimes.

These data indicate that property crimes, like the majority of other crime categories, fluctuate according to socio-demographic variables such as neighborhood characteristics and location. Moreover, the total number of property crimes has declined over the past decade by about 15 percent, with the property crime rate declining by about 25 percent.

Trends in crimes against women

The most serious crimes committed against women include assault, rape, and murder. Most of these crimes are perpetrated by men, consistent with the fact that *most* crimes are committed by men. The UCR provides statistics on the crime of rape, including forcible rape and attempted forcible rape. In 2014, an estimated 84,885 forcible rapes were reported to police, which represents about 38.5 offenses per 100,000 females in the population and a decline over the past decade of about 11 percent. According to NCVS data, rapes have declined about 58 percent from 1995 to 2010. In 1995, the rate was 5.0 per 1,000 persons, falling to 2.1 per 1,000 in 2010 (see Figure 3.6).

An analysis of data on rape and sexual assault shows the following trends:[81]

- An estimated seven of 10 female rape or sexual assault victims report the offender was an intimate partner, relative, friend, or acquaintance.
- Almost two-thirds of rapes/sexual assaults occurred from 6 p.m. to 6 a.m.
- 11 percent of all rapes/sexual assaults include the use of a weapon.
- Over 97 percent of perpetrators of rape/sexual assaults are men.
- Approximately 70 percent of rape/sexual assault offenders are over the age of 21.
- White offenders make up approximately 33 percent of offenders, while black offenders make up 48 percent.
- The lower the family income, the greater the likelihood that a woman will be the victim of a sexual assault or a rape.
- The victimization rate is highest for females between the ages of 16 and 19.

Figure 3.6
1973–2010 rape trends in the United States

Source: Stephanie Coontz and Rachel Adams. 20 April 2015. A Review of National Crime Victim Victimization Findings on Rape and Sexual Assault. CCF (Council on Contemporary Families). Retrieved from https://contemporary families.org/crime-victimization-brief-report/

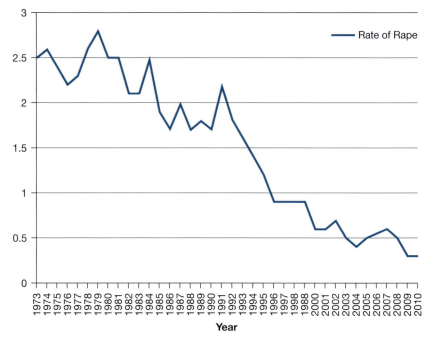

- Black females are three times more likely to become victims of rape or sexual assault than white females.

Other crimes for which women are most often the victim are incest and child sexual abuse. Data on these offenses are notoriously unreliable. Children who are the victims of incest, especially by their father or a close relative, are reluctant to report these acts to police. Families are often complicit in a conspiracy of silence to protect both the offender and the victim in sexual assaults of any kind, since a widespread belief remains that a woman who is the victim of a sexual assault is stigmatized or is even somehow guilty of encouraging the assault. Empirical data clearly demonstrate the error of these assumptions, but their prevalence nevertheless inhibits reporting and skews the data. Despite tendencies to underreporting, however, the incidence of sexual crimes is very high.

Trends in victimization

The National Crime Victimization Survey reports that in 2014, 1.1 percent of all persons age 12 or older in the U.S. (3 million persons) experienced at least one violent victimization and 8 percent of all households (10.4 million households) experienced one or more property victimizations. NCVS data indicate that crime does not occur uniformly; there is a definite relationship between age, race, gender, and the risk of being the victim of a crime. More crimes are committed against men than women, against young rather than older men, against people who live in cities, and against those in working-class areas rather than suburbs or upper-class areas. Although women are more likely to be victims of rape than men, the discrepancy is probably less than the data show, given the reluctance of police to arrest for male rape and of male victims to report the offense. The following is a summary of trends in victimization:

- People between 16 and 24 years old are more likely to be victimized than those of any other age group; approximately one-third of murder victims are under the age of 25. The risk of being a victim declines steadily after age 24, with people over the age of 65 accounting for the fewest incidents of victimization.
- Except for the crimes of rape and sexual assault, men are more likely to be the victims of all crimes and twice as likely to be the victims of violent crimes.
- African Americans experience a higher proportion of victimization than whites across most crime categories.
- The lower the social class, the greater the likelihood that one will be the victim of a crime, especially violent street crime that occurs in many neighborhoods; drug abuse, poverty, and social deprivation are prevalent.

Cross-cultural trends in victimization

The International Crime Victimization Survey (ICVS) was created in 1989 to make cross-cultural comparisons of crime victimization, while accounting for differences in patterns of reporting crime by both victims and police measures. It also aims to create a uniform standard of measurement of crime victimization, to make comparisons easier. The ICVS has conducted surveys in 24 industrialized countries and 46 cities in developing countries since its inception.

What is surprising to many is the revelation from a comparison of cross-cultural data based on victim surveys that U.S. citizens are *not* the most frequent victims of crime among the 17 industrialized nations studied.[82] These findings suggest the hypothesis that, as we pointed out earlier, the FBI, politicians, the media and law enforcement officials exaggerate the frequency and seriousness of crime in the United States, whereas other industrialized countries do not. Some of the more revealing findings from the cross cultural research are that:

- Crime victimization was reported highest (more than 24 percent of those reporting had been victimized in 1999) in Australia, England and Wales, the Netherlands, and Sweden.
- In Canada, Scotland, Denmark, Poland, Belgium, France, and the United States between 10–24 percent of the respondents reported being victimized.
- Finland, Catalonia (Spain), Switzerland, Portugal, Japan, and Northern Ireland had the lowest rates of victimization (below 20 percent).

In terms of crime rate measure (the number of crimes experienced per 100 people), the picture is slightly different: the United States fares relatively worse on incidence rates than on prevalence rates, with incidence being the actual number of victimizations that occurred and prevalence being the per capita rate of victimizations, whereas Denmark and Canada are somewhat lower on incidence. Incidence rates are highest in England and Wales, Australia, and the Netherlands.

According to Kesteren et al., ICVS data indicate the following cross-cultural trends in patterns of crime victimization and risk:[83]

- Crime rose between 1988 and 1991, stabilized or slightly dropped in 1995, then dropped even more in 1999.
- The picture in North America differs from that in Europe. Although ICVS data suggests that crime generally rose between 1988 and 1991, crime levels in North America actually dropped in 1991, whereas in the European countries with four ICVS measures (England and Wales, Finland, and the Netherlands), crime levels were still higher in 1991 than in 1988. Compared to surveys conducted in 1991, the rate of victimization dropped more in 2000 in North America than it did in five of the seven European countries showing similar trends.
- Since 1995, property crime has fallen more consistently than violent crime across all countries.
- Risk of victimization was 60 percent higher in the most urban areas than in the least urbanized ones, with the biggest differentials being for sexual incidents and thefts of and from cars.
- Households with higher incomes were more vulnerable to individual victimization across all crime categories by about a third, compared to poorer ones, with the biggest disparity being for automobile theft.
- The risk of victimization across all ICVS crime categories was well over double for younger respondents compared to that for people aged 55 or more.
- Individuals who went out or spent more time out of the house were at a greater risk for victimization by about 20 percent across ICVS crime categories, than respondents who spent more time at home.
- Individuals who were unmarried were twice as likely to be victims of contact crimes, defined as sexual assault, robbery, and assaults using force, compared to individuals in permanent relationships.
- Men are about 20 percent more at risk of victimization for robbery and assault than women.

Cross-cultural trends in crime victimization are an important source of data for criminologists, as they provide a better understanding of crime in various countries around the world. The study of criminal behavior is not limited to the boundaries of our own society. We can learn more about the phenomena of crime by examining its social correlates in different societies, as well as the various crime control efforts that are used to respond to crime. We will take a closer look at the study of crime in different countries in chapter 18.

SUMMARY

Where do we get our information about crime?

In this chapter, we introduced various data sources that give us information to help us glean a better understanding of crime related facts. Official statistics on crime are compiled by the FBI in the annual Uniform Crime Report (UCR), which presents data on crimes reported to law enforcement authorities by victims and voluntarily submitted by police agencies. In the early 1980s, the FBI began to revise the UCR program by providing a more comprehensive data source that focuses on each incident in a reported crime. Under the new National Incident-Based Reporting System (NIBRS), detailed information is gathered for each reported criminal incident.

What picture of crime do official data sources give us?

Unfortunately, the picture of crime painted by official crime data sources is tainted by the built-in methodological flaws and biases inherent to the reporting of crimes and the representation of facts by law enforcement officials. Many facts about crime fly in the face of commonly held ideas. To differentiate between scientifically reliable data and data generated for political or bureaucratic purposes, we must dispel the "myths that cause crime." By far, the most difficult myths about crime to overcome are those generated by law enforcement officials. While they need not be consciously deceptive, it is in their interests to paint a picture of crime that corresponds with what they need and do. Rules that systematically bias their work and a firm belief in the legitimacy of what they are doing add up to the generation of statistics that are misleading and perceptions of crime that are erroneous.

Is there a typical criminal?

The truth is, there is no typical criminal, nor is there a group of people that are particularly responsible for the majority of crime. In an effort to overcome some of the reporting flaws of official crime reports, researchers developed two alternative crime data sources: the National Crime Victimization Survey (NCVS) and the Self-Report Survey. Both data sources are designed to gather information about criminal activity beyond what is reported to police departments. As we have seen from crime statistics compiled by these two data sources, crime cuts across race, class, gender, and most other socio-economic and demographic variables. We can therefore glean a more accurate picture of who is the victim, who commits criminal acts, and what types of crime are committed from the more systematic and less biased researches summarized in this chapter.

These researches, however, cover only a small segment of the total amount of criminality. In chapters to come, we will build a more comprehensive understanding of crime by discussing a wide variety of criminal acts not included in the official statistics, the victim surveys, or self-report studies. Only then can we gain reliable scientific knowledge, through the accurate representation of facts which are derived from precise observations and logically consistent theories that explain them.

Are there certain crime trends or patterns of offending?

Data compiled for the UCR only focus on street crimes. As we have seen in this chapter, this depiction is distorted in the least, and in many ways misleading. Despite the seriousness and prevalence of corporate crimes, white collar crimes, corruption and political crimes, these types of criminal activities rarely get recorded in official crime reports gathered by police departments. Public scrutiny and media attention continue to focus on the more visible types of street crimes such as murder and assault, which, according to official data sources, have been showing a declining trend over the past several decades.

Who are crime victims and what do they have in common?

As we have seen from data compiled by the NCVS, there is a significant relationship between age, race, gender, and the risk of being the victim of a crime. Men are more likely to be victimized than women, except for the crime of rape, which may be more of a reflection of reporting, rather than actual occurrence. Moreover, data indicates that more crimes are committed against the young rather than older men. Working-class individuals who live in cities also have a greater chance of being victimized as opposed to more affluent residents of suburbs. less than the data show, given the reluctance of police to arrest for male rape and of male victims to report the offense.

CRITICAL THINKING QUESTIONS

1. Close your eyes for a few minutes. Now, picture a crime being committed. What is it? Describe what is happening. Who do you see? What do they look like? Who is the victim? What image do you have of the perpetrator? Where does this image come from?

2. You are watching television one evening and are deciding between two programs: one is profiling a case of corporate fraud amongst top executives and the other is profiling the murder of an actress by her estranged lover. Which one would you choose to watch? What factors influence your decision? Which program is most likely to draw the most viewers? Why?

3. Your best friend is deciding whether to rent an apartment in a major urban city close to work, or live in a condo in a small town and commute every day. His decision is largely influenced by the high crime rate in the city. What can you advise him about official data on crime? How can you go about getting a better picture of the crime problem in that city to help your friend make a more informed decision?

4. Someone knocks at your door one evening and tells you she is conducting a National Crime Victims Survey and ask for your help. Would you participate? Why or why not? Which crimes do victims have the most difficulty reporting to the police? Why?

5. Someone knocks at your door one evening and tells you that she is conducting a self-report study on crime and asks for your help. Would you participate? Why or why not? Which crimes are you most likely to be honest about? Least honest?

E-RESOURCES

For more information about the consequences of adolescent victimization, visit the Office of Juvenile Justice and Delinquency Prevention (OJJDP) website at http://www.ncjrs.gov/html/ojjdp/yv_2002_2_1/contents.html.

For trends in U.S. household victimization, refer to the Bureau of Justice Statistics website at http://www.bjs.gov/developer/ncvs/householdFields.cfm.

Additional data on child victimization can be accessed from the Child Trends Data Bank website at http://www.childtrends.org/databank/.

To find out more about rape and the college campus, see the Association of American Universities report, Sexual Assault Climate Survey (2015), found at https://www.aau.edu/news/article.aspx?id=15696.

Learn more about California's three-strike law by visiting http://www.silicon-valley.com/3strikes.html.

NOTES

1 Surette, Ray. 2015. *Media, Crime and Criminal Justice*, 6th ed. Belmont, CA: West/Wadsworth.

2 Hetsroni, A. 2012. Violent Crime on American Television: A Critical Interpretation of Empirical Studies. *Sociological Mind* 2(2): 144. http://dx.doi.org/10.4236/sm.2012.22018.

3 Federal Bureau of Investigation. 2014. *Crime in the United States, 2014*. U.S. Department of Justice. Retrieved from https://www.fbi.gov/news/stories/2015/september/latest-crime-stats-released/latest-crime-stats-released.

4 Ibid.

5 Op. cit., see 1.

6 Federal Bureau of Investigation. 1984. *Uniform Crime Reporting Handbook*. Washington, D.C.: U.S. Department of Justice, p. 6.

7 Seidman, David and Couzens, Michael. 1974. Getting the Crime Rate Down: Political Pressure and Crime Reporting. *Law and Society Review* 8: 457–493.

8 Federal Bureau of Investigation. 1981. *Uniform Crime Reports Handbook*. Washington, D.C.: U.S. Department of Justice.

9 Op. cit., see 7.

10 Selke, William and Pepinsky, Harold. 1982. The Politics of Police Reporting in Indianapolis, 1948–78. *Law and Human Behavior* 6(3/4).

11 Op. cit., see 7.

12   Shen, A. 2015. What Happens When People Panic About Crime Rates. *ThinkProgress.* Retrieved from http://thinkprogress.org/justice/2015/08/20/3688921/crime-rates-manipulation/. Warner, Bob. 1997. In 25 Years, One Other City Has Had Crime Counts Tossed. *Philadelphia Daily News.*

13   O'Brien, Robert. 1996. Police Productivity and Crime Rates: 1973–1992. *Criminology* 34: 183–207.

14   Carbone-Lopez, Kristin, Slocum, Lee Ann and Kruttschnitt, Candace. 2015. 'Police Wouldn't Give You No Help': Female Offenders on Reporting Sexual Assault to Police. *Violence Against Women,* September 8. doi: 10.1177/1077801215602345.

15   Muncie, J. 2014. *Youth & Crime.* Thousand Oaks, CA: SAGE.

16   Van Wyk, Rich. 2014. Riggs: Apathy Toward Crime Biggest Threat of 2014. *Indiana News Leader.* Retrieved from http://www.wthr.com/story/24475272/2014/01/16/apathy-toward-crime-biggest-threat-of-2014.

17   Herzog, Sergio. 2008. An Attitudinal Explanation of Biases in the Criminal Justice System: An Empirical Testing of Defensive Attribution Theory. *Crime and Delinquency* 54(3): 457–481.

18   Chilton, Ronald, Major, Victoria and Propheter, Sharon. 1998. *Victims and Offenders: A New UCR Supplement to Present Incident-Based Data from Participating Agencies.* Paper presented at annual meeting of the American Society of Criminology, Washington, D.C.

19   Federal Bureau of Investigation. n.d. National Incident-Based Reporting System (NIBRS). Retrieved from https://www2.fbi.gov/ucr/faqs.htm.

20   Office for Victims of Crime, U.S. Department of Justice, Office of Justice Programs, and United States of America. 2014. *Eight Benefits of NIBRS to Victim Service Providers.* Regoli, R. and Hewitt, J. 2008. Crime, Offenders, and Victims. In *Exploring Criminal Justice.* Burlington, MA: Jones & Bartlett Learning.

21   Op. cit., see 14.

22   Biderman, Albert D. and Reiss, Albert J., Jr. 1967. On Exploring the 'Dark Figure' of Crime. *Annals of the American Academy of Political and Social Science* 374: 1–15.

23   Costner, Herbert L., 1967. On Methodology in the Sociology of Crime. Paper presented at the annual meetings of the Pacific Sociological Association.

24   Batley, M. 2015. Sudden Spike in Violent Crime Across US Raises Alarm. *Newsmax.* Retrieved from http://www.newsmax.com/US/crime-violent-homicide-cities/2015/06/04/id/648724/. Wexler, Chuck. *Chief Concerns: Violent Crimes in America: 24 months of Alarming Trends.* Retrieved from http://www.assumption.edu/sites/default/files/public_safety/violent%20crime%20in%20america%20-%2024%20months%20of%20alarming%20trends%202007.pdf.

25   Reiman, Jeffrey and Leighton, Paul. 2016. *The Rich Get Richer and the Poor Get Prison: Ideology, Class and Criminal Justice,* 10th ed. London and New York: Routledge.

26   Barkan, S. and Bryjak, G. 2011. *Fundamentals of Criminal Justice: A Sociological View.* Burlington, MA: Jones & Bartlett Learning.

27   U.S. Department of Justice. 2014. *National Crime Victimization Survey.* Washington, D.C.: Bureau of Justice Statistics.

28   Ibid.

29   Truman, J. and Langton, L. 2015. *Criminal Victimization.* Retrieved from http://www.bjs.gov/content/pub/pdf/cv14.pdf.

30   Ibid.

31   Sheldon, R., Brown, W., Miller, K., and Fritzler, R. 2015. *Crime and Criminal Justice in American Society* 2(27). Long Grove, IL: Waveland Press. O'Brien, Robert M. 2000. Crime Facts: Victim and Offender Data. In Joseph F. Sheley (ed.), *Criminology: A Contemporary Handbook.* Belmont, CA: Wadsworth, pp. 59–83.

32   Maryland Coalition Against Sexual Assault. Reporting Sexual Assault: Why Survivors Often Don't. Retrieved from http://www.umd.edu/ocrsm/files/Why-Is-Sexual-Assault-

Under-Reported.pdf. Patten, D. J. 2015. An Unfinished Journey: The Evolution of Crime Measurement in the United States. *The Hilltop Review* 8(1): 23–35.

33   Simpson, Sally S., Harris, Anthony R. and Mattson, Brian A. 1995. Measuring Corporate Crime. In Michael B. Blankenship (ed.), *Understanding Corporate Criminality*. New York: Garland, pp. 115–140.

34   Elliot, Delbert S., Huizinga, David and Ageton, Suzanne S. 1985. *Explaining Delinquency and Drug Use*. Beverly Hills, CA: SAGE.

35   Porterfield, Austin L. 1946. *Youth in Trouble: Studies in Delinquency and Despair, with Plans for Prevention*. Forth Worth, TX: Leo Potishman Foundation.

36   Wallerstein, J.S. and Wyle, C. 1947. Our Law Abiding Law Breakers. *Probation* 25(March/April): 107–112, 118.

37   Fisher, M. A Guide to the Typical Offenses Handled by Youth Courts. In *Youth Cases for Youth Courts Desktop Guide*. American Bar Association. Retrieved from http://www.americanbar.org/content/dam/aba/migrated/2011_build/public_education/youth cases_youthcourts.authcheckdam.pdf. Marcum, Catherine D., Higgins, George E., Ricketts, Melissa L. and Wolfe, Scott E. 2015. Becoming Someone New: Identity Theft Behaviors by High School Students. *Journal of Financial Crime* 22(3): 318–328. Brooks-Russell, A., Conway, K. P., Liu, D., Xie, Y., Vullo, G. C., Li, K., . . . and Simons-Morton, B. 2015. Dynamic Patterns of Adolescent Substance Use: Results from a Nationally Representative Sample of High School Students. *Journal Of Studies On Alcohol And Drugs* 76(6): 962–970. Mishna, F., Cook, C., Gadalla, T., Daciuk, J., and Solomon, S. 2010. Cyber Bullying Behaviors Among Middle and High School Students. *American Journal of Orthopsychiatry* 80(3): 362–374. Hindelang, M.J., Hirschi, Travis, and Weis, J.G. 1981. *Measuring Delinquency*. Thousand Oaks, CA: SAGE. Short, James F., Jr., and Nye, F. Ivan. 1957. Reported Behavior as a Criterion of Deviant Behavior. *Social Problems* 5: 207–213.

38   Op. cit., see 34.

39   Zatz, Marjorie. 1987. The Changing Forms of Racial/Ethnic Biases in Sentencing. *Journal of Research in Crime and Delinquency* 24: 69–92.

40   Thornberry, Terence and Krohn, Marvin D. 2000. The Self-Report Method for Measuring Delinquency and Crime. *Criminal Justice* 4: 34–82; Gibbons, Donald. 1978. *Delinquent Behavior*, 3rd ed. Englewood Cliffs, NJ: Prentice Hall. Tittle, Charles, Villamez, Wayne J. and Smith, Douglas A. 1979. The Myth of Social Class and Criminality: An Empirical Assessment of the Empirical Evidence. *American Sociological Review* 43: 643–656.

41   Michalowski, Raymond J. 1984. *Order, Law, and Crime*. New York, NY: Random House.

42   Auty, K. M., Farrington, D. P., and Coid, J. W. 2015. The Validity of Self-reported Convictions in a Community Sample: Findings from the Cambridge Study in Delinquent Development. *European Journal of Criminology*, doi 1477370815578198; Cernkovich, Stephen A., Giordano, Peggy C. and Pugh, Meredith D. 1985. Chronic Offenders: The Missing Cases in Self-Report Delinquency Research. *Journal of Criminal Law and Criminology* 76: 705–732.

43   Moskowitz, S. 2013. Sexual Assault Continues to be a Problem on College Campuses. *The Daily Sundial*. Retrieved from http://sundial.csun.edu/2013/11/sexual-assault-continues-to-be-a-problem-on-college-campuses/. Fisher, B., Cullen, F. and Turner, M. 2000. *The Sexual Victimization of College Women*. U.S. Department of Justice, National Institute of Justice and Bureau of Justice Statistics, Washington, D.C. Kanin, Eugene. 1967. Reference Groups and Sex Conduct Norm Violation. *Sociological Quarterly* 8: 495–502.

44   Fedina, Lisa, Holmes, Jennifer Lynne and Backes, Bethany L. 2016. Campus Sexual Assault: A Systematic Review of Prevalence Research From 2000 to 2015. *Trauma, Violence and Abuse*. doi: 10.1177/1524838016631129.

45 Simon, Leonore. 1995. *Validity and Reliability of Violent Juveniles: A Comparison of Juvenile Self-Reports with Adult Self-Reports Incarcerated in Adult Prisons.* Paper presented at the annual meeting of the American Society of Criminology, Boston.

46 Ibid., see 42.

47 Chambliss, William J. 1973. The Roughnecks and the Saints. *Society* 11: 24–31.

48 Jennings, W., Loeber, R., Pardini, D., Piquero, A., and Farrington, D. 2016. *Offending from Childhood to Young Adulthood: Recent Results from the Pittsburgh Youth Study.* New York: Springer Publishing. Bridges, George S. 1987. An Empirical Study of Error in Reports of Crime and Delinquency. In Marvin E. Wolfgang, Terence P. Thornberry, and Robert M. Figlio (eds.), *From Boy to Man, from Delinquency to Crime.* Chicago, IL: University of Chicago Press.

49 Atkinson, P. 2013. *Age and the Decline in Crime.* Tempe, AZ: ASU News. Retrieved from https://asunow.asu.edu/content/age-and-decline-crime. Steffensmeier, Darrell and Allan, Emilie. 2000. Looking for Patterns: Gender, Age, and Crime. In Joseph F. Sheley (ed.), *Criminology: A Contemporary Handbook.* Belmont, CA: Wadsworth.

50 DeLisi, Matt. 2015. 4 Age–Crime Curve and Criminal Career Patterns. In *The Development of Criminal and Antisocial Behavior.* New York: Springer International Publishing. Steffensmeier, Darrell and Streifel, Cathy. 1991. Age, Gender, and Crime across Three Historical Periods: 1935, 1960 and 1985. *Social Forces* 69: 869–894.

51 Farrell, Graham, Laycock, Gloria and Tilley, Nick. 2015. Debuts and Legacies: The Crime Drop and the Role of Adolescence-limited and Persistent Offending. *Crime Science*, 4(1): 1–10. Brame, Robert and Piquero, Albert R. 2003. Selective Attrition and the Age-Crime Relationship. *Journal of Quantitative Criminology*, 19(2): 107–127. Hirschi, Travis and Gottfredson, Michael. 1983. Age and the Explanation of Crime. *American Journal of Sociology*, 89: 552–584; Mulvey, Edward and LaRosa, John. 1986. Delinquency Cessation and Adolescent Development: Preliminary Data. *American Journal of Orthopsychiatry* 56: 212–224. Wilson, Margo and Daly, Martin. 1997. Life Expectancy, Economic Inequality, Homicide, and Reproductive Timing in Chicago Neighborhoods. *British Journal of Medicine* 314: 1271–1274.

52 Agnew, Robert. 2003. An Integrated Theory of the Adolescent Peak in Offending. *Youth & Society* 34: 263–302.

53 Ibid., see 51.

54 Blumstein, Alfred. 2015. Racial Disproportionality in Prison. In *Race and Social Problems.* New York: Springer, pp. 187–193. Chilton, Ronald J. 1987. Race, Age, Gender and Changes in Urban Arrest Rates. *Gender and Society* 1: 152–171. D'Allesio, Stewart and Stolzenberg, Lisa. 2003. Race and the Probability of Arrest. *Social Forces* 81(4): 1381–1397. Milner, Adrienne N., George, Brandon J. and Allison, David B. 2016. Black and Hispanic Men Perceived to Be Large Are at Increased Risk for Police Frisk, Search, and Force. *PLOS ONE* 11(1): 1–13.

55 Chilton, Ronald J. 1987. Race, Age, Gender and Changes in Urban Arrest Rates. *Gender and Society* 1: 152–171.

56 Ibid., see 55.

57 Ibid., see 55.

58 Loury, Glenn C. 2016. Why Are so Many Americans in Prison? Race and the Transformation of Criminal Justice. In Jeffrey Reiman and Paul Leighton (eds.), *The Rich Get Richer and the Poor Get Prison: Ideology, Class and Criminal Justice*, 10th ed. London and New York: Routledge.

59 Heath, B. 2014. Racial Gap in U.S. Arrest Rates: 'Staggering Disparity'. *USA Today*, Nov. 19. Retrieved from http://www.usatoday.com/story/news/nation/2014/11/18/ferguson-black-arrest-rates/19043207/.

60 Greenfield, Lawrence A., and Snell, Tracy. 1999. *Women Offenders.* Washington, D.C.: Bureau of Justice Statistics.

61 Steffensmeier, Darrell and Allan, Emilie. n.d. Gender and Crime—Similarities in Male and Female Offending Rates and Patterns, Differences between Male and Female Offending Patterns. Retrieved from http://law.jrank.org/pages/1256/Gender-Crime.html.

62 Lombroso, Cesare. 1920. *The Female Offender*. New York: Appleton.

63 Ibid.

64 Booth, Alan and Osgood, D. Wayne. 1993. The Influence of Testosterone on Deviance in Adulthood: Assessing and Explaining the Relationship. *Criminology* 31: 93–118.

65 Bottcher, Jean. 2001. Social Practices of Gender: How Gender Relates to Delinquency in the Everyday Lives of High-Risk Youths. *Criminology* 39: 893–932.

66 Schwartz, J. and Steffensmeier, D. 2008. The Nature of Female Offending: Patterns and Explanation. In *Female Offenders: Critical Perspectives and Effective Interventions*. Burlington, MA: Jones & Bartlett Learning. Rowe, David, Vazsonyi, Alexander and Flannery, Daniel. 1995. Sex Differences in Crime: Do Mean and White-Sex Variation Have Similar Causes? *Journal of Research in Crime and Delinquency* 32: 84–100.

67 Reaves, B. 2013. Felony Defendants in Large Urban Counties, 2009—Statistical Tables. Retrieved from http://www.bjs.gov/content/pub/pdf/fdluc09.pdf.

68 Wolfgang, Marvin, Figlio, Robert and Sellin, Thorsten. 1972. *Delinquency in a Birth Cohort*. Chicago: University of Chicago Press.

69 Blumstein, A. et al., (eds.). 1986. *Criminal Careers and Career Criminals*. Washington, D.C.: National Academy Press.

70 Sampson, Robert J. and Laub, John H. 1993. *Crime in the Making: Pathways and Turning Points through the Life Course*. Cambridge: Harvard University Press. Elder, G.H., Jr. 1985. Perspectives on the Life-Course. In G.H. Elder, Jr. (ed.), *Life-Course Dynamics*. Ithaca, NY: Cornell University Press.

71 Calavita, Kitty, Pontell, Henry N. and Tillman, Robert H. 1997. *Big Money Crime: Fraud and Politics in the Savings and Loan Crisis*. Berkeley, CA: University of California, pp. 1, 31.

72 Ibid.

73 Ross, A. 2010. 22 Largest Bankruptcies in World History. Retrieved from http://www.instantshift.com/2010/02/03/22-largest-bankruptcies-in-world-history/.

74 Condon, G.E. Jr. 2014. Disgraced Congressman Randy 'Duke' Cunningham Is a Free Man Again. *The Atlantic*, July 10. Retrieved from http://www.theatlantic.com/politics/archive/2014/07/disgraced-congressman-randy-duke-cunningham-is-a-free-man-again/442878/.

75 Federal Bureau of Investigation. 2014. *Crime in the United States*. Bureau of Justice Statistics, U.S. Department of Justice, Washington, D.C.

76 Ibid.

77 Zahn, Margaret and Riedel, Marc. 1985. *The Nature and Pattern of American Homicide*. Washington, D.C.: U.S. Department of Justice.

78 Ibid.

79 Ibid., see 79.

80 Ibid., see 79.

81 Ibid., see 79.

82 Van Kesteren, J.N., Mayhew, P. and Nieuwbeerta, P. 2000. *Criminal Victimization in Seventeen Industrialized Countries: Key-findings from the 2000 International Crime Victims Survey*. The Hague, Ministry of Justice, WODC. Onderzoek en beleid, nr. 187.

83 Ibid.

CHAPTER OUTLINE

Doing criminology: Research and theory

4

In this chapter we will explore the following questions

KEY TERMS

theory
concepts
operational
 definition
hypotheses
principle of
 falsification
validity
reliability
bias
variable
correlation
causal
 relationship
spurious
 relationship
objectivity
replication
research strategy
research methods
survey
sample
random sampling
ethnography
interview
leading questions
detached
 observation
participant
 observation

Widespread claims about the danger to society of the escalating use of drugs are frequently rooted in ideology. Those who want to advance their own interests and views of right and wrong associate drug use with certain life styles, a youth culture of rebellion, or the routine activities of lower-class individuals. Claims about drugs can also reflect the bureaucratic agendas of law enforcement agencies, politicians, legislators, and other officials seeking to advance their own needs for resources, power, visibility, and prestige. For evidence we can look to the mid-1980s, when cocaine was replaced by its cheaper and more potent form—crack—as the preferred drug among inner-city users. This led to an all-out war on drugs by the federal government.

The reality of drug use in U.S. society has often been tainted by myths promoting an urgent need to combat its explosive growth and harmful social effects. Media, politicians, and legislators ignore historical, medical, and statistical evidence regarding the perceived threat, creating fear and panic greater than the actual social injury of drug use. Researcher Philip Jenkins notes that such drug panics share common patterns in which the drug under public scrutiny "is currently enjoying an explosive growth in popularity; is extremely addictive; and is destructive to the user or to others, threatening health or

Image 4.1 *The U.S. led War on Drugs has been costly, both in terms of dollars spent fighting it and human lives lost or damaged as a result of it. The reach of the War on Drugs now extends well-beyond America's borders, to the poppy fields of Afghanistan and coca groves of Colombia.*
Getty

experiment

experimental group

control group

statistical data

document analysis

historical research

operationalize

independent variable

dependent variable

experimental criminology

encouraging bizarre and violent behavior."[1] Very often, these drug panics are founded on questionable studies easily discredited upon thorough examination.

The danger is that panic can have a direct impact in shaping the law and guiding public policy.[2] The result is that we create policies built on moral opinion and political manipulation, instead of on the empirical evidence of scientific research. This was the finding in Jenkins' 1990s study of public reaction to the alleged explosion and widespread use of the drug "ice," a form of methamphetamine that is smoked, and the ensuing political debates on what to do about this "epidemic."[3] Political and media representation distort the public's understanding of illicit drug use and scapegoat addiction, diverting attention away from larger social problems such as discrimination, poverty, and unemployment.

The value of science is its distinct way of seeing and investigating the world around us. Of course, poets, novelists, filmmakers, painters, musicians, and theologians all provide diverse ways of viewing the world and understanding our surroundings. However, science is unique in that it searches for understanding by building data and theories that have a particular form.

Some people believe science is about predicting and controlling events. Nothing could be further from the truth. The essential methods of science are to create reliable means for gathering data, to construct logically consistent theories, and to test the theories through observation.[4] As a science, criminology strives to achieve these same goals.

In the last three chapters we've presented a large number of facts about crime and criminal law. But the scientific effort does not end with fact-gathering. As mathematician and thinker Henri Poincaré notes, "science is built up of

BOX 4.1: CONSIDER THIS . . .

Creating a fear of youth

Recent trends in media coverage of news stories involving youth crime has created a sense of fear and panic in society that has led the public to be suspicious of youth in general and created stereotypes about young people as dangerous, lawless, and out of control. This stereotype is founded upon the belief that youth represent a threat to the public order of society. Whether or not this representation of the current state of youth in America is truly founded is debatable. While violent crimes committed by youth are undoubtedly a serious matter, the coverage of these cases in the media are grossly disproportionate to the coverage of similar crimes committed by adult offenders, and also neglects the fact that the overwhelming crimes committed by youth are nonviolent.

Very often, people rely on getting factual information from media sources—the news, newspapers, radio, and internet, and indeed the media does shape public views on many issues, especially crime. According to data compiled by the National Crime Victimization Survey (NCVS), at a time when youth crime was at its lowest in 25 years, over 60 percent of those polled felt that juvenile crime was on the rise. The distorted image of youth in America has led to an increased and exaggerated attention to problems like drug use, teen pregnancy, and teen crime, deflecting attention from positive aspects of youth culture, education, and those that are positively involved in their communities and society. In turn, a get tough on youth ideology has spread throughout society and in political arenas for the last decade or so, where zero tolerance, harsher penalties, longer sentences, the elimination of rehabilitation and a decreased reliance on the juvenile justice system as an intervention for young offenders have resulted in more punitive sentencing policies, community surveillance, and profiling of youth by police in particular and by society as a whole. Is this moral panic against youth in today's society warranted or is it an attempt by certain segments of society to extend their control over young people, especially youth who are poor and who are from racial and ethnic minorities? Would research on youth crime give us a different picture than that portrayed by the media? *What do you think?*

Sources

Surette, Ray. 2015. *Media, Crime, and Criminal Justice: Images, Realities and Policies.* Stamford, CT: Cengage.

Youth Crime is a Moral Panic and an Exaggerated Response Based on Media Representation of News Stories About Youth. *The Write Pass Journal.* Retrieved from http://writepass.com/journal/2012/12/youth-crime-is-a-moral-panic-and-an-exaggerated-response-based-on-media-representation-of-news-stories-about-youth/.

Percentage of 8th, 10th, and 12th Grade Students Who Report They Used Any Illicit Drugs Other Than Marijuana[1] in the Past Year, by Race and Hispanic Origin, 2012–2013

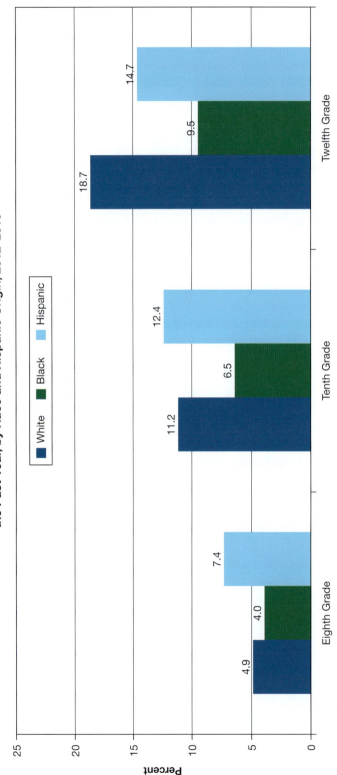

[1]For 12th graders only: Use of "any illicit drug other than marijuana" includes any use of LSD, other hallucinogens, cocaine, or heroin, or any use of other narcotics amphetamines, barbiturates, or tranquilizers not under a doctor's orders. For 8th and 10th graders: Use of "any illicit drug other than marijuana" includes any use of LSD, other hallucinogens, crack, other cocaine, or heroin, or any use of amphetamines or tranquilizers not under a doctor's orders. The use of other narcotics and barbiturates has been excluded because these younger respondents appear to overreport use (perhaps because they include the use of nonprescription drugs in their answers)

Source: Johnston, L. D., O'Malley, P. M., Bachman, J. G., Schulenberg, J. E., & Miech, R. A. (2014). Demographic subgroup trends among adolescents in the use of various licit and illicit drugs: 1975–2013 (Monitoring the Future Occasional Paper No. 18). Ann Arbor, MI: Institute for Social Research. Available at: http://www.monitoringthefuture.org/pubs/occpapers/mtf-occ81.pdf. Tables 4–6

Figure 4.1 Percentage of students who reported using illicit drugs, by race, 2012–2013

Source: Johnston, L.D., O'Malley, P.M., Bachman, J.G., Schulenberg, J.E., and Miech, R.A. 2014. Demographic subgroup trends among adolescents in the use of licit and illicit drugs: 1975–2013 (Monitoring the Future Occasional Paper No. 81). Ann Arbor, MI: Institute for Social Research. Retrieved from www.monitoringthefuture.org/pubs/occpapers/mtf-occ81.pdf.

facts as a house is built up of stone, but an accumulation of facts is no more science than a heap of stones is a house."[5] For facts to become part of the house of science, we must understand how they are *connected*: why is "A" related to "B"? How did it happen that "X" followed "Y" and not "Z"? As we shall see, our observations and theories lead us to ask many different questions about the facts. Asking these questions is a critical step in developing reliable scientific knowledge about crime.

THE SCIENCE OF CRIMINOLOGY

Society, it seems, is fascinated with crime. The popularity of crime-related media entertainment is a testimony to the public's fascination with "the criminal mind," police work, and the apprehension, prosecution, and punishment of people who commit crimes. As a result of media attention, unscientific descriptions and explanations of crime abound. The child molester who engages in deviant sexual acts is depicted as weird, inhuman, and "sick," the murderer is seen as driven by some sort of "evil," and the white-collar criminal is motivated solely by greed. Social policy is often driven by these simplistic, media-generated views of crime (see Box 4.1). It's thus essential for us to develop sound scientific knowledge about crime if we are to avoid social policies based on prejudices and "common sense" explanations that do not consider all the facts.

Criminology and "common sense"

Personal experience and "common sense" about the world are often fine starting points for sociological research. But they can mislead us. In the 14th century, common sense suggested the earth was flat (because it looks flat). Even today, many people believe that when the sun sets, it moves down in the sky. Scientific findings, however, inform us that the earth moves around the sun and gives the illusion that the sun is "setting." Facts about crime can be swayed in a similar way. As Figure 4.1 shows, surveys conducted on high school students show that, contrary to many people's "common sense" ideas about drug use, black high school students are *less* likely to use illegal drugs than are white high school students.

CONSTRUCTING SCIENTIFIC THEORIES

Scientific theories answer questions about how and why we observe what we do, and they also reveal useful relationships in the real world. Theories explain behaviors, establish logical connections between facts, and predict the occurrence of events. They add to our understanding of the social world around us, give meaning, and suggest solutions (see Box 4.2).

BOX 4.2: CONNECTING THEORY TO PRACTICE

Why "just say no"?

An epic crusade against the dangers of drug use began during the 1980s with the efforts of First Lady Nancy Reagan and her "just say no" campaign. This campaign was widely embraced across the United States and encouraged young people to say no to a variety of vices, including taking drugs, having premarital sex, drinking alcohol, and committing violence. The campaign was largely influenced by a National Institute of Health (NIH) theoretical research model supporting substance abuse prevention model developed by University of Houston Social Psychology Professor Richard Evans. Dr. Evans proposed "inoculating" teens with the learning tools and skills necessary to resist peer pressure and other negative social influences.

In 1983, the campaign turned global with the founding of D.A.R.E.—Drug Abuse Resistance Education, designed to discourage children from using illegal drugs, joining gangs, smoking, and drinking alcohol, by teaching them to resist peer pressure, act in their own interests, and educating them about the adverse effects of alcohol, tobacco, and drugs.

At the heart of this and other similar programs is the focus on education to build skills and strategies to resist the temptations of getting involved in crime and delinquency. The focus of these programs lies in the underlying theoretical perspective that crime and deviance are learned behaviors. They are learned by interacting with individuals who engage in the behavior, and by identifying with individuals who value attitudes and beliefs that support the behavior. The most suitable prevention strategies, therefore, should target those most vulnerable to education—children. Moreover, the social pressure to take drugs, join a gang, or get involved in criminal activity is also accompanied by the failure to resist such pressures.

Thus, when it comes to crime prevention, emphasis is placed on teaching children the benefits of staying in school, connecting with positive peer groups, developing positive attitudes, recognizing negative influences, and becoming aware of the risks involved in abusing drugs, smoking, and drinking alcohol. After all, who could forget the painful and poignant message in the unforgettable commercial of Terrie Hall, a famous anti-smoking advocate featured in the Center for Disease Control's advertisement, who "talks" about how she was once a cheerleader and in the homecoming court, but is now dying, her life destroyed by years of smoking that led to 10 cancer diagnoses that left her without a larynx to speak.

The diversity of thinking on crime and deviance is evidenced by the body of literature available on the nature and origins of the behavior. One can only come to this conclusion in the continuing and endless debates on the pros, cons, benefits, and vices of marijuana use and legalization, as we ponder the perplexing question of how something that can be medically prescribed can simultaneously be considered a health hazard. Perhaps this is a testimony to the complexity of the phenomena of crime itself. While criminologists may not agree on the precise cause of crime and deviance, the various schools of thought can help us organize our understanding of this multifaceted social behavior and help us develop strategies at both the individual level, and the societal level.

Sources

Evans, R. I. 1998. An Historical Perspective on Effective Prevention. In W. J. Bukoski and R. I. Evans (eds.), *Cost-Benefit/Cost-Effectiveness Research on Drug Abuse Prevention: Implications for Programming and Policy.* National Institute on Drug Abuse Research Monograph Series No. 176, NIH Publication no. 98–4021. Washington, D.C.: U.S. Government Printing Office.

Frieden, Tom. 2013. Terrie Hall: A Beautiful Woman Who Saved Thousands of Lives. *Huffington Post*, Sept. 19. Retrieved from http://www.huffingtonpost.com/tom-frieden-md-mph/terrie-hall-a-beautiful-w_b_3954443.html.

Smith, Warren Cole. 2014. Marijuana: Can U.S. Just Say No? *Baptist Press*, Oct. 28. Retrieved from http://www.bpnews.net/43608/marijuana-can-us-just-say-no.

Stricherz, Mark. 2014. What Ever Happened to 'Just Say No'? *The Atlantic*, April 29. Retrieved from http://www.theatlantic.com/politics/archive/2014/04/ghost-of-just-say-no/361322/.

A good scientific theory has the following characteristics:

- It is logically consistent. One part of the theory does not contradict another part.
- It is testable. It leads to conclusions that can be refuted or supported by evidence.
- It is valid and reliable. It is consistent with available evidence, and it produces the same results when measured over and over.
- It shows relationships among variables.
- It is objective. It is free of personal biases.

We will now discuss each of these qualifications and what they mean to criminology in particular, beginning with logical consistency.

Image 4.2 *Social policies governing employment background checks and requiring people to disclose personal information are often guided by scientific studies that support the basis of the effort.*

Larry French/Stringer

Theories and concepts are logically consistent

A theory is a comprehensive explanation about certain phenomena or experiences based on facts that have been gathered over a period of time. For example, we can propose the theory that sleep deprivation is a major cause of poor academic performance. Our theory can be based on information gathered over time showing that students who sleep fewer hours the night before a final exam consistently score lower than students who sleep more hours. Theories are made up of concepts—words, phrases, or ideas used to explain a category of individuals or a certain class of events. Concepts are the building blocks of research and theory. A concept can be as tangible as the word "poverty" to describe a category of people living below a specific standard of economic means, or as abstract as the word "prejudice" to describe the attitudes of certain individuals toward a certain racial or ethnic group. In order to gather accurate data and ensure that parts of the theory do not contradict one another, we need to define our concepts as precisely as possible. For a study of violent crime and social class, for example, we would need to begin with a clear definition of what violent crime and social class are. We would want to create an **operational definition**, which defines the concept in such a way that we can observe and measure it. Let's see how this works.

First, what is social class? Sociologists define social class as a person's status, derived from his or her income, wealth, education, occupation, and consumption patterns. This definition highlights the researcher's perspective that class is not just linked to income but also includes education and occupation. Highly successful drug dealers who have a high income thus would not be "upper class" unless they also met the other criteria. On the other hand, a highly successful drug dealer might have very high status in one community, such as among fellow drug dealers, and relatively low status in another, such as among legitimate businessmen and women, thus raising interesting questions about social class for criminological research and theory.

Second, what is violent crime? The FBI uses legal definitions of crime and defines violent crime as robbery, assault, and murder. For some research purposes this might be a perfectly adequate operational definition (especially if we wanted to use FBI data for research purposes). For other purposes, however, a researcher might want a more sociological definition, for example, one that groups such acts according to whether they are physically harmful to others rather than by legal categories. Grouping by legal categories is, obviously, much broader and would include many acts, such as the violation of workplace health and safety regulations, that lead to physical harm but are excluded from the FBI's definition.

Testing theories and hypotheses

Theories must be testable, the second quality of a good scientific theory. By creating operational definitions, we can begin to deduce specific hypotheses from the theory. **Hypotheses** are ideas about the world that we derive from theories and that we can disprove when we test them against observations. For example, we can make a hypothesis that children exposed to violent media are more likely to resolve disputes in a physical, aggressive manner, based on psychological theories about learning violence by imitating observed behavior. To test this hypothesis, we can have a group of children watch some type of cartoon that shows aggressive behavior and observe their interaction with one another. We can then compare their interaction to that of a group of children who have not watched the violent, aggressive program to see whether there is a difference. The results of these observations can enable us to test the accuracy of psychological theories on the effects of media portrayal of violence on imitating behavior. Hypotheses thus enable scientists to check the accuracy of their theories.

We must realize, however, that good theories can never be proven to be absolutely true; otherwise, they would no longer be theories but facts or natural laws. That the sky is blue and not purple or orange is a fact indeed. That a child who throws a ball in the air can be assured it will always come down is a tribute to the natural law of gravity. Good theories, however, must be constructed in a way that makes it possible for us to prove them *wrong*, if they *are* wrong indeed. Karl Popper's famous principle of falsification holds that to be scientific, a theory must lead to testable hypotheses that can be disproved if they are wrong.[6]

Validity and reliability measures

If we want to test theories and hypotheses, we need concepts and measurements that show they meet the third set of criteria for good scientific theories—they are valid and reliable. Validity is the degree to which a measure actually reflects the phenomenon under study. A very simple example comes from our experience of measuring academic performance. A chemistry professor administers a final exam to assess his or her students' understanding of the course material covered in a given semester. The test would be invalid if the questions on it did not reflect the content of the course in terms of lectures, readings, and assignments. Reliability refers to the extent to which a measure is consistent in producing the same results over and over again. Consider a bathroom scale. That scale would be highly unreliable if it gave different readings every time you stepped on it.

Suppose you want to know whether the crime rate in the United States has gone up or down. For years criminologists depended on the Uniform Crime Reports (UCR). As we saw in chapter 3, however, these reports were known to be incomplete, subject to local political events, and sometimes manipulated for political purposes.[7] The newer annual National Criminal Victim Survey (NCVS) provides more comprehensive data which includes, among other things, how many people have been the victims of crime, crime trends, and characteristics of perpetrators. This comprehensive data makes the NCVS a more valid source of information about crime.

When testing a hypothesis, researchers must make sure the findings are consistent with other studies of the same phenomenon or with the same study over time. Comparing UCR data with data from the NCVS, for example, provides a test of the reliability of both these different ways of measuring crime and crime victims. A major cause of unreliability in research is the presence of bias, a distortion that systematically misrepresents the true nature of what we are studying or the results of our study. Bias may creep into research due to the use of inappropriate measures, for example, when survey respondents do not tell the truth. In a classic study on drug use, respondents were asked questions about whether they used illegal drugs (see Table 4.1). Some of the respondents were wired to a machine they were told was a lie detector, while others were not. The subjects who thought their truthfulness was being

Table 4.1 How truthful are respondents on surveys?

Do you ...	Percent answering yes:	
	Subjects not hooked up to a lie detector	Subjects told they were hooked up to a lie detector
Ever drink and drive?	17.2	30.6
Ever smoke pot?	56.9	71.0
Ever use LSD?	19.0	27.4
Ever use cocaine?	25.9	43.5
Ever use amphetamines?	19.0	38.7

Source: Tourangeau, Roger, Smith, Tom W., and Rasinski, Kenneth A. 1997. Motivation to Report Sensitive Behaviors on Surveys: Evidence from a Bogus Pipeline Experiment. *Journal of Applied Social Psychology* 27(3): 209–222.

Note: Criminologists often rely on questionnaire data as a basis for testing theories. One problem that can arise is that the results may be biased because people do not tell the truth. In this study, respondents told that they were attached to a lie detector were much more likely to admit to illegal drug use than those who were not. The findings suggest that people are much more likely to tell interviewers the truth when they believe their responses can be checked.

monitored by the "lie detector" reported higher rates of illegal drug use than the others.

Based on the assumption that actual drug use would be about the same for both groups, the researchers believed the subjects who were not connected to a "lie detector" were understating their actual rate of illegal drug use. They thus concluded that simply asking people about drug use would lead to biased findings because respondents would not tell the truth.

Showing relationships among variables

In addition to being logically consistent, testable, valid, and reliable, scientific theories also show us the relationships among specific concepts or variables. A **variable** is a concept that can take on two or more values.[8] Some familiar variables include gender (male, female, transgender), work status (employed or unemployed), and geographical location (inner-city, suburbs, rural area). We can measure variables either quantitatively or qualitatively. Crime rates, unemployment rates, and drug use frequency are *quantitative* variables; we can attach numbers or quantities to them. *Qualitative* variables include people's attitudes toward drug use, fear of crime, and perception of dangerousness of their neighborhood. These are concepts we measure by asking people questions about their opinions, beliefs, thoughts, or feelings on a certain subject.

Establishing a relationship between two or more variables is at the very heart of criminological (and all other scientific) research. Suppose you want to find out whether there is a relationship between homicide and the level of social disorganization in a neighborhood, as Charis Kubrin did.[9] The first step is to define the two variables: violent crime and social disorganization. Kubrin used the UCR definition of homicide as both murder, the intentional taking of another person's life, and nonnegligent manslaughter, causing someone's death as a result of behavior that, while intentional, was not intended to cause the person's death.

For her measure of neighborhood social disorganization, Kubrin identified a number of variables such as poverty, number of households headed by a single parent, frequency of changing residence, and so on. Her findings generally supported the theory that the higher the level of social disorganization in a neighborhood, the higher the homicide rate.

Notice that what Kubrin explored is the correlation between the two variables: social disorganization and homicide. **Correlation** (literally, "co-relationship") is the degree to which two or more variables are associated with one another. When two variables are correlated, we may be tempted to infer that they have a **causal relationship**, a relationship between two variables in which one is the cause of the other. However, just because two variables are correlated, we cannot assume that one causes the other. Correlation does *not* prove causation.

We can also observe an apparent correlation between two variables that is a result of a spurious relationship. A **spurious relationship** is a correlation between two or more variables that is the result of another factor we are not measuring.[10] In the example above, some criminologists argue that the correlation between social disorganization and violent crime is spurious, and that what causes both is a third variable, a subculture of violence.[11] We must always critically analyze criminological research to ensure that positive relationships are not spurious. Once we have established this, the next goal is to make sure the theory is objective.

Scientific theories are objective

Even if criminologists develop logical and testable theories based on good operational definitions and collect valid and reliable data, like all human beings they have passions and biases that may color their research. For example, criminologists long ignored the criminality of women because they assumed that women rarely committed crime. Until that bias was recognized and corrected, researchers did not have an accurate picture of women and crime. Similarly, criminologists overlooked the crimes of corporations and the state.[12] If in the example above Kubrin had included the violent crimes of large corporations, the correlation she found might have disappeared. In the President's Report on Occupational Safety and Health (1972), for instance, the government estimated "the number of deaths from industrial disease at 100,000":[13]

> numerous studies have documented . . . the fact that much or most of the carnage is the consequence of the refusal of management to pay for safety measures . . . and sometimes of management's willful defiance of existing laws.[14]

Personal values and beliefs may endanger the researcher's **objectivity**, or ability to represent the object of study accurately without being affected by personal bias. Nineteenth-century sociologist Max Weber argued that in order for scientific research to be objective it has to be value-neutral, that is, personal beliefs and opinions should not influence the course of research. The sociologist should acknowledge personal biases and assumptions, make them explicit, and prevent them from getting in the way of observation and reporting.

How can we best achieve objectivity? First, recall the principle of falsification, which proposes that the goal of research is not to prove our ideas correct, but to find out whether they are wrong. To accomplish this, researchers must be willing to allow the data to contradict their most passionately held convictions. Theories should deepen human understanding, not prove a particular point of view.

A second way to ensure objectivity is to invite others to draw their own conclusions about our data. They can do this through **replication**, the repetition of a previous study using a different sample or population to verify or refute the original findings. The original study must spell out in detail the research methods employed, and researchers wishing to replicate a study should have access to the original materials, such as questionnaires or field notes.

Karl Popper described scientific discovery as an ongoing process of "confrontation and refutation."[15] Criminologists subject their work to this process by publishing their results in scholarly journals and other outlets. Once research has been published, other scholars read it with a critical eye, making criticisms, offering suggestions for modifications, or making supportive arguments. Then they may replicate the study in a different setting. Good scientific theories are rooted in the systematic collection and analysis of data that add to our understanding of a specific subject. Let us explore now the various methodologies used by criminologists to conduct scientific research.

CRIMINOLOGICAL RESEARCH METHODS

Criminological research requires a **research strategy,** a clearly thought-out plan that guides the work. For instance, if you want to study the relationship between poverty and crime, you must establish the level of understanding you want to achieve about the subject. Do you want to know how living in poverty can influence an individual's choice to commit crime, or do you want to assess whether involvement in criminal activity creates financial loss and hardship for an individual? Do you want to investigate long-term trends, or do you want to develop an in-depth understanding of the personal experiences of individuals? The research strategy's purpose is to fill gaps in our understanding of the social world and to obtain preliminary knowledge that will help guide our choice of **research methods**—the specific techniques, such as questionnaires, experiments, or surveys, we use for systematically gathering data.

Table 4.2 Some major sociological research methods: how to choose?

Method	When it is appropriate to use
Survey research	When we are looking for basic information about a large population, we conduct survey research by selecting a sample that is representative of the entire population.
Fieldwork	When we want detailed information and when surveys are impractical for getting it (for example, when studying the day-to-day behavior of youth gangs), fieldwork usually allows us to use relatively small samples.
Detached observation	When we need to stay removed from the people we are studying and gather data in a way that minimizes impact on the subjects, we use detached observation.
Participant observation	When we want first-hand knowledge of the direct experience of subjects, including a deeper understanding of their lives, we use participant observation.
Experiments	When we want to test the effect of a variable on human behavior, we conduct an experiment by matching experimental and control groups on relevant variables but provide them with different experiences in the experiment.
Using existing information	When direct acquisition of data is either not feasible or not desirable because the event studied occurred in the past or because gathering the data ourselves would be too costly or difficult, we analyze existing information.

Below we look at a range of research methods, including their advantages and disadvantages. We then discuss how you might prepare a criminological research project.

Criminologists employ a variety of methods to learn about the social world (see Table 4.2). Since each method has strengths and weaknesses, a good research strategy may use several methods. If they all yield similar findings, we are more likely to have confidence in the results.[16] The principal methods are the survey, fieldwork, experiments, and working with existing information.

Survey research

A survey consists of administering a questionnaire to or interviewing a group of people in person or by telephone or email to determine their characteristics, opinions, and behaviors. Surveys are common in sociological research. We can use them to test a theory or simply to gather data. The National Crime Victimization Survey (NCVS) is an example of survey research. It gathers data on crime victimization from a sample of 100,000 citizens and publishes the results through the Bureau of Justice Statistics.

The first step in designing a survey is to identify your population of interest. That is, who makes up the population from which you will draw your data? For the NCVS, who should you survey? All U.S. citizens? Everyone in a certain age group? People in the lower classes? Pet owners? To conduct a good study you'll want to clearly identify the survey population that will most effectively help you answer your research question. The NCVS includes people aged 12 or older in all social classes.

Once you've identified a population of interest, you will usually study a sample of that group, a sub-set or portion of the larger population selected to represent the whole. Researchers seldom have the time or money to talk to all the members of a population, especially if it is a large one, so they sample from it. Thus, the size of the sample selected is an important consideration. Other things being equal, larger samples better represent the population than smaller ones. Ideally, a sample should reflect the composition of the population you are studying. For instance, if you wanted to be able to generalize research data about the population of the United States to draw conclusions about the whole population, you would need to collect correctly proportioned samples from different social classes, neighborhoods, and urban and rural areas.

With proper sampling techniques, criminologists can use relatively small (and therefore relatively inexpensive) samples to represent large populations. A well-chosen sample of 1,000 voters can represent 100 million U.S. voters with a fair degree of accuracy, enabling survey researchers to reasonably predict election outcomes.

To avoid bias in surveys, criminologists often use **random sampling**, in which everyone in the population has an equal chance of being chosen for the study. Typically, researchers draw up a list of everyone in the population of interest. Then they draw names at random until they reach the desired sample size. Moreover, in constructing surveys, criminologists take care to ensure that the questions and their possible responses will capture the respondents' point of view. Poorly worded questions can produce misleading results (see Figure 4.2). Through effective sampling techniques, surveys can save a great deal of time and money.

Figure 4.2 How to make a good survey

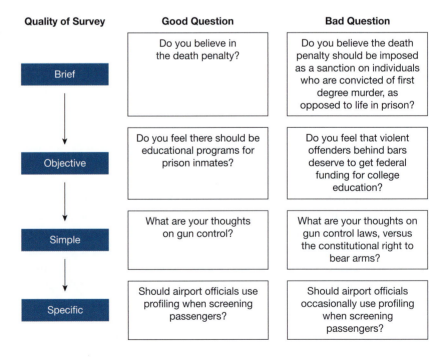

Quality of Survey	Good Question	Bad Question
Brief	Do you believe in the death penalty?	Do you believe the death penalty should be imposed as a sanction on individuals who are convicted of first degree murder, as opposed to life in prison?
Objective	Do you feel there should be educational programs for prison inmates?	Do you feel that violent offenders behind bars deserve to get federal funding for college education?
Simple	What are your thoughts on gun control?	What are your thoughts on gun control laws, versus the constitutional right to bear arms?
Specific	Should airport officials use profiling when screening passengers?	Should airport officials occasionally use profiling when screening passengers?

Fieldwork

Image 4.3 *How do the techniques of field research help us better understand the structure and function of cults and the daily interactions and experiences of group members?*

Artisan Pics/The Kobal Collection/Mountain, Peter

Fieldwork, sometimes called **ethnography**, takes the researcher into the field where people live their lives. It uses in-depth and often extended on-site study to describe a group or community. Criminologists have employed the techniques of fieldwork to study everything from organized crime[17] to graffiti,[18] delinquent gangs,[19] prostitution and drug use among inner-city women,[20] and a host of other criminal and delinquent behaviors.

Most fieldwork combines several different methods of gathering information. These include interviews, detached observation, and participant observation. An **interview** is a detailed conversation designed to obtain in-depth information about a person and his or her activities. In surveys, interview questions can be either open-ended, where there is no definite answer, or closed-ended, where the answer is limited to specific choices such as "agree," "disagree," and "no opinion." In fieldwork, however, questions are usually open-ended to allow the respondent to answer in his or her own words. Sometimes the interviewer prepares a detailed set of questions; at other times, the best approach is to simply have a list of broad topics to cover.

Good interviewers guard against influencing the respondent's answers. In particular, **leading questions**, questions that elicit a particular response, are a danger. Imagine a question on attitudes toward the environment that read, "Do you believe poor neighborhoods, which have high incidences of violent crime, are likely to have high incidences of domestic violence?" The bias in this question is obvious—the stated association of poor neighborhoods with violent crime creates a bias in favor of a "yes" answer. Gathering accurate data depends upon asking questions that are not biased and do not bias the respondent.

Sometimes the study strategy requires that researchers in the field keep a distance from the people they are studying, simply observing without getting involved.[21] The subjects may or may not know they are being observed. This approach is called **detached observation**.

In his study of two delinquent gangs ("The Saints and the Roughnecks"), William J. Chambliss employed detached observation to discover how two delinquent gangs, one middle class and one working class, conducted their "routine activities." Chambliss spent many hours observing gang members without actually being involved in what they were doing.[22] With the gang members' permission, he sat in his car with the window rolled down so he could hear them talk and watch their behavior while they hung out on a street corner. At other times he observed them playing pool while he played at an adjoining table, or followed them in his car as they drove around in theirs, or sat near enough to them in bars and cafés to hear their conversations. Through his observations at a distance, Chambliss was able to observe in detail the kinds of delinquencies the gangs engaged in. He was also able to unravel some of the social processes that led to the delinquent acts and observe other people's reactions to the gang members.

Detached observation is particularly useful when there is reason to believe that other forms of fieldwork might influence the behavior of the people to be observed. It is also a useful technique for checking the validity of what the researcher has been told in interviews. A great deal of sociological information about illegal behavior has been gathered through detached observation.

One problem with detached observation, however, is that the information gathered is likely to be incomplete. Without actually talking to them, researchers cannot check their impressions against the experiences of the people they are studying. For this reason, detached observation is usually supplemented by in-depth interviews. In his study of delinquent gangs, Chambliss periodically interviewed gang members to complement his findings and check the accuracy of his detached observations.[23]

Another type of fieldwork is **participant observation**, a mixture of active participation and detached observation. Participant-observation research can at times be dangerous. Chambliss' research on organized crime and police corruption in Seattle, Washington, exposed him to threats from the police and other organized crime network members who feared he would reveal their criminal activities.[24]

Experiments

Experiments are research techniques for investigating cause and effect under controlled conditions. In a typical experiment, participants are selected who share characteristics such as age, education, social class, and experiences that are relevant to the experiment and then randomly assigned to two groups. The first, called the **experimental group**, is exposed to the independent (or experimental) variable. This is whatever the researchers hypothesize will affect the subjects' behavior. The second group is the control group, where subjects receive no special attention.

In a classic study examining the effect of violent images in the media on viewers' tolerance of real violence, researchers showed one group of undergraduate male students sexually explicit and violent films (the experimental group), while others were shown no films at all (the control group). The students were then interviewed to determine how sympathetic they were to a woman who had been raped. The studies found that students in the experimental group were less sympathetic than those in the control group. The researchers concluded that exposure to violence against women in the media increases men's tolerance of actual violence against women.[25]

Working with existing information

Criminologists frequently work with existing information and data gathered by other researchers, including statistical data, documentary analysis, and historical research.

Image 4.4 *Experiments are often used to determine causal relationships in a controlled environment.*

Patrick Landmann/Science Photo Library

Statistical data include numerical information obtained from government agencies, businesses, and other organizations that collect data for their own or others' use. The Uniform Crime Reports and the National Criminal Victim Survey are two sources of statistical data provided by the government that are invaluable for criminological research. In addition the Bureau of Justice Statistics provides a vast amount of information about police departments, courts, prosecutors, and public defenders' offices.

Document analysis is the analysis of written materials: previous studies, newspaper reports, court records, and other forms of text produced by individuals, government agencies, private organizations, and other sources. However, because such documents are not always compiled with accuracy in mind, good researchers exercise caution in using them. People who keep records are often aware that others will see the records and take pains to avoid recording anything unflattering. The expert researcher looks at such materials with a critical eye, double-checking other sources for accuracy where possible. The diaries and memoirs of politicians are a good example of documents that are an invaluable source of data but must be interpreted with great caution.

Historical research is research based on historical documents. Often such research is comparative, examining historical events in several different countries, looking for similarities and differences. Historical research in criminology often differs from the research conducted by historians. Criminologists usually identify patterns common to different times and places, whereas historians focus on a particular time and place and are less willing to draw broad generalizations from their research. One example of historical research in criminology is studies of law creation.[26]

Historical data requires precautions because it may be incomplete, inaccurate, and sometimes deliberately biased. Gaps in the historical record exist, and it may be difficult or impossible to obtain crucial information. Finally, the researcher must guard against the possibility that words had different meanings in earlier times.[27]

Criminological research seldom follows a "recipe" that indicates exactly how to proceed. Criminologists often have to feel their way as they go, responding to the challenges that arise during research and adapting new methods to fit the circumstances. The following section provides you with a guide to the various stages of criminological research.

A STUDENT'S GUIDE TO CRIMINOLOGICAL RESEARCH

The stages of criminological research can vary, even when researchers agree about the ideal sequence to follow. The ideal process in fact includes six basic steps, according to the scientific method:[28] (1) define the problem, (2) review the literature, (3) formulate a hypothesis, (4) collect and analyze the data, (5) develop a conclusion, and (6) share the results (see Figure 4.3).

Define the problem

The main goal of the scientific method is to answer the question you asked at the beginning of the process, so defining the problem (or the research question) is the most important step. Defining the problem means stating, as clearly as possible, what it is you want to investigate. What exactly do you want to know? Suppose you want to find out whether having a higher level of education reduces a person's chances of becoming involved in criminal activity.

Figure 4.3 The scientific method

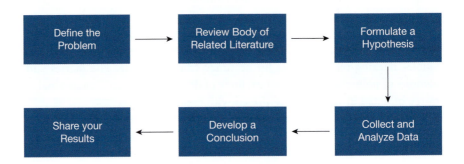

Start by narrowing down key words, definitions, and ideas. Essentially, you must **operationalize** the abstract concepts of education and crime by making them measurable, such as stating educational achievement in terms of years of schooling completed and degrees acquired. Likewise, you must also narrow down our study of criminality. Are you investigating the relationship between educational achievement and violent crime, property crime, or both? Or are you going to narrow your topic even further by choosing a certain category of violent or property crime? Are you studying criminality among a certain class, age, race, or gender of individuals? Are there other social structural variables you want to examine? You must take all these considerations into account before moving on to the second step in the scientific method, reviewing the literature.

Review the literature

Having operationalized your variables, you next review the literature. This means reading and describing other scholarly studies relevant to your topic, always a good idea. If your topic has been researched before, you can add to your own methodology by learning from the various insights into it that already exist in the literature. If, in fact, previous research and experiments have been conducted on your particular topic, you should be able to see what has or has not worked in the past and test your hypothesis in a different way, learning from the outcomes of past efforts. Reviewing the information you have found in the scientific literature will also give you a more in-depth understanding of your topic, making your research stronger, more effective, and scientifically grounded. You will be better able to assess the extent to which your research will add to the existing body of knowledge on your subject.

A literature review will also allow you to see methodological problems that have been encountered by prior researchers so you can refine and amend your own methodology. Comparing your intended research methodology with other

Table 4.3 Important issues a literature review addresses

Is the research question significant and is the work original and important?
Have the instruments used been demonstrated as reliable and valid?
Do the outcome measures relate clearly to the variables with which the investigation is concerned?
Does the research design fully test the hypothesis?
Are the subject's representatives of the population to which generalizations are made?
Did the researcher observe ethical rules?
Has the research reached such a stage that publication is justified and the results are meaningful?

Source: O'Neill, James. American Psychological Association. 2015. *Literature Review Guidelines.* Retrieved from www.apa.org/pubs/journals/men/literature-review-guidelines.aspx.

studies will also give you a context within which to compare and contrast your own findings. The American Psychological Association (APA) outlines several important research issues that a thorough review of the literature can clarify (see Table 4.3).

Formulate a hypothesis

After a thorough examination of the literature, you can begin formulating a hypothesis. Think of your hypothesis as an "educated guess" based on prior observations. It can become part of a theory, or it can become a theory on its own. A hypothesis is therefore a speculative statement about the relationship between certain variables, made in order to draw out and test its conclusion. A hypothesis tells us how one aspect of human behavior affects another. The direction of this relationship determines which variable under study is independent, and which is dependent (see Figure 4.4). The **independent variable** is the variable that we hypothesize has caused or influenced another. The **dependent variable** is the variable we believe is caused by or influenced by the independent variable.

Recall our research topic about the relationship between educational achievement and criminality. In this study, we are interested in the effect education has on crime. Thus, educational achievement is our independent variable, and criminality our dependent variable. Correctly identifying independent and dependent variables is essential to establishing a logical consistency to the research study and clarifying cause-effect relationships. Does the independent variable actually cause or lead to the dependent variable, or is the event connecting the two variables an existing correlation? If we find, for example, that crime goes down as educational achievement goes up, we must also consider that a third variable such as income, may be acting as the causal link, therefore making the relationship between educational achievement and criminality only a spurious relationship.

Figure 4.4
Examples of causal logic: X leads to Y

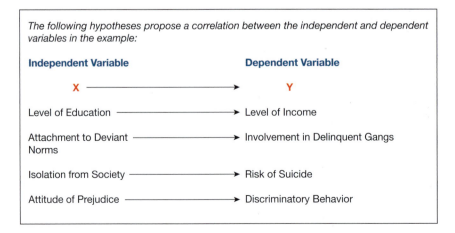

The following hypotheses propose a correlation between the independent and dependent variables in the example:

Independent Variable	Dependent Variable
X	**Y**
Level of Education	Level of Income
Attachment to Deviant Norms	Involvement in Delinquent Gangs
Isolation from Society	Risk of Suicide
Attitude of Prejudice	Discriminatory Behavior

Collect and analyze data

To begin the task of collecting data, first select a representative sample from the population under study.[29] Ideally, social scientists conduct research studies using a random sample, in which, as we said earlier, everyone in the population under study has an equal chance of being selected. For example, if you want to examine the opinion of people in a specific city on the subject of sex offender registration, you can obtain a random sample of residents by using the city telephone directory and a computer-generated sampling technique for randomly selecting names.

Sometimes, however, we cannot obtain a truly random sample. For example, if we wanted to study the social organization of maximum security prisons, then to get a true random selection we would have to ensure that all maximum security prisons, both state and federal, had an equal chance of being selected for the study. For practical and logical reasons, this would not make sense. We would likely have to take into consideration other issues such as geographic location, access, and security.

In your study you must also ensure the reliability and validity of the research.[30] One way to test validity is to make certain the variables you have selected to study are an accurate measure of the phenomena you are researching. For example, let us say you are trying to examine the effects on class participation of enforcing strict attendance policies. Is increased attendance alone a valid measure of class participation? Or, is class participation more accurately measured by an increase in questions, discussions, and comments made by students? Make sure you are measuring what you set out to measure. Equally important, you must also make certain that your research will produce results that are reliable in their measure, meaning that other researchers who replicate your study will get the same results.

After selecting a sample to study and addressing the issues of reliability and validity, you now need to determine how to collect the data based on the type of research questions and hypothesis you've proposed. You must select a research method that is most suitable to gather the data necessary to answer the question you have posed. Choosing a research design depends on how you want to structure your research. It also may be influenced by the particular subject you are studying, the type of information you want, and your own personal preferences. For example, if you are interested in studying the effect of sex offender registration laws on the personal experiences of sex offenders, you may want to capture and record details about the daily hardships, obstacles and difficulties they face by conducting in-depth interviews. This is where a good literature review can give you insights on which path previous researchers have taken to answer your own research question.

The choice of research method will also determine how you analyze your data. Data analysis means "cleaning up" or organizing your data into charts, tables, figures, graphs, or other formats depending on research design. It can also include transcribing recorded interviews, organizing field notes, or recalling information from observation. Your analysis of the data provides the reader with a summary of your observations, comments on your findings, and an assessment of how your data shed light on the question under study.

Develop a conclusion

After collecting and analyzing your data you should begin to draw a conclusion[31] that summarizes what you learned (did the data support your original hypothesis or didn't it?), questions that remain unanswered, benefits and advantages of the research, possible flaws and shortcomings in it, and suggestions or recommendations for future inquiry into the subject. A conclusion is like the final act or scene in a play . . . It ties the beginning to the end. It may not turn out the way the audience wanted or expected, but it puts the entire play in perspective.

Conclusions do not need to answer all questions raised by a particular research subject. The social world is an unstable, unpredictable environment that is very difficult to evaluate. Relationships between variables are, at the least, imperfect. A good scientific conclusion, therefore, will give the research a sense of completeness and value and not try to establish absolute principles. It does not necessarily need to "prove" something but simply comment on the relevance of the results in advancing knowledge about and understanding of the subject.

Share the results

The development of reliable knowledge depends on researchers sharing their results with others. This can be a painful experience; your methods and findings may be criticized for failing to take into account some of the many criteria for good research outlined in this chapter. Nonetheless, sharing the results is imperative. Most criminologists publish the results of their research either in professional journals (such as *Criminology*, *The British Journal of Criminology*, and *Law and Society Review*) or in books. Another way of sharing the results is to present a paper at the meeting of a professional association such as the American Society of Criminology, the Society for the Study of Social Problems, or the Academy of Criminal Justice Sciences. Whatever avenue you choose, the important part of the scientific process is letting other people know what you are doing and the results of your research.

The need to share the results of your work with the academic community places a responsibility on you as a researcher to make sure that your research does not violate any moral or ethical standards. Considering ethical issues that may affect various components of your research project is just as important as using an organized, scientific approach. We turn now to a discussion of ethics in conducting criminological research.

APPLYING ETHICS IN CONDUCTING CRIMINOLOGICAL RESEARCH

Social scientific research is most often conducted on human beings. The value and integrity of criminological research depend on our upholding the highest level of ethical standards and considerations. Issues of confidentiality, privacy, disclosure of research methods, and the protection of human subjects are concerns we must address at the outset of any research endeavor. The researcher's right to know must be balanced against the subject's right to privacy. The social value of gathering data and obtaining information for the purpose of advancing knowledge must be weighed against the duty and obligation of the researcher to be honest, forthright, and value-neutral.

Image 4.5 *In 1971, a team of researchers at Stanford University, under the direction of Dr. Philip Zimbardo, conducted a mock prison experiment to determine the psychological impact of becoming a prisoner and a guard. Participants were randomly assigned the role of guard or inmate. After a few days, the experiment was terminated prematurely because of the authoritarian and abusive treatment of the "prisoners" by those adopting the role of guards. Zimbardo's experiment has been a source of controversy for years. What ethical questions are raised here?*

Philip G. Zimbardo, Inc.

Frank E. Hagan offers an intuitive understanding of the role of the researcher in exercising objectivity and pursuing professional integrity while engaging in scientific research.[32] Hagan suggests that criminologists adhere to a code of professional ethics that will guide them in accepting responsibility for:[33]

- Protecting subjects from harmful procedures.
- Honoring commitments to subjects by respecting mutual agreements.
- Reporting research findings in an objective manner.
- Preserving the privacy and confidentiality of subjects.

We hold criminological research to such rigorous standards because it can and does influence public policy. While these guidelines seem clear cut, they can nevertheless be challenging to follow in real-life situations. The *Academy of Criminal Justice Sciences (ACJS)* has adopted an official code of ethics in conducting scientific research that underlies the values, ideals, and professional responsibility of criminologists in pursuit of their academic endeavors. General principles within this code of ethics call for members of the criminal justice academic and professional community to be "committed to enhancing the general well-being of society and of the individuals and groups within it . . . to avoid incompetent, unethical or unscrupulous use of criminal justice knowledge . . . [and] recognize the great potential for harm that is associated with the study of criminal justice, and . . . not knowingly place the well-being of themselves or other people in jeopardy in their professional work." Table 4.4

Table 4.4 Ethical considerations in conducting your research project

Adhere to the highest possible technical standards in research.
Acknowledge the limitations that may affect the validity of findings.
In presenting research findings, do not misrepresent the findings or omit significant data.
Do not make any commitments to respondents, individuals, groups, or organizations unless there is full intention and ability to honor them.
Human subjects have the right to full disclosure of the purposes of the research as early as it is appropriate to the research process, and they have the right to an opportunity to have their questions answered about the purpose and usage of the research.
Subjects of research are entitled to rights of personal confidentiality unless they are waived.
The process of conducting criminal justice research must not expose respondents to more than minimal risk of personal harm . . . make every effort to ensure the safety and security of respondents and project staff. Informed consent should be obtained when the risks of research are greater than the risks of everyday life.

Source: Academy of Criminal Justice Sciences, *Code of Ethics* 2016. Retrieved from /www.acjs.org/pubs/167_671_2922.cfm.

highlights the guidelines set forth by the ACJS as ethical standards to maintain objectivity and integrity in conducting criminological research.

Adhering to ethical standards of conduct in scientific research is essential. Ethical standards must guide research methodologies that will dictate the course of future developments in criminological inquiry. We turn now to a discussion of the future of criminological theory and research.

LOOKING AHEAD: EVIDENCE-BASED CRIMINAL JUSTICE POLICY

We have mentioned above that one reason reliable data is so critical in criminology is that it has the power to shape and influence the course of crime control policy. But educating policy makers and the public about scientific research findings in criminal justice issues is no easy task. Unless conclusions and suggestions for social change agree with what people already believe, they are often disregarded as irrelevant, flawed, or extremist.

This means future criminology researchers must strive to produce legitimate and consistent results that clearly support the policy changes they recommend. The goal is not to perpetuate policies that are short-sighted, ineffective, or counterproductive but rather to alleviate the problem of crime. This goal can be accomplished only if criminal justice policy initiatives are guided by a thorough review of the literature and driven by research evidence which supports the theoretical wisdom of planned changes and reforms (see Box 4.3). The results of high quality evaluative studies on the best practices in the field of

BOX 4.3: CONNECTING RESEARCH TO PRACTICE

Prime time crime in Washington D.C.

In January 2001, I began working as a Program Analyst for the Court Services and Offender Supervision Agency for the District of Columbia (CSOSA), a federal agency providing treatment and supervision services to pre-trial release, probation, and parole offenders in Washington, D.C. My role as a research specialist there was to evaluate programs and initiatives within the agency and make recommendations for improving its policies and practices for supervising offenders in the community.

In May 2001, the Associate Director of the Office of Community Supervision Services directed me to identify and develop an intervention that would better address the issue of re-arrest among violent and drug-related offenders. He wanted to know how we can better supervise offenders in the community to make them more accountable and responsible citizens, thereby reducing their chances of getting in trouble or being re-arrested. I began addressing this question by developing a profile for a sample of 36 offenders (30 probationers and 6 parolees) under some form of community supervision, who were re-arrested in October, November, and December 2000.

An analysis of the demographic data gathered revealed that the majority of offenders in the sample were young, single, African American males. They were either unemployed or under-employed, with very little education and unstable housing arrangements, making multiple moves in a short period of time. Moreover, the overwhelming majority of offenders in the sample had a history of violent behavior and drug-related offenses. Approximately 60 percent of the offenders under probation supervision had prior convictions for violent offenses, and 93 percent had prior convictions for drug-related offenses. Virtually all those under parole supervision had a violent felony conviction.

The study also examined patterns and trends in the type of re-arrest, day and time of re-arrest, and time frame of re-arrest. More than 80 percent of offenders were re-arrested for violent and drug-related offenses, with almost 90 percent of offenders being re-arrested within the first year of their period of supervision, and over 50 percent within the first six months. Another significant finding was that the vast majority of offenders were re-arrested during the daytime hours and on a weekday.

This research suggested that providing offenders with programming designed to increase accountability and structure in their environment and daily routine was fundamental to reducing re-arrest among violent and drug-related offenders under community supervision. As a result of the findings, CSOSA began designing, developing, and implementing the District of Columbia's first Day Reporting Center Module. The Day Reporting Center Program was designed to be a one-stop place where select offenders on probation or parole supervision would report on a frequent and regular basis, in a non-residential environment. The goal was to provide them with a greater intensity of services, focusing on education, vocational training, job placement assistance, treatment, and drug-screening.

By increasing surveillance and providing a variety of treatment services, the Day Reporting Center Module was designed to give offenders a greater sense of responsibility, make them more accountable for their time and activities, and provide them with the opportunity to become more successful during their period of community supervision . . . a success that will serve the ultimate goal of reducing their re-involvement in criminal activity.

Source

Hass, Aida Y. *Re-Arrest Research Study: Final Report.* (2001). Court Services and Offender Supervision Agency, Community Supervision Services, Washington, D.C. Aida Y. Hass, co-author of this textbook and currently Associate Professor of Criminal Justice at Missouri State University, describes research she conducted as a program analyst with the District of Columbia probation and parole agency, CSOSA.

criminal justice must be integrated into the decision making practices of policy makers and legislators. Only then can criminal justice policy reflect the empirical evidence of what works and what does not work.

Experimental criminology is one relatively new tool for reaching this goal. Experimental criminology relies on transforming subjective evidence into more reliable objective data, by conducting randomized, controlled experiments in a social setting. The idea is to ensure research findings are more valid by using experimentation to create a stronger tie between causes and effects.[34] In a randomized experimental study, researchers Lawrence Sherman and Heather Strang conducted a series of experiments to test the effects of the Restorative Justice Program on offenders with a wide range of offenses, in different correctional settings and at various stages in the criminal justice system.[35] Experiments were designed to evaluate the impact of participating in the Restorative Justice program on adult offenders. The study provides evidence to support the Restorative Justice model as a viable component of criminal justice practice.[36]

For decades the federal government has provided funding for programs and initiatives promising to provide solutions to the problem of crime. Now more than ever, these programs are being held accountable and are required to show demonstrable results in order to ensure continued funding. The effective guidance provided by scientific research in the field of criminology can only be achieved as this field continues to grow and expand in its production of scientifically defensible findings about what works, what does not work, and what is promising.

SUMMARY

How is criminology scientific?

Criminology is a science. It relies on the scientific method to study crime, crime facts, and criminal behavior. Conclusions are made based on observations that are grounded in research methods established for the collection of data and the gathering of facts. This is what differentiates criminology as a science, from the host of commentaries, productions, explanations, and predictions about criminal events that boil down to anecdotal expressions of public opinion, media hype, and political rhetoric.

How do scientific theories help us understand the real world?

When we rely on explanations of phenomena that are arrived at through scientific methods, then and only then, can we truly understand the world around us, and make accurate statements that may not make sense to the casual observer, but that are grounded in sound theories which are based on scientific research. This is the role of criminological theory: to establish an understanding of criminal behavior that accounts for crime causation based on factual scientific data and not just assumptions that represented misguided, biased, and distorted portrayals of individuals who violate the law.

What makes good theories "good"?

We've seen in this chapter that in choosing between alternative theories or explanations for observed data—as we inevitably must—we always prefer those that are scientifically useful—that is, logically consistent, testable, valid, and objective. Scientific theories are systematic expressions of observations that are predictive and tentative. They must be stated in a way that makes them subject to correction, scrutiny, and revision.

What are the various research methods that help us do criminological research?

In this chapter, we have examined the various strategies that are used to conduct scientific research: surveys, fieldwork, observation, experiments, and existing information. Each strategy provides a unique approach to the gathering of data. The selection of a research method must take into consideration practical issues such as time, location, and availability, as well as the design of the project and the personal preference of the researcher.

Are there specific stages to follow when conducting scientific research?

An effective research study must follow the various steps of conducting scientific inquiry, in which you should define the problem, conduct a thorough literature review, formulate a hypothesis, collect, and analyze your data, develop a conclusion, and share your results with other individuals in the scientific community.

When do we have to consider issues of privacy and confidentiality in our research?

Very often, research in the field of criminology uses human beings as the subject of inquiry. For this reason, social scientific inquiry must adhere to the highest standards of ethics in research. Protecting the privacy of research subjects must take precedence over the researcher's desire to obtain data.

How does research guide criminal justice policy?

The end product of the scientific endeavor is a reliable body of descriptions and explanations that can effectively guide criminal justice policy and practice. Yet crime and delinquency are social phenomena that have intrigued scientists and resisted description and explanation for as long as we have kept records. Still, we can draw these guiding principles for our study of crime from the history of science.

CRITICAL THINKING QUESTIONS

1. If some people steal because they don't have enough money to buy what they want, then why do some people who have enough money to buy what they want also steal? How can you use the scientific approach to study this apparent dichotomy?

2. Would most people commit crime if they knew they wouldn't get caught? Does the answer to that question change, depending on the type of crime? Would some people commit murder? What about robbery or rape? What about driving above the speed limit or cheating on taxes? How would you design a survey in which you assess the involvement of college students in certain types of criminal activities? What would their answers tell us about the fear of punishment versus the desire to obey the rules when considering the commission of different types of crime?

3. Crime makes us angry. It hurts, destroys, and often shocks our understanding of the world around us. In light of public opinion and media sensationalizing about crime related facts, how can you be objective in conducting criminological research? How can you set aside your own personal biases to ensure the scientific accuracy of your data? Are some research methods easier to be free of bias more than others? Why?

4. You are conducting a series of interviews with known gang members. What obstacles do you face in conducting such a research study? What steps do you take to ensure the privacy of your subjects? How can you make sure the data you gather remains anonymous? When does the scale of balance tip in favor of ethical research over the dissemination of useful information?

E-RESOURCES

You can learn more about ethics and conduct for engaging in social scientific research by visiting the *Academy of Criminal Justice Sciences* website at www.acjs.org/pubs/167_671_2922.cfm.

Additional information about the growing field of experimental criminology, can be found at the *American Society of Criminology* website at http://exp crim.org/.

Learn more about the steps of the scientific method by visiting www. sciencebuddies.org/science-fair-projects/project_scientific_method.shtml.

Read more about how to develop a research plan at www.library.illinois.edu/ learn/research/researchprocess.html.

NOTES

1 Jenkins, Philip. 1994. The Ice Age: The Social Construction of a Drug Panic. *Justice Quarterly* 4: 7–31.

2 Ibid.

3 Ibid.

4 Kuhn, T.S. 1966. *The Structure of Scientific Revolutions*. Chicago: The University of Chicago Press. Popper, Karl. 1959. *The Logic of Scientific Discovery*. New York: Basic Books.

5 Seriven, Michael. 1959. Explanation and Prediction in Evolutionary Theory. *Science* 130: 477–482.

6 Popper, Karl. 1959. *The Logic of Scientific Discovery*. New York: Basic Books.

7 Chambliss, William. 2001. *Power, Politics, and Crime*. Colorado: Westview Press.

8 Maxfield, Michael G. and Babbie, Earl R. 2015. *Research Methods for Criminal Justice and Criminology*. Stamford, CT: Cengage.

9 Kubrin, Charis E., Stucky, Thomas D., and Krohn, Marvin D. 2009. *Researching Theories of Crime and Deviance*. New York: Oxford University Press.

10 De Vaus, David. 2013. *Surveys in Social Research*, 6th ed. London and New York: Routledge.

11 Hagan, Frank E. 2013. *Research Methods in Criminal Justice and Criminology*, 9th ed. Upper Saddle River, NJ: Prentice-Hall Wolfgang, Marvin and Ferracuti, F. 1967. *The Subculture of Violence: Towards and Integrated Theory in Criminology* London: Tavistock Publications.

12 Ugwudike, P. 2015. *An Introduction to Critical Criminology*. Bristol, UK: Polity Press. Sutherland, Edwin H. 1939. White Collar Criminality. *American Sociological Review*, 5: 1–18; Chambliss, William. 1979. *On the Take: From Petty Crooks to Presidents*. Bloomington and Indianapolis: Indiana University Press.

13 Reiman, Jeffrey and Leighton, Paul. 2016. *The Rich Get Richer and the Poor Get Prison*, 10th ed. London and New York: Routledge.

14 Ibid.

15 Ibid., see 6.

16 Ibid., see 10.

17 Chambliss, William. 1988. *On the Take: From Petty Crooks to Presidents,* 2nd ed, Bloomington and Indianapolis: Indiana University Press.

18 Ferrell, Jeff. 1996. *Crimes of Style: Urban Graffiti and the Politics of Criminality*. New York: Northeastern University Press.

19 Chesney-Lind, M. and Pasko, L. 2013. *The Female Offender: Girls, Women, and Crime.* Thousand Oaks, CA: SAGE. Rodriguez, Luis J. 1993. *Always Running: La Vida Loca: Gang Days in L.A.* Willimantic, CT: Curbstone Press. Jankowski, Martin Sanchez. 1991. *Island in the Street: Gangs and American Urban Society*. Berkeley: University of California Press.

20 Chambliss, W. and Eglitis, D. 2015. *Discover Sociology*. Thousand Oaks, CA: SAGE. Maher, Maggie. 1994. A Change of Place. *Barrons,* March (21): 33–38.

21 Hamm, Mark. 2002. *In Bad Company*. Boston: Northeastern University Press. Chambliss, William. 1988. *On the Take: From Petty Crooks to Presidents,* 2nd ed. Bloomington and Indianapolis: Indiana University Press.

22 Chambliss, William J. 1973. The Roughnecks and the Saints. *Society* 11: 24–31.

23 Ibid; Chambliss, William. 1988. *On the Take: From Petty Crooks to Presidents*, 2nd ed. Bloomington and Indianapolis: Indiana University Press.

24 Chambliss, William. 1988. *Exploring Criminology*. New York: Macmillan.

25 Linz, Daniel G. 1989. Exposure to Sexually Explicit Materials and Attitudes Toward Rape: A Comparison of Study Results. *Journal of Sex Research* 26: 50–84; Linz, Daneil G., Donnerstein, Ed, and Adams, Steven M. 1989. Physical Desensitization and Judgments About Female Victims of Violence. *Human Communication Research* 15: 509–522.

26 Erikson, Kai T. 1966. *Wayward Puritans*. New York: Macmillan. Thompson, E. P. 1975. *Whigs and Hunters: The Origin of the Black Act*. London: Alan Lane. Chambliss, William J. 1964. A Sociological Analysis of the Law of Vagrancy. *Social Problems* 12: 67–77.

27 Foucault, Michel. 1979. *Discipline and Punish: The Birth of the Prison*. New York: Random House. Foucault, Michel. 1980. *The History of Sexuality*. New York: Random House.

28 Perry, J. and Perry, E. 2015. *Contemporary Society: An Introduction to Social Science*. London: Routledge.

29 Bryman, Adam. 2016. *Social Research Methods*, 5th ed. London: Oxford University Press.

30 Ibid.

31 Hagan, Frank E. 2013. *Research Methods in Criminal Justice and Criminology*, 9th ed. New Jersey: Pearson Education.

32 Ibid.

33 Ibid., see 31.

34 Mazerolle, Lorraine, and Bennett, Sarah. 2012. *Experimental Criminology*. Retrieved from http://www.oxfordbibliographies.com/view/document/obo-9780195396607/obo-9780195396607–0085.xml.

35 Rosenblat, Fernanda F. 2015. *The Role of Community in Restorative Justice*. London: Routledge.

36 Ibid.

The criminal justice system in action

PART II

CHAPTER OUTLINE

Law enforcement in America

KEY TERMS

law enforcement/
   police mission

law enforcement
   agency (LEAs)

roles

law enforcement
   officer (LEO)

trust

raw power

authority

stress

culture

socialization

subcultures

police subculture

ethos

worldview

blue wall of
   silence

Sir Robert Peel

beat System

watch and mutual
   pledge system

slave patrols

Marie Owens

Pendelton Act

Alice Stebbens
   Wells

August Vollmer

"We need the police, and the police need us."

Frank Serpico, NYPD (Ret.)

It was February 1971.[1] In a dirty, rundown walk-up apartment building in Brooklyn, a police officer was in serious trouble. As the officer screamed for help, he struggled violently to force open the door to a suspected drug dealer's apartment. Someone on the other side had managed to pin the door partially closed, trapping the officer half in and half out, so that he was unable to raise his weapon or extricate himself. The officer's two partners, rather than jumping in to assist him, stood watching.[2] Then, a gun barked from inside the apartment, sending a bullet into the officer's face, just below his right eye.[3] The officer, dressed in plainclothes, fell backward onto the landing outside the doorway.

Lying bleeding from his wound and near death, the officer's story, and life, could have ended in that dingy apartment building on a cold February day. But it did not. A neighbor's call to report the shooting set in motion a chain of events that ultimately saved the officer's life.[4]

The wounded officer's name: Frank Serpico.

Frank Serpico had always wanted to be a police officer and held in his mind an idealized image of what policing was and who engaged in it.[5] Joining the New York City Police Department in the early 1960s, Serpico quickly realized that being a police officer, and the occupation of law enforcement, was far more complicated and less ideal than he ever imagined.

Frank Serpico is a name you may already be familiar with; in some circles it elicits praise, and in others, it elicits scorn.[6] Serpico is not famous for being shot—that was just an unfortunate footnote to his story. Frank Serpico is famous because he was willing to fight for justice, fairness, and equality by publicly revealing details about systemic, pervasive police corruption within the nation's largest law enforcement agency: the NYPD. Serpico is despised to this day by those, including some fellow police officers, who feel he violated the ironclad rule of law enforcement: you never rat on a fellow cop, or break the blue wall of silence.

Serpico's story, complicated as it is, provides an excellent jumping off point for a general discussion of law enforcement in America, including its history and current issues, because the key elements of Serpico's case remain key concerns to law enforcement right now across the United States. Justice, fairness, equality, corruption—all of those things and more are being discussed now within the context of a national discussion about the role, mission, and actions of law enforcement.

Recently, amidst a series of high profile incidents across the nation that have highlighted just how controversial, complicated, and conflicted law enforcement

Image 5.1 *Former NYPD Detective Frank Serpico broke the NYPD's "code of silence" more than 40 years ago in order to speak out against police corruption. Despite his continuing efforts to create positive police reform, some police officers are still encouraged to turn a blind eye to wrongdoing within their ranks and never question authority, or else face harassment by peers and punishment by superiors.*

Kathy Willens/AP/Press Association Images

can be, Frank Serpico injected a bit of sage wisdom into the conversation. Noting that positive solutions must be found to resolve current policing issues, Frank Serpico justified his view, and urged cooler heads to prevail, by saying: "We need the police, and the police need us."[7]

THE MISSION AND ROLES OF LAW ENFORCEMENT AGENCIES

The police need us. We need the police. These fundamental statements guide the actions and decisions of law enforcement agencies around the United States. Policing and law enforcement comprise Phase I of the American criminal justice system, a system which also includes the courts (Phase II) and corrections (Phase III). Policing and law enforcement are directly influenced by both substantive and procedural criminal law, the subjects of chapter 2.

Law enforcement mission

The law enforcement/police mission is to protect and preserve: (1) life, (2) liberty (freedom), and (3) property. We could also say that, more generally, the law enforcement mission is to protect public safety.

Image 5.2 *Positive interactions between police and citizens should be the norm. Here a mother and her two children discuss neighbourhood crime prevention with a member of the Los Angeles County Sheriff's Department at a National Night Out against crime community fair in Glendale, California.*

iStock/DnHolm

Local, state, and federal law enforcement agencies are united by this shared mission despite differences in how they accomplish it. Thus, whether it is a local police department or a federal law enforcement agency like the FBI, you can be assured they are all fundamentally concerned with protecting public safety or some aspect of it.

Law enforcement roles and responsibilities

In carrying out the mission of keeping citizens, communities, and the nation safe, American law enforcement agencies (LEAs), and agents (police, sheriffs, detectives, special agents, etc.) perform a variety of roles. Roles entail certain obligations, responsibilities, and expectations, which influence how the person performing the role feels and also how people perceive them. Some general roles include parent, brother, sister, and friend. Occupations can also be roles— teacher, firefighter, doctor, ski instructor. Taking on the role of law enforcement officer (LEO) entails some unique responsibilities and obligations.

Law enforcement officers perform a variety of duties in carrying out the law enforcement mission. The law enforcement, or police, role is unique in society. Few occupational roles in America have a more vital mission, or more important responsibilities, than law enforcement officers (see Table 5.1).

Unique aspects of law enforcement and policing

Close examination reveals four unique aspects that set the law enforcement and policing role apart from others. They are: (1) trust, (2) power, (3) stress, and (4) expectations.

Trust

The law enforcement mission and role hinges on trust. Public trust is one of the most defining features of law enforcement. The public trusts that law enforcement agencies, and the people working within them, will perform their duties, and execute their mission, in a way that is consistently fair, impartial, just, honest, and reasonable. Law enforcement legitimacy—the trust and respect

Table 5.1 Summary of the police mission, role responsibilities, and unique factors

Police mission	Protect and preserve life, liberty, and property (i.e., public safety)
Police role responsibilities	crime prevention, law enforcement, criminal investigation, arrest/apprehension
Unique police mission/role factors	1. Trust 2. Power 3. Stress 4. Expectations

of the public which law enforcement depends on to function successfully—depends on positively maintaining this relationship of public trust. In order to carry out their mission, law enforcement officers must have the trust and cooperation of the public. A breakdown or failure of this crucial trust relationship between law enforcement and society can make effective policing difficult, if not impossible.

Power

A second unique aspect of the police mission and role is power. Power is defined in many ways. **Raw power** is the ability to get things done even against the resistance of others.[8] An emperor or dictator often wields power in its most basic, raw form. **Authority**[9] is one of the most important kinds of power. Authority is power that is perceived by others as legitimate. When people think someone has authority, they are far less likely to resist their commands or actions and are far more likely to listen, believe in, and/or do what they are told. In general, authority is a very useful and effective form of power within a large group or society. Parents, principles, coaches, doctors, and law enforcement officers are all examples of people who have authority in American society.

Law enforcement officers possess and wield immense power in the form of authority, which they are legally vested with by a local, state, or the federal government. People are taught to obey and respect law enforcement because of this authority, which also grants law enforcement agencies and officers unique powers.

For example, law enforcement officers can legitimately, and legally, deprive people of their freedom via arrest; they can access sensitive, non-public information; and they can utilize force to accomplish their mission, up to and including utilizing lethal force. Police also have the authority to intervene in social relationships, including those between spouses, co-workers, and parents and their children.

To function most effectively, the law enforcement agencies depend on the public perception that their use of power is legitimate. If they lose legitimacy in the eyes of the public, they also lose the basis for their authority—though they don't lose their legal right to perform their job. A loss of legitimacy negatively impacts how well law enforcement agencies and officers can do their job. When the police lack legitimate authority in the public eye, resistance to police action increases, and so too do conflicts between the police and the public.

Stress

The law enforcement role is characterized by a high level of stress. We all experience stress from time to time for a variety of reasons. You might be feeling stressed right now because your boyfriend or girlfriend is mad at you or because you have to give an oral presentation in class. You might also be stressed out because you have to read this chapter! Stress can occur because

Image 5.3
The law enforcement profession is high stress, particularly during moments of protest and civil unrest, as seen here in this photo of Chilean police clashing with education reform protesters on the streets of Santiago, Chile.

iStock/Evan_Lang

of present circumstances (e.g., something happening now) or future circumstances (e.g., something that might happen). Many people feel stress when they don't get enough sleep, when they are doing something risky or something that makes them fearful, or because of the demands placed on them at work (or school).

Unlike most people, law enforcement officers are constantly under stress for all these reasons (and more) every day. In addition to normal life demands that cause stress (family, friends, health, etc.) law enforcement officers engage in incredibly stressful work in carrying out the law enforcement mission. Every shift, each day, law enforcement officers deal with potentially volatile and dangerous people and situations. They must face risks that few ordinary people would choose to face. They must constantly grapple with the fear of failure and the stress of having to make instantaneous, decisive decisions. They also encounter stress because they must constantly confront the threat of violence— they might be a victim of violence or they might have to use violence against someone else—at any time. Many police officers also work long, rotating day and night shifts, of between 10 to 12 hours. Few, if any, occupational roles place people under similar amounts of stress.

Expectations

Finally, the law enforcement role is unique because of the expectations associated with it. This role practically requires a superhuman being to be performed perfectly. At the least, it requires that each and every law enforcement officer function at their very best every hour, every shift, every day. The public expects, and deserves, nothing less because if law enforcement officers don't perform their very best all the time, crimes may not be prevented. Even worse, lives could be lost, people could get hurt, and others could end up wrongfully imprisoned.

However, it is important to temper our significant expectations about law enforcement with a healthy dose of reality. For example, let's briefly consider our expectations about the characteristics of the "ideal" police officer. If we brainstormed what the ideal police officer would be like, we might say they would be: 100 percent trustworthy and honest all the time; give maximal effort all the time; never take a negative attitude toward their job, co-workers, or citizens; be capable of placing all of their personal baggage, including biases and beliefs, aside; would remain objective and neutral and never allow stereotypes or past experiences to influence their present judgments; they would be completely selfless; always in control of their minds and bodies; and they would always make the correct decision.

How close do you come to meeting all of those ideals?

Most of us would not come close because none of us are perfect; we are all human beings, capable of being flawed, who make mistakes despite our best intentions. The reason we point out these things is to debunk the myth that police officers are inherently different, or better than, the rest of us. Law enforcement officers are just ordinary people with unique histories and personalities; they have feelings, emotions, interests, and hobbies. They have brothers, sisters, and grandparents. They eat and sleep, and they can get tired and crabby just like the rest of us.

What truly differentiates law enforcement officers from the rest of us is not that they are superhuman or superior. Law enforcement officers are neither of those things. They are capable of being as flawed as any person despite their occupation. What truly separates police from ordinary citizens is that they wear a uniform with a badge, carry a gun, and have sworn an oath to uphold the law and protect public safety. Nevertheless, people who work in law enforcement are expected to be better and to do better. These expectations produce stress for law enforcement officers. They also create false impressions about who law enforcement officers are that make it difficult for ordinary citizens to relate to them or accurately evaluate their work.

THE POLICE SUBCULTURE

Culture teaches us how to be human through the process known as socialization. From the time we are born we are socialized (e.g., exposed to and taught) various aspects of culture and social life. In terms of culture, we learn things like language, values, beliefs, norms, knowledge, religion, rituals, food, and music. We also constantly get socialized into other aspects of social life. We learn how our family works and how to behave within it. We get socialized at school, by teachers, friends, and coaches; we learn how to learn, how to play a sport, what it means to be a good friend, or a bad one. Socialization occurs in our workplace too, where we learn how to do a job, and why it's important.

Image 5.4 *Within every culture are thousands of subcultures, which each have their own values, language, and practices. Members of the law enforcement share many subcultural similarities with people who serve in the military, like those engaging in Navy Seal Hell Week training in the image above. Both law enforcement and military personnel emphasize trust among one another and often abide by a strict code of silence.*
Getty

All of our socialization experiences are guided and influenced by the larger culture that surrounds us.

Within a culture, there can also exist many **subcultures**, each with its own distinct values, beliefs, knowledge, and even language (called "argot"). Subcultures aren't bad things (usually), and are, in fact, pretty normal. They are useful ways for people to organize themselves into groups in which everyone has similar desires, interests, or experiences. Surfers have a subculture. Cat lovers, people with tattoos, people who do CrossFit, people who travel all over for summer music festivals—they are all members of subcultures.

In some cases, workplaces and occupations can develop subcultures. People who work as stock traders on Wall Street have their own subculture. Military service members have a subculture, and so too do police and law enforcement officers. The "police culture or subculture" is important to understand. It has both positive and negative implications and plays a vital role in how and why police and law enforcement officers do their jobs as they do.

Throughout the late 1960s and 1970s, researchers Jerome Skolnick,[10] William Westley,[11] and Peter Manning[12] published interesting accounts of what was identified as a distinct **police subculture**, also called the blue fraternity[13] or blue brotherhood,[14] which was argued to have its own **ethos** (fundamental beliefs or spirit) and **worldview** (way of seeing the world and your place in it). At the time, issues of police misconduct were national news due to the Knapp

Commission investigation of police corruption in New York City. Politicians, the public, and researchers were curious about the police and were hoping to find out more about what it was like to be a police officer. The identification of the police subculture emerged as one potential explanation for why cops engaged in criminal behaviors themselves—despite being sworn to uphold the law and protect public safety.

It is important to understand that there is no single, monolithic police subculture. All law enforcement agencies have a subculture associated with them, but they can vary along a spectrum. Some subcultures emphasize more positive qualities,[15] beliefs, or ideas while some emphasize more negative and harmful ones.

In general, when we refer to the police subculture, we are usually discussing it in terms of its negative aspects and impacts on policing. Two key features of a more negative police subculture are (1) the belief that police officers should always look out for and protect their fellow officers, even if they've done wrong, and (2) teaching police officers to have a general distrust of the public. Distrust for the public breeds an "us v. them" mentality that separates police officers from the citizens they serve and can help rationalize misconduct.

Rookie police officers get socialized into the police subculture from the time they enter the police or law enforcement training academy. Ideas about how to police a community and be a police officer are instilled in that setting and then reinforced during field training, when veteran officers pair up with new recruits. Thus, because the police subculture is learned through social interaction, it gets reinforced over time and passed down through each successive wave of new police officers. Obviously, if the subculture promotes negative values and practices, those are passed down and reinforced.

At its very worst, the police subculture can contribute to a criminal mindset and pattern of criminal behavior among law enforcement officers and contribute to an enormous gulf between police officers and the citizens they are sworn to protect and serve. Police officers may learn it is acceptable to use excessive force against certain people or that it's OK to take money, drugs, or property that don't belong to them. Because trust and reliability are so important among police officers, and due to the fact that the police subculture teaches officers to look out for each other no matter what, patterns of criminal or corrupt behavior can develop and persist. This cycle is strengthened when police officers begin associating only with other police officers—a common phenomenon caused by the nature of the work and the fact that police officers may believe no one else could relate to them.

The phrase "blue wall of silence"[16] conveys the notion that what police officers do, whether it is legal or illegal, stays between them and only them. Those who violate this informal code, who go outside the brotherhood and "snitch" or "rat" on other officers who are engaging in corrupt or illegal behavior, become deviants—they cannot be trusted or respected.

The existence of the police subculture is cause for concern since it is often linked to serious issues of police misconduct. It can also lead to issues of

BOX 5.1: WORKING IN . . . LAW ENFORCEMENT

If you are thinking about working in law enforcement, you must prepare mentally and physically for the job and this preparation should begin immediately! The road to a law enforcement career can be a long one, with the hiring process alone taking many months and involving multiple tests, interviews, and phases. The three Ps (Preparation, Practice, and Performance) should guide your efforts as you prepare physically and mentally.

You must be able to answer the following three questions, which will almost certainly arise during any oral panel interview for a law enforcement career: (1) Why do you want to do work in law enforcement, or for this particular agency? (2) What have you done to prepare for a career in law enforcement? (3) What do you know about this agency, the municipality, etc.?

While there is much more to getting a law enforcement career than just answering the three questions above, if you cannot answer those questions in a meaningful, concise manner you should step back and reconsider your intended career path. Moreover, if you find yourself drawn to a law enforcement career because you like the idea of having power, or because you think carrying a gun is cool, or because you want to make people respect you, do not apply for a law enforcement career! Working in law enforcement is, fundamentally, a job that requires an intense amount of sacrifice and compassion. Law enforcement officers are, above all else, public servants sworn to protect and serve their communities—not local politicians, certain segments of the population, or their own interests.

However, if you are attracted to the idea of helping others, are an excellent verbal and written communicator with an ability to think decisively under pressure, and if you embrace the notions of integrity, honesty, and fairness, then a law enforcement career might be for you. But, be forewarned: working in law enforcement is not what you see portrayed in Hollywood movies or television shows. Law enforcement work is 99 percent mundane, consisting of handling minor events, citizen complaints, and a *lot* of paperwork. Every so often something will occur—that remaining 1 percent of the time—that is intense, dangerous, and perhaps even fear inducing. Car and foot chases, fights, and shootouts are the rare exception, rather than the rule.

If you do enter into a law enforcement career, you should be prepared (mentally and emotionally) to start at the bottom. Typically, this entails working as a uniformed patrol officer for at least two years. This may be disappointing news for those of you hoping to be Special Agents or Detectives. You can certainly aspire to those careers, and they are attainable, but not without first building the skills necessary to perform the core functions of those careers—skills that are acquired by putting in time at the entry level!

If you want to work for a Federal law enforcement agency, like the FBI, DEA or U.S. Marshalls service, know that you are very, very unlikely to obtain one of those highly coveted careers without significant prior law enforcement experience at the municipal or state level. Indeed, the average age of first-hire for new, entry-level FBI Special Agents is around 30 years old.[17] Police detectives also tend to be older and more experienced. The reason for this is that solid investigative skills, and the knowledge to perform the job of Detective or Special Agent, are first learned as a young patrol officer!

There are many perks to working in law enforcement. The hours, compensation, retirement benefits, and time off are all quite good in comparison to other careers. Earning a college degree, and continually seeking out new knowledge and education, are both valued and rewarded. Citizens generally respect and value the work law enforcement officers do. Likewise, working in a "helping" profession, of which law enforcement is one, can be incredibly rewarding emotionally and spiritually, even if it is, at the same time, stressful! Best of luck if you choose to pursue a career in law enforcement!

cynicism, emotional distress, burnout, and interpersonal relationship problems in police officers. However, the police subculture does not exist in every law enforcement agency to the same degree. Even within a police department, there will be variation in the extent that individual law enforcement officers accept or reject the police subculture and its more negative aspects. Thus, when cases of police misconduct are uncovered, we often find that a group of officers from the same shift or precinct are involved. The Miami River Cops,[18,19] Philadelphia 39th Precinct[20] and Chicago Area II Violent Crimes Unit[21,22] misconduct scandals are all good examples here.

A BRIEF HISTORY OF AMERICAN LAW ENFORCEMENT

American law enforcement is a continuously evolving field, with modernization spurred by social, political, and technological advances.

"Modern" American law enforcement actually traces its origins to London, England, where, in September 1829, Sir Robert Peel formed the London Metropolitan Police Department (also sometimes called Scotland Yard). Among many innovations, Peel's new LMPD had a centralized, military style command structure. The LMPD was also held accountable to the local government. Strict hiring standards ensured only the most qualified and trustworthy individuals became "bobbies" in the LMPD. Those officers, in turn, were assigned to a beat system of patrol—each officer had an assigned area of responsibility. Many of Sir Robert Peel's innovations drifted across the Atlantic Ocean to America, directly influencing the development of modern American law enforcement.

Prior to Peel's progressive reforms, law enforcement in both England and America was largely dependent on community volunteers; the responsibility for maintaining law and order was considered the obligation of local communities. However, as English and American societies modernized and grew in the 18th and 19th centuries, these volunteer based community methods for maintaining law and order, often called the watch and mutual pledge system, became ineffective.[23] Enforcing the law required the efforts of professional law enforcement officers and agencies.

Image 5.5 *Sir Robert Peel is considered to be the father of modern policing. His successful reforms of the London Metropolitan Police Department influenced the development of modern law enforcement agencies in the United States as well.*

Mary Evans/Interfoto/Sammlung Rauch

In America, modern law enforcement developed differently in different regions. For example, in the American east and in populated areas along the east and west coasts, law enforcement evolved similarly to how it was evolving in London. By the end of the Civil War, every major metropolitan city had a police department modeled, in some manner, after the London Metropolitan Police Department.

In the South, however, the slave system functioned in place of a well-developed criminal justice system. Dr. Samuel Walker, one of the foremost experts on American law enforcement, has argued that southern slave patrols pre-dated modern law enforcement agencies in that region and in the North.[24] Slave patrols, which lasted until the Civil War, were primarily concerned with enforcing laws on behalf of Southern whites and controlling African American slaves. Once the 13th Amendment to the United States Constitution was ratified and abolished slavery, southern communities and states began developing professional law enforcement agencies. Nevertheless, these agencies and officers continued to enforce laws in an unequal and unfair manner, privileging whites over blacks. This issue is also discussed in chapter 7 where we introduce the "convict leasing" system.

The development of law enforcement in the middle and western U.S. territories and states is also unique. Even into the 1890s, someone travelling from an eastern city like Boston or New York through the vast, sparsely populated American west might believe they'd entered another time. Wide-open expanses of territory, ongoing conflicts with Native American tribal bands that refused to surrender to the federal government, and small towns and settlements rife with bandits, cowboys, charlatans, and others seeking to escape the government's reach helped the American west develop into the "Wild West." Outlaws, criminals, horse-thieves, gangs, ne'er-do-wells, con artists, entrepreneurs, and those seeking a fresh start all came together in western towns and settlements creating a unique environment that many writers and movie-makers have portrayed as lawless.

Of course, there were criminal laws governing behavior in the west. The key difference from the development of law enforcement in the east was who was primarily responsible for enforcing those laws and what methods of law enforcement they utilized. There were few large cities, but many small, rural settlements, making large municipal police departments impractical. Law enforcement was primarily carried out by sheriff's and their deputies, deputized posses, bounty hunters, and by federal agents, primarily Deputy U.S. Marshalls. The elite Texas Rangers, formed in 1835, became the first state-wide law enforcement agency in the U.S., though they were the exception rather than the rule. In general, law enforcement in the west was a difficult affair, carried out by rough, gruff, and tough law men.

Modernization continued through the late 19th and 20th centuries (see Table 5.2 for a timeline of key events). Uniformity among police agencies increased. In 1891, **Marie Owens** became one of the nation's first female law enforcement officers. Then, in 1883 the **Pendleton Act**[25] was passed which created the civil service system— greatly improving and standardizing the hiring process for law enforce-ment positions. Also in 1883, the precursor to today's International Association of Chiefs of Police formed, allowing police chiefs and other law enforcement administrators to meet regularly to share ideas and innovations.

After 1900, technology became a key driver of change and innovation in law enforcement, as forensic science, finger-printing, and crime scene photography became more accepted. Radio equipped patrol cars debuted in 1928—while primitive, these early radios improved communication between officers in the field and commanders back at the station. While racial and gender integration in law enforcement took many more decades to occur on what could be considered a wide scale, there were early trailblazers. For example, in 1910, **Alice Stebbens Wells** became the first female police officer hired by the LAPD.

TEXAS RANGERS.

Image 5.6 *Texas Rangers, by Frederic Remington, 1896*
Mary Evans/Everett Collection

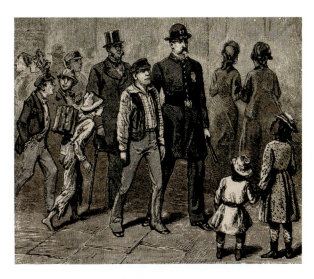

Image 5.7 *A man is arrested in New York and led by a policeman through the streets to the station.*
Mary Evans Picture Library

The 1930s and 1940s witnessed increased academic, political, and social concern with improving law enforcement. **August Vollmer** (1876–1955) authored the **Wickersham Commission Report on Crime** in 1931, which highlighted deficiencies in law enforcement agencies across America, such as a failure to

Image 5.8 *August Vollmer, "father of modern law enforcement."*

Library of Congress Prints and Photographs Division

Image 5.9 *The LAPD's first female officer, Alice Stebbins Wells, in her LAPD uniform.*

Wikimedia Commons

investigate serious crimes like murder and fraud. Vollmer, the first police chief of Berkeley, California, is one of the most notable of America's criminal justice reformers and innovators. He helped professionalize law enforcement and pioneered the field of criminal justice—including teaching courses on criminal justice at the University of California-Berkeley. One of his students, O.W. Wilson (1900–1972), went on to become the police chief in Wichita, KS, and carried on Vollmer's legacy, making numerous contributions to the field of law enforcement in his own right. His book *Police Administration,* published in 1950, was long considered a "must-read" for police administrators and other law enforcement professionals.

TYPES OF LAW ENFORCEMENT AGENCIES

All law enforcement agencies enforce laws and investigate crimes on behalf of governments. In the United States, there are three basic levels of government: federal, state and local. As a result, there are law enforcement agencies at each of these levels—for example, the Federal Bureau of Investigation (FBI), state police, and local sheriff. In addition, military and Native American tribal laws are enforced by military and tribal law enforcement agencies.

Federal law enforcement

Federal law enforcement agencies have the broadest investigatory and arrest powers—they have jurisdiction to investigate and enforce all federal criminal laws, like those detailed in Title 18 of the U.S. Federal Criminal Code, and any crimes occurring on federal property. Moreover, federal law enforcement agencies can be granted jurisdiction over specific types of crime (e.g., terrorism) and can intervene in state and local cases, most commonly when their help is requested.

The scope and mission of each federal law enforcement agency is unique, with a significant degree of variability among agencies. The FBI has the broadest focus, conducting investigations and making arrests in cases involving serial murder, narcotics trafficking, treason, cybercrime, and terrorism (among many crimes). By contrast, the Drug Enforcement Agency (DEA) deals solely with drugs and drug related crimes.

Table 5.2 Timeline of key events in the history of American law enforcement

Year	Event
1829	The London Metropolitan Police Act leads to the formation of the London Metropolitan Police Department by Sir Robert Peel
1838	Boston Police Department, the first large, modern police department, is created
1865	President Abraham Lincoln's assassination leads to the creation of the U.S. Secret Service
1883	Pendleton Act creates a civil service system for hiring and promoting local government employees, including law enforcement officers
1893	National Chiefs of Police Union, precursor to the International Association of Chiefs of Police, is formed
1902	Fingerprinting is utilized for the first time
1907	The Berkeley, California Police Department becomes the first to utilize numerous forensic methods, including blood and soil analysis.
1931	The Wickersham Commission files its report on law enforcement in the U.S. It cites multiple failings in investigation, arrest, and administration and makes numerous recommendations for improvement.
1932	The Federal Bureau of Investigation creates its first Crime Lab under the direction of FBI Director J. Edgar Hoover
1950	O.W. Wilson publishes *Police Administration*
1968	The 9-1-1 emergency response system is created
1994	The COMPSTAT program for tracking crime patterns and improving law enforcement efficiency is introduced
2001	The Sept. 11 terror attacks alter the nature of American law enforcement. Combatting terrorism and mass casualty attacks becomes a key concern.
2002	The Department of Homeland Security is formed in response to Sept. 11 terror attacks.

Most federal law enforcement agencies are organized under the Department of Justice (e.g., the FBI, DEA, ATF, and U.S. Marshalls) or the Department of Homeland Security (e.g., U.S. Secret Service, Immigration and Customs Enforcement, Border Protection). In addition, there are numerous law enforcement agencies situated within other branches of the U.S. federal government, or serving other government agencies, such as the criminal investigations section of the U.S. Fish and Wildlife Service (USFWS).

State and local law enforcement

While federal law enforcement agencies may intervene in state and local matters, the same is not true of state and local law enforcement agencies—their powers and jurisdiction are limited to the state or local level. State police agencies, including state highway patrol, and state Bureaus of Investigation, have the power to investigate crimes and make arrests statewide; they may also run special task forces (like drug task forces).

Local law enforcement agencies include local or county sheriff's departments and municipal police departments—for example the LAPD—as well as campus or university police departments and conservation or wildlife (fish and game) agencies. These agencies enforce state laws, regulations, and local laws and ordinances within a well-defined limited geographic area or area of specialization. For example, university police are tasked with law enforcement only on college campuses, whereas a state highway patrol officer focuses solely on enforcing laws and responding to incidents that occur on state roads and highways. The vast majority of America's more than 1.2 million law enforcement personnel are employed at the local and state levels. As a result, these agencies are the ones most citizens have contact with and are the most visible law enforcement presence in the United States.

LAW ENFORCEMENT STRATEGIES

Have you ever played the game Whack-a-Mole? In that arcade game, the player has a toy mallet which he or she uses to bash toy moles that randomly pop up from the game board—the player earns points for each mole that gets "whacked." Law enforcement has long been like a game of Whack-A-Mole. In other words, law enforcement has traditionally been a reactive endeavor. When a law gets violated and a crime occurs police, detectives, or special agents respond to handle the situation. This is called an "incident" based, or incident driven, law enforcement strategy.

Obviously, there are many times when law enforcement can't be anything but reactive. After all, law enforcement agencies aren't so sophisticated that they can predict all crimes before they occur. There will always be a reactionary or reactive element to law enforcement.

However, over the last 30 years or so, many law enforcement agencies have realized that relying solely on a reactive, incident based strategy is both ineffective and inefficient. Increasingly, law enforcement agencies at all levels are adopting more proactive strategies that rely on building strong law enforcement-citizen partnerships and mining crime data and intelligence to prevent and reduce crime. Below, we briefly detail four major law enforcement strategies that are, or have been, widely used. Each has unique emphases and implications.

Order maintenance policing and zero-tolerance strategies

From the late 1960s through the 1990s, America's economy changed. Industry and manufacturing jobs began moving overseas, where labor and production costs were cheaper. The American economy began its shift toward service and technology-based careers and away from "blue collar" work. These macro-level changes had profound consequences for America's communities, especially those urban ones where blue collar manufacturing and industrial jobs were key staples of employment.

As good jobs departed these communities, so too did the people who could afford to leave and find work elsewhere. This out-migration of people and money, in turn, impacted other businesses—many of which also had to close. Those who could not afford to move out were left behind in rapidly deteriorating communities.

By the late 1970s, many of these urban communities had begun to seriously decay—graffiti, trash, burnt-out cars, and run-down apartment buildings proliferated (just Google "New York City 1980s" for many images). Unemployment and poverty rates rose as did rates of drug use and street crime. Street corners became the haunts of drug dealers and prostitutes. Law and order in these urban spaces began to break down, as the ability of residents to exercise informal social control over their neighbors and surroundings decreased. Many neighborhoods in places now considered vibrant tourist destinations, New York City and Chicago for example, were anything but—fear of crime and victimization kept people away from them; even beautiful Central Park was a place few people dared venture into after dark.

The key question among politicians, policy workers, and the public became: how do we improve these decaying communities? At the time, a lot of focus was paid to the issues of crime and drug use. The dominant thinking became that if those incidents were more aggressively dealt with, major strides could be made in improving the deteriorating communities where those problems appeared most prevalent.

Broken windows theory, developed by sociologists George L. Kelling and James Q. Wilson in 1982, had a profound impact on law enforcement practice during this time and since[35,36] (see Box 5.2). Most directly, broken windows theory led to the law enforcement strategy called **order maintenance** or **quality of life** policing.

BOX 5.2: CONNECTING THEORY TO PRACTICE

Broken windows theory and stop-and-frisk policies

In 1982, *The Atlantic* magazine published an article written by two sociologists, George L. Kelling and James Q. Wilson, titled "Broken Windows: The Police and Neighborhood Safety."[26] At the time, Kelling and Wilson were primarily concerned with the issue of urban crime and neighborhood decay.

Kelling and Wilson utilized the imagery of "broken windows" as a metaphor for the cycle of disorder and crime plaguing inner city communities. According to the authors, small quality of life issues, like broken windows, could very quickly lead to even more serious problems. What was needed in deteriorating neighborhoods was direct intervention—the broken windows needed to be fixed and steps needed to be taken to prevent further decline. If public order was not restored, ever more serious crime and decay would occur. In its most natural incarnations, broken windows theory requires police and community collaboration—

to effectively restore order requires not just the top-down actions of police, but also the bottoms up actions of community members.

Broken windows theory has been extensively cited as a justification for law enforcement strategies like order maintenance and zero tolerance policing. In some cases, highly controversial policies have been implemented based on an interpretation of broken windows theory, with some people interpreting the theory's admonition to restore "order" as a blanket invitation to use any means necessary.

Such has been the case in New York City where, since about 2002, the NYPD has employed a policy known as "Stop-and-Frisk." Ostensibly, the stop-and-frisk policy, which has expanded across the country to cities like Los Angeles[27] and Miami Gardens, FL,[28] is about preventing crimes before they occur. Under stop-and-frisk cops can utilize a murky standard called "reasonable suspicion" to stop and search anyone in a public space. Reasonable suspicion is a far lower standard to meet than probable cause. Reasons for stopping someone under a stop-and-frisk policy can be as mundane as the person acting "furtive" (another murky term).

In 2011, the NYPD made over 685,000 stops under the stop-and-frisk policy;[29] in 2008 the LAPD made over 875,000 stops. Between 2008 and 2014, the small city of Miami Gardens, FL, population 111,378, recorded over 99,000 stops and 57,000 searches—nearly 20 times the number of searches conducted in nearby Miami, FL, which has a population four times larger.

Stop-and-Frisk policies have been widely and fervently criticized by citizens, civil rights groups, policy advocates, researchers, and politicians for condoning and encouraging racial profiling and violating individual constitutional protections against unlawful searches and seizures. Moreover, critics argue that stop-and-frisk policies have not produced the results proponents of the policies hoped for, and have, more than anything, contributed to weakening the relationship between the police and the citizens they serve.

Data do indicate that police have employed stop-and-frisk tactics disproportionately against people of color, specifically African Americans and Hispanics. Over 25 percent of the NYPD's 5 million stops between 2002 and 2012 were of African American men, despite the fact that African American men represent less than 2 percent of the city's population.[30] During the peak of stop-and-frisk in Los Angeles, when Bill Bratton was the city's police commissioner, 23 percent of stops were of blacks who made up just 9 percent of that city's population.[31] In Miami Gardens, one 28-year-old African American man was stopped by police over 250 times in four years.[32,33] According to several Miami Gardens police officers, supervisors in that city used the stop-and-frisk policy to "actively . . . target specific groups" specifically "all black males . . . between the ages of 15 and 30 years old."[34]

The legacy of Broken Windows theory is thus a mixed bag. Certainly, enforcing laws that improve quality of life in communities is essential to the law enforcement mission. Likewise, the goal of preventing crimes before they occur is commendable. However, perversions of the theory, for instance in the form of racially discriminatory stop-and-frisk policies, force us to ask "at what costs?" Broken Windows Theory, as it has been applied both successfully and unsuccessfully, highlights the fundamental point that ideas (theories) have real-world consequences.

Order maintenance policing seeks to remedy problems of urban decay and crime by disrupting the causal chain between those two variables. Broken windows theory argued that things like graffiti, prostitution, open-air drug sales, vagrancy, public intoxication, and other highly visible signs of crime and neglect, like "broken windows," encouraged ever more crime and neglect by sending the message to community residents—good, bad, and indifferent— that nobody cared. Within an atmosphere of "nobody cares," it doesn't take a very big leap of logic to conclude "anything goes." The primary thinking is that small offenses and issues, if left unaddressed, can create opportunities for even more serious crimes to occur.

Thus, order maintenance policing prescribed a remedy for this problematic cycle: "reduce crime by restoring order and restore order by reducing crime."[37] In practice, order maintenance policing encourages law enforcement agencies to vigorously enforce public order crimes, including those that might seem very minor. Graffiti, public drunkenness, public urination, noise violations, prostitution, vandalism—any incident that negatively impacts the quality of life in a community should be taken seriously; arrests and citations should be issued. The goal is to send a dual message. To those engaging in the above listed behaviors, the message is that such behavior is unacceptable and will not be allowed to take place. The hope is that to the law-abiding neighborhood residents the message received would be that law enforcement officers take seriously your quality of life and will work to ensure you feel safe in your own neighborhood.

Closely linked, yet distinct, from order maintenance policing is a broad, ill-defined law enforcement strategy called zero-tolerance policing. Zero-tolerance policing may resemble order-maintenance policing if and when minor offenses that cause disorder in communities are dealt with swiftly. However, the strategy of zero-tolerance policing may also imply simply getting "tough on crime." But even getting tough on crime can mean different things to different people.

In some cases, a zero-tolerance approach to law enforcement may include removing discretion from law enforcement officers in the field—rather than allow officers to decide on a case-by-case basis what action(s) to take with someone suspected of committing a particular crime, the officers must make an arrest regardless of whether it is a first-time offender or any other circumstances. Such an approach is now taken with domestic violence and DUI or DWI situations. Zero-tolerance policing has also been invoked to justify constitutionally suspect practices like New York City's "stop-and-frisk" policy (see Box 5.2).

Both the order maintenance and zero-tolerance law enforcement strategies have been met with criticism, despite data that seems to indicate both strategies have been, at least somewhat, effective in reducing crime.[38,39]

First, critics argue both strategies have distorted, or misapplied, the principles of broken windows theory. Even George Kelling, one of the authors of broken windows, has argued that, in practice, many law enforcement agencies have ignored the community-building and partnership elements of broken windows theory.[40] Instead, law enforcement agencies employing order maintenance and zero-tolerance strategies have relied on an incident drive response pattern, where they resemble an invading army entering communities to "clean them up." Critics argue this does little to provide long-term solutions to crime and disorder and primarily alienates segments the public from the police, especially in predominantly minority neighborhoods. A more general critique relates to the cause of declining crime rates in places enacting the order maintenance and zero-tolerance strategies of broken windows theory. There remains significant debate about whether those declines were solely and directly caused by broken windows theory being put into practice or whether those crime rate declines are actually linked to other intervening causes, such as the aging of the baby boom generation.[41,42,43,44]

Community- and problem-oriented policing (COP and POP)

As previously noted, traditional law enforcement strategies, including most incarnations of order maintenance and zero-tolerance policing, are incident driven—police officers respond to crimes as they occur, moving from incident to incident. Traditional incident-based law enforcement reinforces a divide between citizens and law enforcement officers—keeping them disconnected from each other. Because traditional law enforcement does not encourage or require the development of strong, collaborative working partnerships between community members and law enforcement agencies to solve crime problems, it becomes easier for an "us v. them" mentality to develop within law enforcement officers, who begin to view all citizens with distrust. Likewise, traditional incident-based policing makes it difficult for community members to appreciate the difficulties of law enforcement work or understand how law enforcement officers make decisions. Those things remain shrouded in mystery, which can also lead to distrust and apprehension about who law enforcement officers are and what they do. As sociologist Richard Adams argues, "traditional policing tends to stress the role of police officers in controlling crime and views citizens' role in the apprehension of criminals as minor players at best and part of the problem at worst."[45]

The **community-oriented** and **problem-oriented** law enforcement strategies, often called COP (community-oriented policing) and POP (problem-oriented policing), work to remedy these issues by emphasizing the importance of building and maintaining strong, positive, collaborative relationships between citizens, citizen groups, and law enforcement agencies. The underlying idea is that crime problems are best resolved when law enforcement and the community work together to identify specific crime problems, their causes, and then develop workable solutions to address them.

The COP and POP strategies are closely linked to one another. It may help to think of COP as more of a guiding philosophy that law enforcement agencies can embrace, which subsequently impacts all phases of law enforcement. From a law enforcement perspective, some elements of the COP philosophy include viewing citizens as partners, maintaining open communication between citizens and law enforcement, and more thoroughly integrating law enforcement officers into communities, by introducing things like bike and foot patrols, weekly or monthly police-community meetings, and other partnerships. COP is all about winning over the hearts and minds of the public in order to improve public safety.

POP, meanwhile, can be thought of as a specific method for successfully achieving the goals of the COP philosophy. Its developer, Hermann Goldstein, felt COP lacked an applied focus and was too easily "claimed" by law enforcement agencies who, in reality, continued conducting business as usual. POP is thus more analytical and less theoretical than COP and focuses on locating the root causes of crime problems. Once those causes are located, law enforcement agencies can strategically employ their resources to "solve" (e.g., get rid of or decrease) the problem. POP is accomplished through the four-step Scan, Analyze, Respond, and Assess method, otherwise known as SARA. The **SARA method** relies heavily on criminal intelligence and data analysis (see Figure 5.1 and Box 5.3). Both community and law enforcement input are vital at each step of the SARA process, which is circular. Importantly, POP is an ongoing process—agencies employing POP methods need to regularly ensure that the problem they resolved remains so.

4. Assess: Has the problem been resolved? This step is about measuring effectiveness. More data may need to be collected and new, or revised, strategies employed

1. Scan: Identify and define crime problems

3. Respond: develop and strategically employ plans to resolve the problem

2. Analyze: collect information, intelligence, and data to better understand the problem.

Figure 5.1
POP and the SARA process. SARA: Scan, Analyze, Respond, Assess

BOX 5.3: CONNECTING RESEARCH TO PRACTICE

Improving law enforcement practice through criminal intelligence analysis

Municipal law enforcement agencies across the United States are refashioning their mission and practices to reflect the community oriented policing model (COP), which emphasizes building strong, collaborative partnerships with community members. As a result, these law enforcement agencies are also embracing POP, or the problem oriented policing approach. The systematic application of POP principles directs law enforcement resources to the root cause of crime problems. By addressing the cause of crime incidents at its root, or source, law enforcement agencies can better and more efficiently serve their communities.

Key to the successful implementation of COP and POP strategies is criminal intelligence analysis, a burgeoning academic and professional field. Criminal intelligence analysts leverage various types of data, from crime statistics to informant tips, toward the goal of improving the operations, tactics, and strategies of the law enforcement agency. Criminal intelligence analysis is intellectually rigorous work and requires strong skills in research, data analysis, knowledge of geographic information systems (GIS) and excellent report writing and presentation skills.

Criminal intelligence analysis directly impacts the day-to-day practices of the law enforcement agency. For example, if a CI analyst notices a "hot spot"—or concentration of crimes within a limited geographic area—they can provide this information to police administrators who can then direct law enforcement resources to the hot spot area. The benefits of good criminal intelligence analysis are a more efficient law enforcement agency that is better able to address the needs and concerns of the community it serves. Thus, criminal intelligence analysis truly represents an example of research directly impacting practice.

BOX 5.4: PULLING LEVERS: POP AND FOCUSED DETERRENCE STRATEGIES

Problem Oriented Policing (POP) has many derivatives. One such strategy is called "pulling levers," otherwise known as "focused deterrence." Pulling levers policing is used to target specific criminal offenders or groups of criminal offenders who repeatedly engage in criminal behavior. Pulling levers is based on the ideas of deterrence theory. Essentially, high-risk, habitual offenders—gang members, repeat violent offenders—are targeted by the criminal justice system. They are notified that if they continue offending and are caught, they will face certain, swift, and severe punishment. It is hoped that presenting these offenders with knowledge that repercussions will follow from their continued criminality will deter them from committing more crimes. Conversely, these offenders are also offered positive incentives to desist from criminal conduct, such as access to social services and jobs.

The COP and POP strategies are increasingly popular among law enforcement agencies today, though forms of "neighborhood policing" have existed since the 1960s. More than half of all local law enforcement agencies in the U.S. employ some form of a community-oriented/problem-oriented policing model.[46] Even large cities, where the incident-based crime fighting models have been most entrenched, like Chicago, Los Angeles, and San Francisco, are adopting community and problem oriented policing strategies. San Diego, CA, was one of the first to adopt the principles of COP and POP successfully. They formed both SAFE STREETS NOW! and DART (drug abatement response team) programs, for instance.

BOX 5.5: POP IN ACTION

The City of Fort Collins, CO, a typical college town and home to Colorado State University, successfully employed the POP method to resolve crime and disorder issues in its local downtown area. That area was a frequent congregating point for college students looking to drink, dance, and hang out thanks to its plethora of bars and restaurants. Fort Collins police officers regularly dealt with various complaints, crimes, and municipal ordinance violations including noise complaints, public urination, assaults, public intoxication, underage drinking, DUI, and vandalism. Working collaboratively with local business owners and the University Fort Collins Police were able to find multiple solutions to these problems, including shortening the hours of operation of the local bars, providing more public restrooms, and developing a Campus Ride program to get people safely from the downtown area to the campus.

On a larger scale, the City of San Diego, CA, police department utilized the SARA method to understand and resolve a host of crime related problems.[47] In some areas of the city, police regularly dealt with recurring issues like thefts, muggings, gang fights, and drug dealing. An incident based strategy would simply respond over and over again to those issues, without necessarily resolving any of them. The POP system is a far more intelligent, efficient one. Utilizing POP and the SARA process, police in San Diego were able to diagnose underlying causes for those crimes, direct resources toward crime prevention, and alleviate community concerns. Lo and behold, once police began more rigorously targeting street-level prostitution, other forms of crime in those areas, including thefts, muggings, and drug dealing, decreased.

CONTEMPORARY ISSUES IN LAW ENFORCEMENT

In this section we focus on two contemporary issues in American law enforcement: misconduct and use of force. These issues are consistently occupying our nation's public consciousness and receiving lots of media, political, and public attention—much of it deserved. It is important that we, as educators and students of criminology and criminal justice, understand these issues and their origins so that we can contribute meaningfully to the ongoing dialogue surrounding what should be done about them.

Law enforcement misconduct

Overview

Law enforcement misconduct is a diverse category involving a range of behaviors and activities. In some cases, misconduct can be minor, such as violating an agency regulation against conducting personal business while at work. However, other times misconduct can be extremely serious. Accepting bribes, extorting suspects, assault, homicide, robbery, sexual harassment, stealing, or planting evidence and falsifying reports are just a few examples of serious types of misconduct that have, and do, occur.

Both corruption and use of excessive force (e.g., police brutality) are subtypes of misconduct. (We deal with the issues of use of force and police brutality in the next section.) Corruption can involve many things, like accepting a bribe, pay-off, goods, or services from criminals, suspects, or citizens, extorting someone in a vulnerable position, and attempts to cover up these and other behaviors.

Most commonly, misconduct occurs among individual law enforcement officers, the "rotten apples," or small pockets of them, i.e., "rotten pockets."[48] Television shows like *The Shield* and movies like *Training Day* and *Copland* depict misconduct occurring at those two levels. However, law enforcement misconduct sometimes goes beyond just a few officers and involves an entire unit, precinct, division, or department. When we say "the whole barrel is rotten" we are indicating that misconduct has become systemic—part of the fabric and day-to-day operation of the organization. Unfortunately, far too many examples exist of systemic misconduct. Law enforcement agencies in Miami, New Orleans, Philadelphia, New York, Cleveland, Los Angeles, San Francisco, Chicago, and numerous other cities, counties, and small towns have been scandalized, sometimes more than once, by systemic misconduct issues.[49]

What makes misconduct, in any form, worth discussing is the fact that it violates the mission of law enforcement. Recall that law enforcement agencies and officers are sworn to protect and serve their communities. To accomplish this mission, they are vested with power and trust. Misconduct in any form runs counter to the idea of community service, exploits the power vested in law enforcement agencies and officers, and violates the public's trust.

History

Many people are surprised to learn that law enforcement misconduct is as old as law enforcement itself since it seems like the media is treating it like it is "news." In fact, if you look at history it is fair to say that misconduct is part of the fabric of American law enforcement—it's nothing new, and no less disturbing, despite how saturated the Internet and TV become with stories of misconduct.

And they are saturated. In 2014 and 2015, stories abounded from across the U.S. of misconduct involving law enforcement agencies at every level. There were publicized sex and corruption scandals involving agents of the DEA,[50,51]

FBI,[52] and ATF.[53] U.S. Secret Service Agents—the crème de la crème of federal law enforcement—were the subject of five separate misconduct investigations.[54,55] *Rolling Stone* magazine published an exposé about rogue deputies in the "Panama Unit" of the Hidalgo County, Texas, Sherriff's Office[56] who were caught stealing and dealing drugs. Four police officers in Fort Lauderdale, Florida, were fired after an investigation concluded they violated department regulations by sending lewd, demeaning, and racist text messages to each other about citizens and fellow police officers.

The saying "the more things change, the more they stay the same" applies in relation to law enforcement misconduct. In the 1800s, individual and systemic misconduct was widely known to exist among law enforcement agencies. Corruption was commonplace. At the time, public law enforcement agencies functioned like private security forces for elected politicians. It was not uncommon for a single agency to get a new chief every time a new mayor or city council was elected. For example, between 1879 and 1889, Los Angeles went through 13 police chiefs. At the lowest levels, officers regularly exploited their power and employed violent tactics like "the third degree" to extract confessions from suspects. Even promotions could be purchased for a couple of hundred dollars.

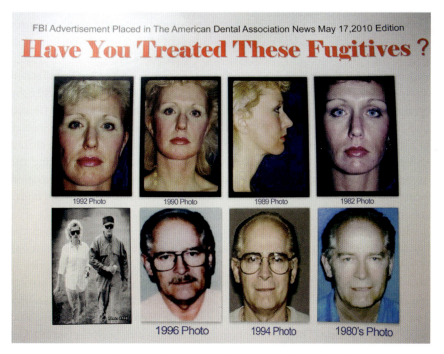

Image 5.10 *A poster featuring fugitives James "Whitey" Bulger and Catherine Greig is seen at the FBI field office in Boston. FBI agents tracked the fugitive Bulger for more than 16 years before finally catching him and his girlfriend in Santa Monica, California in 2011. He was subsequently convicted of multiple charges, including murder, in 2013.*

Michael Dwyer/AP/Press Association Images

Unsurprisingly, since the 1800s, dozens of independent commissions have been convened to investigate allegations of law enforcement misconduct. The NYPD alone has had five separate large-scale investigations of misconduct in its history (see Table 5.3 for a timeline of major events relating to law enforcement misconduct). Federal agencies like the prestigious FBI are not above misconduct scandals either. Recently, the prosecution of Boston's organized crime boss James "Whitey" Bulger included a significant amount of testimony regarding the corrupt activities of several FBI agents, who took bribes and gifts from Bulger in exchange for passing along information about FBI and other law enforcement investigations.

Causes and solutions

Causes of law enforcement misconduct are diverse. On the one hand, it is easy to understand how individual level misconduct can occur given the status, power and discretion law enforcement officers are vested with. President Abraham Lincoln said that "if you want to test a man's character, give him power." Unfortunately, some people are attracted to law enforcement because they want power, not because they want to help others. And, in other instances, changes in policy have allowed poorly qualified candidates at high risk for engaging in misconduct to get hired as law enforcement officers (see Box 5.6).

Because it has long been accepted that "power corrupts, and absolute power corrupts absolutely"[57] and because law enforcement officers are, at root, imperfect people just like you and I, it makes sense that some amount of individual misconduct will occur. Thankfully, individual level misconduct can be mitigated and resolved in a variety of ways. One obvious solution is to ensure that the power and discretion afforded individual law enforcement officers is checked and balanced. Strong leadership and high ethical standards within the agency are crucial. Moreover, uniform, swift, and transparent handling of citizen complaints and allegations about misconduct are also vital in reducing the amount of individual misconduct that occurs. One new technological innovation being utilized today that will hopefully reduce misconduct issues is the body-mounted camera.

But what can be done when misconduct becomes systemic? When the agency's leadership are complicit or unwilling to take action? These questions have been raised repeatedly, especially in New York City and Los Angeles as recently as the mid-1990s. In both cities, major misconduct scandals involving corruption, brutality and other behaviors, were ultimately found to reflect the culture of the agency and the failures of agency leadership to hold officers accountable. The law enforcement subculture in both the NYPD and LAPD socialized new officers into bad behaviors; not surprisingly, as those officers became supervisors, such behavior was considered "normal" operating procedure.

Solutions for systemic misconduct issues are more complicated. Reversing decades of socialization and achieving real progressive change is very difficult.

Typically, when systemic misconduct cases have arisen the Department of Justice (DOJ) gets involved. The DOJ can investigate state and local law enforcement agencies if "a pattern or practice of conduct that deprives persons of rights protected by the Constitution or laws of the United States"[58]

BOX 5.6: THE MIAMI RIVER COPS SCANDAL

In 1985, Miami police detectives were confronted with a puzzle: why did three young men dressed in designer clothes, with cash and handguns in their waistbands, drown in the Miami River? Detectives suspected the three men were drug dealers, probably cocaine smugglers, and that their deaths were anything but accidental. Yet, the fact that they drowned accidentally meant their deaths could not be investigated as a homicide.

A break in the case came when a local security guard notified detectives that around the same time the three men likely drowned, six or seven uniformed Miami Police officers stormed the docks at a nearby boatyard. Detectives called around but nobody could recall any kind of official police operation at the boatyard that night.

Over the next several months, a special task force of DEA agents and local police detectives unraveled what would become known as the Miami River Cops Scandal—one of the largest cases of systemic police misconduct in the history of the U.S. More than eighty Miami police officers were eventually implicated in various types of misconduct. Seven were officially charged with stealing drugs and cash from drug smugglers and for causing the deaths of the three men, as well as plotting to assassinate key government witnesses during their trial.

The Miami River Cops Scandal is infamous not just because of the extent of misconduct—as much as 10 percent or more of the entire department was likely corrupt—but because of the underlying cause. In the 1980s, a new law enforcement mandate was handed down from the highest levels of government: the U.S. was going to get tough on crime and fight a war on drugs. This policy shift placed an immense burden on local law enforcement agencies, who were ill-equipped and poorly staffed to handle such a huge shift in practice.

The City of Miami hadn't hired a new recruit in five years. They then hired 600—doubling the MPD's size. Chief Richard Witt was the Director of Training at the time:

> We recognized that many of them lacked good, basic education . . . many of them lacked good, basic communication skills . . . few of them had any personal discipline. More than one of them had backgrounds for having been gang members while in high school. More than one of them had been identified by a former employer as having committed theft and other kinds of larceny.[59]

Former Miami Police Chief Clarence Dixon aptly summarizes the net effect the new hiring binge to meet bureaucratic demands had on the department: "We ended up scraping the bottom of the barrel to do that, to accomplish what our chief at that time committed us to."[60]

The Miami River Cops Scandal is thus a true example of the fact that policies produce real world consequences.

is suspected. Often, the DOJ will enter into a legally binding settlement with the state or local agency that will require various things. For example, the DOJ might require new policies be enacted for the handling and investigation of complaints. Stricter disciplinary guidelines might need to be developed for guilty officers. The DOJ may also require that data be collected and reported.

Table 5.3 Timeline of major events relating to law enforcement misconduct

Year	Event
1893	The phrase "police brutality" appears for the first time in a *New York Times* article.
1895	Lexow Commission convenes to look into a number of different allegations that corruption was widespread within the NYPD, in the wake of the Tammany Hall public corruption scandal.
1914	Curran Committee investigates NYPD after NYPD Lieutenant kills a New York City elected official.
1932	Seabury Investigation looks into reports of corruption in the NYPD against a national backdrop of similar allegations in other states.
1949	Hefland Commission investigations allegations of bribery, gambling, and corruption within the NYPD.
1968	Kerner Commission concludes that many of the decade's race riots were sparked by conflicts between law enforcement officers and minority communities.
1971–1973	The Knapp Commission finds a systemic pattern of corruption within the New York City Police Department.
1985–1987	The Miami River Cops scandal and trial occur in Miami, Florida.
1991	Black motorist Rodney King is badly beaten by members of the LAPD and LA County Sherriff's Department; the beating is captured on film by a nearby resident.
1991	The Christopher Commission details systemic patterns of excessive force among police officers in the LAPD and cites a failure of management to control such behavior.
1992	Los Angeles experiences several days of violent riots after four white police officers are acquitted in the video-taped beating of Rodney King.
1994	The Mollen Commission again investigates serious claims of misconduct within the NYPD.
1997	The LAPD Rampart Division Scandal breaks; in exchange for leniency, Officer Rafael Perez implicates over 70 officers in misconduct ranging from stealing drugs, to assault, attempted murder, and falsifying reports and testimony. Subsequently, over 100 convictions tainted by the scandal were reversed or thrown out. The City of Los Angeles paid over $125 million to settle lawsuits.
2014–2015	A series of widely publicized incidents of misconduct, police brutality, and other questionable practices, primarily involving white police officers and black or Hispanic suspects, leads to riots in Ferguson, Missouri, Baltimore, Maryland, and other cities.

Beyond the involvement of the DOJ, which is sometimes met with resistance by state and local officials,[61] other solutions for handling systemic misconduct issues include removing the existing leadership. It has also been common in places like New York and Los Angeles to establish an external oversight committee to ensure compliance with new directives and policies. For example, after the Mollen Commission published its findings regarding misconduct in the NYPD in 1994, the City of New York created the Civilian Complaint Review Board (CCRB), which now independently investigates all complaints made against the NYPD. The value of independent oversight commissions is that they can subvert the obstacles created by a subculture that views misconduct as acceptable or tolerable.

Use of force

Overview

Each year, approximately 60 million contacts occur between law enforcement officers and citizens in the U.S. In each of those contacts, law enforcement officers must rely on their training, experience, and discretion to make decisions about what actions they should take. One of the most difficult, and important, decisions any officer will make in his or her career is whether or not to use force in carrying out their duties. Thankfully, less than 2 percent of those 60 million law enforcement-citizen contacts results in any use of force. This means that despite how prevalent stories about citizens being beaten or killed by law enforcement officers are on the news or the Internet, it is actually quite rare for law enforcement officers to utilize force.

The reason for this is that all law enforcement personnel receive training about when force should be used, and how much force should be used, in different scenarios. That training makes very clear that force should not be used unless the situation dictates it is absolutely necessary. Moreover, law enforcement training dictates that whenever possible law enforcement officers should strive to use the least amount of force necessary to control the situation or gain the compliance of the suspect.

The **use of force continuum** is a training tool used to teach rookie and veteran law enforcement officers the basics about the use of force (see Figure 5.2). At the bottom of the continuum, representing the lowest level of force is **officer presence**, which consists of two main components: physical presence and voice. At this level, no physical force of any kind is utilized. The mere presence of a uniformed or credentialed law enforcement officer (or several) is considered a display of force. The uniform, patrol car, and body language of the officer sends clear messages to others about who is in control. At this level officers are instructed on how to utilize their voice (including volume and tone) and voice commands to gain control without resorting to physical force. Officer presence and voice can alter the dynamics of most situations and, generally, are enough to gain control of most people and situations.

Image 5.11 *Less lethal methods for handling encounters with non-compliant citizens are now a common component of a police officer's training. Tasers are one common tool employed by police to end situations without resorting to the use of a gun and lethal force; however, even Tasers have a history of being misused and can kill in certain situations.*

iStock/sean boggs

Of course, all situations are unique and dynamic—on the streets things can change in an instant. Law enforcement officers are taught to look for subtle signs that indicate whether a situation is about to change, such as the tone of a suspect's voice, their hand and body position, etc. In some cases, physical force is necessary to control a suspect or situation. The next level of force above officer presence is called **empty hand control**—this level represents the lowest possible level of physical force. Empty hand control can involve grabbing, holding, striking, kicking, and other combative techniques. Generally, empty hand control is enough to resolve most any situation and is fairly common—you may have seen an officer pin a suspect's arms behind their back? That action represents empty hand control.

After empty hand control, there are a variety of **less lethal methods** officers can use to control people. These methods include pepper spray, batons, Tasers or CEDs (conducted electricity devices), and bean bag rounds (small bean bag projectiles fired from a shotgun). Employing less lethal methods clearly represents an escalation in the amount of force and are not trivial—they are "less lethal" but still capable of killing. For instance, between 2001 and 2012, Amnesty International reports that more than 500 people died after being shocked with Tasers by law enforcement officers;[62] another 27 died in 2015.[63]

In rare instances, the circumstances of a situation might dictate that **lethal force** is required. Lethal force entails an officer drawing and firing their weapon at a suspect or suspects. Lethal force does not have to result in death, though death is a likely outcome. Officers are trained to employ lethal force to protect themselves, fellow officers, or civilians whose lives are in immediate danger. Choosing to use lethal force is a split-second decision. Because of that fact, law enforcement officers are generally given the benefit of the doubt by administrators and the public (including jurors) when they do choose to use lethal force. This does not mean that lethal force incidents are given a free pass— they are all investigated, often very rigorously, by Officer Involved Shooting or Internal Affairs units. However, feeling threatened or in danger is a very subjective emotional state that is hard for others to second guess. People want to believe that police officers would never use lethal force unless they had to and, in most cases, they did have to.

Unless there is evidence that clearly contradicts an officer's statements or recounting of events, most use of force incidents, including lethal force incidents, are likely to be deemed reasonable and justified.

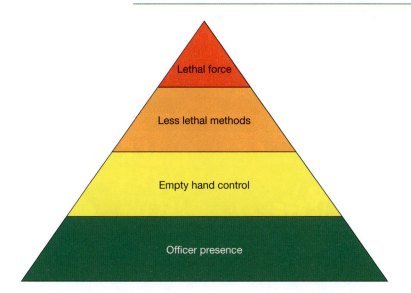

Figure 5.2 The use of force continuum

Current controversies

Controversy surrounds the use of force by law enforcement officers and agencies. Advocacy groups, politicians, researchers, government agencies, and the public have been sensitized to use of force issues thanks to heightened media focus on use of force cases, particularly those involving white police officers and minorities. The proliferation of video recording technologies, in the form of cellphone and surveillance cameras, has allowed interactions between the public and law enforcement—including those resulting in the use of force—to be caught on tape. In certain cases those images have "gone viral" and have allowed people outside law enforcement to review and critique law enforcement actions in ways that might otherwise not be possible.

Over the past several years there have been riots and protests in Ferguson, Missouri, Baltimore, Maryland, and New York City following incidents where law enforcement officers utilized force, including lethal force, to subdue suspected criminals (see Table 5.4 for a timeline of recent high profile cases). Countless articles, opinion columns, and Facebook posts have been written on the topic of use of force. Phrases like "I Can't Breathe"[64] and "Black Lives Matter"[65] have dominated the discourse—*Time Magazine* even published a cover story under the title "Black Lives Matter" for their April 9, 2015, issue.

At the heart of the use of force controversy are important questions that need to be answered: are law enforcement officers utilizing force too quickly in their encounters with citizens? Do minority suspects have force used against them more often than white suspects? Are blacks and Hispanics more likely than whites to become victims of lethal force? Are law enforcement officers trained appropriately in how and when to use force? And, are law enforcement agencies addressing concerns about use of force incidents and practices fairly and transparently in their communities?

Image 5.12 *Minneapolis police guard the entrance to their Fourth Precinct building as Black Lives Matter supporters continued their protest linked to the killing of 24-year-old Jamar Clark, an unarmed black man by a white Minneapolis police officer.*

Jim Mone/AP/Press Association Images

Unfortunately, research and data on law enforcement use of force are not as prevalent as we'd like, which makes it hard for us to definitively answer the above questions at the present time. Initiatives are underway at the state[66] and federal[67] levels to revamp data collection efforts so that we can better answer those questions. Nevertheless, we still know some things that can help us better understand the complicated issue of use of force.

Prevalence of use of force

Current data indicates that use of force is not common in encounters between law enforcement and the public. Less than 2 percent of law enforcement-citizen contacts each year result in any kind of force,[68] which means only about 1.2 million encounters between law enforcement and the public result in force being used. Moreover, data indicate that when force is utilized in those 2 percent of cases, it tends to be low-level force.[69] Thus, lethal force—an officer shooting or otherwise lethally wounding a suspect—is very rare. While exact data are hard to come by, it is likely that fewer than 1,000 or so lethal force incidents occur each year across the United States.[70]

Data on the prevalence of use of force, including lethal force, show us that use of force is not an epidemic—it is not occurring more frequently now than in the recent past.[71] What current data do not tell us is if law enforcement officers are too quick to utilize force when encountering members of the

Table 5.4 Timeline and summary of recent high profile use of force cases

July 2014	43-year-old African American male, Eric Garner[72], dies after being placed in a choke hold by a white NYPD officer on Staten Island. Police believed Garner was illegally selling cigarettes; his death was caught on amateur video.
August 2014	Michael Brown[73], an 18-year-old African American male, is killed by a white police officer in Ferguson, Missouri after an altercation between the two. Witnesses allege Brown was shot after surrendering to the officer and placing his hands in the air. The Department of Justice finds inconclusive evidence to support that version of events, but does find a pattern of racial discrimination and prejudice within the Ferguson Police Department.[74]
November 2014	12-year-old African American boy Tamir Rice,[75] is shot and killed by two white police officers at a playground in Cleveland. The officers were responding to a report of a juvenile with a gun. Within two seconds of arriving on the scene, the officers fired two shots at Rice. His "gun" turned out to be an airsoft pellet gun.
February 2015	Indian citizen Sureshbhai Patel,[76] a 57-year-old grandfather and Indian citizen who had recently arrived in the United States to care for his new grandchild, was left partially paralyzed after being slammed to the ground by a white Madison, Alabama police officer who stopped Patel while he was taking a morning walk in his son's neighborhood. The encounter between Patel, who spoke no English, and the officer was caught on video.
April 2015	50-year-old African American male Walter Scott[77] is shot in the back and killed by a white City of North Charleston, South Carolina police officer. After being pulled over, Mr. Scott fled his vehicle on foot. The officer pursued and caught up to him. An amateur cell phone video captured the next few moments where Mr. Scott, standing before the officer, turns and begins to flee again. Rather than giving chase, the officer draws his firearm and shoots the unarmed Scott in the back, killing him.
April 2015	25 year-old African American male Freddie Gray is arrested by Baltimore City Police officers and placed into the back of a police transport van. During his transport to a central booking facility, Mr. Gray suffers an injury to his spinal cord because he was not properly secured in the van with a seatbelt despite his hands being cuffed behind his back. At various points, personnel transporting Gray made stops throughout Baltimore, but never attend to Gray's injuries. Gray dies April 19 of injuries sustained during his encounter and transportation by police.
May 2015	White Cleveland Police Officer Michael Brelo[78] is found not guilty of two counts of voluntary manslaughter in the deaths of two unarmed African Americans, Timothy Russell and Malissa Williams. Officer Brelo was one of more than a dozen police officers who pursued the couple through Cleveland on the mistaken belief that the couple was armed and had fired shots at police. After cornering the vehicle in a parking lot, Mr. Brelo personally fired 49 shots at the couple, including 15 shots while standing on the hood of their vehicle.

Image 5.13
In this video image, Walter Scott is shot in the back while running away from police officer Michael Thomas Slager in Charleston, S.C., on April 4, 2015.

Feidin Santana/AP/Press Association Images

public, especially minority suspects and people with mental health issues. That question is inherently more difficult, if not impossible, to answer.

Decisions to use force are subjective. Anecdotal evidence from a very small number of high-profile cases, like the shooting of Walter Scott in South Carolina and the high-number of lethal shootings of mentally ill suspects by members of the Albuquerque Police Department[79] indicate there may be truth to the belief that law enforcement officers may resort to using force too quickly, which would reflect upon shortcomings in hiring, training, and administrative oversight. More research is necessary to provide definitive conclusions.

Demographics and use of force

At the heart of the current controversy over the law enforcement use of force is the issue of race. A small number of cases are being cited as evidence that law enforcement agencies and officers are more likely to use force against minority suspects than white suspects. What does the current data say?

First, let's backtrack a bit. According to the latest U.S. Census data,[80] America has a population of over 321 million people. Non-Hispanic and Latino whites comprise the vast majority of America's population: 62.6 percent of the population as of 2014. Blacks make up 13.2 percent and Hispanic or Latino people comprise 17.1 percent of the population.

The idea of **disproportionality** is central to the study of criminology and criminal justice. In essence, when something is disproportional it occurs or is observed more than we would expect it to occur or be observed. When we apply the term to people, it means "the overrepresentation of a particular group of people in a particular group or system."[81] A closely related term is **disparity.** Generally, we use the word disparity to mean "the unequal or inequitable treatment of one group as compared to another."[82]

In terms of criminal justice and law enforcement, if all things were equal or proportional, we would expect whites to represent that vast majority of

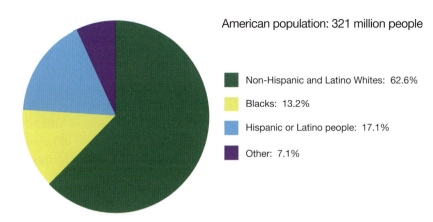

American population: 321 million people

Figure 5.3
Ethnicity of the American population

■ Non-Hispanic and Latino Whites: 62.6%

■ Blacks: 13.2%

■ Hispanic or Latino people: 17.1%

■ Other: 7.1%

people committing crimes, getting arrested and being sent to jail or prison. Hispanics and blacks would represent a very small proportion of people moving through our criminal justice system.

In reality, research shows exactly the opposite to be true. Data show that disparities exist in all phases of the criminal justice system—from law enforcement, to courts, to corrections. In other words, the criminal justice system is not one in which all people are treated equally.

Specifically, people of color are disproportionately more likely to be caught in the net of the criminal justice system than white people. Data reveal that racial minorities, especially young black and Hispanic men, are more likely to be targeted by law enforcement officers for enforcement actions due to both official policies and subjective determinations, sometimes referred to as "racial profiling."

People of color are more likely than whites to be stopped and searched, whether they are in a vehicle or on the street[83] (see Box 5.2). Most important for our discussion, current data shows that blacks and Hispanics are more likely than whites to have force threatened, and used, against them.[84] Findings from official investigations into police use of force, such as the Christopher Commission investigation in Los Angeles following the 1991 Rodney King beating, also provide further evidence that in some places an individual's skin color plays an important role in the use of force and factors into excessive force incidents.[85]

Perceptions of use of force

The current controversy on the use of force is one with multiple facets. On the one hand, use of force is quite rare and incidents of excessive force even rarer still. On the other hand, any incident where force is utilized above and beyond what is reasonable or justifiable is one incident too many.

At a minimum, there exists enough data and anecdotal evidence to warrant concern about the use of force, especially within minority communities.[86] It may very well be that law enforcement agencies and officers resort to using force within those communities far too quickly and apply force excessively.

Indeed, while official data shows that use of force by law enforcement is not common within the grand scheme of all law enforcement-citizen contacts, that official data may not accurately capture the true extent of excessive force incidents. For example, it has been alleged in official reports, as well as anecdotally, that a vast number of excessive force incidents are covered up and hidden by law enforcement officers.[87]

A key driver behind the current concern with use of force, beyond "official data" and report findings, is the increasing perception among many different segments of the American population that use of force by law enforcement agencies may be a real problem in need of our public attention. Within communities of color, this perception has existed for a long time, thanks in part to the fact that laws and law enforcement agencies have upheld discriminatory, racist practices like slavery and Jim Crow laws.[88] Video footage of questionable use of force incidents has been crucial in awakening concern among people outside of those communities.[89]

Unfortunately, while the use of force by law enforcement officers may be "the single most volatile issue facing police departments"[90] today, like many issues, it is one that has existed for quite some time. Decades ago, the Kerner

BOX 5.7: CONSIDER THIS . . .

Repairing the law enforcement–citizen relationship

While rare when considered in light of how many police citizen contacts occur each year (more than 60 million), incidents of police misconduct and use of excessive force—especially those with a racial dimension—have increasingly been showing up in news media reports over the last several years. These incidents have sparked protests, riots, and a significant amount of discussion about things like law enforcement accountability, transparency, justice, and the law enforcement–citizen relationship. Among some communities and groups, particularly minorities with a long history of unequal treatment by law enforcement agencies, the police–citizen relationship is as broken now as it ever has been.

Trust and respect are cornerstones of the law enforcement–citizen relationship. Without the trust and respect of the community, the job of law enforcement officers becomes much more difficult. So, the question is what can be done to rebuild trust and respect among citizens and law enforcement agencies?

Many criminologists, policy analysts,[91, 92] and criminal justice system professionals[93] have been thinking about this question. A starting point would obviously be to re-establish legitimacy, respect, and trust. This could be accomplished in many ways, none of which present a fast or easy fix. Adopting community policing strategies (e.g., COP and POP) and developing strong community engagement and outreach programs are good strategies. The goal should be to build stronger working partnerships with community members to reinforce the idea that law enforcement is best accomplished from the bottom up—with the support and input of every concerned stakeholder—rather than from the top down. Bringing law enforcement agencies and community members closer together will also underscore the mission of law enforcement, which is to protect and serve the community, rather than terrorize and harass it.

Another important strategy that could help mend the law enforcement–citizen relationship would be for law enforcement agencies to embrace greater transparency. Currently, many jurisdictions do not allow the public to review disciplinary records or complaints made against police officers. Keeping that information sealed creates the impression in the minds of citizens, whether accurate or not, that law enforcement agencies have little desire or incentive to ensure that officers who perform their jobs poorly, or who are repeatedly cited in citizen complaints, are held accountable. One option to help resolve this issue could be to funnel all citizen complaints and disciplinary issues to a non-partisan, external committee or review board, as occurs in New York City,[94] and vest that committee with the power to enact discipline, up to and including recommending that criminal charges be filed against officers acting unlawfully.

There are many possible solutions and progressive changes that can be instituted to help improve the law enforcement–citizen relationship. In addition to those mentioned above, others include raising the minimum employment standards, developing more rigorous, continuous educational and training requirements, and mandating recurrent cultural sensitivity training. At the end of the day, it is imperative that law enforcement and citizens work together. Effective law enforcement requires a strong relationship between law enforcement agencies and the communities they serve. That relationship in turn depends on mutual trust and respect.

Commission—which was convened in the wake of numerous race riots across America—concluded that many of the 1960s urban, inner-city race riots "were usually ignited by a minor incident fueled by antagonism between the Negro population and the police."[95] Thus, it remains to be seen what lasting impacts will result from the new public and political awareness about the use of force by law enforcement.

THE FUTURE OF AMERICAN LAW ENFORCEMENT

> *Law and order exist for the purpose of establishing justice ... when they fail in this purpose they become the dangerously structured dams that block the flow of social progress.*
>
> —*Dr. Martin Luther King, Jr. April 1963*

Recent trends in law enforcement signal positive things for the future of American law enforcement. President Obama issued an executive order on December 18, 2014, which created the "President's Task Force on 21st Century Policing." The mission of this task force was to collect data and gather input from professionals and citizens in order to "identify best practices" in policing.[96]

Image 5.14 *U.S. President Barack Obama speaks as Commissioner of the Philadelphia Police Department Charles Ramsey (seated next to him on the right) and others listen during a meeting of his Task Force on 21st Century Policing. President Obama met with the task force "to discuss their recommendations on how to strengthen community policing and strengthen trust among law enforcement officers and the communities they serve."*

Getty

The task force's final report,[97] issued May 2015, identified six key topics or "pillars" and provided recommendations for action under each. The key focal areas identified by the task force included several we have focused on in this chapter, including "building trust and legitimacy," "community policing and crime reduction," and "officer training and education." The task force also recommended the creation of nationwide, federally supported task forces to continue reviewing issues of policing and criminal justice reform as well as important correlates to criminal offending like poverty and education.

The shift toward community and problem oriented policing in America's communities remains a vital step forward in terms of improving American law enforcement. As the Obama policing task force noted, "law enforcement culture should embrace a guardian—rather than a warrior—mindset to build trust and legitimacy . . . with the public."[98] If law enforcement agencies embrace and employ models effectively, antagonisms and conflicts between law enforcement and the public should decrease. However, those macro level changes are not enough to ensure that law enforcement continues to progressively improve into the future.

Steps need to be taken to ensure that hiring practices adequately screen out potentially problematic applicants before they wear a badge. Despite claims regarding the rigorousness of hiring policies, too many individuals still become law enforcement officers despite questionable behavioral and psychological backgrounds.[99] Training must also continuously reinforce principles of cultural sensitivity and best practices regarding the use of force, dealing with people with mental illness, as well as other topics.

Finally, the future of American law enforcement can be a positive one so long as law enforcement agencies embrace notions of fairness, justice, and transparency. This is especially relevant against the backdrop of protests regarding the use of force.

Law enforcement agencies must hold themselves, and individual officers, accountable for their actions while on and off-duty. True leadership occurs when people and organizations set a good example for others to follow.

One author of this textbook was told by a police officer in Miami, Florida: "Everyone loves firefighters, because they only show up to help. But people hate the police, because when we show up something bad is going on and someone is usually going to get in trouble." While law enforcement agencies will never truly escape the perception evinced in the preceding quote, if they

BOX 5.8: CRIME IN GLOBAL PERSPECTIVE

Law enforcement and public order in Europe

The purpose of taking a critical view of the criminal justice system is to encourage outside the box thinking about current practices in order to improve the functioning of the current law enforcement system. In this endeavor, it can sometimes be useful to look at how laws and law enforcement agencies operate in other countries. Perhaps there are methods or strategies that we can learn from and adopt that can improve our system of law enforcement and make it more successful.

Every country has its own way of maintaining law and order. While there is overlap among nations, there is also considerable difference. The actions of law enforcement agencies in America (and elsewhere) are guided by criminal laws. America, more than some countries in western Europe, has a number of criminal laws that prohibit what are called "public order" offenses: things like drug use, prostitution, gambling, etc.

As a result, significant amounts of time and resources are expended by American law enforcement agencies enforcing laws against public order crimes and arresting public order offenders. If you've ever seen an episode of the TV show *Cops*, then you'll have some understanding of just how much time and resources are spent policing things such as drug use and prostitution. In fact, in America the single largest category of arrests made each year is for drug possession.[100]

In several western European countries, however, laws, and law enforcement agencies are not preoccupied with enforcing "public order" laws or arresting public order offenders. Indeed, in countries like the Netherlands, the Czech Republic, and Portugal drug use and possession are not priority number one for law enforcement (and this trend may be expanding to countries like Great Britain[101]). Portugal, for example, which decriminalized all drugs in 2001, has been able to divert many resources previously devoted to drug law enforcement to other drug education and treatment programs.[102] None of those nations has witnessed skyrocketing levels of drug crime, violence, or addiction[103]—arguments that are often central in justifying the existence of harsh U.S. laws and law enforcement practices toward drugs.

Likewise, the legal and law enforcement approach to prostitution and the sex industry throughout Europe is far more tolerant than in the United States. Prostitution is fully or partially legal and regulated in over 60 countries worldwide,[104] including the majority of countries in Europe: Belgium, the Czech Republic, Denmark, France, Italy, Latvia, Luxembourg, the Netherlands, Poland, Portugal, Sweden, Switzerland, Spain, and the United Kingdom. In those countries, engaging in prostitution and purchasing sex are viewed as personal choices, rather than uniformly illegal and morally wrong behaviors that need to be controlled via criminal laws and tough law enforcement practices.

By moving away from the position of blanket intolerance toward "public order" offenses like drug use and prostitution, many European countries have demonstrated there are many ways to engage in law enforcement. Cracking down on public order offenses—the current standard in America—is certainly one strategy. Greater acceptance and tolerance is clearly another. More importantly, by choosing not to waste time, manpower, and other resources enforcing harsh drug and prostitution laws, those European nations noted above can direct more resources to other law enforcement priorities. Further, tolerating people's personal choices may even improve the relationship between law enforcement agencies and the public.

continue the current trend toward improving transparency and accountability when questionable incidents occur, they will ultimately improve public relations.

SUMMARY

In this chapter we have introduced the topic of law enforcement. Space constraints here do not permit a full discussion of every important or interesting facet of law enforcement—that sort of discussion would require its own textbook and several courses. However, in this chapter we have briefly discussed several important topics. Remember that law enforcement is the first phase of the American criminal justice system.

The law enforcement mission is to protect public safety, but more specifically we can say that the law enforcement mission is to protect and preserve life, liberty, and property. This mission directly impacts the law enforcement role, as we discussed in this chapter. That role is both unique and complex, including major responsibilities like crime prevention, law and code enforcement, investigation, and arrest. The law enforcement role is characterized by trust, power, stress, and high expectations.

In this chapter we developed an understanding of the history of modern law enforcement in America and briefly noted that there are a diverse array of law enforcement agencies operating in the United States, including ones at the federal, state, and local levels. The FBI, state police, and county sheriff are all examples of law enforcement agencies working at these different levels. Each has unique responsibilities and exercise jurisdiction over a specific group of offenses or geographic area.

Modern law enforcement agencies, especially local police and sheriff's departments, are adopting new strategies to deal with crime in the 21st century. Two of the most promising including COP (community-oriented policing) and POP (problem-oriented policing). COP and POP are complementary policing strategies that focus on developing strong relationships between the community and police and identify and strategically respond to the root of crime problems. It's very likely that your local police department uses one or both of these strategies in carrying out their mission to protect and serve.

Finally, we discussed two important, current issues in law enforcement: misconduct and the use of force. Along the way, we've also highlighted some interesting case studies, detailed some of the realities of working in law enforcement and many other issues. Most importantly, we noted that there are some possible solutions for addressing these current issues. Among the many strategies we discussed were developing more rigorous hiring standards and better, continuous training, especially on the use of force and dealing with people who are mentally ill.

If you are interested in law enforcement as a vocation or area for further study, this chapter should provide a foundation to pursue either endeavor. Ultimately, understanding where law enforcement fits within the criminal justice system is vitally important as is recognizing that law enforcement is a fundamental topic of concern for criminologists.

NOTES

1 Mass, P. 2005 [orig. 1973]. *Serpico*. New York: William Morrow Paperbacks.
2 Ibid.
3 Ibid.
4 Ibid.
5 Ibid.
6 Kilgannon, C. 2010. Serpico on Serpico. *The New York Times*, Jan. 22. http://www.nytimes.com/2010/01/24/nyregion/24serpico.html?pagewanted=all&_r=0.
7 Serpico, F. 2015. How Police Departments Can Mend the Rift with the Public. *The Nation*, Jan. 7. Retrieved from http://www.thenation.com/article/194425/reforming-police#.
8 Weber, M. 1968. *Economy and Society: An Outline of Interpretive Sociology*. New York: Bedminster Press.
9 Ibid.
10 Skolnick, J.H. 1966. *Justice Without Trial: Law Enforcement in Democratic Society*. New York: Wiley.
11 Westley, W.A. 1970. *Violence and the Police: A Sociological Study of Law, Custom, and Morality*. Cambridge, MA: MIT Press.
12 Manning, P.K. 1977. *Police Work: The Social Organization of Policing*. Cambridge, MA: MIT Press.
13 Severson, L.A. 2007. *Policing in America: A Reference Handbook*. Santa Barbara, CA: ABC-CLIO.
14 Ibid.
15 Paoline, E. 2004. Shedding Light on Police Culture: An Examination of Officers' Occupational Attitudes. *Police Quarterly* 7(2): 205–236.
16 Human Rights Watch. 1998. *Shielded from Justice: Police Brutality and Accountability in the United States*. Retrieved from http://www.columbia.edu/itc/journalism/cases/katrina/Human%20Rights%20Watch/uspohtml/uspo14.htm.
17 Cuthbertson, D. (Special Agent in Charge). 2009. Educating the Next Generation of Homeland Security Professionals. Presentation at the University of Texas at El Paso National Center for Border Security and Immigration Symposium El Paso, TX, Feb. 26.
18 Kissel, T.B. 2000. River of Sleaze. *The Miami New Times*, April 6. Retrieved from www.miaminewtimes.com/news/river-of-sleaze-6378923.
19 PBS Frontline. 1990. When Cops Go Bad. Ep. 901. Original Air Date: Oct. 16, produced by Charles C. Stuart and Marcia Vivancos. Written by Charles C. Stuart.

Transcript available at http://www.pbs.org/wgbh/pages/frontline/shows/drugs/archive/copsgobad.html.

20 Fazollah, M. and Gibbons, T.J., Jr. 1995. 39th District Scandal Nets Another Dirty-cop List At Six, And Still Growing. *The Philadelphia Inquirer*, Aug. 23. Retrieved from http://articles.philly.com/1995–08–23/news/25710780_1_police-corruption-police-corruption-maier.

21 Bandes, S. 1999. Patterns of Injustice: Police Brutality in the Courts. *Buffalo Law Review* 47: 1275–1378.

22 Bandes, S. 2001. Tracing the Pattern of No Pattern: Stories of Police Brutality. *Loyola of Los Angeles Law Review* 34: 665–680.

23 Bacon, S. 1939. The Early Development of American Municipal Policing: A Study of the Evolution of Formal Controls in a Changing Society. Unpublished dissertation, Yale University.

24 Walker, S. 1980. *Popular Justice*. New York: Oxford.

25 The Pendleton Act 1883. 2015. *Digital History*. Retrieved from www.digitalhistory.uh.edu/disp_textbook.cfm?smtID=3&psid=1098.

26 Kelling, G.L. Wilson, J.Q. 1982. Broken Windows: The Police and Neighborhood Safety. *The Atlantic*, March.

27 Fermino, J. 2013. Bill Bratton Expanded Stop and Frisk When He Ran Log Angeles Police Department. *New York Daily News*, City Hall Bureau. Nov. 24. Retrieved from http://www.nydailynews.com/new-york/bratton-article-1.1527258.

28 Weinstein, A. 2014. Meet Miami Gardens, The Stop-And-Frisk Capital of America. *Gawker*, April 29. Retrieved from http://gawker.com/meet-miami-gardens-the-stop-and-frisk-capital-of-ameri-1583348024.

29 Badger, E. 2014. 12 Years of Data from New York City Suggest Stop-and-frisk Wasn't that Effective. *The Washington Post*, Aug. 21. Retrieved from www.washingtonpost.com/blogs/wonkblog/wp/2014/08/21/12-years-of-data-from-new-york-city-suggest-stop-and-frisk-wasnt-that-effective/.

30 New York Civil Liberties Union. 2014. Report: Stop-and-Frisk During the Bloomberg Administration 2002–2013. Retrieved from http://www.nyclu.org/publications/report-stop-and-frisk-during-bloomberg-administration-2002–2013–2014.

31 Op. cit., see 2.

32 Brown, J. 2013. NAACP Calls for Probe of 'Harassment' by Miami Gardens Police. *The Miami Herald,* Dec. 10. Retrieved from http://www.miamiherald.com/news/local/community/miami-dade/article1958372.html.

33 Op cit., see 3.

34 Ibid.

35 Bratton, W.J. 2015. Broken Windows and Quality-of-life Policing in New York City. The City of New York. Retrieved from http://www.nyc.gov/html/nypd/downloads/pdf/analysis_and_planning/qol.pdf.

36 Levy, R. Delgado, J. 2013. McCarthy Touts 'Broken Windows' Crime-Fighting Strategy. *The Chicago Tribune*, March 11.

37 Garcia, R.A. 2013. Order Maintenance Policing for Police Departments. Criminal Justice Systems, Arizona State University School of Criminology and Criminal Justice. Retrieved from http://www.slideshare.net/FitDoc1/ompolicing.

38 Grabosky, P.N. 1999. Zero Tolerance Policing. Australia Attorney General's Department, Office of Crime Statistics, *Trends and Issues in Crime and Criminal Justice* 102.

39 Bratton, W.J. and Kelling, G.L. 2015. Why We Need Broken Windows Policing. *City Journal* (Winter).

40 Morrison, P. 2015. 'Broken Windows' Policing Isn't Broken, Says Criminologist George L. Kelling. *The Los Angeles Times*, Jan. 6.

41 Center for Evidence-Based Crime Policy. 2015. Broken Windows Policing. George Mason University.

42 Seiver, S. 2015. A Millennials Guide to 'Broken Windows.' The Marshall Project. May 20. Retrieved from https://www.themarshallproject.org/2015/05/20/a-millennial-s-guide-to-broken-windows#.iDuVcMSzT.

43 National Bureau of Economic Research. 2015. What Reduced Crime in New York City, May 27. Retrieved from http://www.nber.org/digest/jan03/w9061.html.

44 Bellafante, G. 2015. The Dark Side of 'Broken Windows' Policing. *The New York Times*, Jan. 16.

45 Adams, R.E., Rohe, W.M. and Arcury, T.A. 2002. Implementing Community-Oriented Policing: Organizational Change and Street Officer Attitudes. *Crime & Delinquency*, 48(3): 399–430.

46 Bureau of Justice Statistics. 2015. Community Policing. Office of Justice Programs, United States Department of Justice. Retrieved from http://www.bjs.gov/index.cfm?ty=tp&tid=81.

47 Burgeen, B. and McFherson, N. 1990. Implementing POP: The San Diego Experience. *The Police Chief*, October.

48 Barkan, S. and Bryjak, G. 2011. *Fundamentals of Criminal Justice: A Sociological View*. Sudbury, MA: Jones & Bartlett.

49 Relevant cases include: Chicago Area II Violent Crimes Unit; Philadelphia 39th Precinct; LAPD Rampart Division; Hidalgo County Sherriff's Department; Albuquerque Police Department; City of Miami Police.

50 Perez, E. 2015. DEA Agents Sex Party: Agents Behaving Badly Overseas. *CNN Justice*, March 26.

51 Perez, E. 2015. 2 Former Federal Agents Charged with Stealing Bitcoin during Silk Road Probe. CNN Justice, March 30.

52 Ibid.

53 Perez, E. 2015. DEA Agents Sex Party: Agents Behaving Badly Overseas. *CNN Justice*, March 26.

54 Acosta, J. and Klein, B. 2015. Secret Service Supervisor Accused of Making Unwanted Sexual Advances. *CNN.com*, April 9.

55 Durando, J. 2014. 3 High-profile Secret Service Scandals in 3 years. *USA Today*, March 26.

56 Eells, J. 2015. America's Dirtiest Cops: Cash, Cocaine and Corruption on the Texas Border. *Rolling Stone Magazine*, Jan. 5.

57 Acton Institute for the Study of Religion and Liberty. 2015. Lord Acton Quote Archive. Retrieved from http://www.acton.org/research/lord-acton-quote-archive.

58 The United States Department of Justice. 2015. Addressing Police Misconduct Laws Enforced by the Department of Justice. Retrieved from http://www.justice.gov/crt/about/spl/documents/polmis.php.

59 PBS Frontline. 1990. When Cops Go Bad. Ep. 901. Original Air Date: October 16, 1990. Produced by Charles C. Stuart and Marcia Vivancos. Written by Charles C. Stuart. Transcript available at http://www.pbs.org/wgbh/pages/frontline/shows/drugs/archive/copsgobad.html.

60 Ibid.

61 Weichselbaum, S. 2015. Policing the Police: As the Justice Department Pushes Reform, Some Changes Don't Last. *The Marshall Project*, May 26. Retrieved from https://www.themarshallproject.org/2015/04/23/policing-the-police.

62 Amnesty International Press Release. 2012. Amnesty International Urges Stricter Limits on Police Taser Use as U.S. Death Toll Reaches 500. Retrieved from http://www.amnestyusa.org/news/press-releases/amnesty-international-urges-stricter-limits-on-police-taser-use-as-us-death-toll-reaches-500.

63 *The Guardian.* 2015. People killed by the Police in the U.S. Retrieved from http://www.theguardian.com/us-news/ng-interactive/2015/jun/01/the-counted-police-killings-us-database#.

64 I can't breathe became the slogan of protesters in New York City and elsewhere following the death of Eric Garner. Mr. Garner exclaimed "I can't breathe" while being restrained in chokehold by an NYPD officer.

65 The phrase "black lives matter" saw frequent use after the shooting death of Michael Brown in Ferguson, MO, by a white police office, and other incidents, including the shooting death of Walter Scott in South Carolina, also by a white police officer.

66 California is one example. See: Garza, M. 2015. Public Needs Cold, Hard Numbers on Use of Deadly Force. *The Los Angeles Times,* April 18.

67 H.R. 1447. 2013. Death in Custody Reporting Act of 2013. 113th Congress of the United States of America.

68 Bureau of Justice Statistics. 2015. Use of Force: Summary of Findings. Retrieved from http://www.bjs.gov/index.cfm?ty=tp&tid=703.

69 Smith, M.R., Kaminski, R.J., Alpert, G.P., Fridell, L.A., MacDonald, J. and Kubu, B. 2009. Multi-Method Evaluation of Police Use of Force Outcomes: Final Report to the National Institute of Justice. National Institute of Justice Grant Number 2005-IJ-CX-0056.

70 See data from the FBI UCR program on Justifiable Homicides as well as: Kertscher, T. 2014. Fatal police shootings occur in tiny percentage of arrests in U.S., Milwaukee's police chief says. *Journal Sentinel*/Politifact Wisconsin. Retrieved from www.politifact.com/wisconsin/statements/2014/aug/29/edward-flynn/fatal-police-shootings-occur-tiny-percentage-arres/.

71 Bureau of Justice Statistics. 2015. Use of Force: Summary of Findings. Retrieved from http://www.bjs.gov/index.cfm?ty=tp&tid=703.

72 NBC News 4 New York. The Death of Eric Garner. Retrieved from http://www.nbcnewyork.com/news/local/Eric-Garner-Death-Chokehold-Investigation-272043511.html.

73 Department of Justice. 2015. Department of Justice Report Regarding the Criminal Investigation into the Shooting Death of Michael Brown by Ferguson, Missouri Police Officer Darren Wilson. March 4.

74 United States Department of Justice Civil Rights Division. 2015. Investigation of the Ferguson Police Department. United States Department of Justice. Retrieved from http://www.justice.gov/sites/default/files/opa/press-releases/attachments/2015/03/04/ferguson_police_department_report.pdf.

75 Ohlheiser, A. 2014. Death of Tamir Rice, 12-Year-Old Shot by Cleveland Police, Ruled a Homicide. *The Washington Post,* Dec. 12.

76 Stephens, C. 2015. Indian Grandfather Faces Long Recovery after Police Takedown, Wants to Know 'Why?' Retrieved from http://www.al.com. April 9.

77 *NBC News.* 2015. Walter Scott Shooting. http://www.nbcnews.com/storyline/walter-scott-shooting.

78 Kindy, K. and Kelly, K. 2015. Washington Post/Bowling Green State University Outcomes of Lethal Police Force Study. April 11.

79 Pinto, N. 2015. When Cops Break Bad: Inside a Police Force Gone Wild. *Rolling Stone Magazine,* Jan. 29.

80 United States Census Bureau. 2015. USA Quick Facts. Retrieved from http://quickfacts.census.gov/qfd/states/00000.html.

81 Texas Department of Family and Protective Services. 2015. Disproportionality and Disparity. Retrieved from www.hhsc.state.tx.us/hhsc_projects/cedd/about/.

82 Ibid.

83 Bureau of Justice Statistics. 2015. Use of Force: Summary of Findings. Retrieved from www.bjs.gov/index.cfm?ty=tp&tid=703.

84 Ibid.

85 Human Rights Watch. 1998. *Shielded from Justice: Police Brutality and Accountability in the United States.* Retrieved from www.columbia.edu/itc/journalism/cases/katrina/Human%20Rights%20Watch/uspohtml/uspo14.htm.

86 See FBI Director James B. Comey's remarks at Georgetown University, February 12, 2015, on Hard Truths: Law Enforcement and Race. Retrieved from www.fbi.gov/news/speeches/hard-truths-law-enforcement-and-race.

87 Human Rights Watch. 1998. *Shielded from Justice: Police Brutality and Accountability in the United States.* Retrieved from www.columbia.edu/itc/journalism/cases/katrina/Human%20Rights%20Watch/uspohtml/uspo14.htm.

88 America has a long, well-documented history wherein people with power and high status, often the white majority, have engaged in the unequal treatment and exploitation of people with less power and low-status, often newly arrived immigrants and people of color. Major examples include the treatment of Native Americans, slavery, convict leasing, Jim Crow laws, the internment of Japanese Americans during World War II, and, even more recently, discrimination against Muslim Americans and those of Islamic faith. Often, the criminal justice system and law enforcement agencies have been crucial factors in enabling these forms of racial and ethnic discrimination and prejudice to occur.

89 For example, the shooting of Walter Scott has been one key case. The beating of Francis Pusok by San Bernadino County sheriff's deputies in April 2015 is another.

90 Olsen, R.K. 2004. As cited on the COPS (Community Oriented Policing Services), "Use of Force" webpage maintained by The United States Department of Justice. Retrieved from http://www.cops.usdoj.gov/default.asp?Item=1374.

91 Rahr, S. and Rice, S.K. 2015. From Warriors to Guardians: Recommitting American Police Culture to Democratic Ideals. *New Perspectives in Policing* (April), Harvard Kennedy School Program in Criminal Justice Policy and Management, National Institute of Justice.

92 Police Executive Research Forum. 2007. Strategies for Resolving Conflict and Minimizing Use of Force, J.A. Ederheimer (ed.).

93 Serpico, F. 2015. How Police Departments Can Mend the Rift with the Public. *The Nation,* Jan. 7.

94 New York City Civilian Complaint Review Board. Retrieved from http://www.nyc.gov/html/ccrb/html/home/home.shtml.

95 See the Kerner Commission Report, 1968, p. 40, or Fridell, L.A. 2007. Building Community Trust Around Issues of Force. In J.A. Ederheimer (ed.), *Strategies for Resolving Conflict and Minimizing Use of Force (Critical Issues in Policing series),* Police Executive Research Forum.

96 Community Oriented Policing Services, United States Department of Justice. 2015. President's Task Force. Retrieved from http://www.cops.usdoj.gov/policingtaskforce.

97 Final Report of the President's Task Force on 21st Century Policing. 2015. Office of Community Oriented Policing Services, Washington, D.C.

98 Ibid., p. 1.

99 See the recent case of rookie LAPD officer Henry Solis, recently captured in Mexico after going on the run to avoid prosecution in the murder of a man outside a Pomona, CA, bar.

100 Federal Bureau of Investigation. 2014. Uniform Crime Report 2014. Department of Justice.

101 Travis, A. 2014. Eleven Countries Studied, One Inescapable Conclusion—The Drug Laws Don't Work. *The Guardian,* Oct. 29.

102 Greenwald, G. 2009. Drug Decriminalization in Portugal: Lessons for Creating Fair and Successful Drug Policies. The Cato Institute of Public Policy.

103 Aleem, A. 2015. 14 Years After Decriminalizing All Drugs, Here's What Portugal Looks Like. *Policy Mic,* Feb. 11.

104 ProCon.org. 2015. 100 Countries and their Prostitution Policies. Retrieved from http://prostitution.procon.org/view.resource.php?resourceID=000772#UK.

CHAPTER OUTLINE

Courts

KEY TERMS

adversarial process
jurisdiction
precedents
waiver
judges
attorneys
juries
initial appearance
preliminary hearing
arraignment
plea
plea bargaining
standing mute
nolo contendere
Alford plea
pre-trial motions
jury selection
voir dire
preemptory challenges
opening statements
procedural defense
double jeopardy
entrapment
affirmative defenses

"A BUSY MONTH FOR THE SUPREME COURT . . ."

On June 28, 2015, thousands of jubilant people took to the streets of San Francisco, New York, and other cities across America. The cause of their celebratory marches was a Supreme Court of the United States (SCOTUS) decision handed down two days earlier.

On June 26, SCOTUS ruled that all states must grant marriage licenses to same-sex couples; failure to do so would violate an individual's rights under the 14th Amendment to the United States Constitution. The 14th Amendment, the Supreme Court argued, protects "personal choices central to individual dignity and autonomy, including intimate choices defining personal identity and beliefs."[1] In interpreting the 14th Amendment in this manner and reaching its decision, the Supreme Court effectively ended the legal battle over marriage equality in the United States that had begun over 40 years prior and bolstered the rights of same-sex couples.

However, the Supreme Court was not done. In fact, over a one-week period, June 22–29, 2015, SCOTUS handed down more than a half-dozen important decisions in a variety of cases that will inevitably impact all Americans. For example, on June 25, the court affirmed the legality of the Patient Protection and Affordable Care Act, also known as "Obamacare," which was created to ensure that all Americans have health insurance coverage.[2]

Image 6.1 *Supreme Court of the United States Building, Washington, D.C.*

Wikimedia Commons/350z33/Pine

justification

excuse

self-defense

consent defense

duress defense

intoxication defense

insanity defense

direct appeals

indictment

grand jury

sentencing

capital cases

indeterminate sentences

determinate sentences

three-strikes sentences

truth-in-sentencing

Then, on June 29, SCOTUS reached decisions in two separate and distinct cases. In one, the court rejected a major constitutional challenge to the death penalty[3] and in another it ruled that certain EPA regulations under the Clean Air Act were "unreasonable,"[4] which many view as a setback for environmental protection.

Each of the cases mentioned above demonstrates that there are few court cases or decisions that garner unanimous support. While many people support marriage equality, many others do not. Likewise, there are some who detest Obamacare. The death penalty is a highly contentious issue and regulation of pollution in any form consistently meets with resistance. Ultimately, courts are a forum where grievances can be aired—there will always be some who disagree with whatever decision is reached.

More importantly, these cases, from marriage equality to regulating air pollution, highlight the varied, yet incredibly important role, that courts, especially the Supreme Court of the United States, play in regulating all aspects of social life. In the sections that follow, we'll briefly explore the court system in the United States, which represents the second phase of the American criminal justice system.

FUNCTIONS AND TYPES OF COURTS

Courts represent the second phase of the American criminal justice system. They are a bridge between law enforcement and punishment (i.e., "corrections") and are the place that people go to seek "justice" when they have been wronged.

American courts share many similarities with competitive athletic events. For instance, when you step into a boxing ring, onto a basketball court or a soccer field, your conduct is governed by rules of play specific to that environment. These rules ensure that the event taking place—a boxing fight, basketball game, or soccer match—proceeds in a uniform, fair manner.

The same is true of court environments. Rather than settling scores or righting wrongs on the street, we use the formal legal setting of courts to address wrongs, grievances, and conflicts in a uniform, fair manner. For that reason, American courts utilize an **adversarial process**, where two sides (prosecution and defense), each with different goals and positions, make arguments to support their positions.

Courts serve a multitude of functions, ranging from the more abstract (i.e., finding "justice") to the concrete (i.e., winning a monetary settlement following a lawsuit). Courts may also enable people who were victims of crimes, or relatives of crime victims, to find closure or some semblance of it.

Additionally, courts serve a variety of other functions. For one thing, courts ensure that all people have their "due process" rights upheld, regardless of their gender, race, ethnicity, or social class. As noted at the opening of the chapter, courts can also play a major role in the creation or maintenance of social policies and in refining the meaning or scope of existing laws. All of these functions and more are carried out in different types of courts.

There are many different types of courts in America. Which particular court handles a case is often determined by **jurisdiction**, or the right of a court to hear a case. Jurisdiction is usually linked to geographic boundaries (i.e., the Missouri Court of Appeals for the *Western* District) or to specific subject areas (i.e., appeals, family law, traffic cases, drug cases, etc.).

Jurisdiction helps create and maintain order within the court system. As a result, some courts hear only criminal cases and others hear only civil cases. Further, some criminal courts may only deal with traffic or drug violations, or juvenile offenders. Jurisdiction impacts which level of court hears a case, for example state v. federal courts, and it also determines which court handles appeals. Below we highlight some key distinctions among the various types of courts within the American criminal justice system.

Criminal v. civil courts

As noted in chapter 2, there are two major types of law: criminal and civil. Criminal law is enforced by law enforcement agencies. Typically, when someone commits a crime like rape or murder, they are thought to be victimizing not just the individual victim, but also the state whose law they have broken. Thus, the state ultimately seeks formal justice against criminal wrongdoers inside criminal courts set aside for this purpose.

Conversely, civil or administrative law applies to the interactions of individuals with each other. Civil wrongs are considered private wrongs and are less serious than criminal violations (i.e., you can't be sentenced to prison for a civil wrong). Thus, the state does not seek justice on anyone's behalf. Instead, private individuals must file claims or lawsuits against the person or

Pre-Sentence Investigative Report (PSI)

Victim Impact Statement (VIS)

mitigating factor

aggravating factors

daily docket

long term docket

overloaded docket

jury tampering

jury nullification

corruption

people they feel have wronged them. These civil cases are handled in civil courts. Divorces, land disputes, and breaches of contract are just a few examples of the types of cases handled in America's civil courts.

Federal courts

The federal court system is comprised of district, also known as "trial," courts; appellate, or circuit, courts; and the Supreme Court of the United States (SCOTUS).

Federal district courts are the sites of federal criminal and civil trials. Generally, the jurisdiction of the federal courts is limited to violations of the federal criminal code or any cases involving a Federal law. However, federal courts also deal with bankruptcy, civil rights, and other types of cases.

Federal appellate courts handle appeals once cases have been decided in a district court. There are 13 federal appellate courts in the United States. The ultimate court of appeal in the United States is the Supreme Court.

The Supreme Court hears cases that originated at the state or federal level so long as the case involves a significant constitutional issue. The court also chooses which cases it wants to hear from thousands of submissions. In this regard, the Supreme Court wields immense power since it interprets the meaning of the Constitution and applies its interpretations to legal cases. The **precedents**, or binding legal decisions, reached by the Supreme Court thereby refine the laws of the United States and influence the actions and decisions of all other lower courts.

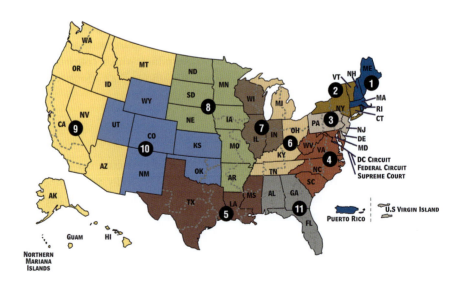

Map 6.1 Geographic boundaries of United States Courts of Appeals and United States District Courts

Most Supreme Court decisions have far reaching consequences for all Americans as well as the entire criminal justice system. This fact means that the Supreme Court is the site of significant political maneuvering.

There are nine Supreme Court justices (eight associate Supreme Court Justices and one Chief Justice), each appointed for life or until they decide to retire. Supreme Court justices are nominated by the president of the United States (POTUS) and then confirmed by the United States Senate. As a result, there is a historical tendency for the sitting president to nominate an individual for a Supreme Court justice position whose political and social views more closely align with those of the president's political party. While Supreme Court justices are not supposed to allow their personal beliefs to influence their legal decisions, the fact that interpreting the meaning of the Constitution and prior case law is subjective inevitably means that a justice's conservative or liberal political tendencies will likely be reflected in their decision making.

State courts

State level courts handle the vast majority of criminal and civil cases in the United States, processing over 100 million cases annually.[5] State court jurisdictions are limited to criminal offenses or civil actions that occur within the state's boundaries. In practice, this means that if a person commits a murder in California, no other state but California can bring them to trial for that murder.

There are several different types of state courts. Municipal courts are the lowest level, typically handling minor criminal, civil, and traffic violations, often without utilizing the jury trial process. In many municipal courts, an individual will stand before a judge, with or without counsel present, and enter a plea to a charge. The judge can then enter a verdict (often a monetary fine).

In some places, municipal courts also process cases involving juvenile offenders; however, most states have entirely separate juvenile court systems with their own rules.

Historically, juveniles have been treated differently by the American criminal justice system, which has attributed to them less culpability for their wrongful actions. Separating juvenile cases from adult ones was a natural outgrowth of a desire in the 1800s to reform our treatment of juvenile offenders and provide for more rehabilitative sentencing.

In 1899, the first juvenile court was created in Cook County, Illinois. Creation of this juvenile court represented the culmination of several decades of work by people like Thomas Eddy and John Griscom, who formed the Society for the Study of Pauperism in New York and strongly believed in finding alternative ways to deal with juvenile delinquents. By the end of World War II in the mid-1940s, all states had separate juvenile justice systems and courts.

Today, juvenile courts play a key role in the adult and juvenile justice systems. On the one hand, juvenile courts divert large numbers of youth from adult courts and provide for more discretion in the handling of their cases. This

Image 6.2 *The original Juvenile Court Building and Detention Home near the corner of Halsted and Des Plaines streets.*

Chicago History Museum/Getty Images

translates into a greater ability for the state to develop rehabilitative sentences that address the needs of the juvenile. More importantly, by separating juveniles, juvenile courts avoid the problem of exposing juveniles, who may not be committed to engaging in serious criminality, to violent or career adult offenders.

Increasingly since the 1980s, however, juveniles have been prosecuted as adults when they have committed serious offenses (crimes like murder, rape, and armed robbery) or when they have become repeat offenders. A state seeking to prosecute a person under age 18 as an adult must do so by obtaining a **waiver** to an adult criminal court. This waiver means the juvenile court system has waived its jurisdiction over the juvenile's case. Once a waiver to an adult criminal court has been approved, the juvenile status goes away, along with all the benefits that accrue from it, and the juvenile can be prosecuted and sentenced like an adult.

State trial courts deal with more serious criminal cases, like those involving felony charges, as well as more serious civil cases. Trial courts are often depicted in television and movies and are probably what you think of when, and if, you think of a courtroom. Depending on the locale, trial courts are also called district, superior, or circuit courts.

Finally, appellate courts, which include courts of appeals and a state's Supreme Court, review judgments and decisions reached in the lower courts. When a case is appealed, the appellate courts can typically do one of several things. They can affirm the original decision, essentially saying that the lower court got things right, or they can reverse the original decision, indicating that the lower court might have gotten something wrong and then send the case back to the lower court. Additionally, the appellate court—particularly the Supreme Court—can enter a new decision in the case.

COURTROOM PARTICIPANTS

Citizens from all walks of life move through America's courts, some as defendants, others as plaintiffs, jurors, or just curious onlookers. Courts are dynamic places that play host to a variety of cases, from the mundane to the very serious. Courts are not, however, chaotic places. There is structure and organization to court life, which is reinforced by the regular participants in unfolding courtroom dramas.

These participants include judges, attorneys, juries, and a host of other civilian and law enforcement support personnel. **Judges** are the referees of the

BOX 6.1: CRIME IN GLOBAL PERSPECTIVE

Going to court in the Czech Republic

There is a huge diversity in criminal justice systems around the world. Few operate in the same way as the American model; all have their own methods and processes and are shaped by different political, economic, social, and cultural forces. Indeed, as an American you might find the criminal justice practices in other nations to be quite strange since you are so accustomed to how things work here.

The Czech Republic, whose capital city is Prague, has a robust, modern criminal justice system. Yet, from an American perspective there are some very interesting differences in how, for instance, court processes play out.

First, in the Czech Republic there is no trial-by-jury system.[6] This is a key difference from the way courts operate in the United States, where trial by jury is constitutionally guaranteed. Instead, in the Czech Republic, all criminal and civil cases are heard by a panel of judges (typically comprising three judges). Interestingly, another important difference from the court system in the United States is that ordinary, non-trained community members, called "laypersons," can be elected to serve on the bench. Often, two laypersons will sit with one professional judge and hear minor cases, called "first instance proceedings," that come before the district and regional courts. Despite their lack of formal training, these laypersons contribute to the court process, including the eventual verdict that is reached.

The Czech Republic is just one country whose criminal justice system practices differ from those in the United States. As you continue learning about the crime and criminal justice in America, consider the pros and cons of the America style of justice and possible alternatives. For example, what do you think are some of the benefits and problems with the American jury trial process versus the Czech "no jury trial" system? Which would you prefer and why?

BOX 6.2: JUDGES PROFILE

Primary role	Highest ranking courtroom participant; act as the court room referee and manage the trial proceedings
No. of judges in U.S.	44,000+
Median salary	$102,000
Prior experience	Most hold law and other advanced degrees, though not always.

courthouse, and, as the most senior officials present, they are able to exert significant influence over the culture of the court proceedings through their influence and leadership.

Judges are trained legal experts who possess law degrees and at some point in the past practiced the law as attorneys. The roles of the judge during trial are straightforward: they manage the courtroom and ensure that all rules and procedures are followed. To call them referees is a fairly accurate way to depict how they must handle the court's other prominent participants—attorneys (i.e., lawyers).

Attorneys include those working as defense attorneys and those working as prosecutors. Defense attorneys include those hired privately, as well as public defenders provided by the state. Their primary responsibilities are to ensure that their client's constitutional rights are protected, to provide guidance to their clients and to ensure their client is well defended against the charges lodged against them. Prosecutors are always employed by the state, since crimes are ultimately considered offenses against the state, as well as the individual(s) harmed. Most cases are prosecuted by deputy or assistant district attorneys at the state level and by deputy or assistant U.S. attorneys at the federal level.

BOX 6.3: ATTORNEY PROFILE

Primary role	To argue for either guilt or innocence on behalf of the client they represent by employing strategies that enhance their position or undermine their opponents
No. of attorneys in U.S.	778,000
Median salary	$114,000
Prior experience	Attend and graduate law school; specialize in trial work; and if interested in criminal law, focus on criminal law and procedure. Becoming a lead prosecuting attorney (DA) requires significant time and experience in the occupation.

Juries, of course, are the fact finders of the courtroom. While in some cases, such as in lower level municipal court proceedings, a judge may weigh the facts of the case, in most criminal and civil trials the jury has the responsibility of listening to the evidence and rendering a verdict. This means, of course, the jurors must determine for themselves what weight and credence to give to the evidence presented to them. Juries, then, play a critical role in the American court system.

Besides the three main courtroom participants—judges, attorneys, juries— there are many more individuals who play key roles America's courts.

BOX 6.4: WORKING IN . . . THE COURTS

Does working in a courtroom environment sound interesting to you? If so, there are many pathways to a career in the courts.

One of the most obvious ways to get into a courtroom career is to go to law school, pass the bar exam in a place you want to live and practice law, and start working as an attorney. Attorneys can specialize in many areas. Criminal defense, prosecution, environmental law, family law, intellectual property, and finance are just a few areas. If you want to work in criminal courts, you can become a defense attorney, an assistant district attorney, or work as a public defender.

Regardless of the legal path you take, it is important to understand a few things about a legal career. First, where you go to law school will have implications for your future career as an attorney. It is important to understand this fact (no matter how dissatisfying it may be) and plan accordingly. Study hard for the LSAT and develop a strong vision for where and what you want your legal career to be. Second, law school costs a lot of money, anywhere from $30,000 to $40,000 per year for three years. While your earnings as an attorney will be very good (median earnings for all attorneys were $113,530 in 2012), expect to pay back a lot of student loans and work some very long hours.

If you think being a judge would be great, you need to go through all of the above steps (i.e., law school, working as an attorney). You then have to prepare extensively for your first judgeship. This means not only being an expert in the law, but also being someone who is politically connected and politically astute, since judges are appointed or elected. Becoming a judge is, in many cases, a life-long career; some people continue serving from the bench into their nineties.

Finally, if law school and working as an attorney seems like more than you want to take on right now, you can work in the courts in many other ways. Law enforcement officers are sometimes assigned to courtroom duty; likewise, probation and parole officers work very closely with the courts and their staff. Or, you could apply to be a court reporter, a court appointed mediator, a court appointed special advocate, working on behalf of children, sometimes called a *guardian ad litem* (GAL). If working in the courts interests you, there are countless ways to make it work. Good luck!

For instance, the court clerk and court reporter are important to the smooth functioning and administration of the court on a daily basis. The court reporter, for example, keeps a written record of everything said or done within the courtroom during proceedings. Bailiffs maintain order in the courtroom. Often, bailiffs are deputy sheriffs or police officers. However, in federal courtrooms you will often find deputy United States marshals protecting the courtroom and its occupants. Box 6.4 provides more information about various courtroom participants and what it takes to get a career in the court system.

CRIMINAL COURTROOM PROCESSES

In America, court processes are highly structured and predictable. This is a positive thing, since we want our courts to be places where all people can seek and find justice fairly and equally. Ensuring that all cases are subject to the same types of rules and that the courts function in a uniform manner, helps alleviate issues of bias and corruption (though it certainly does not mean that bias and corruption cannot occur). Below, we discuss the general processes and events that occur in most American criminal trial courts.

Initial processes and arraignment

Once you get arrested for a committing a crime, you'll be formally processed into the criminal justice system (referred to as "booking"). The first appearance, or **initial appearance,** in court is where you'll hear the charges against you, and often learn if, and for what amount, your bail will be set. If you are granted bail and can post the amount the court has set for it, you'll be able to leave jail; if not, you'll be held over.

In either case, the next process will be a **preliminary hearing**, where, with your attorney present, the court will determine if there exists enough "probable cause" to believe that a criminal offense occurred. In most cases this is just a formality since probable cause would have been established when the arrest was made. However, once the court establishes probable cause the trial date will be set and entered into the court calendar.

The most important initial court process is the **arraignment**; this is where the defendant will once again have the charges against them read aloud and be reminded of their rights. At this point in time, the defendant will enter a plea. A **plea** is the defendant's formal reply to the charges being made against them. You are likely familiar with the pleas of guilty and not guilty. **Plea bargaining** is a process where the prosecutor and defendant reach an agreement that concludes the criminal case prior to trial, often by having the defendant plead guilty to some lesser charge or charges in exchange for leniency or a reduced sentence and subject to the court's approval. (See Box 6.5 for more).

At the arraignment a defendant can also refuse to plead (called "**standing mute**"). Likewise the defendant can plead **nolo contendere** (i.e., no contest). A nolo contendere plea is a strategic plea. It is not an admission of guilt or culpability by the defendant to the charges against them, nor is it a denial of guilt or culpability. Entering a nolo contendere plea does mean the defendant agrees to accept punishment as if they were guilty. So why would someone plead nolo contendere and accept a guilty person's punishment without admitting guilt?

Usually a defendant will enter this type of plea to quickly end a criminal proceeding and keep things that might be revealed at trial from becoming public knowledge. Also, a plea of no contest often results in a punishment far less severe than what would be levied if a person entered a guilty plea or was

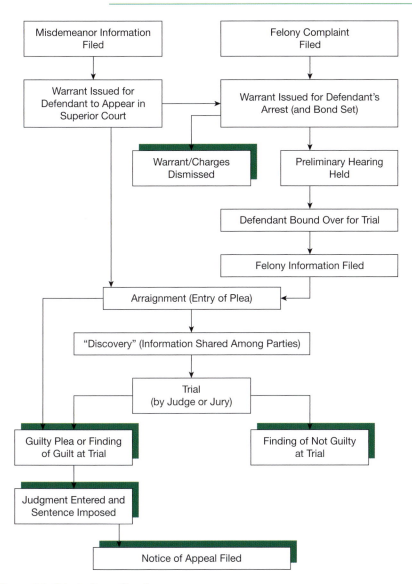

Figure 6.1 Criminal case flowchart

found guilty after trial. Thus for a defendant who is fairly certain they'll be convicted at trial, a no-contest plea is a way to escape the harshest penalties. At the end of the day, they can always say that they were never "convicted" or found "guilty" of the crime. Lastly, a nolo contendere plea protects the defendant from having future legal actions. For example, sometimes after a criminal trial concludes, a defendant will be sued in civil court. If someone had admitted guilt, that is, responsibility, that plea could be used against them. The nolo contendere plea thus protects against such an event because it is not an admission of guilt.

Finally, in some jurisdictions a defendant can enter what is called an **Alford plea**. The Alford plea results in similar outcomes to a plea of nolo contendere, both of which allow the defendant to "save face" by accepting punishment. However, Alford pleas are quite distinct from nolo contendere pleas in terms of their implications further down the road of the legal process. A person entering an Alford plea is positively affirming their innocence but willingly accepting punishment; this is not the case in a plea of no contest. As a result, a defendant who uses an Alford plea is often able to appeal their sentence down the road, unlike someone who enters a plea of nolo contedere.

Pre-trial procedures and motions

Many activities and processes occur after an individual enters a plea. In those cases destined for a criminal jury trial, which comprise about 66 percent of all jury trials each year,[7] two of the most important pre-trial events are the filing of pre-trial motions and jury selection.

Pre-trial motions are written requests submitted by the defense or prosecuting attorneys to the court. Typical pre-trial motions include asking for a dismissal of the case, asking the court to suppress or not allow certain types of evidence, petitioning for a change of venue (i.e., moving the case to a new jurisdiction), or asking for a continuance, which provides more time to get ready for trial. All pre-trial motions are reviewed by the presiding judge, who makes a final determination about whether to grant or deny them.

One of the most important pretrial procedures that occurs in the U.S. is that of **jury selection**. In most criminal trials, a jury is comprised of 12 individuals drawn from the local community—a process carried over from England. There are some instances where juries may consist of fewer than 12 people, though this is rare. Each year in the U.S., over 30 million people are called for jury duty, though only around 8 million ever report to a courtroom and slightly fewer than 2 million are ever "impaneled" or seated for a trial.[8]

In a process known as **voir dire**, the presiding judge, as well as attorneys for the defense and prosecution, question each prospective juror. The judge's goal is to remove any individual who is clearly unfit for jury duty from the pool of prospective jurors. Jurors will usually be asked questions about their occupation, political views, personal relationships, biases, prejudices, experiences, and more in order to determine if they could, potentially, serve on the jury.

The goal of the defense and prosecuting attorneys, however, is to stock the jury with people who will be more favorable to their side. Thus, in reality, jury selection is not at all about finding a group of completely impartial people who can weigh the evidence objectively. Defense attorneys want to stock the jury with people sympathetic to their client and his or her story. Prosecuting attorneys want exactly the opposite. They hope to find people who will, at the very least, be quite skeptical of the defense's claims.

BOX 6.5: CONNECTING RESEARCH TO PRACTICE

Plea bargaining in the courts

If every individual entering a criminal court invoked their constitutional right to a trial by a jury of their peers, the American criminal justice system would come to a screeching halt. Our justice system is simply incapable of processing all criminal, not to mention civil, cases through a complete trial by jury. This is one reason the plea bargaining process, wherein criminal defendants agree to plead guilty to a lesser charge, or set of charges, in order to avoid a trial and earn a less severe punishment, is so important to the continued functioning of our court and criminal justice systems.

At the same time, the plea bargain is a significant weapon in the prosecutor's arsenal. Wielded strategically, the plea bargain can earn a prosecutor easy convictions at minimal cost in time and resources, thus making them look quite successful in the public's eyes. Plea bargains also reduce risk, since jury trial outcomes are difficult to predict. Therefore, plea bargains are safe bets for prosecutors and can seem like a good "deal" to the defendant. On average, nearly 70 percent of criminal cases each year are concluded via plea bargain rather than a trial verdict.[9] Indeed, the vast majority of people convicted of a criminal charge—in some cases as many as 95 percent[10]—are convicted because they plead guilty, many times after agreeing to a deal offered by the prosecutor.

The significance of the plea bargain has attracted a large amount of interest from researchers,[11] as well as criminal justice organizations and advocacy groups. Unsurprisingly, there are those who support the extensive use of plea bargains. This faction argues the practice is fair and cost-efficient.[12]

By contrast, a fairly large and diverse group opposes the practice. Research evidence lends support to their position. First, some research into the plea bargaining process shows that it allows prosecutors to secure convictions in weak cases that would not be likely to result in a guilty verdict at a jury trial[13]. In fact, if not for the coercive power of the plea bargain and the use of threats by prosecutors (e.g., "this is your best option, you better take it") a fair number of criminal cases resulting in plea bargain convictions would likely have to be dropped by the prosecutor for lack of substantial evidence.[14]

Moreover, research shows that people who go to trial, rather than accepting a plea deal, are more likely to receive a harsher punishment.[15,16] This is because prosecutors usually reduce charges in a plea deal, but have no incentive to do so at trial. Thus, prosecutors often utilize the plea bargain like a carrot and stick: take the plea, get the nice carrot, choose to go to trial, and get the stick. Finally, research indicates that race plays a role in the plea bargaining process.[17] Specifically, black defendants are less likely to benefit from plea bargains than whites[18,19] and are less likely to receive reduced sentences as the result of a plea bargain than whites.[20]

Plea bargaining is a key element of the American court system. While research does highlight many potential flaws with the process, it is important to remember that research is ultimately a tool for improving existing systems or policies. Research, as with theory, has real world impacts. Continuing research on the plea bargaining process will ultimately improve that process and strengthen the criminal justice system.

Thus, as a process, jury selection is like a game of chess. Both the defense and prosecuting attorneys can utilize **preemptory challenges** and other tactics to remove jurors who might be more favorable to the opposition. Ultimately, both sides hope to end up with a jury favorable to their cause. Prospective jurors also contribute to this game of strategy, mostly by trying to get kicked out of the jury pool by obviously biasing themselves so that they will not be chosen.

Trial

The average criminal trial is short, lasting only around five days.[21] In that short span of time, many things occur.

Opening statements

At the start of a trial, both sides get to make **opening statements**. Opening statements are arguments made by both the defense and prosecution that summarize the nature of the case, the nature of the evidence (or lack thereof) and provide jurors with a roadmap for how each side will present their case. The prosecution, which must demonstrate beyond a reasonable doubt that the accused person is guilty of committing a crime, always makes their opening statement first. The defense can choose to make an opening statement immediately following the prosecution's, or they can wait until after the prosecution has presented their evidence.

Presenting the prosecution's case

Following opening statements, the prosecution will present its case, which entails presenting many types of evidence to support the argument that the defendant is guilty of committing a crime. Evidence presented might include forensic evidence, eyewitness and expert testimony, statements made by the defendant, police officers, detectives, and more.

Successfully prosecuting a case is much like building a house: you first need to lay a strong foundation, then erect a solid framework, and finally add all the important finishing details. Thus, the prosecution must present their case in a systematic manner. The best prosecuting attorneys are able to build their case right in front of the jury in a manner that is engaging, articulate, and persuasive. Interestingly, while many television shows talk about motive and depict prosecutors spending long amounts of time explaining the defendant's motive before the jury, in reality a prosecutor does not need to prove or demonstrate motive for committing a crime. In other words, all a prosecutor needs to prove beyond a reasonable doubt is that a person did commit the crime, not why they committed it. It certainly helps if a prosecutor can provide jurors with a plausible reason for why someone would commit a crime, but it is not necessary.

Presenting the defense

After the prosecution makes its case, the defendant can present his or her defense. One of the most obvious defenses is to claim complete innocence and/or an inability to have committed the crime you are accused of. Clearly, this defense works well if you can also produce strong testimony and evidence, like an airtight alibi, supporting your claims. Keep in mind that in order to find a person guilty of a crime, a jury must—as they are instructed before the trial begins—find that the evidence supports a finding of guilt "beyond a reasonable doubt." The ultimate goal of any defense, then, is to introduce just enough doubt into the minds of the jurors, even just one juror, to make it impossible for the burden of proof to be met.

Beyond simply claiming no responsibility for the crime, a defendant can present either a procedural or affirmative defense.

Procedural defenses

Procedural defenses often make constitutional rights claims. That is, they argue that the defendant's 5th Amendment due process and other constitutionally protected rights were violated at some point during the investigation and/or prosecution of the case. Remember, the 5th Amendment, along with others from the Constitution and Bill of Rights, are intended to protect people from injustices and ensure that the government operates within the boundaries of the law.

Typical procedural defenses include denial of a speedy trial (6th Amendment), double jeopardy (5th Amendment), illegally obtaining evidence (4th Amendment) and entrapment. Double jeopardy means you cannot be tried twice for the same crime—if you are acquitted, or found not guilty, the state cannot bring you to trial again, no matter what. Protection against entrapment[22] means that your criminal conduct cannot result simply because of the "creative activity of law enforcement" and implies that the prosecution must show beyond a reasonable doubt that you were "independently predisposed to commit the crime."

Affirmative defenses

Another defense strategy is to utilize an affirmative defense. Affirmative defenses come in two general types: those that claim justification and those that claim some type of excuse. In both instances, the defense is not claiming complete innocence, but is instead arguing that other circumstances negate or weaken the defendant's culpability for the crime. Utilizing an affirmative defense requires the defendant to produce evidence to support their claim.

Justification defenses argue: "I did it, but my actions were not criminal." Justification defenses attempt to negate the mens rea principle of criminal law. Two common justifications include (1) self-defense, and (2) consent. Claiming self-defense usually means you utilized a level of force, up to and including lethal force, which you deemed necessary to protect your life or the life of

BOX 6.6: CONNECTING THEORY TO PRACTICE

Self-defense and stand-your-ground laws

In cases when adults claim they committed an act (almost always a violent one) which would normally be a crime (i.e., felony assault or murder) while acting in "self-defense," they are hoping the court, and especially the jury, will accept this justification for their conduct and let them off easy.

Sometimes this is the case, in others it is not. The murder of 17-year-old Trayvon Martin by George Zimmerman in 2012 illustrates a case where the jury accepted Mr. Zimmerman's claim of self-defense. In that case, Mr. Zimmerman claimed he shot Mr. Martin only after the two were engaged in a physical altercation in which Mr. Martin had the upper hand, causing Mr. Zimmerman to fear for his life. Likewise, when a female escort in West Virginia fought off a man who was attacking her and then killed him with his own gun in July 2015, police did not even press charges. Her conduct was deemed to be in self-defense (the man she killed may have been a serial killer).

The conviction of Michael Dunn in February 2014 is an example of a case where a self-defense claim was ultimately rejected by a jury. Mr. Dunn claimed he shot at a group of black teenagers outside a convenience store (and killed one) because he feared for his life and thought the teens had a gun. Witnesses claimed Dunn was simply upset because the teenagers were playing their music too loud.

The operative principle behind the claim of "self-defense" is that there are some moments when every person has the right to stick up for themselves. Getting robbed, assaulted, being threatened with a knife or gun—these are all moments when it may be justifiable to utilize force against another person. The typical standard to judge the validity of a self-defense claim is whether or not the person utilizing the defense was facing imminent danger, or the threat of imminent danger, at the time they acted. Likewise, the level of force utilized by the person claiming self-defense must be commensurate with the threat they faced. Thus, shooting someone just because they were saying mean things to you is usually not an act for which a claim of self-defense will be acceptable.

Box 6.6 Image 1 *Michael Dunn returns to his seat after reading his statement, which included an apology to the Davis family, during his sentencing hearing Friday, October 17, 2014, at the Duval County Courthouse in Jacksonville, Florida. Dunn, convicted of first-degree murder in a retrial in September for fatally shooting 17-year-old Jordan Davis in November 2012 in an argument over loud music outside a Florida convenience store, was sentenced to life in prison without parole.*
Bruce Lipsky/AP/Press Association Images

A few exceptions qualify the above statements. First, some states require that you retreat from danger if retreat is reasonable and possible; using force, especially lethal force, against another person when you could have safely retreated from them usually voids any claim of justifiable self-defense. This is not true if you are in your home. The long-standing *Castle Doctrine*, brought over from English common law, gives everyone the right to defend their home (i.e., their castle) without having to retreat from it. Thus, if a burglar breaks in, you can shoot and kill them, even if they were unarmed. However, once they leave the home and start running away, you cannot pursue and shoot them—this would be considered unreasonable and criminal.

Lastly, some states have taken the premise of the Castle Doctrine—that you are allowed to stand-your-ground—and moved it outside the boundaries of the home. Currently, 33 states have some type of stand-your-ground law on the books. Many people misunderstand the meaning of these modified self-defense laws. Essentially, all these laws do is remove the requirement that you retreat when faced with danger or threat of danger outside the home. Instead, you are allowed to use force to meet that danger even if retreat was possible. All of the other principles and standards of justifiable self-defense still apply: there must have been an imminent threat and your response must have been proportional to that threat.

another person from an imminent threat. Box 6.6 contains more information about self-defense laws in the U.S. A **consent defense,** by contrast, usually requires that you show the person who was injured by your actions actually voluntarily, knowingly, and willingly consented to being injured. This type of defense does not have very wide applicability and does not justify things like having sex with an underage person.

Excuse defenses argue: "I did it. It was wrong. But, I shouldn't be held completely responsible." Commonly utilized excuse defenses include age, duress, intoxication, and insanity.

In previous chapters as well as this one, we've noted that juveniles are often considered less culpable for their criminal actions than adults. Thus age, especially being young, can be, and often is, a defense to prosecution and punishment in adult criminal courts. However, since America got tough on crime in the 1980s, juveniles who commit numerous criminal acts or especially heinous ones, like murder, can be prosecuted and punished like adults.

Utilizing a **duress defense** means arguing that the criminal act you committed had to be committed in order to avoid (or prevent) some more serious type of harm or injury to yourself or someone else. A classic example would be an individual who commits a burglary or robbery after being threatened by a third party with death or serious injury if they refuse to do so. A duress defense undermines both the mens rea and actus reus principles of the criminal law.

Years ago it was much more common than today for people to claim **intoxication** as a means of avoiding full responsibility for their criminal actions.

Now, it is highly unlikely in any state in America that someone who is voluntarily intoxicated (drunk or high on drugs) will be able to use their intoxication as a mitigating factor for their bad behavior. Operation of an automobile or other piece of machinery while intoxicated, especially if such operation results in the death or injury of another person, is a serious felony offense. Still, involuntary intoxication, such as being drugged without your consent, can be a defense to criminal conduct. The logic here is that it would be unfair to criminally prosecute someone for their uncontrollable and unforeseen actions.

You are probably most familiar, through television and movies, with the insanity defense, which also happens to be one of the most controversial defenses that can be raised. The premise behind the insanity defense is that mental illness can function as an excuse for criminal behavior. The logic underlying this premise is that a person suffering from mental illness cannot possess the requisite mens rea necessary to be found guilty of committing a crime. A summary of several different legal "tests" for insanity are contained in Table 6.1. It is worth noting that some tests, like the Durham Rule, are used only rarely, if at all, in today's society (see Box 6.7 for more on the status of the insanity defense today).

It is important to recognize that the insanity defense is not a singular defense, but like all other defenses, it is a strategy of defense. Approaches to presenting and interpreting an insanity defense differ across the United States, but it is common today that anyone enacting such a defense must prove they are insane, rather than forcing the prosecution to prove they are not insane. In a strange paradox, a person can be deemed mentally ill according to medical standards of mental illness, yet still be found sane enough to be held legally culpable for their actions and vice versa: some people can be ruled "sane" by medical professionals and still be found "insane," and therefore non-culpable, within a legal context.

Image 6.3 *Colorado movie theater shooter James Holmes sits in Arapahoe County District Court in Centennial, Colorado prior to being convicted by a jury on 165 criminal counts, including 12 homicides. Holmes attempted to utilize an insanity defense, but legal changes made to that defense after John Hinckley Jr.'s attempted assassination of President Ronald Reagan in the 1980s have made it much harder for criminals to claim insanity as an excuse for their bad behavior.*

RJ Sangosti/AP/Press Association Images

Closing arguments and jury instructions

Once both sides present their cases, the prosecution has the option to rebut, or challenge, any of the defenses claims. After this occurs, both sides will make their closing arguments. Unlike at the start of the trial, in this instance the prosecution makes their closing arguments last. When closing arguments are concluded, the judge will instruct the jury as to their duties. Typical instructions given to jurors before they begin deliberating about a verdict include reminding them of the burden of proof and the elements of the crime that needed to be met.

Table 6.1 Legal tests and rules for insanity

Name of test or rule	Year established or widely adopted	Requirements and/or standards
M'Naghten Rule **AKA The Right v. Wrong Test**	1843	At time of crime, defendant could not: − Understand the criminal nature of their actions − Understand the difference between "right" and "wrong"
Irresistible Impulse	1887	Similar to M'Naghten Rule but also includes the standard that the defendant could not control their impulses to commit wrong-doing
Durham Rule **AKA The Products Test**	1954	A defendant's actions were the product of mental illness or defect Does not require medical diagnosis of mental illness
Model Penal Code Test	1962	Defendant must be medically diagnosed with a "relevant mental defect" And when crime occurred the defendant could not: − Understand the criminal nature of their actions − Or control an impulse leading to their criminal actions

Post-trial

Once the presentation of evidence and argumentation phase of the trial concludes and jurors are given their instructions, they then must debate amongst themselves about what sort of decision they want to hand down. On average, juries only deliberate for about four hours before reaching a decision.[23] As a general rule, the longer a jury takes to reach a verdict, the better the odds are that the defendant will be found not guilty or that a mistrial will be declared. Data indicates, however, that most criminal defendants (over 70 percent) who go through a jury trial process can expect to be convicted.[24]

To be found guilty, nearly all jurisdictions in the United States require a unanimous decision by the 12 jurors. If even one member of the jury is unsure or unwilling to render such a verdict, a "hung" jury results and a mistrial must be declared. A mistrial is not the same thing as being found not guilty. A verdict of not guilty means the defendant must immediately be released from state custody and also means they can never be brought to trial on the same charges again. Thus, a jury trial is very much a high stakes game of chance (see Box 6.8 for more on this topic). A mistrial is in some ways a major blow to the prosecution, since it means they did not prove beyond a reasonable doubt that

213

BOX 6.7: REFORMING THE INSANITY DEFENSE

On July 16, 2015, James Holmes, who was charged with killing 12 people at an Aurora, Colorado movie theatre in 2012, was convicted of 165 counts levied against him, including those 12 homicides. In convicting Mr. Holmes, the Colorado jury rejected his insanity defense.

The insanity defense has received widespread usage for obvious reasons: if you can convince a jury that you are, or were, crazy, mentally ill, or otherwise mentally incompetent when you committed a crime, you just might get away with it. Certainly, crimes—including very awful ones—are committed by people who are legitimately mentally ill. While one could argue that all people who commit very serious crimes like mass murder "must be crazy," there are meaningful differences between being medically crazy and legally crazy.

A key turning point in the use of the insanity defense came in the mid-1980s, following John Hinckley's attempted assassination of President Ronald Reagan. In 1984, Congress passed the Defense Reform Act (DRA, 18 U.S.C. S. 17), which made it much harder for people accused of crimes to utilize an insanity defense. Specifically, following John Hinckley's successful use of the insanity defense during his trial, many states and the federal government shifted the burden of proof from the state to the defendant. In other words, the state no longer had to prove an accused person was not insane. Instead, the defendant had to prove, by the much higher standard of clear and convincing evidence, that they were insane.

Other changes to the insanity defense and related processes following John Hinckley's case included many states strengthening their mandatory commitment policies. Thus, someone found "insane" at trial cannot just be released back into society, but must be committed to a mental hospital and evaluated for a set period of time. Lastly, another important change with respect to criminality and mental illness was the adoption of the "guilty but mentally ill" (GBMI) status. The GBMI status weakens the use of mental illness as an easy out for criminal offenders because it allows the state to require that someone found to be GBMI either be incarcerated and undergo mental health treatment or be confined to a mental hospital, undergo treatment there, and then be transferred to a correctional facility.

the defendant was guilty of committing a crime. However, when a mistrial is declared the prosecution always retains the right to re-file charges and re-try the defendant. In some cases, re-filing of charges may occur immediately; in other cases the prosecution may reserve the right to re-file pending additional investigatory work, which may produce new evidence.

If the trial concludes with a guilty verdict, several additional processes are initiated. First, sentencing (discussed in the next section) must occur. Second, the defense can begin the process of appealing the conviction. All states allow convicted defendants to challenge their convictions via the filing of **direct appeals**, which raise issue with one or several different aspects of the criminal trial. Examples of issues often brought up on direct appeal include the quality of the defense, the nature of instructions given to jurors, the investigatory process, and the handling of evidence.

> ### BOX 6.8: THE HIGH STAKES NATURE OF CRIMINAL TRIALS
>
> Prosecutors are often quite picky about what cases they bring to trial and when they do so. To hedge against losing at trial, which can not only be a public relations but also a political catastrophe for prosecuting attorneys, the prosecutors will often work very closely with law enforcement investigators to ensure the case is as airtight as possible. Relatedly, prosecutors in many jurisdictions, including at the federal level, may first present their case to a grand jury and seek a formal indictment from that entity (this is sometimes a legal requirement as well).
>
> An **indictment** is simply a formal charge or accusation levied against someone suspected of committing a crime. **Grand juries**, which are special juries comprising 6 to 23 members of the public, are often impaneled to hear the prosecution's case against a suspected criminal. Grand jury proceedings are closed to the public and only the state's (i.e., prosecution's) evidence is presented. If a grand jury determines sufficient evidence exists to demonstrate criminal conduct, they will hand down a criminal indictment. Thus, a grand jury can be a crucial tool for the prosecution, helping them to vet their case and determine if it is strong enough to eventually win a conviction at trial.

THE SENTENCING PHASE

The sentencing phase of the post-trial process is a key bridge between court and correctional/punishment phases of the criminal justice system. Sentencing is very important for several reasons. First, it is the opportunity to formally punish a convicted defendant for their conduct. Second, it is an opportunity to provide victims and their families with a sense of closure and justice. Last, the sentencing phase is an opportunity to enact one of the many punishment philosophies (discussed in greater detail in chapter 7), which range from retribution to rehabilitation.

Overview of sentencing

Formally defined, sentencing is the penalty phase of the criminal justice system, occurring after a guilty verdict or plea deal is reached, and involves the court determining what sort of punishment the defendant should receive for their criminal conduct. In most cases, sentencing occurs within 30 days of the conclusion of the trial. However, in complicated or high profile cases, sentencing can take longer than 30 days, while in others, a conviction may carry an automatic sentence, thus occurring almost immediately after the jury renders its verdict. A recent example of this was when former New England Patriots football player Aaron Hernandez was convicted of murder and automatically sentenced to life in prison without parole.

With the exception of capital cases, or cases where a conviction could result in a sentence of death, sentencing is carried out by the presiding judge.

In capital cases, sentencing is handled by the jury, as in the recently concluded case of Boston marathon bomber Dzhokar Tsarnaev. The reason for this difference is to prevent one individual from making a life and death decision. It is thought that having 12 jurors determine when to apply the death penalty will prevent the excessive or abusive application of death sentences.

Types of sentences

Post-conviction sentences can range from a simple fine and/or community service to imprisonment and even death. Alternative or mixed sentences include things like probation, work-release, incarceration in a halfway house. The vast majority of people sentenced are given some kind of probation or alternative/ mixed sentence.

For those defendants destined to be incarcerated, there are two basic sentencing structures that can impact upon their future. **Indeterminate sentences** do not prescribe a fixed or definite period of time that must be served for a given offense. Generally, upper and lower thresholds are set, say from one to five years for drug possession. People sentenced under indeterminate sentencing structures are usually eligible for parole after serving the minimum number of years. Indeterminate sentencing provides judges with far more discretion and the ability to hand out individualized punishments.

Determinate, or fixed, sentences have grown in use since the 1980s. Under determinate sentencing guidelines, judges have less discretion and must usually sentence convicted offenders to a set period of incarceration corresponding to their crime and their criminal history.

To this end, some states utilize mandatory minimum sentences as well as habitual offender sentences, or **three-strike sentences**. The latter are designed to ensure that violent repeat offenders are given an automatic 25-year-to-life prison sentence after being convicted for their 3rd violent felony. **Truth-in-sentencing** regulations, also passed in some states since the War on Drugs and Crime period of the 1980s, are meant to ensure that convicted criminals serve at least 85 percent of their sentence before being released. The goal is to ensure that felony offenders actually get punished for their crimes and cannot exploit the parole system.

The pre-sentence investigative report and victim impact statement

In the vast majority of convictions, a judge is responsible for determining what punishment the convicted offender will receive. Guidelines and regulations often aid the judge in this process. But perhaps two of the most crucial tools aiding the judge in making his or her sentencing decision are (1) the **Pre-Sentence Investigative Report (PSI)**, and (2) the **Victim Impact Statement (VIS)**.

Before the sentencing hearing, the judge will review the Pre-Sentence Investigative Report, a report typically compiled by a parole or probation officer, or other court staff member. The PSI is essentially a background investigation

BOX 6.9: CONSIDER THIS . . .

Sentencing and the Victim Impact Statement

At the conclusion of most criminal cases that end in a guilty verdict, the presiding judge is responsible for giving the convicted person a sentence. Often, a judge's discretion when imposing a sentence is limited by sentencing guidelines and other regulations. However, in instances where a judge is able to devise a sentence within broad parameters, she or he must weigh many factors. As noted, the Pre-Sentence Investigative Report (PSI) is a very important document that helps the judge determine and provide justification for the sentence they inevitably hand down.

Another document and process plays a critical role in sentencing: the Victim Impact Statement (VIS). In some cases, the Victim Impact Statement is included with the PSI; additionally, the judge may allow the victim or their relatives to read their VIS during a sentencing hearing.

Obviously, it is important that the rights of crime victims be respected. Allowing victims to have a voice, to express their feelings to the court, and to provide input regarding sentencing seems like a good idea. However, the VIS is a highly controversial aspect of the sentencing phase of the courtroom process.

Defense attorneys argue that Victim Impact Statements unfairly bias the judge (or jury in capital murder cases) against their client. The premise of their argument is that judges and juries are as susceptible to emotion as any other person, despite the fact that they may be trained or instructed to rise above emotion in making their decisions. Allowing a crime victim to explain in detail all the terrible ways they have been traumatized by the defendant—physically, emotionally, psychologically—is inevitably going to evoke an emotional reaction from those responsible for imposing a sentence on the offender.

Moreover, defense attorneys argue, when victims urge that a specific type of sentence be given, judges and juries are likely to respect these wishes (up to and including giving a sentence of death). Thus, from the defense perspective, the VIS is an inflammatory document and/or process that violates their client's right to a "fair" trial and sentence.

In 1987, the United States Supreme Court agreed with the defense's perspective regarding the VIS. In the capital murder case of *Booth v. Maryland*,[25] the Court ruled that, especially during the sentencing phase of capital cases, reading a VIS aloud to the jury is unconstitutional. Specifically, the Court argued that such an action violates an individual's 8th Amendment protection against cruel and unusual punishment by raising the risk that the jury will impose a death sentence "in an arbitrary or capricious manner."[26]

Just a few years later, however, the Supreme Court again revisited the issue of the Victim Impact Statement in the case of *Payne v. Tennessee* (1991).[27] In this case, several individuals spoke on defendant Payne's behalf during the sentencing hearing, arguing for leniency in his sentencing. He was convicted of two homicides. Also during the sentencing hearing, members of the victim's families spoke and urged that Payne receive the death penalty. Payne claimed the Victim Impact Statements read at his sentencing violated his 8th

Amendment rights. Unlike in *Booth* and another earlier case (*South Carolina v. Gathers*),[28] the Supreme Court ruled this time that the VIS did not violate defendant Payne's constitutional rights. In effect, the Court overruled itself and set a new precedent: the VIS is constitutional.

Today, Victim Impact Statements are commonly utilized in the sentencing phase of criminal trials. One can see how it would be very unpopular to argue against the rights of crime victims to have input into the sentencing proceedings. Yet it is equally clear that the arguments made against the VIS have merit. What do you think about the Victim Impact Statement? How would you feel about them as both a crime victim *and* a criminal offender?

report on the convicted offender. It provides a wide array of descriptive information about the offender and their personal history, as well as their criminal record, drug use history, and their version of events. In most instances, the PSI also contains a professional evaluation of the offender, including their likelihood of reoffending and/or benefitting from different types of sentences, written from the perspective of a trained probation or parole officer. Often, the PSI will highlight both **mitigating factors**, those that would lessen a defendant's punishment, as well as **aggravating factors**, or those that would enhance a defendant's punishment, such as a lack of remorse or a history of similar offending.

Sometimes a PSI will also include Victim Impact Statements. The Victim Impact Statement (VIS) is a written document that provides the victim, or their relatives, an opportunity to explain how they have been affected by the crime. It also includes information about what sort of punishment the victim would like the defendant to receive (see Box 6.9 for more on the Victim Impact Statement). The judge will review the PSI and related information prior to the sentencing hearing and often rely heavily on the information and perspectives contained within it.

CONTEMPORARY COURT ISSUES

All phases of the American criminal justice system deal with their share of issues, the courts included. In the sections below, we briefly highlight three contemporary issues that affect America's court systems at both the state and federal levels.

Overloaded dockets

Overview

Every court in America utilizes a scheduling device known as a docket. A **daily docket** lists the cases that will be heard on a particular day and is usually posted outside each courtroom. The **long-term docket** is a calendar used by court staff to schedule and track the progress of each case assigned to the court.

Legal scholars and others have been writing about the issue of overloaded court dockets since at least the mid-1960s.[29] Essentially, an **overloaded docket** is one with so many cases on it that the court experiences significant difficulties processing all the cases in a timely manner.

Causes

Several factors contribute to overloaded court dockets. First, it is important to think of the criminal justice system as exactly that: a system. Systems are comprised of multiple components, all of which contribute to the healthy, or unhealthy, functioning of the entire whole.

The massive scaling up of America's law enforcement system in the 1980s, when the wars on drugs and crime were initiated, meant more people were getting arrested. Inevitably, this led to a surge in the volume of cases the courts had to handle[30] and, later, a massive increase in the number of people getting incarcerated. For example, from 1978 to 1984, criminal case filings increased 20 percent in the United States, leading at that time to a 3-to-4-year backlog of cases.[31]

Even if cases are settled via plea bargain, and not a jury trial, this still requires courtroom time and the eventual "OK" by a judge, who must read the plea agreement and agree to it. As the saying goes, every person charged with a crime must have their eventual day in court. The real world consequence of this practice, and of getting tough on crime, is a bogging down of a court system that cannot expediently process every case and the overfilling up of America's jails and prisons.

A related cause of overloaded court dockets is that, despite ever increasing workloads, court staffing has not risen commensurately. That is, we have not hired enough judges or other staff to alleviate the massive workload pile up. And, when a judgeship is vacated, both states and the federal government have been slow to fill the vacancies. Thus, in some jurisdictions, judges are still working into their 80s and 90s, while in other states like Nevada, there are half as many judges than are needed to handle the workload on the docket.[32] This led Chief Judge Federico Moreno of the Southern District of Florida to utter the following: "It's like an emergency room in a hospital. . . . The judges are used to it . . . But the question is, can you sustain it? Eventually you burn out.[33]"

Implications

The implications of overloaded court dockets are quite significant. First, courts prioritize cases by their seriousness and importance. Criminal cases always trump civil cases, and serious criminal cases trump minor ones. Because courts are overwhelmed with criminal cases, many civil ones are pushed back . . . and back . . . and back again, sometimes for years.[34,35]

Second, overloaded court dockets negatively impact defendants accused of crimes. Not only do long delays in getting a case through the court system infringe on a defendant's constitutional right to a speedy trial, but they also impact their safety and welfare. Many people awaiting trial or a resolution in their case who are not given bond or cannot post bond (a cash amount that will allow them to leave jail) are held over in jail indefinitely. This means that they may be incarcerated—without having been convicted, let alone sentenced—for months.[36] This problem also affects children.[37] One survey of 2,200 judges specializing in child welfare cases summarized the perspective of those judges: court backlogs and overwhelmed dockets were a serious obstacle to "finding safe, permanent homes for children in foster care."[38]

Finally, overloaded court dockets around the U.S. are forcing prosecutors and judges to make compromises in the name of efficiency that may not be in the best interests of justice. A lack of judges in Riverside, California, led to 18 pending criminal cases, and another 250 awaiting appeal, being thrown out.[39]

Jury tampering and jury nullification

Many people cite the American jury trial process as a victory in the quest for fairness, equality, and justice. Others find fault with a process that is inherently as flawed as human beings, citing numerous instances where all white juries have convicted people of color despite little or no evidence or, in the notorious death of young African American boy Emmett Till, acquitted obviously guilty white suspects of heinous crimes.

In the Emmett Till case, which became a key part of the subsequent American civil rights movement, an all-white, all-male jury in Mississippi ignored significant evidence that several white men had kidnapped young Emmett in the dark of night from his uncle's home because they believed he had insulted the wife of one of the men earlier in the day. They then savagely beat, strangled, and shot Emmett in the head, killing him. His body was weighted down with a cotton gin fan tied around his neck with barbed wire, and his body was thrown into the muddy Tallahatchie River, from which it was later recovered. Emmett Till was only 14 years old when he was murdered. After the white male jury refused to find his assailants guilty, the assailants bragged to the press and openly described the boy's murder—free from the fear of future prosecution or punishment.

Regardless of where you stand on the merits of the jury trial system, one thing is certain: as long as decisions of guilt or innocence have been shouldered by ordinary men and women called for jury duty, others have tried to exploit this process for their own gain.

Jury tampering refers to the act of influencing the decisions of a jury, juror, or group of jurors, through any means outside those explicitly allowed by the court (i.e., evidence and argumentation by attorneys) in order to alter the outcome of a trial. Tampering can therefore take many forms including bribery, blackmail, threats, and physical violence, and can occur through many means, including writing and verbal communication.

Image 6.5 *In this 1955 photo, Mamie Mobley, mother of Emmett Till, pauses at her son's casket at a Chicago funeral home. The 14-year-old Chicagoan was killed in 1955 after reportedly whistling at a white woman during a visit to his uncle's house in Mississippi. Nearly 100,000 people visited his glass-topped casket during a four-day public viewing in Chicago. Images of his terribly battered body and mutilated face helped spark the civil rights movement.*

AP/Press Association Images

Image 6.4 *Emmett Louis Till, 14, photographed not long before he was kidnapped, tortured, and brutally murdered by two white men during his trip to visit family members in Money, Mississippi.*

AP/Press Association Images

Jury tampering is a serious concern in the courts, since it subverts the goal of justice and is considered a criminal act punishable in some places by 20 years or more in prison. While it is hard to say how often jury tampering occurs given the fact that those who engage in it do not want their conduct revealed, but it does happen. As recently as 2014, the federal government filed charges against a man they alleged was engaging in jury tampering in order to sway the outcome of an immigration and naturalization fraud case.[40]

Another contemporary issue that impacts the courts is that of jury nullification. **Jury nullification** occurs when a jury wields its power to decide the outcome of a case to make a social or political statement. That is, a jury can nullify (or subvert) a law that it feels is unfair, immoral, or wrong by choosing to enter a verdict of "not guilty" in any case where a person is charged with breaking that law regardless of how clearly the evidence indicates their guilt. Since double jeopardy rules prohibit a re-trial on the same charges, if a jury purposefully nullifies a law in this manner, the defendant is set free.

Jury nullification has occurred periodically throughout American history. The first noted instance occurred in 1735, when John Peter Zenger,[41] a printer in New York, became the target of a government campaign to squash a newspaper that was printing unfavorable news about New York's governor

William Cosby. Two grand juries refused to indict Mr. Zenger on trumped up charges. Nevertheless, the government pressed its case and brought Zenger to trial, at the conclusion of which the jury again refused to support the government's heavy handed campaign, returning a verdict of not guilty. Since 1735, jury nullification has been used to challenge and undermine laws involving slavery, prohibition, the act of "mercy" killing, and the prosecution of low-level drug offenders.

Jury nullification is not illegal. As Box 6.8 noted, one risk of a trial by jury system is that once a case is given over to a jury, anything can happen. The key question for you to consider is whether or not jury nullification is "right." Should jurors use their power to force changes in the law, or should they confine themselves only to evaluating the hard evidence presented to them?

Corruption

In August 2011, Pennsylvania Judge Mark Ciavarella, Jr. was sentenced to 28 years in prison after being convicted for accepting bribes in exchange for funneling juvenile defendants into several privately run juvenile detention centers in a "kids for cash" corruption scandal that shone a light on the dark side of the American court system. In the aftermath of Ciavarella's conviction, the Pennsylvania Supreme Court voided more than 4,000 convictions that occurred in the judge's courtroom.[42]

Image 6.6 *Luzerne County Judges Mark A. Ciavarella, center, and Judge Michael T. Conahan, far left, leave the William J. Nealon Federal Building and United States Courthouse in Scranton, Pennsylvania, Thursday, February 12, 2009, after pleading guilty to corruption charges.*

Pamela Suchy/AP/Press Association Images

Corruption generally refers to illegal conduct of people who occupy positions of power within society, including government officials, police officers, and business owners and CEOs. Often corruption involves two or more parties engaging in a criminal conspiracy to commit a crime or type of fraud. By its very nature, corruption is difficult to measure since it is predicated upon secrecy and often occurs behind closed doors, out of public view. For those reasons, corruption is an especially troubling crime because its pernicious effects can impact social, economic, and political circumstances, thereby victimizing many people.

Corruption in the court system can take a variety of forms and involve any courtroom participants. It is an especially serious problem in other nations, particularly those that are poor or that have weak or still-developing legal and political systems.[43] Most often, court corruption involves either judges or attorneys taking bribes, or engaging in conspiracies, to profit themselves, as occurred in the Pennsylvania "kids for cash" scandal.

Corruption also occurs frequently when judicial elections are held. A judgeship, like a congressional seat or other political office, is a political position. In their positions at the top of the legal food chain, judges wield considerable power. As a result, various entities will funnel money into judicial campaigns[44] in order to stock the courts with judges whose politics align with their own. In essentially "buying" the election, and the judge, these third parties will often expect and receive special treatment in the future, which obviously undermines the notions of fairness and justice.

SUMMARY

Courts, as the pivotal second phase of the American criminal justice system, are a key bridge between law enforcement and corrections. It is through our nation's criminal courts that the full impact of our criminal laws is felt.

In this chapter we explored many facets of the American court system and highlighted some key differences and intersections with court systems in other countries, like the Czech Republic. You have learned that the primary functions of American courts include acting as a place where people can get "justice" after having been wronged and receive a degree of closure.

In addition to discussing the key courtroom participants and processes, from pre-trial motions and jury selection, we also highlighted important processes like the plea bargain. Plea bargaining is a controversial procedure, with research indicating that people of color and women are treated differently during the plea bargaining process than white men.

Many students are curious about criminal defenses. There are two main categories of defenses: those that make procedural arguments and those that make excuses for criminal conduct. Self-defense is an example of the latter category and, like the claim of insanity, the self-defense defense is pretty controversial today.

Generally speaking, you can claim self-defense if you used force to protect yourself or the life of someone else from an imminent threat. This doctrine has increasingly been applied outside the home to public areas, with many states arguing that individuals no longer have a duty to retreat when faced with an imminent threat in a public space. The fact that people can now stand their ground has created much concern over fears that this extension of self-defense will be abused.

Likewise, there is concern that the two documents used to determine a sentence may also be open to abuse of misuse. The PSI (Presentence Investigative Report) is a large written document that a judge uses to help make a sentencing decision. It contains information on the offense, offender background, conviction history, finances, familial relationships, and more. It's usually prepared by a probation/parole officer. These individuals are often overworked. Moreover, some argue that their official position biases the report and any professional opinion they provide about the sentencing of a defendant. The issue of bias is also present in the discussion surrounding the use of Victim Impact Statements during the court sentencing phase.

Finally, in this chapter we discussed two current issues involving juries: jury tampering and nullification. The American jury trial system is a key cornerstone of the American style of justice. Because the jury process is central to the functioning of the American court system, issues concerning the effectiveness and transparency of jury decisions are taken seriously. Remember that jury tampering occurs when an outside entity or individual attempts to influence a jury decision via threat, bribe, or blackmail, while nullification occurs when a jury wields its decision making power to negate a law or prosecution it feels is unjust.

American courts are not perfect. They struggle with overloaded dockets that sap their efficiency and negatively impact the progress of justice. While corruption in the courts is as unavoidable as corruption in other phases of government, it is crucial to root it out, since its presence is the very antithesis of justice. As you continue learning about the American criminal justice system, keep in mind that the entire criminal justice system—law enforcement, courts, and corrections—is one interconnected, interdependent whole.

CRITICAL THINKING QUESTIONS

1. Given the importance of the Supreme Court and its case decisions, how do you feel about the way that Supreme Court justices are appointed? Do you like the fact that Supreme Court justices are usually chosen because of how their political ideology will mesh with the current president or members of Congress? Should the American people have a larger say in selecting new members to the nation's highest court?

2. American court proceedings differ substantially from those in other countries, like the Czech Republic and China, because of major differences in the legal systems used in those countries. Now that you know more about how American laws and courts function, how do you feel about our method of handling wrongdoing? Where does the American system get things right, where does it fail or fall short? Do you have ideas for how to improve the American legal system?

3. Do you think plea bargaining is problematic? Why? Do you feel anything should be done to reform the plea bargaining process? If so, what?

4. Where do you stand with regard to Victim Impact Statements? In what situations do you support their use? Do you think they should ever be banned or limited? In your opinion, do the VIS's bias sentencing proceedings against the defendant? Does this matter?

5. How do you feel about the insanity defense in the United States as it currently stands? Do you consider the changes made since the 1980s to the insanity defense to be useful and positive changes or not? Do you think the insanity defense should be reformed even further? If so, what do you suggest? If not, why?

NOTES

1   *Obergefell v. Hodges* 14–556, June 26, 2015.
2   *King et al. v. Burwell, Secretary of Health and Human Services et al.* 14–114, June 25, 2015.
3   *Glossip et al. v. Gross et al.* 14–7955, June 29, 2015.
4   *Michigan et al. v. Environmental Protection Agency et al.* 14–46, June 29, 2015.
5   Bureau of Justice Statistics. 2015. State Criminal Courts. U.S. Department of Justice, Office of Justice Programs.
6   Bobek, M. 2006. An Introduction to the Czech Legal System and Legal Resources Online. Retrieved from http://www.nyulawglobal.org/globalex/Czech_Republic.htm#_2.4._The_Judiciary.
7   U.S. Department of State. 2015. Anatomy of a Jury Trial. Retrieved from http://iipdigital.usembassy.gov/st/english/publication/2011/05/20110503110332su0.7537152.html#axzz3h69URLWo.
8   Ibid.
9   U.S. Department of State. 2015. Anatomy of a Jury Trial. Retrieved from http://iipdigital.usembassy.gov/st/english/publication/2011/05/20110503110332su0.7537152.html#axzz3h69URLWo.
10 Bureau of Justice Statistics. 2015. Criminal Cases. U.S. Department of Justice, Office of Justice Programs. Retrieved from http://www.bjs.gov/index.cfm?ty=tp&tid=23.
11 Devers, L. 2011. Plea and Charge Bargaining: Research Summary. Bureau of Justice Assistance, U.S. Department of Justice, Jan. 24.
12 Ibid.
13 Finklestein, M. 1975. A Statistical Analysis of Guilty Plea Practices in the Federal Courts. *Harvard Law Review* 89: 293–315.
14 Ibid.

15 Ulmer, J. Bradley, M. 2006. Variation in Trial Penalties Among Serious Violent Offenses. *Criminology* 44: 631–670.

16 Piehl, A. Bushway, S. 2007. Measuring and Explaining Charge Bargaining. *Journal of Quantitative Criminology* 23: 105–125.

17 Wooldredge, J., and Griffin, T. 2005. Displaced Discretion Under Ohio Sentencing Guidelines. *Journal of Criminal Justice* 33: 301–316.

18 Farnworth, M. Teske, R. 1995. Gender Differences in Felony Court Processing: Three Hypotheses of Disparity. *Women and Criminal Justice* 6: 23–44.

19 Kellough, G. Wortley, S. 2002. Remand for Plea: Bail Decisions and Plea Bargaining as Commensurate Decisions. *British Journal of Criminology* 42: 186–210.

20 Johnson, B. 2003. Racial and Ethnic Disparities in Sentencing Departures Across Modes of Conviction. *Criminology,* 41: 449–490.

21 Ibid.

22 *Sherman v. U.S.* (356 U.S. 369, 1958).

23 U.S. Department of State. 2015. Anatomy of a Jury Trial. Retrieved from http://iipdigital.usembassy.gov/st/english/publication/2011/05/20110503110332su0.7537152.html#axzz3h69URLWo.

24 Ibid.

25 *Booth v. Maryland,* 482 U.S. 496, 107 S.Ct. 2529 (1987).

26 Ibid.

27 *Payne v. Tennessee,* 501 U.S. 808 (1991).

28 *South Carolina v. Gathers*, 490 U.S. 805 (1989).

29 Carrington, P.D. 1969. Crowded Dockets and the Courts of Appeals: The Threat to the Function of Review and the National Law. *Harvard Law Review* 85: 542–617.

30 People for the American Way. 2015. Overloaded Courts, Not Enough Judges: The Impact on Real People. Retrieved from http://www.pfaw.org/sites/default/files/lower_federal_courts.pdf.

31 Sitomer, C.J. 1984. The Litigation Explosion: How Courts can Relieve Overloaded Dockets. *Christian Science Monitor*, Nov. 8. Retrieved from http://www.csmonitor.com/1984/1108/110808.html.

32 People for the American Way. 2015. Overloaded Courts, Not Enough Judges: The Impact on Real People. Retrieved from http://www.pfaw.org/sites/default/files/lower_federal_courts.pdf.

33 Chief Judge Federico Moreno, Southern District of Florida. *The Impact of Judicial Vacancies on Federal Trial Courts.* Brennan Center for Justice, issued 21 July, 2014.

34 Ibid.

35 Palazzolo, J. 2015. In Federal Courts, the Civil Cases Pile Up. *The Wall Street Journal,* April 6.

36 Aborn, R.M. and Cannon, A.D. 2013. Prisons: In Jail, but not Sentenced. *Americas Quarterly*, (Winter). Retrieved from http://www.americasquarterly.org/aborn-prisons.

37 Presutti, C. 2014. Courts Overcrowded With 'Rocket Docket' Migrant Kids. *Voice of America News*, October 16. Retrieved from www.voanews.com/content/courts-immigration-children/2486049.html.

38 Pew Commission on Children in Foster Care. 2004. Overcrowded Court Dockets, Lack of Family Services Keeping Children in Foster Care, Says New Survey of Family Court Judges. Retrieved from www.pewtrusts.org/en/about/news-room/press-releases/2004/07/01/overcrowded-court-dockets-lack-of-family-services-keeping-children-in-foster-care-says-new-survey-of-family-court-judges.

39 Matheny, K. 2010. Court, Jail Overload Is Putting True Justice in Doubt. *USA Today,* Dec. 3.

40   Gerstein, J. 2014. Feds Warn of Jury Tampering in Detroit. *Politico*, Oct. 5. Retrieved from http://www.politico.com/blogs/under-the-radar/2014/10/feds-warn-of-jury-tampering-in-detroit-196591.

41   *Crown v. John Peter Zenger* (1735). Historical Society of the New York Courts. Retrieved from http://www.nycourts.gov/history/legal-history-new-york/legal-history-eras-01/history-new-york-legal-eras-crown-zenger.html.

42   The Associated Press. 2011. Pennsylvania: Former Judge Sentenced in Bribery Tied to Juvenile Court. *The New York Times*, Aug. 11.

43   Transparency International. 2007. Global Corruption Report: Corruption in Judicial Systems. Cambridge University Press. Retrieved from http://siteresources.worldbank.org/INTLAWJUSTINST/Resources/gcr07_complete_final.pdf.

44   Sarokin, H.L. 2014. For Sale—Going Fast: An Independent Judiciary—Buy a Judge Today. *The Huffington Post,* Aug. 7.

CHAPTER OUTLINE

American corrections

- What is mass incarceration and why does the U.S. incarcerate so many people?
- What are the major punishment philosophies and corresponding correctional models?
- What are the characteristics of the "average" offender?
- What is the key difference between prison and jail incarceration?
- What are the primary forms of alternative and community corrections?
- What are the major problems and issues facing the American correctional systems today?

KEY TERMS

mass incarceration

correctional phase

retribution

Mamertine Prison

galley slavery

hulk

transportation

banishment

Enlightenment

Montesquieu

Voltaire

Immanuel Kant

Denis Diderot

John Howard

Cesare Beccaria

Jeremy Bentham

deterrence

deterrence philosophy

ducking stool

Brideswell prisons

William Penn

Great Law of Pennsylvania

rehabilitative punishment philosophy

MASS INCARCERATION IN THE UNITED STATES

Imagine you and some friends are attending a trivia night at a local bar. In the final round, the host asks you to name the country with the highest imprisonment rate in the world. Naturally, your team starts brainstorming possible answer choices. China seems like a natural choice because they have the world's largest population—over 1.35 billion people. How about India? They have the world's second largest population. What about Russia? That is a big country too. You sneak a glance at the team sitting closest to you. You can't tell exactly what they wrote, but it sure doesn't look like Russia. Your team keeps at it, running through country after country: Brazil, Indonesia, Japan, Australia . . . Finally you all give up. Nobody knows the answer, and no one can agree on what country to guess. Instead of writing down an answer, your team draws a big question mark.

When the host of the game finally reveals the winning answer, your mouth gapes open in shock.

The country with the highest incarceration rate in the world is . . . the United States? You can't believe it! But it is true.

Figure 7.1 International comparative incarceration rates for select countries

Sources: 1. Prison Policy Institute. 2012. "States of Incarceration: The Global Context." May 13. www.prison policy.orgglobal/. 2. Bureau of Justice Statistics. 2013. "Prisoners in the United States, 2013." 3. International Centre for Prison Studies.2015. "Highest to Lowest Prison Population Rate." http://www.prison studies.org/highest-to-lowest/prison_population _rate?field_region_taxono my_tid=All. 4. The Sentencing Project. 2013. "Trends in U.S. Corrections." http://sentencingproject.o rg/doc/publications/inc_ Trends_in_Corrections_ Fact_sheet.pdf.

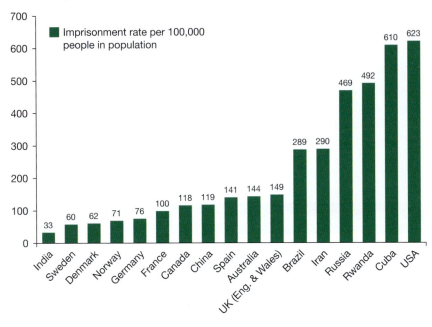

reintegrative philosophy

jails

prisons

community correctional programs

Walnut Street Jail

Dr. Benjamin Rush

Pennsylvania Prison Society (PPS)

Western Pennsylvania State Prison

Eastern Pennsylvania State Prison

Pennsylvania System

New York System

According to the most recent data, for every 100,000 adults in the U.S. population, 623 are incarcerated.[1] This incarceration rate is 5 to 10 times higher than most European nations and quite a bit higher than the incarceration rates for China, India, and Russia (see Figure 7.1). In fact, the nations with the second and third highest incarceration rates in the world—Cuba (510 per 100,000 people)[2] and Rwanda (492 per 100,000 people)[3]—still imprison far fewer people than America.

Even more shocking is what you learn later: for over three-quarters of American history, the U.S. incarceration rate was not astronomically high; it was only about 110 people per 100,000 in the population, a pretty normal figure.[4] Only since the early 1980s has the U.S. jail and prison population soared, increasing by nearly 500 percent.[5]

We use the catchall term "**mass incarceration**" to describe the state of America's correctional system today. Mass incarceration highlights the incredible growth of America's correctional population over the last 40 years; it also hints at how this growth occurred: the phrase "mass incarceration" conjures up an image of herds of people being rounded up and loaded into America's jails and prisons—this image isn't too far from the truth, since many incarcerated people have committed very minor offenses.

Since the 1980s, it is as if a giant corrections fishing net has been thrown indiscriminately over the United States, catching whomever it can. Correctional reformer Marc Mauer paints another vivid picture of mass incarceration when he says: "Imagine the combined populations of Atlanta, St. Louis, Pittsburgh, Des Moines, and Miami behind bars."[6] Mass incarceration is the reality of contemporary American corrections.

In this chapter, we explore the origins and implications of mass incarceration, especially for people of color. We'll also develop our foundational knowledge about what punishment is, and how it works, by learning about punishment philosophy, prisons and jails, and probation and parole. We hope you approach this chapter with your mind wide open—there's a lot to discuss.

SITUATING CORRECTIONS WITHIN THE CRIMINAL JUSTICE SYSTEM

After the court phase is completed and a finding of guilt is made, a punishment is assessed. Today, punishments include fines, probation, imprisonment in jail or prison, and even death. When we study "punishment" we are really looking at one aspect of the third phase of the American criminal justice system broadly referred to as the correctional phase.

This chapter provides a broad overview of the correctional phase of America's criminal justice system. As was the case with developing our knowledge about the criminal law, law enforcement, and the courts, it is vital to understand the basic parameters and contemporary issues associated with corrections in the United States. Many criminologists and criminology students study and publish research on the correctional system. Likewise, numerous organizations, including many prominent non-profit groups, devote their time and energy to advocating on behalf of correctional reform and different populations of correctional "clients" (i.e., offenders). Finally, any person interested in a career working within the American criminal justice system—whether as a police officer, attorney, probation officer or something else—should possess knowledge about what corrections is and how it structures life in America.

THE ORIGINS OF MASS INCARCERATION

As discussed previously in the chapters on policing and courts, the 1980s were a critical decade impacting every phase of the American criminal justice system. The reasons we incarcerate more people today than any other country in the world trace back to that decade.

There is a saying that "history has a way of repeating itself." The more you study history, the more this becomes apparent. One noticeable aspect of American history is that there have been many cycles of progressive, dynamic change either preceded or followed by periods of retraction and conservatism. For example, the progressive social and cultural change of the 1960s and 1970s followed the reserved conservatism of the 1940s and 1950s. In the 1980s, the pendulum swung back again from social progressivism and liberalism toward conservatism. The beauty of hindsight, and historical research, is that trends and patterns over time appear so clearly.

Three Prisons Act
Emmett Till
convict leasing system
pig laws
private prisons
pains of imprisonment
total institution
mortification
prisonization
probation
John Augustus
Total Abstinence Society
parole
discretionary parole
mandatory parole
Alexander Maconochie
marks system
ticket-of-leave
Sir Walter Crofton
Irish System
National Prison Congress
Declaration of Principles
Dorothea Dix
Zebulon Brockway
Elmira Reformatory
disparity
unconditional release
recidivism

**Prisoner Rights
    Movement**

**solitary
    confinement**

Furman v. Georgia

Gregg v. Georgia

In reality, few people in the 1970s could have predicted that policy changes would occur in the 1980s that would set America on a course toward mass incarceration. During the 1970s, in fact, many people and organizations predicted that, if anything, the U.S. would move further away from a reliance on prisons and jails to control people who broke society's rules.[7] In 1973, for example, the National Advisory Commission on Criminal Justice Standards and Goals published a report in which they stated incarceration had "achieved nothing but a shocking record of failure."[8] They went on to recommend that no new adult prisons or jails be built and that some prisons and jails, including those for juveniles, be closed.

Then the 1980s happened. As we detailed in chapter 5, the rise of the New Right and the election of Ronald Reagan reshaped the social and political discussion in America. In the midst of a bad economy, with jobs rapidly moving overseas, high unemployment and rising poverty and crime rates, the Reagan administration sought to shift society's focus away from the structural roots of various problems. It became far easier to paint unemployment and crime as problems linked to individual failures, rather than large-scale political and economic ones.

Within this context Ronald Reagan, and his successor George H.W. Bush, initiated two wars: one against drugs and one against crime. In order to successfully wage war against those two issues, drugs and crime, the Reagan administration recast both as problems linked to personal choices that ultimately reflected the moral failings and bad decisions of individuals. Drug use and crime were completely divorced from larger structural causes, like poverty, unemployment, lack of education, and inadequate social services. Behind the power of political rhetoric and media portrayals, many Americans bought into the idea that the only solution to reduce drug use and crime was to get tougher—to crack down and punish people engaging in those behaviors more harshly. A host of policies reflected this sea change, including those we discussed in the chapters on law enforcement and courts: zero-tolerance and public order policing, determinate sentencing, mandatory minimum sentencing, and, later, three-strikes laws.

As we'll discuss later, parole was significantly altered during this time. The idea of rehabilitating criminals, which is closely linked to the use of parole, was painted as being too soft on crime. In criminology, too, conservatism emerged with the revitalization of rational choice theory (discussed in chapter 8). The result of all of these changes was the widening of a net that increasingly caught people engaging in low-level, non-violent offenses—like drug use and theft—and pulled them into the criminal justice system and, eventually, into America's jails and prisons.

A BRIEF HISTORY OF PUNISHMENT

Understanding modern American corrections requires first appreciating how the punishment of law violators has progressed over time. As with studying the criminal law, policing, and court systems, this means shifting our focus momentarily to the European context. Interestingly, when we study the origins of punishment and compare those origins to the evolution of America corrections today, we find a cyclical pattern. What this means is that old ideas and practices fall into and out of use over time, highlighting the salience of the saying: "what's old is new again."

Punishment as retribution, or "an eye for an eye, a tooth for a tooth"

In order to function cohesively and achieve shared goals, a society must have order and boundaries. Maintaining order and boundaries within a society is at least partially resolved through the creation of laws and the specification of punishments for violating those laws. Throughout much of human history, punishments have been guided by the philosophy, or guiding idea, of retribution. **Retribution** means that punishments should be equal to the severity of the offense. In other words, punishments should be proportional.

Retributive punishment philosophy is old, very old. Sometime around 1780 BC, King Hammurabi of Mesopotamia (modern day Iraq, Syria, southern Turkey, and western Iran) instituted a number of laws, at least 282. These laws were carved into a special stone called a "stele" that French archaeologists uncovered in 1901. Next to each law on the stele was a corresponding punishment that was scaled to "fit" the offense. The punishments varied by type and severity depending on the perceived seriousness of the rule violation. Hammurabi's legal code is the historical basis for the idea of retribution. If you've ever heard the phrase, "an eye for an eye, a tooth for a tooth", then you've been exposed to the idea of retribution.

Image 7.1 *The stone stele of King Hammurabi is one of our earliest known surviving examples of a formal, written legal code. Importantly, next to each law on the stele was a corresponding, scaled punishment. The idea of proportional punishment remains prominent throughout much of the developed world.*

The Art Archive/Musée du Louvre Paris/Gianni Dagli Orti

Punishment in the ancient world

Studying the history of punishment means travelling around the world (at least in our minds) to exotic locales—Egypt, Rome, Greece, Turkey. As long as people have been people, they've been making informal and formal rules and breaking those rules. Punishment, in one form or another, is as old as humanity.

Some of the earliest examples of highly organized punishments can be found in Italy. If you ever get a chance to visit Rome, take a tour of the ancient

Image 7.2 *Mamertine Prison, Rome, Italy*
Wikimedia Commons/Bgabel

Mamertine Prison complex, constructed around the year 640 BC. Scattered throughout the blue waters of the Mediterranean Sea are the decaying, ancient remains of old wooden ships that were powered by people who rowed them by using oars. The Romans and Greeks used those ships, and the manual labor of thousands of criminals and other rule breakers to move them about. **Galley slavery**, as that old form of punishment was called, lasted until better sailing technology came along.

Even after sails replaced people with oars, ships continued to be used as storage places to hold criminals and other unwanted or undesirable people. Author Victor Hugo wrote a book called *Les Misérables*. Jean Valjean, one of the book's main characters, escapes from a decommissioned old ship called a **hulk** early in the story. The British and French used hulks for quite a while to hold prisoners. They were harsh and unpleasant places, to say the least.

Later, England, France, and others nations used ships to simply get rid of criminals and unwanted people like the mentally ill and political activists. **Transportation** was much like **banishment**, an early form of punishment discussed in the Christian Bible, in that rule violators were forced to leave the place they called home. Transportation, however, resulted in hundreds of thousands of prisoners being shipped halfway around the world to often desolate locales like Australia, Africa, America, and even tiny little Devil's Island, located off the coast of French Guiana.

In general, the emphasis of early punishment efforts was to punish for punishment's sake, which is a key aspect of retributive philosophy. People weren't so much concerned with fixing criminals as they were with sending a message to them and others. As a result, punishments around the world were incredibly harsh, brutal, and, often, public. The brutality of punishment only increased as organized religion took hold and introduced the idea that criminals might be possessed by evil spirits, controlled by witches, or performing the Devil's work. Many people were burned alive, hung, decapitated, and tortured to death by having their limbs ripped off. Others were crucified and impaled. Some were drowned or pushed off cliffs. People lucky enough to avoid death often suffered worse fates at the hands of their punishers, who eagerly employed various corporal punishments (corporal means "bodily") such as flogging and placing people in stocks.

Few prisoners were provided decent food, water, or clothing. Getting in serious trouble was, most of the time, a death sentence. The only variable was whether death would be fast or slow. Unless, of course, you happened to be wealthy or well connected. A fundamental aspect of early punishment was that people with more power could avoid the same fate as everyone else. Rarely were the wealthiest or highest status individuals subjected to the same punishments as ordinary people. Many times, they could avoid punishment entirely. Corruption, bribery, and other practices were commonplace throughout most of the world. The twin aspects of early punishment—brutality and corruption—carried over well into the 19th century in Europe and America. Indeed, even into the 1800s in England a person could be put to death for committing any one of over 200 different offenses, including cutting down a tree.[9a]

The Enlightenment, positivism, and punishment

The Enlightenment was an unprecedented period of intellectual, social, and political change across Europe. Taking place from the late 17th through the 18th centuries, the **Enlightenment** ushered in new ways of thinking about and explaining our

Image 7.3 *In this colored woodcut from German artist Tengler, Ulrich, 1447–1511, three defendants are held in the stocks in the Strassbourg town square. For centuries, corporal punishments in Europe and America were frequently used, often in a very public way, in order to deter future criminal or bad behavior.*

Mary Evans/Interfoto/Bildarchiv Hansmann

physical and social worlds. Positivism and positivistic thinking, which emphasize rationality, empirical evidence, and the scientific method, began to grow in popularity and use. In contrast to the "Dark Ages" in medieval Europe, the Enlightenment period was the dawning of a beautiful, sunny day. During the Enlightenment, ideas about criminal behavior and punishment changed dramatically. Emphasis was placed on scientifically understanding the causes of criminal behavior and reforming punishment.

Philosophers and social thinkers from many European countries, including **Montesquieu** (1689–1785), **Voltaire** (1694–1778), and **Immanuel Kant** (1724–1804) revitalized the basic notion of retribution which had been lost over time as societies turned to executions and brutal corporal punishments.

Kant was a particularly strong advocate of matching the harm caused by a crime to the severity of punishment applied to the wrongdoer. Among other things, these Enlightenment thinkers argued that punishments should be proportional and, generally, far more humane than they were. Frenchman **Denis Diderot** (1713–1784) and Englishman **John Howard** (1726–1790) also sought to

Image 7.4 *Charles Louis de Secondat, baron de Montesquieu, French philosopher*

Mary Evans Picture Library

Image 7.5 *Francois-Marie Arouet (Voltaire), the French writer and philosopher*

Mary Evans Picture Library

Image 7.6 *Immanuel Kant, German philosopher*

Mary Evans/Interfoto/Sammlung Rauch

Image 7.7 *Denis Diderot, French encyclopaedist and philosopher*

Mary Evans Picture Library

Image 7.8 *John Howard, British jurist and reformer of the English prisons*

Interfoto/Sammlung Rauch/Mary Evans

Image 7.9 *Cesare Bonesana, Marchese Di Beccaria, Italian economist and jurist*

Mary Evans Picture Library

Image 7.10 *Jeremy Bentham, philosopher and economist*

Mary Evans Picture Library

reform correctional efforts, which were corrupt and brutal. Both the French and English penal systems lacked continuity in administration as well as oversight, and failed to provide inmates with even basic necessities like clean drinking water or edible food. The work of Diderot and Howard lead directly to reforms and the modernization of penal systems in both France and England.

Two especially influential Enlightenment thinkers, whose work continues to influence American correctional efforts, were Italian jurist **Cesare Beccaria** (1738–1794) and English philosopher **Jeremy Bentham** (1748–1832). Becarria published *On Crimes and Punishments* in 1764. In that book, Beccaria suggested that uniformity, equality, and proportionality should guide the application of punishments.

From his perspective, the same crime should receive the same punishment (uniformity), punishments should be applied equally to all people regardless of wealth or status (equality), and punishments should be in proportion to the type of crime committed and the harm caused by it (proportionality/retribution). Many of Beccaria's ideas on punishment, court proceedings, and law have become cornerstones of the modern American criminal justice system and continue guiding our thinking about crime and punishment to this day.

Jeremy Bentham, writing from England, was adamant that human beings were rational, calculating decision makers. Bentham's ideas were based on his assumption that all people wanted to maximize their pleasure and minimize their pain (i.e., hedonism). From his perspective, people decided to engage in criminal behavior after they weighed the risks of criminal action versus the rewards of criminal action. When people determined the rewards outweighed the risks, they would commit crimes. Bentham paired this perspective and understanding of human nature with punishment. He argued that the purpose of punishment should be to raise the risks of engaging in criminal conduct to a point where people would naturally arrive at the conclusion that committing a criminal act just wasn't worth it.

While the idea of using punishment to send a message certainly was not new at the time Bentham formalized his ideas, he was the first person to formalize that idea into a punishment philosophy known as **deterrence**. Since Bentham articulated the idea, the **deterrence philosophy** has guided many modern correctional policies and practices in American and Europe.

EARLY PUNISHMENT AND CORRECTIONS IN AMERICA

Columbus's arrival in the New World in 1492 ushered in an era of colonization that eventually resulted in the formation of the United States of America in 1776. Most colonists hailed from Europe, including England and France. They brought with them religious beliefs, ideas, and laws that influenced all aspects of life in the American colonies. Included among the beliefs and ideas brought over from Europe were those pertaining to law, order, and punishment.

Early American punishment was disorganized and harsh. The colonies each took their own approach to punishment, a trend that carried over to the states after the Revolutionary War. Executions, particularly public hangings, were common in America from its initial settlement through the 1800s and were utilized to punish a wide range of acts including witchcraft, adultery, and homosexuality. American colonists also invented their own creative corporal

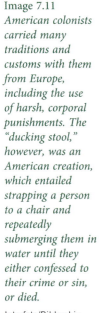

Image 7.11
American colonists carried many traditions and customs with them from Europe, including the use of harsh, corporal punishments. The "ducking stool," however, was an American creation, which entailed strapping a person to a chair and repeatedly submerging them in water until they either confessed to their crime or sin, or died.

Interfoto/Bildarchiv Hansmann/Mary Evans

punishments including branding and the ducking stool, a device where a person was strapped to a chair and repeatedly dunked into a river or pond until nearly (or completely) drowned.

The American colonies were in many ways a social experiment. A large number of American colonists hoped to distance themselves socially and politically from Europe. As a result, American corrections advanced, organized, and formalized faster than correctional efforts in Europe. For example, while the English began developing jails around the 9th century and had built Brideswell prisons, places to house adult and juvenile offenders whose crime was often nothing more than owing a debt, around the 16th century, jails began appearing in American colonies in the late 1500s and 1607s—quite early in the history of the nation. Jamestown colony in Virginia built a jail in 1606. Not long after, Boston followed suit, building its first jail in 1635. If you visit the small New England town of Barnstable, Massachusetts, you can visit the nation's oldest surviving jail, a cedar shingle

Image 7.12 *The Old Jail in Barnstable, MA, now on the National Register of Historic Places, was built in 1690.*

Wikimedia Commons/Kenneth C. Zirkel

structure built in 1690. Thus, prior to most of the Enlightenment advances in Europe, America was already on its way to developing a more sophisticated, uniform system of punishment.

However, problems that plagued correctional efforts in Europe were problems in America too. Corruption allowed influential and wealthy colonists to avoid punishment altogether. Punishments were often not applied equally for the same offense to all offenders. And, far too often, punishments were applied to any undesirable person or population, rather than just serious criminals. As in Europe, correctional facilities were typically dirty, miserable places where inmates were poorly cared for and abused.

Enlightenment ideas trickled over to America beginning in the mid-1700s. However, America had its own Enlightenment-style reformer well before Kant, Bentham, and Beccaria. William Penn (1644–1718), the Quaker founder of the Pennsylvania colony was far ahead of his time. Penn introduced a degree of humanity into the correctional process as yet unheard of in America with passage of his Great Law of Pennsylvania in 1682. Among other things, Penn abolished corporal punishment and emphasized incarceration. He envisioned a person's time incarcerated as an opportunity for self-reflection, soul-searching, and, hopefully, positive change. Those ideas reflected a rehabilitative punishment philosophy that was more than one hundred years ahead of its time. Unsurprisingly, people who are far ahead of their time are often disliked or misunderstood by their contemporaries. As a result, Penn's ideas were quite unpopular.

Image 7.13
William Penn (in white), 1644–1718, the English Quaker founder of Pennsylvania colony, was a key penal reformer in America. His "Great Law" was instrumental in shifting the course of punishment and corrections in America.

The Art Archive/Culver Pictures

When he died in 1718, many of his progressive changes were swept aside and Pennsylvania resorted to relying on corporal punishments, including the death penalty.

MODERN PUNISHMENT PHILOSOPHY AND CORRECTIONAL MODELS

Philosophies provide a rationale, or guide, for action. Punishment philosophies impact how we as a society view criminals and inform our actions in terms of how we deal with them. Punishment philosophies and the models that translate those philosophies into practice are not mutually exclusive. It is often the case, especially in America, that multiple philosophies and correctional models exist simultaneously, often functioning in a supportive or complementary manner.

There are three basic punishment philosophies and corresponding correctional models They are the: (1) retribution and the retributive/isolative/incapacitory/just deserts model; (2) deterrence and the crime prevention model; and (3) rehabilitation and reintegration and the rehabilitative/community model.

Retribution and the retributive/isolative/incapacitory/just deserts model

We previously introduced the origins of the punishment philosophy known as retribution. Retribution is one of the oldest punishment philosophies and is found in nearly every modern nation's approach to punishment, including America's. Among other things, retribution argues that the punishment must fit the crime. This is the idea of proportionality in punishment. From this view, minor crimes receive minor punishments and serious crimes receive the harsh punishments, including death. Unlike other punishment philosophies, retribution does not argue that punishment has a secondary purpose; there is no loftier goal to be achieved via punishment. The only goal of punishment is to hold the offender accountable and ensure justice—however it is defined—is served.

The popularity of retribution and its influence on American correctional practice experienced resurgence in America during the 1980s. As beliefs about criminal behavior and how it could be corrected changed during that decade, people and organizations gravitated toward a retributive philosophy and practice. The retributive philosophy remains popular, but in many ways conflicts with the rehabilitative philosophy discussed below.

In current practice, retribution manifests in various ways. Sentencing offenders to different facilities based on their "threat" or custody level is a clear application of the retributive idea that crimes and criminals should be punished according to offense severity. Minimum-, medium-, maximum- and super maximum-security prisons are a direct result of rehabilitative philosophy. Likewise, the rise in use of solitary confinement and executions since the 1980s highlights a return to retributive ideas about punishing the worst crimes or worst offenders in the harshest way possible. Isolating or incapacitating the worst offenders is in keeping with the basic idea of retribution and James Q. Wilson's argument that sometimes "wicked people exist. [And] nothing avails except to set them apart from innocent people."[9b]

Deterrence and the crime prevention model

Deterrence philosophy overlaps with ideas of retribution, incapacitation, and isolation. Deterrence is about preventing future crime, by the criminal and other societal members (see Table 7.1 for a description of specific v. general deterrence). Executing criminals or secluding them away behind bars or in solitary confinement clearly has the ability to function as a deterrent to future crime. However, deterrence philosophy as envisioned by Jeremy Bentham is much more amenable to the goals of rehabilitation and reintegration than is retribution.

Deterrence philosophy is founded upon the assumptions that human beings are rational decision makers who are motivated to maximize their pleasure and minimize their pain. According to Bentham, people, including criminals, weight the risks and rewards of actions before engaging in them. In general, Bentham and other deterrence theorists would argue that behavior is governed by its results or consequences. Thus, when crimes are committed, it is because the offender decided the reward of committing the criminal act was greater than the risk.

From a deterrence perspective, the goal of punishment is to intervene in, and disrupt, this decision-making process and raise the consequences of criminal behavior to a level that people will find disagreeable. Applied effectively, punishment can serve to deter people from committing crimes by raising the

Table 7.1 Two types of deterrence, general v. specific

	Goals	Examples	Message
Specific deterrence	Prevent future crime committed by a specific individual Show a specific person that their criminal act was not worth it	Expelling a student for cheating on an exam Sentencing someone to a life prison term	Your crime cost you a lot
General deterrence	Prevent future crime among other people Make an example of someone to benefit the greater good	Holding an assembly to discuss cheating, noting the consequences that befell a student who does cheat Publicizing the harsh penalties for committing a certain crime; conducting interviews with incarcerated people who talk about regretting what they did	Crime does not pay, so do not do it

risks associated with criminal conduct to a point where they will decide that committing a certain criminal act isn't worth the risk of getting caught and punished for it. Thus, deterrence philosophy serves the goals of crime prevention and in many ways serves the greater "good" of society by decreasing the number of crimes and criminal offenders. In other words, deterrence philosophy hinges on making an example out of a few people in the hopes that, by applying punishments effectively to them, we can scare not only those individual offenders, but more importantly all other potential offenders, away from ever engaging in that unwanted conduct in the future.

Deterrence plays a significant role in contemporary American correctional practice. Deterrence theory has been used to justify exceptionally harsh punishments and criminal justice policies. Executions, solitary confinement, lengthy prison sentences, forced sterilization campaigns, and many other actions throughout history have been justified on the grounds of deterrence and crime prevention. Many of the criminal justice policies emerging from the 1980s emphasized the "deterrent" value of a particular punishment, for example the death penalty (discussed later in this chapter). Deterrence theory has also led to the implementation of all sorts of crime prevention strategies and educational programs in countries around the world.[10]

Rehabilitation/reintegration and the rehabilitative and/or community model

The ultimate goal of rehabilitative punishment philosophy is to return offenders to a "healthy" state of functioning. Rehabilitative philosophy is quite similar to reintegrative philosophy, which ultimately seeks to return offenders to their communities and society.

Despite the fact that William Penn instituted a variety of progressive changes with a rehabilitative emphasis in Pennsylvania in the late 1600s, rehabilitation as a punishment philosophy is relatively new to punishment and corrections. From the mid-1800s through the 1970s, perspectives on punishment and its ultimate purpose continued shifting further toward rehabilitation. Increasingly, scholars and practitioners emphasized punishment and incarceration as an opportunity to fix criminals and cure them of their criminal ways. This development reflected both Enlightenment and positivistic thinking.

Rehabilitation and deterrence theories overlap. Both are fundamentally concerned with preventing future crime. However, they differ in their methods for achieving this end.

In practice, rehabilitation and reintegration result in rehabilitative and community-based models of corrections. These models emphasize therapeutic, skill-building, and educational interventions as critical components in rehabilitating and successfully reintegrating offenders into society. Deterrence, by contrast, places more emphasis on incarceration and other punitive measures as a way of sending a message and setting an example that "crime doesn't pay." Probation, parole, alternative sentences, and community based correctional programs are all examples of correctional programs founded upon rehabilitative ideas.

While in contemporary American society rehabilitation and reintegration remain influential philosophies, they are no longer the dominant philosophy. By and large, American correctional programs are focused on deterring crime and punishing offenders punitively through long prison sentences. Rehabilitation and reintegration reached their peak appeal during the 1970s. As political and social ideology shifted in the 1980s toward retribution and deterrence, rehabilitation and reintegration were rebranded as being "ineffective," thanks mostly to a few studies that questioned the success of rehabilitative programming.[11]

AMERICAN CORRECTIONAL SYSTEMS

Today's contemporary American correctional system encompasses (1) jails, (2) prisons, and (3) a variety of community correctional programs. These facilities and programs are utilized at local, state, and federal levels to achieve the goals of controlling and punishing offenders, as well as rehabilitating and reintegrating them into communities. At present, approximately 1 in every 35 U.S. adults is under some form of correctional supervision, meaning that they were incarcerated, serving an alternative sentence or on probation or parole.[12] Specifically, 1 in 110 Americans is incarcerated in a jail or prison and 1 in 51 are on probation or parole.[13] Given these stark statistics, it is vital to examine the history, current trends, and issues of America's correctional systems.

Jails in the United States

Current jail populations

America's stable jail population is relatively small and mostly male. Approximately 731,200 people were held in America's jails in the most recent year,[14] though each year jails across America process nearly 13 million people (see Table 7.2 for a listing of some of America's largest jail systems). Most of these people stay in jail for less than a week or two. Many of these temporary jail inmates–male and female—may have been picked up for public drunkenness, vagrancy, or are on a temporary mental health hold for their own safety. Studies of jail inmates indicate that 60–70 percent of the stable jail population at any given time may suffer from one or several forms of mental illness.[15] For example, the Cook County, Illinois, jail surveys new arrestees during the intake-processing phase of jail admission. On average, anywhere from 25–36 percent of new jail arrivals self-report suffering from a mental illness at that one facility.[16,17]

In addition to mental health issues, jail inmates have higher rates of HIV, hepatitis, liver disease, and sexually transmitted infections (STIs) than occur in the general population.[18,19] These higher rates are often linked to issues of serious substance abuse (drugs and alcohol). Some studies report that as many as 68 percent of jail inmates suffer from serious substance abuse issues.[20,21] Physical and mental health and substance abuse issues are, in turn, often linked to larger issues like unemployment and poverty.

Table 7.2 America's largest jail systems

Location	Description
Los Angeles County	• America's largest jail system • Services City and County of Los Angeles • 18,000 inmates • 4 huge facilities
New York City	• Second largest jail system • Services 5 New York City boroughs • 14,000 jail inmates held on the Riker's Island correctional compound • 10 separate jail facilities
Harris County, Texas	• Third largest jail system • Services city of Houston, TX and surrounding areas • 10,000 inmates
Cook County, Illinois	• One of the largest single-site jail facilities • Services the City of Chicago and surrounding areas • 96 acres • Processes over 100,000 people/year

Functions of American jails

Jails serve a variety of functions (see Table 7.3). In general, jails are designed to house relatively minor, non-violent criminal offenders sentenced to less than one year of incarceration. Common offenses that land people in jail include a variety of misdemeanor crimes including minor drug possession, DUI (in some places), petty theft, and simple assault. Jails also hold people prior to and during court proceedings and criminal trials.

As a result, around 60 percent of America's jail population at any given time has not been formally convicted and sentenced for a crime.[22] Since the late 1990s, American jails have also occasionally been used to house excess or surplus prison populations when prison facilities cannot accommodate them; currently over 85,000 prison inmates (5 percent of the total prison population) are held in local or county jails.[23]

Table 7.3 Primary functions of American jails

Hold people sentenced to less than 1 year of incarceration
Hold people prior to, and during court, proceedings, and criminal trials
Hold overflow or surplus prison inmates that cannot be held in state prison facilities
Hold people after conviction, but before final sentencing
Hold people temporarily and those with nowhere else to go (e.g., drunks, the homeless)
Hold state or federal fugitives temporarily until custody transfer to appropriate agency

A brief history of jails

Jails were the first correctional facilities utilized in the American colonies. Over time, as more villages and towns were established, the need for more jails grew. Jails were built in both town and city centers, as well as centralized county locations. Thus, jails quickly became key institutions in American communities. They were not only visible signs of formal social control within communities, but also the site of most individual's first experience with formal punishment for law violation.

Major innovations and changes in America's jails occurred following the Revolutionary War. As America and American cities continued to grow and Enlightenment ideas and positivistic emphases continued to influence social thought, American corrections, particularly jails, began to change for the better.

Philadelphia, Pennsylvania, built the **Walnut Street Jail** in 1773. Like many early jails it was an unsanitary, poorly run place where male, female, and juvenile inmates were thrown together in large rooms. Life at Walnut Street meant going without decent food and inmates were regularly allowed to consume alcohol and use prostitutes.

By 1790, the Walnut Street jail had officially been rebranded as a "prison." Influenced by the ideas of John Howard and Jeremy Bentham, **Dr. Benjamin Rush**, a physician who authored the first American chemistry textbook and signed the Declaration of Independence, worked with the **Pennsylvania Prison Society (PPS)** to improve conditions at Walnut Street. Both Dr. Rush and the PPS were concerned with achieving better treatment for inmates and introducing progressive changes to Pennsylvania's correctional system.

Walnut Street Jail/Prison was remodeled on the basis of Rush and the PPS's ideas. It quickly became one of the most modern, progressive correctional

Table 7.4 Current prison and jail populations in America

	Jails	Prisons
# Facilities	3,200+	1,800+
Total inmates	731,200	1,574,700
Federal total	X	215,866
State or local total	731,200	1,358,875
% Male	86	93
% Female	14	7
% White	X	32
% Black	X	37
% Hispanic	X	22

institutions in the nation. Inmates were kept in single cells and provided adequate food and clothing. They were kept separate from each other based on their gender and offense type. Juvenile offenders were separated from the adults. All convicts were provided medical care and were required to regularly attend religious services. Importantly, charging inmates additional "fees" was no longer allowed, nor was sex, prostitution, or alcohol consumption. Changes at Walnut Street gradually influenced jail construction and reform in other states.

Prisons in the United States

In 2013, there were approximately 1,800 state and federal prison facilities operating across the United States holding over 1.5 million inmates,[24] or 22 percent of the adult population under correctional supervision. The vast majority of prisoners, over 1.2 million, are held in state prisons.[25] Federal prisons account for the second-largest inmate population, while private prisons hold a little over 100,000 inmates. Additionally about 15,000 inmates are held in military and territorial prisons located around the world, including Guam, Puerto Rico, and the U.S. Virgin Islands.[26] Detailed information regarding America's current prison population can be found in Table 7.4.

Functions of prisons

Prisons do not serve as many secondary functions as do jails. Generally, the function of prison is to hold offenders sentenced to more than one year of incarceration, people sentenced to life imprisonment, and people sentenced to death.

As a result, most prison inmates have typically committed felony violations, including serious offenses like homicide, terrorism, robbery, rape, and sexual assault. These individuals are typically classified based on their offense severity and threat level and separated into facilities that differ in their security level (minimum, medium, maximum, and super-maximum security).

A brief history of American prisons

American prisons developed after the Revolutionary War. As the American population grew, so did the number of people committing crimes, including very serious ones. Larger facilities were needed to house these criminals. States responded by building prisons, often in locales far removed from large population centers like cities and towns.

The Pennsylvania System

During the Penitentiary Era (1790–1825) and the Mass Prison Era (1825–1876) of the first phase of early modern corrections (1790–1876), a variety of prison facilities were built. Pennsylvania was one of the first places to develop a statewide prison system. Western Pennsylvania State Prison was built in 1821 near Pittsburgh, PA. Eastern Pennsylvania State Prison, also called "Cherry Hill," was built near Philadelphia on the site of an old cherry orchard. Construction began in 1822, and though Cherry Hill opened in 1829, construction was not completed until 1836. Upon completion, Eastern/Cherry Hill State Prison was one of the most advanced, innovative public facilities (not to mention costliest) in the United States and became the "flagship" institution of the Pennsylvania Correctional System, operating for over 150 years (see Table 7.5).

Table 7.5 Innovations at Eastern PA/Cherry Hill State Prison

Building design	A Central Hub with radiating cell blocks (like a bicycle wheel)—this architectural design was influential throughout Asia, South and Central America
Cells	Eastern had over 400 separate cells to keep prisoners isolated from each other, each with its own small exercise area
Perimeter wall	Eastern has a large perimeter wall to separate the facility from the surrounding area. This feature, which is now a staple of prison design, was new at the time. Most jails had no way of containing inmates should they escape their cell or of keeping unwanted people out.
Central heating	Eastern had a central heating system before most U.S. government buildings, including the Capitol
Hot water	*Flushing toilets*—Eastern has indoor plumbing and flushing toilets before the White House
	Showers—Eastern may have had the first interior showers in the nation

Image 7.14
Hallway of the Eastern State Penitentiary

Wikimedia Commons/Seeminglee

The **Pennsylvania System** of corrections as exemplified by Eastern State Prison was unique in that it emphasized keeping prisoners isolated from each other. Silence was also strictly enforced. Prisoners performed almost every task or activity in their own cell, from eating to exercise to religious worship. They were not allowed contact with visitors, unless those visitors were religious clergymen and could not receive newspapers, letters, or other materials from family or friends. The extensive use of solitary confinement at Eastern State Prison was based on the belief that solitary confinement was a key way to promote rehabilitation.

Interestingly, widespread use of solitary confinement fell out of favor not long after as many correctional officials and citizens viewed it as inhumane and counter-productive to the goal of rehabilitation. Indeed, the New York Prison System (discussed next) was one of the first to do away with solitary confinement. However, solitary confinement reemerged again in the 1980s as America cracked down on criminals and got tough on crime (solitary confinement is discussed in more detail at the end of this chapter).

The New York System

In 1819, Auburn State Prison opened, and it is still in operation today under the name Auburn Correctional Institute (ACI). Auburn State Prison enforced a "congregate and silent" system, also known as the **New York System**. Congregate and silent means that inmates at Auburn were allowed to come into contact with each other, but they were not allowed to speak to each other. Even eye contact between inmates was strictly forbidden and infractions of the silence rule were enforced through corporal punishments, including lashings and

Image 7.15
Aerial view of the Sing Sing prison at Ossining, New York, in 1920.

Library of Congress/George Grantham Bain Collection

beatings. The fact that inmates were allowed into contact with each other differentiated the New York System from the Pennsylvania one.

In 1826, New York opened another prison facility 30 miles north of New York City along the Hudson River. Called Sing Sing Prison, the new facility was built in part by the labor of Auburn State Prison inmates. Sing Sing's close proximity to New York City led to the phrase "being sent up the river," which is still in common usage today. Sing Sing Prison protocols were similar to those enforced at Auburn.

The Federal Bureau of Prisons

The vast majority of all criminal prosecutions occur at the state level. All states have thus developed correctional systems for dealing with the majority of the criminal population. However, individuals can also commit federal offenses by violating federal criminal laws. As a result, the federal government must also have a system for processing and punishing those offenders.

In 1893, the United States Congress passed the "Three Prisons Act." Among other things, this act created the nation's first federal prison system (FPS) and led to the construction of the first federal prisons (Atlanta, Leavenworth, and McNeil Island). The federal prison system was overseen by the Department of Justice, which was established in 1870 with the Attorney General—a position created in 1789—at its head.

As the state and federal prison populations expanded through the early part of the 1900s, it became more apparent that a dedicated agency would be needed to manage the federal prison system. In the mid-to-late 1920s, several individuals, including Assistant Attorney General Mabel Walker and eventual Director of the Bureau of Prisons James V. Bennett, appealed to Congress to create an agency capable of running the federal prison system. In 1930, Congress responded by establishing the Federal Bureau of Prisons within the Department of Justice to centralize oversight and administration of the federal prison system. At the time of its creation, the Federal Bureau of Prisons ran 11 facilities across the nation; by 1980, the number of facilities had grown to 44.[27] Currently, there are over 100 federal prison and correctional facilities spread across America. The rapid growth in the federal prison system since the 1980s is a direct result of many new criminal justice system policies created during the 1980s and 1990s.

Southern prisons

Corrections developed quite differently in the Southern slave states (e.g., Mississippi, Alabama, Georgia, Louisiana) due to the South's unique social and economic characteristics (something true of policing as well). Prior to the Civil War, slavery was the primary method of formal social control and organization— for thousands of African American men, women, and children, slavery was a punishment no different than receiving a sentence of life without parole. Slaves were not free, had no autonomy and were forced to engage in manual labor, which allowed the southern agricultural economy to thrive.

The slave system established clear social and legal boundaries between so-called "decent" whites and blacks; punishments were swift, severe, and often lethal for any blacks violating those boundaries no matter how trivial their transgressions were. Black "criminality" was essentially predetermined by the slave system and its rules, and blacks were not afforded constitutional rights or legal protections. Whites, however, often escaped any punishment, even when they committed atrocious crimes against blacks, including murder (this trend carried through well into the 20th century as the **Emmett Till** case from chapter 6, illustrated). When whites did violate the law, they were entitled to a fair trial and legal representation. Given these circumstances, there was very little need for Southern slave-holding states to worry much about correctional systems since slavery fulfilled all those needs.

The Civil War completely upended the Southern economy and traditional social hierarchy. Slavery was abolished by the 13th Amendment to the Constitution. Formerly sub-human black slaves were now "free" people. In reality, though, former slaves were anything but free. White southerners quickly set about re-establishing social boundaries that put blacks into the same subordinate position they had occupied prior to the Civil War. One solution to achieve this goal appeared in the form of convict leasing. The **convict leasing system** gained immense use in the Southern United States between 1870 and 1930. Under that system, convict labor was utilized to power the post-Civil War economy. Most of the time, the new "convicts" were newly "free" southern blacks.

Across the South, African American men, women, and children were often arrested for minor legal violations and, in some cases, for doing nothing at all. **Pig laws** made theft of items valued at as little as a few cents serious criminal violations, and police officers and sheriffs would sometimes invent charges to arrest African Americans. Once in custody, these individuals were quickly sentenced—though few actually were given trials—and then sold into hard labor in mines, factories, and on farms. Many were coerced into working off their sentences by sheriffs and judges who assessed them high fines and told them they could pay them off through their labor. Convict leasing recreated many of the conditions of the slave system under the guise of legitimate punishment and corrections. Convict leasing also illustrated the dangers of privatizing correctional operations.

Image 7.16 Convicts leased to harvest timber, around 1915, Florida

Library of Congress/State Library and Archives of Florida

Private prisons

Private prisons—for-profit correctional facilities run by private corporations operating under a government contract—actually have a much longer history in American corrections than one might assume. The prison at San Quentin, California, for example, which is now part of the California State Prison System (CSPS), actually began as a for-profit, private prison facility in 1852.[28] Privately run prisons and jails were fairly common in England and France before the Enlightenment; in fact, during the Enlightenment, a key concern of correctional reformers like John Howard and Denis Diderot was getting rid of the rampant corruption linked to jailers and prison wardens charging prisoners fees to be kept incarcerated![29]

Prison privatization reached its zenith in the southern United States from the 1870s through the early 1900s. During that period, southern states like Mississippi and Alabama relied heavily on the convict leasing system. That system led to the full-scale exploitation of African American men and women and essentially replicated the conditions of slavery. Indeed, a key reason private prisons fell out of favor in the United States was because correctional reformers working during the early 20th century utilized the injustices of the convict-leasing system to argue against prison privatization.[30,31] As a result, use of private prisons all but ceased.

Since the 1980s, private prisons have reemerged and currently hold about 8 percent of the U.S. prison population.[32] Thanks to a variety of tough-on-

Image 7.17 *Corrections Corporation of America (CCA) is one of the largest private, for-profit, prison companies in America. The rise of private prisons followed the growth of America's incarcerated population. Thankfully, private prisons are on the decline. In mid-2016, the U.S. Federal government voted to end their use of private prisons.*

Mel Evans/AP/Press Association Images

crime policies that led to more prisoners and longer prison sentences, state and federal prison systems became overburdened. Budgets and facilities simply could not handle the sheer volume of prisoners in need of supervision and control. Private prison companies like Correctional Corporation of America (CCA), GEO Group, and others responded to the need of state and federal prison officials. Those corporations work under contract or receive fees from state governments or the federal government. In return, the private corporations take over the responsibilities of correctional supervision, from building correctional facilities to staffing them and providing inmates with food and health care.

All of this is ostensibly accomplished far more cheaply than would otherwise be possible. However, much of the cost savings stems from paying staff far lower wages and, possibly, by cutting other corners. For example, in 2014, CCA, the nation's largest private prison company, was ordered to pay employees over $8 million in back wages and benefits after it systematically underpaid employees (whose pay rate was guaranteed by contract), some by as much as 30 to 40 percent, at one federally contracted facility in California.[33] Not surprisingly, civil rights groups like the American Civil Liberties Union (ACLU) and some correctional system practitioners are quite concerned about prison privatization and its impacts on the American correctional system.

The prison experience

Criminologists and sociologists have long been interested in understanding the experiences people have, including people in prisons and jails. In general, the prison experience for most inmates is not a pleasant one. Sociologist Gresham Sykes (1958) noted that prison inmates suffer through a variety of serious hardships, which he referred to as the "**pains of imprisonment**."[34] Pains of imprisonment include loss of freedom and independence, loss of important familial, personal, romantic, and/or sexual relationships, inability to access normal goods or services, and loss of personal security. Collectively, these hardships can lead inmates into depression and may make them more susceptible to what sociologist Erving Goffman called "mortification."

Goffman (1961) wrote about the experience of living or working in what he termed a **"total" institution**[35]—a place where "all aspects of life are conducted in the same place, under the same single authority," and where "all phases of the day's activities are tightly scheduled." Examples include jails, prisons, mental hospitals, and even military barracks.

Goffmann argued that one effect total institutions can have on an individual is "**mortification**."[36] Mortification is a process where a person loses their personal identity and connection to roles they had outside the total institution. In some cases, mortification is a necessary process that people enter into willingly. For example, those who join the Army willingly submit to losing their identity and external roles so that they can become a highly functioning soldier. Indeed, the key goal of boot camp is, essentially, to tear people down in order to build them back up.

Prisoners and mental patients, on the other hand, despite the fact that their personal choices may have led to their incarceration, do not willingly enter into the mortification process. The longer one lives within a prison, the more likely they are to lose their identity and any connection they had to who they were outside prison. This can be a painful and sad experience. The mortification process can also be sped up through use of solitary confinement, which isolates prisoners not just from normal society, but all other human contact.

One consequence of mortification may be **prisonization**.[37, 38, 39] Prisonization is a process where inmates adopt the values, beliefs, and argot (language) of the prison subculture. Because the totality of the inmate's world has been reduced to the prison environment and those people within it, it is fairly easy for changes to occur to their self-identity, belief systems, and personal values. The longer one is exposed to the prison world, the more likely they are to become a fully functioning member of the prison subculture. This may be reflected in any number of ways, from getting tattoos, joining a gang and engaging in violence, to developing a mistrust of staff and people on the outside, to forgetting how life outside prison even works. The values of the prison subculture, while not in complete opposition to values in conventional society, do not always mesh well with values considered acceptable in normal society. If fully adopted by the inmate, these values—like being ultra-masculine or hyper-aggressive—can make transitioning back into regular life quite difficult.

Image 7.18 *Prisonization is the process of adopting the prison/inmate subculture. This often contributes to the formation and persistence of prison gangs. Often, prison gangs congeal along racial or ethnic lines, like the white supremacist gang members from a Texas prison pictured above.*

Getty

BOX 7.1: WORKING IN ... CORRECTIONS

The median income for correctional officers, around $38,000 per year, is far lower than the median income for law enforcement officers, attorneys, and other criminal justice system practitioners (in West Virginia starting pay for correctional officers is only $22,584 per year). Federal correctional jobs, and jobs as probation and parole officers, tend to pay more. Be wary of working in privatized correctional settings; private prison staff tend to earn $10,000 to $15,000 less per year than state employees.

Working in corrections is similar in many ways to working in any other criminal justice fields, though the hiring requirements are usually less stringent than entry-level law enforcement careers. Stress and danger are key features of correctional careers, though in comparison to police work correctional jobs are far more predictable. Correctional officers and probation/parole officers are two of the most popular careers; however, you can also work in corrections as a therapist, medical technician, and educator.

Key job functions in correctional careers include supervision of inmates/offenders and enforcement of various correctional rules and regulations. Ideally, the best correctional officers will be excellent communicators, decisive decision makers, possess impeccable integrity, and demonstrate compassion for their "clients." One word of warning before embarking on a career path in corrections: correctional staff tend to have the lowest educational attainment among criminal justice system employees—which may mean that your bachelors or associates degree will make you over-qualified for the position.

CONTEMPORARY PRISON AND JAIL ISSUES

Deaths in custody

A serious issue in jails and prisons is that of deaths in custody. Inmate deaths occur in jails far less frequently than in prisons. This has to do not just with the fact that jails are slightly less violent places than prisons, but also with the fact that prisons hold inmates for very long periods of time. Some people may enter prison at age 20 and live there until their death at age 80.

Each year, around 4,000 inmates die in custody (only around 800 deaths occur in jails).[40] Importantly, the leading causes of death are not murder or suicide, which one would also assume based on TV and movie portrayals of incarceration. In fact, deaths due to heart disease, cancer, liver disease, respiratory disease, and AIDS account for the vast majority of all deaths in custody.[41] This highlights a point we made earlier about inmate populations suffering higher incidents of health-related illnesses, which are often linked to poverty and substance abuse. Of course, it is worth pointing out that most people who die in custody are men (95 percent), which also reflects the gendered nature of incarceration and criminal offending in America.[42]

Violence, gangs, and riots

Prison and jail violence in the form of interpersonal violence (assaults, murders) or self-harm (mutilation, suicide) is an issue that receives a significant amount of attention. Prisons and jails are places prone to violence. This is especially true in prisons where inmates often utilize violence to create and maintain social order and organization. However, in any given year only around 40–80 murders occur in jails and prisons throughout the country.[43]

Gang activity in prisons, and to a lesser extent jails, is a serious concern, especially in medium- and maximum-security state prisons in places like California, Texas, Florida, and New York. The existence of prison gangs, which were first observed in the 1830s, stems from both the realities of life outside prisons and the realities of life inside prisons. Many prison inmates, who are disproportionately minority males, come from communities where gang activity is common; thus, in some places inmates enter prison already affiliated with gangs and indoctrinated into gang culture. Gang life in prison simply reflects life on the outside.

However, the prison environment is also conducive to the formation and persistence of gangs.[44] Gangs can offer protection, a sense of camaraderie, personal relationships, and access to goods and services (i.e., drugs). In fact, *not* being in a gang may be a deviant behavior in some prison environments and expose inmates to more risk. Today, most prison gangs are differentiated by race or ethnicity (see Table 7.6).

Table 7.6 America's 6 largest prison gangs

Gang name	Racial or ethnic affiliation
Neta	Puerto Rican/Hispanic
Aryan Brotherhood	White (non-hispanic)
Black Guerrillas	Black/African American
Mexican Mafia	Mexican American/Hispanic
La Nuestra Familia	Mexican American/Hispanic
Texas Syndicate	Mexican American/Hispanic

Sources: 1. Florida Department of Corrections (www.dc.state.fl.us/pub/gangs/prison.html). 2. Kelley, M.B. 2014. "America's 11 Most Powerful Prison Gangs." *Business Insider*, February (www.businessinsider.com/most-dangerous-prison-gangs-in-the-us-2014–2).

Sexual assault, rape, and sexual violence

Sexual assault, rape, and other forms of completed and attempted sexual violence are very serious issues in America's prisons and jails that effect male and female adult and juvenile inmates. The Prison Rape Elimination Act of 2003 mandated that prison officials keep and report statistics on prison sexual violence.[45,46] However, the FBI did not officially adopt an expanded definition of rape, which defined the act in terms broad enough so that men could be considered rape victims, until 2013.[47] Prior to 2013, the official definition of rape, which guided the collection of data about the crime, limited rape to an act perpetrated against women. Official data indicate that between 3 and 4 percent of adult jail inmates, 4 percent of adult prison inmates, and 8–10 percent of juvenile inmates suffer a sexual assault or attempted sexual assault each year.[48] These figures likely fail to capture the true reality of sexual violence in correctional facilities, due to underreporting by victims who are fearful of reprisals or being deemed a "snitch."

What is especially troubling about the different forms of sexual violence in correctional facilities is that correctional staff are often implicated as the offenders. For example, our most recent data indicate that as many as half of all sexual misconduct and assault incidents involve assailants employed by the correctional facility.[49] This is also true of sexual assault incidents involving juvenile offenders. For instance, in 2012, 1,720 juvenile inmates reported a sexual assault at a juvenile correctional facility.[50] In almost 90 percent of cases the alleged perpetrator was a *female* correctional officer or staff member.[51]

At both the adult and juvenile levels, we know that sexual assaults are sometimes accompanied by violence, especially when the offenders are other inmates. However, it is very important to recognize that more often than not, sexual violence is perpetrated by the *threat* of violence, or by using some other means of coercion (such as offering protection, goods/services, etc.).

Community and alternative corrections

The phrase "community and alternative correctional programs" is used to refer to probation, parole, and a variety of non-traditional punishments (boot camps, treatment programs, etc.). Community-based corrections are increasingly being utilized across America at the state and federal levels. Today, 1 in 51 U.S. adults is on community supervision[52]—mostly via probation or parole—representing 7 out of every 10 criminal offenders.[53]

One reason for this is that community correctional programs are far cheaper to run and thus more budget friendly. Another reason community corrections are more common today is because they can be utilized to divert offenders away from traditional incarceration in jail or prison, thus reducing prison and jail overcrowding which has become a serious problem in some states like California and Texas. Finally, community and alternative correctional programs reflect a rehabilitative and reintegrative philosophy that is gaining more traction as correctional researchers, correctional officials, politicians and the public realize that simply locking people up is not the most effective way to deal with crime problems.

Probation

Probation is a sentence that allows a convicted offender to remain under supervision in the community and avoid incarceration in jail or prison. While on probation, the offender is supervised by a probation/parole officer. It is vital to remember that probation is (1) a conditional sentence that is also (2) revocable; this means that if an offender violates *any* of the conditions of their probation (e.g., don't use drugs, don't associate with certain people), they can have their probation revoked and be sent to jail or prison.

A brief history of probation

The Latin origin of the word probation is "probare" meaning "to prove." Probation, which is similar to the English concept of judicial reprieve, is thus a sentence that allows convicted offenders to "prove" themselves by remaining law-abiding citizens within their communities for a set duration of time. The use of probation in the United States is linked to John Augustus, a Boston boot maker and cobbler born in 1785 and often called the "father of probation." Augustus was a member of the Boston-based Total Abstinence Society (TAS) and was also a devoutly religious man. He was especially concerned with the notion of forgiveness and sought to apply this principle to people suffering from alcoholism. Augustus' beliefs and concerns eventually led him into the Boston court system.

While observing court proceedings, Augustus noticed that a larger number of the individuals appearing in court and being sentenced to jail were suffering from alcoholism. From his view, alcoholism was the root cause of their criminal behavior. This thought led Augustus to make a daring plea to the Boston Police Court judge: would the judge allow Augustus to take charge of one of the drunks and reform him? Likely believing that Augustus would fail and that at the least there was little to lose, the judge agreed. Three weeks later, to the astonishment of the court, Augustus returned with the formerly disheveled man, who was, by all accounts, completely changed in his appearance, demeanor, and attitude.[54] From that initial success, John Augustus decided to dedicate his life to reforming criminal offenders. Others, moved by Augustus' logic—that some offenders might be better served through kindness and leniency than a harsh sentence—joined him in his task.

By 1858, August had personally bailed out and supervised 1,900 men and women.[55] He was so successful that, in 1859, Massachusetts became the first state to pass a probation statute. By 1878, Massachusetts had created the full-time position of probation officer. The idea of probation gained greater currency and by 1900 Vermont, New York, and New Jersey had also adopted the idea of probation. Probation was formally established at the federal level by Congress in 1825, just a few years before the formation of the Federal Bureau of Prisons.

Contemporary probation populations

Today, probation is the most frequently utilized punishment in American corrections. On average, between 80 and 90 percent of convicted offenders receive a probationary sentence.[56] In 2013, more than half of all people (57 percent) under correctional supervision were on probation.[57] Since 1980, the probation population in the United States has grown 34 percent, from 1 million to 3.9 million in 2013.[58] As a result, about 1 in 62 U.S. adults is currently on probation.[59] About one-quarter of the current probation population is made up of female offenders.[60] Relative to their likelihood of offending, women are more likely to receive a probationary sentence than their male counterparts. In terms of race and ethnicity, 54 percent of all probationers are white, 30 percent are black, and 14 percent are Hispanic.[61] Over half (55 percent) of all people on probation in 2013 committed a felony, while 43 percent committed a misdemeanor.[62] Of the people receiving probation in 2013, 66 percent successfully completed their sentence.[63]

Parole

Parole allows convicted offenders to be supervised in the community *after* having already been incarcerated for some period of time. Like probation, parole is conditional and revocable. Prior to the 1980s, most parole was **discretionary**, meaning prisoners could be granted a conditional release from prison by a parole board any time after they became eligible. Discretionary parole typically allows offenders to get out of prison before serving their full sentence, especially when they have demonstrated good behavior. Since the 1980s, discretionary parole releases have decreased. **Mandatory parole** is an automatic release from prison for inmates after serving a specified amount of their sentence without consideration for their behavior or whether they've been rehabilitated. Mandatory parole is closely associated with determinate sentencing structures and has been more widely used since the 1980s.

A brief history of parole

Parole has a more complex history than probation. In the 1830s, **Alexander Maconochie** (1787–1860), the superintendent of Norfolk Island Penal Colony near Australia, began utilizing a "**marks system**." Under that system inmates could earn credits for working and behaving well. With enough credits, inmates could apply for a **ticket-of-leave**, which would allow them to work and live outside the prison grounds before their full term of incarceration was over.[64] For Maconchie, the purpose of incarceration should be to rehabilitate offenders so they could reenter society. Thus, sentences should be flexible enough to allow for rehabilitative practices to be implemented and should also enable prison officials to reward inmates for making progress toward rehabilitation. Creating a system of incentives that could lead to positive rewards was thus a natural outgrowth of Maconchie's personal experiences and ideas about punishment.

Maconchie's mark system influenced **Sir Walter Crofton** (1815–1897), one of the most influential leaders of the Irish Penal System. The "**Irish System**" that Crofton pioneered systematically implemented the notion of early conditional release from prison through a four-phase process[65] (and closely resembles today's discretionary parole). The first phase was the most punitive. Inmates were held in solitary confinement for eight or nine months and given little food. The goal of Phase I was to break inmates down, impress upon them the seriousness of their predicament and spark a desire within them to improve their living conditions. During Phase II, inmates could begin earning marks or credits for good behavior, good work, and other tasks and could also lose marks for bad behavior. Inmates who performed well in the second phase would move on to the equivalent of a "half-way" house where they could continue their rehabilitation, engage in work placement programs and other activities. Assuming all went well, convicts could then earn a ticket-of-leave and a conditional release into the community.

Parole took a while to catch on in America. In 1870, corrections officials from across the United States converged in Cincinnati, Ohio, for the **National**

Prison Congress. In attendance were the warden of Sing Sing Prison, Gaylord Hubbel, and Sir Walter Crofton. In 1863, Hubbell visited Crofton in Ireland to learn more about the Irish System. Over the next few years, Hubbell campaigned in America on behalf of the benefits of the Irish System. His and Crofton's presence at the National Prison Congress had significant ramifications for the future of American corrections.

Generally considered the catalyst for major prison reform and a shift toward a rehabilitative correctional philosophy in America, the National Prison Congress in Cincinnati produced a **Declaration of Principles** meant to guide the organization and administration of correctional systems across America. Among other things, the declaration of principles identified both punishment and incarceration as opportunities to reform criminals and stated that good conduct should be rewarded. Clearly represented in the ideas of the National Prison Congress were those of social reformer **Dorothea Dix** (1802–1887), who published a book detailing the dire circumstances in American prisons and jails prior to the Civil War and strongly advocated for correctional reforms.

Image 7.19 *Dorothea Dix (1802–1887) was a key prison reformer in the period before the Civil War. Her efforts contributed to many of the significant progressive changes enacted during the 1870 Prison Congress in Cincinnati, OH.*

Mary Evans/Everett Collection

In 1876, **Zebulon Brockway**, the head official at the new **Elmira Reformatory** in upstate New York, became the first to implement a parole-like marks system in the United States. Massachusetts then became the first state to pass a parole law in 1884. By 1900, twenty states had some version of a formal parole system. The federal government adopted parole in 1910. By 1944, all states utilized parole.

It is important to understand that probation has a longer history in America than parole. This is because probation's original goal was to go "easy" on first time, non-violent or non-serious criminals. Giving criminals, especially young people and those with substance abuse issues, a second chance to do right is much more palatable to most people. By contrast, allowing criminals, including repeat and perhaps violent offenders, to get out of prison early seems to contradict the retributive element that has been so central to punishment for so long. It is difficult for some people to understand or accept the fairness or necessity of parole, even though its intention—rehabilitation and reintegration—is no different from probation.

Contemporary parole populations

Over 850,000 people were on parole in 2013, the vast majority at the state level, representing about 1 in 286 American adults.[66] Most parolees are men (88 percent). In terms of race and ethnicity, at year-end 2013, 43 percent of parolees were white, 38 percent were black and 17 percent were Hispanic.[67] Slightly more than one-quarter of people on parole had been incarcerated for a violent offense, a third were drug offenders, and one-fifth had committed property crimes.[68] Our most recent data indicate that about 14 of every 100 people on parole fail to reenter society successfully and is returned to incarceration.[69]

Juvenile corrections

Early in American history, juvenile offenders were housed in the same decrepit jails and prisons as adults. It was also common for juveniles to be punished corporally and via the death penalty in the same manner as adults. In the 1800s, this began to change as numerous reformers began advocating for the special treatment of juvenile offenders. While scientific research on human development had not yet provided evidence that youthful offending may be at least partially linked to cognitive and psychological changes, many people were willing to recognize that a lot of juvenile delinquency was linked to large issues like poverty and an unstable home life.

In 1825, the New York House of Refuge was built and others followed, like Jane Addams' Hull House in Chicago, which was built in 1889. The intent behind the creation of these facilities, which were partially modeled after some that existed in Europe, was to separate juveniles, including the poor, homeless and delinquent, from adults. Prior to the creation of houses of refuge, it was very common for all sorts of wayward youth to be thrown into adult jails and prisons. These facilities, many of which were run by volunteers and religious groups, provided a more therapeutic, educational, rehabilitative setting for juveniles. This emphasis on rehabilitation has always been a key characteristic of juvenile corrections in America, setting it apart from adult corrections.

From the mid-1800s through the early 1900s "industrial schools" usurped houses of refuge as the predominant facility type for dealing with juvenile delinquents. These places were more regimented than houses of refuge and focused on work and skill building. Today, there are over 60,000 juveniles housed in a variety of facility types across the U.S.[70]

ISSUES IN MODERN CORRECTIONS

Race, class, gender, and corrections

Currently, there are around 321 million men, women, and children in the United States. According to the most recent data from the U.S. Census, the American population is about evenly split between men and women. In terms of racial or ethnic identity, 63 percent of Americans are non-Hispanic whites, 17 percent are Hispanic or Latino and 13 percent are black/African American. If criminal offending, arrest, and incarceration accurately reflected this basic demographic data, we would expect the vast majority of criminal offenders and incarcerated people to be white men and women. More importantly, we would anticipate that Hispanic and black men and women would represent only a small fraction of criminal offenders and convicts. Unfortunately, this is not the case.

Data consistently show that, compared to their total number in the population, blacks and Hispanics are far more likely than whites to be arrested for crimes, prosecuted, and sentenced to incarceration in America's prisons and jails. While overall whites do comprise the largest number of incarcerated people, Table 7.7 shows just how out of balance imprisonment rates are for other races and ethnicities.

Table 7.7 Race, gender, and U.S. prison populations 2013

Race and gender	Imprisonment rates per 100,000 people
White female	51
Hispanic female	66
Black female	113
All women	65
White male	466
Hispanic male	1,134
Black male	2,805
All men	904

Source: Prisoners in 2013. U.S. Bureau of Justice Statistics.

Among other patterns, Table 7.7 helps us see that, in general, men are far more likely to be incarcerated than women, though between 1980 and 2013, the population of incarcerated women increased 587 percent, highlighting the fact that female incarceration is growing at a rapid rate.[71] The vast majority of prisoners and new prison admissions are young. Incarceration rates are highest for people between the ages of 18 and 39.[72] Men are also more likely to commit crimes and be incarcerated for crime than women. Table 7.7 also shows us, however, that certain types of men and women are more likely to end up behind bars.

Specifically, if you are a black or Hispanic man or woman in the United States, you may be anywhere from 1.5 to 6 times more likely to get incarcerated when compared to your white peers. When we add age into the equation, things get worse, since, by and large, younger people are more likely to get in trouble and get locked up. Thus, some groups, like young black men, are in an especially troubling spot. We now know that one in three young black men born in America will serve time in jail or prison while one in six Hispanic or Latino men will.[73,74] If we consider additional factors like social class (i.e., income, wealth, property ownership) and education, a very clear portrait emerges of America's "typical" inmate: a young minority male from a low-income neighborhood with a low level of educational attainment.

This data illustrates the fact that disparities exist in our criminal justice system and how it functions in relation to race and ethnicity. A **disparity** exists when there is unequal or unfair treatment of one group over another group. The key question is, where does this disparity stem from? The answer is not simple. America has a long history of conflict between different racial and ethnic groups. Conflicts between the dominant Euro-American majority and minority groups have been common throughout America's history, from its first colonization through the forced internment of Japanese Americans during World War II, to 1960s civil rights movements, to today. In America, laws have historically represented the views and values of white society. The police and courts have generally enforced laws on behalf of white society; and the people in positions of power—from police officers to district attorneys to judges—have been white. Racial and ethnic bias is part of the fabric of American society and, as a result, the criminal justice system.

We can point to many examples that support these claims. For instance, racial and ethnic bias has played a key role in the process of criminalizing nearly every major street drug in America, including opium/heroin, cocaine, marijuana, and crack-cocaine. Almost always, the history of drug laws reflects a history of whites linking a new drug problem to a particular minority group. Opium was labeled the "Mongolian Vice" in order to discredit Chinese immigrants who were competing for jobs with whites and European immigrants. Marijuana was linked to Mexican immigrants and Hispanics during the early 20th century. And cocaine, long the drug of choice of respectable middle- and upper-class whites, was rebranded in the post-Civil War period as the drug of choice of free black men. These "negro cocaine fiends,"[75] as they were called, were said to be intent on raping white women in their cocaine-fueled hysteria.

Besides drug laws, we can witness and measure racial disparities in other areas of the criminal justice system. In court proceedings, the plea bargains and sentences handed out to black and Hispanic drug offenders are harsher and more punitive than those given to whites facing similar drug charges.[76,77] Racial minorities are more likely to be the target of police attention and enforcement actions—regardless of if the police have cause to target them. A study of the NYPD stop-and-frisk policy found that blacks and Hispanics made up 80 percent of the people stopped by the NYPD between 2005 and 2008, while whites, who make up the majority of New York City's population, were stopped only 10 percent of the time.[78] Black motorists are more likely to be stopped by police and twice as likely to be arrested than whites;[79] some law enforcement agencies have conducted covert surveillance of Muslim groups not known to be engaging in any criminal activity[80] and some states, like Arizona, have passed unconstitutional legislation essentially condoning racial profiling—where law enforcement use race or ethnicity as a key factor guiding their law enforcement decisions and actions.[81,82,83]

Today, 60 percent of people incarcerated are people of color;[84] of that, 37 percent are black.[85] One in ten black males in their thirties is incarcerated, which means about 3 percent of the *entire* adult black male population was incarcerated in 2013.[86] Due to police corruption and abuse-of-force scandals, some communities in America do not trust the police and view them more as a criminal element or occupying military force than as a force for good. The consequences of racial and ethnic bias within America's criminal justice system are significant and troubling, and they impact the legitimacy and effectiveness of every phase of the criminal justice system.

In America, the highly unjust, discriminatory convict-leasing system was used by southern states following the Civil War and into the 20th century to reconstitute African American slave labor. Throughout the 20th century and even today, prisoners across the United States can be sentenced to "hard labor," or more generally put to work producing goods for sale. Some state prisoners make license plates or office furniture, while others, like those sentenced to Louisiana's maximum-security state prison, Angola, work in fields planting and harvesting crops. The irony that most of Angola's prisoners are African American men who are legally obligated to work at tasks their ancestors were once forced to complete during slavery is a glaring one.

Prisoner reentry and recidivism

For some individuals, correctional institutions are the final stop on their journey through the criminal justice system and life—they may never reenter society again. For the majority, however, correctional facilities are just a stopping point; some will serve their sentence and punishment, reenter society, and never offend again. Others, however, are not so lucky and will repeatedly enter correctional facilities for varying lengths of time over their life course.

Most prisoners in America get a chance to reenter society through parole or through unconditional release, meaning they served their time and will not be supervised on the outside. Some prisoners reentering society may have committed minor drug offenses or thefts, while others may have committed robbery, rape, and murder. How inmates reenter society, and what condition they are in when they do, are key issues in modern corrections. As Travis (2005) noted: "Reentry is not a goal . . . Reentry is not an option. Reentry reflects the iron law of imprisonment: they all come back."[87]

In any given year nearly as many people leave prison as enter it. In 2013,[88] 631,200 people entered America's prisons and 623,337 left. Of those who left, 173,824 left unconditionally—they were not subject to ongoing monitoring or treatment. Unconditional release occurs once a prisoner has served their complete sentence, thus it differs from mandatory parole in that people on mandatory parole are still subject to supervision in the community. The key issue with prisoner reentry is whether or not the formerly incarcerated person is able to integrate back into society and avoid reoffending.

Recidivism is the "actual occurrence and likelihood that someone will reoffend." In an ideal world, recidivism would be very low or non-existent— we would like all people punished to learn from their mistake and live a healthy, positive, and productive life. In reality, recidivism is a real concern. Research shows that within three years of being released, 67 percent of offenders commit another crime and are re-arrested. Within five years more than three-quarters of offenders recidivate. More than one-third (36 percent) of offenders who get released are re-arrested within the first six months on the outside! Whether the individual committed a property, violent, sex, or drug crime seems not to matter. In America, many criminals get punished, get out, and get caught breaking the law again. This cycle of offending and incarceration is concerning and contributes to America's world leading correctional population.

Research also demonstrates that offenders re-offend regardless of whether they spent time in a rehabilitative environment or a more punitive one. There are numerous reasons for this. Ex-convicts struggle finding employment post-incarceration because they often lack a decent work history, have low educational attainment, and are viewed by employers as untrustworthy. Not being able to find a job also impacts an ex-convict's ability to secure stable housing. Thus, ex-offenders are in many ways set up to fail when they emerge from prison. It is no surprise that many revert to criminal behavior, including theft, drug use, and violence.

We also know that those prisoners who do successfully reintegrate into normal society are able to do so when their personal deficits have been adequately addressed. Most offenders have little or no formal education, for instance. Many more have few useful work skills. Others suffer from learning, substance abuse, cognitive, behavioral, emotional, and psychological issues. When correctional programs and staff work with offenders to fix or improve these problems— through education, therapy, substance abuse treatment, job placement, skill building, and other practices—the offenders are much more likely to have success reentering society. In sum, it is important that correctional programs and systems pay as much attention to the reentry aspect of incarceration as they do the punishment phase, in order to improve communities and reduce America's correctional population.

BOX 7.2: CONSIDER THIS . . .

The lifelong impact of a criminal record and incarceration

It is easy enough for most people to grasp the awful implications of being incarcerated: living each and every day inside a small concrete and steel cell, eating mediocre food, having every part of one's entire life regimented and controlled up to and including when you can bathe, exercise, and even see the sun and the sky. Just thinking about what it would be like to be incarcerated is enough to keep most people from committing a crime. Yet, few people have a solid grasp of the long-term impacts of incarceration.

In America, there is a strong belief that "if you do the crime, you should do the time." Punishment for rule violation is widely considered fair and just. For that reason, courts sentence hundreds of thousands of people to terms of incarceration each year (not to mention those people given other "non-custodial" sentences). However, attached to the notion that people who engage in wrongdoing should be punished is the implicit assumption that once you serve your punishment you will have paid your debt to society. Ostensibly, this means that you should not keep getting punished for the same thing for the rest of your life. In reality, however, this is exactly what occurs.

To begin with, simply having a criminal record, whether you served time in jail or prison or not, can close off many opportunities. A criminal record can keep you from getting a job because many employers are hesitant to hire someone with a checkered past (especially if you committed theft or a violent crime). Indeed, some entire career fields will forever be off-limits if you have a felony conviction (like childcare, teaching, and many public service careers). Buying a home or going to college may be impossible, because many loan and financing programs, including the Federal Student Loan program, are not available to people with felony convictions, including for things like drug possession. Accessing state and federal social welfare programs, things like food stamps, Medicaid, and public housing, are also likely to be off limits to someone with a criminal record. In many places, a felony conviction keeps you from being able to own a gun. And, in 14 states, a felony conviction can keep you from voting in a national election for the rest of your life (this is called felony voter disenfranchisement). Due to the racial dynamics of mass incarceration, this means that in some states, like Florida, one in four adult African Americans is permanently disenfranchised.[89]

Now, imagine you not only have a criminal record, but also served time behind bars. Data show the vast majority of criminal offenders are young when they are first convicted, in their late teens through their 20s. Let's think about the long-term implications of getting incarcerated as a young person. If you get put away for five, ten, fifteen or twenty years at age 20, then you miss out on a time in life when most other young people are going to college, gaining work experience and starting careers, finding their partners and beginning their families, buying their first home, saving money, etc. Despite how hard we might try, we cannot get back time that has already gone by.

Thus, it is important that you consider the true reality of running afoul of the law. Criminal convictions and punishments are not one-off events; it is a myth that you serve your time and then reenter society with a clean slate. Some people, no matter how hard they try, can never outrun their criminal past despite their best intentions and desires to do so. For far too many Americans, a conviction for something as minor as possession of crack-cocaine or marijuana results in a life-long punishment.

Solitary confinement, wrongful imprisonment, and the death penalty

Solitary confinement

Solitary confinement, wrongful imprisonment, and the death penalty are three of the most controversial issues in contemporary American corrections. Around the country, civil rights and non-profit advocacy groups, politicians, correctional officials, and the public are debating these topics.

Our knowledge of solitary confinement's effects on the human mind and body reveal that it is, in many ways, a modern corporal punishment. Keep in mind that solitary confinement has a long history in America dating back to the Pennsylvania system of corrections. However, even in the 1800s correctional practitioners at Auburn State Prison in New York noted that solitary

Image 7.20 *A solitary confinement cell known all as "the bing," at New York's Rikers Island jail. Inmates are often confined in these cells for 23 hours a day and are denied interactions with other people. They may even have reading materials and other sources of stimulation taken away. Solitary confinement is never a punishment bestowed following trial; it is an administrative punishment, which means there is little or no oversight of its use.*

Bebeto Matthews/AP/Press Association Images

confinement seemed to produce detrimental effects and limited positive gains. As American corrections continued progressing through the 1870 National Prison Congress, rehabilitation emerged as the guiding punishment philosophy. Solitary confinement was considered antithetical to the rehabilitative mission. This belief lasted through the 1970s and the **Prisoner Rights Movement**, which utilized 8th Amendment arguments against "cruel and unusual" punishments to improve conditions and treatment in many American correctional facilities. Then, as the 1980s ushered in a new socio-political ideology, criminal justice system policies and practices changed. Retribution and deterrence through harsh punishment reemerged. Solitary confinement came back into style.

Today, solitary confinement is often referred to by the more innocuous title of "administrative segregation" or ad-seg. Nevertheless, its basic premise is the same: confine inmates by themselves for up to 23 hours per day in small cells, often without windows. Inmates in ad-seg are deprived most human contact; they are deprived of reading materials; clocks and their visitation, canteen and other privileges are curtailed or completely cut off. Those states and correctional administrators who make extensive use of solitary confinement argue it is necessary to punish certain offenders for violating prison rules or committing violence against other inmates and staff. Many believe it is useful for encouraging offenders to turn over a new leaf and is, thus, a rehabilitative technique—an idea pioneered by Sir Walter Crofton in the Irish Prison System.

The problem with solitary confinement is that it is used far too often for far too long to deal with inmates who often suffer from mental illness or whose only offense was not being 100 percent compliant with prison staff. In some cases, inmates have been kept in solitary confinement for 10 or 20 years straight. We know from research that even short-term solitary confinement, even just a day, can initiate a process of physical and mental decay that may be irreversible (see Box 7.3 for more).

The new executive director of Colorado's prison system, Rick Raemisch, voluntarily experienced solitary confinement for 20 hours after the man he replaced, Tom Clements, was shot and killed at his home by an inmate recently released from solitary confinement.[90] Within hours of being put in a solitary cell, Director Raemisch admitted he began feeling "twitchy" and "paranoid."[91]

Sarah Shourd was held as a political prisoner in Iran for 14 months. The entire time, 24 hours per day, she was kept in solitary confinement. She described her experience in an opinion column in the *New York Times:*

> After two months with next to no human contact, my mind began to slip. Some days, I heard phantom footsteps coming down the hall. I spent large portions of my days crouched down on all fours by a small slit in the door, listening. In the periphery of my vision, I began to see flashing lights, only to jerk my head around to find that nothing was there. More than once, I beat at the walls until my knuckles bled and cried myself into a state of exhaustion. At one point, I heard someone screaming, and it wasn't until I felt the hands of one of the friendlier guards on my face, trying to revive me, that I realized the screams were my own.[92]

As a result of Chief Raemisch's and Sarah Shourd's widely published experiences and the mounting research evidence, some states, like New York and Colorado, have begun to abandon the use of solitary confinement altogether. In other states, prisoners are suing state correctional officials for violating their 8th Amendment protection against cruel and unusual punishment. Sarah Shourd aptly summarized the root of their argument when she said: "you don't have to beat someone to inflict pain and suffering."[93]

Wrongful imprisonment

The issue of wrongful imprisonment is also important to consider. The idea of punishing a person (adult or juvenile) for a crime they did not commit—including subjecting them to solitary confinement or death—runs counter to the ideas of fairness and equality that form the foundation of the American criminal justice system. We know that innocent people have been convicted of crimes they did not commit. In fact, some cases, like that of the Central Park Five, have garnered international attention.

According to The Innocence Project,[94] which works to free people who have been wrongly convicted of crimes through the use of advanced DNA testing

BOX 7.3: CONNECTING RESEARCH TO PRACTICE

The toll of solitary confinement

On February 23, 2014, the *New York Times* opinion section published a column called "My Night in Solitary."[95] The author of the column described how, during an experiment that lasted just under 24 hours, he began to feel the negative physical, psychological, and emotional toll that solitary confinement can produce on the human mind, body, and spirit. What made the opinion column unique and powerful was that it was written by Colorado's newly appointed Executive Director of Corrections, who concluded he would work diligently to reform and significantly limit the state's use of solitary confinement (called "administrative segregation").

Solitary confinement may be a punishment worse than death. Typically, inmates in solitary confinement are cut-off completely from the world around them and all human contact. Research and interviews with inmates have revealed that emotional and psychological damage can begin to accrue over short periods of time. Over extended periods—some inmates have been isolated in solitary confinement for over twenty years[96,97]—solitary confinement can produce serious and irreversible mental, emotional, and physical harm. Among the findings of various studies about solitary confinement's short and long term impacts on inmates are the following: anxiety, nervousness, headaches, insomnia, nightmares, nervous breakdowns, confusion, oversensitivity to stimuli, anger and mood swings, social withdrawal, hallucinations, depression, and suicidal ideation. Utilizing a punishment that produces these effects is clearly counterproductive to the idea of "corrections." What is worse is that many inmates are put in solitary and then released into society with no effort made to treat these issues.

Research into the effects of solitary confinement has been vital in raising awareness of the toll solitary confinement exacts on the inmates and has been vital in helping reform the use of solitary confinement in state and federal correctional institutions. First-hand accounts by people like Colorado's Executive Director of Corrections Rick Raemisch and former political prisoner Sarah Shourd about what living in solitary confinement is like, coupled with the work of advocacy groups like Solitary Watch, the ACLU, the National Religious Campaign Against Torture, and the Center for Constitutional Rights has further shifted the discussion about the constitutionality and humanity of solitary confinement.

and other legal means, over 330 people have been exonerated (found to have been wrongfully convicted) since 1989.

That means that, at a minimum, 329 people have been locked up in America despite not having anything to do with the crime they were accused of. Of course, we only know these 329 people were innocent thanks to advanced technologies and the dedication of professionals who believed in their innocence. What is especially frightening is that 20 of the convicted persons were on death row awaiting execution when they were freed. On average, those individuals known to be innocent lost 14 years of their lives behind bars. And, because

Image 7.21
In 1989, five Black and Hispanic teenage boys were arrested, interrogated, and eventually convicted for raping a white woman. Years later, the actual rapist who was serving time in prison confessed to the crime.

Bebeto Matthews/ AP/Press Association Images

most were young at the time of their conviction—in their 20s and 30s—they missed out on opportunities to get an education, begin a career, and start a family, all things most of us take for granted.

We know several things about the causes of wrongful convictions and imprisonment.

First, we know that race of the alleged suspect plays a big role. Of the 329 people freed since 1989, nearly 70 percent have been people of color (205 black, 24 Hispanic or Latino). In some places, law enforcement and prosecuting attorneys have far too quickly and enthusiastically determined that a person of color—any person of color—is the most likely suspect when a crime is committed.

Over the years, police corruption scandals have revealed that police officers in cities like New York,[98] Los Angeles,[99] Chicago,[100] and Philadelphia[101,102] have coerced suspects into signing false confessions, pressured witnesses into making incorrect suspect identifications, planted evidence to implicate a person they knew was innocent, and more. Other causes leading to wrongful imprisonment include inaccurate or deceitful informant testimony, faulty forensic evidence, and eyewitness misidentification.

Wrongful imprisonment is the sort of issue that most people easily recognize as one needing a swift and speedy response. Too often, however, state officials are reluctant to admit that any prosecutorial mistakes were made. Some note that the "innocent" person pled guilty and that no truly innocent person would ever do that. Indeed, 31 of the 329 people freed since 1989 pled guilty to the crime(s) they were charged with. However, research evidence shows that most people who confess to some crime they did not commit do so after being questioned for hours on end, without legal counsel present. Many report feeling like saying they "did it" seemed like their best option in the moment and others report that being told that if they confessed everything would be all right. The psychology of false confessions is complicated, yet also simple: most people at some point in their life have admitted to doing something they didn't actually do. The key difference is that fudging the truth in most cases does not result in one's freedom being taken away.

When people are proven to be innocent state officials can publicly proclaim their innocence. They can also provide short-term support in the immediate aftermath of a prisoner's release: housing, transportation, medical care, and money for food. Keep in mind that even though a person may be legally innocent, the social stigma of incarceration and the effects of prisonization, may keep them from successfully reintegrating back into society. Thirty U.S. states currently have laws that provide financial compensation to wrongfully convicted and imprisoned people.

But what price tag do you place on human life? How much should each year lost be worth? What do people who fell victim to the criminal justice system deserve to get? Those are not easy questions to answer, though most people would likely agree that the wrongfully imprisoned should receive a pretty hefty payday for their troubles. At this point, however, most states only value each year lost to wrongful imprisonment at around $50,000 to $60,000.[103] This means that in most states someone incarcerated 20 years for a crime they did not commit would receive, at most, $1.2 million *before* taxes.

The death penalty

In the last section we discussed wrongful imprisonment. In the history of American corrections, it is fairly safe to assume that far more than 329 people have been wrongfully convicted and imprisoned for crimes they did not commit. Undoubtedly, some people have also been executed despite being innocent. Most European countries no longer utilize the death penalty for a variety of legal and moral reasons. In other countries around the world, the death penalty is used to punish seemingly harmless acts that have been defined as "crimes," including practicing sorcery in Saudi Arabia, drug smuggling in Indonesia, and homosexuality in several African countries like Mauritania and Sudan.[104]

America falls somewhere between those two poles, vacillating between abolition and use, though only very serious crimes, like first degree murder, felony murder, and treason are typically eligible for the death penalty. America is also unique in that in capital cases—those where the death penalty may be applied—the jury, not the judge, must decide to sentence the convicted offender to death. The recent trial of Boston marathon bomber Dhozkar Tsarnaev[105] illustrates this process, which is a reversal of usual sentencing procedures and is intended to ensure balance and fairness in the application of the death penalty.

In the long history of the death penalty in America, prisoners have been hanged, shot, gassed, electrocuted, and, since 1977, injected with a lethal cocktail of drugs in an attempt to make execution more "humane." Over time, 19 states have decided that the death penalty is, in fact, not humane, including most recently Maryland and Connecticut, which got rid of the death penalty in 2013 and 2012 respectively.

Still, the vast majority of American states and the federal prison system allow the death penalty. Currently, over 3,000 people are on death row in America, a 497 percent increase since 1968 when only 517 people were awaiting execution.[106] America's use of the death penalty parallels that of China, Iran, and Vietnam.

The best way to describe the death penalty in America is "manic." Throughout history, as correctional philosophies and emphases have changed, so has use and acceptance of the death penalty. Since the 1980s, the death penalty experienced a resurgence of sorts as getting tough on crime and punishing offenders more harshly gained support. At various points in time, the death penalty has also been challenged on legal grounds as being "cruel and unusual."

Table 7.8 Important death penalty cases

Case	Year	Issue	Summary of Supreme Court actions
Furman v. Georgia (408 U.S. 238)	1972	Challenges the constitutionality of the death penalty under the 8th Amendment protection against cruel and unusual punishment by specifically challenging the wording of Georgia's death penalty statute.	Suspends all use of the death penalty in the United States until 1977, at which time the issue would be reconsidered. States immediately begin drafting new statutes.
Gregg v. Georgia (428 U.S. 153)	1976	Constitutionality of the death penalty	Finds that newly revised death penalty statutes in various states whose statutes were previously found to be unconstitutional are now constitutional. Also finds that the death penalty, as a general punishment, is constitutional and not a violation of the 8th Amendment.
Coker v. Georgia (433 U.S. 584)	1977	Use of the death penalty in rape cases	Bans use of the death penalty when the adult victim of a rape was not killed during the crime
Ford v. Wainwright (477 U.S. 399)	1986	Use of death penalty against people with mental illness	Bans the execution of people who are "insane" and requires adversarial process for determining mental competency
Thompson v. Oklahoma (487 U.S. 815)	1988	Use of death penalty against juveniles	Applying the death penalty to anyone age 15 or younger when they committed their crimes is unconstitutional
Atkins v. Virginia (536 U.S. 304)	2003	Use of death penalty against people with mental illness	Applying the death penalty to people with mental retardation is a violation of the 8th Amendment protection against cruel and unusual punishment and is therefore unconstitutional
Roper v. Simmons (543 U.S. 551)	2005	Use of death penalty against people under age 18	Applying the death penalty to people who committed their crime while under the age of 18 is cruel and unusual punishment and unconstitutional

Throughout the 1960s and 1970s the U.S. Supreme court considered the death penalty no less than seven times. In what became the landmark case *Furman v. Georgia* (1972)[107] the Supreme Court banned the use of the death penalty in America until 1977 due to what it considered the unconstitutionality of existing state death penalty statutes. This encouraged states to re-draft their death penalty statutes, rather than abolish the death penalty altogether. In *Gregg v. Georgia* (1976),[108] a second landmark case, the Supreme Court ruled the new state death penalty statutes were constitutional and it lifted the moratorium on the death penalty. Immediately thereafter, on January 17, 1977, Gary Gilmore was killed by firing squad in Utah. Then, in December 1982, Charlie Brooks became the first person ever executed by lethal injection in Texas.

Since the 1980s, the Supreme Court has been asked to further define the scope of the death penalty and when it can and cannot be applied. The most important cases are summarized in Table 7.8. It is important to realize that the death penalty continues to attract the attention of legal scholars with important cases occurring in 2002,[109] 2005,[110] and 2007.[111] Two of those cases dealt with using the death penalty on the mentally ill and one banned use of the death penalty for anyone under age 18 (see Box 7.4).

The death penalty is important to discuss because it draws together other pressing issues in corrections. For example, Illinois abolished the death penalty in 2011 after releasing 13 "innocent" people from death row in the early 2000s while also executing 12 "guilty" people.[112] Most recently, Alfred Dewayne Brown was released in June 2015 from death row in Harris County, Texas, after the "Texas Court of Criminal Appeals overturned . . . his conviction . . . because prosecutors withheld a phone record that supported his alibi."[113]

A key question for you to consider in light of these facts is: should the death penalty ever be utilized if we cannot be absolutely certain that (1) innocent people will not be executed, or (2) that prosecutors will not cut corners or withhold potentially exonerating evidence?

Moreover, there are countless examples of executions going wrong, leading to horrific and painful deaths for the offender. Even the more "humane" lethal injection method has not always been humane. In 2009, it took executioners in Ohio hours to find a vein in Romell Broom's arms where he could be injected; over 18 attempts were made until the executioners gave up;[114] Mr. Broom remains on death row in Ohio while the Ohio Supreme Court considers the constitutionality of attempting to execute him a second time.[115] In 2014, Clayton D. Lockett's botched execution in Oklahoma made national head-lines.[116] It took executioners in his case one hour to find a usable vein for the injection and then another 43 minutes for him to die, during which time he was incorrectly pronounced to be unconscious.[117] He died visibly in pain, writhing on the gurney. Thus, another important question to consider in light of every American's 8th Amendment protection against cruel and un-usual punishment is: should the death penalty be used if it causes pain to the offender?

BOX 7.4: JUVENILES AND THE DEATH PENALTY

George Stinney Jr. holds the infamous title of youngest person executed in the United States since 1900. Stinney, an African-American, was 14 years old when he was executed in South Carolina in 1944 for killing two white girls following "a one-day trial and 10-minute jury deliberation."[118]

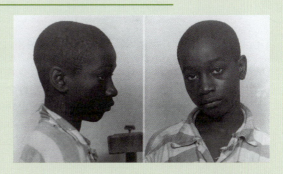

Box 7.4 Image 1 *George Stinney mugshot, 1944*
Wikimedia Commons/State of South Carolina

Since 1944, Stinney's case has attracted attention from around the world. Many argue it illustrates the dire consequences that result when a criminal justice system fails to uphold the principles of fairness, equality, and justice. Others highlight how Stinney's arrest by white law enforcement officers and his subsequent conviction and sentencing by an all-white jury reflect long-standing issues of racism and discrimination with the criminal justice system. Lastly, some hold up Stinney's execution as a prime example for why the death penalty should be abolished.

Recent developments lend support to all of the positions above. In December 2014, a South Carolina appellate judge exonerated George Stinney Jr., vacating his murder conviction after more than 70 years.[119,120]

In closing, it is important to recognize that George Stinney Jr. was not the only juvenile executed in America. According to the Death Penalty Information Center,[121] 22 juveniles were executed between 1973 and 2003, including 13 in Texas alone. The 2005 U.S. Supreme Court ruling in *Roper v. Simmons* finally outlawed the use of the death penalty against anyone who committed their crime before the age of 18.

It is also important to consider the death penalty in light of race. Just as blacks and Hispanics are overrepresented as inmates they are also over-represented on death row across America. In one review of all the death penalty studies conducted, it was found that the race of the victim significantly influenced whether the jury assessed the death penalty. People who murder white people were far more likely to receive a death sentence than people who murder blacks or Hispanics.[122] There have only been 31 executions of white defendants when the victim was black, yet over 290 executions of black defendants when the victim was white.[123]

More recently, studies from around the country conducted between 2005–2014 have found that jurors in death penalty cases are anywhere from three to four times more likely to assess the death penalty when the victim was white than when the victim was a person of color, no matter how similar the cases were in all other regards.[124] Thus, you might consider: should the death penalty be utilized if it is not utilized fairly and equally?

BOX 7.5: CONNECTING THEORY TO PRACTICE

Does the death penalty actually deter crime?

One of the most prominent arguments in support of the death penalty is that it helps deter, or prevent, more violent or serious crime from occurring. The logic underling this argument stems from philosopher Jeremy Bentham's deterrence theory. Deterrence theory assumes that human beings are rational, calculating decision makers who weigh the costs and benefits of acting before doing so. From this perspective, punishment can influence the decision making process by elevating the costs of criminal behavior or action well above the rewards.

Thus, very harsh punishments like long prison sentences, corporal punishments, solitary confinement, and the death penalty are believed by some to deter not just the individual wrongdoer, but all other potential wrongdoers. Proponents of the death penalty in particular argue it not only serves as a specific deterrent because it incapacitates (i.e., kills) the individual criminal, but that it also serves the larger purpose of being a general deterrent by showing the rest of society that if they commit the same act they too could be executed.

So, does the death penalty actually deter crime? Research data indicate it does not, or that, at most, its deterrent effect is minimal.

For example, if the death penalty were truly a deterrent to the commission of very serious crimes, like homicide, we would expect that places with the highest number of executions and greatest use of the death penalty would have lower overall violent crime and homicide rates. In fact, what we find in America is that the opposite appears true. We consistently find that murder rates are highest in the South, where 80% of all executions take place and that murder rates are lowest in the Northeast, where the death penalty is used least often.[125]

Moreover, the very nature of the act of criminal homicide seems to contradict the notion of deterrence through the death penalty. If someone is truly intent on committing a first-degree, premeditated homicide of the sort that could result in a death sentence, the threat of the death penalty is not likely to dissuade them.

Thus, in one survey,[126] 88 percent of criminologists said that existing research does not support the idea that the death penalty deters crime. A 2009 survey of police chiefs[127] from across America indicated that out of numerous options for deterring crime, the vast majority felt the death penalty was the least effective. Even 62% of ordinary non-expert U.S. citizens,[128] when surveyed about the death penalty and its deterrent value, said they didn't think it was much of a deterrent at all. Finally, if the death penalty were truly a deterrent to crime commission we would expect that in places where the death penalty is used most often, murder rates would be lowest since the death penalty would supposedly convince people not to commit such a crime.

While the U.S. continues to utilize the death penalty at far higher rates than most other comparable nations, there is increasingly recognition among experts, policy analysts, police

Chiefs and even the public that the death penalty is not a good deterrent to crime. Thus, in 2012 the National Research Council advised states that deterrence "should not factor into policy decisions" about whether to keep or abolish the death penalty.[129] Therefore it is worth asking: if the death penalty does not truly deter crime, and if most people do not believe it can deter crime, what purpose does it serve other than fulfilling a desire for vengeance? *What do you think?*

Lastly, it is worth pondering the notion that the death penalty helps prevent crime through deterrence. At issue is whether people will be less likely to commit serious crimes, like criminal homicide, if they know they could be sentenced to death if they get caught and convicted. On this point we also have some telling data, as Box 7.5 demonstrates.

THE FUTURE OF AMERICAN CORRECTIONS

Our job in corrections is to protect the community, not to release people who are worse than they were when they came in.

Rick Raemisch[130]

In discussing contemporary American corrections, correctional system researcher and reform advocate Marc Mauer wrote:[131] "We have embarked on a great social experiment. No other society in human history has ever imprisoned so many of its own citizens for the purpose of crime control." Mr. Mauer is right: America incarcerates more people than any other nation in the world, including China and India, which have populations in the billions. Many experts agree that America's "great social experiment" with mass incarceration has demonstrated one thing very clearly: incarceration alone does not solve crime problems[132] and may, in fact, make them worse.

How? First, by incarcerating large numbers of people, especially people of color, and saddling them with a criminal record, we close off many legitimate opportunities for them to be successful. A criminal record and history of incarceration function like a non-curable disease—no matter where you go or what you do, they follow you around, keeping you from being all you could be. Arrest, conviction, and incarceration affect every aspect of life: education, employment, housing, access to loans and credit, even one's ability to vote or receive public assistance are negatively impacted. This feeds a cycle that traps people for life. An entire generation of Americans—young black and Hispanic men in particular—have grown up and been caught in this cycle. Their children, if they have any, are likely to face similar struggles as well. Rather than incarceration curing crime in America, it has helped to ensure that crime continues to be a problem, especially in some neighborhoods and regions of this country.

But what does the future hold? How might American corrections change for the better? As Dr. Martin Luther King Jr. and other civil rights crusaders pointed out long ago, true change can only occur when people are willing to stand up repeatedly and demand change. It is possible that a popular social movement around reforming the correctional system could occur. But it is unlikely to mirror the size and magnitude of the civil rights or other historical social movements. Still, if people speak up and demand change, politicians may listen (as was the case with crack-cocaine sentencing). Popular demand for

BOX 7.6: CRIME IN GLOBAL PERSPECTIVE

The future of corrections?

Increasingly people in the U.S.—from ordinary citizens to politicians in the highest offices—are asking critical questions about the current state, and future, of the American correctional system. This is a positive, progressive trend. So, what might the future of corrections look like?

For starters, many progressive correctional reformers argue that the American correctional system must begin diverting low-level, non-violent offenders from terms of incarceration.[133] This will entail expanding the use of alternative sentences,[134] uniquely crafted to address the competing needs of punishment, rehabilitation and reintegration. In general, the sentiment increasingly seems to be that incarceration should be a last, not a first, resort for dealing with criminal offenders.

In the future, the American correctional system should also try to adopt many of the progressive changes already instituted in a host of European countries. In nations like Norway and Sweden, prisoners are treated humanely—like people—rather than like some disposable or expendable entity. Unsurprisingly, use of the death penalty and solitary confinement is rare.

The logic, exemplified in places like Norway's Halden Prison,[135] is to minimize the pains of imprisonment and reduce the impact of the prisonization process, while providing a wide range of therapeutic and rehabilitative services aimed at helping the convicted offender. At Halden Prison inmates are able to sleep on comfortable beds, rather than concrete or steel bunks, access private showers, and even cook their own meals. While this might seem the opposite of punishment from an American perspective, the strategies employed at Halden Prison and elsewhere throughout Europe signal the ascendance of an enlightened approach to crime and criminality.

In closing, we might consider whether we, in America, want our prisons and jails to be simply harsh, cold warehouses for holding society's outcasts and rule-breakers, or whether a vast reimagining of the purpose and nature of corrections—along the lines of that which is taking place in Europe—might yield more benefits, and positive results, in the long term.

action and political will do not always go hand in hand, but they present the two most viable ways for serious changes to occur within the correctional system.

What types of change might be beneficial in America? Reforming our sentencing structures is one starting point. Locking up people for drug use, for example, has been one of the key factors leading to over-incarceration in America. Experiments with drug decriminalization in other countries, like Portugal, have shown that decriminalizing drugs has few negative side effects and many benefits, such as encouraging more drug users to seek treatment. Ensuring that sentences are more fair across the board, and equally applied, are two other key changes. Finally, placing greater emphasis and directing more resources toward rehabilitative programs and services, including mental health and substance abuse treatment, job skill building, and education, are important. Equally important is addressing the structural causes of crime in our neighborhoods and communities—too few jobs, poor schools, and lack of services.

Our European friends are leading the way on all these fronts—emphasizing rehabilitation and compassion. They are deescalating their War on Crime and deemphasizing the notions of combat and victory so central to waging such a war. In warfare, there are always opposing forces. There is always an enemy. When we apply the language of war to something like crime, we inadvertently label an entire group of people, our people, American citizens, the "enemy." Given that fact, it is not surprising that for the last thirty years we have treated criminals like enemy combatants. That strategy has not worked. As a student of criminology you now know why it has not worked. You also have a solid grasp of what could work. We hope you take your knowledge, educate others, and promote positive social change in whatever way possible.

SUMMARY

In this chapter, we introduced the topic of American corrections, focusing on jails, prisons, and alternative corrections (recall the key difference between jail and prison incarceration is the duration of time one spends in either place; jail incarceration is for one year or less, while prison incarceration is for one year or more). Our discussion was substantial and wide-ranging, beginning with a brief look at mass incarceration, the term used to characterize America's correctional philosophy and system.

The roots of mass incarceration lie in policy changes adopted in the late 1970s and throughout the 1980s and 1990s, including waging a War on Drugs, reforming sentencing guidelines to remove discretion from judges, creating mandatory minimum sentences, the abolition of Federal parole and more. Mass incarceration is not a positive thing—nor is the fact that America incarcerates more people than any other nation something to be proud of.

When America embarked down the path of mass incarceration, it moved away from the rehabilitative philosophy and medical/treatment model of corrections. Mass incarceration and rehabilitation do not align. Indeed, mass incarceration is closely linked to a retribution and incapacitory philosophy, in addition to a tough-on-crime deterrence approach to handling criminal law violations. Importantly, as more people and politicians have begun to realize that mass incarceration is not a solution to crime, more and more states have adopted elements of the rehabilitative focus while also creating more community corrections programs.

This slow shift back toward rehabilitation and alternative sentences is important, particularly when one looks at who is most likely to be the recipient of those long, harsh prison terms. The "average" offender is a young person of color, often with little education, who grew up and lived in a poor community. Young black men in particular are vastly overrepresented in our correctional populations. Hispanic men, women, and black women are also overrepresented in comparison to whites. This raises serious questions about how our criminal justice system functions, and where and how we are applying our criminal justice system resources.

We have pondered what the future of American corrections could look like and how it could get there. The information in this chapter represents a very brief primer on this important topic. There are many issues and topics we could not discuss. We hope you will seek out and explore the world of corrections in more detail on your own and through the numerous online resources we have provided.

CRITICAL THINKING QUESTIONS

1. Why do you think the U.S. incarcerates so many people? How do you feel about this? What are two solutions to this issue in your opinion?

2. Do you believe that a person can be deterred from committing crime? In what situations do you think deterrence works best and where is it least likely to succeed?

3. How do we address the issue of racial disparities in our correctional populations? Is there a simple fix? If not, what areas of society and/or services, programs need to be addressed in order to ensure that black and Hispanic Americans are not being overrepresented in America's prisons and jails?

4. You've learned there are serious lifelong impacts of having a criminal record and even more substantial impacts from having been incarcerated. What can we do as communities, states, and a society to ensure that people who have been punished for a crime and return to society hoping to succeed are not confronted with insurmountable obstacles to success and punished for the rest of their lives?

NOTES

1   Bureau of Justice Statistics. 2013. Prisoners in the United States, 2013. Retrieved from http://www.bjs.gov/content/pub/pdf/p13.pdf.

2   International Centre for Prison Studies. 2015. Highest to Lowest Prison Population Rate. Retrieved from http://www.prisonstudies.org/highest-to-lowest/prison_population_rate?field_region_taxonomy_tid=All.

3   Prison Policy Institute. 2012. States of Incarceration: The Global Context. May 13. Retrieved from http://www.prisonpolicy.org/global/.

4   Garland, D. 2001. The Meaning of Mass Imprisonment. *Mass Imprisonment: Social Causes and Consequences.* Thousand Oaks, CA: SAGE.

5   The Sentencing Project. 2013. Trends in U.S. Corrections. Retrieved from http://sentencingproject.org/doc/publications/inc_Trends_in_Corrections_Fact_sheet.pdf.

6   Mauer, M. 2001. The Causes and Consequences of Prison Growth in the United States. In D. Garland (ed.), *Mass Imprisonment: Social Causes and Consequences.* Thousand Oaks, CA: SAGE, pp. 4–14.

7   Rothman, D.J. 1971. *The Discovery of the Asylum. Social Order and Disorder in the New Republic.* Boston, MA: Little and Brown.

8   National Advisory Commission on Criminal Justice Standards and Goals. 1973. The Criminal Justice Standards and Goals of the National Advisory Commission Digested from a Strategy to Reduce Crime. Complete report available at https://www.ncjrs.gov/pdffiles1/Digitization/54466NCJRS.pdf.

9a   Hale, B. 2009. The 222 Victorian Crimes that Would Get a Man Hanged. *The Daily Mail*, Aug. 2. Retrieved from http://www.dailymail.co.uk/news/article-1203828/The-222-Victorian-crimes-man-hanged.html.

9b   Wilson, J.Q. 1976. *Thinking About Crime.* New York: Basic Books.

10   For example, many countries and states are utilizing various high-tech crime detection and surveillance technologies, in addition to building architecture and environmental design strategies to deter or reduce crime. In some places, like Washington, D.C., and Camden, NJ, these changes have arguably reduced crime, possibly due to a deterrent effect. However, research from England, which has made extensive use of CCTV surveillance cameras to reduce crime, shows that deterrence may not be so easily achieved. Deterrence theory has also informed related ideas like Routine Activities theory (discussed in chapter 8), which in turn has informed the development of self-defense, sexual assault awareness, and other crime prevention programs.

11   Martinson, R. 1974. What works? Questions and Answers about Prison Reform. *The Public Interest* 35: 22–54.

12   Correctional Populations in the United States, 2013. Dec. 2014. U.S. Department of Justice, Office of Justice Programs, Bureau of Justice Statistics. NCJ 248479.

13   Ibid.

14   Ibid.

15   Ibid.

16   Cook County, IL Sheriff's Office. 2015. Office of Mental Health Police and Advocacy. Retrieved from http://www.cookcountysheriff.org/MentalHealth/MentalHealth_main.html.

17   See also: Ford, M. 2015. America's Largest Mental Health Hospital is a Jail. *The Atlantic Monthly*, June 8. Retrieved from http://www.theatlantic.com/politics/archive/2015/06/americas-largest-mental-hospital-is-a-jail/395012/.

18   Bureau of Justice Statistics. 2006. Medical Problems of Jail Inmates. U.S. Department of Justice, Office of Justice Programs. NCJ 210696. Retrieved from http://www.bjs.gov/content/pub/pdf/mpji.pdf.

19   Bureau of Justice Statistics. 2014. Mortality in Local Jails and State Prisons, 2000–2012. U.S. Department of Justice, Office of Justice Programs. NCJ 247448. Retrieved from http://www.bjs.gov/content/pub/pdf/mljsp0012st.pdf.

20   Bureau of Justice Statistics. 2005. Substance Dependence, Abuse, and Treatment of Jail Inmates, 2002. U.S. Department of Justice, Office of Justice Programs. Retrieved from http://www.bjs.gov/content/pub/pdf/sdatji02.pdf.

21   Casa Columbia. February 2010. Behind Bars II: Substance Abuse and America's Prison Population. Retrieved from http://www.casacolumbia.org/addiction-research/reports/substance-abuse-prison-system-2010.

22   Rennison, C.M. and Dodge, M. 2015. *Introduction to Criminal Justice: Systems, Diversity, and Change.* Thousand Oaks, CA: SAGE.

23   Correctional Populations in the United States, 2013. U.S. Department of Justice, Office of Justice Programs, Bureau of Justice Statistics Dec. 2014. NCJ 248479.

24   U.S. Bureau of Justice Statistics. 2014. Prisoners in 2013. U.S. Department of Justice, Office of Justice Programs. Retrieved from http://www.bjs.gov/content/pub/pdf/p13.pdf.

25   Ibid.

26   Ibid.

27   Federal Bureau of Prisons. 2014. History. Retrieved from http://www.bop.gov/about/history/.

28   Private Prisons and Jails in the United States. 2014. Findlaw. Retrieved from http://civilrights.findlaw.com/other-constitutional-rights/private-jails-in-the-united-states.html.

29   Fitzsimmons, M. 2013. Punishment and Profits: A Brief History of Private Prisons in Oklahoma. *Oklahoma Policy Institute.* Retrieved from http://okpolicy.org/punishment-and-profits-a-brief-history-of-private-prisons-in-oklahoma.

30   Zimmerman, J. 1951. The Penal Reform Movement in the South During the Progressive Era, 1890–1917. *The Journal of Southern History,* 17(4): 462–492.

31   Mancini, M.J. 1978. Race, Economics and the Abandonment of Convict Leasing. *The Journal of Negro History,* 63(4): 339–352.

32   U.S. Bureau of Justice Statistics. 2014. Prisoners in 2013. U.S. Department of Justice, Office of Justice Programs. Retrieved from http://www.bjs.gov/content/pub/pdf/p13.pdf.

33   Private Prison Company Pays $8M in Back Wages. 2014. *CBS Los Angeles.* Retrieved from http://losangeles.cbslocal.com/2014/08/19/private-prison-company-pays-8m-in-back-wages/.

34   Sykes, G.M. 1958. *The Society of Captives: A Study of a Maximum Security Prison.* Princeton, NJ: Princeton University Press.

35   Goffman, E. 1961. *Asylums: Essays on the Social Situation of Mental Patients and Other Inmates.* New York: Anchor Books.

36   Ibid.

37   Clemmer, D. 1940. *The Prison Community.* Boston: Christopher.

38   Irwin, J. and Cressey, D. 1962. Thieves, Convicts, and the Inmate Subculture. *Social Problems* 54: 590–603.

39   Thomas, C.W. 1977. Theoretical Perspectives on Prisonization: A Comparison of the Importation and Deprivation Models. *Journal of Criminal Law and Criminology* 68(1): 135–145.

40   Bureau of Justice Statistics. 2014. Mortality in Local Jails and State Prisons, 2000–2012. U.S. Department of Justice, Office of Justice Programs. NCJ 247448. Retrieved from www.bjs.gov/content/pub/pdf/mljsp0012st.pdf.

41   Ibid.

42   Ibid.

43   Ibid.

44   See: Wood, G. 2014. How Gangs Took Over Prisons."*The Atlantic Monthly*, Oct. Retrieved from http://www.theatlantic.com/magazine/archive/2014/10/how-gangs-took-over-prisons/379330/.

45   Bureau of Justice Statistics. 2015. Prison Rape Elimination Act (Sexual Violence in Correctional Facilities). Retrieved from http://www.bjs.gov/index.cfm?ty=tp&tid=20.

46   The National Prison Rape Elimination Act Resource Center. 2015. Prison Rape Elimination Act. Retrieved from http://www.prearesourcecenter.org/about/prison-rape-elimination-act-prea.

47   Federal Bureau of Investigation. 2013. UCR Program Changes Definition of Rape Includes All Victims and Omits Requirement of Physical Force. U.S. Department of Justice. Retrieved from https://www.fbi.gov/about-us/cjis/ucr/crime-in-the-u.s/2013/crime-in-the-u.s.-2013/violent-crime/rape.

48   Bureau of Justice Statistics. 2014. "Sexual Victimization Reported by Adult Correctional Authorities, 2009–11." U.S. Department of Justice, Office of Justice Programs. Retrieved from http://www.bjs.gov/index.cfm?ty=pbdetail&iid=4882.

49   Ibid.

50   Bureau of Justice Statistics. 2013. Sexual Victimization in Juvenile Facilities Reported by Youth, 2012. U.S. Department of Justice, Office of Justice Programs. Retrieved from www.bjs.gov/content/pub/pdf/svjfry12.pdf.

51   Ibid.

52   U.S. Bureau of Justice Statistics. 2014. Probation and Parole in the United States 2013. U.S Department of Justice, Office of Justice Programs.

53   Ibid.

54   New York City Department of Probation and Parole. 2015. History of Probation. Retrieved from http://www.nyc.gov/html/prob/html/about/history.shtml.

55   Ibid.

56   U.S. Bureau of Justice Statistics. 2014. Probation and Parole in the United States 2013. U.S Department of Justice, Office of Justice Programs.

57   Ibid.

58   Ibid.

59   Ibid.

60   Ibid.

61   Ibid.

62   Ibid.

63   Ibid.

64   American Probation and Parole Association. 2015. History of Probation and Parole: Parole's Historical Roots. Retrieved from www.appa-net.org/eweb/Resources/PPPSW_2013/history.htm.

65   Ibid.

66   Bureau of Justice Statistics. 2015. Probation and Parole in the United States 2013. U.S. Department of Justice, Office of Justice Programs. NCJ248029. Retrieved from http://www.bjs.gov/content/pub/pdf/ppus13.pdf.

67   Ibid.

68   Ibid.

69   Ibid.

70   The Sentencing Project. 2015. Juvenile Correctional Populations. Retrieved from http://www.sentencingproject.org/map/map.cfm.

71   The Sentencing Project. 2015. Incarcerated Women. Retrieved from http://www.sentencingproject.org/doc/publications/cc_Incarcerated_Women_Factsheet_Dec2012final.pdf.

72   U.S. Bureau of Justice Statistics. 2014. Prisoners in 2013. U.S. Department of Justice, Office of Justice Programs. Retrieved from http://www.bjs.gov/content/pub/pdf/p13.pdf.

73   Bureau of Justice Statistics. 1997. Lifetime Likelihood of Going to State or Federal Prison. U.S. Department of Justice, Office of Justice Programs. NCJ 160092. Retrieved from http://bjs.gov/content/pub/pdf/Llgsfp.pdf.

74   NAACP.org. 2015. Criminal Justice Fact Sheet. Retrieved from http://www.naacp.org/pages/criminal-justice-fact-sheet.

75   *The New York Times,* 8 Feb., 1914.

76   VERA Institute of Justice. 2014. Race and Prosecution in Manhattan. Retrieved from http://www.vera.org/pubs/special/race-and-prosecution-manhattan.

77   Savitsky, D. 2009. The Problem with Plea Bargaining: Differential Subjective Decision Making as an Engine of Racial Disparity in the United States Prison System. Doctoral Dissertation, Cornell University. Retrieved from http://ecommons.cornell.edu/bit stream/1813/13836/1/Savitsky,%20Douglas.pdf.

78   Center for Constitutional Rights. 2009. Racial Disparity in NYPD Stops and Frisks. Retrieved from http://ccrjustice.org/home/get-involved/tools-resources/publications/report-racial-disparity-nypd-stop-and-frisks.

79   Bureau of Justice Statistics. 2013. Police Behavior During Traffic and Street Stops, 2011. U.S. Department of Justice, Office of Justice Programs. NCJ 242937. Retrieved from http://www.bjs.gov/content/pub/pdf/pbtss11.pdf.

80   American Civil Liberties Union. 2015. Factsheet: The NYPD Muslim Surveillance Program. Retrieved from https://www.aclu.org/factsheet-nypd-muslim-surveillance-program.

81   U.S. Department of Justice, Civil Rights Division. 2011. Maricopa County Sheriff's Office Findings Letter. December 15. Retrieved from http://www.justice.gov/crt/about/spl/documents/mcso_findletter_12–15–11.pdf.

82   NAACP. 2014. NAACP Files Legal Challenge to Arizona Racial Profiling Law. Retrieved from http://www.naacp.org/news/entry/naacp-joins-legal-challenge-to-arizona-racial-profiling-law.

83   Badger, E. 2014. The Long, Halting, Unfinished Fight to End Racial Profiling in America. *The Washington Post*, December 4. Retrieved from http://www.washingtonpost.com/blogs/wonkblog/wp/2014/12/04/the-long-halting-unfinished-fight-to-end-racial-profiling-in-america/.

84   U.S. Bureau of Justice Statistics. 2014. Prisoners in 2013. U.S. Department of Justice, Office of Justice Programs. Retrieved from http://www.bjs.gov/content/pub/pdf/p13.pdf.

85   Ibid.

86   Ibid.

87   Stohr, M.K. and Walsh, A. 2014. *Corrections: The Essentials.* Thousand Oaks, CA: SAGE, p. 194.

88   U.S. Bureau of Justice Statistics. 2014. Prisoners in 2013. U.S. Department of Justice, Office of Justice Programs. Retrieved from http://www.bjs.gov/content/pub/pdf/p13.pdf.

89   Staples, B. 2014. Florida leads the pack in Felon Disenfranchisement. *The New York Times*, Nov. 7 Retrieved from http://takingnote.blogs.nytimes.com/2014/11/07/florida-leads-the-pack-in-felon-disenfranchisement/.

90   Raemisch, R. 2014. My Night in Solitary. *The New York Times* (Opinion Section), Feb. 20.

91   Ibid.

92   Shourd, S. 2011. Tortured by Solitude. *The New York Times,* November 5.

93   Ibid.

94   The Innocence Project. 2015. Retrieved from http://www.innocenceproject.org/free-innocent.

95   Raemisch, R. 2014. My Night in Solitary. *The New York Times* (Opinion Section), Feb. 23.

96   Jennings, D. 2009. Thousands of Texas Inmates Held in Administrative Segregation —One for 24 Years. *The Dallas Morning News,* July 16.

97   Solitary Watch. 2015. How Long are People Held in Solitary? Retrieved from http://
      solitarywatch.com/facts/faq/.

98   Human Rights Watch. 1998. *Shielded from Justice: Police Brutality and Accountability
      in the United States.* Retrieved from https://www.hrw.org/legacy/reports98/police/
      toc.htm.

99   Ibid.

100   Ibid.

101   Ibid.

102   Solotaroff, P. 2015. Why is this Man Still in Jail? *Rolling Stone Magazine,*
      March 2.

103   The Innocence Project. 2015. Compensating the Wrongly Convicted. June 4.
      Retrieved from http://www.innocenceproject.org/free-innocent/improve-the-law/
      fact-sheets/compensating-the-wrongly-convicted.

104   Rupar, T. 2014. 10 Countries where Homosexuality may be Punished by Death.
      The Washington Post, Feb. 24.

105   Seelye, K.Q., Goodnough, A. Bidgood, J. 2015. Death Sentence for Boston Bomber,
      Dzhokhar Tsarnaev, Unsettles City He Tore Apart. *The New York Times*, May 16.

106   Death Penalty Information Center. 2015. Death Row Facts. Retrieved from
      http://www.deathpenaltyinfo.org.

107   *Furman v. Georgia, 408 U.S. 238* (1972).

108   *Gregg v. Georgia, 428 U.S. 153 (1976).* See 3.

109   *Atkins v. Virginia, 536 U.S. 304* (2002)

110   *Roper v. Simmons, 543 U.S. 551* (2005)

111   *Panetti v. Quarterman, 551 U.S. 930* (2007)

112   Death Penalty Information Center. 2015. http://www.deathpenaltyinfo.org.

113   Ibid.

114   Associated Press. 2014. Ohio Supreme Court to Rule on Second Execution of Romell
      Broom. *The Guardian,* June 3.

115   Ibid.

116   Eckholm, E. 2014. One Execution Botched, Oklahoma Delays the Next. *The New
      York Times*, April 29.

117   Mencimer, S. 2014. Grisly New Details Emerge in Probe of Botched Oklahoma
      Execution. *Mother Jones,* Sept. 5.

118   Reuters. 2014. Judge Overturns 1944 Conviction of George Stinney, Executed at 14
      After Three-Hour Trial.

119   Ibid.

120   Bever, L. 2014. It Took 10 Minutes to Convict 14-year-old George Stinney Jr.
      It Took 70 Years After his Execution to Exonerate him. *The Washington Post*,
      Dec. 18.

121   Death Penalty Information Center. 2015. http://www.deathpenaltyinfo.org.

122   United States General Accounting Office, Death Penalty Sentencing, February
      1990.

123   Death Penalty Information Center. 2015. Facts about the Death Penalty. Retrieved
      from http://www.deathpenaltyinfo.org/documents/FactSheet.pdf.

124   Ibid.

125   Death Penalty Information Center. 2015. Facts about the Death Penalty. Retrieved
      from http://www.deathpenaltyinfo.org/documents/FactSheet.pdf.

126   Radelet, M. and Lacock, T. 2009. Do Executions Lower Homicide Rates? The Views
      of Leading Criminologists. *Journal of Criminal Law & Criminology* 99: 489.

127   Dieter, R. 2009. *Smart on Crime: Reconsidering the Death Penalty in a Time of
      Economic Crisis.* The Death Penalty Information Center, October. http://www.
      deathpenaltyinfo.org/documents/CostsRptFinal.pdf.

128   Gallup Polling Agency. 2004, 2006, 2011. Death Penalty. Retrieved from http://www. gallup.com/poll/1606/death-penalty.aspx.

129   Nagin, D. and Pepper J. Deterrence and the Death Penalty. Committee on Law and Justice at the National Research Council, April 2012.

130   Raemisch, R. 2014. My Night in Solitary. *The New York Times* (Opinion Section), Feb. 23.

131   Mauer, M. 2001. The Causes and Consequences of Prison Growth in the United States. In D. Garland (ed.), *Mass Imprisonment: Social Causes and Consequence.* Thousand Oaks, CA: SAGE, pp. 4–14.

132   Stemen, D. 2007. Reconsidering Incarceration: New Directions for Reducing Crime. VERA Institute of Justice, Jan.

133   Turner, N. and Wetzel, J. 2014. Treating Prisoners Like People. *National Journal,* May 22.

134   The Sentencing Project. 2011. The Science of Downsizing Prisons—What Works? Retrieved from http://sentencingproject.org/wp-content/uploads/2016/02/The-Science-of-Downsizing-Prisons-What-Works.pdf.

135   Gentleman, A. 2012. "Inside Halden, the Most Humane Prison in the World." *The Guardian,* May 18.

An overview of criminological theory

PART III

CHAPTER OUTLINE

Crime as rational behavior: classical and rational choice theory

8

In this chapter we will explore the following questions

- How did people explain criminal behavior in the past?
- In what ways did the Enlightenment change society's view of crime?
- What does classical theory tell us about why people break the law?
- Do individuals actually choose to engage in criminal activities?
- How did rational choice theory expand our understanding of crime causation?
- Does crime always make sense?
- What are the policy implications of classical and rational choice theories?

KEY TERMS

exorcism
Enlightenment
Classical School of Criminology
hedonism
positivism
rational choice theory
offense-specific
offender-specific
situational choice theory
routine activities theory
situational crime prevention
general deterrence
determinate sentencing
specific deterrence
mandatory minimum sentences
truth-in-sentencing guidelines

Do individuals who break the law act recklessly and impulsively, or are their actions based on reasoning and calculations of risk and yield? Harry King was a well-known "boxman"; his specialty was opening safes. He enjoyed his life of crime and accepted prison sentences when they came as "the price you pay." With money he got by robbing grocery stores, banks, and restaurants, King would spend tens of thousands on a weekend in Las Vegas, buy his current girlfriend a house, cash down, wear expensive suits, and lavish money on friends and strangers alike. If arrested, he relied on lawyers to get him out on bail. If he had no money, he would immediately commit another "caper" to get the ten or twenty thousand dollars to pay the bail bondsman's fee, compensate his lawyer, and make whatever bribes to judges and prosecutors he needed to have his case "fixed."[1]

Harry King hardly fits the popular image of a desperate and irrational criminal. On the contrary, he very carefully calculated his criminal endeavors, weighing the benefits from his thefts against the consequences of getting caught and doing time in prison. King doesn't blame his behavior on circumstances or his upbringing, but rather explains:

> I never could blame my life on my parents. I mean, I could sit down and talk about it and say if it hadn't been for my mother I wouldn't have been

a thief . . . I can't say that . . . if you're built one way you're going to live that way . . . you know? There's nothing going to change it. It's just like why don't you go opening safes? I didn't know how to steal when I started, but I was inclined that way, or I wouldn't have done it.[2]

Image 8.1 *Harry King was a professional thief. As a safecracker, he ranked high within the criminal hierarchy of burglars. His exploits were well-planned and carefully executed . . . not your typical criminal.*

iStock/ReeseImages

Harry King's career seems to support the theory that crime is rational behavior, and therefore, in order to deter criminals, we must make the consequences of crime—punishment—outweigh its benefits. In a study examining restrictive deterrence and the cultivation of cannabis, researchers used data collected from an anonymous web survey which included participants recruited on a voluntary basis through advertisement on various websites related to marijuana use and production. Using negative binomial regression on 337 cases, researchers measured the relationship between criminal justice sanctions and the behavior of growers to determine whether the threat of sanctions impacted the size of cultivation site and the number of co-offenders. They found some evidence that the severity of punishment reduces the size of cultivation of marijuana among growers. Their finding seems to support a rational choice model of criminal behavior, where the decision to engage in criminal actions is influenced by the offender's perception of the cost of the crime. The study suggests that we approach the study of criminal behavior using the individual rational actor as the starting point.[3]

As we've seen in chapter 4, theories answer questions, clarify relationships between events, and provide causal explanations for them. They tell us why or how the facts we observe are as they are. In this chapter, we begin to answer our questions about crime and its causes by looking at the theory of crime that is most closely linked to the concept of punishment in our society. We will study criminal behavior from the point of view that individuals *choose* to engage in it, and that to stop it we must influence this choice. We begin with the story of how criminological theory emerged.

EARLY EXPLANATIONS OF CRIME

Before the birth of scientific criminology, explanations of crime were based on concepts like sin, evil, or utilitarianism, the idea that people calculated the relative likelihood of pleasure and pain in deciding how to act. In England as recently as the 19th century, criminal indictments accused the defendant of "being prompted and instigated by the devil and not having the fear of God before his eyes."[4]

EXORCISMO.
CUADRO DE D. SERAFIN MARTINEZ DEL RINCON, PREMIADO CON MEDALLA DE TERCERA CLASE. — (DIBUJO DEL MISMO AUTOR.)

Image 8.2 *Before criminology offered scientific explanations of criminal behavior, people blamed crime on evil spirits and demonic possession.*

Mary Evans Picture Library

The Middle Ages and the Renaissance

Throughout history, explanations of crime and deviance centered on moral and religious ideas of good and evil. For cosmic events such as plagues, wars, and floods that bring devastation to many, and for single acts of violence that affect a few, society has sought explanations in the form of some sort of evil or the vengeful actions of angry gods.

Thus efforts to control and prevent crime and deviance also focused on supernatural intervention to remove the evil forces residing within the individual.[5] In the Middle Ages and the Renaissance in Europe, individuals often brought loved ones believed to be tormented by some form of evil or demon to the church, hoping members of the clergy would perform an **exorcism**, a practice of prayers and rituals that literally evicted the demon from the individual's body. Other attempts to control crime and deviance included surgical penetration of the skull to allow the release of evil spirits residing within the individual's mind. Since criminal behavior was regarded as being caused by demons and other wicked spirits, the punishment of those determined to be guilty of criminal acts was seen as directed toward those evil forces and not the individual. Thus, punishments were harsh and severe, including physical torture to force confession, beatings, and other forms of corporal punishment, public humiliation, and death.

Religious explanations of crime and deviance dominated social thinking until the era known as the Enlightenment ushered in new methods of scientific inquiry.

Image 8.3 *John Locke was an English philosopher and physician, and is widely regarded as the Father of the Enlightenment. Locke questioned principles of knowledge and truth, laying the foundation for modern liberalism. Locke's writing influenced other great Enlightenment philosophers such as Voltaire and Rousseau.*

Interfoto/Sammlung Rauch/Mary Evans

The Enlightenment

The 17th- and 18th-century period of the Enlightenment, also known as the Age of Reason, inspired innovative thinking and a search for truth using philosophical reasoning.[6] European philosophers such as Jean-Jacques Rousseau (1712–1778), Voltaire (1694–1778), and John Locke (1632–1704) challenged the prevailing social institutions of education, law, and religion on the grounds that they perpetuated ignorance and superstition while inhibiting progress. Hallmarks of the Enlightenment Era include ideas about the intricate yet comprehensible nature of the universe and about how we can understand it through intellectual reasoning and scientific inquiry.

The Enlightenment had a significant impact on moral and social reform. It encouraged the use of logic, reason, fairness, and justice, leading writers and scholars to challenge existing authority as they extended the concept of human rights to include common citizens. No longer was the government or the church the ultimate source of knowledge and understanding. Fate was in the hands of each individual, with personal choices defining human destiny. As social and government institutions came under drastic reform, the practices defining crime and punishment were no exception.

Image 8.4 *Portrait of Voltaire.*

Mary Evans/Iberfoto

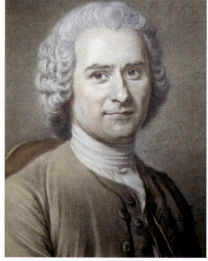

Image 8.5 *Jean-Jacques Rousseau, French philosopher.*

Interfoto/Sammlung Rauch/Mary Evans

PRINCIPLES OF CLASSICAL THEORY

One challenger to traditional explanations of crime was Cesare Beccaria, who in 1764 published his classic work, *Essay on Crimes and Punishments.*

Image 8.6
The rational behavior of criminals is portrayed in Ocean's 13, *a Hollywood movie about a very calculated, scrupulously thought-out heist of a gambling casino.*

Warner Bros./The Kobal Collection/Gordon, Melinda Sue

Cesare Beccaria and the idea of free will

Rather than seeing crime as a manifestation of sin, or of demons in possession of a person's mind and soul, Cesare Beccaria (1738–1794) looked for a more practical explanation: crime was wrong and immoral behavior driven by personal human choices.

Beccaria noted that all individuals possess free will and are therefore capable of making rational choices and calculated decisions. They will always look out for their own benefit, which may include engaging in crime and deviance. In this proposition Beccaria saw the relationship between crime and the law. According to Beccaria, the function of the law is to preserve the social order and curb the deviant and criminal behavior that individuals with free will and rational choice might commit in the pursuit of personal pleasure. With both individual actors and the social order seeking to satisfy their opposing goals, a clash of interests is inevitable. However, because human behavior is rational, it is also predictable and therefore controllable by punishment. The right punishment, or even just the threat of it, is enough to control the rational decision whether to engage in criminal behavior. The question is, what punishment is right?

We can think of Beccaria's writings as a philosophy of punishment rather than as a theory of crime. Beccaria argued against the cruel and arbitrary

Figure 8.1 Beccaria on punishment . . . A means to an end?

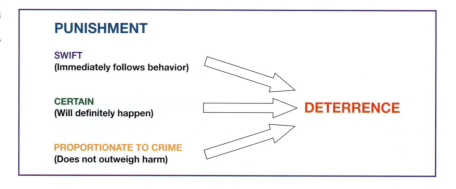

punishments that existed during his time, maintaining that physical torture and capital punishment were not only uncivilized and motivated only by a desire for revenge; they also did not deter crime. In Beccaria's view, then, punishment is a means to an end—crime prevention—and not an end in itself. For punishment to effectively deter crime, Beccaria argued, it must be swift, certain, and proportionate to the crime[7] (see Figure 8.1). Let us see why.

We can associate punishment with a particular behavior only if the consequence is *swift,* immediately following the behavior itself. A child who breaks the family's rule by grabbing a cookie before dinner gets an immediate time-out of ten minutes, effectively associating the time alone with the deed itself. Waiting several hours to impose the punishment weakens the link between the punishment and the behavior.

For punishment to be *certain*, the actor must believe the consequence will actually happen if the behavior takes place. Punishments that are threatened but not enforced will have little deterrent effect on an individual's behavior (see Box 8.1).

BOX 8.1: CONNECTING THEORY TO PRACTICE

Does punishment certainty stop criminals?

Throughout our lives, society and its various institutions have established rules and guidelines to help us understand what is expected of us. Without them, we would be in a state of chaos and confusion, unable to function in the environment around us. Whether you are starting a new job, shopping at a grocery store, beginning a new semester in college, or visiting a State park, your behavior is governed by formal and informal rules about what you can and cannot do. As important to governing our behavior as understanding the rules is knowing what will happen if we violate them.

If we are *certain* of the consequences, we feel a level of safety and control. Imagine your boss telling you that when you come to work on time, and do your job well, sometimes you get paid and sometimes you don't! Or, what if your professor said sometimes she will grade tests and sometimes she won't count them at all! How would that make you feel about going to work every day or doing the readings for your class? We can make a rational decision about how to behave only if we truly know with some level of assurance, the outcome. Thus the quality of punishment most closely associated with inhibiting a behavior is *certainty*.

Over the past several decades, the theoretical concept of certainty in punishment has been put to the test in criminological research examining the practical application of theory to various punishment outcomes. In a macro-level analysis by the Institute of Criminology at Cambridge University, researchers examining offense rates of a specific population found that an increased likelihood of certainty of apprehension and punishment was associated with declining crime rates. Moreover, leading scholars on deterrence theory, Daniel Nagin and Greg Polansky, conclude that "punishment certainty is far more consistently found to deter crime than punishment severity, and the extra-legal consequences of crime seem at least as great a deterrent as the legal consequences." Other micro-level studies on deterrence using scenario-based self-report research techniques to examine the effect of punishment certainty on individual choices consistently find that individuals are less likely to engage in criminal acts such as petty theft, tax evasion, and drunk driving, if their perception of risk of arrest is high.

During the 1990s, the crime rate in Texas fell to the lowest rate since 1974. Some have attributed the decline to significant changes in sentencing practices, prompted by an expansion of prisons to accommodate more offenders. Longer sentences became a certainty for violent criminals, under guidelines that required them to serve 75 percent of their sentences instead of 30 percent before release. Between 1990 and 1999, the certainty of serving time and expected sentence length for murder went up 213 percent, for rape 243 percent and for aggravated assault, 300 percent. Moreover, new crime prevention strategies aimed at expanding the number of jail and prison beds available, making it more difficult to be released on bond, and limiting the use of early release, increased the probability of serving time in prison after being arrested and convicted of a crime. In fact, the ratio of prisoners to population in Texas rose 143 percent during the 1990s.

With more offenders behind bars, and with time served tripling on average, should we be surprised to see a decline in the crime rate? Is the decline a side effect of having more criminals off the street, or are the tougher punishments affecting the rational choices of potential offenders by allowing them to take certainty into account?

Sources

Kleiman, Mark A.R. and Hollander, Kelsey R. 2011. Reducing Crime By Shrinking the Head Count. *Ohio State Journal of Criminal Law* 9(1): 89–106.

Loughran, Thomas E., Brame, Robert, Fagan, Jeffrey, Piquero, Alex, Mulvey, Edward P., and Shubert, Carol A. 2015. *Studying Deterrence Amongst High Risk Adolescents.* Office of Juvenile Justice and Delinquency Prevention, U.S. Department of Justice, Washington, D.C.

Muhlhausen, David. 2010. Theories of Punishment and Mandatory Minimum Sentences. *The Heritage Foundation.* Retrieved from http://www.heritage.org/research/testimony/theories-of-punishment-and-mandatory-minimum-sentences.

Reynolds, Morgan O. 2000. Certainty of Punishment Equals Less Crime. *Human Events* 56(46): 15.

Wright, Valerie. 2010. Deterrence in Criminal Justice Evaluating Certainty vs. Severity of Punishment. *The Sentencing Project.* Retrieved from http://www.sentencingproject.org/publications/deterrence-in-criminal-justice-evaluating-certainty-vs-severity-of-punishment/.

Finally, punishment must be *proportionate* to the crime, not only in quantity but also in quality, meaning the consequences of criminal behavior must somehow be related to the weight or seriousness of the crime. Punishments that outweigh the harm caused by an individual's actions are not only unjust but fail to serve the goal of deterrence. Punishments must be severe enough only to outweigh the benefits or pleasure derived from engaging in the criminal act.

Beccaria also advocated equity and fairness in the treatment of those accused of a crime, urging citizens to protect one another by discouraging a vigilante type of justice. Instead, he called for a system of justice that protected the rights of the accused, presuming their innocence until the necessary requirements for guilt were established in a court of law. Beccaria's theories and proposals paved the way for many legal and social science writers who followed him, including Jeremy Bentham.

Jeremy Bentham and the Classical School

The writings of the English jurist Jeremy Bentham (1784–1832) characterized what we today call the **Classical School of Criminology**. The Classical School believed people calculate the rewards and risks of their actions and decide how to act based on what they believe will bring them the most pleasure and least pain. Let us take a closer look at the basic ideas of classical theory.

In his *Introduction to the Principles of Morals and Legislation*, Bentham describes human nature as governed by the desire to maximize pleasure and minimize pain, a principle also called **hedonism**.[8] Inspired by Enlightenment thinking, Bentham believed all human beings are fundamentally rational and therefore will weigh the pain caused by punishment against the benefit or pleasure derived from the criminal act. Bentham therefore agreed with Beccaria that the goal of punishment should be to deter individuals from future crimes. He also agreed that in order for punishment to have a deterrent effect, it must be swift and certain and strike a careful balance by being painful enough to outweigh the rewards associated with the criminal endeavor.

In Bentham's view, human beings are in a constant dialog with themselves, weighing the possible consequences of their actions before following through with their behavior. To a large extent, we do engage in this dialog, countless times a day. Should I eat dessert, or will that ruin my diet? Should I go out with my friends, or will that not give me enough time to study for finals? Should I buy that expensive phone, or will it break my budget? The scenarios we play out in our minds are driven by our desire to increase our happiness and reduce our distress (see Table 8.1).

However, because we are all different and each attach different meanings to our experiences, Bentham argues that the value we associate with any given pleasure, as well as our desire to avoid pain, is governed by the sensation's intensity, duration, certainty, and immediacy.[9] *Intensity* of pleasure or pain is the degree to which an act is pleasant or painful, time and time again. *Duration*

Table 8.1 Calculating pleasure versus pain

When you . . .	. . . what do you take into consideration?
Prepare for an exam	Doing well in school versus staying home and missing a party you were invited to
Get to work late	Catching up on much needed sleep versus possibly getting fired
Stay out drinking with your friends	Socializing and having fun versus missing class the next day and losing attendance points
Go jogging for two miles	Having a healthy, lean body versus being tired and sweaty
Make an extravagant purchase	Watching your favorite movie on your new flat screen TV versus going into debt and not having enough money to spend on necessities
Have a second helping of dessert	The taste of chocolate in your mouth versus the extra hour at the gym you will have to spend to burn it off
Abuse illegal drugs	Getting high, partying, and gaining peer approval versus risking your health and ruining your chances for a good career if you get caught

Image 8.7 *Police stand over David Sweat after he was shot and captured near the Canadian border Sunday, June 28, 2015, in Constable, New York. Sweat is the second of two convicted murderers who staged a brazen escape three weeks earlier from a maximum-security prison in northern New York. His capture came two days after his escape partner, Richard Matt, was shot and killed by authorities.*

AP/Press Association Images

Image 8.8 *On July 28, 2015, 51-year-old Joyce Mitchell, a training supervisor at Clinton Correctional Facility, was arraigned at the Plattsburgh County Court on charges of smuggling tools to two inmates to assist them in their daring escape from the upstate New York Maximum Security Prison. Mitchell reportedly smuggled in hacksaws in hamburger meat. What hedonistic calculations did this correctional worker fail to make in her decision to assist the inmates with their escape?*

AP/Press Association Images

is a function of how long it lasts, and *certainty* refers to the probability it will happen. Finally, *immediacy* describes the closeness between the act and the associated pleasure or pain.

Bentham expands our understanding of how hedonism influences our rational decisions. He shows us a glimpse of the human struggle to do the right thing, while at the same time balancing the need to maximize pleasure and minimize pain.

EVALUATING CLASSICAL THEORY

Classical theory and the works of Beccaria and Bentham shaped the course of criminological theory for hundreds of years, and they continue to play an important role in debates about the origins of criminal behavior and the social response to it. But critics observed that they could not entirely account for criminal behavior, because individuals do not always weigh the costs and benefits of their actions. Classical theory approaches the study of criminal behavior from a simplistic view that places too much emphasis on the value of free will and personal choice in the decision to engage in crime. We can hardly imagine how situations riddled with such emotions as jealousy, anger, and rage can escalate into violence as the product of a rational calculation of pleasure and pain.[10]

Classical theory emerged during a time when society was redefining the value of punishment as a deterrent. While it made sense for the cost of crime to outweigh the benefits, classical theorists overlooked the simple fact that people don't always agree on what constitutes pleasure and pain. There is no universal formula that policy makers can employ to determine what and how much punishment is painful enough to deter crime or to make it less attractive or pleasurable.[11] For example, it may be worth the risk of spending six months in jail for an unemployed, homeless youth to steal money from a cash register at a convenience store, but not worth the risk for a college student to cash a stolen check and receive the same or similar consequences.

Finally, classical theory has been criticized for its failure to take into account the wide array of variables that affect an individual's decision to engage in crime. These include innate differences in biological and psychological makeup, as well as variations in the social experiences that shape us. Some people are quick to anger while others are patient until sufficiently provoked. It is this need to identify and isolate individual traits that create variations in criminal behavior that inspired the rise of positivist theories.

Positivism uses the scientific method to research biological, psychological, and social variables within the individual, and in his or her immediate social environment, as the root causes of criminal behavior.[12] Positivist theorists focused on forces beyond the individual's control—heredity, genetics, psychological trauma, abuse, socialization, peer influences, economic deprivation—as contributing to crime and delinquency. Rejecting the notion of free will and choice, positivist theories argued that the only solution to the problem of crime was to address the conditions that lead to criminality. Essentially, individuals who broke the law were in need of rehabilitation, as they were victims of the circumstances that led to their involvement in crime.

We will discuss positivist theories in greater detail in chapters to come. For now, we turn to an examination of rational choice theory, which, ironically, represented a reaction against positivism and led to a resurgence of classical ideas about personal responsibility and choice.

PRINCIPLES OF RATIONAL CHOICE THEORIES

In the 1970s, positivism in turn came under attack on the grounds that it shifted responsibility for crime from the individual to experience and the social environment, placing a greater burden on society to correct those conditions. A surge of research studies showed the apparent failure of offenders to change and become rehabilitated, regardless of the interventions tried.[13] At the same time, growing public fear of crime and a movement to get tough on crime and criminals swung the pendulum back to focus on individual choice and personal responsibility. Criminal justice policies began once again to reflect the idea that individuals are accountable for their criminal choices, and punishment became viewed as the deserved outcome of offenders' poor decisions.[14] Classical theory was reborn in the *rational choice* model. What did this theory add to our understanding of crime causation?

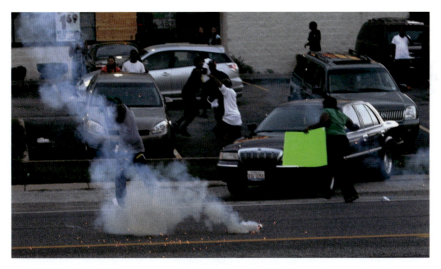

Image 8.9 *On August 10, 2014, Ferguson, Missouri, became a battleground of protests and civil disorder. The unrest was sparked by the fatal shooting of Michael Brown by a police officer. Curfews were set and riot squads were called on as residents took to the streets in protest, rioting and looting, and acts of violence including assault and arson. How does rational choice theory explain this type of mob behavior?*

St Louis Post-Dispatch/ABACA/PA Images

Rational Choice Theory

Rational choice theory emerged in the late 1970s and early 1980s to resurrect some of the major ideas of classical theory and its emphasis on the conscious decision to engage in criminal behavior.[15] Rational choice theory retained the classical school's central notion of free will, but it recognized that certain circumstances may affect the exercise of personal choice. It views criminals as reasoning human beings who evaluate the total circumstances before choosing to participate in acts that violate the law, including their own *personal circumstances* (experiences, needs, wants, desires); *situational factors* (type of security barriers, efficiency of law enforcement); *risk of getting caught*; seriousness of expected punishment (such as life in prison); and *value of expected yield* (monetary gain or benefit, desired approval by a group). Thus, rational choice theory sees the decision to commit crime as influenced by two types of variables, those related to the offense, offense-specific, and those related to the offender, offender-specific. Table 8.2 lists a variety of questions this theory suggests an individual may contemplate in evaluating the cost and benefit of a criminal enterprise.

We are still left with the question, what places individuals in circumstances where they make such choices? If you are running behind in paying your bills and are short on cash, do you go out and rob a bank, sell drugs, or commit a theft? What makes these options for some individuals? Two variations of rational choice theory offer us some answers: situational choice and routine activities.

Table 8.2 Rational choice theory: variables in evaluating criminal choices

Thinking about committing . . .	Offender-specific variables	Offense-specific variables
Theft from a retail store	How desperate am I for money or other items of value?	How much will I benefit from this crime?
Burglarizing a home	Am I physically and mentally capable of carrying out the crime?	Do I have what I need to successfully carry out this crime: equipment, weapons, look outs, a method of escape/getting away?
Fencing stolen property	Is there a better, more legitimate alternative I can resort to?	Will anyone be watching? (occupants, neighbors, crime watch groups)
Stealing a car	What do I do if I get caught?	How effective are the police in this neighborhood?
Committing armed robbery	Am I willing to handle the punishment that may come with this crime?	Are there other barriers such as dogs, alarms, or fences to overcome?

Situational choice theory

Situational choice theory argues that the individual decision to engage in criminal activities is shaped by the opportunities, risks, and benefits—the *situation*—attached to certain types of crimes.[16] Situations will vary according to time, location, personal circumstances, who is there, and what is going on.[17] These variables provide individuals with a context within which they rationally calculate the decision to violate the law. Crime is thus not just a matter of motivation or opportunity, but rather a complex interaction between the two.[18] *Motivation* is as diverse as human beings are and may flow from temptation, peers, boredom, or provocation.[19] *Opportunity* is equally distinct and takes into account the opportunity for financial reward, knowledge of criminal techniques, and personal experiences.

To choose to engage in certain types of criminal behavior, an individual must see the criminal enterprise as paying off despite possible risks like getting caught. Researchers note that individuals will continue to engage in illegal activities only if they perceive the enterprise as attractive.[20] Moreover, studies suggest the existence of a self-gratifying opportunity will increase the chances of an individual's decision to engage in a criminal act[21] (see Box 8.2).

Can someone choose to traffic marijuana across the Mexico border into the United States without knowing the intricate mechanisms necessary to carry out this form of illegal activity? Can someone wake up one day disillusioned with the government and bent on destruction, and instantly decide, "I am going to become a paramilitary special tactics official in a terrorist organization"?

These examples sound extreme, but the point is criminal opportunities are created by a knowledge of the necessary skills and techniques, an understanding of the limitations and risks, and possession of a way to avoid detection. Studies show training in effective criminal techniques often precedes the decision to carry out a crime.[22] Certainly, skill, knowledge, and understanding motivated Dennis Nikrasch to steal $6 million dollars from Las Vegas casinos in the late 1990s through an intricate scheme that included rigging mechanical slot machines. Investigators still wish they knew how he did it.[23]

Routine activities theory

Routine activities theory, the second variation of rational choice theory, argues that victim and offender lifestyles contribute to both the amount and type of crime within society.[24] The volume and distribution of certain types of predatory crimes, such as robbery, depend on three characteristics of the average U.S. lifestyle as shown in Figure 8.2.[25]

(1) **Presence of motivated offenders**—a large population of individuals who are unemployed, underemployed, or idle and who want money or other valued goods

BOX 8.2: CONSIDER THIS . . .

College girl . . . Call girl?

How far will people go to violate the law when a lucrative criminal opportunity presents itself? What variables are likely to influence their choices?

An unlikely offender, a college teacher with a master's degree from Yale University and a doctorate in social anthropology, found herself in desperate need of money when her boyfriend ran off after emptying her checking account. With bills to pay and rent due, she began looking for part-time work to supplement her meager salary. Her story is not uncommon, but the type of work the teacher chose was: she became a high-priced prostitute working for an escort service.

Her clients were diverse. Some were single, some married, some led fulfilling lives, and others were socially inept. Some were polite and courteous, others were rude and abusive. They met her at bars, in motels, in their homes, on boats, and in malls. They engaged in a variety of activities including conversation, dining at fine restaurants, attending parties, and having sex. The clients all had one thing in common: they could afford to pay $200 an hour for her services.

In a revealing first-person account told to *Boston Magazine*, the teacher explains her actions:

> They used the time in a variety of ways, and that is my usual response when someone—and someone will, inevitably, in any conversation about the profession— says something judgmental about the perceived degradation of exchanging sex for money. Because, in my experience, that doesn't make sense. You think I'm just manipulating semantics here, don't you? I'm not: Hear me out. Many people are paid by the hour, right? An employer hires a consultant, for example, on the basis of certain areas of expertise the consultant can offer. The employer—or client— pays for the consultant's time by the hour. A call girl is a consultant, using her expertise and experience in seduction and giving pleasure to fulfill a verbal contract with a client who is paying her by the hour. She is a skilled professional possessing knowledge for which there is a demand and for which the client is willing to pay her a predetermined rate.

Did it make sense for this university professor to become a prostitute? Was her decision rational? *What do you think?*

Sources

Angell, Jeannette. 2004. *Call Girl: Confessions of an Ivy League Lady of Pleasure*. New York: Perrenial Currents.

Angell, Jeannette. Confessions of an Ivy League Call Girl. *Boston Magazine*, Aug. 2004. Retrieved from http://www.bostonmagazine.com/2006/05/confessions-of-an-ivy-league-callgirl/.

Image 8.10 *How do the location, hours of operation, and type of products sold here make this store a possible crime target?*
iStock/Stele10

(2) **Availability of suitable targets**—individuals, homes, vehicles, grocery stores, and convenience markets that are easily accessible and provide the goods motivated offenders want
(3) **Absence of capable guardians**—individuals such as homeowners, police, and friends, and barriers such as security alarms and locks, that can discourage the decision to engage in crime.

Routine activities theory sees criminal behavior as the dynamic interplay between opportunity and the lifestyle of both victim and offender.[26] Individuals who live in high-crime neighborhoods and do not take measures to protect themselves and their property increase their risk of victimization, while at the same time providing motivated offenders with a suitable target. Those who go to an ATM alone at night carrying expensive valuables such as jewelry increase their risk of victimization and provide motivated offenders with an easy target for perpetrating a crime.

Opportunity is also affected by the offender's lifestyle and routine activities. Individuals who live in urban communities where crime and poverty abound are more likely to learn about criminal opportunities through family, friends, peers, and their own experiences. Weapons, drugs, and a culture that tolerates violence and predatory behavior act as facilitators and may escalate a motivated offender's desire to seek a suitable target.[27]

The propositions made by rational choice theory can have a profound impact on the crime control strategies and practices we as a society choose. But does research support the finding that crime is rational behavior? Let us turn now to an evaluation of classical and rational choice theories.

Figure 8.2
Routine activities
theory's three
variables

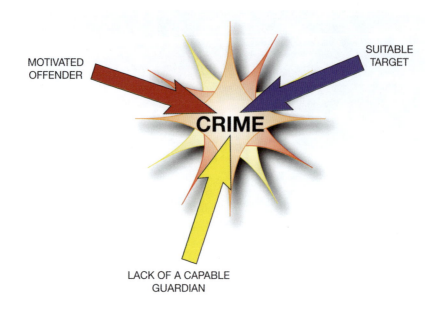

MOTIVATED
OFFENDER

SUITABLE
TARGET

CRIME

LACK OF A CAPABLE
GUARDIAN

EVALUATING RATIONAL CHOICE THEORY

Does crime make sense? Do offenders really make active decisions to engage in criminal behavior based on a cost-benefit analysis of a criminal opportunity? The elaborate financial schemes of corporate executives, the intricate mechanisms behind technology scams, and the market analyses and profit-and-loss assessments made by international drug cartels are all testimony to the rational, calculated decisions some offenders undertake when engaging in criminal activities. The decision to commit a burglary is guided, theorists say, by careful considerations about the best house to target, patterns of vacancy established by occupants and neighbors, methods and ease of entry, type of goods inside, and means of getting out quickly.[28]

More difficult to explain, however, are the acts of violent offenders that often seem the product of desperation, poor judgment, irrational thinking, emotions, misguided beliefs, and mental instability. On June 9, 2015, Gypsy Blancharde, age 23, had her boyfriend Nicholas Godejohn, age 26, stab her mother to death in her home in Springfield, Missouri. Police traced the murder weapon to Godejohn's home in Big Bend, Wisconsin. Godejohn claimed to have mailed the knife to his home after the murder to avoid getting caught with it. Blancharde made suspicious Facebook posts about the murder, which prompted friends and neighbors to contact the police. Are these acts of violence the calculated decisions of rational individuals who somehow benefit from their crimes? Rational choice theorists would argue they are.

Crime expert Richard Felson argues that even violent forms of criminal behavior take on very specific meanings and motives for the offender and are not the product of some type of mental breakdown, emotional hysteria, or randomly unbalanced decisions.[29] Violent crime is a matter of personal choice, involving very intricate planning, victim selection, a clear definition of motive, an assessment of risk involved, and a level of reasoning that takes into consideration the consequences of the act.[30] Felson argues that violence, while it may appear to be the irrational behavior of deranged individuals, actually serves very specific goals:[31]

1. *Violence as a means of control.* Violent offenders often perpetrate their crimes as a way of controlling the victim's life, behavior, and sense of freedom or independence. This is often the case with perpetrators of spouse abuse and domestic assault.
2. *Violence as a means of revenge.* Acts of violence may be committed to punish or get back at someone for real or perceived harm done. A type of vigilante justice, violence can be used by individuals who feel they have been wronged, injured, or mistreated, where the system of justice has not intervened in an appropriate manner.
3. *Violence as a means of deterrence.* Individuals may resort to violence if they feel threatened by the hostile or provocative actions of another and believe a violent response is necessary to make it cease.
4. *Violence as a means of establishing reputation.* Violence can often serve to establish a certain image, establish worth, make a statement, or gain the approval of others. Teenagers seeking the approval of and membership in a street gang sometimes engage in random attacks on individuals.

Yet, we are still left with a certain uneasiness about the purely rational nature of criminal behavior. Are famous actors and actresses, political figures, corporate executives, athletic superstars, and military heroes rational when they sabotage their careers, jeopardize their reputations, and face legal consequences, as well as public disproval and shame, by taking drugs, stealing, lying, cheating, and committing acts of violence and abuse? Was New York Giants superstar Plaxico Burress thinking rationally when he decided to carry a concealed weapon, without a permit, getting arrested after accidentally shooting himself in the thigh at a Manhattan nightclub in November 2008, almost one year after leading his team to victory in Super Bowl XLII?[32] Skeptics of rational choice theory argue to the contrary.

Critics say rational choice theory oversimplifies the complexity of human interaction with the social environment. Faced with certain circumstances and situations, such as peer pressure, abuse, anger, and frustration, do some individuals even have the choice to reason effectively? When 39-year-old Claire MacDonald snapped and killed her husband one evening after suffering several years of physical, emotional, and sexual abuse, jurors agreed she had no choice and acquitted her of murder charges.[33]

Moreover, rational choice theory fails to explain the impact of socialization, poverty, and social structure on crime. A study surveyed households in a small Virginia city, in neighborhoods with low and high crime rates, to test the effect of routine activities on patterns of property crime victimization. Findings indicated routine activities theory explained 28 percent of variation in crime rates and types of crime in high-crime neighborhoods, but only 11 percent of variation in low-crime neighborhoods. High-crime neighborhoods are socially disorganized and characterized by higher rates of unemployment, poverty, family disruption, and residential mobility, thus increasing the likelihood of crime and victimization. These dynamics, the researchers argue, create a larger population of motivated offenders, reduce guardianship over property and individuals, and contribute to the presence of suitable targets.[34]

Other critics of rational choice theory argue that it does not account for certain characteristics that may influence reasoning. Individual choices, they say, are often influenced by moral judgment, personal temperament, and character, which are not related to rationality. Many individuals turn away from crime to adhere to higher standards of what they view as right. By the same token, others may engage in criminal activities due to personal characteristics that make them more excitable, impulsive, and unthinking,[35] or through a combination of personal characteristics and external variables such as the influence of drugs and alcohol. A study examining the effects of alcohol and anger on cognitive functioning showed they increased aggression, and diminished the ability to distinguish between success and failure, risk and reward, and cost and benefit in the decision to engage in violent behavior.[36] Thus, a true empirical test of rational choice theory must take into account the range of human emotions, reasoning capabilities, individual psychology, and social experiences that influence the immediate decision to engage in criminal behavior. With these limitations in mind, we next ask, what implications does rational choice theory have for reducing crime?

Table 8.3 The classical and rational choice perspective

What is crime?	Crime is rational behavior
WHY does crime occur? **(theory)**	• Individuals choose to engage in criminal behavior
	• People make choices based on hedonistic calculations
	• Rational human beings act to maximize benefit and reduce cost
	• Crime occurs when it is a more attractive alternative than law-abiding behavior
	• The decision to violate the law takes into account the range of constraints and opportunities
	• The lifestyle of individuals contribute to both the amount and type of crime they engage in
WHAT is the solution to crime? **(policy)**	• Make crime a less attractive alternative by increasing its cost to individuals
	• Deter criminals by enacting punishments that are precise and certain

PRACTICAL APPLICATION OF CLASSICAL AND RATIONAL CHOICE THEORIES

Table 8.3 summarizes the classical and rational choice theories. Together these ideas form a single perspective that focuses on the act of committing a crime, as opposed to other variables such as the individual's state of mind, environmental influences like peer pressure, or experiences that teach individuals deviant norms and values. The cause of crime is rationally calculated choices between the risk and the possible benefit. The challenge for crime control, then, is how to make criminal behavior a less attractive alternative. How can we convince potential offenders that crime does *not* pay? Crime prevention policies and procedures that rely on the classical/rational choice perspective focus on two types of intervention: situational crime control and deterrence strategies. We first take a look at situational crime control policies.

Image 8.11 *American youth Michael Fay stirred up controversy when in May 1994 he was caned in Singapore for theft and vandalism. U.S. President Bill Clinton made an appeal for clemency to the President of Singapore on behalf of Fay, claiming the punishment was excessive for a teenager committing a non-violent crime. Based on rational choice theory, would Fay have committed this crime if he had known the consequences of his actions?*

Tan Ah Soon/AP/Press Association Images

Situational crime control

Assuming ordinary people engage in criminal acts after assessing the costs and benefits, crime control policies based on situational crime prevention try to make crime a more difficult and costly alternative. They consider the characteristics that put people and places at greater risk of being crime targets, the situations

Image 8.12 Stores all over the country install hi-tech security cameras that are visible to would be shoplifters in the hopes this will influence their decision to steal. Is this an effective deterrence strategy?

iStock/Tzido

or mechanisms that allow potential offenders to prey upon these targets, and the immediate variables that can trigger criminal acts.[37]

Developed in the early 1970s, situational crime prevention began as a method of reducing crime in high-risk neighborhoods, such as public housing, by increasing surveillance.[38] Since then, it has focused on altering the physical and social environment within which crime takes place.[39] This strategy includes (1) increasing the effort necessary to commit the crime, such as installing immobilizers in cars or adding a photo to a credit card; (2) increasing the perceived risk of committing crime by forming neighborhood watch groups or improving street lighting; (3) reducing the potential rewards of the criminal act, such as by placing ink tags on garments sold in retail stores; (4) reducing situations that provoke anger and aggression by, for example, limiting the capacity of bars and nightclubs to avoid excessive crowding; and (5) removing rationalizing excuses for committing crime by setting clear rules and employing clear reminders such as *we prosecute shoplifters.*[40]

Deterrence strategies

The second type of crime control strategy inspired by classical and rational choice theory focuses on punishment as deterrence. Criminologists distinguish between two types of deterrence: general and specific. The idea behind **general deterrence** is that individuals will refrain from crime if they fear apprehension and punishment. In other words, the choice to commit a deviant or criminal act will be affected by the threat of punishment. Thus society should identify which behaviors are acceptable, which are not, and what social sanctions and punishment result from the latter.[41] General deterrence is meant to reduce deviance by setting standards that tell everyone, "this is what happens when you break the law"[42] (see Table 8.4).

General deterrence strategies thus focus on preventing individuals from choosing criminal activity by influencing their rational decision-making process. Random traffic stops looking for drunk drivers, police visibility in high-crime neighborhoods, special law-enforcement task forces designed to uncover drug trafficking and gang activities, and even warnings about movie copyrights and prosecution of shoplifters are all strategies to inform the public of the consequences of violating the law.

Table 8.4 Which punishment would stop you from . . .

Stealing from your employer?
Sexually assaulting a date?
Cheating on your taxes?
Speeding in a residential neighborhood?
Lying under oath?
Accepting a bribe?
What characteristics of the punishment give it deterrent value?

Determinate sentencing, which mandates a fixed sentence for every type of offense, is another general deterrent. If I know the punishment for trafficking drugs is a definite 10 years in prison, I may be less willing to engage in that behavior than if the punishment can range from 5 to 10 years. Policies that increase the visibility of crime's consequences, such as sex offender registration, are also designed to make the public aware of the shame of criminal behavior and its aftermath.[43]

In contrast to general deterrence, **specific deterrence** strategies focus on deterring particular offenders by administering punishment that is severe enough to affect rational decision making and prevent future offenses.[44] The intent is to teach criminals a lesson. Stiff fines and harsh **mandatory minimum sentences** that require jail terms for offenses like domestic abuse and driving while intoxicated are specific deterrence policies, for example. Another is **truth-in-sentencing guidelines** that require offenders to serve more than 80% of their sentence in prison before they can be released.

Consider the specific deterrence practices of Sheriff Joe Arpaio of Maricopa County in Phoenix, Arizona, who runs a jail holding roughly 8,000 inmates. Sheriff Arpaio houses offenders in tents in the Arizona desert where summer temperatures reach 120 degrees, requires chain-gang prisoners to perform community work normally worth thousands of dollars, serves two cold meals a day of food that is surplus and often rotten, and makes inmates wear pink underwear. Arpaio defends his system by arguing that he is teaching a lesson so vivid offenders won't want to come back.[45]

Image 8.13 *How are these prison conditions examples of specific deterrence strategies?*
Eduardo Barraza/Demotix/Press Association Images

Another specific deterrence practice designed to divert juvenile offenders gained popularity in the 1970s when a group of inmates serving life sentences at Rahway State Prison in New Jersey began a program called *Scared Straight.* This program was designed to bring youth offenders inside prison walls for a guided tour and a confrontational lecture by inmates, which gives a realistic and aggressive depiction of prison life, including incidents of assault, rape, and murder. For a time *Scared Straight* served as a model for similar programs that hoped to turn juvenile offenders and at-risk youth from their delinquent ways. While these programs were well meant, critics point to studies showing they have no deterrent value and may in some cases increase the likelihood of offending.[46] Researchers question the merit of using scare tactics as a method for deterring future criminal behavior. That leaves us with the question, how *does* deterrence work?

To be deterred from crime, potential offenders must be convinced they will get caught and suffer the legal consequences. There cannot be any hope of getting off lightly or finding a legal loophole.[47] The punishment must be imposed with certainty, so rational individuals will refrain from criminal activities. When they weigh the cost and benefits of committing a crime, they take into consideration their perceived possibility of getting caught, as well as the possibility of gain from the act.[48]

Deterrence also works when would-be offenders fear formal and informal sanctions. Studies show individuals who take into account the shame, embarrassment, and rejection by family, friends, and peers, that their criminal involvement may bring, are more likely to refrain from criminal activity.[49] Box 8.3 discusses other policies and practices designed to deter crime.

BOX 8.3: CONNECTING RESEARCH TO PRACTICE

A closer look at deterrence

What is it that stops us from engaging in certain types of behavior? Is it possible that we refrain from certain types of behaviors because the consequences are undesirable? So, for example, some people stop smoking when their doctor says they are at risk of getting lung cancer; some people might skip dessert to knock off those extra pounds; a teenager may come home just one minute before curfew to avoid losing car privileges; a businessman files taxes on time to avoid penalties. Unattractive consequences, therefore, seem to have a deterrent effect . . . they stop undesirable behavior. Are certain crimes and behaviors more susceptible to deterrence than others? Does general deterrence work as intended?

The relationship between crime rates and deterrent measures is often difficult to establish. Most studies rely on official statistics on crime, which, as we saw in chapter 3, can be skewed due to reporting problems, biased police practices, and organizational and political interests. It is also difficult to measure the effects of informal social controls, such as anti-crime campaigns and the fear of public exposure and losing the respect of family and peers.

Research examining the relationship between increases in penalty and reduction in crime has generally been ambiguous. As a matter of fact, over the past several decades, studies indicating that more punitive measures have led to decreases in crime have been repeatedly challenged and refuted in many cases. There is little supportive evidence that capital punishment decreases homicides, or that policies imposing three-strikes laws and mandatory minimum prison sentences, reduce crime such as illegal drug use, assault, rape, and domestic violence. On the other hand, there are findings that suggest that some types of crimes like tax evasion, speeding, shoplifting, and littering, are significantly deterred by the perceived likelihood or risk of apprehension and the severity of punishment associated with the behavior.

Is it therefore quite plausible that there are some types of crime or a certain category of offenders that are more easily deterred than others? Studies examining the relationship between punishment severity and DUI have been successful in establishing that deterrence measures seem to effect would be drunk drivers. Relying on a rational choice model of deterrence, researchers tested the effects of harsher punishments on deterring driving under the influence. Findings suggest that increasing penalties for individuals with prior DUIs reduced recidivism by 17 percent, while enhanced penalties for aggravated DUI reduced recidivism by 9 percent. In another study, researchers used a quasi-experimental time-series design to determine the effects of statutory changes in DUI penalties for first time offenders over a period of time. Results indicate that mandatory fine policies are associated with an average reduction in fatal car accidents by drunk drivers. Moreover, mandatory minimum jail policies are associated with a decline in single-vehicle fatal crashes.

These findings, while persuasive, still do not isolate the deterrent effects of punishment alone on criminal behavior. Numerous studies show fear of punishment alone does not account for declines in the rate of criminal activity, which are also affected by psychological variables, environmental pressures such as poverty, unemployment, and peer influences, certain values and beliefs, and misperceptions about crime and its consequences. If the relationship between crime and punishment were that simple, capital punishment, the ultimate criminal sanction, should have the strongest deterrent effect of any punishment on would-be murderers. However, at best, if murder rates decline shortly after a widely publicized execution, they would eventually go up again to even higher levels and then back down, with no net deterrent effect. Relying on deterrent strategies alone is therefore not sufficient. Since punishment does not remove the underlying cause of criminal motivations and actions, it alone will not deter them.

Sources

Hansen, Benjamin. 2015. Punishment and Deterrence: Evidence from Drunk Driving. *American Economic Review* 105(4): 1581–1617.

Wagnaar, Alexander, Mildred M. Maldonado-Molina, Darin J. Erickson, Ma Linan, and Amy L. Tobler. 2007. General Deterrence Effects of U.S. Statutory DUI Fine and Jail Penalties: Long-term Follow-up in 32 States. *Accident Analysis & Prevention* 39(5): 982–994.

Wright, Valerie. 2010. Deterrence in Criminal Justice: Evaluating Certainty vs. Severity of Punishment. The Sentencing Project. Retrieved from http://www.sentencingproject.org/publications/deterrence-in-criminal-justice-evaluating-certainty-vs-severity-of-punishment/.

The debate about whether deterrence strategies reduce crime will continue to rest on the shoulders of classical and rational choice theories. We can take from these theories many practical ideas for controlling crime and making it less attractive, but they do not supply us with a complete explanation of why crime occurs or how to prevent it. We have yet to address the situation, heredity, social learning, pressure and stress, and so on. We go on to address more promising theories in the following chapters.

SUMMARY

How did people explain criminal behavior throughout history?

Before the science of criminology emerged, explanations of crime and deviance focused on moral and religious definitions of right and wrong. Crime and deviance were seen as the manifestation of evil and attributed to the supernatural forces of demons and spirits.

In what ways did the Enlightenment change society's view of crime?

During the Enlightenment of the 17th and 18th centuries, scholars and philosophers developed a more logical understanding of crime based on the human capacity to choose. Challenging existing authority, they focused attention on principles of fairness and justice and sought to account for crime as a human decision based on rational thought processes.

What does classical theory tell us about why people break the law?

Classical theory, as characterized by English jurist Jeremy Bentham, argues that human beings are rational actors who weigh the potential pleasure of engaging in crime against the potential pain of apprehension and punishment. The goal of punishment in classical theory is to deter individuals from crime by influencing their perception of the associated punishment. The ability of the law to control human behavior is increased if punishment is swift, certain, and severe enough to outweigh the benefits of the crime.

Do individuals actually choose to engage in criminal activities?

According to classical theory, individuals are the product of their own free choices to do whatever they want. Thus, individuals actually choose to engage in crime and deviance of their own will, according to the hedonistic principle of maximizing pleasure and minimizing pain.

How did rational choice theory expand our understanding of crime causation?

Rational choice theory elaborated on the relationship between personal circumstances, situational factors, and risk of getting caught in a person's evaluation of the expected benefits of a criminal act. One variation, situational choice theory, placed the decision to violate the law within constraints and opportunities that vary according to time, location, personal circumstances, who is there and what is going on. Another variation, routine choice theory, proposed that lifestyle and opportunity both contributed to the amount and type of crime within society, creating variations among motivated offenders, suitable targets, and the lack of capable guardians.

Does crime make sense?

If all offenders were like Harry King in the chapter opening story, making rational decisions based on a calculation of the cost and benefit of their criminal activities, the answer would be yes. The truth, however, is that crime does *not* always make sense. It does not always include careful assessment of the risks, or a full understanding of the benefits. While offenders often do reason about motive, goal, means, and outcome, classical and rational choice theories fail to account for variables such as socialization, personal characteristics, moral upbringing, and environment.

What are the policy implications of classical and rational choice theory?

Policies stemming from classical and rational choice theory focus on the *act* of crime and try to alter the circumstances affecting an individual's decision to engage in criminal or deviant activity. Thus the goal of crime control strategies is to make the criminal act a less attractive alternative to the rational individual. This is accomplished by two means: situational crime control strategies that focus attention on the physical, social, and environment context within which criminal opportunities arise, and deterrence strategies aimed at getting tough on crime and criminals, convincing them that crime does not pay.

CRITICAL THINKING QUESTIONS

1. The Enlightenment brought about great changes in thinking about a variety of social issues, including crime and punishment. What trends in our current social and political climate may inspire similarly new thinking about crime causation and appropriate response to criminal behavior? What ways of reasoning about crime and justice may become obsolete? On what types of punishment currently in practice may we look back in decades to come and think "I can't believe we used to do that?"

2. You are an overworked, underpaid employee in the stock room of a major grocery store chain. You are working hard to pay off student loans, yet your extra efforts, working overtime and filling in whenever other workers slack off, are hardly recognized by company executives. Your co-worker has devised a scheme to embezzle money from the store over a period of six months that will land each of you about $50,000, after paying off the necessary employees to make sure the scheme will work and reduce the

risk of getting caught. Suppose for half a minute you consider going along with the plan. What dilemmas does it pose? What choices do you make? Are you thinking rationally? What makes your thinking rational? What elements of hedonism are included in your deliberations?

3. What characteristics of a college campus increase the likelihood of criminal opportunities? Who are the motivated offenders? Who and what are the suitable targets? Why is there a lack of capable guardians? What can *decrease* the likelihood of victimization in such an environment?

4. The debate about what type of criminal punishment works is endless. Where do you stand in this debate? Do you think people would reconsider their criminal actions if the punishments included cutting the hands off thieves, flogging vandals, publicly shaming perpetrators of fraud, and castrating rapists? Would potential murderers think twice if they had seen a televised execution? Why or why not? How would you defend these types of punishments in light of spontaneous crimes that occur in the heat of the moment?

E-RESOURCES

Learn more about the influence of the Enlightenment on the philosophy of punishment and law in the United States by visiting http://www.international. ucla.edu/asia/article/29410.

To read more about the bizarre murder story of Dee Dee Blancharde, visit http://fox4kc.com/2015/06/16/investigators-uncover-a-web-of-deception-in-springfield-murder-investigation-that-has-metro-connection/.

You can learn more about the positivist approach in studying criminal behavior at http://law.jrank.org/pages/777/Crime-Definition-positivistic-approach.html.

Does punishment deter? Read more on this debate at the *National Center for Policy Analysis* website http://www.ncpa.org/pub/bg148.

Visit the *Center For Problem-Oriented Policing* website at http://www.popcenter.org/ to learn more about situational crime prevention.

NOTES

1   King, Harry and Chambliss, William J. 1982. *Harry King: A Professional Thief's Journey.* New York: Macmillan.
2   King, Harry and Chambliss, William J. 2004. *A Professional Thief's Journey.* An Author's Guild Back Print Publication, p. 4.
3   Nguyen, Holly, Malm, Alli and Bouchard, Martin. 2015. Production, Perceptions, And Punishment: Restrictive Deterrence In The Context Of Cannabis Cultivation. *International Journal of Drug Policy* 26(3): 267–276.
4   Chambliss, William J. 1988. *Exploring Criminology.* New York: Macmillan.

5   Huff, Ronald C. 2008. Historical Explanations of Crime. In Robert D. Crutchfield, Charis E. Kubrin, George S. Bridges, and Joseph G. Weis (eds.), *Crime Readings,* 3rd ed. California: Sage.

6   Baronov, D. 2015. *Conceptual Foundations of Social Research Methods.* London: Routledge.

7   Learn more about Beccaria at http://www.newworldencyclopedia.org/entry/Cesare_Beccaria.

8   Bentham, Jeremy. 1967. *A Fragment on Government and an Introduction to the Principle of Morals and Legislation,* edited by Wilfred Harrison. Oxford: Basil Blackwell.

9   Bentham, Jeremy. *An Introduction to the Principles of Morals and Legislation.* Retrieved from http://www.utilitarianism.com/jeremy-bentham/index.html.

10   Hayward, K. 2007. Situational Crime Prevention and its Discontents: Rational Choice Theory versus the 'Culture of Now'. *Social Policy & Administration* 41(3).

11   Maitama, Kabiru, Mohd, Faridahwati, and Shamsudin, Ajay C. 2015. Does Self-Regulatory Efficacy Matter? Effects of Punishment Certainty and Punishment Severity on Organizational Deviance. doi: 10.1177/2158244015591822.

12   Shelden, R., Brown, W., Miller, K., and Fritzler, R. 2015. Theories of Crime. In *Crime and Criminal Justice in American Society.* Long Grove, IL: Waveland Press, pp. 60–85.

13   Reiman, J. and Leighton, P. 2015. Making Rehabilitation Corrections' Guiding Paradigm. In *Rich Get Richer and the Poor Get Prison.* London: Routledge, pp. 180–185.

14   Cornish, D. and Clark, R. 2014. *The Reasoning Criminal: Rational Choice Perspectives on Offending.* New Brunswick, NJ: Transaction Publishers.

15   Miller, J. 2014. *The Encyclopedia of Theoretical Criminology.* Hoboken, NJ: John Wiley & Sons.

16   Cornish, Derek and Clarke, Ronald V. 1987. Understanding Crime Displacement: An application of Rational Choice Theory. *Criminology* 25(4).

17   LaFree, Gary and Christopher Birkbeck. 1991. The Neglected Situation: A Cross-National Study of the Situational Characteristics of Crime. *Criminology* 29: 1.

18   Clarke, Ronald V. *Situational Crime Prevention: Everybody's Business.* Paper presented at the 1995 Australian Crime Prevention Council conference.

19   Eck, John E. and Weisburd, David, L. 2015. Crime Places in Crime Theory. *Crime Prevention Studies* 4: 133.

20   Pezzin, Liliana. 1995. Earnings Prospects, Matching Effects, and the Decision to Terminate a Criminal Career. *Journal of Quantitative Criminology* 11: 29–50.

21   Perry, Simon and Hasisi, Badi. 2014. Rational Choice Rewards and the Jihadist Suicide Bomber. *Terrorism and Political Violence* 27(1): 53–80.

22   Cherbonneau, Michael and Copes, Heith. 2006. Drive it Like You Stole it: Auto Theft and the Illusion of Normalcy. *The British Journal of Criminology* 46: 193–211. Jacobs, Bruce. 1996. Crack Dealers' Apprehension Avoidance Techniques: A Case of Restrictive Deterrence. *Justice Quarterly* 13: 359–381.

23   Learn more about this case by visiting http://www.idxinc.com/counterfeit.htm.

24   Daigle, Leah and Muftik, Lisa R. 2015. *Victimology.* Thousand Oaks, CA: Sage.

25   Cohen L.E. and Felson, Marcus. 1979. Social Change and Crime Rate Trends: A Routine Activities Approach. *American Sociological Review* 44(4): 389–406.

26   Andresen, Martin A. and Farrell, Graham. 2015. *The Criminal Act: The Role and Influence of Routine Activity Theory.* New York: Palgrave Macmillan.

27   Clark, M. 2010. Drugs and Alcohol in Relation to Crime and Victimization. In S. Shoham, P. Knepper, and M. Kett, (eds.), *International Handbook of Victimology.* Boca Raton: CRC Press, pp. 251–272.

28   Blevins, Kristie R., Kuhns, Joseph B., and Suengmug, Lee. Aug. 2012. *Understanding_Decisions_To_Burglarize_From_The_Offender's_Perspective.* UNC Charlotte, Department of Criminology and Criminal Justice.

29 Felson, Richard and Messner, Steven. 1996. To Kill or Not to Kill: Lethal Outcomes in Injurious Attacks. *Criminology* 34: 519–545.

30 *Homicide: Behavioral Aspects-Victim/Offender Relationships.* Retrieved from http://law.jrank.org/pages/1322/Homicide-Behavioral-Aspects-Victim-offender-relationships.html. Decker, Scott. 1996. Deviant Homicide: A New Look at the Role of Motives and Victim-Offender Relationships. *Journal of Research in Crime and Delinquency* 33: 427–449.

31 Op. cit., see 28.

32 Eligon, J. 20 August 2009. Burress Will Receive 2-Year Prison Sentence. *The New York Times.* Retrieved from http://www.nytimes.com/2009/08/21/nyregion/21burress.html?_r=0.

33 Abused Wife Cleared of Husband's Murder. *The Sydney Morning Herald.* Retrieved from http://www.smh.com.au/news/National/Abused-wife-cleared-of-husbands-murder/2006/03/03/1141191843495.html.

34 Moriarty, Laura and Williams, James E. 1996. Examining the Relationship Between Routine Activities Theory and Social Disorganization: An Analysis of Property Crime Victimization. *American Journal of Criminal Justice* 21(1): 43–59.

35 Walsh, A. and Ellis, L. Psychosocial Theories: Individual Traits and Criminal Behavior. In *Criminology: An Interdisciplinary Approach.* Thousand Oaks, CA: Sage, pp. 169–198. Retrieved from http://www.sagepub.com/sites/default/files/upm-binaries/13434_Walsh_Chapter_7.pdf.

36 Gan, G., Sterzer, P., Marxen, M., Zimmermann, U. S. and Smolka, M. N. Neural and Behavioral Correlates of Alcohol-Induced Aggression Under Provocation *Neuropsychopharmacology.* doi:10.1038/npp.2015.141.

37 Smith, Martha. 14 April 2011. *Situational Crime Prevention.* Retrieved from http://www.oxfordbibliographies.com/view/document/obo-9780195396607/obo-9780195396607-0040.xml.

38 Eck, J. Preventing Crime at Places. In L. Sherman, D Gottfredson, D MacKenzie, J. Eck, P. Reuter and S Bushway (eds.), *Preventing Crime: What Works, What Doesn't, What's Promising.* Retrieved from https://www.ncjrs.gov/works/chapter7.htm.

39 *Twenty-Five Techniques of Situational Prevention.* 2015. Center for Problem Oriented Policing, Community Oriented Policing Services, U.S. Department of Justice. Retrieved from http://www.popcenter.org/25techniques/.

40 Scott, R. 2015. Twenty-Five Techniques of Situational Prevention. *Center for Problem-Oriented Policing.* Albany, NY: University of Albany. Retrieved from http://www.popcenter.org/25techniques/.

41 Walker, S. 2010. Deter the Criminals. In *Sense and Nonsense About Crime, Drugs, and Communities: A Policy Guide.* Boston, MA: Cengage Learning, pp. 122–145.

42 Van Den Haag, Ernest. 1982. The Criminal Law as a Threat System. *Journal of Criminal Law and Criminology* 73: 709–785.

43 Prescott, J., and Rockoff, J. 2008. Do Sex Offender Registration and Notification Laws Affect Criminal Behavior? In *Law and Economics Working Papers. University of Michigan Law School.*

44 Anderson, J., Johnson, J., Haskell, H. and Barach, P. 2014. The Classical School of Thought. In *Criminological Theories.* Burlington, MA: Jones & Bartlett Publishers, pp. 63–80.

45 Information retrieved from the Maricopa County Sheriff's Department website at http://www.mcso.org/.

46 Schembri, Anthony J. Florida Department of Juvenile Justice. *Scared Straight Programs: Jails and Detention Tours.* Retrieved from http://www.djj.state.fl.us/Search?q=scared%20straight.

47 Pratt, Travis C., Cullen, Francis T., Blevins, Kristie R., Daigle, Leah E. and Madensen, Tamara D. 2006. The Empirical Status of Deterrence Theory: A Meta-Analysis.

In Francis T. Cullen, John Paul Wright and Kristie R. Blevins (eds.), *Taking Stock: The Status of Criminological Theory,* Vol 15. New Brunswick, NJ: Transaction Publishers.

48 Zettler, Haley R., Morris, Robert G., Piquero, Alex R. and Cardwell, Stephanie M. 2015. Assessing the Celerity of Arrest on 3-Year Recidivism Patterns in a Sample of Criminal Defendants. *Journal of Criminal Justice* 43(5): 428–436. Cellini, S., and Kee, J. (2010) Cost-Effectiveness and Cost-Benefit Analysis. In *Handbook of Practical Program Evaluation.* San Francisco, CA: Jossey-Bass, pp. 493–530.

49 Tangney, J., Stuewig, J. and Mashek, D. Moral Emotions and Moral Behavior. In *Annual Review of Psychology* 58. Retrieved from http://www.annualreviews.org/doi/pdf/10.1146/annurev.psych.56.091103.070145. Grasmick, Harold and Bursik, Robert. 1990. Conscience, Significant Others, and Rational Choices: Extending the Deterrence Model. *Law and Society Review* 24: 837–861.

CHAPTER OUTLINE

Biological theories: crime is in the brain

9

Could there be a biological basis for repeat violent offending? According to Adrien Raine, Criminology Professor at University of Pennsylvania, the answer is unequivocally yes! Raine spent years studying the brains of violent criminals, serial killers, and psychopaths. His research findings suggest that biological dysfunctions within the human brain are causal variables of violent offending and should therefore be taken into account in our approach to crime prevention and rehabilitation.[1] Can such claims indeed mediate criminal justice policy and practice? This seemed to be the case in the infamous 1979 shooting deaths of San Francisco Mayor George Moscone and fellow Councilman Harvey Milk.

By all accounts, Daniel White, former police officer and San Francisco City Councilman, was a good man and an upstanding member of the community who became a disgruntled victim of dirty politics in city hall. White's rage and frustration eventually turned deadly, when in 1979, he shot the Mayor and City Councilman. The line of defense and the outcome of this case were landmarks in the field of criminology and our understanding of crime causation. White's guilt was never in question; at issue instead was his degree of responsibility and criminal intent. Based on the argument of diminished capacity, caused by White's suffering from a combination of emotional and physiological variables, his defense attorneys built a case for a lesser charge than first-degree murder. Experts testified that he suffered from various symptoms of depression, compounded by the effects of consuming large amounts of refined sugar in common snack foods such as Ho-hos and Twinkies prior to the shootings. In

Image 9.1 *Criminologist Adrien Raine was the first to use imaging technology to study the brains of violent murderers. He is fully convinced, based on extensive research that while there are social and environmental variables that mediate criminal choices, biology can be a major driving force behind violent crime . . . How could this be possible?*
Adrien Raine

dizygotic twins
behavioral genetics
XYY syndrome
reductionism

a pivotal moment in legal history, and what some would argue was a miscarriage of justice, jurors agreed with what became known as White's "Twinkie defense" and convicted him of voluntary manslaughter instead of the more serious charge of murder.[2]

What do we make of such explanations of violence and aggression? Is it possible that the structure and function of the human body can drive an individual towards criminal behavior? Are violence and aggression waiting within us to manifest as criminal behavior given the right triggers from the environment? What does the science of criminology have to say about this matter?

Studies on the biological basis of human behavior attempt to draw a link between biological traits such as impulsivity, aggression, and intelligence and criminal behavior. Do criminals have certain common traits more often than non-criminals? Researchers note that certain biological characteristics are strongly correlated with the likelihood of criminal offending.[3] These include such variables as male sex hormones, maternal smoking during pregnancy, certain brainwave patterns, and low blood sugar. A growing body of literature has found evidence of a link between low monoamine oxidase (MAO) activity and anti-social behavior.[4] MAO is an enzyme found throughout the body. These enzymes work to maintain a balance of chemicals within the brain, chemicals that affect mood and behavior. MAO activity is measured in the blood and is referred to as platelet MAO. In a study of 483 school children around the age of 15, researchers examined the relationship between levels of MAO activity, personality, and traffic behavior. Their findings reveal that risky traffic behavior such as drinking and driving were strongly correlated with impulsivity and agreeableness, personality traits associated with low platelet MAO activity.[5]

This chapter examines perspectives within criminology focusing on the innate biological characteristics of the human body that interact with forces in the environment to shape human behavior. Is it possible that we are ruled by instinct and nature, with biology and environment competing for control of our actions? Or, do we dismiss claims that reduce criminal behavior to uncontrolled, predetermined responses by the human organism? We first examine the basic premises of the biological perspective, to understand its distinct contribution to criminological theory.

MAJOR PRINCIPLES OF THE BIOLOGICAL APPROACH

The **biological perspective** on crime is built upon the foundation of positivism, which presumes criminal behavior is caused by biological forces beyond an individual's control (see chapter 9). Biological positivism rejects the notion of rational choice and free will and instead uses the scientific method to examine the basic controls of thought, behavior, and action. These are its fundamental assumptions:

- The brain controls the human mind and personality.
- The basis of human behavior is linked to a person's biological constitution.
- Differences in behavior between gender and racial groups, including differences in types and rates of criminality, are in part due to biological differences between them.
- Human behavior, including a predisposition to criminality, may be inherited. Thus, criminal tendencies can be passed down from generation to generation.
- Much of the way we behave as human beings is linked to instinctive behavioral responses similar to those of other biological organisms. Like animals, we have a desire to dominate, protect, make acquisitions, and reproduce.
- What makes us different from other biological organisms is that our conduct, while linked to basic primitive instincts, has been disguised by modern symbolic forms of expressive behavior. A man who holds the door open for a woman or rushes to carry a heavy bag for her is practicing chivalry, a symbolic disguise for the instincts of domination and protection.
- Not all human beings are equally evolved on the developmental scale of evolution and natural selection. Those who are less evolved may behave in ways that reflect their less primitive state of development.
- Any comprehensive explanation of crime causation must take into account the dynamics of biology and social environment. Biology and the social environment are not mutually exclusive.

In the sections to come, we will take a close look at various competing approaches linked to specific fields within the biological and biomedical sciences, previewed in Table 9.1. We begin with an examination of early biological theories of criminal behavior.

Table 9.1 Biological perspectives on criminal behavior

Early biological theories	Biochemical variables	Neurocriminology	Heredity and genetics
• Criminal anthropology • Phrenology • Atavism • Body type	• Nutrition • Blood glucose • Hormones • Contaminants	• Neurological impairment • Brain chemistry • Attention Deficit Hyperactivity Disorder (ADHD)	• Criminal families • Twin studies • Adoption studies • Chromosomes

EARLY BIOLOGICAL THEORIES

We find the earliest thoughts on the association between physical features and personality in the Greek civilization, which embraced a culture of inter-connection between mind and body.[6] Later, scientific criminology developed in parallel with other sciences. It emerged during the Enlightenment of the 18th century, with the arrival of a naturalistic way of looking at the universe that focused on science instead of superstition, and the then-revolutionary idea that we should test our theories with observation and experiment. Behavioral science first looked to biology and medicine for its framework. Not surprisingly, then, people interested in studying crime hypothesized that criminality was biologically determined. The search was on for physical and biological characteristics that would differentiate criminals from non-criminals.

Criminal anthropology proposed a relationship between physical features and criminal behavior that we can trace to the work of European anatomist and physiologist, Franz Joseph Gall (1758–1828). Gall founded the school of anatomy known as **phrenology,** which suggested the constellation of bumps on the head indicated biological differences in the way people behaved.[7] Gall's approach focused on the idea that the brain is the organ of the human mind and personality, and that particular mental functions were associated with certain regions within it. Gall believed under-development of a specific brain region was associated with weakness in a particular aspect of the personality, and that we could predict the development of personality and mental capacity by the underlying shape of the skull.[8]

Image 9.2 *Franz Gall founded the study of the relationship between human physical features and criminal behavior. How do you think society reacted to the emergence of phrenology?*

Photo Researchers/Mary Evans Picture Library

Image 9.3
How do you think Cesare Lombroso was influenced by Darwin's theory on the evolution of human beings?

David Gifford/Science Photo Library

Gall's claims were disputed by religious leaders and the scientific community alike. His research did not survive careful empirical testing, and phrenology died an early death. Seventy years later, however, the idea that criminal behavior was rooted in biological characteristics was revived by the Italian physician Cesare Lombroso.

Lombroso began his work in light of discoveries spearheaded by Charles Darwin's influential work, *On the Origin of Species*, published in 1859.[9] Darwin reasoned that if species survived because of their fitness for the conditions of life, at any point in time other species would be disappearing because they were unfit. Applying this logic to humans, Lombroso hypothesized that some human beings were carrying within them biological characteristics suitable for pre-civilized peoples (aggressiveness, impulsiveness, insensitivity to pain) but unfit for contemporary society. These "throwbacks" to an earlier form of human being could be identified, Lombroso believed, by certain physical features that had survived the cycle of evolution. By studying the post-mortem bodies of Italian prisoners, he developed a set of these characteristics, which he called "anomalies": low cranial capacity, a receding chin, long arms, insensitivity to pain, and so on (see Table 9.2). Lombroso used the term **atavism** to suggest that these individuals were inherently criminal due to their primitive biological states, which rendered them incapable of functioning according to the norms and standards of a complex society.[10]

Unfortunately, Lombroso did not look among non-criminals for the characteristics he found among prisoners. When later researchers, especially the English prison physician Charles Goring, replicated Lombroso's study in 1913, their findings did not confirm Lombroso's theory. Goring concluded criminals could be

Table 9.2 Atavistic features of Lombroso's Primitive Menu

Atavistic features of Lombroso's Primitive Man
Large jaw
Exceptionally long arms
Protruding chin
Large teeth and fleshy lips
Eyes too close together or too far apart
Crooked nose
Index finger longer than the middle finger
Eyes of different hues
Attached ears that lack lobes
Excessive body hair

Source: Adapted from Lombroso, Cesare, and Gina Lombroso-Ferrero [1911] 1972. *Criminal Man*. Montclair, NJ: Patterson Smith.

characterized by generally defective physiques and intelligence, but these differences did not support the theory of a "criminal type" with specific physical markers.[11] Failure to find any support for Lombroso's theory of atavism ultimately brought about its demise.

In the 1930s, Harvard anthropologist Ernest Hooton tried once again to establish a connection between biological features and criminality.[12] This time the research to test the theory was impressively massive. Hooton compared 14,000 prisoners and 3,000 non-prisoners on numerous physical attributes. He concluded criminals were both physically and mentally inferior to non-criminals and that these differences were inherited. Different types of offenders were also thought to differ significantly from one another. For example, Hooton thought murderers and bank robbers had different body types.

Hooton's research contains many shortcomings that undermine its validity. His data can tell us only about people in prison, obviously a small proportion of the total criminal population, and one that is also overwhelmingly lower-class. Any possible generalizations are thus limited at best. Hooton's measures of "inferiority" also reflect his own bias rather than objectively measuring cultural or intellectual inferiority. Tattooing, eye color, low forehead, and narrow jaws are hardly evidence of inferior physical types, as he suggests. Finally, Hooton made two fundamental methodological errors: (1) he assumed that because two factors occur together, one must cause the other, and (2) he compared a large number of prisoners with a relatively small number of non-prisoners, instead of using samples whose proportions reflected their relative proportions in the population as a whole. That would necessitate drawing a non-prison sample of hundreds of thousands for a reliable comparison.

In 1949 a student of Hooton's, William Sheldon, published *Varieties of Delinquent Youth* in which he described three basic body types and their corresponding temperaments: endomorph, ectomorph, and mesomorph[13] (see Table 9.3). Endomorphs, according to Sheldon, are short and round, inclined to put on fat, relaxed, extroverted, and tend to prefer a comfortable and easy life. Mesomorphs are athletic, muscular, strong, and aggressive in personality. They are also assertive, seek and need vigorous physical activity, and enjoy risk-taking behavior. Ectomorphs are lean, fragile, and slender. In temperament, ectomorphs are introverted and shy with a tendency toward physical and psychosomatic disorders.

Sheldon classified 200 boys sent to a rehabilitation home in Boston and compared them with two hundred college students assumed to be non-delinquent. Sheldon found the delinquent youths were decidedly more mesomorphic than non-delinquents. He argued that the mesomorph is more likely to have a higher pain threshold and be more physically aggressive and callous than either the ectomorph or endomorph. He concluded that there is a strong correlation between body type and personality.

Another pair of Harvard criminologists, Sheldon and Eleanor Glueck, replicated Sheldon's findings. They compared 500 incarcerated delinquents

Table 9.3 Sheldon's three body types

Sheldon's three body types		
Body type	Physical attributes	Temperament
Endomorph	Short, round, pudgy	Sociable and relaxed
Ectomorph	Lean, thin, fragile	Shy and reserved
Mesomorph	Muscular and athletic	Aggressive and assertive

Source: Adapted from Sheldon, William 1949. *Varieties of Delinquent Youth*. New York: Harper and Brothers.

aged 9–17 with 500 youths in the same age group who were not incarcerated and added a fourth body type to Sheldon's three: a balanced type for boys whose physiques conformed to none of the original categories. The Gluecks' research led them to conclude that "among the delinquents, mesomorphy is far and away the most dominant component, with ectomorphic, endomorphic and balanced types about equally represented."[14]

The studies conducted by Sheldon and the Gluecks appear to consistently find physical differences between youths officially labeled delinquent and groups not labeled delinquent. However, these findings must be approached with caution. Selecting a sample of persons labeled delinquent and comparing them to a sample of persons not so labeled does not necessarily assure us that we are comparing delinquent and non-delinquent populations. The sample college students compared with delinquents come from a population often engaged in unreported delinquent and criminal acts, from illegal drinking and drug use to stealing, vandalism, and even rape. How many college students are guilty of crimes but escape the label of delinquency is unknown. What we do know from self-report and participant observation studies is that people who are not incarcerated for crime or delinquency report a very high rate of delinquent and criminal acts (see chapter 3). Thus it is possible that what these researchers are actually comparing are delinquents in institutions with delinquents *not* in institutions, and if there really is a difference in body type between the two groups, the interesting question is why institutionalized youths are more mesomorphic than non-institutionalized youths.

We can only conclude that neither mesomorphy nor any other physical or biological characteristic is correlated with crime or delinquency. Indeed, over a hundred years of research has failed to establish any physical difference between criminal and non-criminal populations, from bumps on the head to atavisms to body and temperament types. Should we thus abandon the biological line of inquiry completely, or can we look more deeply into the underlying principles of biological theory to understand the interrelationship of nature and nurture?

Let us take a closer look at the biological perspective by examining the effects of chemical and environmental variables on human behavior.

BIOCHEMICAL VARIABLES AND CRIME

Early biological theories rested upon the foundation that variations in individual constitutions alone accounted for the difference between criminals and non-criminals. Recognizing the fallacy of this approach, researchers began to advance a **biosocial approach** to the study of human behavior that acknowledges the interaction between social environment and variations in individual constitutions as contributing factors in how people act and react (see Figure 9.1). Biological theories began to expand our understanding of crime causation by examining the impact of biochemical, neurological, and genetic variables on human reaction to environmental stimuli.[15] Let's start with biochemical factors that affect the ability to think and behave, beginning with nutrition.

Figure 9.1 Nature or nurture . . . What drives our actions?

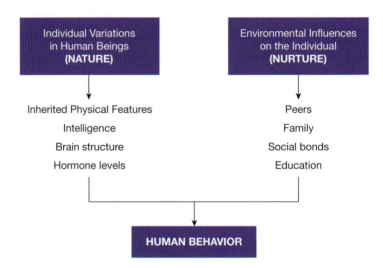

Nutrition

Criminological research has taken seriously the popular phrase "you are what you eat," and has examined the role of vitamin deficiencies, food allergies, and diet, particularly in relationship to juvenile delinquents. Evidence supports the value of a balanced diet in alleviating the symptoms of behavioral and mood disorders such as depression, hyperactivity, and aggression.[16] Too much or too little of substances such as sodium, potassium, iron, mercury, and amino acids can lead to an increase in aggression, hyperactivity, depression, memory loss, abnormal sexual behavior, and learning problems.[17] Ingesting high quantities of refined sugar, white flour, and saturated fat may also put individuals at a greater risk of developing mental disorders such as schizophrenia and dementia.[18]

Given these tentative conclusions, criminologists point to the need for further exploration into the link between diet and certain behavioral disorders that lead to violence and crime, and between diet and reduced aggression, irritability, impulsivity, and anti-social behavior.[19] We also need to evaluate the relationship between nutritional deficiencies and social class. Poorer children and adolescents may be at a greater risk of inadequate nutrition given the expense of buying the varieties of food necessary for a well-balanced diet. The wide availability and relative low cost of fast foods may also lead to excessive chemical additives and sugar in the diets of lower-class individuals.

Blood glucose

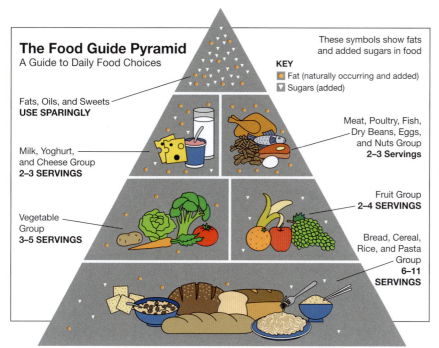

Figure 9.2
What fuels our brain?

Source: USDA Center for Nutrition Policy and Promotion (CNPP). 2015. "Food Guide Pyramid." Retrieved from www.cnpp.usda.gov/FGP

To date, evidence about the impact of blood glucose (sugar) on levels of behavior—especially violent, aggressive behavior—is inconclusive. Studies have examined the effects of **hypoglycemia**, a condition that occurs when blood glucose falls below the necessary level for the brain to function effectively (see Figure 9.2). Hypoglycemia can be caused by too much production of the hormone insulin in the body, or by inadequate diet. Individuals experiencing low blood sugar become irritable, excitable, and confused, and often lack proper judgment.[20] Several studies have linked hypoglycemia to outbursts of aggression, violence, and assault.[21] Research has also found a higher incidence of hypoglycemia in repeat violent offenders.[22] We must also evaluate these findings in the context of their interaction with environmental variables. An individual experiencing symptoms of hypoglycemia, if untreated, may continue to exhibit signs of irritability, poor self-control, and lack of reasoning, which can affect his or her job performance, relationships, and other social circumstances.

Hormones

Studies of differences between male and female rates of criminality have focused on the biological differences between the sexes, rooted in sex-based hormones. Research about the male hormone **testosterone** shows no consistent relationship to aggressiveness or sexual aberrations, although some studies support the finding that an elevated level of male hormones can in fact lead to aggressive behavior.[23] However, testosterone levels naturally vary daily and seasonally, making comparisons difficult. Even with some evidence suggesting a relationship between elevated levels of testosterone and behavioral measures of aggression, we cannot assume this condition alone causes criminal behavior. We must instead consider the dynamic interaction between hormonal levels and other physical and social variables.

Research on variations in female hormones as possible links to antisocial and aggressive behavior began in the early 1970s. Studies attempted to show that females are more likely to exhibit poor impulse control, anxiety, depression, and antisocial behaviors just prior to or during their menstrual cycle.[24] The use of this condition, commonly referred to as **premenstrual syndrome (PMS)**, as a possible defense strategy to reduce the culpability of female offenders in criminal cases has been debated among criminologists and in the courtroom.[25] While evidence does support the theory that elevated levels of female hormones prior to and during menstruation can contribute to an increase in psychological and physical stress, there is little agreement about whether PMS is linked to criminality.

Contaminants

Research has linked long-term exposure to certain environmental pollutants such as copper and mercury to the onset of physical, mental, and behavioral disorders. Lead (in paint, water, and soil) and other environmental contaminants can affect the development, growth, and behavior of children and adolescents by causing learning and reading problems, hearing impairment, and brain damage. Exposure can even result in death.

The presence of high levels of lead inside buildings, schools, and apartments has been linked to an increase in antisocial behaviors and juvenile delinquency.[26] Researchers note a positive relationship between concentration of lead in the air and the occurrence of violent crime[27] (see Box 9.1). A recent study at the University of Cincinnati that examined longitudinal data found evidence to support a direct link between prenatal and early-childhood lead exposure and an increased risk for criminal behavior later in life.[28] In the study, after age 18, individuals with elevated levels of lead in their blood before birth and during early childhood had higher rates of arrest for violent crimes than other individuals in the population. It is also important to note that these types of pollutants and toxins are disproportionately found in poor neighborhoods.

The evidence from these and similar studies support the need to develop an integrated understanding of criminal behavior that incorporates research

Image 9.4 *Where is this apartment building that has been condemned for high levels of lead toxins likely to be, and who has been affected by its contamination?*
Chitose Suzuki/AP/Press Association Images

on the effects of individualized components on human behavior and their connection to environmental experiences. We turn now to a discussion of another perspective that examines the effects of brain activity on human behavior, the field of neurophysiology.

BOX 9.1: CONSIDER THIS . . .

Decades of decline in crime rates: is it cleaner air?

The last two decades have marked an unprecedented decline in crime rates across the United States, with incarceration rates also reaching an all-time high. While the link between the two may be logical, researchers and critics note that this is too simplistic of an explanation. Many competing propositions have emerged that attempt to make sense and explain why crime rates have gone down: improved economic opportunities, policing practices, expansion in rehabilitation programs, an aging population, and a declining use of alcohol and drugs. A growing body of research literature, however, points to another completely different source explaining the declining crime trend: the removal of leaded gasoline from the market under the Clean Air Act passed by Congress, which required leaded gas to be phased out by the mid-1980s.

Since then, studies citing the harmful effects of lead poisoning have become abundant. Such poisoning has been found to cause increased depression, aggression, and antisocial behavior. Research studies on the effect of lead on children link it to lower levels of intelligence and learning disabilities, as well as impulsivity and behavioral problems that last into adulthood.

Harvard graduate and Economist Jessica Reyes proposes that the removal of leaded gasoline across the country took lead levels in blood down to a fraction of previous levels. Those who were children when leaded gasoline use peaked in 1973 reached their most crime-prone years around the same time crime topped off in the United States—the early 1990s. Since then, U.S. crime rates, especially for violent crime, have been dropping steadily. Similar findings were reported in a comparison study of nine countries throughout the world, which found that dropping world crime rates were consistent with government-enforced removal of lead from consumer gasoline and paints.

Could the Clean Air Act and similar remedies to remove lead and toxic substances from consumer markets have done more to lower crime rates in the United States than any criminal justice policies have in the past? *What do you think?*

Sources

Chettiar, Inimai M. 2015. The Many Causes of America's Decline in Crime. *The Atlantic*. Retrieved from http://www.theatlantic.com/features/archive/2015/02/the-many-causes-of-americas-decline-in-crime/385364/.

Drum, Kevin. 2013. Lead: America's Real Criminal Element. *Environment*. Retrieved from http://www.motherjones.com/environment/2013/01/lead-crime-link-gasoline.

Meyer, Jim. 2011. Get The Lead Out: Clean Air Tied to Decline in Violent Crime. *Grist Newsletter*. Retrieved from http://grist.org/clean-air/2011–10–18-get-the-lead-out-clean-air-tied-to-decline-in-violent-crime/.

NEUROCRIMINOLOGY

Ever wonder why some people enjoy riding roller coasters, jumping out of airplanes, and wrestling wild animals? Have you noticed how some children, when reprimanded, will cower in fear, while others stand up to authority in defiance? Certainly, we've heard that people are "wired" differently, and that's what makes us act differently and react differently to environmental stimuli. Is there something about the structure and function of some people's brains that makes them more prone to violence and aggression? This question is explored by the growing field of neurocriminology, which relies on the science of neurophysiology to understand, predict, and prevent crime.[29] They work in three main areas of research: neurological impairment, brain chemistry, and attention deficit hyperactivity disorder (ADHD). Let's first take a look at the research on neurological impairment.

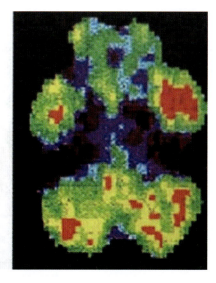

Image 9.5 *The field of neurocriminology is revolutionizing our understanding of what causes crime by allowing us to "see" the brains of violent criminal offenders.*

Public domain

Neurological impairment

Abnormalities within the brain are either inherited or acquired, from poor blood flow to the brain, a head injury, or other trauma. Using **brain imaging** techniques, scientists have been able to capture three-dimensional images of the brain. These allow us to examine the structure and function of various regions and identify tumors, lesions, and developmental deficits. Studies support the finding that individuals who exhibit antisocial behavior, aggression, and violence show significant structural and functional deficits within the prefrontal regions of the brain.[30] They affect the ability to communicate effectively, control impulses, develop social skills, and reason abstractly.

Research indicates that impairments in the regions of the brain responsible for self-control, reasoning, and problem-solving have been linked to violent, aggressive behavior.[31] Criminologists note that at the core of such behavior is an underlying disregard for the rules and guidelines of moral reasoning. Evidence shows a significant number of individuals who exhibit these types of behavior suffer neurological impairment that severely affects their level of cognitive ability and understanding.[32]

Criminologists who study the brain caution that we must view structural and functional deficits as only partial contributors to criminal behavior. If we ignore the social, economic, and political components of crime causation, we reduce every criminal event to the behavior of individual criminals, as though they exist separately from, and are unaffected by, their environment.

Brain chemistry

Research has established a connection between the chemical composition of the brain and the development of different behaviors in response to our surroundings (see Box 9.2). Chemical compounds within the brain called neurotransmitters are responsible for activating and controlling emotions, moods, drives, and other mechanisms of human response. Some neurotransmitters such as dopamine and serotonin affect our ability to tolerate excitement, manage stress, and deal with anxiety. The reason some of us enjoy horror movies while others have to cover our eyes, why many of us panic when speaking in public while some actually embrace it, and why most of us stay up all night before taking an exam is that these chemical compounds vary in their level from individual to individual. The appropriate level of neurotransmitter function within the brain maintains a balanced level of excitement-seeking activity. Individuals without the proper level of chemical stimulation will be unresponsive to normal levels of excitement and thrill, and will seek alternative measures of stimulation within the environment.[33]

BOX 9.2: CRIME IN GLOBAL PERSPECTIVE

Low serotonin levels and the angry brain . . . A study from the U.K.

In 1973, researchers tested the effects of serotonin on behaviors in rats and mice, isolating rats for four weeks and then measuring their serotonin levels. Serotonin is a neurotransmitter manufactured by the brain that affects sleep, mood, sexual function, and appetite, among other functions of the central nervous system. Medications such as Prozac and Zoloft control serotonin levels in the brain to control anxiety and depression. When placed with mice, the rats with significantly lower serotonin rates attacked and killed them, while rats with steady serotonin rates ignored the mice, and rats with higher rates introduced were actually friendly towards them. Rhesus monkeys that had poor impulse control and habitually violent behavior were also found to have low brain serotonin.

A recent study at the University of Cambridge examined how fluctuations in the levels of serotonin in the brain affect regions that allow people to regulate emotions such as anger and sadness. The study used volunteers with normal or healthy serotonin levels that were altered chemically through the manipulation of diet. Individuals whose serotonin levels were depleted were then exposed to photos of faces with angry, sad, and neutral expressions, as their brains were scanned using *Functional Magnetic Resonance Imaging* (fMRI). The study revealed that low levels of serotonin within the brain weakened the brain's ability to communicate emotions from one region of the brain to the other, making it difficult for the prefrontal cortex to control emotional responses to anger. Moreover, sensitivity to serotonin depletion increased the chances of an aggressive response in individuals who might have been predisposed to aggression, according to responses on a personality questionnaire.

Dr Molly Crockett, researcher at Cambridge's Behavioural and Clinical Neuroscience Institute, notes "we have known for decades that serotonin plays a key role in aggression, but it's only very recently that we've had the technology to look into the brain and examine just how serotonin helps us regulate our emotional impulses . . . by combining a long tradition in behavioural research with new technology, we were finally able to uncover a mechanism for how serotonin might influence aggression."

Other international studies report similar findings, linking serotonin levels and aggressive behavior and suggesting violent offenders may need medicinal intervention. In a study at the University of Helsinki in Finland, eight hundred test subjects, including a group of alcoholic, impulsive, and habitually violent Finish offenders and their relatives and other male cohorts, were tested for serotonin turnover rates. The alcoholic offenders were found to have low serotonin turnover in the brain, which researchers associated with low impulse control and a history of suicide attempts. The offenders were also prone to hypoglycemic levels of blood glucose, which researchers concluded played a further role in escalating impulsive behavior into more excitable, aggressive behavior patterns. Another study at the University of Groningen in the Netherlands found "serotonin deficiency appears to be related to pathological, violent forms of aggressiveness, but not to the normal aggressive behavior that animals and humans use to adapt to everyday survival." These results seem to conclude that medicinal intervention to regulate serotonin levels will help keep aggressive offenders from engaging in future impulsive, violent crimes.

Sources

Crockett, Molly. 2011. Serotonin Levels Affect the Brain's Response to Anger. *University of Cambridge*. Retrieved from http://www.cam.ac.uk/research/news/serotonin-levels-affect-the-brain%E2%80%99s-response-to-anger.

Sloan, Falishia. 2007. Lack of Serotonin Leading Violent, Aggressive Behavior. *Journal of Young Investigators* 17. Retrieved from http://www.jyi.org/issue/lack-of-serotonin-leading-violent-aggressive-behavior/.

Valzelli, L. 1973. The 'Isolation Syndrome' in Mice. *Psychopharmacologia* 31: 305–320.

Wlassoff, Viatchaslav. 2014. Serotonin and Behavior. Biopsychosocial Health. *Brain Blogger*. Retrieved from http://brainblogger.com/2014/06/11/serotonin-and-behavior/.

Images 9.6 and 9.7 *How are these individuals—mountain climbers and gang members—both thrill seekers? How is their nature (their level of brain chemicals) influenced by their nurture (their social experiences, opportunities, peer interactions)?*

iStock/guvendemir; iStock/shironosov

Evidence suggests abnormally low levels of neurotransmitters in the brain are associated with impulsive, aggressive responses.[34] People with abnormal levels of the neurotransmitter monoamine oxidase tend to be more defiant of authority, impulsive, and hyperactive and are also more likely to engage in risky behavior.[35] Within this context we can see why some individuals, through their social learning experiences and available network of social contacts and means, may seek to jump out of an airplane, while others may join a drive-by shooting. Once again, we can see the interaction between nature and nurture.

Attention deficit hyperactivity disorder (ADHD)

Over the past several years we've seen a surge of diagnoses of the neurological condition known as attention deficit hyperactivity disorder (ADHD). Children who are merely unable to sit still, do not pay attention in school, and are easily distracted are often misdiagnosed with ADHD and inappropriately treated with stimulant medication such as *Ritalin*, *Focalin*, and *Strattera*. Experts in the medical community refer to this incorrect diagnosis as SIH, or socially induced hyperactivity, a behavior that is learned and has no clear neurological basis. There are three marked characteristics of a true ADHD diagnosis: poor attention skills, deficient impulse control, and hyperactivity.[36] Table 9.4 outlines some of the behavioral manifestations of these three characteristics.

Image 9.8 *How do hyperactivity, distractibility, and poor attention span contribute to delinquent behavior? What role might parents, teachers, and peers play in this process?*

iStock/BraunS

Table 9.4 How do those with ADHD behave?

Symptom: poor attention skills	Symptom: deficient impulse control	Symptom: hyperactivity
Has a hard time keeping eye contact	Interrupts peoples' conversations	Is unable to sit still for a period of time
Mind wanders during a conversation	Is very impatient	Always wants to be "on the go"
Gets easily bored during group play	Jumps from one thought, idea, or activity, to another	Has excessive movement
Has trouble focusing on assignments, homework, tasks	Blurts out information	Has awkward, aggressive motor skills
Is easily distracted by sounds or by others	Constantly needs to be told what to do	Runs around, fidgets

Source: Adapted from Adler, Lenard, and Florence, Mari. 2006. *Scattered Minds: Hope and Help for Adults with ADHD.* London: Penguin Books.

The causes of ADHD are not yet fully known, although experts point to neurological damage, allergic reactions, prenatal consumption of alcohol or drugs, prolonged exposure to environmental contaminants such as lead, and even inherited genetic tendencies.[37] ADHD is a lifelong disorder that begins in early childhood and continues through adolescence and adulthood. In the early years, it has been linked to poor academic performance, bullying, defiance of authority, and lack of response to treatment or discipline. Adolescents and adults with ADHD continue to suffer in their personal and social lives from difficulties in maintaining relationships, risk-taking behavior, erratic work performance, and low self-esteem.

Research has attempted to link ADHD with the onset of delinquency among juveniles. We know children with ADHD are more likely to be suspended from school, get into fights, use drugs and alcohol, and have multiple arrests throughout their lives.[38] Early detection and treatment of ADHD symptoms is thus imperative.[39] We also know this biologically based human characteristic can be compounded by the reactions of others and the reinforcement of negative labeling.

We've seen from our look at neurophysiology and biochemistry that innate differences among individuals produce behavioral differences in violence, aggression, and criminality that are mediated by our environment and our experiences. We turn now to the unanswered question: What may individuals inherit that produces a biological predisposition to criminal behavior?

HEREDITY, GENETICS, AND CRIME

Does criminality run in some families, like blue eyes, curly hair, or tall stature? Are certain people predisposed to violence and aggression simply because they were born that way? How have criminologists attempted to isolate the variable effects of inheritance on crime?

Criminal families

The exploration of criminal behavior and inherited characteristics began in the late 1800s when researchers started to study families that exhibited criminal tendencies through several generations. One study in 1877 traced six generations of the Juke family[40] and attempted to demonstrate a genetic basis for the family's anti-social behavior. Of 709 family members identified, 76 were criminals, 128 were prostitutes, and 206 were on public welfare. However, a closer look establishes no scientific basis for any influence of inheritance. The Juke Family study is inherently flawed because any claim to have found criminal tendency in a family lineage must compare the frequency of criminality between groups of descendants *in the same family*. Herein lays the major flaw, as the Juke family lineage was compared to the descendants of Jonathan Edwards, a Puritan preacher who was a former president of Princeton University and whose descendants included several United States presidents and vice presidents, successful entrepreneurs, and wealthy business owners.

An equally famous family study was the Kallikak family study conducted in 1912.[41] Its subjects were the descendants of Martin Kallikak, who had an illicit encounter with a mentally impaired bar maid during the Revolutionary War before returning home to later marry a Quaker woman (see Figure 9.3). Following the offspring of both unions, researchers found numerous paupers, criminals, alcoholics, and mentally deficient persons from the illegitimate union, but few, if any, from the second. Ignoring all the differences in social and economic circumstances experienced by the children of these two unions (and concealing the fact that some of the photographs of the "deficient" Kallikaks were altered to make them appear moronic and shifty), the study concluded that a genetic cause of antisocial behavior had been established.

The implications of such research had a profound impact on social policy. They largely contributed to the eugenics movement in the 1920s and early 1930s, in which science and policy merged in an attempt to improve the human race through breeding.[42] According to this theory, individual worth and potential were genetically determined; to improve the quality of life in the United States, society needed to improve the quality of the individuals in it. Individuals, classes, races, and countries in power were obviously superior to those at the bottom of the status hierarchy, who had only their defective genes to blame.

Today we can see the weaknesses of both the family studies and the eugenics philosophy. The fact that family members inhabit similar environments as well as having similar genes makes it impossible to conclude that similar behavior is the product only of genetics and not also of the environment. But the history and impact of the eugenics movement demonstrates that theories need not be accurate to affect thousands of people (see Box 9.3).

How then can we accurately explore the link between heredity and criminal behavior? We turn now to an examination of twin studies, which attempt to separate the variables of nature and nurture.

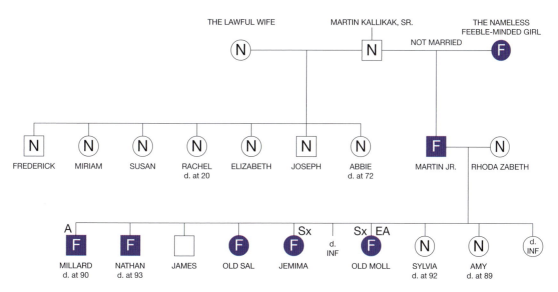

Figure 9.3 The Kallikaks: a family of criminals?

Source: Goddard, Henry Herbert. 1912. *The Kallikak family: a study in the heredity of feeble-mindedness*. The Macmillan Company.

Note: N = normal, F = feeble-minded.

BOX 9.3: CONNECTING THEORY TO PRACTICE

Are defective genes inherited? Policy implications of trait theory

Even when theories have been discredited, practices based upon them may continue to exist. In the early 1970s, evidence came to light that involuntary sterilizations might still be occurring in the United States, for the purpose of social control. In a 1972 federal case looking into the sterilization of two African American children in Alabama, the court remarked:

> Over the past few years, an estimated 100,000 to 150,000 low-income persons have been sterilized annually under federally funded programs ... there is uncontroversial evidence in the record that minors and other incompetents have been sterilized with federal funds and that an indefinite number of poor people have been improperly coerced into accepting a sterilization operation under the threat that various federally supported welfare benefits would be withdrawn unless they submitted to irreversible sterilization.

Emphasizing savings in welfare payments and vague standards like "fitness for parenthood," these practices targeted the same group at risk from the earlier eugenicists—low-income minority women. Physicians themselves acknowledged the common practice of performing elective hysterectomies on poor African American and Hispanic women as part of standard obstetrics and gynecology training in teaching hospitals. A rural doctor in South Carolina refused all medical treatment to his financially dependent female patients when they declined sterilization after their third child.

Only if we believed the children of minorities and the poor were destined (or predestined) to poverty, public welfare, and crime would such policies ever make any sense. Both past and present abusive practices see the poor, the illiterate, and the unemployed as the *source* of poverty, illiteracy, and unemployment, instead of the more complex social conditions that deny individuals the opportunity to succeed.

Sources

Kaelber, Lutz. 2012. Eugenics: Compulsory Sterilization in 50 States. *Social Science History Association*. Retrieved from http://www.uvm.edu/~lkaelber/eugenics/

Roberts, Dorothy. 2000. Black Women and the Pill. *Family Planning Perspectives* 32(2). Retrieved from http://www.guttmacher.org/pubs/journals/3209200.html.

Ross, Loretta J. 2006. The Color of Choice: White Supremacy and Reproductive Justice. In *Color of Violence: the INCITE! Anthology*. Boston, MA: South End Press.

Silliman, Jael, Fried, Marlene Gerber, Ross, Loretta and Gutierrez, Elena R. 2004. *Undivided Rights: Women of Color Organize for Reproductive Justice*. Boston, MA: South End Press.

Twin studies

While family studies have been abandoned, criminologists' efforts to identify genetic influences on crime go on. One continuing problem, however, is our inability to control for variations in social experiences. If we could create an experiment in which genetically identical persons grew up in different controlled environments, we might be able to distinguish genetic from environmentally produced similarities and differences in behavior. Fortunately, nature provides researchers with part of this experiment, in the form of identical twins.

Monozygotic or identical twins are the product of a single egg and sperm and therefore are 100 percent genetically similar. Dizygotic or fraternal twins, on the other hand, are the product of two eggs and two sperm and have the same genetic similarity as any two siblings (approximately 50 percent).

Images 9.9 and 9.10 *How might their similarity in appearance affect the way identical twins are treated, as opposed to the experiences of fraternal twins?*

iStock/praetorianphoto; iStock/DragonImages

This biological fact led researchers to look at how similarly identical twins behave, compared to fraternal twins. Since both types of twins are raised together and exposed to similar environments, greater similarity in behavior among identical twins could be the result of greater similarity in genetic makeup. The first study to report greater concordance in criminal behavior among identical twins was conducted in 1929. Researchers identified prisoners who had a twin and then tried to determine whether the twin was also in trouble with the law. Of thirteen identical pairs studied, ten (77%) were *concordant*; that is, both twins were criminals, while among the seventeen pairs of fraternal twins located, only two pairs (12%) were concordant. The study concluded that the significantly higher level of concordance for identical twins was due to heredity rather than environment.[43]

The vast majority of twin studies report greater similarity in criminal behavior for identical twins than for fraternal twins. Moreover, psychiatric problems such as antisocial personality and conduct disorder are more likely to exist in pairs of identical twins than fraternal twins.[44] Identical twins are also more likely to exhibit behavioral correlates of criminality such as impulsivity, aggression, and lack of emotions, than fraternal twins.[45]

We should not interpret these findings as conclusive evidence that inherited traits are the sole cause of the more frequent similarities in behavior among identical twins. The reason is that we still cannot control for, and therefore remove as a possible factor, the environmental impacts on two individuals who look to the outside world like the same person.[46] While most siblings grow up in the same family and have generally comparable environmental and social backgrounds, identical twins have unique experiences. Often dressed alike, treated alike, and able to confuse friends and teachers, identical twins may experience an environment significantly more similar than same-sex fraternal twins, and any similarity in their behavior may be explained by this fact rather than by genes.

Adoption studies

Another way to examine the impact of heredity on criminal behavior is to compare adopted children with both their genetic and their rearing parents. If adopted children are more similar in behavior to their genetic (though absent) parents than to their adopted parents, it would provide support for the argument that criminal traits are inherited.

One of the largest adoption studies of its kind was conducted in Copenhagen, Denmark, where 1,145 males born between 1927 and 1941 and adopted by non-family members were compared with both their biological and adopted fathers. Researchers concluded that the criminality of the adoptees' biological fathers was of greater importance in predicting their criminality than was their adoptive fathers' criminality, and that the probability of criminality increased for boys whose adoptive and biological fathers were both criminals[47] (see Table 9.5).

Table 9.5 The XYY phenomenon: what are the findings?

• XYY men tend to be taller than comparable XY men
• XYY men convicted of crimes are more likely to be guilty of property offenses and less likely to have committed violent offenses than convicted XY men
• The families of XYY inmates tend to have less history of crime or mental illness than the families of XY inmates
• The prevalence of XYY men appears to be higher in mental-penal institutions than in the general population

Source: Adapted from Jamieson, Anne K. Are XYY Males More Prone To Aggressive Behavior Than XY Males? *Science Clarified: Science in Dispute.* Retrieved from www.scienceclarified.com/dispute/Vol-1/Are-XYY-males-more-prone-to-aggressive-behavior-than-XY-males.html.

Evidence from adoption studies seems to support a genetic basis to criminal behavior. Adopted individuals whose biological parents have criminal tendencies also engage in criminal behavior.[48] Nonetheless, while these studies are more successful than others in separating environmental and genetic influences, they too have serious problems. Children are often placed in adopted homes not in the random ways that are best suited for experimentation, but in ways authorities deem best for each child. The attempt to match adoptive parents with genetic parents may also reduce environmental differences between the two sets of parents to less than we might expect.

Chromosomes

In the mid-1960s, developments in the field of **behavioral genetics**, the study of the role of genetics in human behavior, led to the identification of an anomaly in the structure of the male chromosome and the propensity for violence and aggression. The average person possesses 23 pairs of chromosomes, one pair of which determines the person's sex. Two X chromosomes is the common configuration for females, and an X and a Y produce a male. Occasionally, a person is born with too few or too many chromosomes, and this variation can occur in any of the 23 pairs. Down's syndrome is caused by an extra non-sex-related chromosome, resulting in a total of 47. Klinefelter's syndrome is a condition of certain males who possess an extra X chromosome (XXY) and appears to be related to some mild mental deficiency, and mild degeneration of certain sex characteristics. Another, rarer, variation is the possession of an extra Y chromosome—**XYY syndrome**—seen in a minute number of men.

The link between XYY syndrome and criminal behavior was first studied in 1965, when researchers examined 197 maximum-security prisoners at an institution in Scotland for mentally disturbed patients with violent or criminal histories. Though the expected number of XYY men in the general population is 0.15 percent, the study revealed the incidence of the XYY anomaly among the prisoners to be about 3.5 percent.[49] The response to these findings was immediate. Hundreds of studies in prisons and mental hospitals followed as researchers claimed they too had found a larger-than-expected percentage of XYY men.[50] The media also focused on these reports. Richard Speck, the murderer of eight Chicago nursing students in 1968, was falsely reported as having the XYY variation. The California Center for the Study and Reduction of Violence announced in 1972 that it would begin measures to screen junior high school boys for the XYY chromosome as one part of its research in the prevention of violence. A few states passed laws to screen delinquent boys for data to use in sentencing decisions, and in 1968 a group of doctors started a massive screening of newborn males at the Boston Hospital for Women.

Since then, many studies have attempted to link the genetic abnormality to a predisposition to criminal behavior.[51] They have been inconclusive, providing little evidence that males with the XYY chromosome are generally more violent than males without it. More importantly, the underlying explanation for the supposed relationship between this biological oddity and crime is based on a stereotypic and unsupported view of men that assumes men are innately (chromosomally) more aggressive than women. Only if we assume the single Y of the normal male causes aggression in men (and its absence explains the lack of aggression in women) could we predict an extra Y would make a man "extra male," or extra aggressive.

Behavioral genetics research will undoubtedly continue, but we must for now dismiss the notion that we have found a single cause of serious criminal behavior in the genetic code of a very small percentage of males. While certain traits may be consistent among men with XYY syndrome (see Table 9.5), we can in fact reasonably ask whether there is any actual "syndrome" here at all. Certainly a significant number of XYY men (about a quarter million in the United States alone) lead perfectly normal and uneventful lives.

We must also weigh the influence of innate traits against that of environmental variables. Indeed, in our effort to understand human nature, it is unlikely that we will ever be able to isolate it from our everyday social interactions and learning experiences. With that in mind, we turn now to an evaluation of the biological perspective, to assess how it contributes to our understanding of the causes of crime.

EVALUATING BIOLOGICAL THEORY

The biological perspective has provided us with an array of research studies. Their basic premise is that criminality—as well as other behaviors like conformity and teamwork—is largely a product of constitutional variations and biological conditions that profoundly affect our actions. Whether the studies focus on heredity, genetics, biochemical influences, or brain structure, their underlying message is the same—human behavior, while subject to environmental stimuli and social experiences, is mediated by biological factors. We are not all the same, and we will not respond to the world in similar ways.

But these theories fall short of explaining the diversity and complexity of criminal behavior;[52] they reduce it to an uncontrolled and predetermined response. Not only is this an inaccurate depiction of crime in general, it distorts the relationship of biology to human behavior. We *are* biological creatures, but that does not mean we are ruled by our biology, or that biology and environment compete for control of our actions. Many biological theorists argue that biological, and in particular genetic traits, are innate and permanent. Sociobiologists believe certain human traits such as aggression are universal and the natural product of evolution, and still others argue that specific individuals' genetic code predisposes them to maladaptive behavior.

There is, in fact, no persuasive evidence to support the conclusion that we are biologically programmed for certain types of behavior such as aggression simply because we are often aggressive. Genetic potentials do not lead to inevitable outcomes. Violence, sexism, and racism are biological only in the sense that as humans we are capable of them, just as we are biologically capable of nonviolence, equality, and justice. The fact that we are affected by gravity does not mean we must seek an explanation of crime in gravitational forces. The fact that learning relies on biochemical processes does not mean those processes predetermine what we learn or what we will do with it.

Moreover, research methods in biological theories are fundamentally flawed.[53] The studies do not account for the scope and variety of criminal behavior, generally focusing on street crimes involving violence and aggression and failing to address the criminality of the middle and upper classes. Small sample sizes, sampling bias, flawed statistical procedures, and lack of generalizability make it difficult to draw any reliable connection between biological explanations and criminal behavior.

Finally, a major concern about the biological perspective on crime is its implications for how we treat those who violate the law. If we determine that behavior is entirely controlled by the brain, instead of responding to criminal behavior after it has occurred we must turn to crime prevention programs that identify those at risk for committing crime before it happens. The potential for class, sex, and race bias here is profound.[54] It is a short leap to the assumption that some individuals are biologically inferior, and that we are justified in treating them in an inhumane manner.[55] While these problems make it difficult for us to conceive of any potential benefit we may derive in terms of social policy, nonetheless, we turn now to the policy implications of biological theories of criminology.

PRACTICAL APPLICATION OF BIOLOGICAL THEORY

Table 9.6 summarizes the biological approach to the study of crime and crime causation. For the biological theorist, the starting point for the study of crime is the individual, and his or her physical or genetic codes are the ultimate components of analysis. The characteristics of society are the sum of the characteristics of its individual members. Crime and even war, the most organized form of aggression, are the product of clusters of hostile, aggressive individuals. Economics, politics, culture, and social relations are all reduced to the sum total of the individuals and their biological make-up. Some would argue that this form of analysis is **reductionism**, the attempt to study the whole (society) by reducing every event to the behavior of its parts (people), as if the parts exist separately from and are unaffected by the whole.

Table 9.6 The biological perspective

What is crime?	• Criminal behavior is an instinctive response to environmental stimuli
What is crime occur? (theory)	• Because the brain is the organ of human behavior, any disturbance of the brain structure or function (neurological impairment, chemical imbalances, exposure to toxins, genetic defects) will result in a disturbance of behavior
What is the solution to crime? (policy)	• Monitor infants and children to address potentially harmful developmental conditions • Identify symptoms of behavioral disorders in children and adolescents through neurological examination • Intervene on behalf of individuals identified with behavioral disorders by altering or modifying their social environments to reduce violence-inducing experiences

What then can we say of the policy implications of the biological approach? Do we abandon its potential contribution to the domain of criminal justice practice? The science of criminology would suggest that we shouldn't. To do so would be to ignore a major aspect of human behavior that relies on our innate biological drives and predispositions, those components of our being that make us unique as individuals, different from one another.[56]

In order for criminology to be an effective science, we must recognize that variations in human behavior are a complex interplay between individuals and their social, political, and economic environments.[57] What makes each person unique in his or her response to the surrounding environment? This is the starting point of the biological approach's response to criminal behavior.

Policies guided by biological theory try to alter human behavior by implementing the medical model of identification, prevention, and treatment. Several strategies have been suggested for the early diagnosis and treatment of potentially harmful conditions that can have long-term effects on physical and social development:[58]

- Implementing screening clinics for the early identification of neurological disorders and other harmful conditions. This strategy includes pre- and post-natal care of pregnant women and their newborn children, especially those identified as at risk for exposure to environmental variables that can be violence-inducing, such as alcoholism, drugs, abuse, and criminality among other family members.

- Monitoring children in the early stages of development to screen and test for the possibility of learning disabilities, hypoglycemia, lead exposure, ADHD, and other conditions that result in behavioral changes and conduct disorders.

- Intervening early in the lives of children identified with behavioral and conduct disorders to minimize their exposure to environmental variables that may heighten the effects of their biological condition. This may include drug-based treatment, behavior modification therapy, school-based intervention, educational enrichment programs, and family counseling.

- Supporting research on the origins of aggressive behavior that integrates the role of environmental variables. Further study of the link between sensory stimulation and the need for excitement can help criminal justice professionals develop youth programs that replace criminal activities like running with a gang, taking drugs, and getting into fights with after-school competitive sports, rock-climbing, hiking, and other exciting sports and activities (see box 9.4).

BOX 9.4: CONNECTING RESEARCH TO PRACTICE

Building teens through positive adventures

Teenagers today, especially urban youth, face the challenges of growing up in an environment where drugs, gangs, and violence are often the realities of daily living. Building resilience is often equated with social immunization from the effects of low self-esteem, isolation, depression, and feelings of inadequacy. Outward Bound is an example of a program that for decades now has targeted endangered teens that are consistently making bad choices as a result of negative influences in their lives. The goal of this program is to give at-risk youth an alternative to delinquency through an adventurous outdoors sports and education program. By taking them on expeditions into the wilderness to participate in challenging sports and activities, the program aims to help them realize their positive potential and develop responsibility, leadership, effective decision-making skills, and a dedication to service. Outward Bound currently works with over 70,000 teachers and students throughout the world each year.

Throughout the years, Outward Bound and similar outdoor adventure programs have been examined and evaluated by countless research organizations and University studies trying to determine the impact this type of intervention has on changing the lives of youth by helping them cope with the difficulties and challenges of life. Researchers at the University of Otage in New Zealand examined the role of participation in an Outward Bound experience in enhancing the resilience of youth. In their initial study, they found that participation in the outdoor adventure did indeed increase resilience amongst youth. In a follow up study, they found that resilience was maintained five months following the voyage. Researchers at Texas State University examined the impact of the Positive Youth Development (PYD) approach on 159 urban youth in the United States. The PYD approach uses mentor sponsored wilderness expeditions that are structured around building positive, meaningful, and supportive relationships through the experiences of outdoor wilderness adventures. Findings from the study indicate that this type of programming can be a strong asset-building experience for at-risk youth facing multiple life challenges.

In a meta-analysis of the research literature summing up major findings showing the overall effectiveness of adventure programming, researchers found that adolescents who participate in outdoor wilderness type adventure programs are 62 percent better off on various indicators than those who do not. Moreover, annual evaluation studies and program accountability reports consistently show findings that support the long term positive impact of programs such as Outward Bound, in keeping youth offenders crime-free for at least one year. In addition, while the value and impact of traditional educational programs tend to decline over time, researchers note that participation in adventure education and Outward Bound programs, show both immediate and long-term positive effects in eighteen-month follow-up studies. Scholars agree that more research on variations in outcomes according to differences in participants and programs is needed to assess the overall effectiveness of outdoor wilderness adventure programs.

Sources

Cason, Dana, and H.L. Gillis. 1994, May. A Meta-Analysis of Outdoor Adventure Programming with Adolescents. *Journal of Experimental Education*, 17(1): 40–47. Retrieved from http://jee.sagepub.com/content/17/1/40.short

Comprehensive Accountability Report 2010–2011. Florida Department of Juvenile Justice. Retrieved from http://www.djj.state.fl.us/research/reports/research-reports/car.

Hayhurst, Jill, Hunter, John A., Kafka, Sarah, and Mike Boyes. 2015. Enhancing Resilience in Youth Through a 10 Day Developmental Voyage. *Journal of Adventure Education and Outdoor Learning*, 15(1): 40–52.

Norton, Christine Lynn and Watt, Toni T. 2014. Exploring the Impact of a Wilderness-Based Positive Youth Development Program for Urban Youth. *Journal of Experimental Education*, 37(4): 335–350.

Outward Bound. 2015. *Outcomes.* Retrieved from http://www.outwardbound.org/about-outward-bound/outcomes/.

The biological perspective has reminded us to consider the individual in our study of crime, along with the dynamics of social structure and the impact of environmental variables. In this chapter, we focused on those unique characteristics that originate with the human brain. In the next chapter we turn to an examination of another component of individual variation, the human mind.

SUMMARY

What are the basic assumptions of biological theories of criminal behavior?

Biological theories assume human behavior is intricately linked to our biological constitution, with the brain being the central control for personality (see Table 9.6). Thus, they suggest, a predisposition to criminality may be inherited and criminal tendencies can be passed down from generation to generation. Finally, the biological perspective argues that those who are less fully evolved may behave in ways that reflect their less primitive state of development.

Are certain physical features or body types related to criminality?

Lombroso's theory of atavism suggests that criminals are primitive human beings, identified by a set of physical anomalies such as low cranial capacity and insensitivity to pain. Other criminologists such as Sheldon and the Gluecks conducted studies to correlate body type with delinquency. Early studies of physical features and criminal body types have been widely criticized and ultimately dismissed for their fundamentally flawed research design and sampling procedures.

Do certain chemicals in the body make people more aggressive?

Theories stemming from biochemistry research focus on aspects of nutrition, blood glucose, hormones, and contaminants as factors in human behavior. Research on the impact of nutrition has shown that changes in diet can alleviate the symptoms of a variety of behavioral and mood disorders and patterns of behavior such as aggression, hyperactivity, depression, memory loss, abnormal sexual behavior, and learning disorders. Several studies have linked hypoglycemia or low blood sugar to outbursts of aggression, violence, and assault. Research data has, however, found no consistent relationship between varying levels of the male hormone testosterone and criminal behavior. An elevated level of female hormones prior to and during menstruation, known as Premenstrual syndrome (PMS) has been shown to increase psychological and physical stress among women, which may affect their behavior and cognitive reasoning capacity. Finally, evidence suggests that early exposure to certain environmental contaminants such as lead is linked to an increase in risk for criminal behavior later in life.

Could problems in the brain lead someone to commit murder?

Studies focusing on the structure and function of the brain focus on three main areas: neurological impairment, brain chemistry, and attention deficit hyperactivity disorder (ADHD). Studies support the finding that individuals who exhibit antisocial behavior, aggression, and violence show significant structural and functional deficits within certain regions of the brain. Evidence also links abnormally low levels of neurotransmitters in the brain with impulsive, aggressive responses to certain environmental stimuli. Finally, research on the life-long disorder ADHD has attempted to link this physiological condition with the onset of delinquency among juveniles. Children with ADHD are more likely to be suspended from school, get into fights, use drugs and alcohol, and have multiple arrests throughout their lives.

Can criminal tendencies be passed down from generation to generation?

Criminological research has had tremendous difficulty separating the variable effects of heredity on human behavior from the effects of environmental factors. Studies of criminal families have largely been discredited as methodologically flawed and racist in their policy implications. The vast majority of twin studies report greater similarity in criminal behavior for identical twins than for fraternal twins. However, we must view these findings with caution because we cannot control for the similarity of twins' environmental experiences. Adoption studies seem to support the finding that adopted individuals whose biological parents have criminal tendencies also become involved in criminal behavior. These studies are more successful in separating environmental and genetic influences, but they too suffer some problems, including fewer environmental differences between adoptive and genetic parents than we might expect in agency adoptions that try to match parents' characteristics. Studies attempting to link the genetic abnormality known as XYY syndrome to a predisposition to criminal behavior in males have been inconclusive.

If crime is in the brain, how do we respond to criminal behavior?

Crime prevention strategies in the biological perspective are designed to identify and treat harmful conditions that can have long-term effects on physical and social development. They include screening for the early identification of neurological disorders and other harmful conditions; monitoring children for learning disabilities, hypoglycemia, lead exposure, ADHD, and other conditions; minimizing exposure to environmental variables among children identified with behavioral disorders; and finally, supporting research that integrates the role of environmental variables in the onset of violence and crime.

CRITICAL THINKING QUESTIONS

1. Let us say you were interested in studying the body types of male criminals convicted of violent crimes. You develop a scale from 1 to 10 that ranks individuals on objective physical measures, with 1 being the least muscular, and 10 the most. You administer this scale on a sample of maximum security prisoners across the United States and find that about 75 percent of your sample rank above a 7. What conclusions do you draw? Do your findings support a biological theory of criminal behavior? What other variables would you take into consideration? What are the implications of your findings?

2. Economists have attempted to link the decline in crime rates during the 1990s to a rise in abortions resulting from the 1973 ruling in *Roe v. Wade*, legalizing abortion.[59] The argument is based on the assumption that the majority of abortions occurred among lower-class, poor, unwed teenagers, who, if they did carry their infants to term, would have produced a class of potential criminals. What do you think about this argument? How can the science of criminology shed light on it? What do scientific research methods tell us about the simultaneous occurrence of two unrelated phenomena?

3. Researchers who combine the fields of biology and sociology argue that biological traits may predispose individuals to certain patterns of behavior, but environmental factors influence the nature and extent of their influence. If this is true, what can we do to help children diagnosed with ADHD? What components of their social environment need to be modified to limit the detrimental effects of their biological condition?

E-RESOURCES

Born to be violent? Get more information on this perspective and the growing field of neurocriminology by listening to an interview with criminologist Adrien Raine found at http://www.npr.org/2014/03/21/292375166/criminologist-believes-violent-behavior-is-biological.

To read more about the various regions of the brain as control centers for pleasure, pain, emotions, reactions, and phrenological mapping, visit http://www.phrenology.com/index.html.

Learn more about the relationship between diet and its impact on behavior at "Nutrition and the Brain," found at http://faculty.washington.edu/chudler/nutr.html.

For additional information on the effects of hormones on stress and aggression, visit the American Psychological Association website at http://www.apa.org/monitor/nov04/hormones.aspx.

Get a variety of literature, resources and publications about ADHD from the National Institute of Mental Health at http://www.nimh.nih.gov/search.jsp?query=adhd.

More details about brain imaging techniques and research can be found at http://www.nida.nih.gov/NIDA_notes/NNVol11N5/Basics.html.

NOTES

1   Raine, Adrien. 2013. *The Anatomy of Violence*. New York: Random House.
2   Schneider, Tod. 1 Sept. 2013. The Twinkie Defense Revisited. *Safe School Design*. Retrieved from http://www.todschneider.com/personal-health/the-twinkie-defense-revisited/.

3   Theories of the Causes of Crime. 2009. In *Strategic Policy Brief*. Retrieved from http://www.justice.govt.nz/justice-sector/drivers-of-crime/publications-and-background-information/documents/spb-theories-on-the-causes-of-crime.

4   Bortolato, M. and Shih, J. 2012. Behavioral Outcomes of Monoamine Oxidase Deficiency: Preclinical and Clinical Evidence. National Institute of Health.

5   Ratchfor, M. 2009. Platelet Monoamine Oxidase Activity & Antisocial Behaviors: A Multi-Faceted Meta-Analysis. Florida State University Libraries.

6   Physical Attractiveness and Criminal Behavior. In Richard A. Wright, and Mitchell J. Miller, (eds.), 2004. *Encyclopedia of Criminology*. Retrieved from http://cw.routledge.com/ref/criminology/physical.html.

7   The Founder of Phrenology: Franz Joseph Gall. Retrieved from http://www.phrenology.com/franzjosephgall.html.

8   Ibid.

9   The Complete Work of Charles Darwin Online. Retrieved from http://darwin-online.org.uk/.

10 Lombroso, Cesare. 1972. Introduction. In Gina Lombroso-Ferrero (ed.), *Criminal Man According to the Classification of Cesare Lombroso*. Montclair, NJ: Patterson Smith.

11 Beirne, Piers. 1988. Heredity Versus Environment: A Reconsideration of Goring's 'The English Convict.' *The British Journal of Criminology* 28: 315–339.

12 Lee, Bandy X. 2016. Causes and Cures II: The Biology of Violence. *Aggression and Violent Behavior* 25: 204–209.

13 Sheldon, William. 1949. *Varieties of Delinquent Youth*. New York: Harper and Brothers.

14 Glueck, Sheldon and Eleanor Glueck. 1950. *Unraveling Juvenile Delinquency*. New York: Commonwealth Fund.

15 Piquero, Alex R. 2016. *The Handbook of Criminological Theory*. United Kingdom: Wiley Blackwell.

16 Raine, Adrian, Portnoy, Jill, Liu, Jianghong, Mahmood, Tashneem and Hibbeln, Joseph R. 2015. Reduction in Behavior Problems with Omega-3 Supplementation in Children Aged 8–16 Years: a Randomized, Double-blind, Placebo-controlled, Stratified, Parallel-group Trial. *Journal of Child Psychology and Psychiatry* 56(5): 509–520. Rao, T., Asha, M., Ramesh, B. and Rao. K. 2008. Understanding Nutrition, Depression and Mental Illness. *Indian Journal of Psychiatry* 50(2).

17 Konofal, Eric, Cortese, Samuele, Lecendreux, Michel, Arnulf, Isabelle and Mouren, Marie Christine. 2005. Effectiveness of Iron Supplementation in a Young Child with Attention-Deficit/Hyperactivity Disorder. *Pediatrics* 116: 732–734.

18 Gold, S. 2015. Eat Your Way to Happy: The Mood-Boosting Benefits of Food. In *Yoga Journal*. El Segundo, CA: Cruz Bay Publishing.

19 Zaalberg Ap, Wielders, Jos, Bulten, Erik, Staak, Cees van der, Wouters, Anouk and Nijman, Henk. 2015. Relationships of Diet-related Blood Parameters and Blood Lead Levels with Psychopathology and Aggression in Forensic Psychiatric Inpatients. *Criminal Behavior and Mental Health*. doi: 10.1002/cbm.1954.

20 Johnson, Melissa. 2015. 10 Warning Signs of Low Blood Sugar. *Everyday Health*. Retrieved from http://www.everydayhealth.com/specialreport/diabetes/signs-of-low-blood-sugar.aspx. Kirkman, C. 2014. Hypoglycemia Symptoms. In *Diabetes Self-Management*. Braintree, MA: Madavor Media.

21 DeWall, C. Nathan, Deckman, Timothy, Gailliot, Matthew T., and Bushman, Brad J. 2014. Sweetened Blood Cools Hot Tempers: Physiological Self-Control and Aggression. *Aggressive Behavior* 37(1): 73–80. Gatti, Uberto, and Rocca, Gabriele. 2013. Human Violence Between Biology and Environment: Criminology Towards a 'New' Biosocial Approach. *Italian Journal of Criminology*, 7(1): 22–33.

22 Virkkunen, Matti. 2009. Reactive Hypoglycemic Tendency among Habitually Violent Offenders. *Nutrition Reviews Supplement* 44: 94–103.

23 Van Goozen, Stephanie, Matthys, Walter, Cohen-Kettenis, Peggy, Thijssen, Jos and van Engeland, Herman. 1998. Adrenal Androgens and Aggression in Conduct Disorder Prepubertal Boys and Normal Controls. *Biological Psychiatry* 43: 156–158.

24 Dalton, Katharina. 1971. *The Premenstrual Syndrome*. Springfield, IL: Charles C. Thomas.

25 D'Emilio, J. 2012. Battered Women's Syndrome and Premenstrual Syndrome: A Comparison of Their Possible Use as Defenses to Criminal Liability. *St. John's Law Review* 59(3).

26 Reyes, Jessica W. 2015. Lead Exposure and Behavior: Effects on Antisocial and Risky Behavior among Children and Adolescents. *Economic Inquiry* 53(3): 1580–1605.

27 Zahn, M., Brownstein, H. and Jackson, S. 2014. *Violence: From Theory to Research*. New York: Routledge.

28 Reyes, J. 2012. Lead Exposure and Behavior: Effects on Antisocial and Risky Behavior among Children and Adolescents. Amherst, MA: Amherst College. Retrieved from http://www1.amherst.edu/~jwreyes/papers/LeadBehavior.pdf.

29 Pallone, Nathaniel and Hennessy, James. 1998. Brain Dysfunction and Criminal Violence. *Society* 35: 21–27.

30 Yang, Y. and Raine, A. 2009. Prefrontal Structural and Functional Brain Imaging findings in Antisocial, Violent, and Psychopathic Individuals: A Meta-Analysis. *Psychiatry Research: Neuroimaging* 174(2).

31 Bannon, Sarah M., Salis, Katie L. and O'Leary, Daniel. 2015. Structural Brain Abnormalities in Aggression and Violent Behavior. *Aggression and Violent Behavior,* 25: 323–331. McMurtry, R. and Curling, A. 2008. *Review of the Roots of Youth Violence*. Toronto, Canada: Queen's Printer.

32 Umbach, Rebecca, Berrvessa, Colleen M. and Raine, Adrian. 2015. Brain Imaging Research on Psychopathy: Implications for Punishment, Prediction, and Treatment in Youth and Adults. *Journal of Criminal Justice* 43(4): 295–306. Fabian, J. 2010. Neuropsychological and Neurological Correlates in Violent and Homicidal Offenders: A Legal and Neuroscience Perspective. *Aggression and Violent Behavior* 15(3).

33 Jazaeri, S., and Habil, M. 2012. Reviewing Two Types of Addiction–Pathological Gambling and Substance Use. *Indian Journal of Psychiatry* 34(1).

34 Coccaro, Emil F., Fanning, Jennifer R., Phan, K. Luan, and Lee, Royce. 2015. Serotonin and Impulsive Aggression. *CNS Spectrums* 20(3): 295–302. Seo, D. and Patrick, C. 2008. Role of Serotonin and Dopamine System Interactions in the Neurobiology of Impulsive Aggression and its Comorbidity with other Clinical Disorders. *Aggressive Violent Behaviors* 13(5): 383–395.

35 Roohi, J., DeVincent, C., Hatchwell, E. and Gadow, K. 2009. Association of a Monoamine Oxidase-A Gene Promoter Polymorphism with ADHD and Anxiety in Boys with Autism Spectrum Disorder. *Journal of Autism and Developmental Disorders* 39(1).

36 Adler, Lenard and Florence, Mari. 2006. *Scattered Minds: Hope and Help for Adults with ADHD*. London: Penguin.

37 Attention Deficit Hyperactivity Disorder. 2016. *National Institute of Mental Health*. Retrieved from http://www.nimh.nih.gov/health/publications/attention-deficit-hyperactivity-disorder-easy-to-read/index.shtml.

38 Ibid.

39 Halperin, J., Bedard, A. and Curchack-Lichtin, J. 2012. Preventive Interventions for ADHD: A Neurodevelopmental Perspective. *Neurotherapeutics* 9(3).

40 Estabrook, Arthur. 1916. *The Jukes in 1915*. Washington, D.C.: The Carnegie Institute.

41 Goddard, Herbert H. 1912. The Kallikak Family: A Study in the Heredity of Feeblemindedness. New York: Macmillan.

42 Rafter, Nicole H. 1997. *Creating Born Criminals*. Urbana: University of Illinois Press.

43 Lange, Johannes. 1930. *Crime as Destiny*. New York: Charles Boni.

44 Burt, Alexandra. 2015. Evidence That the Gene–Environment Interactions Underlying Youth Conduct Problems Vary Across Development. *Child Development Perspectives* 9(4): 217–221. Eysenck, M. 2014. Forms of Psychopathology. In *Individual Differences: Normal and Abnormal*. Abingdon, England: Psychology Press, pp. 111–139.

45 Tartakovsky, Margarita. 2013. Surprising Myths and Facts About Antisocial Personality Disorder. World of Psychology. *Psych Central*. Retrieved from http://psychcentral. com/blog/archives/2013/04/06/surprising-myths-facts-about-antisocial-personality-disorder/. Viding, Essi, Blair, James, Moffitt, Terrie and Plomin, Robert. 2005. Evidence for Substantial Genetic Risk for Psychopathy in 7-Year-Olds. *Journal of Child Psychology and Psychiatry* 46: 592–597.

46 Lyons, Michael J. 2007. A Twin Study of Self-Reported Criminal Behavior. In Gregory R. Brock and Jamie A. Goode, (eds.), *Genetics of Criminal and Anti-Social Behavior*. Retrieved from http://www3.interscience.wiley.com/cgi-bin/bookhome/114298845/.

47 Hutchings, Barry and Mednick, Sarnoff A. 1977. Criminality in Adoptees and Their Adoptive and Biological Parents: A Pilot Study. In Sarnoff Mednick and Karl O. Christaiansen (eds.), *Biosocial Bases of Criminal Behavior*. New York, NY: Garner Press.

48 Tehrani, J., and Mednick, Sarnoff. 2000. Genetic Factors and Criminal Behavior. *Federal Probation* 64: 24–28.

49 Jacobs, P.A., Brunton, M. and Melville, M. 1965. Aggressive Behavior, Mental Subnormality and the XYY Male. *Nature* 208: 1351.

50 A summary of studies can be found in Katz, Jack and Chambliss, William J. 1991. Biology and Crime. In J.F. Sheley (ed.), *Criminology*. Belmont, CA: Wadsworth.

51 Raine, Adrian. 2013. The Psychopathy of Crime: Criminal Behavior as a Clinical Disorder. San Diego, CA: Academic Press Inc; Wilson, Jeremy. 2011. Debating Genetics as a Predictor of Criminal Offending and Sentencing. *Student Pulse* 3(11).

52 Race and Crime—Bio-psychological Theory. 2016. Retrieved from http://law.jrank. org/pages/1911/Race-Crime-Bio-psychological-theory.html.

53 Rafter, Nicole. 2008. The Criminal Brain: Understanding Biological Theories of Crime. New York: NYU Press.

54 Cullen, Francis T. and Chouhy, Cecilia. 2015. The Role of Theory, Ideology, and Ethics in Criminal Justice. In Thomas G. Blomberg, Julie M. Brancale, Kevin Beaver and William D. Bales (eds.), *Advancing Criminology and Criminal Justice Policy*. New York: Routledge.

55 Wiarda, H. 2014. Political Culture, Political Science, and Identity Politics: An Uneasy Alliance. Farmham, England: Ashgate.

56 Pinker, Steven. 2002. *The Blank Slate: The Modern Denial of Human Nature*. New York: Viking Press.

57 Walsh, Anthony and Wright, John P. 2015. Biosocial Criminology and its Discontents: A Critical Realist Philosophical Analysis. *Criminal Justice Studies* 28(1): 124–140. Wright, John Paul, Tibbetts, Stephen G. and Daigle, Leah E. 2008. *Criminals in the Making: Criminality Across the Life-Course*. Thousand Oaks, CA: SAGE.

58 Blomberg, Thomas G., Brancale, Julie M., Beaver, Kevin, and Bales, William D., (eds.), *Advancing Criminology and Criminal Justice Policy*. New York: Routledge.

59 Lott, J. 2008. The Myth About Abortion and Crime. *Fox News*. Retrieved from http:// www.foxnews.com/story/2008/07/07/myth-about-abortion-and-crime.html.

CHAPTER OUTLINE

Psychological theories: crime is in the mind

10

In this chapter we will explore the following questions	KEY TERMS

- How does a diseased mind affect the way we think and act?
- Is criminal behavior related to a defect in personality?
- Do crime and delinquency stem from the inability to control certain impulses?
- Is crime a symptom of mental illness?
- What happens when we process information incorrectly?
- Do some individuals imitate aggressive behavior?
- How is crime rewarding to some people?
- If crime is in the mind, what can we do to prevent it?

KEY TERMS

psychopath

antisocial personality disorder (APD)

maladaptation

psychoanalysis

id

ego

superego

neurosis

phobias

kleptomania

psychosis

cognitive theory

behavior theory

behavior modeling

static factors

dynamic factors

cognitive behavioral therapy

cognitive skills training

cognitive restructuring

aversion therapy

token economics

Is it possible that components of our personality affect the way we think, how we react, and the way we treat others? If so, what life experiences shape the development of our minds? What aspects of growth and development affect the mental processes that determine personality? Criminological research has a long history of associating components of human behavior with certain personality characteristics.[1] Studies analyzing the offending behaviors and personalities of murderers, rapists, arsonists, and other types of criminals consistently find evidence to link the structure of an offender's personality to the methods and behaviors of the criminal act. Components of personality such as impulsivity, agreeableness, conscientiousness, self-confidence, and sensation-seeking were found to be directly correlated to the motive behind the rape, the selection of the victim, and the method of operation, producing three distinct patterns of offending.[2]

These findings suggest that in the identification, diagnosis, and treatment of rapists and other sex offenders we must take into account the integral link between personality traits and patterns of offending.[3] The findings can also play an important role in crime prevention, and in law enforcement's investigation of complaints and apprehension of criminal suspects.[4]

Image 10.1 *Who would have known that this elegant, attractive ice-cream parlor owner killed both her ex-husband and lover, dismembered them with a chainsaw, froze them in a freezer, and later took concrete mixing classes to learn how to hide the bodies in concrete in a cellar beneath her store?*

Dieter Nagl/AFP/Getty Images

What the eye sees is not always what the mind reveals. We can clearly understand this concept when we consider the horrific acts of Estibaliz Carranza who in 2012 plead guilty to the brutal and cold-hearted murders of her ex-husband and boyfriend. We can also see this when on May 27, 1991, in the early morning hours, police officers were dispatched to an old neighborhood in a Milwaukee suburb after witnesses reported seeing a young Asian teen running around naked, frightened, and bleeding. Police officers arriving on the scene were met by 31-year-old Jeffrey Dahmer, a white male, who told them it was just a lover's quarrel and that there was nothing wrong. Police escorted the boy back to Dahmer's apartment. Dahmer later strangled the boy and dismembered his body, keeping parts of it to eat and saving his skull as a trophy. One year later, Dahmer was convicted of the murder of 15 young men.[5]

What police didn't know was that Dahmer was on probation for a prior sexual offense—sexually assaulting a 13-year-old boy, a pattern of behavior that marked an integral component of Dahmer's personality and a link to his progressive acts of violence, assault, and murder. His murder spree spanned more than a decade and included a ritual of luring unsuspecting victims, mostly Asian and African American, into his apartment, drugging them, engaging in sexual acts, sometimes torturing them, and then killing them, usually by strangulation.

For years, the acts of Jeffrey Dahmer confounded human understanding and became the subject matter of crime stories in both academic literature and the media. All painted the same picture of a monster, a fiend, and a psychopath. However accurate these labels may be, they do not tell us much about the mind of a serial killer like Jeffrey Dahmer. How can we understand such uncommon acts? What light can the science of criminology shed?

In this chapter, we explore the various explanations of criminal behavior that stem from the psychological perspective. Is crime an uncontrolled or symbolic expression of basic human urges? Does criminality stem from disturbances in childhood relationships that are necessary for the adequate development of inhibitions?

MAJOR PRINCIPLES OF THE PSYCHOLOGICAL APPROACH

We often turn to the field of psychology for answers when unexpected and explosive acts of violence are committed by individuals who by all indications have led seemingly normal lives.[6] The psychological perspective in criminology is not concerned with how we collectively arrive at definitions of normal and abnormal behavior. There is a general assumption within this field of study that normalcy is defined by social consensus. That is, we as a society can reach general agreement about which behaviors fall within the realm of the typical, and which fall outside it.

Our starting point for understanding the cause of criminal behavior from the psychological perspective is the individual actor. The primary component within individuals that dictates all major aspects of behavior is the personality, that element of our being that dictates, motivates, and drives our mind.[7] Various explanations tell us how inappropriate, dysfunctional, or abnormal mental processes can affect the personality and create disruptive, deviant, and criminal behavior patterns. What are these defective mental processes and how do they come about?

The mind is complex, with the ability to reason, believe, imagine, create, and engage in a variety of other mental processes. With this complexity, there are various sources of disturbances to the mental processes of the mind. These sources are distinct, yet all equally important in providing us with an understanding of their impact on human behavior. In this chapter, we identify four sources of defective mental processes: a pathological personality, mal-adaptation, faulty cognitive processes, and inappropriate learning and conditioning. Table 10.1 provides a summary of these distinct approaches to the understanding of crime causation, and we'll explore each in this chapter. We will also evaluate their merit in explaining criminal behavior. Let us begin by taking a look at the emergence of the term *psychopath*.

Table 10.1 Psychological perspectives on criminal behavior

Pathological personality	Maladaptation	Cognition	Behaviorism
• The Psychopath • Anti-Social Personality Disorder	• Psychoanalysis: id, ego, superego • Mental Disease: Neurosis • Mental Disease: Psychosis	• Social perception and the processing of information	• Modeling and imitation • Stimulus-response conditioning

PATHOLOGICAL PERSONALITY: THE PSYCHOPATH

The term **psychopath** found its way into the clinical literature in the early 1940s with the publication of *The Mask of Sanity,* which describes individuals with this type of personality as incapable of experiencing genuine emotions.[8] Psychopathic individuals are described as fully comprehending their social environments and often seeming on the surface to be genuine, sincere, and even intelligent. There is nothing remarkable about their appearance or

Image 10.2 *Notorious serial killer Charles Manson was believed by many to be a psychopath. Friendly and charming, he was also capable of committing horrific acts of brutality without guilt or remorse.*

AP/Press Association Images

demeanor. They can be polite, carry on a conversation, and even seem happy and content.

Deep inside, however, psychopaths lack the ability to identify with or understand how others think and feel. Consequently, they are self-centered, shallow, and detached from others. Their lack of affect or emotions dominates their personality. With prolonged interaction, especially on an interpersonal level, it becomes clear these individuals are chronic liars, do not feel guilt or shame, are reckless and irresponsible, are incapable of maintaining long-term relationships, and engage in ongoing antisocial and disruptive behavior.[9]

Not all psychopaths evolve into criminals. However, psychopathic criminals are viewed by experts as perversely cruel, committing their acts without any regard to the consequences on their victims.[10] Whether it is brutality in the form of torture and rape, or scamming an elderly person out of their life savings, there is a wanton disregard for the pain and suffering they are causing their victim. Experts disagree about the origins of the psychopathic personality. Some studies suggest that environmental variables such as traumatic childhood experiences of neglect, violence, and abuse can play a role in the development of psychopathic traits.[11] Research on inmates with psychopathic personality traits shows that these offenders show a significantly lower rate of accuracy in identifying facial affect than the control group, indicating that they are incapable of accurately identifying certain emotions.[12] Other studies point to the evolution of inherited neurological defects in the brain as the origin of psychopathy. These deficits are primarily in the *amygdala*, the part of the brain associated with emotional learning and reaction, and the *prefrontal cortex*, associated with impulse control, reasoning, and the ability to adapt.[13]

The term psychopath was abandoned by the American Psychiatric Association (APA) in the late 1960s and replaced by **antisocial personality disorder (APD)**.[14] Table 10.2 lists the behavioral characteristics of individuals with APD, including a persistent pattern of violating social norms and a disregard for the rights of others that begins in early adolescence and continues through adulthood. APD is a chronic type of mental illness in which an individual's perception of the social world around them, including ways of thinking and reacting to others, is dysfunctional.[15] Individuals with APD will lie, cheat, manipulate situations, become violent, and even break the law in the selfish pursuit of their own immediate wants and desires. It is not very surprising that some of them come into contact with the criminal justice system at some point in their lives. Studies of inmate populations have shown that the overwhelming majority of offenders classified with a mental disorder suffer from APD.

Researchers also note that individuals diagnosed with APD exhibit both high rates of criminality and repeat patterns of chronic offending.[16]

Researchers who study pathological personalities have found that personality traits such as a consistent failure to abide by social norms, a disregard for the feelings of others, and a lack of remorse for harmful actions predispose individuals to delinquency and crime. We turn now to a discussion of other forms of mental disorders that also put people at odds with society, categories of mental illness that manifest in forms of maladaptive behavior.

MALADAPTATION

How do we respond to circumstances in our social environment? For example, if you have been standing in line for a long time and someone cuts right in front of you, how do you react? Do you get angry and frustrated? How do you manage your anger? Do you politely indicate you are first or push the person out of the way?

The ways in which we react to and manage certain frustrations, disappointments, and hostile situations are all forms of *adaptation*. We learn to act and react in ways that make us better suited to our social environments. Unlike small children, who may first encounter the concept of sharing at preschool or a day-care facility, we do not forcibly take something we want from someone, and we do not bite or hit them when they refuse to give it to

Table 10.2 Signs and symptoms of anti-social personality disorder

• Disregard for right and wrong
• Persistent lying or deceit
• Using charm or wit to manipulate others
• Recurring difficulties with the law
• Repeatedly violating the rights of others
• Child abuse or neglect
• Intimidation of others
• Aggressive or violent behavior
• Lack of remorse about harming others
• Impulsive behavior
• Agitation
• Poor or abusive relationships
• Irresponsible work behavior

Image 10.3
What skills must children develop in order to adapt to this type of structured environment? What happens if they don't develop these skills?

iStock/Pamela Moore

ID... what do
I want?

EGO... how can
I get it?

SUPEREGO... what
is the right way?

Figure 10.1
Freud: one
personality,
three parts

us. That would represent maladaptation, an inappropriate way of coping with the social environment. Why do some individuals exhibit maladaptive behavior?

Psychoanalysis

Modern explanations of the origins of disturbances in patterns of behavior are rooted in the works of Sigmund Freud (1856–1939). Freud founded the psychoanalysis perspective, a method of understanding human behavior by examining drives and impulses within the unconscious mind.[17] His theory divided the human mind into three components: the *id,* the *ego,* and *superego* (see Figure 10.1). According to Freud, we are born with the id, that part of our personality that seeks instant gratification for our immediate need and wants. The id represents our biological drives for comfort, shelter, food, and sex. It does not consider the feelings of others or the reality of the situation when seeking pleasure or satisfying desire. When a baby gets hungry, angry shrieks of protest will send mom into a frenzy, whether she is sleeping in the middle of the night or sitting in a quiet church service.

Over the next few years, a baby begins to learn that wishes cannot always be granted immediately. The second part of the personality, the ego, develops to take into consideration the reality of situations. The ego creates a sense of balance for the unlimited desires of the id by guiding behavior within the boundaries of what is socially acceptable. A four-year-old child who is hungry will consider that mom is cooking dinner, so there is no need to cry or have a tantrum. Instead of acting upon the impulsive and selfish desires of the id for instant gratification, the child may ask for a small snack and then simply wait for the appropriate time to eat.

The appropriateness of our behavior in a given situation is judged by the superego, that aspect of personality that develops around the age of five or six and is the result of the morals and values instilled within us by parents, teachers, and other significant individuals we interact with. The superego is often referred to as our conscience. It is that aspect of personality that determines right and wrong, the watchful eye of the mind that will keep our behavior in line whether we think others will find out about it or

Image 10.4 *Mom has already said no going out tonight . . . What will this teen's superego have to say about her actions?*

iStock/deimagine

not. Suppose the child who wants a snack sneaks into the kitchen to get one anyway when mom refuses. In this situation, a properly developed superego will urge the ego to stop, because the behavior is inappropriate.

A poorly developed superego can be the result of different variables, including inappropriate socialization, unhappy experiences in childhood, and a weak ego damaged by a traumatic event (see Box 10.1). Under Freud's model, an inadequate superego will render the individual incapable of making appropriate moral judgments. Thus, in the struggle between the instinctive needs of individuals and the obstacles presented by social norms, the ego will submit to the unlimited desires of the id, without any consideration for the boundaries set forth by conventional society. An individual driven by a desire for the comforts and pleasures of material goods may decide to steal in order to get what he or she wants. The ego will present the reality of the situation: you don't have enough money, your job doesn't pay well, getting an education will take too long, selling drugs is a bit risky, stealing is quick and easy, and so on. Without a properly developed superego, the individual is likely to act instinctively to meet immediate needs, with little consideration of the consequences of the behavior or the wrongfulness of the act.

BOX 10.1: CONSIDER THIS . . .

Twenty-four years of rape, abuse, and imprisonment

How can a father violate his role as protector and guardian of his own child? When does an individual's sense of right and wrong become so jaded that they cross the lines of humanity to commit acts of abuse, rape, and incest upon their own daughter? The tale of horror began in August of 1984, when Josef Fritzl decided to lock his 18-year-old daughter, Elisabeth, in a windowless cellar of his home in Amstetten, Austria. On Sunday, April 27, 2008, 24 years later, the world was shocked, saddened, and outraged when 73-year-old Austrian Josef Fritzl was arrested for the crime of murder by neglect, enslavement, deprivation of liberty, multiple counts of rape and incest, and coercion. For over two decades, Fritzl held his daughter captive, raping her and fathering seven children with her; one child died of respiratory problems a few months after he was born. Fritzl had refused to seek medical attention for the infant. Three of her children were raised by Fritzl and his wife Rosemarie in the home upstairs. The other three were locked up in the basement with their mother. A jury took just four hours to find Fritzl guilty on all charges. He was sentenced to life imprisonment.

While the trial may have been quickly over and Fritzl continues to pay for his crimes today, the psychological impact on his victims cannot be easily erased. How does one erase, cope with, and heal from such a traumatic ordeal? In the years following the trial and conviction of her father, Elisabeth Fritzl and her children relied on the therapeutic intervention of numerous medical, psychological, and psychiatric care providers as they learned to adjust to seeing sunlight, interacting with other individuals, and walking in rooms with open spaces and ceilings higher than five feet six inches—the height of the underground cellar. They also received medical attention for vitamin deficiencies, anemia, and other physical ailments.

Austrian officials provided them all with new identities and enforced a country-wide no-fly zone over their new location. With this new beginning, Elisabeth and her children had to learn how to live again physically, psychologically, and emotionally. They not only had to learn how to walk in an upright normal position, but also had to be counseled on how to react to and cope with the dimming of lights and shutting of doors. Although their true nightmare was over, they have had to receive therapy for the continued experiences of panic attacks, anxiety, and anger.

It is difficult to assess and even imagine what the long-term effects of years of abuse and neglect can be. Experts note that "time does not heal all wounds. Elizabeth and her three children have been traumatized beyond belief, in ways that most of us cannot comprehend and never will." Psychoanalysis theory maintains that an individual's personality can be damaged by traumatic experiences in childhood development. With this understanding, can we predict the long-term effects this ordeal might have on the victims? What types of intervention would you recommend to avoid the onset of anti-social behavior in the victims? *What do you think?*

Box 10.1 Image 1 *Elisabeth Fritzl was imprisoned for 24 years in this basement cellar by her father, who raped and abused her and fathered her seven children. How does the experience of years of rape and abuse affect an individual's personality?*

Anonymous/AP/Press Association Images

Sources

Austria's House of Horrors. 2015. *Time Magazine*. Retrieved from http://content.time.com/time/photogallery/0,29307,1735500_1580982,00.html.

Mitchell, Juliann. 2008. Josef, Rosemarie, and Elizabeth Fritzl: The Sadist, The Silent, and The Survivor. Retrieved from http://blogcritics.org/josef-rosemarie-and-elizabeth-fritzl-the/.

The Children of Josef Fritzl: 5 Years Later. *Newsdesk International*. 25 April 2013. Retrieved from https://newsdeskinternational.wordpress.com/2013/04/25/the-children-of-josef-fritzl-5-years-later/.

In a healthy individual, the ego has the challenging task of balancing the reality of the situation with the wants and needs of the id, while staying within the boundaries of acceptable behavior as defined by superego. A disturbance in the development of these three components of personality will create a conflict that can manifest as criminal behavior, a form of maladaptation that balances desires with available choices. We turn now to a form of maladaptation resulting from personality disturbances created by mental illness.

Neurosis

A **neurosis** is a form of mental illness manifested by behavior expressing fear, tension, anxiety, and emotional distress.[18] Individuals who suffer from neurosis are well in touch with reality. In fact, they recognize the symptoms of their disorder but simply cannot help themselves. They adapt to their environment in ways inconsistent with the norms and standards of acceptable behavior, so their actions often seem unreasonable, bizarre, disruptive, and inexplicable. Some examples of neuroses include depression, acute or chronic anxiety and panic attacks, irrational fears or **phobias**, and obsessive-compulsive tendencies.

Neurotic individuals develop behaviors to manage and cope with their disorders. Someone with an irrational fear of heights may avoid taking the elevator or traveling by airplane. This can be a very disruptive form of adaptation if it interferes with that person's job or choice of where to live, go on vacation, and the like, but if the alternative will create an unbearable state of panic and anxiety, it is not an option. While most neuroses do not lead to criminal behavior, some can. Individuals suffering from **kleptomania**, the obsessive compulsion to steal, may shoplift items despite their lack of financial need.

Many individuals with neurosis will go through life without any major disturbance in their social interactions and adapt to conventional social norms and roles. Their patterns of maladaptive behavior will in all likelihood go unnoticed by most of those who come into contact with them. The situation is very different, however, when someone suffers from a psychosis.

Psychosis and other major mental disorders

A **psychosis** is a major form of mental illness manifested by the inability to comprehend reality, think clearly, and respond appropriately.[19] Symptoms of psychoses include disorganized and confused thoughts, extreme and unfounded paranoia, mistaken perceptions, hallucinations, and social withdrawal. Individuals may hear voices that command them to do certain things or think they are a spy for the federal government or carry out the work of the devil. They are unaware of their faulty thought processes and their distortion of reality, which makes it very difficult for them to function properly in society and often disrupts every aspect of life, including the ability to work, maintain meaningful relationships, and carry out responsibilities.[20] Table 10.3 provides a brief overview of some of the major mental disorders and their corresponding behavioral components.

Table 10.3 Patients of major mental disorders: who are they and how do they act?

Type of disorder	Characteristics
Schizophrenia	• Distorted sense of reality • No logical relationship between thoughts and feelings • Experience delusional thoughts and ideas • Often have hallucinations in the form of hearing voices or seeing visions
Bipolar disorder	• An elevated "manic" mood marked by irrational behavior such as an increase in spending and risk taking behavior, feelings of grandiosity, and tendency towards extravagance • Manic phase is followed by a period of depression where the individual experiences feelings of guilt, worthlessness, and loss of hope
Psychotic depression	• Marked by feelings of extreme sadness, failure, hopelessness, or rejection • The feelings are inconsistent with environmental variables and rather originate from thoughts, feelings, and ideas that are untrue or unfounded • Thoughts of persecution, paranoid fears of illness, and self-blame for circumstances beyond their control are common
Schizoaffective disorder	• Have symptoms of schizophrenia and a mood disorder such as depression or bipolar disorder • Are unable to distinguish between the real world and what is imagined • Cannot establish concrete thoughts
Dissociative identity disorder	• Have two or more distinct personalities that are often in conflict with one another • Individual is incapable of accounting for gaps in times and experiences • Changes in personality is often associated with a stressful event or emotional experience

Source: Sadock, Benjamin, and Virginia Sadock. 2014. *Synopsis of Psychiatry*, 11th ed. Philadelphia, PA: Lippincott Williams and Wilkins.

The association between crime and psychotic disorders has been researched extensively. Studies show that offenders committing violent crimes often suffer from mental illness, and the presence of a psychotic disorder places individuals at a greater risk for criminal behavior.[21] Delinquents also have higher rates of clinically diagnosed psychotic disorders than adolescents in the general population.[22] In a study of over 79,000 offenders incarcerated between September 1, 2006, and August 31, 2007, researchers found inmates diagnosed with major psychotic disorders such as bipolar disorder and schizophrenia had a significantly higher rate of recidivism over the six-year study period. Prisoners with major psychiatric illnesses were more likely to have had multiple prior incarcerations than inmates not so diagnosed.[23]

We must interpret these research findings with some caution. The presence of mental illness alone does not establish a causal link between criminal behavior and the presence of psychosis; there may be intervening social variables. For example, mentally ill individuals may be more susceptible to weakened social ties, unemployment, poverty, and low educational achievement, any of which may increase their likelihood of involvement in criminal activity.[24] Moreover, the behavior and demeanor of a mentally ill individual may make him or her more likely to be confrontational when approached by law enforcement officers, inflating their rate of arrest in crime statistics.[25]

Criminal behavior associated with the presence of a neurotic or psychotic condition is marked by unconscious turmoil that results in disturbances to the personality. We turn now to another explanation of criminal behavior—that it results from faulty cognitive processes.

Cognition and criminality

Suppose your grades are slipping in one of your classes, you are put on academic probation, and you're in danger of losing your financial assistance if you do not bring up your grades. One of your classmates works as a student assistant to the professor in whose class you are having difficulty. When you tell her of your predicament, she says she is willing to help you out by getting you a copy of the next exam. What do you do in this situation? How do you perceive the option to cheat? Which variables come into play in your solution to this problem?

The branch of psychology that studies the mental processes of understanding, perceiving, interpreting, and manipulating information is **cognitive theory**.[26] Cognitive processes have three major components: perception, judgment, and execution (see Figure 10.2). *Perception* is the accumulation of data we perform when we seek out, recognize, understand and recall certain stimuli and information. *Judgment* is a process of organizing and evaluating the information to make a decision. *Execution* is simply acting on the decision.

According to cognitive theory, individuals who properly process information by having a clear understanding of environmental stimuli and who better evaluate choices are more likely to make better decisions in difficult situations. The opposite is also true. Suppose someone is facing financial hardship after being laid off from work during difficult economic times. Cognitive processes will begin to take place when the individual realizes bills are piling up, foreclosure on the family home is imminent, and child care

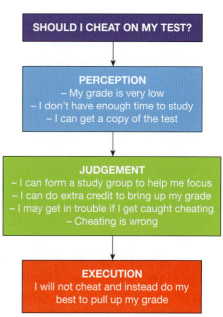

Figure 10.2
Cognitive processes in the decision to cheat

expenses continue to mount. What to do? An individual who processes information appropriately is more likely to explore a range of options that may include getting a loan to pay off bills, refinancing the mortgage to reduce monthly payments, and temporarily taking a lower-paying job to make ends meet. An individual who processes information inappropriately may see criminal activity as a suitable means to meet immediate financial needs. This error in cognitive processing can result from a number of factors including lack of development of appropriate moral reasoning, personal values that emphasize survival over adherence to social norms, and faulty calculation of the long-term consequences.[27]

Distortion in cognitive processes has been used to explain a wide variety of criminal behavior such as domestic violence and rape. Research on the behavior patterns of child molesters notes that they perceive children as desiring sexual contact with adults, believe sexual contact is beneficial to the child, feel entitled to sexual activity with the child, and feel a need to control their social environment, which they see as dangerous and threatening.[28]

Various behavior modification treatments attempt to undo errors in cognitive thinking. Box 10.2 discusses the various techniques of cognitive behavior treatments for effective long term prevention of criminal offending. We turn now to another form of disturbance to personality—faulty mental processes that develop through learning experiences.

BOX 10.2: CONNECTING THEORY TO PRACTICE

Restructuring distorted thinking—cognitive behavior therapy in action

When faced with multiple failures at a task, do you stop trying or do you continue your attempts? When you approach a problem, do you see multiple solutions or are your choices either/or? When you experience pain or happiness, do you feel in control of those emotions or are those experiences imposed on you? How does one begin to think in a way that positively affects choices and actions? What is the true meaning of cognitive change?

Cognitive behavior therapy (CBT) refers to a category of clinical intervention that targets the way an individual thinks. They are premised on the belief that cognitive processes govern mood and behavior and therefore, changes in thinking mechanisms will result in changes in feelings and behaviors. Researchers note that the goal of cognitive behavioral intervention is to change the way an individual perceives, reflects upon, and, in general, thinks about his/her life circumstances. Cognitive behavioral therapy is therefore designed to help people become more aware of those thought processes that lead to maladaptive behaviors and make the necessary changes in order to achieve positively valued goals.

Treatment interventions for sexual offenders are designed to prevent attacks from recurring by emphasizing the control of deviant arousal patterns and correcting cognitive distortions.

In their seminal work on sex offender therapy, researchers Barry Maletzky and Cynthia Steinhauser published a 25-year follow up on 7,275 sex offenders treated with behavior modification in a northeastern United States clinic. The patients included child molesters, pedophiles, rapists, and exhibitionists. These are some of the behavior modification techniques used to alter their thoughts and reactions to certain stimuli:

- *Aversive conditioning*: A negative stimulus (such as an offensive odor) is paired with the onset of sexual arousal to an offending scenario (such as child pornography).
- *Plethysmographic biofeedback:* The plethysmograph measures volume changes of the penis. This allows the offender to reduce arousal to deviant thoughts or images using objective evidence from visual cues that indicate when arousal is increasing or decreasing.
- *Aversive behavior rehearsal*: This technique is used primarily for the crime of exhibitionism. Offenders are required to perform an actual offense before therapeutic staff who are instructed not to respond, and the offender becomes conditioned not to be aroused by the offending behavior.
- *Masturbatory reconditioning*: The role of sexual fantasies plays a major part in patterns of sexual offending. In this technique, offenders are reconditioned to change the themes of their sexual fantasies by becoming aroused to consensual, non-deviant sexual scenarios.
- *Vicarious sensitization:* Stimuli such as a video can make an offender more cognitively aware of negative effects on the victim of a sexual crime.
- *Relapse prevention:* Identifying thoughts or events that trigger offending behavior may inhibit patterns of offending before they begin.
- *Cognitive restructuring:* Group therapy is used to discuss and correct thinking errors offenders make to rationalize, minimize, or justify their actions. All offenders do not share the same distortions and can therefore recognize the errors in each other's thinking in a group setting.

Treatments were administered at the clinic on an outpatient basis. Telephone follow-up interviews were given over the course of the study between 1973 and 1997. Police records were also reviewed and, in some cases, plethysmographs were checked.

Overall, the treatments appeared generally effective over the time period. According to Maletzky and Steinhauser's data, the rate of reoffending for those who did not prematurely drop out of treatment was 1.7 percent of 5,606 participants, versus 8.1 percent of the 1,669 participants who did quit early.

The benefits of cognitive behavior treatment for sexual offenders have been well documented in the empirical literature. Researchers also note that behavioral modification treatments are most effective when customized to individual offenders and their circumstances.

Sources

Clark, Patrick. 2010. Preventing Future Crime with Cognitive Behavioral Therapy. *NIJ Journal* 265. National Institute of Justice, Office of Justice Programs, Washington, D.C.

Lamont, William M. and Marshall, Liam E. 2014. Psychological Treatment of Sex Offenders. *Psychiatric Clinics of North America* 37(2): 163–171.

Maletzky, Barry M. and Steinhauser, Cynthia. 2002. A 25-Year Follow-Up of Cognitive/Behavioral Therapy with 7,275 Sexual Offenders. *Behavior Modification* 26(2): 123–147.

BEHAVIORISM AND CRIMINALITY

Much of what we do is the result of learning. What we watch on television, the way our parents handle problems, and the reactions we get from others all serve as learning experiences from which we develop our various patterns of behavior. **Behavior theory** says that human actions are derived from learning experiences that include observing others and getting reinforcement for certain behaviors. Let us first turn to the concept of observation and see how it affects our learning.

Modeling

Children learn from their parents all the time. Without the input of any lecturing, instructing, or admonishing, a child will learn what to think and how to act, just by watching the behavior of mom and dad. For example, a child may grow up in a home where parents make derogatory statements about certain racial groups, participate in racist rallies and meetings, and forbid their children to have friends who are minorities. Such experiences can lead the child to grow up with similar attitudes and behavior patterns. This type of learning is called **behavior modeling**, learning by watching, listening, and copying what we see and hear.

Prominent theorist Albert Bandura noted that individuals become violent and aggressive

Image 10.5 *Even though this child is actually playing, what role does the social learning mechanism of modeling play here?*

iStock/Jaimie D. Travis

Image 10.6
What impact might this type of sporting event have on the behavior of observers?

Jens Meyer/AP/Press Association Images

through life experiences that teach them to act that way.[29] These experiences can be very personal, such as being physically abused as a child or growing up in a neighborhood where assault and homicide were common occurrences, or less personal, like viewing violent interactions in films or television and by playing video games (see Box 10.3). For example, a child who watches his mom being slapped by his dad when dinner is not ready may in turn slap his classmate at daycare when he doesn't get a toy back immediately. Another child watches a cartoon where an angry character hits another on the head with a hammer and then gets up immediately, without being injured or hurt. The next day, the child recalls the cartoon and decides to hit his classmate on the head with a block. In both cases, the children responded in a violent manner. Table 10.4 summarizes the various sources from which we model our behavior.

BOX 10.3: CONNECTING RESEARCH TO PRACTICE

Media violence and behavior . . . Lessons learned from research

The global entertainment market has experienced unprecedented growth over the past decade or so. Media technology is now more than ever available to people of all ages and social backgrounds, worldwide, in various forms. Today, it is estimated that over 98 percent of U.S. homes own televisions, VCRs or DVD/DVR players, video game systems, computer devices, and electronic tablets of some kind.

In a study by the Parents Television Council (PTC), researchers found that "the volume and degree of violent content shown on broadcast and cable television are virtually indistinguishable" and "broadcast TV shows consistently underrated graphically-violent content as appropriate for 14-year-old children, even though similar content on the cable networks was rated for mature audiences only." Moreover, viewers watching certain programs are exposed to bladed weapons or guns every 3 minutes. Violent content includes exposure to instances and occurrences of physical torture, mutilation, dismemberment, graphic killings, child molestation, and rape. The study concludes that broadcast television, contrary to popular belief, is not a safe media environment for children.

The empirical literature presents clear and compelling evidence of the link between media violence and aggression. Psychologists have performed hundreds of studies testing the effects of media violence and aggressive behavior. Longitudinal findings suggest that:

- Exposure to media violence is a contributing factor to the development of aggression.
- Early childhood exposure to media violence is strongly correlated with aggressive behavior for both males and females in adulthood.
- Identification with same sex aggressive characters on television can be a predictor of adult aggression in both males and females.
- Men who report to be high television violence viewers as children are three times as likely to have been physically confrontational with their spouses, have responded to an insult by shoving a person, or to have been convicted of a crime.

- Women who report to be high television violence viewers as children are four times as likely to have punched, beaten, or choked another adult.

So, with this research evidence at hand, what can be done? In response to the growing body of evidence, media outlets have developed several mechanisms to warn people about the content they will be watching. The Motion Picture Association of America (MPAA) has a full-time board stationed in Los Angeles, California that reviews and rates each movie based on how most parents would respond to it. Upon review and a group discussion and vote, the film is given its rating. Violent content is one of the main factors the board must consider when viewing any film.

Video games are given similar ratings by the Entertainment Software Rating Board (ESRB) so consumers can make informed decisions about their software purchases. Computer and video games with the "Mature" rating may contain "intense violence" and/or "blood and gore," and most stores and other outlets are not allowed to sell them to anyone under 18 without a parent's or legal guardian's consent.

In 1999, the Federal Communications Commission (FCC) announced it would begin requiring television manufacturers to install *V-Chips* into their product (the V stands for "violence"). Parents program the chip with a code to block certain television programming based on its content as set forth by FCC programming ratings. As of January 1, 2000, all television sets 13 inches or larger sold in the United States must include a V-Chip. As of March 1, 2007, all televisions and set-top boxes are required to have digital tuners, and therefore need the new version of the V-Chip.

According to a 2003 study on V-Chip usage, only 27 percent of all parents in the research sample of parents who owned the V-Chip actually used it. Those who did not use it cited difficulty in understanding how to program it, and the inability to get it to work properly. Another study conducted in 2004 found similar results. Of 1,001 parents of children between the ages of 2 and 7, only 15 percent had used the V-Chip. Some stated they were not even aware that their television sets had the device. In April of 2007, the FCC released a report on the use of V-Chip technology, citing the need to make parents more aware of the device and its usage through education.

Sources

American Psychological Association. 2003. *Childhood Exposure to Media Violence Predicts Young Adult Aggressive Behavior, According to a New 15-Year Study.* Retrieved from http://www.apa.org/news/press/releases/2003/03/media-violence.aspx.

Entertainment Software Rating Board. 2015. *Game Ratings and Descriptor Guide.* Retrieved from http://www.esrb.org/index-js.jsp.

Huesmann, L. R., Moise-Titus, J., Podolski, C., and Eron, L. D. 2003. Longitudinal Relations Between Children's Exposure to TV Violence and Their Aggressive and Violent Behavior in Young Adulthood: 1977–1992. *Developmental Psychology* 39: 201–221.

Motion Picture Association of America. 2015. *How Movies Are Rated.* Retrieved from http://www.mpaa.org/film-ratings/.

Parents Television Council. 2013. *An Examination of Violence, Graphic Violence and Gun Violence in Television.* Retrieved from http://w2.parentstv.org/main/Research/Studies/CableViolence/cableviolence2013.aspx.

V-Chip: Viewing Television Responsibly. 2012. Federal Communications Commission, Washington, D.C. Retrieved from http://transition.fcc.gov/vchip/.

Table 10.4 Whom do we observe?

Family, peers, co-workers, television figures, political leaders, etc.	
Positive role modeling	Negative role modeling
sharing	apathy
cooperation	verbal abuse
peaceful conflict resolution	hostility
honesty	aggressive conflict resolution
accepting responsibility	manipulation
caring for the feelings of others	deception
respecting authority	blaming others
working hard	praising violence
commitment to community	rebellion

Research studies show a strong correlation between exposure to violence and hostility and aggressive behavior.[30] Children who see repeated patterns of abuse at home are more likely to exhibit aggressive tendencies throughout their lives and more likely to be abusive in their own relationships.[31] Moreover, studies on the effects of violent video games on behavior show a positive relationship between playing violent video games and having hostile thoughts, acting aggressive, and engaging in delinquency.[32] Children who are exposed to violent content in video games become more aggressive over a period of time than their counterparts who have less exposure, even when controlling for how aggressive the children are at the beginning of the research study. In 2001 12-year-old Lionel Tate, who weighed 170 pounds, was charged with murder in the beating death of his six-year-old cousin Tiffany. Young Lionel claimed it was an accident. He didn't mean to kill his cousin; he was imitating the pro wrestling moves he had been watching. He thought it would be all right to body-slam her, and that she could get up and walk away unhurt, just like they do on television.[33]

Researchers note that the observation of violence, hostility, and aggression leads us to model those patterns of behavior, communicating to us that this is an acceptable way of interacting. Moreover, prolonged exposure to violence desensitizes us to its emotional impact. If we see someone getting slapped, punched, beaten, or killed over and over again, whether at home, in our neighborhood, or on television, it becomes an almost ordinary event.[34] Modeling of aggressive, violent behavior also occurs, and is likely to persist and be repeated, if the outcome of the encounter is positively reinforced, such as by showing it as acceptable or making the aggressor a hero. Let's look at the effects of positive and negative reinforcement on modeling.

Stimulus-response conditioning

Image 10.7 *How do you think this dog learned to shake hands at his owner's command? Did the anticipated reward have anything to do with it?*
iStock/PhotoTalk

Behavior theory is based on the assumption that actions are learned and maintained by the results or consequences they produce.[35] Thus, behavior is more likely to persist the more it is rewarded. Think for a moment about someone starting a new diet and exercise program. How long do you think the person will continue that program if it does not produce the intended consequences of losing weight or having a healthier body?

Behavior can be reinforced in direct or indirect ways (see Figure 10.3). Direct reinforcement occurs when the behavior itself is rewarding. When you exercise and eat well, you feel better and your body is healthier. *Direct reinforcement* also occurs when the behavior is praised by another person, for example, someone notices you working out at the gym and tells you you're looking great. *Indirect reinforcement* occurs when you see someone else's behavior producing positive results. When you attend your high school reunion in 20 years and that chubby kid that everyone picked on is now lean and physically fit, you may decide to follow his or her diet and exercise regimen.

Patterns of delinquent and criminal behavior often persist because of rewards associated with them as well. Reinforcement and punishment also influence the extent to which an individual exhibits a behavior that has been learned. Studies of gang affiliation and membership indicate that individuals join a gang to gain a sense of respect, belonging, and acceptance. Behaviors such as assault, robbery, vandalism, and homicide are not only accepted but praised as demonstrations of loyalty to the norms and values of the gang. These rewards

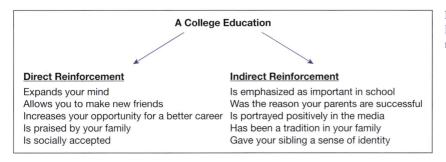

Figure 10.3
Direct and indirect
reinforcement

for criminal acts further reinforce the gang member's reputation for violence and sense of group identity.[36] Research on the effects of rewarding and punishing violence in video games shows those individuals who played games where violence is praised or rewarded exhibit more hostile thinking and aggressive behavior than individuals who play games where violence is punished.[37]

Human behavior, according to the behavioral perspective, is thus a response to the environment. The presence or absence of a behavior in the future depends on the balance between the rewards and punishments associated with it now. A child who jokes around in class and receives praise and admiration from peers may continue to be the class clown, despite being punished by the teacher. The reward associated with the behavior is greater than the punishment. Violence, aggression, and criminal behavior can be rewarded in many ways. The association between criminal activities and the rewards of excitement, thrill, money, praise, and group membership will increase the individual's participation in these activities, despite the risks of punishment and social disapproval.

While all this makes sense, behavioral theory does not account for the role cognitive variables play in the way we interpret outcomes as positive or negative. Why is the approval of peers, for example, more rewarding to some individuals than the approval of parents, or vice versa? Why does someone resort to gang membership as a source of unity and belonging, as opposed to joining an athletic team or school club? In fact, the psychological perspective in general says very little about the effects of social structures on personality, modeling, and behavior. With this in mind, we turn now to an evaluation of the contribution psychological theories have made to our understanding of criminal behavior.

EVALUATING PSYCHOLOGICAL THEORY

The psychological perspective in many ways provided us with an understanding of crime that fills a void in the literature. It helps us comprehend behaviors that environmental variables alone cannot explain. Psychological theories paved the way toward an understanding of the role of personality in shaping human behavior, as well as the influence of role models on learning and the effects of rewards on its persistence. Now, when we read headlines about an ordinary

Image 10.8 *How can psychological theories help us understand why Kisha Holmes, a 35-year-old mother of three, killed her children then herself, in an apparent murder-suicide?*
David Tulis/AP/Press Association Images

mother like Kisha Holmes who killed her three children, and wonder, *what was she thinking?*, we can develop a scientific understanding of what she really *was* thinking, and an understanding of the faulty thought processes that compelled her to kill her children and then kill herself.[38]

Despite these contributions, psychological theories of criminal behavior have been criticized on several grounds. One major shortcoming is their reliance on research conducted on criminals and delinquents within a clinical or institutional setting and rarely in their homes, on the streets, or in their neighborhood. This approach overlooks the influence that jail, detention, or a mental hospital may have on an individual's mental state and thought processes.[39]

The psychoanalytic approach has been regarded by critics as being fundamentally flawed, relying on empirical evidence that is based on unconscious memories triggered during therapy.[40] These memories can often be the result of prompting or suggestions made by the clinician, rather than objective data. Moreover, to say that certain unconscious memories from early traumatic childhood experiences are later on expressed through behavioral symptoms and disturbed personality traits adds little to our scientific understanding of crime and delinquency. That is, if we find someone that exhibits symptoms of antisocial behavior, low self-esteem or other negative disposition, then we are to say that they had experienced some trauma during childhood. This prediction, however, is difficult to make with any true empirical accuracy.

Moreover, psychological theories attribute variations in human behavior to differences in personality, without accounting for social conditions such as poverty, lack of opportunity, and cultural differences that influence how individuals see the world around them and react to different situations.[41] Thus, these theories fail to explain variations in crime rates among different groups. Why do men commit far more crimes than women? Are men more likely to suffer mental illness then women, or is the difference more a product of how the two genders are socialized?[42] With their emphasis on an individual level of explanation, psychological theories also fail to account for changes in crime trends over time. It is very difficult to argue that criminal behavior declined during certain time periods because people were more mentally balanced.

This brings us to the final criticism of psychological theory. By what standards are we measuring normality?[43] Psychological theories interpret behavior based on the assumption that we arrive at the definition of normal by social consensus. But social structure plays a role in imposing labels and legal definitions on the behavior of certain individuals. As we've seen in chapter 2, whether we define behaviors as normal or abnormal, legal or criminal, depends on who has the power to define, not on what the majority thinks. We cannot assume that because someone does something others consider abnormal, there is anything wrong or different about that individual's personality.

Moreover, many individuals who violate the norms of society and engage in horrible acts of violence and crime are not diagnosed with any type of psychological disorder[44] (see Box 10.4). Psychological theories rely on the assumption that individuals commit crime because they have some type of personality or mental problem; cure these individuals and the crime problem will go away. With a cautious eye on this reasoning, we turn now to a brief overview of crime control strategies offered by the psychological perspective.

BOX 10.4: CRIME IN GLOBAL PERSPECTIVE

The Abu Ghraib prison guards

Abu Ghraib was a United States Army detention center for prisoners captured in Iraq from 2003 to 2006. Located 20 miles west of Baghdad, Iraq, the prison held as many as 3,800 detainees. The prison was operated and run by U.S. Army soldiers as well as private contractors. It was also the site of one of the largest and most disturbing scandals in U.S. military history that marked a systematic failure of military tactics, leadership, and humanity. We as a country learned of this when in 2004, photographs were released showing the graphic acts of torture and abuse perpetrated by U.S. soldiers at Abu Ghraib.

The world was shocked and horrified at the evidence of physical, psychological, and sexual abuse of prisoners that included forced nudity, torture, rape, assault, humiliation, and homicide. Photos released for the world to see and ponder included American soldiers punching, slapping, and kicking detainees; arranging detainees in sexually explicit positions; forcing detainees to wear women's underwear and masturbate themselves while being videotaped; positioning a detainee on a box and attaching wires to his finger, toes, and penis to deliver electric shocks; and taking photos with a detainee with a dog collar around his neck.

The U.S. military has a rigorous screening process in place for those who want to enlist. It includes criminal and financial background checks, physical and mental aptitude testing, drug and alcohol abuse history screening, chronic sexual disease history screening, and moral character screening. After these tests, the military still holds the right to refuse service enlistment to anyone with questionable character, behavior or personality issues, or a conscientious objection to war.

So, how could at least six members of the 372nd Military Police Company perpetrated such atrocious crimes against the prisoners detained at the Iraqi Abu Ghraib military war prison? By all accounts, these soldiers were put through a rigorous testing process to make sure they would never perpetrate these kinds of heinous acts. Still, they *did*.

Behavioral assessments alone cannot determine the risk for potential future criminal behavior. Many other individual factors can contribute to whether a person is prone to deviance and/or violence. To assess risk based solely on one set of factors is to turn a blind eye to many other potential causes, and ultimately, to other potential treatments and crime prevention measures. While psychological testing can be a useful tool in evaluating potential criminals, it should not be the only tool we rely upon, a lesson painfully learned at Abu Ghraib.

Sources

Iraq Prison Abuse Scandal. 2015. *CNN Library*. Retrieved from http://www.cnn.com/2013/10/30/world/meast/iraq-prison-abuse-scandal-fast-facts/index.html.

Military Selection and Psychological Testing. 2010. *Psychology*. Howard University, Washington, D.C. Retrieved from http://psychologytec.blogspot.com/2010/03/military-selection-and-psychological.html.

Powers, Rod. 2009. United States Military Enlistment Standards. Retrieved from http://usmilitary.about.com/od/joiningthemilitary/a/enlstandards.htm.

PRACTICAL APPLICATION OF PSYCHOLOGICAL THEORY

Table 10.5 summarizes the psychological approach to the study of crime and crime causation. For the psychologist, crime control strategies based on the psychological perspective focus on two techniques: identifying and treating emotional problems and conflicts before they manifest as criminal behavior, and treating individuals who have already violated the law and are suffering some type of psychological disturbance.[45]

Predicting criminality before it occurs

Policies that try to predict future criminal behavior do so by identifying risk factors such as early childhood aggression, truancy in school, and teenage alcohol and drug abuse as indicators.[46] Policy makers rely on studies showing

Table 10.5 The psychological perspective

What is crime?	• Crime is purposeful behavior that is a response to certain felt needs
What does crime occur? (theory)	• Because the personality controls motivation and all aspects of human behavior, any disturbance of the mental processes affecting personality (personality disorder, mental illnesses, errors in cognitive development, inappropriate modeling) will result in a disturbance of behavior
What is the solution to crime? (policy)	• Early detection of behavior symptoms of psychological problems that may be predictive of future criminal behavior • Therapeutic intervention and treatment of individuals identified with a psychological disorder to correct the faulty thought process or minimize its impact on behavior

children who display early signs of aggression and disruptive behavior are likely to persist in these patterns of behavior as adults.[47]

Programs to identify early warning signs of interpersonal conflicts, anger, depression, substance abuse, and other symptoms of psychological problems are meant to help us identify a condition and intervene with therapy and counseling to avoid its escalation into violence and crime.[48] When a problem is suspected, parents, teachers, school-based clinicians, employers, and social welfare and juvenile justice agencies are encouraged and often required to make a referral to individual or group counseling, substance abuse treatment, mental health assessment, or family therapy.[49]

We can divide strong predictors of future involvement in criminal activities[50] into two categories: *family factors* such as coercive or inconsistent parenting techniques, and *child factors* such as hyperactivity and conduct disorder. Within each category, static factors are experiences in the past that cannot be reversed or altered. Dynamic factors are capable of changing over time with treatment or counseling. Table 10.6 summarizes these factors. The task of predicting criminal behavior is only one step to take in the direction of crime prevention, according to the psychological perspective. A variety of programs, which we look at next, are designed to intervene on the behalf of individuals who have already become engaged in criminal activity.

Responding to criminality after it occurs

Psychological theories say behavior, including criminal behavior, originates within the mind.[51] Correcting inappropriate behavior therefore focuses on correcting faulty mental processes. Psychologically based treatment practices operate at several levels, including school based counselors, private clinicians, and mental health practitioners in institutional settings such as a mental hospital or prison. Interventions range from individual counseling to behavior modification therapy.

According to the literature, criminal behavior is often connected to deep-rooted, unconscious hostilities and anxieties that, if left in the hidden mind,

Table 10.6 Behavior predictors of future criminality

	Family factors	**Child factors**
Static risk	• Parental involvement in criminal activity • Complications during pregnancy	• Age of onset of delinquency • Age of onset of alcohol and drug use
Dynamic risk	• Parental mental health • Parental management • Family structure • Adverse family environment	• Lack of self control • Developmental delay • Aggression • School related problems such as truancy • Involvement with alcohol and drugs • Experiences of abuse and maltreatment

Source: Leschied, Alan, Debbie Chiodo, Elizabeth Nowicki, and Susan Rodger. 2008. Childhood Predictors Of Adult Criminality: A Meta-Analysis Drawn From The Prospective Longitudinal Literature. *Canadian Journal of Criminology and Criminal Justice,* July 2008.

will interfere with any effort at rehabilitation.[52] Mental health experts often work with offenders through counseling sessions to uncover repressed memories from traumatic childhood experiences that may be driving their delinquent or criminal behavior. Critics note, however, that it is often difficult to find objective evidence that demonstrates the authenticity of repressed memories that come back through therapy.[53]

Other programs focus on treatment methods aimed at correcting how people process information. Individuals who are easily excited and quick to become hostile and aggressive need to learn how to manage frustrating situations by approaching them as problem-solving experiences. When someone cuts in front of you in a long line, you can look at that situation in two very different ways: on the one hand, you can take it as an insult, challenge, or form of disrespect that sends you into a quick moment of anger that may affect how you react; on the other hand, you might see that person's actions as simply accidental or maybe the person does not understand the norm of waiting in line.

Cognitive behavioral therapy programs are made up of two major components: cognitive skills training and cognitive restructuring. **Cognitive skills training** helps offenders become more effective problem-solvers by teaching them how to cope with anger, resist peer pressure, respect the feelings of others, exert better self-control, accurately assess the consequences of behavior, and understand moral reasoning. Techniques such as role play, listening to others talk, and following instructions during an exercise are often employed in a group setting. **Cognitive restructuring** focuses on changing faulty thought processes called criminal thinking errors.[54] These errors may include rationalizing deviant and criminal behavior and lacking appreciation for the crime's consequences on the victim. Some correctional programs require that offenders come face to face with their victims, to hear how their behavior has affected their lives.[55] Research studies indicate that cognitive behavioral therapy programs have had positive results in reducing delinquent and criminal activities among juveniles and adults.[56]

Practices stemming from the psychological perspective on criminal behavior can also focus on "unlearning" faulty patterns of behavior.[57] We have seen in this chapter that much of what we do stems from what we observe others doing, and that certain behavior patterns we model persist because of the rewards they produce. One technique to correct a faulty connection between inappropriate behavior and a rewarding result is **aversion therapy**,[58] which pairs a stimulus that brings pleasure with an unpleasant response. For example, a child molester may be allowed to look at a sexual image of a child while simultaneously receiving a mild electric shock. This conditioning is repeated several times until the pedophile no longer associates the image with pleasure, but rather with disapproval or dislike. While this method may produce the desired results, they may be short-lived, because conditioning can wear off or become reversed once again.

Many group homes for juvenile delinquents use an intervention called **token economics**.[59] Program participants earn tokens or points for good behavior like following directions and attending class, and likewise lose them for inappropriate behavior such as disrespecting authority or fighting. Tokens can be used to buy items from a store, watch television, or get a weekend pass to go home. Earning them is therefore associated with positive rewards and becomes an incentive to increase the frequency of desirable behavior.[60]

While these techniques are effective in gaining compliance and reducing problem behavior in an institutional setting, researchers caution about their limitations in the real world. Ordinary compliant behavior does not always produce the immediate rewards of points and tokens in the social environment. A juvenile who earned tokens for attending class at the group home will probably not get the same type of reward for going to school. How will this change in environmental response change the thinking and behavior of the individual? Will he or she continue to go to school? Indeed, our thoughts and actions are intertwined, yet they are both inherently connected to aspects of the social environment. In what ways does the social environment affect the way we think and act? We turn to an exploration of this question in the next chapter.

SUMMARY

How does a diseased mind affect the way we think and act?

A diseased mind alters the way in which individuals experience the social world around them. Early thoughts on the relationship between personality and criminal behavior focused on the diseased mind of the psychopath. Unable to identify with others or understand how they think and feel, psychopaths are self-centered individuals who do not feel guilt or shame, are reckless and irresponsible, are incapable of maintaining long-term relationships, and engage in ongoing antisocial, disruptive behavior.

Is criminal behavior related to a defect in personality?

Individuals suffering from antisocial personality disorder (APD) exhibit a persistent pattern of violating social norms marked with a disregard for the rights of others that begins in early adolescence and continues through adulthood. They are not concerned with right or wrong, especially when pursuing their own immediate wants and desires. They will lie, cheat, manipulate situations, become violent, and even break the law to advance their own interests.

Do crime and delinquency stem from the inability to control certain impulses?

Sigmund Freud founded the psychoanalysis perspective, a method of understanding human behavior by examining drives and impulses within the unconscious mind. His theory of human behavior centered upon the division of the human mind into three components: the *id,* the *ego,* and *superego.* Under Freud's model, an inadequately developed superego will render the individual incapable of making appropriate moral judgment and therefore more likely to submit to the impulsive desires of the id and violate the rules.

Is crime a symptom of mental illness?

Certain types of mental illness can result in maladaptive behavior. Individuals suffering from neuroses such as phobias and compulsive disorders often experience fear and anxiety in the face of certain social stimuli that make them adapt to their environment in unacceptable and often bizarre or disruptive ways. Individuals suffering from psychoses such as bipolar disorder and schizophrenia are unable to comprehend reality, think clearly, and respond appropriately. Studies show that the presence of a psychotic disorder places individuals at a greater risk for criminal behavior.

What happens when we process information incorrectly?

The way individuals perceive their environment and appropriately judge their behaviors is the subject of cognitive theory. Cognitive processes have three major components: perception, judgment, and execution. When we have a clear understanding of environmental stimuli (perception), we are better able to evaluate choices (judgment), and are therefore more likely to make better decisions in difficult situations (execution). Distortion in cognitive processes has been used to explain a wide variety of criminal behavior such as domestic violence and rape.

Do some individuals imitate aggressive behavior?

By observing the behavior of individuals that play an important role in our lives, we learn how to think and act. This type of learning is called behavior modeling. Theorist Albert Bandura notes that individuals become violent and aggressive through life experiences that teach them to act that way. Research studies support this claim, showing a strong correlation between exposure to violence and hostility and aggressive behavior.

How is crime rewarding to some people?

Studies show that patterns of delinquent and criminal behavior often persist because of rewards associated with them such as money, prestige, and peer approval. Human behavior therefore reflects a balance between the rewards and punishments associated with it.

If crime is in the mind, what can we do to alter the human personality?

According to the psychological perspective, criminal behavior is linked to the drives and motives within the human mind. Correcting inappropriate behavior therefore requires correcting faulty mental processes, through the early detection of psychological problems that may predict future criminal behavior. Once a problem has been detected, counseling or therapy helps individuals learn how to manage their disorder or minimize its impact on their behavior.

CRITICAL THINKING QUESTIONS

1. Society sometimes reacts to crimes that are particularly difficult to comprehend by arguing that the perpetrator is insane—that no one in his or her right mind would torture and kill a child or rape an elderly woman. What types of criminal acts are the most difficult for you to understand? Can you identify a purpose or motive for the behavior? What elements make these crimes difficult to explain from the standpoint of rational choice? How can the psychological perspective help us understand "insane" behavior?

2. Psychological theories help us understand the mental processes behind human drives and motives. What role does this type of explanation play in the development of a criminal defense? What standards of responsibility do we place on individuals who suffer a mental disorder? Would it be fair to judge them by the same criteria as those who do not suffer from a mental disorder? Is someone "less guilty" because he or she is mentally ill?

3. How do you think information about the mental health status of a suspect or offender should affect the decision of law enforcement officials in handling a particular case? In what ways could such information be helpful? What obstacles or detriments may it pose?

4. Do individuals adapt to their environment, or does the environment affect the way in which individuals adapt? Why do some people cope with stress, conflict, and trauma in positive ways such as joining a support group,

picking up a hobby, or getting counseling, while others engage in maladaptive behaviors such as turning to drugs or alcohol or becoming hostile and abusive? Could the environmental experiences of these two types of individuals have been different? What different environmental factors affect the way we manage and adapt to certain difficult situations and experiences?

E-RESOURCES

Learn more about the life and crimes of Jeffrey Dahmer by visiting http://www.biography.com/people/jeffrey-dahmer-9264755.

Visit the Mayo Clinic website at http://www.mayoclinic.org/diseases-conditions/antisocial-personality-disorder/basics/definition/con-20027920 to get more information on the signs and symptoms of anti-social personality disorder.

Additional information on the treatment of obsessive-compulsive disorder can be found at http://www.psychologytoday.com/search/site/ocd%20treatment.

Research on the relationship between childhood psychiatric disorders and adult criminality can be found at http://ajp.psychiatryonline.org/doi/full/10.1176/appi.ajp.2007.06122026.

Read more about the field of forensic psychiatry by visiting the Forensic Psychiatry Resources on the web at http://www.psymeet.com/psymeet/index.shtml.

NOTES

1   Groth, N., A. Burgess, and L. Holmstrom. 1977. Rape: Power, Anger, and Sexuality. *American Journal of Psychiatry* 134: 1239–1243. Anderson, W.P., Kunce, J.T. and Rich, B. 1979. Sex Offenders: Three Personality Types. *Journal of Clinical Psychology* 35: 671–676.

2   Hoberman, Harry M. 2016. Personality and Sexual Offending. In Amy Phenix, and Harry M. Hoberman (eds.), *Sexual Offending: Predisposing Antecedents, Assessments, and Management.* New York: Springer, pp. 119–184.

3   Sizemore, O.J. 2013. The Role of Perpetrator Motivation in Two Crime Scenarios. *Journal of Interpersonal Violence* 28(1): 80–91.

4   Phenix, Amy and Hoberman, Harry M. 2016. *Sexual Offending: Predisposing Antecedents, Assessments, and Management.* New York: Springer.

5   Chua-Eoan, Howard. 2009. Crimes of the Century: The Top 25. *Time.com.* Retrieved from http://content.time.com/time/specials/packages/completelist/0,29569,1937349,00.html.

6   Greenemeier, L. 2011. What Causes Someone to Act on Violent Impulses and Commit Murder? *Scientific American.*

7   Shelden, R., Brown, W., Miller, K. and Fritzler, R. 2015. Theories of Crime. In *Crime and Criminal Justice in American Society: Second Edition.* Long Grove, IL: Waveland Press, pp. 61–86.

8   Cleckley, Hervey. 1982. *The Mask of Sanity*, Revised Edition. Mosby Medical Library.

9   Furnham, A. 2016. Psychopaths at Work. In *Psychology Today*. New York: Sussez Publishers.

10 Moscovici, C. 2011. What is a Psychopath? In *Dangerous Liaisons: How to Recognize and Escape from Psychopathic Seduction*. Lanham, MD: Hamilton Books.

11 Craparo, G., Schimmenti, A. and Caretti, V. 2013. Traumatic Experiences in Childhood and Psychopathy: A Study on a Sample of Violent Offenders from Italy. *European Journal of Psychotraumatology* 4.

12 Blair, R. 2013. Psychopathy: Cognitive and Neural Dysfunction. *Dialogues in Clinical Neuroscience* 15(2); Koenigs, M. 2012. The Role of Prefrontal Cortex in Psychopathy. *Reviews in the Neurosciences* 23(3).

13 Shaffer, Catherine, McCuish, Evan, Corrado, Raymond R., Pehnken, Monic P. and Delisi, Matt. 2015. Psychopathy and Violent Misconduct in a Sample of Violent Young Offenders. *Journal of Criminal Justice* 43(4): 321–326.

14 American Psychiatric Association. 2014. Diagnostic and Statistical Manual of Mental Disorders, 5th ed. Retrieved from http://dsm.psychiatryonline.org/doi/book/10.1176/appi.books.9780890425596.

15 Blough, P. 2013. Mental Health Education. Retrieved from http://rehinge.com/resources/education/.

16 Gregory, Sarah, Fytche, Dominic, Simmons, Andrew, Kumari, Veena, Howard, Matthew, Hodgins, Sheilagh and Blackwood, Nigel. 2012. The Antisocial Brain: Psychopathy Matters: A Structural MRI Investigation of Antisocial Male Violent Offenders. *Journal Of American Medical Association: Psychiatry* 59(9). Graeve, C. 2007. An Exploratory Look at Career Criminality, Psychopathy, and Offending Persistence: Convergence of Criminological and Psychological Constructs. Iowa State University. Retrieved from http://lib.dr.iastate.edu/cgi/viewcontent.cgi?article=16045&context=rtd. Wiesner, M. Kim, H., and Capaldi, D. 2005. Developmental Trajectories of Offending: Validation and Prediction to Young Adult Alcohol Use, Drug Use, and Depressive Symptoms. *Development and Psycholpathology* 17(1).

17 Freud: Conflict and Culture. 2009. Library of Congress, Online Exhibit. Retrieved from http://www.loc.gov/exhibits/freud/.

18 Horney, K. 2013. *Neurosis and Human Growth: The Struggle Toward Self-Realization*. London: Routledge.

19 Latour, C., Perez, R., Kathol, R., Huyse, F. and Cohen, J. 2010. *The Integrated Case Management Manual: Assisting Complex Patients Regain Physical and Mental Health*. New York: Springer.

20 Understanding Psychosis. 2013. *Mind*. Retrieved from http://www.mind.org.uk/media/519359/understanding-psychosis-2013.pdf.

21 Skeem, Jennifer L., Winter, Eliza, Kennealy, Patrick J., Louden, Eno, Jennifer and Tatar II, Joseph R. 2014. Offenders with Mental Illness Have Criminogenic Needs: Toward Recidivism Reduction. *Law and Human Behavior* 38(3): 212–224.

22 De Hart, Dana, Lynch, Shannon, Belknap, Joanne, Dass-Brailsford, Priscilla and Green, Bonnie. 2014. Life History Models of Female Offending: The Roles of Serious Mental Illness and Trauma in Women's Pathways to Jail. *Psychology of Women* 38(1): 138–151. Copeland, William E., Miller-Johnson, Shari, Keeler, Gordon, Angold, Adrian and Costello, E. Jane. 2007. Childhood Psychiatric Disorders and Young Adult Crime: A Prospective, Population-Based Study. *American Journal of Psychiatry* 164: 1668–1675.

23 Baillargeon, Jacques, Binswanger, Ingrid A., Penn, Joseph V., Williams, Brie A. and Murray, Owen J. 2008. Psychiatric Disorders and Repeat Incarcerations: The Revolving Prison Door. *American Journal of Psychiatry*. DOI appi.ajp.2008.08030416.

24 Social Determinants of Mental Health. 2014. *World Health Organization, Geneva*, Switzerland. Canadian Population Health Initiative. 2009. Mental Health, Delinquency, and Criminal Activity. *Canadian Institute for Health Information*.

25 Schulenberg, J. 2015. Police Decision-Making in the Gray Zone: The Dynamics of Police-Citizen Encounters with Mentally Ill Persons. In *Criminal Justice and Behavior.*

26 Cherry, K. 2015. What is Cognitive Psychology? In *About Health.* Retrieved from http://psychology.about.com/od/cognitivepsychology/f/cogpsych.htm.

27 Nentjes, Lieke, Bernstein, David, Arntz, Arnoud, Breukelen, Gerard and Slaats, Mariette. 2015. Examining the Influence of Psychopathy, Hostility Biases, and Automatic Processing on Criminal Offenders' Theory of Mind. *International Journal of Law and Psychiatry* 38: 92–99.

28 Sigre-Leiros, Vera, Carvalho, Joana and Nobre, Pedro J. 2015. Rape-related Cognitive Distortions: Preliminary Findings on the Role of Early Maladaptive Schemas. *International Journal of Law and Psychiatry* 41: 26–30. Retrieved from http://www.science direct.com/science/journal/01602527/41/supp/. C. Marziano, Vincent, Ward, Tony, Beech, Anthony, Pattison, Philippa. 2006. Identification of Five Fundamental Implicit Theories Underlying Cognitive Distortions in Child Abusers: A Preliminary Study. *Psychology, Crime and Law* 12: 97–105.

29 Bandura, Albert. 1971. *Psychological Modeling: Conflicting Theories.* New Brunswick, NJ: Transaction Publishers.

30 Gunderson, J. 2006. Impact of Real Life and Media Violence: Relationships Between Violence Exposure, Aggression, Hostility, and Empathy Among High School Students and Detained Adolescents. Retrieved from http://utdr.utoledo.edu/cgi/viewcontent.cgi?article=2373&context=theses-dissertations.

31 Edleson, J. 2011. Problems Associated with Children's Witnessing of Domestic Violence. National Resource Center on Domestic Violence. Retrieved from http://vawnet.org/print-document.php?doc_id=392&find_type=web_desc_AR.

32 Hollingdale, J. and Greitemeyer, T. 2014. The Effect of Online Violent Video Games on Levels of Aggression. *PLOS ONE* 9(11).

33 Youth Who Killed Girl By Imitating Wrestling Moves Is Offered Plea Bargain; May Be Set Free. *Jet,* Jan. 2004.

34 Orue, I., Calbete, E., Thomaes, S., Orobio de Castro, B., and Hutteman, R. 2011. Monkey See, Monkey Do, Monkey Hurt: Longitudinal Effects of Exposure to Violence on Children's Aggressive Behavior. *Social Psychological and Personality Science* 2(4): 432–437.

35 Gazzaniga, M. 2013. *Fundamentals of Psychology: An Introduction.* Cambridge, MA: Academic Press.

36 Sharkey, J., Shekhtmeyster, Z., Chavez-Lopez, L., Norris, E., and Sass, L. 2011. The Protective Influence of Gangs: Can Schools Compensate? In *Aggression and Violent Behavior.*

37 Reilly, R. 2014. Violent Video Games Makes Children Grow Up into Aggressive Adults, Study Claims. *Daily Mail.* Retrieved from http://www.dailymail.co.uk/science tech/article-2588864/Violent-video-games-makes-children-grow-aggressive-adults-study-claims.html.

38 Schrade, Brad. 2015. What Went Wrong For Kisha Holmes? *The Atlantic Journal Constitution.* Retrieved from http://investigations.myajc.com/kishaholmes/.

39 Collier, L. 2014. Incarceration Nation. *American Psychological Association* 45(9).

40 McLeod, Saul. 2015. Psychoanalysis. *Simply Psychology.* Retrieved from http://www.simplypsychology.org/psychoanalysis.html.

41 Pressley, Michael and McCormick, Christine B. 2007. *Child and Adolescent Development for Educators.* New York: Guilford Press.

42 Addis, M. 2008. Gender and Depression in Men. *Clinical Psychology: Science and Practice* 15(3): 153–168.

43 Schram, P. and Tibbetts, S. 2013. Psychological/Trait Theories of Crime. In *Introduction to Criminology: Why Do They Do It?* Thousand Oaks, CA: SAGE, pp. 136–161.

44 Halicks, Richard. 2004. Iraqi Prisoner Abuse: People Will Do What They're Told. *Atlanta Journal-Constitution,* May 9:1E.

45 Ou, Suh-Ruu and Arthur J. Reynolds. 2010. Childhood Predictors of Young Adult Male Crime. *Child Youth Services Review* 32(8): 1097–1107.

46 Loeber, R., Farrington, D., and Petechuk, D. Child Delinquency: Early Intervention and Prevention. Child Delinquency Bulletin Series. U.S. Department of Justice. Retrieved from https://www.ncjrs.gov/html/ojjdp/186162/contents.html.

47 Pardini, Dustin and Frick, Paul J. 2013. Multiple Developmental Pathways to Conduct Disorder: Current Conceptualizations and Clinical Implications. *Journal of the Canadian Academy of Child & Adolescent Psychiatry* 22(1): 20–25. Petras, H., Kellam, S., Brown, C., Muthen, B., Ialongo, N., and Poduska, J. 2009. Developmental Epidemiological Courses Leading to Antisocial Personality Disorder and Violent and Criminal Behavior: Effects by Young Adulthood of a Universal Preventive Intervention in First- and Second-Grade Classrooms. In *Drug and Alcohol Dependence.*

48 Allison, Jennifer. 2016. Alternative Dispute Resolution Research. *Harvard Law School Library.* Retrieved from http://guides.library.harvard.edu/ADR.

49 Ibid.

50 Farrington, D. 2011. Family Influences on Delinquency. In *Juvenile Justice and Delinquency.* Burlington, MA: Jones & Bartlett Publishers, pp. 203–222.

51 Mlodinow, Leonard. 2013. Subliminal: How Your Unconscious Mind Rules Your Behavior. New York: Pantheon. Bargh, J. and Morsella, E. 2008. The Unconscious Mind. *Perspectives on Psychological Science* 3(1).

52 Cinnamon, Grant C.B. 2015. Psychopathy and Criminal Behavior. In Wayne Petherick (ed.), *Applied Crime Analysis: A Social Science Approach to Understanding Crime, Criminals, and Victims.* Elsevier Academic Press.

53 Hopper, Jim. 2015. Recovered Memories of Sexual Abuse. Scientific Research and Scholarly Resources. Retrieved from http://www.jimhopper.com/memory/.

54 Kenne, D. 2010. *Examination of Thinking Error and the Responsivity Principle in a Cognitive-Behavioral Intervention for Offenders: Implications for Criminal Justice Policy.* Akron, OH. University of Akron.

55 Zehr, Howard. 2014. *The Little Book of Restorative Justice.* New York: Good Books.

56 Cerda, Magdalena, Tracy, Melissa, Keyes, Katherine M. and Galea, Sandro. 2015. To Treat or to Prevent?: Reducing the Population Burden of Violence-related Post-traumatic Stress Disorder. *Epidemiology* 26(5): 681–689; Clark, P. 2010. Preventing Future Crime with Cognitive Behavioral Therapy. *National Institute of Justice Journal* 265.

57 Dombeck, Mark and Jolyn Wells-Moran. 2015. Techniques for Unlearning Old Behaviors. Psychological Self-Tools. *Centersite.net.* Retrieved from http://www.centersite.net/poc/view_doc.php?type=doc&id=9732&cn=353.

58 Walton, Jamie S., and Chou, Shihning. 2015. The Effectiveness of Psychological Treatment for Reducing Recidivism in Child Molesters: A Systematic Review of Randomized and Nonrandomized Studies. *Trauma Violence Abuse* 16(4): 401–417.

59 James, S. 2011. What Works in Group Care? A Structured Review of Treatment Models for Group Homes and Residential Care. *Child and Youth Services Review* 33(2).

60 Doll, C., McLaughlin, T., and Barretto, A. 2013. The Token Economy: A Recent Review and Evaluation. *International Journal of Basic and Applied Science* 2(1).

CHAPTER OUTLINE

Sociological theory: crime is in the structure of society

In this chapter we will explore the following questions

- How do criminologists explain trends and variations in criminal behavior?
- Where does the sociological approach search for the cause of crime?
- What is the social structure and how does it affect our behavior?
- Are certain places more conducive to crime than others?
- Can certain types of frustrations lead to crime?
- Do all subcultures go against the dominant norms of society?
- If crime is acquired behavior, what can we change about the social structure to prevent it?

KEY TERMS

sociological theories

sociological perspective

Émile Durkheim

social structure approach

social process approach

social conflict approach

social disorganization theory

Chicago School

social ecology

concentric zones

social pathology

environmental criminology

anomie

general strain theory (GST)

culture conflict theory

conduct norms

subculture

focal concerns

delinquent subcultures

O n May 17, 2015, a meeting of a coalition of motorcycle clubs took place at the Twin Peaks Restaurant in Waco, Texas. Sometime during that event, a confrontation between two rival motorcycle gangs erupted in violence outside of the restaurant. What began as a fist fight between two members turned into several minutes of shooting, confusion, and chaos. When police arriving at the scene asked everyone who had a weapon there to raise their hand, nearly every single biker there did. A police report documenting the incident described it as a combat scene where people were running around screaming, guns, chains, clubs, and knives were all over the place, shots were being fired, and bloodied bodies were everywhere. The incident led to the death of nine people and resulted in several injuries. The incident led to the arrest of 177 people and over 430 weapons being confiscated.[1]

How can we explain the variations in type and distribution of criminal behavior from place to place, individual to individual and group to group? Why is it that four of five offenders are male, men are more likely to be victims of violent crime than women, urban communities experience higher rates of crime, minorities are arrested at a disproportionate rate, and theft is the most common category of crime?[2] What is it about the social environment that creates trends and variations in the distribution and content of criminality? The makeup of a community or neighborhood, the availability of jobs, and the

Image 11.1 *Nine people were killed and over twenty were injured when two rival motorcycle gangs collided outside of a restaurant in Waco, TX. What aspects of the social environment may have contributed to the melee that broke out that night?*

Jerry Larson/AP/Press Association Images

reaction
   formation
subculture of
   violence theory
differential
   opportunity
techniques of
   neutralization
drift
Chicago Area
   Project (CAP)
weed and seed
   program

individual's cultural background, desire for wealth and success, and access to education are all dynamics that affect behavior.

For the first time ever in 2001, the United States Surgeon General produced a research report on youth violence. According to that report, most youth violence begins in early adolescence; 30–40 percent of male youth and 15–30 percent of female youth report having committed a serious violent crime by the age of 17. The study describes certain "pathways" to violence that include both personal characteristics and environmental conditions that place children at risk for the onset of deviant behavior. Personal characteristics such as gender, aggression, attitudes toward school, and drug use interplay with environmental conditions such as ties to delinquent peers, involvement with a gang, socioeconomic status, and poverty to produce violent behavior. These results suggest we should direct intervention and prevention efforts at the immediate environment of at-risk youth—family, school, peer group, neighborhood, and community—in order to identify those variables and conditions contributing to the onset of criminal behavior.[3]

Criminologists explain trends and variations in criminal behavior by analyzing how social forces influence human behavior. Biological and psychological traditions examine criminal behavior by looking at the specific traits that make criminals different from non-criminals. In this chapter, we examine theories that search for the origins of criminal behavior *outside* the individual, collectively known as **sociological theories**. What is the sociological approach, and what aspects of society do we study in our search for a better understanding of crime and its origins?

THE SOCIOLOGICAL PERSPECTIVE

Have you ever looked at pictures of your parents when they were your age and wondered how they ever survived without laptops, electronic tablets, and smartphones? Now imagine your grandparents at your age, and think how they must have been dazzled by the first computer, color television, and microwave ovens. Our social environment is constantly changing and we must adapt to the emergence of new technology, different ways of thinking, and changing expectations for the roles we play.

The **sociological perspective** explains patterns in human behavior by examining those aspects of society that affect the way people think, act, and react. What happens when there are more people than jobs? How does a single mother who barely makes ends meet afford to take care of her children? When a teenager runs away from his abusive, dysfunctional family, where does he go and whom will he turn to on the streets? How does a person survive in a neighborhood where gunshots are fired every day? Does marriage affect people in different ways?

Sociologist **Émile Durkheim** helped develop the sociological approach.[4] Durkheim studied many aspects of society such as religion, education, crime, and suicide. He focused on describing how different parts of society functioned to make society "work." According to Durkheim, all aspects of society served a specific function which contributed to the order of social life, and even to crime. Crime is an objective indication of what is wrong and immoral in society.

Image 11.2 *How might the social forces of economic depression and unemployment affect the behavior of these individuals?*

Rick Bowmer/AP/Press Association Images

It lets us know what needs to change, the ways in which rules and regulations should be established, and how we should move towards becoming a better—more ordered—society.[5]

Crime is a social fact; it exists outside the individual traits and variations in human thought and action. We find the starting point for the study of crime, therefore, not within the individual, but rather within the society in which the individual lives—a society made up of groups, organizations, and institutions. Crime develops from the various dynamics, relationships, and interactions that take place within the social environment. By studying these, we can develop a more comprehensive understanding of the characteristics of criminal behavior, estimate trends and rates of criminal activities, and question the larger social forces affecting criminal choices.

ONE PERSPECTIVE, THREE APPROACHES

While all sociological theories share a common theme in the study of crime, we can divide the sociological perspective into three distinct approaches: social structure, social process, and social conflict. Let us look at what makes each approach unique and different from the others.

The **social structure approach** looks for the origins of crime within the immediate environment. What holds society together and what breaks it apart? What social and economic conditions are people exposed to on a daily basis? The social structure approach examines conditions of life such as poverty, deprivation, frustration, lack of opportunity to succeed, and deviant cultural values, and analyzes their influence on the development of criminal behavior.[6] We will examine this perspective in more detail in this chapter.

The **social process approach** sees crime as the product of the various interactions that take place between individuals and the social environment.[7] Problems within society do not alone cause crime—it is the way we react to and deal with these problems that forms the starting point for the study of criminal behavior. Crime is the outcome of inappropriate or faulty social processes that contribute to crime. We will examine this approach in greater detail in the next chapter.

Finally, the **social conflict approach** to the study of crime examines the fundamental distribution of wealth and power within society. It sees the law as a mechanism of social control in which society's dominant classes—those with the most wealth and political power—are able to coerce the rest into compliance. Power relationships in society determine who has the power to create the law, which acts will be defined as crime, and which individuals will be treated as criminals.[8] We will talk more about conflict theory in chapter 13. For now, let us take a closer look at the social structure approach.

MAJOR PRINCIPLES OF THE SOCIAL STRUCTURE APPROACH

Theories stemming from the social structure approach search for the cause of criminal behavior in the immediate conditions of society. With a quick glance at the world around us, we can easily see major differences between the environments under which people live: some are poor, some are rich; some drop out of high school and others have college educations; some live in the city, others in suburban neighborhoods; some have high paying jobs and others struggle to make ends meet. The social structure approach looks at these variations in the economic and social environments and highlights those that contribute to socioeconomic disadvantage.[9] They include poverty, lack of educational opportunities, limited employment options, poor or deteriorated neighborhoods and housing, dysfunctional family conditions, social injustices, and exposure to conflicting value systems.

We find the root cause of crime, according to the social structure approach, in these formal and informal structures of society that produce conditions leading to criminal behavior.[10] While individuals are responsible for their own actions and should be held accountable for them, in this view the social environment creates certain conditions of imbalance, discord, and chaos that provide the causal link from which criminal behavior occurs.[11]

Thus, in order to understand crime, we must direct our attention to the environmental forces driving individuals toward criminal activity. According to the social structure approach, crime is an acquired pattern of behavior—individuals are a product of their social environment and the conditions which limit and impose upon their opportunities, experiences, choices, and ways of thinking.

Within the social structure approach, there are three major theoretical perspectives: social disorganization, strain theory, and culture conflict (see Table 11.1). While each offers a unique understanding of the specific aspects of the environment that contribute to crime and delinquency, they all share a common understanding of criminal behavior as largely a phenomena of the socially and economically disadvantaged members of society. We turn now to a discussion of these theories, beginning with social disorganization.

Table 11.1 Social structure theories of criminal behavior

Social disorganization theory	Strain theory	Culture conflict theory
• The Chicago School • Environmental criminology	• Anomie • General strain	• Subcultures • Differential opportunity • Drifting

SOCIAL DISORGANIZATION THEORY

Some criminologists make a link between high rates of crime and the social and economic conditions of urban communities. They point to the disordered nature of certain neighborhoods where overcrowding, increased transience, the presence of business and retail stores alongside residences, and lack of cohesion contribute to a deteriorating social life.[12] This approach to the study of crime is known as social disorganization theory.

Image 11.3 *What aspects of the social environment may contribute to the high rate of crime found in this urban community?*
iStock/shakzu

Under these conditions, the social structure begins to collapse, failing to provide the necessary elements of a healthy community, such as adequate education, proper housing, meaningful employment, access to healthcare, and a positive family life. Some of the groundbreaking studies of social disorganization theory are found in the tradition known as the Chicago School.

The Chicago School

Between the 1920s and 1940s, criminological research was dominated by the University of Chicago, where the works of Robert Park and Ernest Burgess began an ecological approach to the study of crime.[13] Social ecology is a method of analysis that studies how the environment adapts to the human interactions and natural resources within it.

Park and Burgess aimed to explain the distribution of crime rates by thinking of cities as made up of concentric zones, identified by the rate and incidence of

Image 11.4 *When we observe children playing in a bounce house, we can see that this type of environment makes them more hyper, playful, and active. But consider the effect of the children playing on the bounce house itself. How many children can this structure hold before it collapses? Do they need to take their shoes off to avoid tearing the fabric? The effect of various interactions on the social structure is considered by social ecologists.*
iStock/Kali Nine LLC

certain social characteristics within the city such as immigration, residential mobility, housing structure, and family income (see Figure 11.1). Park and Burgess used this model to explain why crime was concentrated in certain parts of inner city zones where the structure is weak and disorganized due to high rates of poverty and unemployment, rapid social change, competition for limited resources, and conflict between different cultural values.[14] These conditions produce personal and group interactions marked by strained relationships, deteriorating values, lack of family solidarity, and community fear. Individuals living under such conditions, which become a breeding ground for criminal activity, are exposed to social pathology and turn to deviant behavior and crime.

The concentric zone model was used by researchers Clifford Shaw and Henry McKay to study juvenile arrest rates in Chicago.[15] Shaw and McKay were interested in studying how crime and delinquency were normal responses to social, economic, and cultural characteristics of certain communities. Using official data spanning three distinct time periods marked by high rates of immigration (1900–1906, 1917–1923, and 1927–1933), they illustrated the distribution of delinquency rates among juveniles within different ecological environments. Rates of juvenile delinquency remained stable over time and corresponded to certain inner city urban zones, despite changes in immigrant populations (for example, from German to Italian). Areas farther from these zones had lower rates of crime and delinquency. These findings support the theory that crime is a characteristic of certain ecological conditions within the social environment of urban communities, rather than a consequence of

Figure 11.1
A concentric zone model

Source: Bunyi, Joan. 1 May 2010. Concentric Zone Model. Retrieved from www.lewishistorical society.com/wiki/tiki-read_article.php?articleId=16

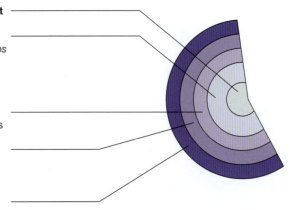

The Concentric Zone Model:

1. **Central Business District**

2. **Transitional Zone**
   ***Recent Immigrant Groups**
   – Deteriorated Housing
   – Factories
   – Abandoned Buildings

3. **Working Class Zone**
   – Single Family Tenements

4. **Residental Zone**
   – Single Family Homes
   – Yards/Garages

5. **Commuter Zone**
   – Suburbs

individuals' characteristics. It is in the structure of neighborhoods within the inner city where deviant norms and values, impoverished lifestyles, unemployment, culture conflict—social disorganization—perpetuate criminal behavior.

Shaw and McKay laid the foundation for the development of social disorganization theory in a theoretical movement that spanned over seven decades of research. We turn now to a brief look at the legacy of the Chicago School in the field of environmental criminology.

BOX 11.1: CONNECTING RESEARCH TO PRACTICE

Does collective efficacy really deter crime?

The tradition of social disorganization theory has been to focus on location and neighborhood-specific aspects as they relate to criminal activity. Structurally disorganized neighborhoods lack the formal and informal controls needed to prevent crime and delinquency. Public order crimes such as public intoxication, graffiti, and vandalism are an invitation to potential offenders that say residents within these neighborhoods are apathetic about their community and will not intervene on the behalf of victims, question strangers, or call the police when suspecting a crime.

In a long-term National Institute of Justice study, researchers re-examined the effect of neighborhood disorder in Chicago communities as a pathway to predatory criminal behavior. The study proposed that both crime and disorder stem from structural characteristics specific to certain neighborhoods. These include concentrated poverty, unemployment, residential mobility, high population density, and the absence of social resources. Using a method known as *systematic social observation*, researchers videotaped blocks of over 23,000 streets in 196 neighborhoods with different racial, ethnic, social, and economic compositions. What were they looking for? Signs of disorder, recorded and measured by visual cues such as trash and litter on the streets, graffiti, abandoned cars, syringes, loitering, people intoxicated or consuming alcohol on the street, evidence of gang membership such as young people in groups, and observed drug transactions.

Findings suggest that disorder and crime both stem from similar structural characteristics of certain neighborhoods. While bearing no direct causal link, disorder and crime are inherently connected in that they both reduce *collective efficacy*, the "cohesion among neighborhood residents combined with shared expectations for informal social control of public space." Collective efficacy is a significant deterrent to crime and disorder in neighborhoods and communities. In a 2011 study by Maxwell et al., researchers found that collective efficacy had a positive influence on Chicago area neighborhoods over a ten-year time period, with neighborhoods characterized by the lowest levels of collective efficacy having the highest rates of homicide and rape. In neighborhoods with low levels of collective efficacy, rates of violence and the amounts of disorder were high, even after controlling for socio-demographic characteristics. They conclude that its absence is the single most long term predictive influence on rates of crime and disorder.

These findings suggest that policies aimed at reducing community disorder *indirectly* reduce crime by increasing neighborhood stability and enhancing collective efficacy. Tough law enforcement practices and procedures attempting to "clean up the streets" by eliminating violence and disorder are often insufficient without a comprehensive understanding of the link between crime, disorder, and collective efficacy.

Sources

Maxwell, Christopher D., Garner, Joel H., and Skogan, Wesley G. 2011. Collective Efficacy and Criminal Behavior in Chicago, 1995–2004. Final Report submitted to U.S. Department of Justice, Washington, D.C.

Sampson, Robert J. and Raudenbush, Stephen W. 2001. Disorder in Urban Neighborhoods—Does It Lead to Crime? *Research in Brief*. U.S. Department of Justice, Office of Justice Programs, National Institute of Justice, Washington, D.C.

Skogan, Wesley G. 2000. *Public Involvement: Community Policing in Chicago*. U.S. Department of Justice, Office of Justice Programs, National Institute of Justice, Washington, D.C.

Environmental criminology

Are certain places more prone to criminal activity than others? If so, what is it about these places that make them crime magnets? These questions are the subject of contemporary criminological research, which draws a link between criminal behavior and the geographic location and physical features of specific neighborhoods[16] (see Box 11.1). During the mid-1980s studies in environmental criminology emerged to highlight the importance of deteriorated conditions within communities as contributing to high rates of criminal activity.[17] Environmental criminologists analyze the immediate context within which criminal behavior occurs in order to understand how environmental variables, potential offenders, and targeted victims interact. Within this approach, there are three basic premises:[18]

- Criminal behavior is significantly influenced by the immediate nature of the environment in which it occurs.
- The distribution and pattern of criminal activity is not random but rather vary according to time, place, and situation. Certain times, places, and situations facilitate criminal opportunities.[19]
- Understanding the role of environmental variables in the pattern and distribution of criminal activity is essential to controlling and preventing crime.

The central theme behind the study of crime and environmental variables lies in the basic premise that disorganized neighborhoods send a message to would-be criminals that this is a vulnerable target for crime because we, as a

Table 11.2 Anatomy of dangerous persons, places, and situations

Type of variable	Characteristics
Space	• Presence of blind spots due to excessive trees, shrubs, bushes • Rundown or abandoned buildings and apartments • Bars on windows, broken windows, boarded up windows • Dirty, littered parks, and other public spaces • Excessive graffiti on public buildings • Poor street lighting
Time	• Businesses open late/all night • Increased nighttime activities, especially on weekends
Offender	• Network links to other offenders • Lack financial resources • Unemployed • Have nothing to lose • Triggering event prompts frustration, anger
Target/victim	• Large numbers of single-parent families • Regularized/predictable patterns of movement • Loss of trust in social institutions such as law enforcement, government, and education • Little sense of community • High degree of residential instability • Fear of crime • High rates of unemployment
Social control	• Lack of informal surveillance by family, peers, neighbors due to weak social ties • Limited social control efforts by schools, recreation centers, and churches due to atmosphere of fear and mistrust • Absence of sufficient formal social control resources (law enforcement)

Source: Andreson, Martin. 2014. *Environmental Criminology: Theory, Research, and Practice*. New York: Routledge.

community, either don't care, are afraid, or also involved in criminal activity.[20] Researchers have identified five components that help to predict the likelihood of a criminal event—space, time, the offender, the victim, and social control (see Table 11.2).

Environmental criminology thus helps us gain a better understanding of patterns and trends in crime. This in turn becomes a useful tool in the development of policies and interventions that target specific crime-prone situations. Studies have shown that changing or altering certain temporal or spatial patterns, such as putting in a street light in a dark neighborhood, can have a significant impact on reducing criminal activity.[21]

Places sustain criminal activity because of the structure of their environment. People may come and go, but crime rates will always remain high. This is the basic idea behind social disorganization theory and environmental criminology. At the end of this chapter, we will examine the merits of this theory. Another approach to the study of criminal behavior focuses on the specific mechanisms whereby individuals react and adjust to the structure of their environment. Let's now look at strain theory.

STRAIN THEORY

In 1938, Robert Merton, arguing against the idea that criminality was the result of variations in individual traits, proposed that conditions within the social structure created situations to which criminal activity was the response.[22] What are these situations and why is crime a response to them?

Anomie

Merton was interested in why rates of deviant behavior differed among different societies and between certain groups within the same society.[23] He argued that the key lies in anomie, a state of normlessness and confusion that leads to strain. Anomie results from the discrepancy between the cultural norms that define success in life (goals) and the legitimate and appropriate ways to achieve it (means).[24]

Think for a moment about how we define success in our society. Perhaps you see a nice home and car. What about fancy clothes or a flat-screen television? How about the latest smartphone and electronic gadget? Whatever the case, through various institutions like family, education, and media, our culture constantly bombards us with messages of success that revolve around the acquisition of material goods. People from all walks of life feel pressured to keep up, get ahead, and stay on top of things; but how? The culturally accepted means is through education, hard work, and perseverance. The problem, however, is that the access to these avenues is not equally distributed to all members of society, even though the message of achievement and success is spelled out loud and clear—to everyone.[25] How do people deal with this apparent dilemma?

Image 11.5
How does society define success for us? What happens when we can't all shop in Beverly Hills?

iStock/littleny

Anomie leads to frustration and resentment, to which people react in different ways. Many will continue to run the "rat race" their entire lives, working hard to pursue the "American dream" and hoping to one day pay off their debts, buy a nice car, and own their own home. These individuals are *conformists*. Some who are *ritualists* may simply give up, settling for a minimum-wage job just to make ends meet. Others, recognizing their limited opportunities, will become *innovators*, turning to other avenues such as stealing or selling drugs to get what they want. Table 11.3 describes the various adaptations people make to the discrepancy between culturally desired goals and legitimate means of achieving them.

Merton's theory helps us understand how the strain between culturally defined success and the legitimate means of achieving it leads to deviant behavior patterns. Once again, the roots of crime lie within the social structure and not within individuals or their unique qualities. But what about individuals who commit criminal acts despite their access to legitimate avenues of success—Ivy League thieves, millionaire murderers, or well-educated bank robbers? What about the variety of crimes committed by successful business owners and corporate executives who by all accounts have all the necessary means to achieve the American dream? (See Box 11.2.) We turn now to a discussion of general strain for a possible explanation.

General strain

In 1992, Robert Agnew broadened anomie theory by developing the concept of general strain. **General strain theory (GST)** maintains that various sources of strain and frustration exist within the social structure that are not the result of economic failure.[26] Individuals who experience certain types of strain,

Table 11.3 Ways of adapting to a frustrating social structure

Culturally desired goals	Legitimate means	Adaptation	Who am I?
Accepted	Accepted	Conformity	I am ambitious, motivated, and hard-working. I go to school to get an education so that I can get ahead in the workforce and make more money so that I can afford to travel, buy the things that I want, and live the American dream.
Accepted	Rejected	Innovation	I live in an inner-city deteriorated neighborhood with my mom and five siblings. I drop out of school to get a job and help my mom out with finances. I turn to drug trafficking which makes a lot more money and gives me a better life.
Rejected	Accepted	Ritualism	I work at a factory from nine to five. I gave up on achieving success a long time ago. I'm just happy to have a job to make ends meet. I'll probably never own a home or drive a car that runs well. These are the facts and there's nothing I can do to change them.
Rejected	Rejected	Retreatism	I have given up on life in general. I just don't care anymore about anyone or anything. I spend most of my days drunk and high on drugs. I peddle for money to buy food and drugs; and live on the street.
Rejected *but* Substituted	Rejected *but* Substituted	Rebellion	I am dissatisfied with the way society is structured so I'm going to change things my way. I am a political activist whose goal is to achieve social justice and egalitarianism.

BOX 11.2: CONSIDER THIS . . .

Successful businessmen turn fraudsters

What do Martin Grass, Dennis Kozlowski, Jeff Skilling, Bernie Madoff, and Raj Rajaratnam all have in common? They were all successful, wealthy, business executives running multi-million prominent corporations, and by all accounts living the American dream. They were also all convicted of serious corporate crimes and sentenced to lengthy prison terms.

Martin Grass was the CEO of Rite-Aid Corporation and headed the third largest pharmaceutical corporation which was founded by his father. He was also fined $500,000 and sentenced to eight years in prison in 2003 for conspiring to falsely inflate the value of the company by directing an accounting fraud scheme. Dennis Kozlowski was the chief executive of Tyco International, a worldwide security and fire protection corporation. In 2005, Kozlowski was convicted of crimes related to the fraudulent receipt of $81 million in unauthorized bonuses, and the payment of a $20 million investment banking fee to a former Tyco director. He was sentenced to eight years and four months to twenty-five years in prison for his role in the scandal.

And who could forget Jeff Skilling, former CEO of Enron Corporation, formerly one of the world's major providers of electricity, natural gas, communications, and paper and once claiming over $110 billion in revenues. Skilling was directly involved in fraudulent transactions that led to the company's financial collapse and the loss of millions of dollars to investors and the loss of over 20,000 jobs to employees. Skilling, convicted in 2006 on 35 counts of fraud, insider trading, and other crimes related to the scandal, was sentenced to a twenty-four-year and four-month federal prison term.

Then there's Bernie Madoff, founder of the Wall Street firm Bernard L. Madoff Investment Securities LLC (BMIS). It was a small, penny-stock trader Madoff began with the $5,000 he earned working as a lifeguard and installer of sprinkler systems. With help from his accountant father-in-law, the company grew enough to compete with other investment companies on the New York Stock Exchange floor, developing innovative computer software that helped create what eventually became known as the NASDAQ.

However, on December 11, 2008, Madoff was arrested and charged with securities fraud. He pleaded guilty in what was soon revealed as the largest investor fraud scandal ever committed by a single person, with an estimated loss to investors of almost $65 billion. On June 29, 2009, Madoff was sentenced to 150 years in federal prison, with billions of dollars in restitution to be paid to his victims.

And what about Raj Rajaratnam, who was sentenced to an eleven-year prison term for his conviction in 2011 on nine counts of securities fraud and five counts of conspiracy. Founder of the prominent Galleon Group hedge fund, Rajaratnam made about $64 million in illegal profits by trading in eBay, Google, and Goldman Sachs stocks.

How can we explain the 47-count indictment handed down in May of 2015, to 14 defendants, including presidents and vice presidents, who participated in a 24-year scheme to make illegal profits within the international soccer association known and respected worldwide as FIFA (Fédération Internationale de Football Association), by engaging in racketeering, wire fraud, and money laundering, to name just a few of their offenses. What could have driven these men, who by all means, had legitimate access to achieve personal success, business advantage, and material wealth? What other variables could come into play in the decision to commit fraudulent criminal actions by these business executives? Could it be greed, arrogance, or a lust for power? What about financial stress, mismanagement, or corporate misguidance? *What do you think?*

Sources

Creswell, Julie and Thomas, Landon. 2009. The Talented Mr. Madoff. *The New York Times,* Jan. 24. Retrieved from http://www.nytimes.com/2009/01/25/business/25bernie.html?em.

Tobak, Steve. 2013. What Makes Rich and Powerful Executives Commit Fraud? *FOXBusiness.* Retrieved from http://www.foxbusiness.com/business-leaders/2013/07/05/what-makes-rich-and-powerful-executives-commit-fraud/.

United States Department of Justice. 2015. Nine FIFA Officials and Five Corporate Executives Indicted for Racketeering Conspiracy and Corruption. Office of Public Affairs, *Justice News,* May 27. Retrieved from http://www.justice.gov/opa/pr/nine-fifa-officials-and-five-corporate-executives-indicted-racketeering-conspiracy-and.

especially if repeated over time, may cope by turning to delinquency and crime.[27] According to Agnew, there are three types of strain: failure to achieve positively valued stimuli, loss of positively valued stimuli, and presence of negative stimuli (see Figure 11.2). In practical terms these may include losing a loved one, getting fired, ending a relationship, feeling pressure to perform on the job, or being discriminated against.

Strain and frustration can create hurt and disappointment in some, while others become angry and resentful. Feelings of injustice can lead to a desire for revenge, which some may use to rationalize criminal activities. Studies show individuals who experience racial discrimination have higher rates of violent crime.[28] Those who blame others for their own misfortunes may turn to delinquency and crime. Consider the following events in the life of a teenager:

Image 11.6 *How can we explain the criminal activities of wealthy business woman Martha Stewart, who had both fame and fortune?*
David Handschuh/AP/Press Association Images

A 14-year-old boy lives with his mother and her alcoholic boyfriend; his father left them several years earlier. His mother is diagnosed with cancer and spends her last days in great pain in the hospital. One Saturday morning, the hospital calls and tells the boy to rush over, as his mother is dying. On the way, the mother's boyfriend insists on stopping at the liquor store to buy some alcohol. The boy begs him not to, but he does so anyway; his mother dies 10 minutes before they arrive and he never says goodbye. The boyfriend is uncaring and the boy runs away from home. He spends a year moving from one foster home to another. He becomes angry, hurt, and resentful. He turns to drugs and alcohol to find some relief from his pain. He begins to steal to support his habits.

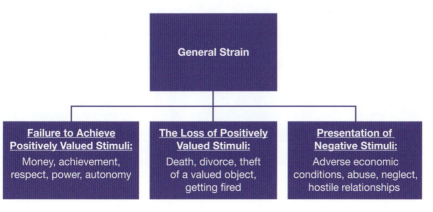

General Strain

Failure to Achieve Positively Valued Stimuli:	**The Loss of Positively Valued Stimuli:**	**Presentation of Negative Stimuli:**
Money, achievement, respect, power, autonomy	Death, divorce, theft of a valued object, getting fired	Adverse economic conditions, abuse, neglect, hostile relationships

Figure 11.2
Sources of strain: what hurts?

Some people accept responsibility for their negative circumstances and actively seek to change them in a positive manner. They often have a positive outlook on life, are emotionally strong, communicate effectively, have positive social support systems, and are financially capable.[29] Someone who has been discriminated against and has good financial resources is more likely to hire an attorney to right the wrong than resort to violence for revenge. But because of their circumstances, their negative experiences, their lower tolerance for frustration, their lack of ability to handle stress in a legitimate way such as through counseling or recreational activities, and their personal relationships or social support networks, some individuals with certain value systems use crime and delinquency as coping mechanisms.

What are these value systems and how are they acquired? We examine this question through a discussion of culture conflict theories.

CULTURE CONFLICT THEORY

If you found a hundred-dollar bill on the floor of a grocery store, would you keep it or turn it in? Let's say you are taking a test and your classmate is cheating; would you tell the instructor? How do you feel about legalizing marijuana? Is prostitution a criminal act? Do you believe people deserve the right to marry someone of the same sex? If your class took an opinion poll on each of these issues, our guess is there would be more disagreement than consensus. We are all different in some way, and our ideas and opinions will often disagree.

Image 11.7 *How do you suppose the differences in cultures found here can affect the ways people think and act?*

iStock/Nikada

BOX 11.3: CRIME IN GLOBAL PERSPECTIVE

When murder is defined as honor

Imagine that a father murders his pregnant daughter by dragging her into the street and then instigating and participating in her killing? This happened not too long ago in Lahore, Pakistan, where a 25-year-old young woman chose to marry the man she loved, despite pressure from her family to marry her cousin. Farzana Parveen was stoned to death by her father, two brothers, the cousin she was supposed to marry and several other men. When asked why, her father told police that she had insulted the family by marrying without their consent, and that this brought shame and dishonor that could only be restored by killing her.

An *honor killing* such as this is an act of murder in which a woman is killed for her actual or perceived immoral behavior. Such behavior can include being unfaithful in marriage, refusing to submit to an arranged marriage, wearing make-up or short skirts, asking for a divorce, flirting with or receiving phone calls from men, and dinner on time. In some cultures, a woman raped by a man is also accused of committing an immoral act that brings shame to the honor of the family and perhaps the wider community. If her execution is considered deserved, it is usually carried out by one or more of her fellow family members.

Honor killings result from a tradition that sees murder as justified when an individual has brought shame to the family name, a dishonor that can be removed only by killing the offender. In the Turkish province of Sanliurfa, one young woman was publicly executed by having her throat slit in the town square. Apparently a love song had been dedicated to her over the radio. Within such traditions, cultural norms become intertwined with deviant behavior and crime becomes a matter of social definition.

Sources

Ahmed, Beenish. 2015. Telling the Stories of the Victims of 'Honor Killings.' *Think Progress*, June 17. Retrieved from http://thinkprogress.org/world/2015/06/17/3670460/honor-crimes/.

McCoy, Terrence. 2014. In Pakistan, 1,000 Women Die in 'Honor Killings' Annually. Why Is This Happening? *The Washington Post,* May 28. Retrieved from http://www.washingtonpost.com/news/morning-mix/wp/2014/05/28/in-pakistan-honor-killings-claim-1000-womens-lives-annually-why-is-this-still-happening/.

Najam, Adil, and Owais Mughal. 2008. Jahalat: There is no Honor in Murder; Criminality is not Culture. *All Things Pakistan,* Aug. 30. Retrieved from http://pakistaniat.com/2008/08/30/honor-honour-killing-pakistan/.

Culture conflict theory emerged in the works of Thorsten Sellin, who argued that we find the root cause of criminal behavior in the clash of those values by which we decide what constitutes acceptable and unacceptable behavior.[30] Cultural diversity is particularly common in modern, industrialized society, especially within inner-city communities. According to culture conflict theory, this vast diversity produces a clash in values because different people are socialized in different ways. Thus, **conduct norms**, those rules of acceptable behavior we learn early on in life, will vary. Consider an Armenian in his eighties who visits his grandson in the United States for the first time to attend his wedding. The elderly man accompanies his grandson to the local grocery store, where he repeatedly picks up different types of fruits and tastes them. He explains his behavior by fervently defending his right to taste the merchandise to see whether it is good before buying it, arguing with a store employee that this is the normal practice in his own country.

The law emerges to ensure that all people adhere to a common set of rules about right and wrong. For Sellin, however, the law's definitions of right and wrong are based on middle-class values—values that are not equally shared by all members of society. Crime, therefore exists because there is disagreement over what is acceptable behavior. Consider, for example, cultures where people commit murder in the name of family honor and tradition (see Box 11.3). Sellin argued that the more diverse society becomes, the more likely conflict and disagreement will exist, and therefore, the more likely deviance and crime will also increase. The question is, why and how do some individuals adhere to norms and values that support criminal behavior? We turn now to a brief look at the concept of delinquent subcultures.

Subcultures

In 1958, Walter B. Miller developed a theory of delinquent behavior that attributes crime to a lower-class culture.[31] Miller studied gangs in Massachusetts for three years, observing that urban youth learn values conducive to criminal activity from their exposure to a lower-class **subculture**, a group within the larger social culture that has a distinct set of norms and a unique pattern of behavior. The dominant values of mainstream, middle-class society—working hard, getting an education, and abiding by the rules—become less meaningful among the urban poor who are exposed to the daily hardships of deteriorated living conditions, economic struggle, and limited resources.[32] It is very difficult to convince an urban youth to stay in school and get an education in hopes of going to college, when his biggest problem is getting up every morning and hoping to survive the day without getting shot.

According to Miller, members of the lower class have different **focal concerns**, values, and behaviors that emerge to meet the specific conditions of the lower-class environment and that may result in deviant activities and violence. Table 11.4 illustrates these concerns. The concern with *toughness*, for example, may lead to fighting in order to gain respect, whereas a concern with *autonomy* can justify disobedience or disregard for the law.

A theory of **delinquent subcultures** was articulated by Albert Cohen in his 1955 publication of *Delinquent Boys*.[33] In this now-classic study Cohen examines the delinquent activities of youth, arguing that a delinquent subculture emerges from the common need to resolve similar problems. Lower-class youth engage in delinquent activities as a means of compensating for their lack of legitimate opportunities within the dominant social structure. They often feel rejected by parents, teachers, and society in general. They are well aware of their failure

Table 11.4 Focal concerns . . . what do the urban poor worry about?

Concern	Context
Trouble	Getting in and out of trouble is a main concern of the lower class subculture; fighting, handling conflicts and disputes with aggression, drinking, and running into cops are all a part of the daily routine.
Toughness	Value is placed on being tough, both physically and in attitude. Masculinity is equated with fighting prowess, strength, and athletic capability.
Smartness	Lower class members equate smartness with being savvy or streetwise, outwitting the opponent at any contest, game, or transaction. Gambling, con-games, and outwitting police become survival techniques.
Excitement	The definition of excitement within the lower class subculture centers upon the available activities that can deliver a "high" or "rush." Participating in a drive-by shooting, taking drugs, and being in a high speed police chase are all considered forms of excitement.
Fate	The outlook of individuals from the lower class is connected to the concept of destiny, luck, and inevitability. This type of attitude encourages risk taking behavior as there is some higher power that is always in control of the outcome of events.
Autonomy	The independence from all sources of authority is a major concern of the lower class subculture. Adherences to rules and being coerced or controlled by others are all signs of weakness.

Source: Miller, Walter B. 1958. Lower Class Culture as a Generating Milieu of Gang Delinquency. Journal of Social Issues 14: 5–19.

and of the relative impossibility of achieving anything close to the American dream. Thus, in a process Cohen refers to as **reaction formation**, lower-class youth reject the mainstream culture and develop hostility toward its norms and values.

Consequently, their disadvantaged social and economic position makes them vulnerable to joining gangs and participating in non-conformist, lawless behavior.[34] These youths adhere to the norms and values of a delinquent subculture, one that emphasizes negative, spiteful, destructive, and generally "hell-raising" behavior—values directly opposed to the dominant culture. Essentially, society at large is the enemy, and all acts that go against its norms—whether theft, vandalism, or assault—are defined as positively valued and desirable forms of behavior.

In 1967, Franco Ferracuti and Marvin Wolfgang elaborated on the concept of culture conflict and crime by developing the **subculture of violence theory**.[35] Wolfgang and Ferracuti observed that violent behavior is not evenly distributed within the social structure; rather, for some individuals it is a learned pattern of behavior and an adaptation to certain environmental stimuli—anger, frustration, conflict, or provocation.

Image 11.8 *Throwing punches at a hockey game is the norm. Ever wonder why? Isn't it rare for a fight to break out at a basketball or baseball game, even when players disagree or certain calls by the referee are so close? What makes hockey players so prone to violence? Could there possibly be a subculture unique to this sport?*

Claudio Bresciani/TT News Agency/Press Association Images

In a study of 588 criminal homicides in Philadelphia, Wolfgang and Ferracuti found non-white males ages 20–24 committed homicide at a rate of 92 per 100,000, compared to 3.4 for white males ages 20–24.[36] They concluded that violence is most prevalent among a homogeneous group within the larger urban community, because in this subculture's value system, violence is an acceptable means of behavior in a variety of circumstances.[37]

The basic premise of Wolfgang and Ferracuti's subculture of violence theory is that some individuals within certain groups—such as males, African Americans, and southerners—regard violence as a normative, acceptable, and even required means of upholding certain values such as honor, masculinity, and courage. Research shows violence is often a means of gaining status and approval among peers.[38] Thus, it becomes a tradition and an expectation within circumstances the group defines, and non-violence is a rejection of the group's norms with negative consequences such as exclusion or ostracism.

Wolfgang and Ferracuti never explained why violence becomes part of the normative structure for certain groups of individuals. Could it be that some individuals resort to violence and criminal activity simply because the opportunity presents itself to them, over and over again, and therefore the violent response becomes embedded as regular, ordinary, or routine? We explore this question by looking at differential opportunity.

Differential opportunity

We can all agree with some certainty that most people would not know how to organize a drug-trafficking operation, join the underground nicotine market, connect with international terrorists, or set up a methamphetamine lab. It's safe to say that even if life becomes difficult and education and a good career seem too far away, these illegitimate avenues are not readily available to most people.

Researchers Richard Cloward and Lloyd Ohlin noted that Merton's strain theory was correct in its observation that legitimate opportunities for success were not evenly distributed within the social structure.[39] However, the distribution of crime and delinquency also depend on the presence of illegitimate opportunities.[40] Indeed, frustration and strain contributed to the evolution of delinquent and violent subcultures; but it is variable access to illegitimate opportunities that contributes to the development of crime and delinquency, hence the term **differential opportunity**.[41]

Cloward and Ohlin developed a typology of three different delinquent subcultures: criminal, conflict, and retreatist.

(1) *Criminal Subcultures*—These gangs are predominantly present in long-standing, steady neighborhood environments where adolescent offenders have close access to adult criminals who teach them the successful path of criminal enterprise, including the necessary skills and techniques, the proper criminal associates and friendships, and even the right lawyers, politicians, and corrupt police to connect with. Criminal activities are generally organized and well planned and often include extortion, fraud, theft, and other income-generating illegal activities.

(2) *Conflict subcultures*—Within this subculture, status is derived from engaging in violent activities. Unstable, disorganized neighborhood communities provide little access to legitimate opportunities for success, and few opportunities for illegitimate activities. There is little or no network of criminal enterprise between adults and delinquent youth, and therefore adolescents turn to the random and disorganized acts of teen gangs that include fighting, assault, vandalism, and arson. Violence is a means of survival and gaining respect.

(3) *Retreatist subcultures*—Some youth who face blocked access to legitimate opportunities are not tough enough to survive within the conflict subculture and do not have the knowledge of criminal enterprise prevalent in the criminal subculture. They gain peer approval by remaining in a continuous state of oblivion or drug-induced high, adopting a disorganized lifestyle marked by hustling through prostitution, pimping, drug selling, and petty theft.

Cloward and Ohlin brought together the concepts of subculture and social disorganization to explain emerging and adaptive patterns of delinquent behavior. Their theory had significant impact on social policy and the creation of programs meant to increase educational and employment opportunities for disadvantaged youth (See Box 11.4). Differential opportunity theory also raised some very important issues not brought to light by other culture conflict theories.

BOX 11.4: CONNECTING THEORY TO PRACTICE

Juvenile delinquents ... Give them something to do

On September 22, 1961, President John F. Kennedy made battling juvenile delinquency a national priority by signing the *Juvenile Delinquency and Youth Offenses Control Act*, stating that:

> The future of our country depends upon our younger people who will occupy positions of responsibility and leadership in the coming days. Yet for 11 years juvenile delinquency has been increasing. No city or state in our country has been immune. This is a matter of national concern and requires national action.

This legislation made the Federal government a more active participant in assisting local and state governments to control and prevent juvenile delinquency at its very source—the community. The resulting Mobilization for Youth Program began the organization of neighborhood councils to correct conditions leading to poor education, poor health, idleness, despair, and ultimately juvenile delinquency. This national effort and its pilot projects began what came to be called "community action."

Community action agencies were established across the United States to continue and expand the work begun by President Kennedy. With the goal of eliminating social conditions that contributed to delinquency and crime, these agencies provided many needed programs and services within disadvantaged communities. They expanded opportunities for job training and access to education and promoted economic development, community health care delivery centers, legal services, youth recreational and mentoring programs, senior citizen centers, and other innovative practices.

Adopting Cloward and Ohlin's ideas on dealing with juvenile delinquency, the initiatives begun by the Kennedy administration were indeed an effort at providing disadvantaged youth with resources to combat the effects of poverty, unemployment, and deteriorated living conditions and empowering communities into action. However, they were also a direct challenge to the unbalanced distribution of resources within the United States.

Sources

John F. Kennedy: Remarks Upon Signing the Juvenile Delinquency and Youth Offenses Control Act. 2009. *The American Presidency Project*. Retrieved from http://www.presidency.ucsb.edu/ws/index.php?pid=8347.

Vinovskis, Maris A. 2005. *The Birth of Head Start: Preschool Education Policies in the Kennedy and Johnson Administrations.* University of Chicago Press.

For Cloward and Ohlin, participants in deviant subcultures were still members of the larger culture, and their beliefs and values were not always counter to the dominant value system within society. Given that these individuals know right from wrong and understand the value of conventional behavior, how do they justify their criminal actions? How do they explain their loyalty to norms that goes against those of mainstream society? Researchers Gresham Sykes and David Matza provide an answer to these questions in their concept of delinquency and drift.

Drifting

The concept of justifying criminal behavior was articulated by Gresham Sykes and David Matza in their 1957 publication "Techniques of Neutralization: A Theory of Delinquency."[42] **Techniques of neutralization** are rationalizations people use to justify their criminal acts (see Figure 11.3). Sykes and Matza note there is a difference between a subculture of delinquency and a delinquent subculture. A delinquent subculture sets up its own moral system that completely replaces the dominant social system of beliefs and values. The subculture of delinquency exists when individuals form groups whose members share common values and beliefs that don't necessarily agree with the dominant culture, yet retain certain elements of it. These can include various groups and organizations that are protesting against war, embracing sexual freedom, and defying the establishment.[43] Thus, when individuals adhere to a subculture

Image 11.9 *When given the opportunity to choose between right and wrong, how do individuals who choose to do wrong justify their actions?*

iStock/hoozone

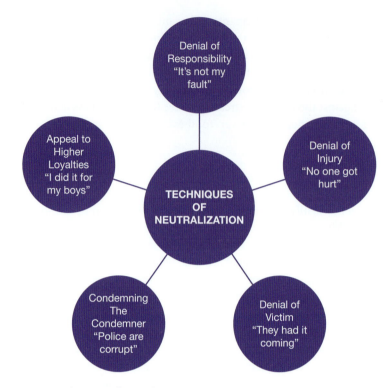

Figure 11.3 Techniques of neutralization

of delinquency, they must develop various rationalizations to justify their deviant acts that are inconsistent with some of the values and beliefs of the larger dominant culture that they also adhere to.

In his 1964 publication of *Delinquency and Drift*, Matza suggested that individuals **drift** from conventional, law-abiding behavior to delinquent and criminal behavior by gradually altering their way of thinking and reacting to their acts using neutralization techniques.[44] A necessary condition of drifting is the experience of injustice and despair within your social environment, which creates a disconnect with society and diminished loyalty to its values. An inner-city youth who is failing in school, repeatedly demeaned by his parents, and bullied by his peers may become lonely and isolated. When a criminal opportunity presents itself, such youths may justify such acts as spray-painting graffiti, robbing a convenience store, or selling drugs by neutralizing their loyalty to the dominant value system and regarding their actions as convenient, appropriate, and right given their situation, thereby reducing their feelings of guilt.[45]

Research studies find support for Sykes and Matza's contentions.[46] Neutralization techniques are highly correlated with involvement in gang activities.[47] Moreover, youth engaged in delinquent acts use techniques of neutralization to protect their self-concept, especially when they are more attached to their parents.[48] In a study of 27 male offenders who had committed violent crimes, the subjects used a series of justifications for the harm they caused the victim, believing the victim either provoked the act or deserved the harm, or the act was not intended or blameworthy.[49]

While these studies confirm the basic premises set forth by Sykes and Matza, we would still like to know how the individual pondering criminal choices interacts with the social environment to make a decision. Consider individuals who share similar adverse experiences and negative conditions within the social structure—why do some rationalize their drifting into a delinquent subculture while others do not engage in criminal activities at all? We will explore this dilemma in our next chapter on social process theories. For now, we turn to an evaluation of the social structure approach and its merits in explaining crime and delinquency.

EVALUATING SOCIAL STRUCTURE THEORIES

The root cause of criminal behavior, according to the social structure approach, lies in the conditions of the social environment that produce poverty, inequality, and injustice. Within this perspective, we identified three distinct approaches to the study of crime: social disorganization, strain, and culture conflict. Each provided us with a unique understanding of the problems within the social structure that contribute to patterns of crime and delinquency. To ensure we have a critical understanding of each theory, we now look at their various shortcomings.

Social disorganization theory provided us with an ecological approach to the study of crime that emphasizes ills within the social environment assumed to be the cause of crime and delinquency. Some, however, would argue to the contrary—that it is the presence of violence, fear, and crime that lead to the deterioration of neighborhoods and the presence of high rates of poverty and unemployment.[50] It is in fact very difficult to distinguish whether crime and delinquency are *symptoms* of social disorganization or actual *components* of it. This problem reveals the flaw in social disorganization theory: We cannot isolate aspects of social disorganization as sources of crime and delinquency when crime and delinquency are basic components of social disorganization; the consequence of a phenomenon cannot also be its cause.

The ecological approach of social disorganization theory uses crime statistics as evidence that some places are more crime-prone due to the structure of their social environment. However, as you may realize from our discussion of bias in official crime statistics in chapter 3, high reported rates of crime in these areas may simply reflect increased police visibility and activity. Researchers note this presence also leads to an overestimation of criminal behavior among certain racial and ethnic minorities.[51]

Social disorganization theory also fails to account for the presence of criminal activities within affluent neighborhoods. Murder, rape, robbery, assault, and drug use clearly occur in areas *not* characterized by social disorganization.

How do we account for crimes such as securities fraud, identity theft, and embezzlement that are committed more frequently by individuals from well-established communities and social environments? Clearly, social disorganization theory does not adequately account for this variety of criminal behavior.

The concept of strain has also been widely criticized as an oversimplified explanation of crime that focuses on a disjunction between aspiration and opportunity. Empirical evidence suggests strain is not always consistent with delinquent behavior.[52] Moreover, if crime were merely a consequence of economic deprivation, then only the economically deprived should become criminal. If matters were that simple, we could solve the problem of crime and delinquency by giving everyone equal access to legitimate means of achieving success. How then do we explain the criminal behavior of individuals who are not economically disadvantaged? The flaw in strain theory is its narrow focus on limited economic opportunity, with little attention to other influences such as poor socialization or a psychiatric disorder.

Moreover, we know that not all individuals who experience strain and frustration adapt by engaging in criminal acts. Some individuals adapt to the disjunction between goals and means by rejecting the goals set forth by society, yet reluctantly accepting the means in the adaptation Merton identified as ritualism. Why do individuals adapt to strain in different ways? Merton never answers this question. Thus, strain theory fails to account for variations in crime and delinquency among individuals with common socioeconomic characteristics; it does not explain the subjective effects of the intensity or frequency of strain or individual differences in coping strategies.[53]

The final group of theories we discussed in this chapter came to us from the culture conflict approach, based on the assumption that crime is a reflection of norms and values in conflict with the dominant social structure. This method of analysis fails to recognize one very important fact that the definition of right and wrong is subject to social interpretation and therefore cannot be used as a standard to measure crime and delinquency. In a classic critique of cultural deviance theory, Ruth Kornhauser explains:

> In cultural deviance models, there is no such thing as deviance in the ordinary meaning of that word. If conformity is defined as obedience to the norms of one's own culture and deviance as violation of those norms, then human beings apparently lack the capacity for deviance. Except for the idiot and the insane, we cannot know what they are about, the universal experience of mankind is conformity to the norms of the groups into which they have been socialized, and to which they owe allegiance. People never violate the norms of their own groups, only the norms of other groups. What appears to be deviance is simply a label applied by an outgroup to the conforming behavior to the conforming behavior endorsed in one's own subculture.[54]

Table 11.5 The social structure perspective

What is crime?	• Crime is acquired behavior
Why does crime occur? (theory)	• Because aspects of the social environment are pathological due to disorganization, strain, and culture conflict, individuals exposed to such conditions will acquire patterns of criminal behavior
What is the solution to crime? (policy)	• Alter the structure of the social environment to eliminate its pathological conditions • Improve individuals' quality of life, increase their opportunity for legitimate activities, and transform crime-prone neighborhoods and communities through a collaborative effort between law enforcement, community networks, and social service agencies

Saying rates of crime and delinquency are higher among those whose norms emphasize violence and toughness is like saying those who are successful work hard and working hard therefore explains their success. This type of circular reasoning merely describes; it does not explain the behavior itself. Why do some people work hard for years to achieve success while others are unable to delay their immediate needs for money and other desired goods? The culture conflict approach also neglects variables like self-control that may prevent involvement in criminal behavior.[55]

Finally, culture conflict theories have been criticized for bias against certain racial and ethnic groups. To say we find certain violent subcultures more often among African American youths, for example, and that this is why crime is higher in areas that are predominantly African American, is not only biased but also fails to recognize the structural barriers within the social environment that create inherent inequalities for certain groups. We discussed these barriers in greater detail in chapter 10.

Despite their shortcomings, social structure theories have had a significant influence on the development of social policies that acknowledge the role of environmental variables in the development of crime and delinquency. We turn now to a discussion of the policy implications of social structure theories to assess their impact on crime control programs and strategies.

PRACTICAL APPLICATION OF SOCIAL STRUCTURE THEORY

Table 11.5 provides a summary of the social structure approach to the study of crime and crime control. The social structure paradigm in criminology has influenced a variety of intervention strategies aimed at combating the effects of environment on behavior and life experiences, including the war on poverty during the 1960s and *weed and seed* programs in the early 1990s. The legacy of social structure theory began during the 1930s when Clifford Shaw attempted to put theory into practice by establishing the Chicago Area Project.

The Chicago Area Project

In the 1930s, the Chicago Area Project (CAP) was founded by sociologist Clifford Shaw to address the problem of juvenile delinquency in some of the poorest communities in Chicago.[56] Its central goal was to assist neighborhoods in organizing their communities by making residents more aware of criminal activity, improving the physical environment and quality of life within their community, and creating positive role models for youth.

The CAP aimed at strengthening communities by doing three things:

(1) Developing academic, educational, and recreational programs designed to provide underprivileged youth with the opportunity to participate in positive and structured activities, sports, academic enrichment, employment training, and mentoring programs.

(2) Mobilizing citizens to take pride in their neighborhoods and participate in efforts at cleaning up parks, picking up trash, renovating rundown buildings, removing graffiti, and improving the overall appearance of their community, all to encourage residents to collaborate in solving common problems.

(3) Intervening on the behalf of troubled teens who had already become part of the juvenile justice system in order to connect them to the proper community agencies and resources to improve their social environment and provide them with alternatives to drug abuse, gang involvement, and truancy.

The CAP continues to serve the members of its community today, with over forty affiliate organizations, partners, and special projects throughout the city of Chicago.[57] Its core ideas are modeled in programs across the country, including public housing tenant boards, neighborhood watch groups, community action programs, and youth initiatives. These programs are driven by urban planning, self-sustenance, community improvement, and alternatives to crime and delinquency. We turn now to a national initiative that also rests upon the foundations of social structure theories, the war on poverty.

War on poverty

In 1964, President Lyndon B. Johnson declared a "War on Poverty" in his first State of the Union address, declaring poverty a priority in the public policy arena.[58] For the next decade, the federal government, in collaboration with state and local governments, non-profit organizations, and other citizen action groups, created a series of legislative acts aimed at improving the welfare of citizens across the United States. These are some of the strategies developed by the war on poverty:

- Economic Opportunity Act (1964)
- Job Corps
- Volunteers in Service to America (VISTA)
- Upward Bound
- Head Start
- legal services
- Neighborhood Youth Corps
- Community Action Program (CAP)
- College Work-Study Program
- Neighborhood Development Centers
- small business loan programs
- rural programs
- migrant worker programs
- remedial education projects
- local health care centers
- Food Stamp Act (1964)
- Elementary and Secondary Education Act (1965)
- Higher Education Act (1965)
- Social Security amendments creating Medicare/Medicaid (1965)
- creation of the Department of Housing and Urban Development (1965)
- Model Cities Act (1966)
- Fair Housing Act (1968)
- urban renewal projects

The philosophy behind the war on poverty and its initiatives rested on decades of research about the detrimental effects of poverty on individuals, and the need for social reform to counter the effects of deteriorated living conditions. Legislators recognized the need for massive social reform to reach generations of poverty-stricken individuals who embraced values and behaviors that kept them in a cycle of poverty.[59] They were heavily influenced by the Chicago School and drew upon the research and premises of opportunity theory, emphasizing systematic change in urban ghetto communities to help eliminate criminal opportunity structures.

Weed and seed

Another national policy initiative resting on the theoretical foundation of the social structure approach is the **weed and seed program**. In 1991, the U.S. Department of Justice initiated this innovative program aimed at preventing and controlling violent crime, drug abuse, and gang activities in targeted neighborhoods by combining law enforcement efforts with community revitalization.[60] The program employs a strategy of "weeding" out violent criminals and drug traffickers and "seeding" communities with much-needed social services and neighborhood restoration programs. This strategy is used to accomplish three goals:

(1) Develop a comprehensive strategy to control and prevent violent crime, drug trafficking, and gang activity through the collaborative efforts of law enforcement and the prosecutor's office.
(2) Coordinate existing community resources and build new initiatives to restore communities and provide intervention, treatment, and prevention of violent crime and drug abuse.
(3) Use a community-oriented policing approach to mobilize neighborhood citizens to assist law enforcement in identifying violent offenders, gang members, and drug traffickers.

An evaluation of weed and seed programs in various jurisdictions shows a persistent pattern of long-term decrease in criminal activity in targeted communities.[61] More research needs to be conducted to account for differences in results across jurisdictions. Today, weed and seed initiatives are implemented in over 150 communities across the United States, integrating law enforcement and community action to improve the structure of urban environments and reduce criminal activity. These programs are based on findings that crime control efforts must address the underlying factors making some communities susceptible to high levels of crime.[62]

Indeed, social action is essential to changing environment. In the chapter to come, we explore the concept of social action further in a discussion of social process theories.

SUMMARY

How do criminologists explain trends and variations in criminal behavior?

Criminologists explain trends and variations in criminal behavior by examining the effects of the social structure, the socialization process, and conflicts inherent to social institutions, on patterns of human behavior.

Where does the sociological approach search for the cause of crime?

The sociological perspective explains patterns in human behavior by examining those aspects of society that affect the way people think, act, and react. Thus, this approach looks for the causes of crime *outside* the individual.

What is the social structure and how does it affect our behavior?

The social structure is the foundation upon which society is built. It includes the social and economic conditions to which people are exposed on a daily basis. Harsh conditions such as poverty, deprivation, frustration, the lack of opportunity to succeed, and deviant cultural values can influence the way people think and act.

Are certain places more conducive to crime than others?

Social disorganization theory argues that crime is a characteristic of certain ecological conditions within the social environment of urban communities, rather than a consequence of the distinct qualities of certain types of individuals. It is the structure of neighborhoods within the inner city, where deviant norms and values, impoverished lifestyles, unemployment, culture conflict—social disorganization—perpetuate criminal behavior. Thus, some places draw more criminal behavior because of their geographic location and physical features.

Can certain types of frustrations lead to crime?

According to strain theory, variations in the structure of society creates anomie, or strain due to the discrepancy between the cultural norms that define success in life and the legitimate and appropriate ways to achieve success. Anomie leads to frustration and resentment, to which people react in different ways. Some adapt by accepting the culturally defined goals but rejecting the legitimate means. This adaptation is referred to as innovation and often includes criminal and deviant activities such as stealing or selling drugs.

Do all subcultures go against the dominant norms of society?

Culture conflict theory finds the root cause of criminal behavior in the clash of values about what is right and what is wrong. Subcultures are groups within the larger social culture that have a distinct set of norms and a unique pattern of behavior. Not all subcultures go against the dominant norms of society. However, deviant subcultures emerge among urban youth who learn values conducive to criminal activity from their exposure to a lower-class subculture. Moreover, individuals adhering to a subculture of violence regard violent behavior as a normative, acceptable, and even required means of upholding certain values such as honor, masculinity, and courage, and they rationalize their behavior accordingly.

If crime is acquired behavior, then what can we change about the social structure to prevent it?

The solution to crime, according to social structure theories, is social policies and programs that alter social-environment variables contributing to the development of crime and delinquency. Crime control strategies influenced by this theory have focused on interventions that improve individuals' quality of life and enhance the neighborhoods and communities in which they live.

CRITICAL THINKING QUESTIONS

1. Imagine a society where no one was very wealthy or very poor. All homes had the same value and cars the same price. Everyone had a job that was equally rewarded and there was no unemployment. Would such an environment lead to criminal activity? If so, what types of crimes would be committed and how would we explain their cause?

2. Have you ever thought about the expression the "black sheep of the family"? What does that phrase mean? How do we account for individuals who deviate from social norms despite being raised in a positive, nurturing, and pro-social environment?

3. How would you describe the social structure of the neighborhood you grew up in? What aspects of it contributed to the way people acted and the dynamics of group behavior there? Were delinquency and crime a problem in your neighborhood? Why or why not?

4. We live in a society where the value of entertainment far exceeds the value of saving lives. How does this make you feel? How do you overcome feelings of strain and frustration to avoid *retreatism* and *rebellion*? What keeps us going as *ritualists* and *conformists*? When and why do some cross the line to *innovation*?

E-RESOURCES

Learn more about Émile Durkheim and the foundations of sociological theory by visiting http://routledgesoc.com/profile/%C3%A9mile-durkheim.

You can get more information about the study of the environment as related to human interactions at the *Institute for Social Ecology* website, http://www.social-ecology.org/.

Visit the Griffith Criminology Institute website at https://www.griffith.edu.au/criminology-law/griffith-criminology-institute/research/environmental-criminology-and-crime-analysis for additional facts on this field of study.

For an excellent study on urban subcultures, see *Code of the Street: Decency, Violence, and the Moral Life of the Inner City* by Elijah Anderson, referenced at https://www.amazon.com/Code-Street-Decency-Violence-Moral/dp/0393320782/189–5128427–4381961?ie=UTF8&*Version*=1&*entries*=0.

Read more about the programs and initiatives of the Chicago Area Project by visiting http://www.chicagoareaproject.org/.

NOTES

1   Fernandez, Manny, Stack, Liam, and Blinder, Alan. 2015. 9 Are Killed in Biker Gang Shootout in Waco. *The New York Times,* May 17. Retrieved from http://www.nytimes.com/2015/05/18/us/motorcycle-gang-shootout-in-waco-texas.html?_r=0.

2   National Criminal Justice Reference Service. 2015. Bureau of Justice Statistics, U.S. Department of Justice, Washington, D.C. Retrieved from https://www.ncjrs.gov/.

3   United States Department of Health and Human Services. 2001. *Youth Violence: A Report of the Surgeon General.* Washington, D.C.: United States Department of Health and Human Services. Retrieved from http://www.surgeongeneral.gov/library/youth violence/toc.html.

4   Carls, Paul. Émile Durkheim (1858—1917). Internet Encyclopedia of Philosophy. Retrieved from http://www.iep.utm.edu/durkheim/.

5   Elwell, Frank W. 2003. *The Sociology of Emile Durkheim.* Retrieved from http://www.faculty.rsu.edu/~felwell/Theorists/Durkheim/index.htm.

6   Akers, Ronald, L. 2011. *Social Learning and Social Structure: A General Theory of Crime and Deviance.* Piscataway, NJ: Transaction Publishers.

7   Huck, Jennifer L. and Morris, Carrie. 2014. *The Encyclopedia of Criminology and Criminal Justice.* New Jersey: Blackwell Publishing.

8   Chambliss, William J. 2001. *Power, Politics and Crime.* Boulder, CO: Westview Press.

9   Brown, S., Esbensen, F. and Geis, G. 2015. *Criminology: Explaining Crime and Its Context.* New York: Routledge.

10 Anderson, Elijah. 2009. *Against the Wall: Poor, Young, Black, and Male (The City in the Twenty-First Century).* University of Pennsylvania Press.

11 Ibid.

12 Morgan, Rachel E. and Iasinski, Jana L. 2016. Tracking Violence Using Structural-Level Characteristics in the Analysis of Domestic Violence in Chicago and the State of Illinois. *Crime & Delinquency.* Published online before print 19 Jan., 2016, doi: 10.1177/0011128715625082.

13 Park, Robert and Burgess, Ernest. 1925. *The City.* Chicago: University of Chicago Press.

14 Brown, Nina. 2009. Robert Park and Ernest Burgess: Urban Ecology Studies, 1925. *Center for Spatially Integrated Social Science.* Retrieved from http://www.csiss.org/classics/content/26.

15 Shaw, Clifford R. and McKay, Henry D. 1942. *Juvenile Delinquency in Urban Areas.* Chicago: University of Chicago Press.

16 Eck, John E. and Weisburd, David L. 2015. Crime Places in Crime Theory. *Crime and Place: Crime Prevention Studies* 4:1–33.

17 Byrne, James and Sampson, Robert. 1985. *The Social Ecology of Crime.* New York: Springer Verlag.

18 Randa, R. 2014. Environmental Criminology. *The Encyclopedia of Criminology and Criminal Justice.* Hoboken, NJ: Blackwell.

19 Andresen, Martin. 2014. *Environmental Criminology: Evolution, Theory and Practice.* London and New York: Routledge.

20 Ibid.

21 Weisburd, David L. and McEwen, Tom. 2015. *Crime Mapping and Crime Prevention.* Retrieved from http://papers.ssrn.com/sol3/papers.cfm?abstract_id=2629850.

22 Merton, Robert K. 1938. Social Structure and Anomie. *American Sociological Review* 3(5): 672–682.

23 Merton, Robert K. 1996. On Social Structure and Science. In Piotr Sztompka (ed.), *Essays by Robert K. Merton.* Chicago: University of Chicago Press.

24 Ibid., see 22.

25 Cullen, F., Jonson, C., Myer, A. and Adler, F. 2011. The Origins of American Criminology. Piscataway, NJ: Transaction Publishers.

26 Agnew, Robert. 1992. Foundation for a General Strain Theory of Crime And Delinquency. *Criminology* 30(1): 47–87.

27 Agnew, Robert. 2001. Building on the Foundation of General Strain Theory: Specifying the Types of Strain Most Likely to Lead to Crime and Delinquency. *Journal of Research in Crime and Delinquency* 38: 319–361.

28   Bryant, W. 2011. Internalized Racism's Association with African American Male Youth's Propensity for Violence. In *Journal of Black Studies*.

29   Sharpe, Tanya. 2015. Understanding the Sociocultural Context of Coping for African American Family Members of Homicide Victims: A Conceptual Model. *Trauma, Violence, and Abuse* 16(1): 48–59.

30   Sellin, Thorsten. 1938. *Culture Conflict and Crime*. New York: Social Science Research Council.

31   Miller, Walter B. 1958. Lower Class Culture as a Generating Milieu of Gang Delinquency. *Journal of Social Issues* 14: 5–19.

32   Anderson, Elijah 2003. *A Place on the Corner: A Study of Black Street Corner Men*, 2nd ed. Chicago: University of Chicago Press.

33   Cohen, Albert. 1955. *Delinquent Boys*. New York: Free Press.

34   Ibid.

35   Ferracuti, Franco and Wolfgang, Marvin. 1967. *The Subculture of Violence: Toward an Integrated Theory of Criminology*. London: Tavistock.

36   Wolfgang, Marvin E. 1958. *Patterns in Criminal Homicide*. Philadelphia: University of Pennsylvania Press.

37   Ibid, see 34.

38   Pokhrel, P., Sussman, S., Black, D., and Sun, P. 2010. Peer Group Self-Identification as a Predictor of Relational and Physical Aggression Among High School Students. In *The Journal of School Health*.

39   Cloward, Richard A. and Ohlin, Lloyd E. 1960. *Delinquency and Opportunity: A Theory of Delinquent Gangs*. Glencoe, IL: Free Press.

40   Thompson, W. and Bynum, J. 2013. Sociological Explanations of Juvenile Delinquency: Social Strain and Cultural Transmission Theories. In *Juvenile Delinquency: A Sociological Approach*. Upper Saddle River, NJ: Pearson.

41   Ibid., see 38.

42   Sykes, Gresham and Matza, David. 1957. Techniques of Neutralization: A Theory of Delinquency. *American Sociological Review* 22(6): 664–670.

43   Matza, David and Sykes, Gresham. 1961. Juvenile Delinquency and Subterranean Values. *American Sociological Review* 26(5): 712–719.

44   Matza, David. 1964. *Delinquency and Drift*. New York: John Wiley and Sons.

45   Dong, Beidi and Kroh, Marvin D. 2016. Dual Trajectories of Gang Affiliation and Delinquent Peer Association During Adolescence: An Examination of Long-Term Offending Outcomes. *Journal of Youth and Adolescence*. Retrieved from http://link.springer.com/article/10.1007/s10964–016–0417–2.

46   Alleyne, E. and Wood, J. 2010. Gang involvement: Psychological and Behavioral Characteristics of Gang Members, Peripheral Youth and Non-gang Youth. In *Aggressive Behavior*. Canterbury, England: University of Kent.

47   Ibid.

48   Ibid., see 45.

49   Pressner, Lois. 2003. Remorse and Neutralization Among Violent Male Offenders. *Justice Quarterly* 20(4): 801–825.

50   Grinshteyn, Erin G., Eisenman, David P, Cunningham, William E., Andersen, Ronald and Ettner, Susan L. 2016. Individual- and Neighborhood-Level Determinants of Fear of Violent Crime Among Adolescents. *Family and Community Health* 39(2): 103–112.

51   Rinehart, Tammy K., Burruss, George and Weisburd, David. 2015. St. Louis County Hot Spots In Residential Areas (SCHIRA) Final Report: Assessing The Effects Of Hot Spots Policing Strategies On Police Legitimacy, Crime, And Collective Efficacy. Retrieved from http://opensiuc.lib.siu.edu/cgi/viewcontent.cgi?article=1002&context= ccj_reports&sei-redir=1&referer=https%3A%2F%2Fscholar.google.com%2Fscholar %3Fq%3Dhigh%2Bcrime%2Brates%2Band%2Bpolice%2Bvisibility%26btnG%3D

%26hl%3Den%26as_sdt%3D0%252C26%26as_ylo%3D2015#search=%22high%20 crime%20rates%20police%20visibility%22.

52   Felson, Richard B. and Kreager, Derek A. 2015. Group Differences in Delinquency What Is There to Explain? *Race and Justice* 5(1): 58–87.

53   Ousey, Graham C., Wilcox, Pamela and Schreck, Christopher J. 2015. Violent Victimization, Confluence of Risks and the Nature of Criminal Behavior: Testing Main and Interactive Effects from Agnew's Extension of General Strain Theory. *Journal of Criminal Justice* 43(2): 164–173.

54   Kornhauser, Ruth. 1978. *Social Sources of Delinquency*. Chicago: University of Chicago Press, p. 29.

55   Turanovic, Jillian J., Reisig, Michael D., and Pratt, Travis C. 2015. Risky Lifestyles, Low Self-control, and Violent Victimization Across Gendered Pathways to Crime. *Journal of Quantitative Criminology* 31(2): 183–206.

56   Matsueda, R. (ed.). 2012. The Criminologist: The Official Newsletter of the American Society of Criminology 37(5).

57   What is CAP? *The Chicago Area Project*. Retrieved from http://www.chicagoarea project.org/about.html.

58   *Community Action: Nearly 50 Years Moving Forward*. 2013. Annual Report. Retrieved from http://www.cap-dayton.org/contentmgr/documents/COMACT1945Annual Report_Revised_FIN_Web2.pdf.

59   Lewis, Oscar. 1998. The Culture of Poverty. *Society* 35(2): 7.

60   Office of Justice Programs. Weed and Seed. U.S. Department of Justice. Retrieved from https://www.justice.gov/usao-ndca/weed-and-seed.

61   Ibid.

62   Hoffman, J., Knox, L. and Cohen, R. 2011. *Beyond Suppression: Global Perspectives on Youth Violence*. Santa Barbara, CA: ABC-CLIO.

CHAPTER OUTLINE

Social process theories: crime is socialized behavior

In this chapter we will explore the following questions

- What is the social process approach?
- How are we socialized?
- Do individuals learn to become criminal? If so, who are their teachers?
- What do social learning, social control and labeling theories tell us about the specific mechanisms by which individuals learn crime?
- Does the social process approach tell us everything we need to know about crime?
- How do social process theories guide our understanding of criminal justice policy?

KEY TERMS

social process

socialization

agents of socialization

social learning theory

differential association

differential learning

differential reinforcement

differential association-reinforcement

differential identification

reference groups

social control theory

containment theory

external containment

internal containment

social bonds

labeling or "societal reaction" theory

Chris Harper-Mercer had a strong contempt for religion. He was not alone. Apparently, there was an anti-religion internet group he belonged to that "doesn't like organized religion" either. Harper-Mercer, age 26, also blogged about his fascination with Nazi memorabilia as well as the terror tactics of the Irish Republican Army, writing, "seems like the more people you kill, the more you're in the limelight."[1] On October 1, 2015, armed with three pistols and a rifle, Harper-Mercer went to Umpqua Community College in Roseburg, Oregon, and began a shooting rampage that left 13 people dead and several others wounded. Survivors tell that Harper-Mercer asked people one by one if they were a Christian. Those who answered "yes" were shot in the head. Those who answered "no" or didn't answer were shot in the leg. What questions do Harper-Mercer's actions raise in our minds? How could this individual develop a hatred that is so strong? Why would someone take the lives of innocent people they have never met before? What breakdown in self-control could justify such actions?

The array of college campus and school shootings over the past several years has left us with many questions about apparently inexplicable violence, as the images of students running away in a panic on April 20, 1999, at Columbine High School in Jefferson County, Colorado, continue to haunt us.

Image 12.1 *Photo of a shooting victim being wheeled away by paramedics from the scene where a gunman opened fire at Umpqua Community College in Roseburg, Oregon, 2015.*
Mike Sullivan/AP/Press Association Images

primary deviance

secondary
   deviance

stigmatization

deviance
   amplification

youth mentoring
   initiatives

Head Start

diversion

This attack remains one of the deadliest high school shootings in U.S. history. Why did Columbine students Eric Harris and Dylan Klebold go on a shooting rampage that day, killing 12 students and a teacher and wounding 24 others, before turning their weapons on themselves and committing suicide? Why did Harris and Klebold do it? Were they alienated from family and peers, social isolates who lacked the appropriate bond to society? Did they act upon a self-image imposed upon them by their social environment? Did they have a long-term pre-disposition to commit their crime, or was it an explosive act precipitated by something that triggered a gruesome response to social pressure?

Criminologists often face the daunting task of explaining a variety of criminal events. In many circumstances the search for the cause leads to the usual suspects: poverty, drugs, unemployment, social inequality, criminal subcultures, and mental illness. However, none of these was an issue for Klebold, Harris, or Ford. In a research study conducted by Akers and Silverman, a social learning model is used to explain terrorism as a form of violence, arguing that the exposure of individuals to definitions that favor radical militant ideologies justifies, rationalizes, and excuses their deviant attitudes and actions.[2] Akers and Silverman argue that the socialization of individuals into deviant attitudes and beliefs that support violence serves to define and justify their behavior as morally right, appropriate, and acceptable.[3] Let us turn now to an exploration of the social interactions that take place as part of the learning process, and how they may contribute to crime and delinquency.

MAJOR PRINCIPLES OF THE SOCIAL PROCESS APPROACH

This chapter introduces a way of understanding crime that goes beyond the theories we have presented thus far. At one end of the spectrum in chapters 9 and 10, we saw that 200 years of research have failed to discover significant personality, biological, anatomical, or psychological traits common to individuals who engage in criminal behavior. Criminal behavior is not a characteristic of individuals, but rather a legal category created by lawmakers who define particular types of behavior as criminal.[4] In chapter 11, we looked at the other extreme, which seeks the cause of crime in the "pathologies" of society. These theories focus on problems such as poverty, unemployment, and injustice, and portray the criminal as a product of his or her social environment. Yet most people who live in poverty do not make crime a part of their way of life, and many of the most harmful crimes, such as white-collar crimes, war crimes and genocide are committed by people of privilege (see chapter 17).

Criminology came of age when it abandoned both biological-personality theories and societal pathology theory. Criminologists then turned to an examination of the *social processes* that led to patterns of criminality in different social groups. These offer us an explanation of criminal behavior that transcends time, place, setting, and individual characteristics and looks at the often-overlooked quality of human interactions.

From the **social process** perspective, criminality is not an innate human characteristic. Instead, everyone has the potential to commit criminal acts, as a consequence of social learning, social ties or bonds, labeling, and other social processes. In other words, *crime is socialized behavior*. Social process theories differ on the precise mechanisms, but they all agree that crime is learned in the process of lifelong interactions between individuals and their social environments.

Socialization is the process through which people learn the skills, knowledge, values, motives, and roles of the groups to which they belong, or the communities in which they live.[5] It is "the medium for transforming newcomers into bona fide members of a group."[6] Socialization shapes our behavior and is one reason that simply living in a violent neighborhood does not by itself produce violent individuals. Criminologists therefore focus a great deal of their research on the **agents of socialization**, that is, the groups and individuals who are the main influences on the process of socialization.[7] They include the family, peer groups, media, educational and religious institutions, and authority figures.

The effect of socialization on crime is clear. We can be socialized to *conform* to generally held values and norms, or to *violate* them. The question is, what makes the difference?

Criminologists' efforts to answer this question have generated three major theories in criminology: social learning, social control, and labeling. We'll look at each in some detail in this chapter, but briefly, **social learning theory** maintains that we learn criminal behavior in the same way we learn any other behavior:

Table 12.1 Social process theories

	Social learning theory	Social control theory	Labeling theory
	Differential learning	Integration	Stigmatization
Socialization process involved in learning criminal behavior	• Association • Reinforcement • Identification	• Social containment • Social bonds	• Primary deviance • Secondary deviance

we acquire the norms, values, and patterns of behaviors conducive to crime. **Social control theory** focuses on the interaction between an individual's personality and his social environment, through which he forms, or fails to form, the appropriate bonds to society. **Labeling theory** says that deviance is not a type of behavior but rather a name or labels by which society makes certain behaviors undesirable. Table 12.1 provides a summary of these three social process theories, and presents the various processes involved in learning criminal behavior, which we will discuss below.

SOCIAL LEARNING THEORIES

The theories we discuss in this part of the chapter focus on the processes involved in learning criminal behavior. The modeling, imitating, and adopting of criminal behavior patterns is discussed in the context of three learning components: differential association, differential reinforcement and differential identification. We turn first to the concept of differential association.

Image 12.2 *Active learning in a classroom takes place through an interactive process of communication.*

iStock/Steve Debenport

Differential association

One of the earliest and most influential social learning theorists was Edwin Sutherland. Sutherland noted that other explanations of criminality, focusing on individual traits and socioeconomic variables such as poverty and unemployment, fail to recognize one very important fact: that all significant aspects of human behavior are learned.[8] The key to understanding criminality, Sutherland believed, is to examine the various learning experiences individuals have that put them into contact with values, attitudes, and beliefs that favor criminal behavior.

Sutherland's starting point was to see society not as a harmonious collection of people who agreed on what behavior was right, but rather as different groups and social classes with very different beliefs about right and wrong. From there it was logical to argue, as Sutherland did, that people are exposed to a variety of behavior patterns, some labeled criminal and some not. This led Sutherland to the general principle of **differential association**: criminal behavior results from having more contact with individuals who hold attitudes favorable to criminal behavior than with individuals who hold attitudes that discourage it. In Sutherland's words:

> Criminal behavior is learned in association with those who define such behavior favorably and in isolation from those who definite unfavorably . . . a person in an appropriate situation engages in such criminal behavior if, and only if, the weight of the favorable definitions exceeds the weight of the unfavorable definitions.[9]

We can think of this theory as proposing a balance between associations with attitudes favorable and those with attitudes unfavorable to the violation of criminal law. The scale will "tip" toward the side that "weighs more" (see Figure 12.1).

Sutherland died in 1950, but his work was continued by Donald Cressey. Both Sutherland and Cressey highlighted **differential learning** as the socialization mechanism whereby we learn criminal behavior. The basic principles of the differential learning process are as follows:[10]

- *Criminal behavior is learned.* This assumption is clear: criminality is a by-product of socialization and not caused by any innate characteristic within the individual. It is not something we are born with or acquire from the environment. Crime is a function of learning processes that can affect any one at any time.
- *A person learns criminal behavior by interacting with others.* This proposition says that learning criminality is an interactive process in which we must associate with other individuals who serve as the "counselors" or "mentors" of our criminal behavior.
- *A person learns criminal behavior through a process of communication within intimate personal groups.* This principle underscores the importance

Figure 12.1
According to differential association theory, behavior is the outcome of which side weighs more.

Source: iStock/Dmitrii Guzhanin

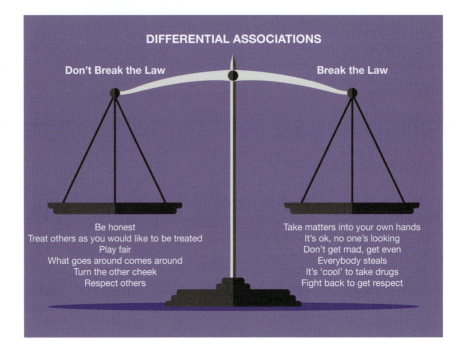

DIFFERENTIAL ASSOCIATIONS

Don't Break the Law

Break the Law

Be honest
Treat others as you would like to be treated
Play fair
What goes around comes around
Turn the other cheek
Respect others

Take matters into your own hands
It's ok, no one's looking
Don't get mad, get even
Everybody steals
It's 'cool' to take drugs
Fight back to get respect

of communicating ideas with those individuals who have the greatest influence on how we see and interpret events in our lives. Our relationships with family, friends, and peers are the primary mechanisms by which we learn and become socialized, and therefore, their influence far outweighs the effects of other forms of communication such as radio, television, video games, and the Internet.

- *Learning criminal behavior means acquiring the techniques of committing the crime, as well as the associated motives, drives, rationalizations and attitudes.* Learning means understanding, not just simple imitation. The novice criminal must learn not only how to commit specific crimes, but also how to react to violating the law, the proper language associated with the specific acts, and ways to rationalize the behaviors he or she is engaging in.

- *Our behavior is motivated by whether we view legal codes as favorable or unfavorable.* Learning criminality is a violation of society's norms, and therefore, individuals experience what Sutherland calls culture conflict: being exposed to a variety of opposing definitions about what is right and wrong.

- *A person learns to become criminal when he or she perceives the consequences of violating the law as more favorable than unfavorable.* Here, according to Sutherland, is the key to becoming a law violator. In an intimate group setting the individual is constantly bombarded with thoughts and ideas about emulating the criminal behavior, while at the same time isolated from thoughts and ideas that affirm the virtues of abiding by the law.

Image 12.3
How does differential association theory help explain the learning processes involved here?

iStock/wundervisuals

- *Differential associations may vary in frequency, duration, priority, and intensity.* Sutherland defined *priority* in terms of how early in life the associations occur; *duration* describes how long the associations last; *frequency* is how often they occur; and *intensity* refers to the amount of prestige attributed to the person or persons from whom the learning occurs.
- *The process of learning criminal behavior relies on all the mechanisms operating in any other learning process.* It involves interacting with the instructor, observing, listening, understanding, practicing, imitating, following directions, etc. Once again, differential association theory emphasizes the learning aspect of criminality and sees it as a process like learning how to read, bake a cake, or ride a bicycle.
- *General needs and values do not explain criminal behavior, because non-criminal behavior expresses those same needs and values.* Sutherland dismisses personal frustrations or desire for money or material goods as primary motives of criminality, because these same drives also prompt people to get a job, work hard, and save. Instead, we learn criminality through a process of socialization and association with individuals who foster criminal attitudes and behaviors.

Differential association theory meets several criteria of good scientific theory extremely well. It explains a wide range of behaviors in a single, straightforward way. It is very general and seeks to account for all criminal behavior. Because we can look at real events and experiences to see whether the theory is correct, we can verify it by experiment.

The ultimate question the theory must face, then, is this: does it fit the facts we know about crime and criminal behavior? Past research studies suggest it does:

- Children who associate with aggressive peers are more likely to engage in aggressive behavior themselves. A study conducted by Hektner et al. examined the behavior of 118 second-graders who participated in a six-week summer school program that paired moderately aggressive children with non-aggressive peers. It found that aggressive children had lower levels of disruptive behavior when their teammate was non-aggressive, regardless of whether the teammate was a friend. Moreover, the highest level of aggressive behavior occurred in pairs of aggressive teammates who were friends.[11]
- Studies show that individuals who engage in deviant behaviors are also likely to agree with norms, values, and attitudes that support their acts. Moreover, acts of deviance are generally supported by motivations that are consistent with the deviant acts.[12]
- Parents engaged in criminal activities are likely to produce children who continue the same patterns of criminality. Research using a three-generation study design supported the finding that there is continuity in patterns of anti-social behavior passed down from generation to generation.[13]
- A study conducted on 1,492 youths between the ages of 18 and 24 used questionnaires to explore subjects' attitudes toward deviance and also the attitudes of their peers. The study revealed that having delinquent friends who support criminal attitudes is strongly related to the development of a long-term criminal career.[14]

Differential association theory succeeded in moving sociological theory away from a view of criminality as a function of personality, neighborhood, or class. But it does have some weaknesses. It proposes that exposure to long-term crime-inducing stimuli causes people to commit criminal acts, but it doesn't take into account short-term triggers that prompt individuals to commit crimes impulsively or opportunistically. It also doesn't explain why some individuals who have never come into contact with criminal associations also commit crimes, or why others, even when surrounded by norms, values, and definitions favorable to rule violation, are able to resist and abide by the standards of conventional society.

Differential reinforcement

Recognizing the limitations in the theory of differential association, social scientists tried to fill the gaps. Robert Burgess and Ronald L. Akers published an article outlining their differential association-reinforcement theory of criminal behavior.[15] They drew upon concepts of psychology to argue that criminal behavior, like any other learned behavior, is a function of social and environmental rewards and punishments. They emphasized the idea that we are more likely to repeat behavior that results in a reward and less likely to repeat behavior that results in punishment. Essentially, Burgess and Akers built on Sutherland's original theory of differential association by adding the psychological component of **differential reinforcement**, whereby individuals learn to define their behavior according to the rewards or punishments attached to it. Thus, the behavior that results in a greater reward will more likely persist over the behavior that results in a lesser reward, whether that behavior is deviant, criminal, or both.[16]

For example, teenagers who join a street gang whose members value stealing, fighting, and getting high on drugs, will be encouraged to engage in these activities, as they are positively rewarded by the group members themselves. According to Akers, therefore, individuals engage in behaviors and activities that are positively rewarded by groups with whom we most intimately interact and identify, whether they are criminal or deviant groups, church groups, peer groups, school groups, or others.

While promising, Akers' theory suffers some of the same pitfalls as does Sutherland's original theory of differential association. For one thing, it generally neglects the role of opportunity in criminal behavior by assuming that individuals who learn to become criminal must have interacted with other individuals who engage in such behavior. Nor does Akers' theory explain why some individuals manage to escape the effects of seeing deviant behavior positively reinforced and choose instead to conform to law-abiding behavior. On the flip side, how do some individuals engage in criminal acts when they have never had criminal contacts?

Finally, the theory cannot be proven false.[17] By definition, behavior is strengthened by reinforcement. If a behavior is repeated, then the experience was reinforcing. If the behavior is *not* repeated, then the experience was *not* reinforcing. We have no independent measure of whether a particular experience of behavior is reinforcing. The logic of the definition is infallible, and therefore, it is also inadmissible as scientific explanation no matter what empirical research reveals.

Differential Identification

Daniel Glaser added to social learning theory the concept of **differential identification**.[18] Glaser argued that the degree to which individuals symbolically identify with criminal or non-criminal behavior patterns determines whether they will commit criminal acts, and not the frequency or intensity of associations they have.[19] Differential identification thus focused attention on an individual's susceptibility to environmental pressures. It said the learning of criminality through differential association is mediated, or modified, by individual factors that intervene between social contact and criminal behavior. The individual becomes an active participant in the learning process, making a voluntary, subjective choice to identify with criminals or non-criminals, whichever he desires to copy. For example, certain groups in high school that are perceived to be the most popular will influence the behavior of other students who admire them and may copy their style of dress or join their clubs in order to become more like them. Glaser refers to these groups as **reference groups**, composed of those whom we most admire, respect, and emulate. While this argument has the merit of linking criminal behavior theory to an impressive body of social psychological theory, it still leaves unclear why some individuals admire or favor criminal groups over other types of reference groups.

SOCIAL CONTROL THEORY

A somewhat different twist in criminological theory tries to answer the question why people *don't* commit crime, rather than why they *do*. Since, as we have seen, virtually everyone commits crime, the question might seem a bit silly. Perhaps it is. Nonetheless, if we assume there is always something to be gained by committing criminal acts, but some people nonetheless refrain from doing so, then the question makes sense.

Social control theory examines the element of socialization that builds our mechanisms of social control and allows us to refrain from engaging in indulgent, norm-violating behavior. It directs us to understanding conformity, rather than deviance, on the grounds that the root cause of deviant behavior is the absence of those social controls that allow most individuals to control their passions and impulses and obey the rules of society. Essentially, social control theorists assume all people have the potential to deviate from the norms of society—drink under age, cheat on their taxes, and drive above the speed limit— and therefore, we must understand criminal behavior in the context of the social relationships, values, and beliefs that tie individuals to society, limiting their chances of becoming involved in crime.[20] We turn now to an examination of *social integration*, the process by which we develop social bonds with conventional society, and internalize a sense of responsibility to abiding by the rules, simply because we have a greater stake in it.

Containment

Walter C. Reckless observed that prevalent sociological theories did not explain how individuals who face social pressures to commit crime also fail to resist such pressures. He developed a theory to answer this question that he called **containment theory**.[21] According to containment theory, individuals must become socialized to resist the "pushes" and "pulls" imposed upon them by individual and environmental factors.[22] Pushes include various aspects of our experiences and personal characteristics that make us more vulnerable to committing a crime. These may include a biological predisposition to aggression, psychological maladjustment, membership in negative peer groups, and exposure to a deviant subculture, or the experience of strain or deprivation.[23] Pulls signify the perceived rewards of engaging in criminal acts such as financial gain, sexual gratification, or peer approval.[24] So, for example, we might be tempted to rob a bank because we are hanging out with a group of peers who are encouraging the behavior (push) and we also want the immediate financial rewards associated with the crime (pull). Social containment is therefore a

Figure 12.2

Which have more of a deterrent effect: internal or external containments?

Source: iStock/karinsasaki

barrier or obstacle that neutralizes the effects of pushes and pulls. According to Reckless, containment is both external and internal (see Figure 12.2).

External containment represents "the holding power of the group"[25] or the "watchful eyes" around us that we take into consideration before we decide to engage in certain acts. External containments set our limits and boundaries by continually reassuring us someone or something is evaluating our decision to act in certain ways. As Reckless put it, external containment is "the society, the state, the tribe, the village, the family, and other nuclear groups [that] are able to hold the individual within the bounds of the accepted norms and expectations."[26] For example, if you believe your partner will disapprove of your cheating on your income taxes, you will be motivated not to do it.

Conversely, **internal containment** "represents the ability of the person to follow the expected norms, to direct himself."[27] Internal containment comes from within us, and we develop it by being successfully socialized into the approved norms, values, and standards of society. It is our desire for socially approved goals, a commitment to the beliefs of society, a healthy and positive self-image, and the ability to manage strain and frustration. No longer do we always need to look over our shoulders to walk the straight and narrow path, rather we search within ourselves to resist the temptations of crime, no matter how much gain they seem to offer. According to Reckless, internal containment is much stronger than external. "As social relations become more impersonal, as society becomes more diverse and alienated, as people participate more and more for longer periods of time away from a home base, the self becomes more and more important as a controlling agent."[28]

Social control mechanisms, both external and internal, undoubtedly do inhibit some crime. We all have observed containment theory's two general standards of conduct in action: I do not steal cars because it is wrong, I cannot act that way, or I'm better than that (internal containment), or I do not steal cars because I will get caught, I will lose the approval of significant individuals, or I will lose my position in society (external containment). However, social control theory does not provide all the answers we seek.

Social bonds

In his 1969 publication *Causes of Delinquency*, Travis Hirschi proposed that it is not the number or quality of their associations that keeps people from committing criminal acts. Rather it is their close interpersonal attachments to people who disapprove of criminality.[29] Our successful integration into society includes the development of these **social bonds**, or ties between individuals and conventional social groups within society, such as friends, family, teachers, co-workers, neighbors, and church members.[30] On the other hand, weak social bonds with members of the law-abiding community will increase the likelihood that a person will get involved in criminal behavior. Thus, while we are all vulnerable to engaging in criminal behavior, it is our fear of damaging our relationships with individuals to whom we are bonded that keeps us from doing so.[31] Hirschi proposed four components of the social bond (see Figure 12.3):

- *Attachment* is a person's shared interests with others in society. Hirschi emphasized the importance of attachment to family, especially to parents, as essential to this element of the social bond. Other important attachments are those to peers and schools.
- *Commitment* is the amount of effort and energy an individual puts into conventional activities with others in society. Commitment values hard work, education, and personal success, and working toward these goals by, for instance, going to school or having a job.
- *Involvement* describes how an individual spends his or her time in conventional activities. Idleness will encourage deviation toward criminal behavior, while actively participating in sports, school clubs, community organizations and events, and religious groups, will leave little opportunity for law-breaking.
- *Belief* is sharing with members of society an understanding of moral values such as honesty, equity, social responsibility, and respect.

Figure 12.3
Elements of the social bond: successful social bonds = conformity

Social bond theory appears consistent with the experiences of many people who commit crimes. In fact the chief merit of control theory may be its proposition that individuals engaging in crime and delinquency are generally detached from conventional society, with weak social bonds. Research findings seem to support the basic proposition:

- Attachment to family, peers, and school has been found to be a major variable in the ability of children and adolescents to develop positive affection, respect for authority, and the social skills necessary to manage stress and avoid alienation. A study on the interrelationship of family and peer experiences in predicting adolescent problem behaviors was conducted on an 18-year longitudinal sample using 198 adolescents from both traditional and non-traditional families. The study found that the most powerful predictors of teen drug use and delinquent behavior were similar behaviors by peers.[32]

- Commitment to educational achievement has been linked to a decrease in the likelihood of youth becoming involved in illegal drinking, drugs, and other forms of delinquency, and an increase in the likelihood of attending school. Children with lower academic performance committed more, and more serious, crimes, and re-offended more frequently than children with higher academic performances.[33]

- Studies conducted on after-school programs available to teens have consistently shown that kids involved in sports, supervised activities, school clubs, and other school-sponsored events are less likely to engage in illegal activities than kids who are not involved in such programs. Analyses of the National Education Longitudinal Study of 1988 suggested that regular participation in extracurricular activities from 8th to 12th grade predicts academic accomplishments, as well as pro-social behaviors in young adulthood.[34]

- A belief in society's moral values has also been linked to the likelihood of refraining from criminal activity. The more likely a person is to value honesty, morality, and ethical behavior, the less likely that person will behave in manners inconsistent with those beliefs.[35]

Image 12.4 *Herbert Diess, CEO of Volkswagen Corporation, apologized at the beginning of a Volkswagen press conference in the media preview of the Tokyo Motor show in Tokyo, Japan, on October 28, 2015. U.S. authorities found Volkswagen diesel vehicles had software installed that allowed the cars to cheat emissions tests, emitting pollutants at levels many times higher than advertised.*

AP/Press Association Images

While control theory will continue to hold its place as a prominent perspective in criminological literature, it falls short of answering some very important practical questions. For example, how do we account for the fact that many offenders have strong attachment to family, friends, co-workers, and peers, yet nevertheless risk damaging this social bond to engage in criminal activities? Many crimes have been committed by people described as "very close" to their family. Indeed, they are not at all the loners detached from society that social bond theory describes. Moreover, research indicates that individuals committed to success and achievement, but unable to achieve it through conventional means, often engage in criminal activities to obtain their goals (see Box 12.1). Another shortcoming of social bond theory is the fact that many criminals, while actively violating the law, will acknowledge their belief in society's general principles of morality and even express remorse for their actions.

BOX 12.1: CONSIDER THIS . . .

Committed to social norms: what happened?

In 1999, Enron Corporation became one of the largest companies selling gas and electricity in the United States. Behind the profits, however, were suspect corporate strategies and irregular accounting procedures that treaded on the boundaries of fraud. As early as 1996, Andrew Fastow, the Chief Financial Officer (CFO) of Enron, began creating off-book business entities the firm used to avoid paying taxes and create the illusion that Enron was making huge profits each quarter when it was actually losing money. Corporate executives and other Enron insiders were trading millions of dollars of Enron stock, making huge profits for themselves, at the expense of company workers, stockholders, and investors.

Box 12.1 Image 1 *Washington D.C.: probe of Enron Corporation collapse—staff for the House Energy and Commerce Committee sift through Enron Corporation documents at the Ford House Office Building.*

Scott J. Ferrell/Congressional Quarterly/Getty Images

The distortion and manipulation of accounts could not be sustained and finally led the company's finances into a downward spiral. Enron filed for bankruptcy on December 2, 2001. When the scope of its top managers' wrongdoing was revealed, the value of the company's stock shares dropped down to pennies. The former Chairman of the Board and Chief Executive Officer, Kenneth Lay, and the former Chief Operating Officer and Chief Executive Officer, Jeffery Skilling, went on trial for their part in the Enron scandal in January 2006. They were indicted on 53 criminal counts including insider trading, securities fraud, money laundering, wire fraud, bank fraud, conspiracy, and making false statements. Both were found guilty, and on October 23, 2006, Skilling was sentenced to 24 years and 4 months in federal prison, and ordered to make restitution of Enron's squandered pension funds, in the amount of $26 million. Lay died of a heart attack that summer, before he could serve any time. Andrew Fastow plead guilty to two counts of fraud for his role in the accounting scandal and on December 26, 2006, was sentenced to six years in prison, followed by two years of probation.

How can criminological theory account for individuals like Fastow, Lay, and Skilling, who appear to spend the majority of their time and effort engaging in conventional activities, who adhere to the values and norms of society, and who have developed social bonds and networks of attachment to family, friends, peers, and business associates, yet who go beyond the boundaries of social control to violate the law? How do the basic tenets of social control theory hold up to the observable facts in this case? Has emphasis on profit become so integral to the fabric of U.S. financial institutions that it can jeopardize and even neutralize the controlling effect of conventional social bonds and attachments? *What do you think?*

Source

Behind the Enron Scandal. *TIME Online.* Retrieved from http://www.time.com/time/2002/enron.

Di Meglio, Francesca. 2012. Enron's Andrew Fastow: The Mistakes I Made. *Bloomberg Business,* March 22. Retrieved from http://www.bloomberg.com/bw/articles/2012–03–22/enrons-andrew-fastow-the-mistakes-i-made.

Enron Fast Facts. *CNN Library.* Retrieved from http://www.cnn.com/2013/07/02/us/enron-fast-facts/.

Thus while lack of social control may pave the way for the onset of criminality, there must be other forces in play that account for persistent patterns of deviant behavior. We turn now to an examination of these dynamics.

LABELING THEORY

Sex offenders are among the most despised criminal offenders. Many people believe they are dangerous predators who cannot be rehabilitated and want to see them locked up forever. Highly publicized sex crimes have led all 50 states to pass central registration laws requiring convicted sex offenders to register with the state or local law enforcement agency, which in turn disseminates the information to the public. These laws focus on controlling released sex offenders at the expense of their individual rights. The emphasis seems to have shifted from solving and punishing crimes to identifying dangerous people and depriving them of their liberty before they can do harm.[36]

The requirement that sex offenders must fulfill registration and notification laws has the net effect of branding them with a deviant label for life, preventing them from ever being able to properly function as members of society, make new friends, hold a job, develop a relationship, or just start over. Winick notes that sex offender registration results in the offender's rejection by the community, threats, harassment, shame, isolation, and feelings of hopelessness that are difficult to overcome.[37] Many people will react by saying "they deserve it" or "society must be defended." However, the idea behind labeling theory suggests this may not be the case.

In the 1960s Howard Becker built upon the sociological theories of Frank Tannenbaum, Edwin Lemert, and Alfred R. Lindesmith, applying their ideas and research methodologies to the study of deviant behavior among jazz musicians. In *Outsiders: Studies in the Sociology of Deviance*,[38] Becker called for criminology to recognize the basic fact that deviance or crime was a label attached to people by those with the power to do so, rather than a characteristic of the person. According to Becker, "social groups create deviance by making the rules whose infraction constitutes deviance, and by applying those rules to particular people and labeling them as outsiders ... deviance is not in the quality of the act the person commits, but rather a consequence of the application by others of rules and sanctions."[39]

This perspective came to be known as **labeling or "societal reaction" theory** and led criminologists to examine the process by which laws are made and by which people are labeled deviant. Most importantly, it resurrected Edwin Sutherland's idea that criminology was not just the study of criminal behavior but also the study of why acts get defined as criminal and what kinds of acts are punished.

Clarence Schrag summarized the basic propositions of the labeling perspective as follows:[40]

- No act is inherently criminal. It is the law that makes an act a crime.
- Criminal definitions are enforced in the interest of powerful groups by their official representatives, including the police, courts, correctional institutions, and other administrative bodies.
- People do not become criminal by violating the law. Instead, they are designated as criminal by the reactions of authorities who confer upon them the status of outcast and deprive them of some social and political privileges.
- Only a few people are caught violating the law, although many may be equally guilty.
- Criminal sanctions vary according to characteristics of the offender, and for any given offense they tend to be most frequent and most severe among males, the young, the unemployed or underemployed, the poorly educated members of the lower classes, members of minority groups, transients, and residents of deteriorated urban areas.
- The criminal justice system is built on a stereotyped conception of the criminal as a pariah—a willful wrongdoer who is morally bad and deserving the community's condemnation.
- Individuals labeled criminal begin to view authorities and society in general as the enemy, and their subsequent behavior is an outcome of this negative interaction

In this sense, no act is objectively deviant or criminal until it receives the subjective definition by society as such. Hence, no individual is deviant or criminal until reacted to and symbolically labeled as such by society. These reactions and definitions are shaped by those individuals, called "moral entrepreneurs" by Becker, who determine and define the content of the criminal law and sanctions according to their values and standards of right and wrong.[41] Moreover, labeling theory notes that criminal law is applied differently, to the benefit of those with social and economic power in society. The likelihood of an individual's being charged and prosecuted has more to do with her socioeconomic standing than with her actions.[42] Labeling theory also concludes that police, courts, and corrections officers are not only biased and selective in their application of negative labels, but actually perpetuate criminality by imposing a deviant identity upon the individuals they are supposed to treat or correct.

Primary and secondary deviance

Labeling theory represents the first attempt to distinguish between primary and secondary deviance.[43] According to Edwin Lemert, primary deviance *refers to an offender's original act of violating the law*. This violation can occur for many reasons—to meet an immediate need, adhere to a subculture, deal with frustration, or respond to deviant association. Primary deviance can go relatively unnoticed. We can find out that a President of the United States smoked marijuana in his youth, a famous ballplayer was convicted of assault, or an admired movie star used to be a thief. Because the behaviors were somehow excused, dismissed, or quickly forgotten, they had little impact on the future of the individual. However, if the event came to the attention of agents of social control (such as police) who applied a negative label to the behavior *and* to the individual, its consequences would undoubtedly determine the course of her future.

Secondary deviance is the continued pattern of offending based on an individual's adjustment to society's negative social reaction.[44] Understanding secondary deviance is the key to understanding why some individuals refrain from engaging in future acts of criminality, while others react to the negative label attached to them by continuing on the path of recurrent deviance (see Figure 12.4). When primary deviants learn, accept, and internalize a deviant self-concept bestowed on them by society, they develop behavior patterns that live up to their new expected role. Secondary deviance thus becomes a self-fulfilling prophecy that results from being *stigmatized*.[45]

Figure 12.4 Secondary deviance: how it occurs

Stigmatization

For better or for worse, our behavior as human beings is to a great extent controlled by the reactions of others. Throughout our lives, we are showered with a variety of symbolic labels that help us define who we are. We are "athletic," "talented," "smart," "pretty," "a troublemaker," "bad," or "anti-social" according to parents, siblings, teachers, friends, and peers. In fact, these are not mere descriptions that come and go without leaving their mark. Rather, such labels confirm and define our identity and bestow upon us a variety of attitudes and behaviors consistent with them.

Stigmatization occurs when a negative label applied to an individual has an enduring effect on that person's self-identity. The perception of an individual as a social deviant will negatively affect his treatment at home, school, work, and other social contexts.[46] The stigmatized individual will turn to others similarly labeled for support, friendship, and interaction, which reinforces a new personality, attitudes, and actions consistent with criminal behavior. Stigmatized individuals will come to interact and identify with other outcasts and social pariahs who affirm, approve, and facilitate their behavior. Figure 12.5 summarizes this interactive process of labeling. Moreover, research suggests the application of a negative label can create deviance amplification, whereby the activity labeled as deviant is amplified by the spiraling effect of negative social reaction.[47] The social deviant becomes isolated from society and reacts by becoming more actively deviant. The increase in deviant activity draws further disapproval from society, and the whole process continues to perpetuate itself.

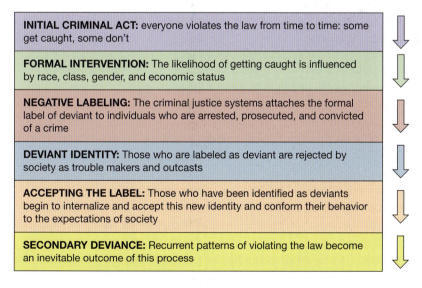

Figure 12.5 The labeling process

Labeling theory constituted a fundamental challenge to the prevailing models of the time. If we accept the labeling school of thought, we cannot keep looking for the causes of criminal behavior in the individual offender. Instead we must look to the system of justice that defines acts as criminal and labels some people criminal and not others. We have already encountered the concept of discretion (arrest bias, reporting errors, and politically motivated data reports) throughout the criminal justice process in chapter 3. According to labeling theory, the way this discretion is used proves that deviant labels are applied to those who are powerless and unable to defend themselves.[48]

Labeling theory forces us to consider the context within which criminal acts take place, with research studies putting a greater burden on society for the perpetuation of crime and deviance (see Box 12.2). Nevertheless, it has been criticized on several points. First of all, it fails to explain the original act of violating the law. Why does the primary deviance occur? Labeling theory relies on the notion that recurrent patterns of deviant behavior are primarily caused by the offender's acceptance of a deviant self-image. Many criminals and delinquents do not claim to have a deviant identity.[49]

Finally, labeling theory has been criticized for its unequivocal contention that the criminal justice system perpetuates crime and deviance. It is almost unreasonable to argue that formal intervention will *always* lead to more crime, while lack of formal intervention will *always* lead to less crime. Community sanctioning, informal processing, restorative justice, and other non-stigmatizing methods of correction have been attempted time and again yet have failed to produce the outcome that labeling theory predicts.

BOX 12.2: CONNECTING RESEARCH TO PRACTICE

The Saints and the Roughnecks

"The Saints and the Roughnecks" is a research study conducted through observations and interviews with two delinquent gangs. The Saints were a group of eight promising young men from "good" white upper-middle class families. They were active in school affairs, received good grades, and played on athletic teams. At the same time, they were some of the most delinquent boys at Hannibal High. However, their technique for covering truancy was so successful that teachers did not even realize that the boys were absent from school much of the time.

The local police also saw the Saints as good boys who were among the leaders of the youth in the community. On rare occasions when they were stopped in town for speeding or running a stop sign, the Saints were always polite, contrite, and plead for mercy. Although constantly occupied with truancy, drinking, wild driving, petty theft, and vandalism, none of them was officially arrested for any misdeed during the two years they were observed.

Although their rate of delinquency was about equal to that of the Saints, the Roughnecks were constantly in trouble with police, who suspected that they were engaged in criminal activities. They knew this partly from catching them, mostly from circumstantial evidence, and also because they shared the view of the community in general that this was a bad bunch of boys. Because they were constantly involved with the police, teachers also saw the boys as heading for trouble.

What was the cause of this disparity in treatment between the Saints and the Roughnecks, and what was the result? Why did the community, the school, and the police react to the Saints as though they were good, upstanding, non-delinquent youths with bright futures but to the Roughnecks as though they were tough, young criminals who were headed for trouble? Why did the Roughnecks and the Saints in fact have quite different careers after high school careers which, by and large, lived up to the expectations of the community?

The community responded to the Roughnecks as boys in trouble, and the boys agreed with that perception. Once their pattern of deviance was reinforced, the boys acquired an image of themselves as deviants, selecting friends who affirmed that self-image. As that self-conception became more firmly entrenched, they also became willing to try new and more extreme deviances. With their growing alienation came freer expression of disrespect and hostility for representatives of the legitimate society. This disrespect increased the community's negativism, perpetuating the entire process of commitment to deviance.

The discovery, processing, and punishing of some kinds of criminality and not others means that visible, poor, non-mobile, outspoken, undiplomatic, "tough" kids like the Roughnecks will be noticed, whether their actions are seriously delinquent or not. Their noticeable deviance and the reaction to it will have been so reinforced by police and the community that their lives will be effectively channeled into careers consistent with the self-image they developed in adolescence. Other kids, like the Saints, who establish a reputation for being bright, reasonably polite, and involved in respectable activities, who are mobile and moneyed, will be invisible when they engage in delinquent activities. When it is time to leave adolescence most will follow the expected path, settling into the ways of the middle class.

This study makes a very important finding: labeling, stigma, and negative self-images are powerful forces in determining who we are and what we become. The practical implication of the study on the Saints and the Roughnecks guides us in the direction of labeling theory's emphasis on secondary deviance as a product of social reaction. The inescapable lesson is, the less formal intervention by the Criminal Justice System in the minor crimes of juveniles the better off they, and society, will be.

Source

Chambliss, William J. 1973. The Saints and the Roughnecks. *Society* (November–December): 24–31.

EVALUATING SOCIAL PROCESS THEORIES

Despite their shortcomings, social process theories have brought us closer to understanding crime within the context of socialization. If we understand human behavior as a function of structure, context, interaction, and interpretation, social process theories provide us with a clear picture of the many causes of crime. We must incorporate the effect that family, peers, education, societal reaction, and role have on the development of human behavior and not rely on personal traits or environmental variables alone to explain crime. The multi-faceted views we find in social process theory help explain a wide variety of deviant behaviors across all class structures.

Research has also found social process theory to be consistent with some basic facts: that people move in and out of delinquency and crime as youths and adults, that almost everyone commits some crime at different times in their lives, and that often this is a transitory event. But social process theories share the same fundamental flaw as earlier theories: they fail to recognize that crime is politically defined behavior embedded in the structure of society.

The harshest lesson for any science to learn is that not all questions can be scientifically answered. We must develop our science in different directions if we are to overcome the shortcomings of conventional approaches to crime. In the next chapter we turn to yet another approach to the study of crime and criminality, but first we turn to a brief examination of the policy implications of social process explanations of crime and delinquency.

We've outlined the three levels of the social process approach to the study of criminal behavior. Table 12.2 summarizes the social process perspective's definition of crime, explanation of why the behavior occurs, and solutions offered in terms of prevention. Public policies influenced by the social process approach advocate programs to counter the socialization of individuals into deviant behavior patterns. These policies have the goal of encouraging positive associations, building pro-social bonds, encouraging self-control, and providing alternatives to formal sanctioning. We will focus on three policies that highlight how the social process perspective has shaped criminal justice policy: youth mentoring initiatives, Head Start, and diversion.

Table 12.2 The social process perspective: definition, cause, and solution to crime

What is crime?	Crime is socialized behavior
Why does crime occur? (theory)	Interactions between the individual and their social environments include social processes whereby individuals learn to become deviant and criminal. These social processes are: • **Social Learning Theory**: differential learning • **Social Control Theory**: inadequate social integration • **Labeling Theory**: stigmatization
What is the solution to crime? (policy)	Develop policies to counter the learning effects of those social processes, to encourage positive associations, build social bonds, encourage self-control, and inhibit the damaging effects of negative labels

Youth mentoring initiatives

Youth mentoring initiatives replace the law-and-order model characteristic of crime-prone neighborhoods, drawing upon community resources to provide at-risk youth constructive alternatives to criminal activity. These programs operate on the premise that reaching out to troubled teens through nurturing, mentoring, and education will reverse the detrimental experiences and negative social influences that led to their involvement in crime, and break the cycle of delinquency and violence. They focus primarily on youth identified by family members, schools, or government agencies as at risk for becoming involved in of delinquency and crime. In 1997, a collaborative effort between local faith-based institutions and juvenile justice and law enforcement organizations in 15 cities laid the foundation for the National Faith-Based Initiative for High-Risk Youth which provided vulnerable teens with a productive alternative to delinquency and violence by matching them with mentors according to skills, needs, and interests.[50] The goal was to offer the opportunity for learning positive social skills in order to better handle conflict, improve educational outcomes, and reduce the likelihood of substance abuse, teen pregnancy, and truancy.

The Youth and Congregations in Partnership (YCP) is an example of a youth mentoring program. Established in 1997 by District Attorney Charles Hynes, in Brooklyn, NY, the YCP is a community-based alternative to incarceration that offers youth offenders a second chance to benefit from the help and care of a volunteer mentor from the faith community.[51] Program participants between the ages of 13 and 22 are referred to the Kings County (Brooklyn) District Attorney's Office by the courts, social service agencies, and other organizations for troubled youth. The program continues to operate today on the premise that these young people are amenable to rehabilitation in an enriched social environment that encourages positive support and learning. By providing troubled teens with positive role models to offer support and friendship, and someone who accepts, understands, and respects them, the program aims to develop their self-worth, accountability, and respect for others.[52] Classes help teens learn anger management and conflict resolution skills and techniques, go through substance abuse recovery, and receive mental health counseling. The program also provides educational support, career counseling, and recreational development.

Head Start

Mounting evidence suggests that early-childhood experiences are paramount in the social and developmental growth of children.[53] One of the best-known social policy initiatives aimed at strengthening the socialization process of low-income children is **Head Start**, which emphasizes developing pro-social bonds early in life, an emphasis made by social control theory.

Head Start is a federally mandated program created in 1965 as part of President Lyndon Johnson's War on Poverty. It focuses on providing

Image 12.5 *Head Start educational programming prepares young children for success in school and life though interactive and developmental learning.*

Tim Kimzey/AP/Press Association Images

comprehensive services to assist preschool children from low-income families, to increase their attachment to conventional norms and values, and to solidify their bonds to society. Administered by non-profit organizations and local schools, Head Start services are designed to help end the cycle of social and economic disadvantage by providing a program that serves the physical, emotional, and psychological needs of young children. Programming focuses on four major areas of growth: education, health and nutrition, social services, and cognitive development. Parental involvement is an essential component.

The educational element of Head Start emphasizes acquiring the intellectual skills necessary to become successful in school, with special attention to the development of math and reading skills. The health and nutrition component emphasizes the identification and prevention of health-related problems early in life. Resources are offered to participating families to provide children with immunization, medical treatment, dental hygiene, mental health counseling, and nutritional services. Families are taught the skills necessary to ensure the safety of their children and reduce the risk of injury. Moreover, the Head Start program is mandated to conduct an initial screening to identify developmental, sensory, or behavioral problems in the child, to better provide appropriate community services.

Head Start is now also available to the parents of preschoolers enrolled in the program. By attending classes that improve parenting skills, promote literacy, reduce domestic violence, promote health and nutrition, and identify community outreach resources and social service agencies, parents take on a more active and supportive role in their child's preparation for school and general well-being.

Diversion

A final policy offshoot of social process theory's perspective on the negative effects of labeling is diversion. **Diversion** programs are designed to prevent youth and adult offenders from being formally processed through the criminal justice system. In 1967, when the labeling perspective was raising serious questions about secondary deviance and social reaction, the President's Commission on Law Enforcement and the Administration of Justice report called for the creation of youth services bureaus to develop alternative sanctioning within local communities.

The goal of diversion is to reduce the need for formal sanctioning by the criminal justice system as a solution to the social problem of crime.[54] It assumes that formal processing, including arrest, trial, and incarceration, may actually produce more harm than good by stigmatizing first-time offenders for relatively minor violations of the law. Diversion programs therefore provide remedial actions for youth and adult offenders within the informal context and setting of the community.

The diversion process usually assembles a panel of experts who determine offenders' eligibility and amenability to diversion on a case-by-case basis. Offenders must successfully complete the diversion program requirements, which often focus on some element of rehabilitation, including substance abuse treatment, outpatient mental health screening and evaluation, educational and vocational training, anger-management program training, and a variety of other services tailored to fit the specific needs of the offender. A diversion agreement may also include some form of restitution, where the judge orders the offender to make a monetary payment to the victim for the harm resulting from the offense.[55] Restitution can also be a court order to do some type of service to the community as a form of repayment for crimes committed. For example, a youth who has been caught spray-painting graffiti in a public place can be ordered to spend a certain amount of hours doing volunteer work within the community such as picking up trash at a park, cleaning up a church, or working at a shelter in lieu of receiving a formal court-ordered sentence.

And now we turn back to the puzzling question that began this chapter: why did Eric Harris and Dylan Klebold go on a shooting rampage at Columbine High School in April of 1999? How can the social process perspective shed some light on their acts of violence and retaliation? On the surface, Harris and Klebold appeared to be two average, intelligent kids from good homes whose adult members were by all accounts highly regarded members of the community. As the investigation into their crime got deeper, however, a picture formed of a troubled pair of teenagers, angry at the world, and out for revenge.

Police investigations centered on the discovery of a website created by Eric Harris, where he expresses hostility toward Littleton residents, with his anger directed mostly at teachers and students from Columbine High School. He claimed to want revenge against those who angered, irritated, or annoyed him over the years. His desire for revenge is expressed in terms of blowing up the city and shooting everyone he can.[56] Harris and Klebold even posted the results of their experimentation with pipe bombs on the website. Many teachers claimed that Harris and Klebold had shown various signs of disturbing behavior, and although they reported their concerns, no action could be taken by authorities, as no crime had actually been committed. What's even more bizarre is their parents' claim that they were never informed of their sons' anger, rage, and anti-social behavior. Harris's parents were also never aware of the complaints made about their son to police, by the parents of another student at Columbine, who was apparently threatened by him.

Eric Harris and Dylan Klebold were undoubtedly the products of the negative effects of strained relationships, alienation from family, school, and peers, and the feeling of rejection and isolation by members of society. As a matter of fact, this was no small scale plot for getting back at a few individuals who wronged them. Their plans for revenge were much grander than that. In a note left by Harris, he blames their deadly scheme on the parents, teachers, and students of Columbine High. He points the finger at students for their rejection, ridicule, and non-acceptance of individuals who are "different." In turn, parents and teachers are blamed for making the students behave that way, and not teaching them any better. Harris and Klebold were acting upon their rage and anger with nothing to lose and revenge as the only force driving their behavior. A journal chronicling their plot stated their intention to kill as many people as possible, with Columbine being just the beginning of their lethal rampage that would leave a path of deadly destruction throughout the community of Littleton.

The extent of the wrongs the teenage boys perceived to be done to them was clearly the foundation that served to trigger their anger, hostility, and isolation. At the heart of this perception are their feelings of being wronged and rejected by members of society who essentially labeled and treated them like outcasts. They turned to each other as a means of affirming their antagonistic attitudes, as their attachments to conventional norms, values, activities, and relationships had been strained over the years, if not completely severed. Moreover, Harris and Klebold developed associations that made it possible to carry out their plans. Police investigations revealed that a close friend of Dylan Klebold was responsible for purchasing the weapons used in the attacks. Robyn K. Anderson was an 18-year-old student and close friend of Klebold at Columbine High. Although Anderson made the purchase, she had no knowledge of their plans to use the weapons in the massacre. Moreover, police believe that Harris and Klebold had used the internet to learn the techniques of how to make pipe bombs and other explosive devices and where to go to purchase materials.

The foundation of policy initiatives stemming from the analysis of events relating to the Columbine shooting have focused attention on the need for preventive strategies, rather than imposing restrictions and control mechanisms such as limiting access to school property, reducing student gatherings, operating metal detectors, and installing security cameras in schools. Instead, policy initiatives developed to identify students who have been socialized into deviant behavior patterns and provide them with programs and services designed to encourage and promote academic success, appropriate conflict management, and mental and emotional enhancement (see Box 12.3).

BOX 12.3: CONNECTING THEORY TO PRACTICE

Reacting to school violence through collaboration

The Columbine tragedy was a testimony for the need to integrate community resources by developing a comprehensive plan for preventing school violence by embracing key sectors within the social domain of youth, including the school, mental health and social service agencies, juvenile justice components, and law enforcement.

As a means of providing schools with the tools necessary for developing a comprehensive plan for the prevention of violence and other behavioral problems, the U.S. Departments of Justice and Education, along with the American Institutes for Research, developed a report, "Safeguarding Our Children: An Action Guide," outlining three levels of policy response:

Tier 1: build a school-wide foundation for all children
This tier provides the framework for schools to develop strategies to improve the academic performance and behavior of students. Several components must be put into place in order to make this task complete, including the modeling of caring, supportive, and respectful behavior by school teachers and staff; developing programs that reinforce adequate conflict resolution skills; initiating learning techniques that are both child and family focused; and collaborating with community agencies to create the most effective and engaging curricula.

Tier 2: intervene early for some children
This tier involves the early identification of students at risk for severe academic or behavioral difficulties. It includes the training of teachers, counselors, and other staff to recognize early warning signs of potential problems and to act upon those signs by making appropriate referrals. Early intervention includes the creation of services and support mechanisms that address risk factors and build protective measures for them. This includes the development of interventions such as anger management training, structured after-school programs, mentoring support, group and family counseling, educational enhancement, and tutoring.

Tier 3: provide intensive interventions for a few children
Intensive intervention is called upon for students whose needs are not fully met by early intervention methods. They tend to be more specific and tailored to the student's needs, strengths, and weaknesses. Intensive intervention involves a planning process that includes the child and family, community agencies, and school staff to create a unique set of school and community services that meet the specific needs of the child and family. Services are provided to children identified as experiencing significant emotional and behavioral problems.

Intensive intervention programs include day treatment programs which provide students and families with intensive mental health and special education services; multi-systemic therapy, focusing on the individual youth and his or her family, the peer context, school/vocational performance, and neighborhood/community supports; or treatment foster care, an intensive, family-focused intervention for youth whose delinquency or emotional problems are so serious and so chronic that they are no longer permitted to live at home. To be effective, these approaches generally require the collaboration of schools, social services, mental health providers, and law enforcement and juvenile justice authorities.

The key to such policy measures is to provide strategies to design and implement effective plans to reduce behavioral problems that may escalate into acts of violence by providing children with access to the services they need, to enhance and enrich their socialization experiences. The value of early intervention and preventative approaches is demonstrated in the empirical literature. However, these policies must be balanced against the detrimental effects of profiling and labeling students as potential trouble makers. Warning signs and checklists must be approached with caution to identify children who are socially withdrawn, feeling rejected or isolated, and performing below their academic level of functioning, without running the risk of unfairly labeling children who are simply not reflecting some desirable image. Indeed, the very policy initiatives stemming from the social process perspective must strike a balance between intervention and the caution against too much involvement in the lives of individuals, in order to create a healthy, positive social environment that fosters learning experiences that promote conventional law abiding behavior.

Sources

Dwyer, K. and Osher, D. 2000. *Safeguarding Our Children: An Action Guide.* U.S. Departments of Education and Justice, American Institutes for Research. Washington, D.C.

Welton, Evonn, Vakil, Shernavaz, and Ford, Bridgie. 2014. Beyond Bullying: Consideration of Additional Research for the Assessment and Prevention of Potential Rampage School Violence in the United States. *Education Research International.* Retrieved from http://www.hindawi.com/journals/edri/2014/109297/abs/.

Also, see the Center for Effective Collaboration and Practice website at http://cecp.air.org/default.asp.

SUMMARY

What is the social process approach?

The social process suggests that criminal behavior is a function of the various interactions that take place between individuals and their social environments. These interactions are seen as the core of socialization, and form the foundation upon which all aspects of human behavior are learned. Inadequate socialization is therefore the key to understanding criminality. From this perspective, any person, regardless of age, race, gender, or socioeconomic class, has the potential to deviate from the law. The specific mechanisms of social learning will dictate the course of behavioral choices that individuals will make in various situations.

How are we socialized?

Socialization occurs from the moment we are born. It is a lifelong process whereby we learn how to live and interact with others on a daily basis. By communicating with individuals that are close to us—classmates, friends, family, and peers, we learn the various norms, rules, beliefs, and values that govern our behavior. Through these interactions, we learn the complex meanings and shared understandings of our culture, which guide and shape the roles we play in society. Our socialization can have a positive or negative impact on our lives. Agents of socialization can transmit deviant norms, beliefs, and values, and therefore play a critical role in determining the outcome of our behavior, by teaching individuals to embrace attitudes and behaviors that support crime and delinquency.

What do social learning, social control, and labeling theories tell us about the specific mechanisms by which individuals learn crime?

Social process theories explore three distinct social processes by which individuals are socialized to criminal behavior: differential learning, inadequate social integration and stigmatization. *Social learning theory* stresses the mechanisms involved in learning criminality through differential associations with individuals who favor definitions of crime over definitions that emphasize law abiding behavior, the differential reinforcement of rewards and punishments, and the differential identification with criminal v. non-criminal reference groups.

Social control theory analyzes human behavior from the aspect of those mechanisms of internal and external constraints that are created by the social bonds that exist between individuals and conventional society. The positive integration of individuals into society forms the basis for social control that inhibits criminal behavior. On the contrary, weak social bonds create a lack of integration which in turn allows individuals to behave in anti-social ways.

Labeling theory finds the cause of criminal behavior in the negative reactions by society to the behavior of some individuals. Formal negative labels such as "delinquent" or "criminal" are attached to individuals and serve to isolate them from mainstream society. Their apparent rejection from society has a spiraling effect whereby the individual comes to internalize the negative label and becomes stigmatized, identifying with the new deviant identity, and behaving in ways that are consistent with the expectations of that label.

Does the social process approach tell us everything we need to know about crime?

Social process theories have been criticized for focusing too much attention on aspects of social learning, while ignoring individual variations amongst people and also neglecting the influence of social-structural variables that contribute to crime and delinquency. Not all individuals exposed to deviant social learning processes will develop patterns of criminal behavior, and some become deviant who have not been so exposed. Differential association theory therefore fails to explain why some individuals who are surrounded by deviant norms and values, continue to hold on to conventional attitudes and behaviors.

Social control theories have also been criticized on similar grounds. Attributing crime and delinquency to the absence of those social bonds or socialization processes that encourage law-abiding behavior does not tell us very much about why some individuals who do have conventional ties and attachments to society, nevertheless break the law.

Moreover, the labeling approach, while shedding some light on the emergence of continued patterns of criminal behavior, tell us little about the original cause of primary deviance. There is also a lack of empirical support for the claim made by labeling theory that contact with the criminal justice system alone serves to perpetuate criminality. If that were true, then career criminals who generally escape formal sanctions would desist from their criminal activities.

How do social process theories guide our understanding of criminal justice policy?

Despite its shortcomings, the social process perspective has served as the cornerstone for the development of criminal justice policy. Social process theories have guided policy in the direction of enhancing the learning experiences of individuals to increase self-control and promote the positive integration of individuals into society by encouraging healthy social bonds. The basic ideologies behind this perspective has laid the groundwork for policies and practices that emphasize an improvement in teaching positive values, the mentoring of youth to encourage control and accountability, and the re-orientation of criminal justice towards community intervention as a response to crime and delinquency.

CRITICAL THINKING QUESTIONS

1. Do you think negative labels cause crime or does getting involved in criminal behavior result in the negative label? In either case, how can an individual escape the spiraling effects of internalizing a deviant status? What labels have significant people in your life attached to you? How did these labels affect the image you had of yourself, your identity, and your behavior?

2. How much of our behavior is really socialized. Is most of what we do learned behavior or do we do it instinctively? Try to remember what activities you engaged in last weekend. Besides, sleeping, breathing, and occasionally sneezing, is there much else we can attribute to nature, or is most of it a product of our nurture?

3. What type of social bonds do you experience? Have your attachment, commitment, involvement, and belief in conventional activities and groups contributed to your positive integration into society? How could things have been different in the absence of these pro-social bonds?

4. Why do we refrain from engaging in particular types of criminal activities, such as rape, assault, and murder? Why do we try to drive the speed limit, pay our taxes, and avoid parking in a disabled parking space? What mechanisms of social control govern our behavior in these examples? Are they internal or external containments? Do different types of containment prevent different types of crime?

E-RESOURCES

For more information on the Head Start initiative, visit http://www.acf.hhs.gov/programs/ohs.

Details on diversion programs can be found at the U.S. Department of Justice website at http://www.ncjrs.gov/html/ojjdp/9909–3/div.html.

Additional information about the Columbine shootings can be found at http://www.disastercenter.com/killers.html.

More Statistics on school violence can be found in the National School Safety Center Report, http://www.schoolsafety.us/.

For the full report, "Safeguarding Our Children: An Action Guide," see http://www.ed.gov/admins/lead/safety/actguide/action_guide.pdf.

NOTES

1 Perez, Chris, Fears, Danika and Musumeci, Natalie. 2015. Oregon Gunman Singled Out Christians During Rampage. *The New York Post,* Oct. 1. Retrieved from http://nypost.com/2015/10/01/oregon-gunman-singled-out-christians-during-rampage/.
2 Akers, Ronald L. and Silverman, Adam. 2004. Toward a Social Learning Model of Violence and Terrorism. In Margaret A. Zahn, Henry H. Brownstein, And Shelly L. Jackson (eds.), *Violence: From Theory to Research*. Cincinnati, OH: LexisNexis-Anderson Publishing.
3 Ibid., see 1.
4 Chambliss, William. 1988. *Exploring Criminology*. New York: Macmillan.
5 Mohanty, Jayashree, Keokse, Gary and Sales, Esther. 2006. Family Cultural Socialization, Ethnic Identity, and Self-Esteem: Web-based Survey of International Adult Adoptees. *Journal of Ethnic and Cultural Diversity in Social Work* 15: 153–172. Arnett, Jeffrey J. 1995. Adolescents' Uses of Media for Self-Socialization. *Journal of Youth and Adolescence* 24: 519–533.
6 Long, Theodore E. and Hadden, Jeffrey K. 1985. A Re-Conception of Socialization. *Sociological Theory* 3: 39–49.
7 Beaver, K., Barnes, J.C. and Boutwell, B. 2014. *The Nurture Versus Biosocial Debate in Criminology: On the Origins of Criminal Behavior and Criminality*. Thousand Oaks, CA: SAGE.
8 Sutherland, Edwin. 1939. *Principles of Psychology*, 3rd ed. New York: Lippincott.
9 Ibid., see 6.
10 Sutherland, Edwin and Cressey, Donald. 1970. *Criminology*, 8th ed. Philadelphia: Lippincott.

11 Volkow, N. 2004. *Director's Report to the National Advisory Council on Drug Abuse.* Bethesda, MD: National Institute on Drug Abuse. Retrieved from https://archives. drugabuse.gov/DirReports/DirRep204/DirectorReport6.html.

12 Jetten, Jolanda and Hornsey, Matthew J. 2014. Deviance and Dissent in Groups. *Annual Review of Psychology* 65: 461–485.

13 DeLisi, M. and Vaughn, M. 2014. *The Routledge International Handbook of Biosocial Criminology.* London: Routledge.

14 Cullen, T. and Wilcox, P. 2010. *Encyclopedia of Criminological Theory.* Thousand Oaks, CA: SAGE.

15 Burgess, Robert and Ronald Akers. 1966. A Differential Association-Reinforcement Theory of Criminal Behavior. *Social Problems* 14: 363–383.

16 Watts, Amanda C., Wilder, David A., Gregory, Meagan K., Leon, Yanerys and Ditzian, Kyle. 2013. The Effect of Rules on Differential Reinforcement of Other Behavior. *Journal of Applied Behavior Analysis* 46(3): 680–684.

17 Hirschi, Travis. 1969. *Causes of Delinquency.* Berkeley: University of California Press.

18 Glaser, David. 1960. Differential Association and Criminological Prediction. *Social Problems* 8: 6–14.

19 Ibid., see 15.

20 Tittle, Charles R. 2000. *The Nature of Crime: Continuity and Change.* National Institute of Justice, Washington D.C.

21 Reckless, Walter C. 1967. *The Crime Problem,* 4th ed. New York: Appleton-Century-Crofts.

22 Ibid., see 18.

23 Kennedy, Jay P. 2015. Losing Control: A Test of Containment Theory and Ethical Decision Making. *International Journal of Criminal Justice Sciences* 10(1): 48–64.

24 Cardwell, Stephanie L. 2013. *Reckless Reevaluated: Containment Theory and its Ability to Explain Desistance Among Serious Adolescent Offenders.* Retrieved from http://www. mhsl.uab.edu/dt/2013/Cardwell_uab_0005M_11076.pdf.

25 Flexon, Jamie L. 26 March 2014. Containment Theory. *The Encyclopedia of Theoretical Criminology.* Wiley Online Library. DOI 10.1002/9781118517390.wbetc023.

26 Ibid., see 21.

27 Ibid., see 21.

28 Lux, Jennifer L. 22 January 2014. Walter Reckless. *The Encyclopedia of Criminology and Criminal Justice.* Wiley Online Library. DOI: 10.1002/9781118517383.wbeccj500.

29 Ibid., see 17.

30 Bouffard, Jeffrey A. and Petkovsek, Melissa A. 2014. Testing Hirschi's Integration of Social Control and Rational Choice: Are Bonds Considered in Offender Decisions. *Journal of Crime and Justice* 37(3): 285–308.

31 Valdimarsdottir, Margaret and Bernburg, Ion G. 2016. Community Disadvantage, Parental Network, and Commitment to Social Norms. *Journal of Research in Crime and Delinquency* 52(2): 213–244.

32 Ramirez, R., Hinman, A., Sterling, S., Weisner, C. and Campbell, C. 2012. Peer Influences on Adolescent Alcohol and Other Drug Use Outcomes. *Journal of Nursing Scholarship* 44(1).

33 Cook, Philip J. and Kang, Songman. 24 February 2014. Birthdays, Schooling, and Crime: Regression-discontinuity Analysis of School Performance, Delinquency, Dropout, and Crime Initiation Retrieved from https://www.aeaweb.org/articles?id= 10.1257/app.20140323

34 Davis, J. 2009. *The Influence of Social Capital Factors on African-American and Hispanic High School Student Achievement.* Orlando: University of Central Florida.

35 Hirtenlehner, Helmut and Kunz, Franziska. 2015. The Interaction Between Self-control and Morality in Crime Causation Among Older Adults. *European Journal of Criminology* 13(3): 393–409. doi:10.1177/1477370815623567

36 Rice, Marnie and Harris, Grant T. 2016. *The Sex Offender Risk Appraisal Guide*. New York: Springer.

37 Winick, B.J. 1998. Sex Offender Law in the 1990s: A Therapeutic Jurisprudence Analysis. *Psychology, Public Policy, and Law* 4: 505–570.

38 Becker, Howard. 1963. *Outsiders: Studies in the Sociology of Deviance*. New York: Free Press.

39 Ibid.

40 *Crime and Justice: American Style*. 1971. Rockville, MA: National Institutes of Mental Health, pp. 90–92.

41 Ibid, see 38.

42 Cuevas, C. and Rennison, C. 2016. *The Wiley Handbook on the Psychology of Violence*. Hoboken, NY: John Wiley and Sons.

43 Lemert, Edwin M. 1951. *Social Pathology: A Systematic Approach to the Theory of Sociopathic Behavior*. New York: McGraw-Hill.

44 Ibid.

45 Ibid, see 43.

46 Belmi, Peter, Barragan, Rodolfo C., Neale, Margaret A. and Cohen, Geoffrey. 2015. Threats to Social Identity Can Trigger Social Deviance. *Personality and Social Psychology Bulletin* 41(4): 1–18. doi: 10.1177/0146167215569493.

47 Wiley, Stephanie A. 2015. Arrested Development: Does the Grade Level at Which Juveniles Experience Arrest Matter? *Journal of Developmental and Life-Course Criminology* 1(4): 411–433.

48 Farrington, David and Murray, Joseph. 2014. Labeling Theory: Empirical Tests. *Advances in Criminological Theory*, Volume 8. New Brunswick, NJ: Transaction Publishers.

49 Frauley, J. 2015. *C. Wright Mills and the Criminological Imagination: Prospects for Creative Inquiry*. Farnham, England: Ashgate.

50 Sider, R. 2007. *Just Generosity: A New Vision for Overcoming Poverty in America*. Ada Township, MI: Baker Books.

51 Goodman, J. 2015. *Prison Diversion Programs in New York Face New Scrutiny After Police Officer's Killing*. The New York Times.

52 Ibid.

53 Vazsonyi, A.T., Roberts, J.W., Huang, L. and Vaughn, M. G. 2015. Why Focusing on Nurture Made and Still Makes Sense: The Biosocial Development of Self-control. In *The Routledge International Handbook of Biosocial Criminology*. New York: Routledge, pp. 263–279.

54 Bynum, J.E. and W.E. Thompson. 1996. The Family and Juvenile Delinquency. *Juvenile Delinquency* 3: 430.

55 Galaway, Burt and Hudson, Joe. 1990. *Restorative Justice: International Perspectives*. New Jersey: Criminal Justice Press.

56 Björkqvist, K. 2015 'White Rage': Bullying as an Antecedent of School Shootings. *Journal of Child and Adolescent Behavior* 3(175): 2.

CHAPTER OUTLINE

Sociological theory: crime is from conflict inherent to society

13

In this chapter we will explore the following questions

- How does conflict theory describe the social order?
- What is the relationship between power, politics, and the economy?
- Does conflict lead to crime?
- Is it possible that the criminal justice system perpetuates human suffering?
- Why is there a huge gap in crime statistics between men and women?
- Where do contradictions in the social structure come from?
- Can radical criminology offer a peaceful solution to crime?

KEY TERMS

social conflict approach

functional-conflict theory

power-conflict theory

radical theory

mode of production

proletariat

bourgeoisie

egoism

altruism

left realism

receptive deprivation

peacemaking criminology

feminist theory

power-control theory

structural contradictions theory

restorative justice

In June of 2015, Texas police officer Eric Casebolt resigned from his post just days after footage of him dragging a young teenage girl in a bikini to the ground at a pool party in McKinney, Texas, and pulling his gun on several others, went viral. Police were called to the scene after a resident in the neighborhood reported a disturbance at the Craig Ranch North Community Pool. Accounts of the events that took place that day were varied dramatically. Some claim there was racism involved on the part of police officers on the scene, claiming that they were cursing at African American teens, and taking things way too far in their use of force. Others maintain that law enforcement handled things properly and that it was the teens who were not following directions.[1]

According to research conducted by Bowling Green State University Criminologist Philip M. Stinson, more police officers in the United States have been prosecuted for on-duty shootings in 2015 than have been since 2005.[2] Conflict between law enforcement and citizens is not a new phenomenon, however. Over two decades ago, in the midnight hours of a March day in 1991, Rodney King, an African American male in his mid-twenties, along with two passengers, entered a freeway in the San Fernando Valley area of Los Angeles. A California highway patrol car pursued King's speeding vehicle. A freeway chase began between the police and King, who eventually exited the freeway into a residential neighborhood where police cornered his vehicle.

Image 13.1 *A neighborhood pool in McKinney, Texas, became the site of hostility between law enforcement and minority teens in June of 2015. Video capturing the encounter shows a police officer slamming a 15-year-old unarmed teenager to the ground. This scene is just one example of the different forms of conflict that exist in society.*

Ron Jenkins/AP/Press Association Images

Several Los Angeles Police Department officers arrived at the scene. The three men were ordered to exit the vehicle and get down on the ground. King's two passengers complied and were taken into custody without incident. After initially remaining in the car, King finally came out but was described as acting "bizarre." When officers attempted to restrain and handcuff him, he became agitated and resisted. King was shot with a Taser and was subsequently beaten several times with police batons and repeatedly stomped and kicked by police officers while he was on the ground. Following the incident, captured on tape, four officers were charged with using excessive force.[3]

On April 29, 1992, a jury acquitted three of the officers on all charges and was hung on one of the charges for the fourth.[4] The news of their acquittal sparked one of the longest and most devastating race riots in U.S. history. Angry citizens took to the streets, looting, setting fires, destroying property, assaulting, and protesting what they considered an unfair, biased verdict. At the end of the almost week-long rampage, over 50 individuals were dead and more than 2,380 injured; property damage amounted to nearly $1 billion.[5]

Commentators, political activists, scholars, and ordinary citizens have since debated the reaction to the acquittal of the police officers in the King case. Was it an outcry against racism and bias inherent in the criminal justice system?[6] Would the outcome have been different if Rodney King were white? What if the jury had not consisted of 11 whites and one person of Filipino descent? Was there an inherent bias in the Los Angeles police department against certain types of suspects? Do law enforcement practices include a certain level of racial profiling?

In a classic study on racial profiling, researchers at the George Washington University in Washington, D.C., examined these issues. Using data from a national survey, they found nearly 75 percent of African American men between 18 and 34 said they were victims of profiling.[7] Moreover, research studies have found a strong link between police use of force and certain neighborhood contexts where larger minority-group representation, lower socioeconomic status, and increased conflict create the perception that more drastic interventions are needed.[8] Studies show that officers are significantly more likely to use force during citizen encounters in disadvantaged neighborhoods, even taking into account individual factors such as the suspect's resistance.[9] What do such findings suggest about our perception of criminal behavior? Do the law and the various agents of social control operate in the interests of justice and equity? Or are they an instrument of bias and oppression? We turn to the conflict perspective in this chapter for an exploration of these questions.

MAJOR PRINCIPLES OF THE SOCIAL CONFLICT APPROACH

In this chapter, we will take a look at the third major sociological approach to the study of crime, social conflict. Recall from chapter 8 that the **social conflict approach** examines the fundamental distribution of wealth and power within society. The Rodney King incident and ensuing riots are an example of one of the many levels of conflict inherent to society. Conflict occurs between adversaries, family members, citizens and police, religious groups, political opponents, and various other groups. It can be a source of unrest and destruction, but it can also be the impetus for social change.

A theory of criminal behavior that purports to explain all criminality must account for the incidence of the entire range of criminal acts. White collar, corporate, state organized, and political criminality is widespread. Mass political movements are also a mainspring of vast amounts of criminal behavior. The American revolutionaries who terrorized the British were criminals by the law of the land, as were the workers who fought for their right to collectively bargain and strike, and the women in Western societies who for centuries have committed criminal acts in the course of opposing oppressive and discriminatory laws that prevented them from voting or inheriting property. They are joined by the students who violate trespass and other laws while demonstrating against war or apartheid, the farmers who mobilize civil disobedience and are beaten, jailed, and killed, and the civil rights activists who protest segregated schools, buses, housing, and restaurants. We cannot casually dismiss these criminal actions while focusing just on mugging, burglary, and assault. Indeed, we can explore the possible connections between varieties of criminality only by seeking the link between social class, crime, and the need for social control. We must now approach our understanding of crimes such as burglary, robbery, arson, and assault as expressions of outrage against greater social ills and injustices—racism, exploitation, inequality, and discrimination.

The data and observations we've used in evaluating theories of crime in the last few chapters show that we must somehow integrate the political nature of criminal law with the social character of criminal behavior. This will help us understand why the official crime rate for certain types of crime is higher for some classes and groups of people than it is for others, why black under-class males have a higher official crime rate for burglary, assault, and robbery while white upper-class males have a higher official crime rate for corporate, political,

BOX 13.1: CRIME IN GLOBAL PERSPECTIVE

Who is defined criminal in Pakistan?

Set in Lahore, Pakistan, the novel *Moth Smoke* is a realistic portrayal based on factual accounts that illustrate how the wealthy yet corrupt members of the ruling classes within this society are able to insulate themselves from the very laws that bind the subordinate classes. The story describes the life experiences of Darashikoh "Daru" Shezad. Daru is a young banker who despite his education lacks the connections to become a part of the elitist class. His life takes a downward spiral when he gets fired from his job in Lahore for being late to work and keeping a wealthy customer waiting. When he tries to get a job at another bank, he is told there are enough applicants with more wealth and power than the salaries being offered, who are hired out of respect and to gain their families' business.

Desperate, Daru turns to drugs, alcohol, and robbery. When he first holds a gun in his hand he experiences an overwhelming sense of power. For the first time he feels in control of his life rather than a victim of his vagrant status. For a short while, Daru is reunited with Ozi, a childhood friend who is a part of the upper echelon of Pakistani society. However, their friendship crumbles under the strain caused by Daru's declining social status as well as his attraction to Ozi's wife Mumtaz. Daru's life becomes filled with disillusion as he not only goes on trial for a murder committed during a robbery but is also framed for a hit-and-run crime committed by his friend Ozi, who is able to escape sanction due to his privileged status.

Moth Smoke describes how the ruling classes within Pakistani society are able to create laws, escape punishment, get good jobs, accumulate wealth, and perpetuate their privileged status. The rest of society is forced to obey their rules, accept lower-class status, and serve as scapegoats for the wealthy, perpetuating their subordinate positions. The story of Daru describes how the criminal justice system in Pakistan operates as a tool of oppression. It reinforces the ruling class' privileged status while keeping the lower class under its control.

Sources

Birua, Vidisha. Crime and Social Control in Pakistani Society. *Journal of Criminal Justice and Popular Culture* 14(2): 227–236. Retrieved from http://ebookmarket.org/pdf/crime-and-social-control-in-pakistani-society-a-review-of-30818064.html.

Hamid, Mohsin. 2001. *Moth Smoke*. New York: Picador.

and white-collar crimes, and why white male college students are rarely arrested for rape despite the fact that 20 percent of female college students experience date rape on college campuses.

Criminologists who view crime as an outcome of social and economic contention are known as *conflict theorists*. They try to explain crime by understanding the social, political, and economic structure of society and the role this structure plays in the distribution of power. Conflict theory argues that the root cause of crime is the social conflict created by the unequal distribution of wealth and power in society. According to this approach, the political and economic structure of society allows the criminal justice system to operate in favor of those who have the power to define the law.[10] Moreover, the wealthy and privileged use the law as a tool to control the less advantaged members of society who threaten their position, by defining their acts as criminal (see Box 13.1).

How do the social, political, and economic structures of society create social conflict that allows these dynamics to occur? What is the relationship between group power and the shaping of criminal law? How does a capitalist economic structure influence crime rates? What role does the criminal justice system play in perpetuating criminal behavior? The various branches of conflict theory (see Table 13.1) attempt to answer these questions. We turn now to a closer look at the emergence of conflict theory for a better understanding of the origins of crime.

Table 13.1 Social conflict theories of criminal behavior

Radical theories	Contemporary radical theories	Feminist theories	Structural contradictions
• Marx and Engels • William Bonger • William Chambliss	• Left Realism • Peacemaking Criminology	• Marxist Feminism • Radical Feminism • Socialist Feminism • Multiracial Feminism • Liberal Feminism	• Conflicts and contradictions • Crime in Capitalist Societies

THE EMERGENCE OF CONFLICT THEORY

The origins of conflict criminological theory date back to World War II and have often been described as a reaction to mass changes taking place around the world in both the political arena and the economy.[11] The civil rights movement in the United States showed us people struggling for their rightful place in society, with breaking the law and going to prison as their only means of exercising their rights.

Image 13.2
How did the
violation of criminal
laws during the civil
rights movement
affect our
understanding and
definition of crime?
Who are the
criminals in this
photo?

Mary Evans/Everett
Collection

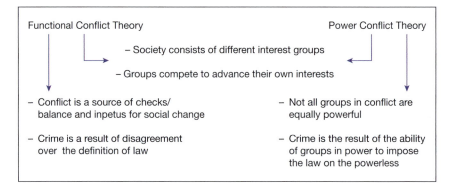

Figure 13.1 Functional-conflict versus power-conflict

Aware that not all crime was contained in the violence and property offenses of urban ghetto youths, criminologists had to recognize that the legal system did not always express the values and norms of the community.[12] Two different forms of conflict theory emerged: a functional-conflict approach and a power-conflict approach (see Figure 13.1). Let's look at what makes each one unique.

Functional-conflict theory

Functional-conflict theory views society as consisting of different groups of individuals who have very different goals and interests in life. Think about the advertisements you see on television. One moment, you see a commercial about a weight-loss product, and the very next ad is promoting a delicious calorie-rich dessert. During a football game, you will see countless commercials

Image 13.3
Society includes groups and individuals with opposing points of view . . . Opposition can unite, divide, or bring about social change.

Olivier Douliery/Abaca USA/PA Images

for beer, and during prom season or homecoming, you will see a plethora of public service ads warning about the dangers of drunk driving. Why is that? These messages reflect the natural human diversity in our society and the need to meet the different goals and interests that are a function of it.

According to functional-conflict theory, this diversity also puts people in conflict with one another. Different groups continually seek to achieve their own goals—through lobbying, media, and petitions—and to hinder the efforts of their opponents. Functional-conflict theory sees this process as a system of checks and balances that gives society stability while at the same time nurturing the underlying forces for social change.[13]

Theorists George Vold (1958) and Austin Turk (1969) took on the challenge of applying functional-conflict theory to criminology.[14] Vold described society as "held together in a shifting but dynamic equilibrium of opposing group interests and efforts."[15] According to Vold, groups with the authority to define the law will impose definitions that represent their own interests. Thus, crime is a consequence of a disagreement between different interest groups over the definition of law. Austin Turk echoed this idea when he described social order as "an always tenuous approximation of an order, more a temporary resolution of conflicting notions about right and wrong and of incompatible desires."[16] Turk saw criminal behavior as something that occurs in the course of interaction that takes place between individuals, whereby crime is a label imposed by some individuals on others. Therefore, no act is inherently criminal. The question that remained unanswered, however, was *how* some groups achieved the power to impose definitions on others.

While the functional-conflict perspective articulates the nature of group conflict in society, it mistakenly treats all conflict as equal. It views conflicts arising from differences in culture, for example, as similar to those arising from structural variations in power, such as between classes or genders. So it is power-conflict theory instead that highlights the connection between group conflict and the distribution of economic, social, and political resources.

Power conflict theory

Power-conflict theory is an elaboration of Max Weber's sociology of law as applied to criminology. The starting point for this perspective is the recognition that not all groups in conflict are equally powerful, and that the task for sociological understanding is to explain which groups are able to force their will on other groups. In 1938, researcher and scholar Thorsten Sellin observed that the cultures brought from Europe in massive waves of immigration in the late 1800s were repressed by the dominant culture of the United States, just as the cultures the fascists defined as "alien" were decimated in the name of "law" and "progress" because one group had the power to use the law to the detriment of others.[17] In contrast to Vold and Turk, Sellin believed it is not sufficient to merely point out that conflict and power struggles are ubiquitous in human social relations; we must go on to describe and explain who wins and who loses in the struggle.

Power-conflict theory aims to develop a radical vision for structuring society in the direction of equity and justice, rather than building upon the existing differentials in power distribution. A body of other research on law and crime (which we look at below) supported the power-conflict approach and contributed to the ongoing search for criminological theories that better fit the reality of the times. Thus conflict criminology has undergone several phases in the ensuing twenty years. We turn now to a discussion of the specific components of this radical approach in criminological theory.

RADICAL CRIMINOLOGICAL THEORIES

Over the years, the conflict approach has developed under various names such as "radical," "critical," "Marxian," and "the new criminology." To avoid confusion, we will use the term **radical theory** to refer to all the theories within this tradition, which originate with the propositions made by Marx and Engels.[18]

Marx and Engels on capitalism

Karl Marx and Friedrich Engels are considered the founders of modern socialism.[19] Their many writings span a variety of different topics that present a complex analysis of society and history in terms of class relations.

Marx and Engels' philosophy of thinking centered upon the nature and organization of labor in society, and how this determines the course of human relations. Marxist theory begins with the observation that every human group faces the same fundamental problem: how to organize its labor.[20] Unless they convert the natural environment to useable products—food, shelter, clothing—human beings cannot survive. There are an infinite number of ways people may organize their labor. In Marxist theory, the way they choose is called the **mode of production**. The mode of production may allow each member to seek, horde, and consume everything he or she acquires. Or a group might organize the production and distribution of products equally among all the members regardless of how much each person contributes to acquiring them. Groups of people may take most of the production for themselves and redistribute only enough to keep those who produce alive. If there is an unlimited supply of people producing, they can organize the distribution so some people consume all and others die for lack of food, shelter, and clothing. Every historical era contains examples of how human groups organize the acquisition and distribution of the products of labor. Most, but not all, societies have created modes of production that result in social classes with different shares of the goods.

Image 13.4 *Great thinkers Karl Marx and Frederick Engels laid the groundwork for the development of radical criminological theories.*

Mary Evans Picture Library

According to Marx and Engels, the uneven division of labor in society is the central feature of capitalism, where labor itself becomes a valuable commodity.[21] The working class or **proletariat** sells their labor to the **bourgeoisie**, the class of individuals who own the means of production—land, factory, business or enterprise—the capitalists. The proletariat greatly outnumbers the bourgeoisie. Under capitalism, people are compensated with less than the value of the commodity they are producing, in order for the wealthy capitalists to make a *profit*. If this were not the case, commodities would be priced too high for consumers to purchase. Can you imagine paying even more than $4.00 for a cup of coffee?

Marx believed the long-term effect of capitalism is to produce a capitalist class that was rich and powerful, and a working class that was impoverished and relatively powerless. Thus, one of the problems facing every society with an unequal distribution of wealth and power is that those social classes receiving more of the products will strive to retain their privileged position, while those who receive less will strive to increase their share. This simple and obvious fact bestows on every class society a fundamental contradiction: the need to maintain class relations that inevitably produce antagonisms and conflicts between the classes. The people with the control over a greater proportion of the resources generally also have access to more effective tools of physical coercion. One solution, then, is for the upper class to enforce the continuation of the unequal distribution of goods by coercion. A cleverer way to organize people to accept an unequal distribution of goods, however, is to convince them that this is the right and proper way for the world to be ordered.

The law therefore becomes the principal source of both legitimation and coercion. It is the law that maintains inequality in the distribution of the products of a people's labor. The law defines the rights, duties, and responsibilities people have to one another and to various institutions within society. One facet of the law central to maintaining existing social relations, including inequality, is the definition of some acts as criminal and the punishment of people who engage in those acts. Thus in the Marxist tradition, law in capitalist societies is a reflection of class struggle that attempts to maintain both the institutions that facilitate the accumulation of capital and a relative level of social peace. Crime, on the other hand, is a reaction of the oppressed working class to the disadvantaged conditions under which capitalism forces them to live.[22] It is a mechanism by which the worker compensates for being exploited, deprived, and living in distress and despair. Crime can also be a symbol or expression of rebellion and hostility toward the ruling classes of society.[23] Figure 13.2 highlights the various components of Marx and Engels' views on capitalism. The two did not elaborate too much on crime and the law. However, they laid the foundation upon which other theorists built their research on the relationship between crime, law, and the economy.

Figure 13.2 Marx and Engels: the cycle of capitalism

Willem Bonger on the economic culture

In 1916, Dutch criminologist Willem Bonger published a classic work titled *Crime and Economic Conditions*[24] that began from the Marxist position outlined above. Bonger applied this perspective to crime and theorized that crime varied depending on the degree to which a society was structured around capitalist or communist modes of production. More than anything else, the capitalist mode of production relies on competition to make a profit. In the struggle for survival, not everyone will come out on top; someone must win and someone must lose, and the winner wins at the expense of the loser. A neighborhood deli must compete for customers with the deli that just opened down the street. In order to get more business and increase its profit, each deli must develop strategies to "steal" customers from the other.

According to Bonger, the prevailing personality type produced by capitalism is what he calls **egoism**—a personality that strives for self-attainment and

Image 13.5 *Sales and other tactics retail stores use to attract customers are characteristic of economic competition to increase merchandise sales and make a profit. The winner of this competition, according to Bonger, is the one who makes the most profits.*
iStock/P_Wei

places only secondary importance on providing support or aid to one's neighbors.[25] The resulting emphasis on profit and greed make people less likely to abide by the law in their effort to gain economic advantage, even if their actions may hurt someone along the way. More importantly, Bonger argued that in an economic system based on capitalist principles, those who ultimately gain control of the means of production are those who behave in the most egoistic fashion. Bonger believed that in societies whose economies are built primarily on socialism, crime rates are very low. The emphasis on equality and sharing produces **altruism**, or the sacrifice of self to help others, and competition is replaced by cooperation and the desire for peace and harmony among different groups in society.

In support of his theory Bonger presents a summary of the existing anthropological data comparing societies with different modes of production. In the data Bonger found pre-industrial capitalistic societies without exception had ongoing problems of deviance, crime, and violence. By contrast, communistic societies revealed a consistent tendency to be harmonious, relatively free of conflict, crime, violence, and disruptive forces.[26] Subsequent research surveying hundreds of later anthropological studies also supports Bonger's proposition that societies based on equality and sharing manifest a much lower incidence of conflict and crime than do societies based on acquisitiveness and personal accumulation.[27]

Bonger argued that crime was inherent in capitalist economies. The potential to break the law is characteristic of all individuals in a capitalist economy, regardless of their social or economic status. However, Bonger argued that although the economically advantaged commit crimes, they do not suffer the same legal consequences as do the economically disadvantaged, because the law is designed to control the poor in the interest of the wealthy. How and why is the law designed to favor the ruling classes of society? The work of William Chambliss provides an answer.

William Chambliss on law and politics

Hundreds, even thousands, of local, state, and federal laws are passed each year, some out of the specific need or interest of a particular individual or group. This was the case when the federal government enacted "Megan's Law," requiring all states to develop procedures for notifying residents about sex offenders living in their neighborhoods (see Box 13.2). Some laws emerge because a group of individuals lobbies for the specific interests of a significant segment of society, such as those in favor of gun control. Still others simply develop out of legislative debates that represent the views of individual law makers and congressional committees. Regardless of origin, laws emerge from conflict-ridden situations that arise between different groups within society.[28]

The process of law creation is a complex one, but we highlight one area here—its relationship to power. A prominent study by Chambliss and Seidman sees the connection between law and power as the key to understanding the origin of criminal behavior.[29] In stratified societies, where social status depends on economic privilege and political authority, the dominant groups must enforce the norms and rules of conduct most likely to guarantee their advantaged positions. They are able to do this through the criminal law.

History shows that in adjudicating disputes between classes, the state will usually be persuaded by the interests and actions of the dominant economic class. Thus, what makes the behavior of some individuals "criminal" is the state's ability to enforce the will of the dominant classes through the coercive but legitimate power of the law.[30] In an analysis of the development of vagrancy law in England in the mid-1300s, Chambliss shows how wealthy landowners benefited from its passage, which forced would-be beggars to accept low-wage jobs as serfs instead of committing what the law had made a criminal act.[31]

When you came home past your curfew in high school, what made your behavior "criminal" was the ability of your parents (the dominant class in your house and the one that defined the rules) to enforce their definition of a curfew on you, the subordinate member of the household. Similarly, for Chambliss, crime is rooted in social conditions that empower the wealthy to define as criminal those acts that go against their own interests. At the same time, the government, law enforcement, and the criminal justice system as a whole perpetuate criminal activity by providing a distorted sense of the reality of crime as primarily a problem of poor, urban minority youth.[32] This not only deflects attention from the harmful and dangerous crimes committed by the

BOX 13.2: CONSIDER THIS . . .

The power of voice

In the summer of 1994, Jesse K. Timmendequas lured 7-year-old Megan Nicole Kanka into his New Jersey home by telling her he wanted to show her his puppy. Once she entered her neighbor's house, he sexually assaulted and murdered her. Timmendequas had previously been convicted of raping a five-year-old girl and had also attempted to sexually assault another seven-year-old girl. Why did his neighbors not know about this?

Grief-stricken and angry, Megan's family started lobbying for stricter laws regarding registration of sexual offenders. Only three months later New Jersey signed what became nationally known as "Megan's Law." This legislation required the active notification of residents about the presence of registered sexual offenders who live in their neighborhoods. Active notification requires police to go door-to-door informing residents of an offender's presence and/or sending out letters alerting neighbors. The Kankas, along with other parents whose children were murdered by repeat offenders, then lobbied federal lawmakers to pass a federal version of Megan's Law. In May 1996, the federal government passed a version of Megan's Law requiring law enforcement departments within each State to develop policies regarding the release of information about registered sex offenders to communities. Moreover, individuals convicted of sexual crimes against children are required to notify local law enforcement of any change of address or employment after they are released from prison.

The parents who lobbied for Megan's Law had lived a nightmare many parents fear. Their personal experiences and suffering allowed them to attract the attention of media as well as lawmakers. This gave them the power they needed to get such laws passed on a state and federal level. Does our society allow all victims of crime to lobby successfully to get such laws passed? *What do you think?*

Sources

State of California Department of Justice, Office of the Attorney General, 2014. About Megan's Law. Retrieved from http://www.meganslaw.ca.gov/homepage.aspx?lang=ENGLISH.

Welchans, Sarah. 2005. Megan's Law: Evaluations of Sexual Offender Registries. *Criminal Justice Policy Review* 16(2): 123–140.

Zgoba, Kristen, Melissa Dalessandro, Bonita Veysey, and Philip Witt, Philip. 2008. *Megan's Law: Assessing the Practical and Monetary Efficacy.* Retrieved from http://www.ncjrs.gov/pdffiles1/nij/grants/225370.pdf.

rich and privileged, but also endlessly expands crime control strategies—building more prisons, hiring more police, and making tougher laws—that continue to fail while diverting resources away from education, social services, and healthcare.[33] Table 13.2 summarizes the propositions offered by Chambliss and Seidman.

Chambliss laid the foundation for a critical approach to the study of crime, one that emphasizes the reality of crime as manipulated by the vested interests of politicians, media, law enforcement, and prison industries.[34] Essentially,

Table 13.2 Class interest, class conflict, the law, and crime

Proposition	Observation
Complex societies consist of a variety of groups that live under different conditions and have different life experiences	People live in different environments that range from urban ghettos to suburbs to high-rise apartments in Beverly hills
The conditions under which we live affect our values and norms.	People have different concerns such as survival, making ends meet, buying a new car, getting a promotion, attending college. These different concerns lead to a diversity in values and norms.
Complex societies are thus composed of a very different and often conflicting set of values and norms.	People do not agree about, for instance, lying or cheating to get ahead v. maintaining honesty and integrity, or establishing a reputation by being tough v. gaining respect by being respectful.
The likelihood that the law will reflect your norms and values is not evenly distributed in society but is instead related to your political and economic position.	The AARP (American Association of Retired Persons) is one of the most powerful lobby groups in the United States; those 65 and older are also the largest group of voters.
The higher a group's political and economic status within society, the greater the likelihood its norms, values, and interests will be reflected in the law	The NRA (National Rifle Association) is one of the most politically and economically advantaged interest groups in the United States; its views are more likely to be represented in the legislature than the views of gun control advocates

Source: Adapted from Chambliss, William J. and Seidman, Robert T. 1971. *Law, Order and Power*. Reading, MA: Addison-Wesley.

Image 13.6 *Thousands of people are killed or injured each year from post-collision fires caused by defective designs in auto fuel systems. Manufacturers continue to produce these vehicles, avoiding newer, safer designs that are not as cost-effective. Why aren't they held accountable for the resulting injuries and loss of life?*

iStock/shaunl

criminal law perpetuates the existing social and economic order. Contemporary radical theories emerged to build upon these concepts, taking a more practical approach to the study of crime. We turn now to an exploration of these theories.

CONTEMPORARY RADICAL THEORY

Radical criminological theories contend that crime and the criminal justice system are products of, and affected by, capitalism. Capitalist societies are riddled with conflicts and contradictions that create a disharmony in social relations. Essentially the criminal law serves as a tool by which those with political power and economic advantage can coerce the poor into compliance by engaging in certain patterns of behavior that maintain the status quo. What are these behaviors and how do they maintain the status quo? Let's take a closer look at the theories, beginning with left realism.

Left realism

Left realism emerged in the 1980s partly in reaction to radical criminology's failure to provide a practical understanding of street crime, and its portrayal of criminals as political dissenters reacting against the alienation caused by capitalism.[35] Left realism provides us with a more concrete approach. According to this perspective, crime has a profound impact on criminals, victims, and society in general, and we should focus our attention on the consequences of street crime on its victims, who often share the same backgrounds as their criminal perpetrators.[36]

Prominent theorist Jock Young, a major contributor to the development of left realist thought, argued that the most probable source of criminal behavior is relative deprivation, feeling deprived relative to similar social groups around you. Relative deprivation occurs when people become disillusioned due to the experience of social inequality and injustice. Criminal behavior becomes a means by which individuals tip the scale toward fairness and justice, in the absence of real solutions for being degraded and exploited. We see this in the criminal acts of rioters reacting to the perceived injustice of the Rodney King verdict discussed earlier in this chapter.

Moreover, we should view the criminal justice system not simply as an agent of oppression in the hands of the powerful, but rather as a mechanism by which both victim and offender can achieve social justice. For left realists, the causes of crime lie in the social forces that perpetuate deprivation and social conflict and impose social and economic hardships on some individuals. Thus, crime control strategies should focus on a unified, cooperative effort between law enforcement and the public.[37] Box 13.3 discusses the emergence of community policing and some findings on its successful implementation as a crime control strategy.

BOX 13.3: CONNECTING RESEARCH TO PRACTICE

The "community" in community policing

In May 2015, the Final Report of the President's Taskforce on 21st Century Policing stated:

> Trust between law enforcement agencies and the people they protect and serve is essential in a democracy. It is key to the stability of our communities, the integrity of our criminal justice system, and the safe and effective delivery of policing services.

The report identifies the need to build trust and foster legitimacy between law enforcement and the community in order to increase the positive relationship between police and citizens. Moreover, policies affecting citizens should reflect community values and strategies that aim to improve the law enforcement/public relations and increase community engagement.

Several decades earlier, community policing was founded as an approach to crime control that makes law enforcement and the community partners in addressing neighborhood conditions that create fear, tension, and social disorder. Unlike other strategies, community policing encourages police officers to become a part of the communities they are policing, for example by having more police on foot patrol and establishing smaller sub-stations in high-crime areas.

The community policing approach was developed to reduce the adversarial side of the relationship between residents and police. Its goal is to form collaborative partnerships between law enforcement officers and the individuals, businesses, and organizations they serve, creating a team effort to keep communities safe. It changes the role of police officers from mere enforcers of the law to supportive community members who solve crime problems, participate in neighborhood safety meetings, and serve their communities.

There are over 12,000 police departments nationwide that have adopted community-policing strategies. Over the years, research findings have found a positive influence on residential communities throughout the United States. There is less fear of crime and improved communication between residents and law enforcement. Moreover, police are better informed about the problems and concerns of the neighborhoods they are patrolling. Residents in turn are more informed about the specific steps police are taking to address their concerns. They have more confidence in police and feel their community is a better place to live.

Sources

Ahlin, Eileen, Beckman, Karen, Gibbs, Jennifer, Gugino, Mathew and Varriale, Jennifer. *Trends in Research on Community Policing 2000–2004: A Review of the Published Literature.* 2007. Paper presented at the annual meeting of the American Society of Criminology, Atlanta, GA.

Office of Community Oriented Policing Services. U.S. Department of Justice, Washington D.C. Retrieved from http://www.cops.usdoj.gov/about.

President's Task Force on 21st Century Policing. 2015. Final Report of the President's Task Force on 21st Century Policing. Washington, D.C.: Office of Community Oriented Policing Services.

Left realist theory does a good job of unifying structure and action. Crime is a dynamic process that includes actions committed by an offender, the impact of those actions on the victim, formal reaction by the state, and informal reaction by society (see Figure 13.3). We will discuss the impact of left realism on applied research and policy development in sections to come. For now, we turn to a discussion of peacemaking criminology, which also has a profound impact on the direction of criminal justice policy and practice.

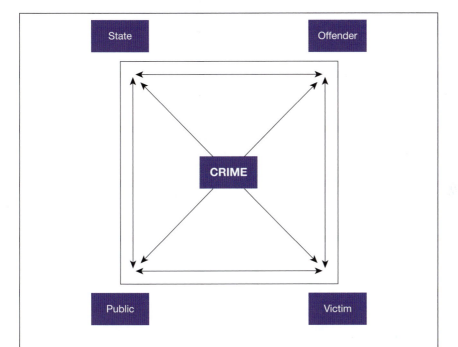

When examining a crime, one must consider the 4 following aspects:

• **The state** – as an agent of formal social control, the state decides what is "criminal" and what is not. It is thus necessary to consider criminal acts within the context of the state.

• **The Offender** – it is also important to consider why people offend. What conditions serve as the initial motive for committing a crime and what makes them continue to commit crime? What makes some people drift in and out of criminal behavior?

• **The public** – we must also consider the social dynamics that shape and influence public perception, attitude, and response to crime.

• **The victim** – the victim ultimately determines if a crime has been committed and therefore must also be taken into consideration.

Figure 13.3 The square of crime

Source: Bowman, Alan. 2006. Revision: AQA Sociology A2—Crime and Deviance—Left Realist Criminology. Retrieved from www.thestudentroom.co.uk/wiki/Revision:AQA_Sociology_A2_-_Crime_and_Deviance_-_Left_Realist_Criminology

Image 13.7 This statue is a symbol of our justice system's embodiment of fairness and equity in the treatment of those accused of a crime. Has the concept of "blind justice" closed our eyes to injustices that have an oppressive effect on the accused? Should true justice also incorporate the circumstances and status of the offender?

iStock/Piotr Adamowicz

Peacemaking criminology

John Doe is accused of trafficking marijuana across the border from Mexico, a federal offense. His court indictment reads, the *United States v. John Doe,* implying, even if unintentionally, that John Doe has become the adversary of the entire country. Our criminal justice system is an adversarial one, from the beginning moments of investigation and arrest, throughout the trial process and sentencing. The accused is up against the upholder of the law, in a battle where who wins and who loses often depends on variables that are hardly related to the facts or circumstances surrounding the case. Variables such as the offender's socio-economic class often overshadow the interests of achieving justice and fair treatment (see Box 13.4).

Peacemaking criminology emerged in the early 1990s as a philosophical movement rooted in Christian teaching and the ideology of religious figures such as Gandhi and Buddha.[38] It provides us with a better understanding of the role the criminal justice system plays in perpetuating conflict and suffering. According to this perspective, crime is a form of suffering, a means by which people react to conditions of hardship, injustice, and oppression. To make matters worse, the adversarial nature of the criminal justice process adds to this suffering. Consider, for example, a single mother of three small children whose live-in boyfriend is arrested for manufacturing meth-amphetamines in her basement. Imagine the profound hardship on her children if the mother were also arrested and sentenced to prison. What good would come of this? Some would say this punishment would teach her a lesson; but at whose expense? Could this lesson worsen the continuing cycle of crime and suffering to which her three children may fall victim?

Peacemaking criminologists emphasize the need to treat crime and crime control strategies as social issues involving citizens and criminal justice agents. They call for a transformation of the criminal justice system and various other social institutions from ones that add to human suffering and misery, to ones that focus on forgiveness, repair, and healing. We will elaborate a great deal on the policy implications of peacemaking criminology later in this chapter. For now, we turn to an examination of Feminist theories for another critical examination of crime and justice.

BOX 13.4: CONNECTING THEORY TO PRACTICE

The Rich Get Richer and the Poor Get Prison

Studies have repeatedly shown that individuals from all social classes commit crime. However, society's disadvantaged classes experience higher rates of arrest, criminal charges, and convictions, spend more time in prison, and are more often denied parole. This apparent bias within the criminal justice system has led to the publication of such works as *The Rich Get Richer and the Poor Get Prison.* In this work, author Jeffery Reiman illustrates conflict theory's argument that the criminal justice system is used as a means to keep disadvantaged classes in society from gaining social and political power.

Reiman argues that the rhetoric surrounding crime suggests members of the lower class are responsible for most criminal acts, in spite of the fact that wealthy white-collar criminals and powerful corporations commit many of the most devastating and harmful criminal activities. Yet media, politicians, and social propaganda continue to reinforce and exploit the idea that young, inner-city, urban minorities should be feared the most.

Moreover, Reiman notes that the processes of law formation, police arrest, judgments, and sentences are all misguided. Instead of addressing the most dangerous or harmful crimes, the criminal justice system still focuses on criminalizing the behavior of, arresting, and convicting the poor. This emphasis diverts valuable resources away from social programs that can address the poverty, unemployment, discrimination, and inequality disadvantaged groups face, in turn sustaining a socio-economic system that perpetuates crime and violence and a growing distrust of the criminal justice process.

Source

Anderson, Jennifer. 2014. Racial Bias and the Criminal Justice System: Research for a Fairer Future. *Social Science Space*. Retrieved from http://www.socialsciencespace.com/2014/11/racial-bias-and-the-criminal-justice-system-research-for-a-fairer-future/.

Chambliss, William J. 2001. *Power, Politics and Crime*. United Kingdom: Westview Press.

Reiman, Jeffrey and Leighton, Paul. 2016. *The Rich Get Richer and the Poor Get Prison*, 10th ed. London and New York: Routledge.

FEMINIST THEORIES

Until the 1970s, criminological theory and research focused almost exclusively on male criminality. One of the most profound developments in the understanding of crime causation was the emergence of feminist theory. Feminist perspectives in criminology directed our attention to the role of gender and gender relations in ordering social life.[39] With the development of research on the criminal behavior of women and girls, we are now in a better position to develop social policies that address the specific needs of female offenders, understand the dynamics of female victimization, and elaborate on the huge gap in crimes rates between males and females.

Image 13.8
How does the subordinate status of females in the work place influence the gender gap in crime rates between men and women?

iStock/mediaphotos

Types of feminist theories

Various branches of feminist criminology have emerged over the years. While each has its unique approach, they all include gender stratification, the unequal access to wealth, power, and prestige on the basis of sex, as an integral component in the study of crime.

Marxist feminist theory

Marxist feminist theory, in the tradition of Marxism, sees the capitalist economic structure as the source of gender inequality. According to this perspective, the division of labor in capitalist society has traditionally allowed men to adopt a primary role within economic production. A historical look at the development of capitalism reveals that men were the primary workers in farms, factories, and other labor markets, forcing women to become economically dependent on men. Moreover, changes in the social and economic position of women such as the rise in divorce, an increase in female headed households, and the concentration of women in low paying jobs, has contributed to women's involvement in criminal activity, especially property crimes, to compensate for their disadvantaged position in society.[40]

Radical feminist theory

Radical feminist theory examines the role of patriarchy in the exploitation of women by men. Patriarchy exists mainly because women are physically smaller and in most cases weaker than men, and because women are the child bearers and this makes them dependent on men for help during their childbearing years. The role of men in the structure of the household allows them to dominate women in many ways, including through violence, aggression, and sexuality.

Radical feminist theory explains violent female crime as a product of the violence women experience from men. Moreover, the exploitation of women by men can lead to other forms of deviant behavior, especially in young girls, such as running away, using alcohol, and turning to drugs or prostitution.[41]

Socialist feminist theory

Socialist feminist theory encompasses ideas from Marxist and radical feminist perspectives by emphasizing the importance of both capitalism and patriarchy on the subordination of women in society.[42] The economic and social organization of gender roles affects the life experiences of women and their opportunities in society. This in turn has a direct impact on both the amount and types of crimes they commit. According to socialist feminist theory, the distribution of power created by the economic and social order diverts women into offenses such as shoplifting and prostitution, while men are responsible for the majority of violent street crimes such as assault and homicide.[43]

Multiracial feminism

Another feminist framework emphasizes the consideration of race in addition to economic and social class as an important variable in the study of women and crime.[44] Multiracial or multicultural feminist theory examines the disadvantaged conditions of African-American women who experience subordination not only because of gender and class, but also due to race. The interconnection of these three variables helps us understand why African-American women have higher rates of criminality than white women.[45]

Liberal feminist theory

Liberal feminist theory emphasizes the role of gender role socialization in patterns of criminal behavior. Men are socialized to adopt roles that increase their opportunities within society, while women are socialized to believe they have certain limitations,[46] which in turn affects the manner in which women engage in criminal activities.[47] When the socialization of men and women becomes less diverse, according to this view, the genders become more similar —occupying economically lucrative positions, getting a college education, heading a household, and being politically active–and the crime rate of men and women should also become more similar. As we have seen in chapter 3, however, this has not been an accurate prediction. While the rate of female criminality has increased at a much greater rate than that of men, a huge gap in criminality continues to exist between the genders, especially with regard to violent crime. We will discuss this controversy in greater detail in the sections to come.

Feminist theory on the victimization of women

The emergence of feminist theories in the 1970s brought about significant changes in our understanding of violent crimes against women. These theories examined the role of inequality in the victimization of women, as well as the effect of such crimes as rape and sexual assault on the emotional and behavioral development of female victims. In a classic study on the relationship between rape and inequality, researchers Julia and Herman Schwendinger suggest rape is a consequence of female powerlessness under capitalist development.[48] Women constitute a reserve labor force that elevates men to a position of political and economic domination, rendering women powerless and men able to take advantage of their powerlessness to act violently towards them.

The Schwendingers support their argument in part with survey data from four non-industrialized societies that shows rape is (a) not universal, and (b) linked to the economic system; the emergence of exploitive modes of production either created or increased the prevalence of sexual inequality, violence against women, and rape. Recent research has focused on the role of patriarchy in creating a culture where the exploitive treatment of women is regarded as socially acceptable,[49] and violence against women is a product of social conditions that create gender inequality and leave women relatively powerless.

A growing body of feminist literature has also directed attention to the role of victimization in the onset of delinquency among juvenile girls. Studies show that delinquent girls and young women are disproportionately victims of domestic assault, rape, and incest prior to their offending.[50] Moreover, the vast majority of females in prison have been the victims of violence and sexual abuse.[51] Childhood sexual abuse is also significantly correlated with female offending behavior.[52] The victimization girls and young women experience serves as a catalyst for finding an escape, and turning to the streets opens the door for a variety of delinquent and criminal behaviors such as prostitution and drugs. Researchers note that gender-specific differences in victimization between male and female delinquents is an important variable in the treatment of female offenders by the juvenile and adult systems of justice and the development of gender responsive programming and approaches to female criminality.[53]

Feminist theory on female criminality and the gender gap in crime rates

From the very beginning, feminist theorists such as Freda Adler[54] and Rita J. Simon[55] have tried to understand why a gender gap exists in the rate of criminality between men and women, especially with regard to violent crime. Even as the gender socialization of men and of women has grown more similar over the years, the gender ratio in crime statistics has remained about the same, with men committing far more crimes than women. What could explain this gap?

Criminological research in this area has focused on two broad categories of explanation.[56] One line of study has explored the role of gender stratification within crime networks. Despite changes in gender role socialization, femininity is still associated with being nurturing and cooperative, and masculinity with

Image 13.9
How has the changing role of women in the workforce affected the type of crimes they commit?

iStock/Susan Chiang

being aggressive and protective. Research shows these attitudes also exist within the criminal world of offenders. A study of female gang members shows girls are reluctant to fight rival gang members unless absolutely necessary, and this reluctance was due to their understanding of female gender roles. The gang members referred to themselves as "ladies," not "dudes."[57]

Another area of research explores the impact of family class structure on the gender distribution of delinquency and crime. **Power-control theory** distinguishes two types of family structures: *patriarchal*, where the father usually works outside the home and the mother is responsible for taking of the children, and *egalitarian*, where both parents work outside the home and children receive less care and nurturing from their mothers.[58] Within a patriarchal family structure, boys are encouraged to be "real men," adopting attitudes that encourage aggressive, macho behavior, while girls are encouraged to be "ladylike," acting in a cooperative, submissive manner. Within egalitarian households, sons and daughters are treated more alike and expectations about their behavior are the same. Power-control theory suggests gender differences in criminality are more characteristic of patriarchal than egalitarian households. Research has produced mixed results, with some studies finding that gender differences in delinquency are *not* higher in patriarchal families[59] and others that female criminality is higher in households characterized by a more egalitarian structure.[60]

With these and many other research studies on female offenders, feminist theory brought a distinct awareness of the role of gender to the analysis of criminal behavior and to our understanding of how gender relations shape the dynamics of crime and criminal justice.[61] We turn now to another critical perspective that also highlights inequality, conflict, and contradiction within society.

CRIME AND STRUCTURAL CONTRADICTIONS

The various structural analyses of crime and criminal law we've looked at so far have provided us with a theoretical framework that accepts that criminality is widely distributed in the social structure and that different types of criminality characterize different social classes or groups. It avoids the errors in other explanations of crime by not seeking to explain individual adaptations but rather linking characteristics of the social structure with differences in crime rates and the distribution of crime.

One thing missing from these theories, however, is a description of the specific characteristics of social structures that can explain how laws and criminal behaviors are produced. For this we turn to an analysis of the social structure, and the various *contradictions* inherent to different forms of political, economic, and social relations.

Structural contradictions theory seeks to answer questions about why criminal behavior exists, why it is distributed as it is, and why it varies from place to place and from one historical period to another. We do not seek to answer why Jessica steals and Bob makes airplanes; why one politician accepts bribes and another does not; or why one manager violates health and safety regulations and another promotes the rules. Instead, we seek to understand the larger relationship between crime and social structure.

Contradictions and conflicts

A contradiction exists in a given set of social relationships (political, economic, and ideological) when these relationships simultaneously maintain the status quo and produce the conditions necessary to transform it. The owner of a coffee shop must make a profit in order to pay the rent for his store. In order

Figure 13.4
Conflicts, contradictions, dilemmas, and resolutions

Source: Chambliss, William J. 1993. On Lawmaking. In William J. Chambliss and Marjorie Sue Zatz. *Making Law: The State, the Law and Structural Contradictions.* Indiana University Press.

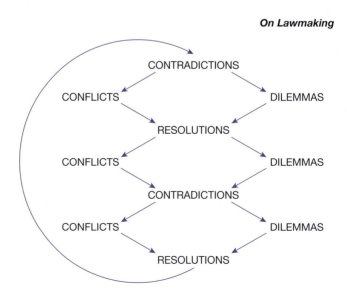

On Lawmaking

to make a profit, he must increase coffee sales. Too much increase, however, means that customers will stop buying their coffee at his shop. An alternative would be to decrease the wages of his employees who are actually selling the coffee and running the shop. Workers become dissatisfied, complain, don't have enough money to buy what they need and live a good life, and seek some type of change. These contradictions inevitably lead to conflicts between groups, classes, and strata. Workers go on strike; women demonstrate against unequal pay; farmers march on Washington; small landowners take up arms against agribusiness; religious cults barricade themselves against federal agents.

Every historical era has its own unique contradictions and conflicts. The most important derive from the way the social, economic, and political relations are organized. How people make a living; the work they do; the way they organize their labor to produce the things that are useful and necessary for survival; how they distribute the results of their labor and organize power relations; these are the most basic characteristics of any human group.

According to structural contradictions theory, the types, amount, and distribution of crime in a particular time and place depend on the existing contradictions, the conflicts that develop as people respond to them, and the mechanisms institutionalized for handling the conflicts and dilemmas the contradictions produce. Workers are paid less or laid off because of downsizing, yet they still have to pay a house mortgage; a business owner must charge more for retail merchandise because the cost of production has gone up. Yet, it is the same workers who are underpaid or unemployed that must pay the higher prices for the merchandise they want. Criminal laws emerge, change, and develop as people attempt to respond to conflicts generated by contradictions in the political and economic organization of their world.

Crime in capitalist societies

The capitalist economy depends upon the production and consumption of commodities by large numbers of people. Thus it presents a two-fold problem: how to make people work to produce the commodities, and how to make people desire them. Some commodities are essential for survival: food, clothing, shelter. If the only means of obtaining these essentials is to work for someone who owns them, people will generally choose to work rather than starve or freeze to death. But capitalism does not depend on the production and consumption of necessities alone. It depends on the production and consumption of goods and services that have little or nothing to do with survival. For capitalism to develop, people must thus be motivated to work in order to purchase commodities that are not essential.

There are many ways people are taught to want non-essential commodities: advertising, socialization into a world in which the acquisition of non-essential commodities bestows status and a sense of personal integrity on those who can display them; the necessity to accumulate property in order to stave off the possibility of falling below the level of consumption necessary for survival.

Creating the desire to consume, however, simultaneously creates the seeds of discontent and the possibility that people will discover ways to increase consumption without working. If, instead of spending eight hours at a boring, tedious, and sometimes dangerous occupation, someone can obtain the money necessary for purchasing commodities by theft, fraud, trickery, or bribery, then some people will choose that option. In an effort to avoid this possibility the people who own the means of production and those who manage the state pass laws making such acts illegal. In this way they try to reduce the attractiveness of alternative routes to consumption.

Other forces push people to discover alternative ways of accumulating capital. Not everyone has an equal opportunity to consume the products they are taught to want. In capitalist economies there are vast differences in the wages people receive and the wealth they can accumulate. Some jobs pay only enough for survival. How, then, can a set of social relations be sustained that requires the vast majority of people to spend most of their lives working at tasks they find unsatisfactory, in order that we may have a large enough population of consumers to fuel the engines of capitalist production and consumption?

People must work for wages in order to have the power to consume, and they must consume in order for the economy to survive. This, too, creates its own contradictions. There is only one source of profit for the capitalist: the difference between what the capitalist pays the worker and the price for which the capitalist sells the product of that worker's labor. If the worker is paid the full amount for which the product is sold, then there is no profit and the economic system comes to a grinding halt. Without an accumulation of surplus capital to re-invest, the economy collapses. If, on the other hand, the worker is not paid enough to survive, the population is decimated and there is no one to purchase the commodities produced. Thus a fundamental *wages, profits, and consumption contradiction* explains a large part of the history of modern capitalism. Workers seek higher wages and owners seek to pay the minimum amount.

From the point of view of crime, the conflicts culminate in criminal behavior on the part of both workers and owners. Owners cut corners (violate health and safety regulations, illegally deal in the stock market, ignore Securities and Exchange regulations); workers steal from employers, supplement their wages by selling illegal drugs, illegally strike and organize, and join illegal political groups. The state sits squarely in the midst of the contradiction: although generally influenced more by owners than workers, it cannot allow the ongoing conflict to destroy either capitalism or democracy. It responds by passing laws to keep workers from disrupting production or stealing property and to keep owners from disregarding the health and safety of workers and consumers. It also prohibits economic activities that undermine the state's own interests (such as avoiding taxes by laundering money through overseas banks) or that give one group of capitalists an advantage over another (such as insider trading).

Image 13.10
Structural contradictions theory helps us understand strikes and protests as outcomes of the conflicts and dilemmas that arise between workers and management.

Xinhua/SIPA USA/PA Images

Capitalism also fosters a fundamental *wages-labor supply contradiction.* The owners pursuing the logic of capitalist economies will strive to pay workers as little as possible. It is not possible, however, to pay nothing, unless an over-abundance of labor, as in slave labor, allows for workers to be used up and replaced by others flowing in. In advanced industrial societies much of the needed labor requires skills that take time to learn. However, if there is full employment under capitalism, workers have an advantage in the struggle for increased shares of profits with owners. If there is a reserve labor force—that is, if a significant proportion of the labor force is unemployed or under-employed—then when the demands of labor threaten the profits of the owners, the owners can turn to the reserve army to replace the workers. The reserve army, however, forms an underclass that cannot consume but nonetheless is socialized into a system in which consumption is the necessary condition for happiness. Criminal behavior offers a solution for the underclass: what they cannot earn legitimately they can earn illegally.

EVALUATING SOCIAL CONFLICT THEORIES

Critics of radical criminology accuse this perspective of being more a commentary on the unbalanced state of capitalist society than a theoretical understanding of crime causation.[62] They argue that radical criminology assumes crime exists predominantly under capitalist economic modes of production and would virtually disappear under socialism. This assumption, however, neglects to explain relatively low crime rates in capitalist societies such as Japan and the conflicts and struggles within oppressive socialist and communist nations such as China. Critics also fault radical criminology for overemphasizing class relations in the development of criminal behavior, neglecting many other variables that should be factored in.[63] Crime in general is condemned by society, even by the socially isolated and exploited members of the working class. Thus, it is incorrect to say criminal behavior is a means of protesting the unfair distribution of wealth and power in society. Defenders of radical theory note that these criticisms are directed at Marxist traditions and do not apply to the many branches of radical theory that have developed since and that take a more structural and practical approach.

Feminist criminology has been criticized as more descriptive than empirical, focusing too much attention on the victimization of women and their subordinate status in society rather than developing a theoretical understanding of female criminality. Other critics note that feminist theory has failed to develop an adequate understanding of the continued gender gap in crime statistics.[64] Moreover, there seems to be a contradiction in the basic premise of feminist theory relative to the conflict perspective in general. If power relations shape the course of criminal behavior, then why do men, who invariably have more power than women, commit more crimes?[65] Nevertheless, despite these criticisms, we cannot neglect the valuable contribution of feminist theory in bringing gender to the forefront in the study of crime and criminal justice and developing a feminist orientation in criminology.

PRACTICAL APPLICATION OF SOCIAL CONFLICT THEORY

At the core of the various theories within the conflict perspective is the notion that conflict is inherent to society and is a major driving force behind criminal behavior. The sources of conflict vary, but conflict theories generally focus on the unequal distribution of social, political, and economic power. Table 13.3 summarizes conflict theory's contribution to the definition and cause of crime, as well as the approach to its resolution.

Table 13.3 The conflict perspective

What is crime?	• Crime is socially created behavior
Why does crime occur? (theory)	• Conflicts and contradictions within society create imbalances of power, and the State allows the ruling classes to define as criminal those actions/behaviors that go against their own interests
What is the solution to crime? (policy)	• Redistribute the wealth in society so as to eliminate class struggle
	• Implement principles of conflict resolution and cooperative criminal justice alternatives that emphasize social equity, gender equality, equal justice for all, and an awareness of social issues when dealing with crime

Policy implications of conflict theory can fall under various extremes. At one end of the spectrum, reducing conflict and crime can call for the radical restructuring of society, to eliminate the competition and greed that exist under capitalism and replace it with a more equitable distribution of wealth and power. Some conflict theorists, however, recognize the need for more practical solutions, such as increasing public awareness of criminal justice issues such as the consequences of crime on both victims and offenders, the role of gender socialization in female criminality, and the recognition of structural contradictions in the development of social policies.

The most successful application of conflict theory comes to us from the principles of peacemaking criminology and its call for the resolution of conflict through the development of programs that emphasize repair and reconciliation within the criminal justice system. Criminologists embracing this concept point to the failure of harsh penalties such as imprisonment in reducing crime within society.[66] What then is the alternative?

Crime control strategies have historically and traditionally focused on developing coercive forms of punishment designed to inhibit potential criminal behavior.[67] These have not only failed to reduce crime but have also produced a class of alienated individuals unlikely to ever become integrated into society as productive, law-abiding citizens. An alternative approach to offender rehabilitation is known as restorative justice. What is restorative justice and how does it work?

What is restorative justice?

Restorative justice is an ideological model of justice that brings together the offender, the victim, the community, and the criminal justice system in responding to delinquency and crime.[68] The restorative justice movement began in Canada in 1974, when a court ordered two juveniles who robbed and vandalized 21 homes in Ontario to visit and make a personal apology to each victim, as well as pay for the damages.[69] During the late 1970s and early 1980s the restorative justice philosophy was first embraced in the United States by the juvenile courts, as a method of informally processing first-time, non-violent juvenile offenders.

Since the 1990s, restorative justice practices began to spread throughout the court system as a sentencing alternative designed to allow offenders to repair the harm caused by their criminal acts and provide a forum for bringing equity and justice to all individuals affected by the crime. The restorative justice model is designed to offer offenders a learning experience that both increases their sense of responsibility and makes them more accountable for their acts. It thus makes community reintegration a more practical option than making criminal choices.

Restorative justice is more than just a treatment philosophy or justice initiative; it is a working process that draws on various program guidelines and components.

How does restorative justice work?

Restorative justice is designed to give offenders a second chance at a clean record. The process begins when juvenile and adult offenders convicted of non-violent crimes are referred by the State's Attorney to participate as an alternative to formal court proceedings. Offenders agree to fulfill all requirements of the program, and in exchange for their successful completion, all charges are dismissed.[70]

The restorative justice approach views crime within its social context. Thus, the various program components are designed to identify and challenge the root causes of the criminal behavior in order to break the cycle of deviance. There are three general goals: repairing harm to the victim and the community, encouraging dialog between victims, offenders, and community citizens, and transforming the role of community and government.[71] Table 13.4 provides

Table 13.4 Restorative justice in action

Program goal	Program practice
Repair harm	• **Restitution**: offenders are required to make full monetary compensation to the victim for any loss or damage caused by the criminal act. • **Community Service**: offenders are required to perform a set amount of volunteer hours serving nonprofit organizations within the community where the crime was committed. • **Letter of apology**: offenders are required to write a formal letter of apology to their victims expressing their regret and remorse for the criminal act.
Encourage dialog	• **Victim impact panel**: offenders are required to participate in a face-to-face meeting of various crime victims from the community who explain the struggle and hardship caused by crime. • **Victim empathy course**: offenders are required to complete a course curriculum designed to teach them how their actions affected the lives of their victims and encourage them to respect others and accept responsibility for the consequences of their actions. • **Reparative board**: volunteer members of the community are trained to become citizen participants on a reparative board. The board meets once a month and plays an active role in monitoring the progress of offenders in the program and holding them accountable.
Transform community and government	• **Respect essay**: offenders must prove to reparative board members that they understand the consequences of the crime and recognize the need to become responsible, law-abiding citizens. • **Prison tour**: offenders are often required to participate in a tour of a State Correctional Institution. The Department of Corrections collaborates with the restorative justice program in order to provide offenders with the opportunity to see the potential consequences of criminal choices. • **Alternative dispute resolution**: restorative justice programs collaborate with the courts, social service agencies, and local universities to provide offenders and crime victims with workshops and consultation meetings to mediate conflicts, discuss family issues, and encourage dialog.

Source: Hass, Aida and Corno, Jessica. 2010. Forgiveness, Repair And Healing: An Examination of the Greene County Missouri Restorative Justice Program with Implications for Peacemaking Criminology. *International Journal of Conflict and Reconciliation* Winter 2010.

an overview of the various practices of restorative justice as they pertain to each goal.

Over the past several years jurisdictions across the United States have reported significant benefits of restorative justice programs, including reductions in recidivism and a high rate of programmatic success.[72] The literature paints a picture of moderate to significant success in increasing offender accountability and reintegration into the community, providing victims with the opportunity to participate in the justice process, ensuring the community becomes more engaged in ensuring the welfare of all its members, and reducing recidivism by helping offenders improve their skills and become more responsible citizens.

SUMMARY

How does conflict theory define the social order?

Conflict theory views society as consisting of different groups that have competing goals and interests. This diversity in goals and interests creates conflict within society.

What is the relationship between power, politics, and the economy?

The social, political, and economic structures of society create imbalances between groups whereby some have more wealth and power than others. Those with more wealth and power will use their privileged positions to influence the legal system to control the acts of the less advantaged members of society, who threaten their position.

Does conflict lead to crime?

Radical conflict theory maintains that crime is an outcome of the social and economic contention between different groups within society. Thus, crime is rooted in the conflict created by the unequal distribution of wealth and power, and in social conditions that empower the wealthy to define as criminal those acts that go against their own interests.

Is it possible that the criminal justice system perpetuates human suffering?

Contemporary theories in conflict criminology argue that the criminal justice system and its various components often reinforce the cycle of oppression experienced by both victims and offenders. Instead of contributing to deprivation and conflict, the theories suggest, the criminal justice system should entail unified crime control strategies that emphasize resolution and cooperation.

Why is there a huge gap in crime statistics between men and women?

Some criminologists explain the gap in crime statistics between men and women as a function of gender stratification in the development of criminal roles within crime networks. Others point to the impact of family class structure, either patriarchal or egalitarian, on the gender distribution of delinquency and crime.

Where do contradictions in the social structure come from?

Contradictions within the social structure occur when the goals, rules, and social processes creates situations that produce antagonistic social relations, between political rivals, employers and employees, customers and owners, clients and service providers, corporate executives and stock holders. These contradictions inevitably lead to conflicts between groups struggling against one another at the social, political, and economic levels.

Can radical criminology offer a peaceful solution to crime?

Contemporary radical theories call for an emphasis on social justice and an awareness of the inherent relationship between crime and social conflict. Thus, solutions to crime emphasize the need to repair conflict-ridden situations and relationships. Agents of criminal justice must play a unified and cooperative role in the rehabilitation of alienated individuals and restoration to victims of crime.

CRITICAL THINKING QUESTIONS

1. Suppose you were on a jury trying the case of an individual accused of robbing a bank at gunpoint, although the gun was not loaded. The accused managed to get away with $5,000 before getting caught. He is a Hispanic male in his mid-20s who has been struggling to find a job during economically challenging times. He has no prior criminal record, except for some traffic violations and driving with a suspended license. How would your knowledge of the conflict perspective influence your perception of this case?

2. Research studies show that education within prisons is a strong correlate of successful reintegration into society upon release. Why do you think society is so opposed to providing offenders in prison with adequate access to educational programming, especially at the post-secondary level? How would radical criminology guide our understanding of this issue and shed some light on a possible resolution?

3. Which argument is more convincing, that men commit more crime than women because of biological differences in temperament, or that men commit more crime than women because of differences in the gender roles they play in society? What social changes do you think would narrow the gender gap in crime statistics?

4. Suppose your home was vandalized by two reckless youth claiming to be "just having fun." They spray-painted your walls, ruined several of your

shrubs, and broke a couple of windows. Which would you rather see: (1) the two youths go to juvenile detention for 6 months and pay a fine; or (2) they write you a formal letter of apology, do 100 hours of community service cleaning up parks in your neighborhood, pay you for all the damage they did to your property, and attend a victim impact panel where you can tell them in person how their actions affected you? Which alternative is more popular in our society? Why do you think this is the case? How can criminology address this issue and shed some light on how to change society's view?

E-RESOURCES

For a critical examination of the criminal justice system visit the Critical Criminology Division of the American Society of Criminology website at http://www.critcrim.org/.

Learn more about the policy implications of left realist criminology at http://www.historylearningsite.co.uk/sociology/crime-and-deviance/left-realism-and-crime/.

You can read more about gender inequality and stratification by visiting the Cornell University Center for the Study of Inequality website at http://inequality.cornell.edu/.

Additional information about the restorative justice model and peacemaking criminology can be found at http://www.cehd.umn.edu/ssw/rjp/.

NOTES

1 Fantz, Ashley, Yan, Holly, and Shoichet, Catherine E. 2015. Texas Pool Party Chaos: Out of Control Police Officer Resigns. *CNN, June 9*. Retrieved from http://www.cnn.com/2015/06/09/us/mckinney-texas-pool-party-video/.

2 Stinson, Philip M. 2015. Police Crime: The Criminal Behavior of Sworn Law Enforcement Officers. *Sociology Compass* 9(1): 1–13.

3 Chandler, D. L. Rodney King Riots in Los Angeles Began on This Day in 1992. *NewsOne*. Retrieved from http://newsone.com/2423835/rodney-king-riots-2/.

4 Gray, Madison. 2009. The L.A. Riots: 15 Years After Rodney King. *Time, July 14.* Retrieved from http://www.time.com/time/specials/2007/la_riot/article/0,28804,1614117_1614084_1614831,00.html.

5 Gooding-Williams, R. 2013. *Reading Rodney King/Reading Urban Uprising*. Abingdon: Routledge.

6 Cannon, Lou. 1999. *Official Negligence: How Rodney King and the Riots Changed Los Angeles and the LAPD*. New York: Basic Books.

7 Weitzer, Ronald and Tuch, Steven. 2002. Perceptions of Racial Profiling: Race, Class and Personal Experience. *Criminology* 40: 435–456.

8 Hays, Zachary R. 2011. *Police Use of Excessive Force in Disorganized Neighborhoods: A Social Disorganization Perspective*. El Paso: LFB Scholarly Publishers.

9 Weitzer, Ron. 2015. American Policing Under Fire: Misconduct and Reform. *Social Science and Public Policy* 52(5): 475–480. Sun, I., Payne, B. and Wu, Y. 2008. The

Impact of Situational Factors, Officer's Characteristics, and Neighborhood Context on Police Behavior: A Multilevel Analysis. *Journal of Criminal Justice,* 36(1).

10   Chambliss, William J. and Seidman, Robert. 1971. *Law, Order and Power.* Reading, MA: Addison-Wesley.

11   Chambliss, William J. 1988. *Exploring Criminology.* New York: Macmillan.

12   Ibid.

13   Deflam, Mathieu. 2015. Deviance and Social Control. In Erich Goode (ed.), *The Handbook of Deviance.* Hoboken, NJ: Wiley and Sons.

14   Vold, George. 1958. *Theoretical Criminology.* New York: Oxford University Press.

15   Ibid., p. 204.

16   Turk, Austin. 1969. *Criminality and the Legal Order.* New York: Rand McNally, p. xii.

17   Sellin, Thorsten. 1938. *Culture, Conflict and Crime.* New York: Social Science Research Council.

18   Russell, Stuart. 2002. The Continuing Relevance of Marxism to Critical Criminology. *Critical Criminology* 11: 113–135.

19   Blundenden, Andy. 2004. *Marx/Engels Selected Works,* Volume One. Moscow: Progress Publishers.

20   Marx, Karl. 1887/2008. *Capital (Das Kapital)* Misbach Enterprises.

21   Tucker, Robert C. 1978. *The Marx-Engels Reader,* 2nd ed. New York: W.W. Norton & Company.

22   Marx, Karl and Engels, Friedrich. 1887/1993. Crime and Primitive Accumulation. In David F. Greenberg, (ed.), *Crime and Capitalism: Readings in Marxist Criminology.* Philadelphia: Temple University Press.

23   Engels, Friedrich. 1887/1993. The Demoralization of the English Working Class. In David F. Greenberg, (ed.), *Crime and Capitalism: Readings in Marxist Criminology.* Philadelphia: Temple University Press.

24   Bonger, Willem. 1916. *Criminality and Economic Conditions.* Boston: Little, Brown.

25   Moxon, D. 2014. *The Encyclopedia of Theoretical Criminology.* Hoboken, NJ: John Wiley & Sons.

26   Ibid., see 22.

27   Lynch, Michael J. and Michalowski, Raymond. 2006. *Primer in Radical Criminology: Critical Perspectives on Crime, Power and Identity,* 4th ed. Criminal Justice Press.

28   Chambliss, William J. 1993. On Lawmaking. In William J. Chambill and Marjorie Sue Zats (eds.), *Making Law: The State, the Law and Structural Contradictions.* Indiana University Press.

29   Chambliss, William J. and Seidman, Robert T. 1971. *Law, Order and Power.* Reading, MA: Addison-Wesley.

30   Chambliss, William J. 1978. Toward a Political Economy of Crime. In Charles Reasons and Robert Rich, (eds.), *The Sociology of Law.* Toronto: Butterworth.

31   Chambliss, William J. 1964. A Sociological Analysis of the Law of Vagrancy. *Social Problems* 12: 67–77.

32   Chambliss, William J. 2001. *Power, Politics and Crime.* United Kingdom: Westview Press.

33   Reiman, Jeffrey and Leighton, Paul. 2016. *The Rich Get Richer and the Poor Get Prison,* 10th ed. London and New York: Routledge.

34   Banks, C. 2016. *Criminal Justice Ethics: Theory and Practice.* Thousand Oaks, CA: SAGE.

35   Young, Jock. 1986. The Failure of Criminology: The Need for a Radical Realism. In Roger Matthews, and JockYoung, (eds.), *Confronting Crime.* Beverly Hills, CA: SAGE.

36   Currie, E. 2010. Plain Left Realism: an Appreciation, and Some Thoughts for the Future. In *Crime, Law, and Social Change.* New York: Springer.

37 Hughes, G. and Edwards, A. 2013. *Crime Control and Community*. New York: Routledge.

38 Pepinsky, Harold and Quinney, Richard. 1991. *Criminology as Peacemaking*. Bloomington: Indiana University Press.

39 Gabbidon, S. 2015. *Criminological Perspectives on Race and Crime*. New York: Routledge.

40 Mukherjee, S. and Scutt, J. 2015. *Women and Crime*. London: Routledge.

41 Kendall, D. 2012. *Sociology in Our Times*. Boston, MA: Cengage Learning.

42 Messerschmidt, James W. 1986. *Capitalism, Patriarchy, and Crime: Toward a Socialist Feminist Criminology*. Totowa, JJ: Rowman and Littlefield.

43 Radical Women. 2001. The Radical Women Manifesto: Socialist Feminist Theory, Program Organization and Organizational Structure. Seattle, WA: Red Letter Press.

44 Hondagneu-Sotelo, P., Zinn, M., Messner, M. and Denissen, A. 2015. *Gender Through the Prism of Difference*. Oxford, United Kingdom: Oxford University Press.

45 Roberts, D. 2014. The Social and Moral Cost of Mass Incarceration in African American Communities. *Stanford Law Review* 56 (5).

46 Adler, Freda. 1975. *Sisters in Crime: The Rise of the New Female Criminal*. New York: McGraw-Hill.

47 Kruttschnitt, C. 2013. Gender and Crime. *Annual Review of Sociology* 39.

48 Schwendinger, Julia R. and Schwendinger, Herman. 1983. *Rape and Inequality*. Newbury Park, CA: SAGE.

49 Khan, A. 2015. A Chronicle of the Global Movement to Combat Violence against Women: The Role of the Second-Wave Feminist Movement and the United Nations: The Perspective of Bangladesh. *Journal of International Women's Studies,* 16(2). Bridgewater, MA: Bridgewater State University.

50 Rose, S. 2014. Gender Violence: The Problem. *Challenging Global Gender Violence: The Global Clothesline Project*. New York: Palgrave Macmillan.

51 Ibid., see 37.

52 Ogloff, J., Cutajar, M., Mann, E., Mullen, P., Wei, F., Hassan, H. and Yih, T. 2012. Child Sexual Abuse and Subsequent Offending and Victimization: A 45-Year Follow-up Study. *Trends and Issues in Crime and Criminal Justice* 440.

53 Garcia, Crystal A. and Lane, Jodi. 2010. *Looking in the Rearview Mirror: What Incarcerated Women Think . . . Feminist Criminology* 5(3): 227–243.

54 Ibid., see 44.

55 Simon, Rita J. 1975. *Women and Crime*. Lexington, MA: Lexington Books.

56 Hsieh, M. and Schwartz, J. 2016. Female Violence and Gender Gap Trends in Taiwan: Offender-Behavioral Changes or Net-Widening Enforcement Explanations? *Feminist Criminology*.

57 Miller, Jody and Decker, Scott H. 2001. Young Women and Gang Violence: Gender, Street Offending, and Violent Victimization in Gangs. *Justice Quarterly* 18: 115–140.

58 Hagan, John. 1989. *Structural Criminology*. New Brunswick, NJ: Rutgers University Press.

59 Blackwell, B. and Kane, K. 2015. Power-Control Theory. In *Encyclopedia of Crime and Punishment*. New York: John Wiley & Sons.

60 Matos, R. 2015. Trajectories and Identity of Young Women in Prison: An Empirical Analysis of Gender, Youth, Crime and Delinquency. In Robert Carneiro (ed.), *Youth, Offense and Well-Being*. Universidade Católica Portuguesa, pp. 177–193.

61 Connell, R. 2014. *Gender and Power: Society, the Person and Sexual Politics*. New York, NY: John Wiley & Sons.

62 Klockers, Carl B. 1979. The Contemporary Crises of Marxist Criminology. *Criminology* 16: 477–515.

63 Taylor, I., Walton, P. and Young, J. 2013. *Critical Criminology*. Abingdon, England: Routledge.

64   Steffensmeier, D, Schwartz, J. and Roche, M. 2013. Gender and Twenty-First-century Corporate Crime: Female Involvement and the Gender Gap in Enron-era Corporate Frauds. *American Sociological Review* 78(3).

65   Chesney-Lind, M. and Pasko, L. 2013. *The Female Offender: Girls, Women, and Crime.* Thousand Oaks, CA: SAGE.

66   Taylor, R. 2011. Why Has Prison Emerged as a Prominent Form of Punishment for Most Crime and what are its Functions in Relation to Wider Society? *Internet Journal of Criminology,* online. Retrieved from http://www.internetjournalofcriminology.com/ Taylor_Prison_and_its_Functions_IJC_August_2011.pdf.

67   Taylor, Mark Lewis. 2001. *The Executed God: The Way of the Cross in Lockdown America.* Minneapolis, MN: Fortress Press.

68   Van Ness, D. and Strong, K. 2013. *Restoring Justice: An Introduction to Restorative Justice.* Abingdon, England: Routledge.

69   Johnstone, G. 2013. *Restorative Justice: Ideas, Values, Debates.* Abingdon, England: Routledge.

70   Wilson, H. and Hoge, R. 2013. The Effect of Youth Diversion Programs on Recidivism. *Journal of Criminal Justice and Behavior* 40(5): 497–518.

71   Wachtel, Ted. 2016. Defining Restorative Justice. *International Institute of Restorative Justice.* Retrieved from http://www.iirp.edu/what-is-restorative-practices.php.

72   Bazemore, Gordon and Shiff, Mara. 2015. *Restorative Community Justice: Restoring Harm and Transforming Communities.* London and New York: Routledge.

Typologies of criminal behavior

PART IV

CHAPTER OUTLINE

Interpersonal crimes of violence

In this chapter we will explore the following questions

- What is criminal homicide?
- Why do people kill?
- What constitutes an assault?
- Does assault occur more often between strangers or acquaintances?
- Is rape a sexual act?
- Why is robbery a violent crime?
- What is the motive behind stealing by force?
- What are hate crimes?

KEY TERMS

homicide

murder

malice
aforethought

criminal
homicide

first-degree
murder

premeditation

second-degree
murder

manslaughter

voluntary or
nonnegligent
manslaughter

involuntary or
negligent
manslaughter

primary
homicides

expressive
homicide

non-primary
homicide

instrumental
homicide

serial murder

mass murder

assault

battery

Who is more likely to hurt us, a stranger, a coworker, a neighbor, a friend, or an intimate partner? Michael DeMaio, age 55, lived with his wife, Dianne DeMaio, a mother of three children, in an affluent neighborhood in Greenwich, Connecticut. On September 10, 2013, at around six in the evening, police were dispatched to their $7.3 million mansion. Police arriving at the scene found Dianne DeMaio in an upstairs closet, lying on the floor motionless in a pool of blood, with significant injuries to her head. Her mother was in the house and told officers that Michael DeMaio was a monster and that he had attacked her. Michael DeMaio told police that he had gotten into an argument with her when he viciously beat her with a baseball bat in the head, claiming he was really angry and just "lost it." Dianne DeMaio was transported to the hospital in critical condition, with possible permanent brain damage due to her injuries. Her husband was charged with attempted murder and first degree assault.[1]

Research on violence against women has proliferated in the past 20 years. The U.S. Department of Justice estimates approximately 1.3 million women and 835,000 men are physically assaulted each year by an intimate partner, and intimate partner homicides make up 40 to 50 percent of all murders of women in the United States.[2] The National Institute of Justice reports that over 60 percent of women who report being raped, physically assaulted, and/or stalked were victimized by a current or former spouse, cohabiting partner, boyfriend, or date.[3]

Image 14.1
What patterns of interaction trigger a violent attack?

iStock/John Gomez

aggravated assault

simple assault

stalking

domestic violence

intimate partner violence

tension building phase

acting out phase

honeymoon phase

child maltreatment

physical abuse

neglect

sexual abuse

emotional abuse

forcible rape

attempted rape

statutory rape

sexual assault

acquaintance rape

What social dynamics place women at greater risk of being victimized by someone with whom they are so closely connected? A study by researchers at the University Illinois found exposure to domestic violence during childhood increased the risk of victimization of both sexual assault and domestic violence. Domestic violence victimization was also significantly related to having increased education and employment skills, more children, and clinical depression.[4] A team of researchers at the National Institute of Justice examined the risk factors associated with intimate partner violence and found that almost half of women killed by an intimate partner did not recognize the danger they were facing in the abusive relationship.[5] The implications are that we need to do more research to identify demographic, social, and environmental variables associated with intimate partner violence, and that prevention strategies should focus on teaching women how to protect themselves and identify risk factors in an abusive relationship.

Violence can take many forms and result in varying causes and consequences ranging from financial loss to emotional and physical injury and death. Michael DeMaio's violent attack on his wife is a form of assault that takes place in a domestic or intimate setting. This chapter focuses on different types of interpersonal violent crimes including homicide, rape, robbery, assault, and hate crime. We will describe and explain these behaviors according to their legal definitions, the factors that motivate these crimes, aspects of the situation that led to them, and characteristics of the victim and the offender. In chapters to come, we will examine other forms of violent crimes such as genocide, ethnic cleansing, terrorism, corporate crimes of violence and state organized crimes of violence. While these categories of crime result in destruction, harm, and death, they are not considered forms of interpersonal violence. For now, we turn to the first category of interpersonal violence, homicide.

HOMICIDE

Image 14.2
Outbursts of violence such as this June 2015 shooting at a South Carolina Church are often spontaneous actions that take the lives of several victims.

Stephen B. Morton/AP/Press Association Images

On June 17, 2015, 21-year-old Dylann Roof opened fire on worshippers during a prayer service at Emanuel African Methodist Episcopal Church, killing nine people and injuring others. After a massive manhunt for the shooter, Roof was captured the next morning. Roof confessed to the murders and claimed later that he was trying to initiate a race war. Several days after the shooting, investigators traced a website called *The Last Rhodesian* to Roof. The website contained photos of Roof displaying symbols of white supremacy and a manifesto claiming his hatred of African Americans and other groups. Roof was charged with 33 federal counts, including murder, hate crimes, and other civil rights violations.[6] Anger, hostility, hatred, and conflict could all have been variables that led up to this criminal event. What other factors are at work in the crime of homicide? What makes some homicides distinct from others? Let us turn now to a closer examination of this crime category by defining homicide.

Defining homicide

Homicide is the willful killing of one human being by another. It is not always a criminal offense; homicide committed in self-defense is often deemed justifiable and therefore legal. **Murder** is an *unlawful* form of homicide, the intentional killing of one human being by another without legal justification or excuse. A murder is committed with **malice aforethought**, a depraved state of mind that shows a willful and intentional disregard for human life. Thus, criminal justice officials use the term **criminal homicide** to describe the act of murder. Murder is the most serious of all violent crimes and the only crime punishable (in some states) by death.

rape shield laws

date rape

spousal-marital rape

gang rape

same-sex rape

power rape

anger rape

sadistic rape

power-assertive rapist

power-reassurance rapist

anger-retaliatory rapist

anger-excitation rapist

lust rapists

righteous rapists

peer rapists

fantasy rapists
control and anger
supremacy rapists
robbery
institutional
   robbery
personal robbery
hate crimes

The law categorizes the severity of murder by looking at the degree of motive or intent. **First-degree murder** is the unlawful killing of a human being by another with malice aforethought *and* **premeditation**—planning, plotting, and deliberating before committing the act. Premeditation can be proven by the simple passage of time, or anything else that demonstrates the individual had the opportunity to think about the intent to kill and to retreat from those thoughts. The following case illustrates some of these elements of first-degree murder.

One night while his wife Denise Amber Lee was tied up in the back seat of his Camaro, Michael Lee King borrowed a shovel, a flashlight, and a gas can from his cousin Harold Muxlow. That same evening, while driving, Janet Kowalski stopped at a light and noticed a car pull up next to her. The passenger-side window was slightly down and Kowalski heard screaming and a woman's hand "slapping the left passenger window like she was trying to get out." Kowalski called 911 from her car and informed the police of what she had seen. Later that evening, police entered King's home to find a roll of duct tape on the kitchen counter as well as a pillow and blanket on the floor of the bedroom, along with balled-up duct tape with long strands of light brown hair. After a manhunt that included canine teams, helicopters, and dozens of officers, King was arrested near Interstate 75. The body of Denise Amber Lee was found buried off the interstate, and her husband was charged with abduction and premeditated murder. Clearly, this was a crime he had thought about and planned, making sure he had what he needed earlier that day.[7]

Although it may sometimes be difficult to prove premeditation, the distinct features of second-degree murder make it easier to understand what premeditation means. **Second-degree murder** is the unlawful killing of a human being with malice aforethought, but *not* with premeditation. It is regarded as a "crime of passion," in which no time for deliberation elapses between the thought to kill and the killing itself. Second-degree murder implies a degree of impulsiveness or provocation. This was the case in the conviction of Tari Ramirez, who stabbed his girlfriend Claire Tempongko several times in front of her two children. Jurors agreed with defense attorneys that Ramirez acted on the spur of the moment, enraged after Tempongko told him she had aborted their unborn baby.[8]

The third category of murder, **manslaughter**, is criminal homicide that occurs without malice aforethought *or* premeditation. There are two types of manslaughter: voluntary and involuntary. **Voluntary manslaughter** is an unjustified killing that arises out of an intense conflict that provoked violence. Voluntary manslaughter can also occur during the commission of a felony. For example, a burglar sneaks into a building with the intent to steal. Startled by a security guard, he begins to run, knocking the guard down a flight of stairs and killing him. Without the presence of a deadly weapon that would have suggested he had intent to kill, the burglar will most likely be charged with voluntary manslaughter.

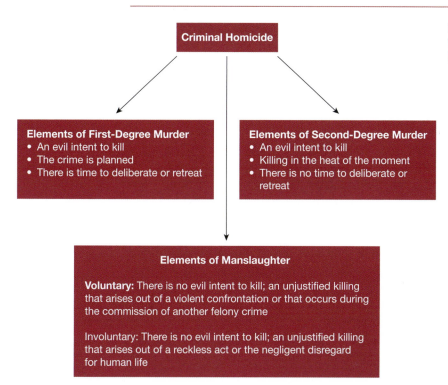

Figure 14.1
Types of criminal homicide

Criminal Homicide

Elements of First-Degree Murder
- An evil intent to kill
- The crime is planned
- There is time to deliberate or retreat

Elements of Second-Degree Murder
- An evil intent to kill
- Killing in the heat of the moment
- There is no time to deliberate or retreat

Elements of Manslaughter

Voluntary: There is no evil intent to kill; an unjustified killing that arises out of a violent confrontation or that occurs during the commission of another felony crime

Involuntary: There is no evil intent to kill; an unjustified killing that arises out of a reckless act or the negligent disregard for human life

Involuntary or negligent manslaughter is the unlawful killing of another person by a person's own negligent disregard of his harmful acts. This category includes homicides that occur during non-felony violations, making it distinct from voluntary manslaughter. For example, a driver who is speeding through a neighborhood where children are playing and causes a fatal accident can be charged with involuntary manslaughter. Figure 14.1 provides a summary of the categories of criminal homicide.

Understanding homicide

The many legal categories of criminal homicide are a testament to the complex relationships we recognize between cause, motive, and situation in this form of violent behavior. Research has also focused on understanding four distinct *patterns* of homicide: (1) chronic offending and the subculture of violence; (2) situational homicide; (3) serial killing; and (4) mass murder. We start by examining homicide within the context of the subculture of violence.

Chronic offending and the subculture of violence

Subcultures are groups of people who share norms, values, and beliefs that differ significantly from those of the dominant culture. In the United States the Amish, whose values forbid the use of modern technology like electricity, automobiles, and farm machinery, are a subculture, although not a criminal one. Members of fundamentalist sects of the Church of Latter Day Saints who continue to practice polygamy are another, but unlike the Amish, they embrace norms that are in violation of the law.

Subcultures exist to manage and cope with problems and situations that are not common to mainstream society. Sociologists Marvin Wolfgang and Franco Ferracuti suggest that problems unique to lower-class urban youth help create a subculture of gangs, delinquency, and violence. Among other responses, this subculture demands that its members make a violent response to social situations like disputes or damage to their reputation.[9] A confrontation between two gangs in Texas illustrates the dynamic of subcultural violence. The 2015 deadly encounter between two rival motorcycle gangs that took place at a Waco, Texas restaurant was a result of growing suspicion and animosity between the Bandidos and the Cossacks. This incident of deadly violence which resulted in nine deaths and numerous injuries is typical of conflict resolution in a gang subculture, which emphasizes toughness, aggression, and brutality.[10]

Classical sociological research on urban gangs suggests a pattern of subculture norms that help explain the persistence of violence in urban areas. Researcher Albert Cohen found gang delinquency was one way that lower-class youth responded to shared problems associated with being poor and being constantly judged (in school, for example) by white middle-class standards that contradicted their experiences and opportunities.[11]

In an extensive participant-observation study of low-income black Philadelphia neighborhoods, Elijah Anderson discovered the dominant culture to which most residents belonged was what he called a culture of "decent people:" adults and youth alike embraced the dominant non-violent, law-abiding culture of U.S. society. But alongside the "decent people" culture there existed a subculture of "the street." Street families:

> often show a lack of consideration for other people and have a rather superficial sense of family and community . . . the seeming intractability of their situation, caused in large part by the lack of well-paying jobs and the persistence of racial discrimination, has engendered deep-seated resentment and anger in many of the poorest blacks, especially young people.[12]

The "code of the street" is the result of this resentment and anger, and of alienation from the institutions of the larger society, especially the police. In poor urban neighborhoods the police are seen as oppressors representing the interests and values of white society. Equally important, residents feel they cannot depend on police to settle disputes or come to the aid of victims of violence. Individuals must therefore protect themselves by demanding respect and, if offended, seeking vengeance.

The contributions of subculture of violence and other theories help us understand why homicide becomes a way of life in certain neighborhoods, for certain people, and in certain situations, guiding the direction of policy development strategies (see Box 14.1).

Violent environments, violent role models, and violent attitudes and belief systems are the breeding ground for a violent mode of response. Whether the cause is defending yourself, avenging a drug deal gone bad, defending someone's honor, getting respect, settling an argument, or obtaining an expensive pair of shoes, violence is the answer.[13] Criminologists have identified four stages in the development of chronic violent offending (see Table 14.1). The first stage, *brutalization*, describes the cumulative and prolonged exposure to violence as a means of communication and conflict resolutions. As the individual progresses to the stages of *belligerency, violent performance* and *violent personality,* the predominant means by which to achieve one's goals becomes the exertion of force upon others, with violent acts becoming purposeful attempts to injure

BOX 14.1: CONNECTING THEORY TO PRACTICE

Public policy and the subculture of violence

Criminological studies have shown that higher rates of interpersonal violence are reported among certain ethnic and racial groups, and within certain geographic locations such as the inner city and the south and west. The subculture of violence theory of criminal behavior posits that some individuals adhere to the values, norms, and attitudes of a street subculture and therefore turn to violence, assault, and homicide as a means of resolving conflicts. The public policy implications for intervention and prevention are that we need to change the social values of high-risk populations to counter the negative effects of their prevailing street subculture. Programs of the U.S. Department of Justice's Office of Juvenile Justice and Delinquency Prevention (OJJDP) attempt to do just that.

OJJDP programs target youth most at risk for truancy, gang activity, alcohol and drug abuse, and involvement in the criminal justice system, providing education and literacy resources, substance abuse counseling, housing, and preparation for the workforce. Another OJJDP policy initiative focuses on reducing youth gangs in targeted neighborhoods, suppressing gang crime and violence, and reintegrating known gang members into non-gang lifestyles. The model uses a five-pronged approach, emphasizing the following variables:

- **Primary prevention** targets the entire population in high-crime, high-risk communities. The key component is a one-stop resource center for prenatal and infant care, after-school activities, truancy and dropout prevention, and job programs.
- **Secondary prevention** identifies young children ages 7–14 at high risk and, drawing on the resources of schools, community-based organizations, and faith-based groups, intervenes with appropriate services before early problem behaviors turn into serious delinquency and gang involvement.
- **Intervention** targets active gang members, close associates, families, and gang members returning from confinement with aggressive outreach and recruitment activity to help youth make positive choices.

- **Suppression** focuses on identifying the most dangerous and influential gang members and removing them from the community.
- **Reentry** targets serious offenders returning to the community after confinement and provides appropriate services and monitoring. Of particular interest are "displaced" gang members who may attempt to reassert their former roles.

These programs have shown positive results in reducing crime and gang-related activities and in making significant improvements in the physical appearance of neighborhoods and public housing.

Sources

Harries, Kieth D. 1997. *Serious Violence: Patterns of Homicide and Assault in America.* Springfield, IL: Charles C. Thomas Publishers.

Rosenfeld, Richard. 2010. *Understanding Homicide and Aggravated Assault.* Presentation at the Conference on the Causes and Responses to Violence, Arizona State University. Retrieved from https://www.researchgate.net/publication/255576102_Understanding_Homicide_and_Aggravated_Assault.

U.S. Department of Justice, Office of Juvenile Justice and Delinquency Prevention. 2015. *OJJDP How OJJDP Is Promoting Youth Justice and Safety.* Retrieved from http://www.ojjdp.gov/newsletter/249506/index.html.

whoever gets in the way, ultimately conferring a sense of power upon the individual perpetrator.

While the escalation of violence is understandable in the context of these stages, it is far less clear why homicide sometimes occurs without them. Let's take a look now at the types of homicide that arise out of a specific type of interaction or situation.

Situational homicide

As we noted in chapter 3, most homicides arise from interpersonal conflicts or hostilities between an offender and victim who are acquaintances, relatives,

Table 14.1 Stages of chronic offending

Stage	Description
Brutalization	Offenders are forced at an early age to submit to authority through coercion; they are taught by others to resort to violence to achieve their goals and are often witness to the brutalization of others
Belligerency	Offenders internalize the idea that violence is the only means to get what they want and are thus convinced it is an acceptable response in dealing with others
Violent performance	Offenders commit violent acts upon individuals in order to seriously injure the victim
Violent personality	The use of violence is reinforced as the offender comes to be defined by others as a violent person, conferring upon him or her a sense of power

Source: Athens, Lonnie H. 1989. *The Creation of Dangerous Violent Criminals.* New York: Routledge.

or friends. Thus, we can best understand some patterns of homicide within the situation, or context, of the victim-offender relationship. Dwayne Smith and Robert Nash distinguished between two classifications of homicide: primary and non-primary.[14] **Primary or expressive homicides** are the most common and occur between family members, friends, and acquaintances. They are called expressive, because they usually spring from some type of interpersonal conflict or dispute based on jealousy, hatred, anger, rage, or frustration. Love triangles, financial disagreements, and domestic disputes are situational contexts within which expressive homicide often takes place.[15]

Non-primary or instrumental homicides occur during the course of another crime, or in the pursuit of some other valued goal. They are less common, and usually the victims and offenders have no prior relationship—circumstance brings them together, and killing is not the offender's primary motive. An incident that begins as a robbery but in which the victim presents a great deal of resistance may turn deadly when the offender panics, for example. These types of homicide are called instrumental, because the violence is a means to an end such as obtaining money, eluding the police, eliminating a witness, or getting away from a botched rape.[16]

Studies have examined the relationship between homicide rates and the presence of firearms. Researchers note that disputes often escalate into violence, and the availability of a gun often influences whether the outcome is deadly.[17] Cities, states, and regions where there are more guns have elevated rates of homicide, especially firearm homicide.[18] Other countries report similar trends. Box 14.2 discusses international trends in homicide rates and firearm ownership.

Serial murder

Popular U.S. culture has a fascination with notorious serial killers. Entertainment media, books, and documentaries portray the dark shadows of a crime that brings shock, fear, and confusion to neighborhoods and police departments across the country. **Serial murder** is the killing of several individuals in at least three separate events. The most common stereotype of a serial murderer is of a shady, low-life, bloodthirsty individual. However, many have been well-educated, charismatic, and attractive people like Ted Bundy, who in the 1970s killed what may have been dozens of young women across the United States. While their true profile runs the gamut of physical, social, and psychological

Image 14.3 *Ted Bundy is a notorious U.S. serial killer who confessed to the murder of 30 women between 1974 and 1978. He graduated in 1972 with a degree in psychology from Washington University. By all accounts, Bundy was a sweet-talking, charming, handsome young man who had been accepted to law school, not the person we typically think of when we hear the term serial killer.*

AP/Press Association Images

BOX 14.2: CRIME IN GLOBAL PERSPECTIVE

Around the world ... Trends in homicide rates and gun ownership

According to statistics compiled by federal law enforcement agencies such as the ATF (Bureau of Alcohol, Tobacco, and Firearms), there are more guns in the United States than there are people, with gun manufacturers nearly doubling their production from 5.6 million guns in 2009 to 10.9 million guns in 2013, with a 112.6 per capita rate of gun ownership in 2014.

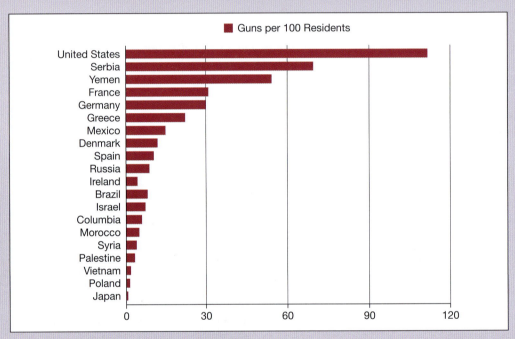

Box 14.2 Figure 1 *Gun ownership around the world*

   While the United States has the highest per capita rate of gun ownership in the world, countries such as Australia, Canada, and Japan have enacted strict gun control laws banning most private firearm ownership. In Great Britain, when sixteen children were killed by a gunman who opened fire at Dunblane Primary School in 1996, parents and outraged citizens called upon Parliament to radically reform gun laws. Within months, private gun ownership had been basically outlawed. What is the relationship between enacting laws restricting firearm manufacture and ownership, and the prevalence of firearm deaths? Figure 2 charts the number of firearm deaths per 100,000 people against the percentage of households in each country in which guns are privately owned.

   From this graph, we see that the data presented would indicate that from a global perspective, gun ownership equals fewer homicides. However, a closer examination reveals that the data presented does not take into account the fact that cross-country data can often be misleading in its presentation of facts. For example, what if in fact, countries with

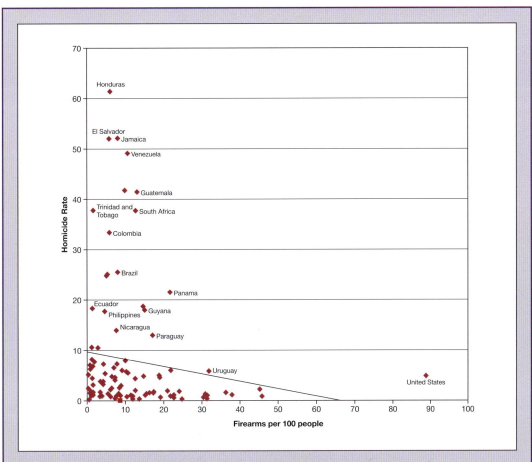

Box 14.2 Figure 2 *Gun ownership and homicide rates for countries covered by the Small Arms Survey*
Scott J. Small Arms Survey, 2012.

higher homicide rates are the ones that frequently adopt stringent gun control laws? Moreover, perhaps gun control actually lowers homicide rates, but not by enough to reduce rates to the same levels predominant in the majority of countries that do not have the same laws; this would then falsely appear that stricter gun control laws resulted in higher rates of homicide.

In his 2015 address to the nation, President Obama said: "We as a country will have to reckon with the fact that this type of mass violence does not happen in other advanced countries. It doesn't happen in other places with this kind of frequency." Later in 2016 during an emotional plea to support gun control legislation to curb violence and mass shootings by expanding the background check system, Obama urged, "We know we can't stop every act of violence, every act of evil in the world. But maybe we could try to stop one act of evil, one act of violence."

Despite many mass shootings in the United States in the past several years, debate rages between those for and against gun control laws. Many people feel private gun ownership is protected by the 2nd Amendment to the U.S. Constitution and that it is the criminals who illegally own guns who perpetrate gun violence. They say social and cultural factors other than gun ownership influence violent crime rates in other countries.

Meanwhile, according to the *Center for Disease Control*, the rate of death by firearm in the United States is more than eight times higher than in comparable developed nations. Other studies have shown that people living in houses containing privately held firearms are more susceptible to violence, particularly violence involving guns. Based on all the evidence, private ownership of firearms does at the very least seem to have a direct relationship with homicide rates. Thus, the debate continues, and those who support gun control laws call for massive gun law reform across the United States.

Sources

Bradner, Eric and Krieg, Gregory. 2016. Emotional Obama calls for 'sense of urgency' to fight gun violence. *CNN*, Jan. 5. Retrieved from http://www.cnn.com/2016/01/05/politics/obama-executive-action-gun-control/index.html.

Centers for Disease Control and Prevention. 2016. Retrieved from http://www.cdc.gov/index.htm.

Crime Prevention Research Center. 2015. Comparing Death Rates From Mass Public Shootings And Mass Public Violence In The Us And Europe. Retrieved from http://crimeresearch.org/2015/06/comparing-death-rates-from-mass-public-shootings-in-the-us-and-europe/.

Ingraham, Christopher. 2015. There are Now More Guns Than People in the United States. *The Washington Post*, Oct. 5. Retrieved from https://www.washingtonpost.com/news/wonk/wp/2015/10/05/guns-in-the-united-states-one-for-every-man-woman-and-child-and-then-some/

Small Arms Survey. 2015. Retrieved from http://www.smallarmssurvey.org/publications/by-type/yearbook/small-arms-survey-2015.html.

traits, all serial killers are particularly adept at leading a double life, putting up a front of normalcy that shields them from suspicion and makes them even more difficult to apprehend.[19]

The popular image of serial murder is riddled with misconceptions about both the crime and the offender. The idea that serial killers are psychotic or anti-social, that they are an imminent threat, and that they are somehow lashing out at individuals in a "cry for help," all run counter to what we know. Researchers have identified various myths surrounding the crime of serial murder and their perceptions of serial killers.[20] The following statements dispel some of these myths:

- Serial murder is not occurring at epidemic proportions.
- Serial killers do not have a distinct appearance.
- In most cases, serial killers are sane; they know the difference between right and wrong.
- Serial killers are generally not sociopaths incapable of abiding by the norms of society.
- Serial killers are not primarily motivated by pornography.
- Traumatic childhoods are not at the root of most serial killers' problems.
- Identifying serial killers before they strike is not always a straightforward task.
- Most serial killers are not sexual sadists.

- Victim selection is not always based on family resemblance.
- While serial killers thrive on the attention they get and on the cat-and-mouse chase with law enforcement, they do not want to be apprehended.

In reality, serial killers can be anyone: young or old, male or female, of diverse ethnic background, operating alone or with a partner, from any walk of life. Researchers have developed typologies of serial murderers based on their pattern of offending and motive.[21] Criminologists recognize that differences exist within each category of serial murder. Nevertheless, they find a general similarity in the repetitive crime patterns of serial killers with regard to the types of victims selected, the motivation for the crime and the method of carrying out the murder.[22] Table 14.2 provides a summary of the different categories of serial homicide, with specific examples of each type.

Despite making up a very small proportion of the overall homicide statistics, serial murders receive an ordinate amount of attention in the media. We turn now to another pattern of homicide that is also fairly uncommon, mass murder.

Table 14.2 Four types of serial killers based on motive

Motive	Example
Visionary/missionary serial killer: feels compelled to kill based on hearing voices or having visions, or is on a "mission" to rid the world of evil	Joseph Kallinger (who died in 1996) constantly heard voices from a floating head that followed him around and stated that God told him to kill young boys; he was arrested and sentenced to 40 years in jail for robbery plus a life sentence for the murder of Maria Fasching. In jail Joe had constantly expressed his desire to kill every person on Earth and often told people he would become God after he died.
Comfort serial killer: motivated by financial or material gain; the killing is secondary to the primary motive of personal gain	Dorothea Puente, a sweet-looking elderly lady, was sentenced to life in prison without the possibility of parole in 1993 at the age of 64. Puente was convicted of the murders of three of the tenants who lived in her Sacramento home. She took in elderly and disabled boarders, then killed them and buried them in her back yard to collect their government checks to buy luxuries.
Thrill-motivated serial killer **Hedonistic**: motivated by excitement and pleasure derived from inflicting pain upon the victim.	On February 25, 2005 Dennis Rader (also discussed in chapter 3) was arrested and charged with killing 10 people in Sedgwick County, Kansas. Known as the notorious BTK killer; which stands for Bind, Torture, and Kill, Radar described what occurred when he killed/attempted to kill each of his victims. He told the judge he committed these murders because he wanted to satisfy sexual fantasies.
Power: seeks to exercise authority, often playing cat-and-mouse games with victim.	Charles Cullen attended Mountainside School of Nursing in New Jersey. He got a job at St. Barnabas Medical Center in Livingston, N.J. In 2003, Cullen admitted to police that he had murdered as many as 45 patients during his 16 years of working at various hospitals in New Jersey and Pennsylvania. He was sentenced to 18 life sentences in March of 2006 for killing 13 patients and attempting to kill two others by lethal injection

Source: Hickey, Eric W. 2005. *Serial Murderers and Their Victims*. Belmont, CA: Wadsworth.

Mass murder

The U.S. Bureau of Justice Statistics defines **mass murder** as the killing of three or more individuals in a single event. Mass murders are uniquely shocking because of the number of victims; they make people feel vulnerable as traditionally safe places such as restaurants, schools, or office buildings erupt in spontaneous violence. Mass murderers are also unique offenders in that they are easily apprehended or stopped; most commit suicide, are shot down by law enforcement officers, or stay at the scene of the crime until caught.[23] Victims can be randomly selected or be part of a target group.

Mass murders vary in motive, degree of planning, and victim-offender relationship.[24] Criminologists have identified four distinct categories. Table 14.3 provides a summary with examples from case profiles.

Data on mass murderers is difficult to gather since most perpetrators commit suicide at the scene of the crime. Research shows, however, that the majority are not madmen.[25] Instead, most mass murders are the result of the accumulation

Table 14.3 Four types of mass murderers based on motive

Motive	Example
Revenge: the murderer wants to get even with a particular individual or a category of people such as women, racial or ethnic minorities, or religious groups	Marc Lepine (who died in 1989) was found guilty of murdering fourteen women and wounding ten women and four men at an engineering school. After killing the students, Lepin killed himself. He left behind a letter stating that feminists had ruined his life, and a list of nineteen women he wanted to kill because of their feminist beliefs.
Love: the murderer wants to "save" loved ones from some type of threat or imminent danger	Andrea Yates, convicted of first-degree murder for the 2002 drowning of her children in the bathtub, was sentenced to life in prison with the possibility of parole after 40 years. Yates drowned each of her five children, covered them with a sheet, and then called her husband and told him to come home. Yates claimed her children were bad and she was trying to save them from going to hell. She was found to suffer a recurring severe case of postpartum psychosis and in 2006 the verdict was overturned on appeal and she was found not guilty by reason of insanity.
Profit/personal gain: murderer seeks some material outcome or benefit	In January 1948 Sadamichi Hirasawa went to a branch of the Teigin Bank at Shiina in Tokyo. He said he was a public health official and gave all sixteen people there a pill and a few drops of liquid that was later found to be a cyanide solution. While everyone was incapacitated Hirasawa took all the money available at the bank. Ten of the sixteen victims died at the scene and two died at the hospital. Hirasawa was sentenced to death but died of natural causes in a prison hospital in 1987.
Terror: the murderer intends to create fear and panic or send a message or warning to society	In January 1971 Charles Manson, Patricia Krenwinkel, Susan Atkins, and Leslie Van Houten were each found guilty of murder and conspiracy to commit murder and were sentenced to death for the killing of five people, including pregnant [actress] Sharon Tate. The Charles Manson "family" were inspired by Manson's doomsday ideology to attack high-profile celebrities in an effort to gain attention for his beliefs.

Source: Fox, James Alan and Levin, Jack. 1996. *Overkill: Mass Murder and Serial Killing Exposed*. New York: Plenum.

of anger, rage, and frustration. Factors like personal failure, social ridicule, isolation, and loss can all contribute to a culmination in mass murder. Whether a disgruntled employee, frustrated student or political dissenter, the mass murderer wants to send out a message, make a point, or be heard, with devastating consequences. Despite their rare occurrence, mass murder cases inspire countless news stories, documentaries, and entire Hollywood productions. We turn now to a form of interpersonal violence that stirs very little public attention, yet is far more common than mass murder or any other category of homicide, the crime of assault.

ASSAULT

Assault is the attempted commission of bodily injury to another human being. Assault can also mean putting an individual in fear of imminent bodily harm, injury, danger, or threat. An assault can therefore include threats, taunting, intimidation, and harassment; it requires no physical contact.

Many people confuse assault with the crime of battery, defined as unwanted, non-consensual physical contact. According to the FBI, assault with battery is the most common violent crime in the United States. For the sake of simplicity, we will consider the category of criminal assault to include assault *and* battery of the victim.

Criminal assault is a complex pattern of behavior to investigate because it has the potential to escalate to homicide.[26] Offenders who commit certain categories of assault are regarded as having the potential for lethal violence.[27] There are two categories of assault: aggravated and simple. Aggravated assault is the attempt to commit, or the commission of, serious bodily harm or injury upon an individual. It usually includes the use of some type of weapon or deadly force that can cause grave injury or death. A person can be convicted of aggravated assault even for an act that results in no physical harm, such as holding someone at gun point. Simple assault is the attempt to commit, or the commission of, less serious physical injury and usually does not include the use of a weapon.

The number of assaults is much higher than the number of homicides in the United States, according to the Bureau of Justice Statistics. The profile of the typical offender in aggravated assault is African American, male, 15 to 34 years old, of lower socioeconomic status, with a prior history of arrest for other crimes.[28] The majority of offenders were victims of or witnesses to violence in their childhoods. They commit aggravated assault on strangers and non-strangers alike, usually in the victim's home or on a street nearby, or at a friend's or neighbor's home. Victims of simple assaults, on the other hand, are more likely to be non-strangers. Most assaults follow a pattern of spontaneous violence triggered by an argument or altercation.[29]

In recent years, stalking has become regarded as a step in the continuum of violence that can lead to a more serious, even deadly encounter between victim and offender. Stalking includes any unwanted contact between two individuals that communicates a threat or places the victim in fear or distress. Patterns of stalking can include such behaviors as following someone, repeatedly watching the person, making unwanted phone calls, and sending unwanted letters or messages. A national study conducted by the U.S. Department of Justice suggests an urgent need for a more widespread understanding of and response to this crime.[30]

How do patterns of violence emerge between individuals? Is the continuum of violence more likely to escalate between strangers or acquaintances? We turn now to an examination of assault that distinguishes between two categories: assault between strangers and assault between non-strangers.

Understanding assault between strangers

Assaults that occur between strangers tend to fall into two categories of violence, mentioned before in our discussion of homicide: *instrumental* and *expressive*.[31] An instrumental assault occurs as a means toward achieving an end and is usually preceded by some degree of planning, such as in a robbery in which the offender becomes familiar with the store in advance and prepares for the crime by assessing the type of force necessary.

The other type of assault between strangers is a somewhat more spontaneous act of violence, called expressive because it usually includes an escalation of emotions in an argument or a slight that ends up in a violent confrontation. It often occurs in everyday setting such as a bar, restaurant, or sporting event where people find themselves in conflict with strangers.

Understanding assault between non-strangers

Patterns of violence between non-strangers are much more difficult to study because victims are reluctant to report a crime committed by someone they know or live with. For years, criminology lagged behind in researching the type of violence that occurs within the intimate setting of the family. The first study to compile national data on family violence was conducted in 1975 by researchers at the University of New Hampshire. The *National Survey on Family Violence* (NSFV) was conducted on a representative sample of 2,146 families. The second NSFV was conducted in 1985 on a representative sample of 4,032 families.[32] Using a *Conflicts Tactic Scale* to measure the context of disagreements and how they are resolved, the 1985 study concluded that the rate of violence between spouses was 161 per 1,000 couples, a rate slightly lower than in the 1975 NCVS survey.[33] Next we examine two patterns of violence within the intimate setting of a family: intimate-partner assault and child maltreatment.

Intimate partner assault

The U.S. Office on Violence Against Women (OVW) defines domestic violence very broadly as a "pattern of abusive behavior in any relationship that is used by one partner to gain or maintain power and control over another intimate partner."[34] The OVW definition includes behavior that is coercive, manipulative, intimidating, and harassing, as well as behavior that is violent. **Intimate partner violence** is a more restrictive definition that criminologists use when they study spouse abuse or domestic violence (see Table 14.4 for the major types of intimate partner violence).

More than 9 of 10 victims of domestic violence are women; more than 9 of 10 perpetrators are men.[35] This does not mean men are never victims of violence and abuse at the hand of their female partners, but female violence against men is much rarer than male violence against women.[36] Domestic violence occurs in all racial and ethnic groups, cuts across all socioeconomic classes, and is a global issue that is the subject of a great deal of research and policy-making.[37]

Domestic violence is a behavioral pattern that emerges over time and continues to have long-term negative effects beyond the specific outburst of violence. In a classic study, Lenore Walker examined its impact on 1,500 battered women.[38] She found the overwhelming majority described a similar cycle of behavior in their interaction with their intimate partners, which she referred to as the *cycle of violence*. She identified three stages within this cycle (see Figure 14.2):

The **tension building phase** begins with the normal or routine interactions between intimate partners. A breakdown in communication leads to the building

Table 14.4 Categories of domestic violence

Type of violence	Description
Physical abuse	Hitting, slapping, shoving, grabbing, pinching, biting, hair-pulling, etc. Physical abuse also includes denying a partner medical care or forcing alcohol and/or drug use.
Sexual abuse	Coercing or attempting to coerce any sexual contact or behavior without consent. Sexual abuse includes, but is certainly not limited to, marital rape, attacks on sexual parts of the body, forcing sex after physical violence has occurred, or treating someone in a sexually demeaning manner.
Emotional abuse	Undermining an individual's sense of self-worth and/or self-esteem. This may include but is not limited to constant criticism, name-calling, or damaging one's relationship with his or her children.
Economic abuse	Making or attempting to make an individual financially dependent by maintaining total control over financial resources, withholding someone's access to money, or forbidding attendance at school or employment.
Psychological abuse	Causing fear by intimidation; threatening physical harm to self, partner, children, or partner's family or friends; destroying pets and property; and forcing isolation from family, friends, or school and/or work.

Source: United States Department of Justice, Office on Violence Against Women, 2015.

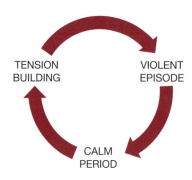

Figure 14.2 The cycle of violence

of tension, anxiety, and fear in resolving conflicts and arguments and dealing with everyday matters of disappointment, disagreement, and life stresses. Tensions continue to escalate as the relationship becomes characterized by the abuser's desire for power and control in dealing with the situation, leaving the victim in continuous fear of causing an outburst. In the **acting out phase**, an explosive incident occurs in which the abusive partner begins to dominate his/her victim by verbally assaulting, threatening, hitting, or attacking. It may appear to be a loss of control over emotions, but in reality, the abusive partner is beginning to take control of the victim, in an effort to dominate the situation, the immediate environment, and the outcome. The victim is left hurt, betrayed, confused, and afraid. The final phase, the **honeymoon phase**, is characterized by remorse, apology, and the apparent end of violence. This stage is the abuser's attempt to "make it up" to the victim. It may include showering the partner with love and affection or just withdrawing from violent behavior. The batterer will do anything to gain the approval and forgiveness of the victim, in an attempt to reestablish trust and security. The promise to never act out again and get help gives the victim hope that things will get better and reaffirms the intimate-partner relationship. When violence escalates over time and without intervention, this stage becomes progressively shorter and may disappear completely.

Let's turn now to a closer look at the second form of violence that occurs within an intimate family setting, child maltreatment, to see whether there are patterns of similarity between it and domestic violence.

Child maltreatment

The term **child maltreatment** describes any act or failure to act on the part of a parent or caretaker that results in the emotional harm, physical injury, sexual exploitation, or death of a minor child, or puts the minor child at risk of imminent danger.[39] The Child Abuse Prevention and Treatment Act (CAPTA) provides states with guidelines for defining child maltreatment, in order to ensure they do all that is necessary to protect the well-being of the child. Most states incorporate within their definitions these different forms of child maltreatment:[40]

- **Physical abuse**—Physical abuse is the physical injury to a child that results from the non-accidental infliction of harm without reasonable explanation. It can include burning a child or hitting, punching, kicking, or beating with hands, belt, stick, or other object. It can also include actions that put a child at great risk of physical harm or injury, such as Michael Jackson's

Image 14.4 *In November 2002 while at a hotel in Berlin, Michael Jackson dangled his nine-month-old baby by the arm from a fourth floor balcony as he greeted fans gathered below. Child abuse experts criticized Jackson's behavior as careless at the least, with some calling for his arrest for reckless endangerment. Did Jackson's actions constitute child maltreatment?*

AP/Press Association Images

dangling his baby from a hotel balcony before crowds of observers (see Image 14.4).

- **Neglect**—Although not all neglect qualifies as a violent crime, some forms of child neglect clearly are. Withholding of adequate food, clothing, shelter, medical care, or supervision can lead to violent consequences for the child due to adults' failure to assume their responsibilities.[41]

- **Sexual abuse**—The CAPTA definition of child sexual abuse includes the employment, use, persuasion, inducement, enticement, or coercion of any child to engage in, or assist any other person to engage in, any sexually explicit conduct or simulation of such conduct for the purpose of producing a visual depiction of such conduct; or the rape, and in cases of caretaker or interfamilial relationships, statutory rape, molestation, prostitution, or other form of sexual exploitation of children, or incest with children.[42]

- **Emotional abuse**—Most definitions of emotional abuse to a child incorporate elements of parents' or caretakers' behavior that cause or can cause serious mental injury including depression, anxiety, withdrawal, and aggression. Often, emotional abuse is associated with traumatizing forms of punishment such as locking a child in the closet or using verbally abusive or derogatory language.[43]

The U.S. Department of Health and Human Services estimates there are 905,000 victims of child maltreatment each year, about half of them cases of neglect. The most vulnerable children are under three. While male offenders account for the majority of child sexual abuse, females represent the majority of perpetrators in child maltreatment cases in general.[44] Other than the physical effects of abuse resulting in bodily injury and death, victims of child maltreatment endure long-term emotional trauma and often have behavioral problems in school, become involved with alcohol and drugs, are susceptible to teen pregnancy and promiscuity, and have a greater likelihood of juvenile delinquency.

RAPE AND SEXUAL ASSAULT

We turn now to another category of interpersonal violence that also has devastating effects on its victims. **Sexual assault** is a crime that includes the use of physical violence, threat, or intimidation to commit a sexual act on the victim. Sexual assaults contain an element of denigration in that the perpetrator often sees the victim as "deserving it" or as being inferior.

Rape is the most serious type of sexual assault. For more than eighty years, the FBI Uniform Crime Report defined **forcible rape** as "the carnal knowledge of a female by force and against her will." In 2011, FBI Director Robert S. Mueller III, approved the redefinition of rape as "penetration, no matter how slight, of the vagina or anus with any body part or object, or oral penetration by a sex organ of another person, without the consent of the victim." The UCR distinguishes between forcible rape and other types of sexual assaults including **attempted rape** or the attempt to commit a rape by force or threat of force, and **statutory rape** or sexual intercourse with a minor under the age of consent (in most states the age of consent is sixteen; in some it is eighteen). In many cases, the crime is defined in terms of degrees of severity, as measured by the resulting physical and psychological injury to the victim, the relationship between the victim and offender, the number of offenders, and the age of the victim.[45] Regardless of its definition, rape is about power, not sex. It is the use of force and coercion to take control over the victim.

Traditional rape laws essentially allowed the focus of prosecution to become an attack on the victim's character, past sexual behavior, and general credibility.[46] Feminist groups and other reformers have criticized these laws for the past two decades, on the grounds that they place the burden of proof on the victim instead of the defendant, adding to the trauma and to victims' unwillingness to report the crime. Statutory definitions of rape have undergone revisions over the years, as part of a national effort to increase the public's awareness of the crime, offer support and social services to the victim, and aid the apprehension and prosecution of the rape offender.[47] Policy changes over the past several decades include:

Image 14.5 *How does society's perception of the crime of rape affect the treatment of rape victims?*

Michael Debets/Demotix/Press Association Images

- Replacing the single criminal act of rape with a series of offenses graded according to the presence or absence of aggravating circumstances, such as the presence of a weapon or resulting injury to the victim.
- Making obsolete the legal requirement that the victim must physically resist the attacker.
- Eliminating the legal requirement for victims to testify about the attack at trial.
- Developing rape shield laws to protect the victim by restricting the defense's ability to use irrelevant evidence regarding the victim's past sexual behavior or reputation.[48]
- Requiring the use of anonymous "Jane Doe kits," which collect forensic evidence in a numbered, sealed envelope in case the victim later decides to press charges.[49]
- Broadening the scope and meaning of the crime of rape to include date rape, spousal rape, same sex rape, and gang rape.

How have the dynamics of change in the legal definition of rape affected the nature, meaning, and extent of this crime? Let us take a closer look at the various categories of rape.

Defining rape

The vast majority of rapes occur between victims and offenders who have some prior relationship. Research shows that acquaintance rape, while the most common form of the crime, is probably the least likely to be reported to the police. Victims either are unaware a crime has been committed, mistakenly believe they may have precipitated their own victimization, have been under the influence of alcohol, are too embarrassed or ashamed of the incident, or do not believe anything can be done about it.[50] Nevertheless, the emotional and psychological impact and trauma to the victim in these cases are significant and can have long-term negative consequences. We can better understand the crime of rape by identifying the various contexts within which it can take place.

Date rape

Date rape is sexual intercourse forced on a person by an acquaintance acting as an escort during some type of social engagement. Most empirical research on date rape has focused on the social relationships of college dating. In a classic study on rape, Kent State University psychologist Mary P. Koss surveyed 6,059 college students and found one of every eight females had been compelled to have sexual intercourse through the use or threat of force.[51] Moreover, the overwhelming majority of victims, 90 percent, knew their assailants.

More recent data from a study conducted by National Institute of Justice estimates that approximately 5 percent of college women will become the victims of a rape or an attempted rape in any given academic year.[52] A majority of these rapes go unreported, as women who are forced to have sex with someone they know and with whom they are likely to continue to interact are reluctant to report the crime to police, for fear of retaliation, shame, and the lack of sufficient evidence to prove a crime was committed.

A growing concern on college campuses is "date rape drugs" such as GHB (Gama Hydroxybutyric Acid) and rohypnol, or "roofies," hypnotic drugs with powerful sedative effects. These odorless, tasteless drugs are usually added to alcohol in clubs, in bars, at fraternity parties, or on a date, to sedate women with the intention of having sexual intercourse without their consent and against their will. These drugs induce drowsiness, blackout, and loss of memory. Because of its powerful side effects and widespread abuse, rohypnol was included in the Drug-Induced Rape Prevention and Punishment Act of 1996.[53] In response to publicity by women's groups about the frequency with which these drugs are misused and their dangers, a pharmaceutical company, Hoffman-La Roche, changed the formula for rohypnol to include a dye that makes a drink turn green if the drug is added to it.

College and university campuses have responded to the growing problem of sexual assault by both educating men and women about personal safety issues and raising awareness of the socio-cultural dynamics on campuses that may contribute to sexual violence and rape.[54] Researchers note the prevalence of rape on college campuses is largely the result of the social organization of college life and peer group interactions at fraternity houses, athletic events, parties, and other social gatherings conducive to sexual assault on young women.[55] Studies also show rape on college campuses to be largely a product of sexual misconceptions by male college students about female sexual behavior, the prevalence of alcohol use among college students, and the notion of sexual conquest as a means of social approval by male peers.[56] To effectively change these dynamics, many colleges have implemented peer discussion groups, counselors and campus programs to educate students on some of the misconceptions that can lead to sexual violence. These programs are designed to increase communication in order for women, especially, to be aware of the dangers and recognize the situations in which sexual assault and rape may occur.

Spousal rape

The recognition that **spousal** or **marital rape** is a crime is another by-product of rape law reform, which expanded the common law definition of rape to include forced sexual intercourse in a marriage relationship. Laws criminalizing this form of sexual assault were first passed in 1976, with Nebraska being the first state to abolish the marital exemption to rape laws. Today, spousal rape is illegal in every state. However, debates still spark over whether a man and woman entering a marital contract are fundamentally agreeing to a sexual relationship. If we believe they are, then spousal rape will continue to be a challenging crime to prove.

From a procedural standpoint, the standard of evidence required to convict a husband of spousal rape is usually higher than for any other form of rape, often requiring proof of violence or injury. In addition, punishment for spousal rape is often less severe. Many women are reluctant to report marital rape for fear of jeopardizing their marriage, losing their homes and families, suffering public humiliation and retaliation by their husbands, and not having sufficient evidence to be taken seriously by authorities. Unfortunately, victims of spousal rape suffer just as much trauma as victims of stranger rapes.[57] Research indicates that repeated sexual abuse in spousal rape is accompanied by longer-lasting trauma that results from the social stereotypes surrounding this crime, and the lack of social support to help victims overcome feelings of betrayal, guilt, shame, and fear.[58]

Gang rape

Gang rape is the rape of a victim by more than one assailant. Offenders charged with gang rape include those who actually engage in non-consensual sexual intercourse with the victim, as well as those who use force or threat of force to facilitate the actions of others and make the victim submit. Although gang rape often occurs between victims and offenders who have some type of prior relationship, this type of rape is very different from individual acquaintance rape. Sometimes the expression of power and male sexual dominance over a woman is used as an affirmation of acceptance and membership into a group of men such as a street gang, social club, or college fraternity.[59]

BOX 14.3: CONSIDER THIS . . .

When "good guys" rape

At campuses across the country, women are attacked and sexually assaulted during football games, at parties, and inside fraternity houses by groups of young men who claim to be having a good time. In many cases, these attacks are perpetrated by members of the university's athletic teams, students often perceived by their peers as beyond reproach and looked upon fondly by the academic and social community.

In a classic 1980s study, researcher Mary Koss examined 6,059 students at 32 universities across the country. She found that 1 in 12 male college students admitted committing acts that state statutes legally define as rape or attempted rape, but only 1 in every 100 admitted actually committing rape or attempted rape. Koss notes their denial of criminal behavior is largely due to a lack of understanding of the social and legal consequences of their acts, along with the scapegoating of women as "sluts" or "whores" who "deserve" or "ask for it," to absolve assailants' feelings of guilt or responsibility.

Studies also show justification of rape can be heightened by the unique culture of university athletes. Participation in an all-male group or activity such as a sports team can often insulate men from feelings of guilt and responsibility for treating a woman with disrespect and brutality. Male bonding is a primary element in gang rapes, connecting aggression with sexuality and fueling each group member's sense of power and dominance, especially in front of his "brothers." Moreover, the attention and special privilege granted to many collegiate athletes can often allow them to feel they are above the law, in too bright a light to be dimmed by a single victim's accusation.

How can we condone a culture that seems to overlook or underplay the prevalence of rape by supposedly "good guys"? How can criminology advance the understanding of acquaintance rape among college students? *What do you think?*

Sources

Finley, Laura. 2016. Sexual Assault: Among College Athletes Favourite Crimes. *CityWatch*, Jan. 14. Retrieved from http://www.citywatchla.com/archive/5717-sexual-assault-among-college-athletes-favorite-crimes.

Hammond, E. M., Berry, M. A. and Rodriguez, D. N. 2011. The Influence of Rape Myth Acceptance, Sexual Attitudes, and Belief in a Just World on Attributions of Responsibility in a Date Rape Scenario. *Legal and Criminological Psychological Society* 16(1): 242–252.

Koss, Mary P., Gidycz, C.J. and Wisniewski, N. 1987. The Scope of Rape: Sexual Aggression and Victimization in a National Sample of Students in Higher Education. *Journal of Consulting and Clinical Psychology* 55: 162–170.

McMahon, Sarah. 2004. *Student-Athletes, Rape-Supportive Culture, And Social Change.* Department of Sexual Assault Services and Crime Victim Assistance, Rutgers, the State University of New Jersey.

Strasser, A. and Culp-Ressler, T. 2013. How the Media Took Sides in the Steubenville Rape Case. Retrieved from http://thinkprogress.org/health/2013/03/18/1732701/media-steubenville/.

Physical resistance is more difficult in a gang rape attack and often can lead to the use of excessive violence and restraint. The victim also suffers the added humiliation of knowing people stood by and failed to help or stop the rape. Men who participate in gang rape often use peer approval and the affirmation of their masculinity to justify a behavior they are not likely to engage in if acting alone.[60]

Gang rape is difficult for victims to prove, since the bond that exists between the group members often supersedes their willingness to cooperate or testify against their friends. According to research studies, rapes perpetrated by multiple assailants often take on a new meaning as a symbol of masculinity and dominance. Gang rapists often rape for each other, to prove their manhood or feel a sense of belonging with "the boys." It can be the spontaneous act of males egging each other on, or it can start out as a dare, joke, or even a rite of passage.[61] Box 14.3 illustrates some of the dynamics of gang rape in cases where college athletes are the perpetrators.

Same-sex rape

For many years, the definition of common law rape was limited to the sexual assault of a female by a male offender. Only recently has publicity increased our awareness of **same-sex rape**, or sexual violence and abuse perpetrated by men against men and women against women.[62] In same-sex rape, neither the perpetrator nor the victim is always gay or lesbian.

Same-sex rape follows the same pattern as heterosexual rape. It is an attempt to control, dominate, and overpower the victim, forcing him or her to submit to sexual acts using fear, threat, intimidation, and violence. Survivors of same-sex rape go through the same emotional turmoil and issues dealt with by survivors of opposite-sex rape. However, they also have to deal with the additional stereotypes held by society that an individual cannot be raped by somebody of the same sex. Victims of same-sex rape must also face the trauma of remaining silent for fear that others will see their victimization in a negative homophobic light.[63] In some instances, offenders will use this fear to persist in their pattern of abuse, under the threat of exposing the victim's real or supposed sexual orientation to family, friends, peers, and co-workers.[64]

Understanding rape and sexual assault

Criminologists consider rape a violent form of coercive behavior, not an expression of sexual desire. Several researchers have attempted to develop a typology of rapists according to the motivation of the offender and the meaning attached to their crime. Nicholas Groth conducted one of the first systematic efforts to study patterns of rape and identified three motivations: power, anger, and sadism.[65] In his analysis of 348 convicted rapists serving time in prison, Groth found that over half the offenders (55%) reported they raped their victims to dominate and exert control over the women; he called this category of offense **power rape**. Groth noted that the power rapist does not set out to hurt the victim, in contrast to the offender in **anger rape**, who impulsively assaults his victim as a means of releasing anger or hostility. Anger rapists made up about 40 percent of Groth's sample and usually carried out their attacks in a brutal, violent manner. The last category of rapists, only 5 percent of Groth's sample, was primarily motivated by an erotic expression of power and anger. In **sadistic rape** the male offender derived sexual pleasure from the torture of the victim and the exertion of power and dominance.

Several other typologies have emerged to expand upon the work of Groth. Robert Hazelwood and Ann Burgess offer a similar categorization based on motivation that classifies rape offenders into four categories.[66] The **power-assertive rapist** spends a great deal of effort planning his crime and even seduces his victim. The rape is an expression of masculine power and often includes the use of a great deal of force or violence to overpower the victim. The **power-reassurance rapist** acts out of a general sense of sexual inadequacy. He usually attacks victims who are strangers, often after a period of stalking them, and often attempts to continue contact with them after the attack in a socially inappropriate expression of sexuality. The **anger-retaliatory rapist** attacks his victim by surprise and somewhat spontaneously, using direct physical force and carrying out the attack as an expression of anger and hostility. The attack becomes a source of release to the perpetrator, since the victim is often the source of his rage or a symbolic representation of it. Finally, the **anger-excitation rapist** usually takes time to plan and execute his attack, usually on a stranger. The primary motive is to inflict pain and to humiliate and degrade the victim. The offender gains sexual stimulation from hurting the victim and therefore often uses forms of torture for gratification, sometimes recording these activities.

Drawing upon research conducted on sixty-one incarcerated serial rapists, Dennis Stevens offers an alternative typology based on motivation, victim selection, style of attack, and degree of violence.[67] **Lust rapists**, the largest category in the sample, are predatory rapists who generally do not use violence and select their victim based on availability. **Righteous rapists** contend the victim bears primary responsibility for the sexual encounter and view their own behavior as based on victim consent. **Peer rapists** blame their actions on associating with "bad company" and membership in groups that define rape as acceptable behavior. This is often the case in gang rapes. **Fantasy rapists** are motivated by thoughts and ideas from their past that often include violent scenarios they want to carry out, in which the sexual act is secondary. For rapists motivated by **control and anger**, rape is secondary to the violence expressed during the attack. Finally, **supremacy rapists** are primarily motivated by the satisfaction gained from inflicting pain and suffering on the victim. Control and anger and supremacy rapists are the most violent of all types of rapists.

A survey of the literature indicates that the crime of rape includes a cognitive component, whereby perpetrators justify the crime according to their perception and interpretation of the situation and their attitude toward the victim. Offenders use the following themes to minimize their offense and promote denial:[68]

- *Women are seductresses.* They entice men through their sexuality.
- *No means yes.* While women may protest a man's sexual advances, they really want them.
- *Women like it.* Most women eventually give in to the forced sexual intercourse, relax, and enjoy it.
- *Only bad girls get raped.* Nice girls avoid circumstances than can lead to a rape.
- *Rape is not really a crime.* It is a minor wrongdoing based on a misunderstanding.

Many of these justifications are an extension of various myths regarding the context of sexual violence, and they often reflect social and cultural biases about the role of women in society. Studies on the myths surrounding the crime of rape confirm that many people believe women bring false charges of rape to get back at men, draw attention to themselves by wearing suggestive clothing, engaging in certain activities, and secretly want to be raped but simply say no so as not to appear promiscuous.[69] These myths have the compound effect of minimizing the perceived trauma and injury to the victim, diffusing responsibility for the crime from the offender to the victim, and undermining efforts to reduce the negative impact of rape by prosecuting offenders and shielding the victim from further humiliation and scrutiny by the criminal justice system.

The social and emotional stigma associated with the crime of rape takes something away from the victim that is very difficult to restore. We turn now to another category of violent crime that involves a different aspect of taking: the violent crime of robbery.

ROBBERY

The Uniform Crime Report defines **robbery** as "the taking or attempting to take anything of value from the care, custody, or control of a person or persons by force or threat of force or violence and/or by putting the victim in fear." The ultimate goal of the robber is to take something of value, but in the view of the criminal justice system, robbery is not about the value of the stolen items. It is considered a violent crime because it includes a face-to-face confrontation between victim and offender in which the victim's life is placed in jeopardy. Thus, the severity of punishment is usually related to the amount of force used during the robbery.[70]

Image 14.6 *Since robbers select victims who are vulnerable and most likely to produce a better yield, the use of ATMs in isolated, poorly lit places, and at night make for a quick and relatively easy target for robbery.*

iStock/Michael Luhrenberg

Robberies are more likely than any other type of violent crime to include the use of a weapon, especially firearms. According to the UCR, a firearm is used in about 43 percent of all robberies. Moreover, robberies are more likely than other crimes to include multiple assailants, as well as victims and offenders who are strangers. Stranger attacks more commonly occur in public locations, implicate multiple offenders, include weapons, and often result in greater physical harm to the victims than acts by offenders known to them.[71] The group nature of robbery is best illustrated in the typical robbery of a bank or convenience store, in which one or two people may enter the targeted place and another waits outside as look-out or drives a getaway car.

As in most violent crimes, in robbery the majority of offenders arrested are disproportionately young African American males. These data may be somewhat misleading, though, since only about 25 percent of offenses known to the police result in an arrest.[72] The NCVS indicates about 40 percent of robberies are not reported to police, with men less likely to report being robbed than women.[73]

Most robbers are not specialists who engage in robbery as their sole criminal activity. The majority are amateurs who engage in a variety of criminal behavior ranging from theft and burglary to fraud.[74] However, especially among repeat offenders, robbery has some potential to escalate in violence over time. Research indicates that the typical robbery is a spontaneous violent attack that occurs as an opportunity presents itself, with little planning and no thought about how to avoid getting caught.[75] The exception is the professional robber, who commits this crime as a source of livelihood. Professional robbers carry out their crimes using a great deal of planning, including the rational decision to select a particular target, choose a time to commit the crime, anticipate possible resistance, and determine how to escape.[76]

Defining robbery

Robberies that occur in commercial settings such as banks, gas stations, pawnshops, and jewelry, liquor, and other retail stores are **institutional robberies**.[77] Commercial outlets like these are preferred targets for their easy access and availability of quick cash.[78] Often, businesses in remote areas and poorer neighborhoods are at greater risk, due to their low level of customer activity and insufficient security.

The overwhelming majority of robberies are **personal robberies**, occurring in a residential setting or on the street; street robberies are commonly referred to as *muggings*. A street robbery by a single assailant will often include the use of a weapon, usually a gun. In a street robbery by multiple assailants, the attackers usually overpower the victim in order to take his or her possessions by force. The majority of street robberies occur on an individual's way to his or her car, in parking lots, at or near an ATM, on subways, and in train stations. Robbers select victims who are more vulnerable and most likely to produce a better "yield."[79] A study conducted by criminologist Jody Miller found that robbers choose victims they perceive as likely to offer the least resistance.[80]

Personal robberies also occur in residences. Least prevalent of all robberies are home invasions, in which armed robbers force their way into someone's home, restrain the occupants, and proceed to take their personal belongings and ransack the residence. Homes selected for invasion are often located in a neighborhood that is socially disorganized, where security measures are least effective and precautions least likely to exist.[81]

Understanding robbery

Studies indicate that financial need is the stated motive of the majority of all convicted offenders.[82] Robberies motivated by financial gain usually occur either to meet the offender's immediate need for cash or to support a certain type of lifestyle. In a classic study conducted by researcher Floyd Feeney, a robber describes his financial need in this way:

> I needed the money for food. I tried welfare. I tried to borrow money from all the people that I could borrow from. I didn't have any sources of money. I was just flat broke. I was getting it out of savings and borrowing money from my mother, but I was getting kind of run out because she was starting to need more. I didn't even think about how much I wanted to get. I just felt that anything I got would help. [83]

Table 14.5 Robbery as a response to norm violations within the street subculture

Type of violation	Description
Market-related offenses	Emerge when there are disputes between street rivals, partners in trade, or generalized predators
Status-based offenses	Occur when aspects of the individual's character and personality have been challenged, disrespected, or offended
Personalistic offenses	Result from incidents where an individual was personally harmed, injured, or violated, where the incident creates a challenge to personal autonomy and belief in justice

Source: Jacobs, Bruce A. and Wright, Richard. 2006. Street Justice: Retaliation in the Criminal Underworld. *The British Journal of Sociology* 58: 506–507.

Robbers often see their takings as quick easy money to pay off a debt, buy food, make a rent payment, or purchase drugs. Such robberies are often associated with a particular criminal lifestyle that values lawless, reckless behavior, and a street culture inhospitable to conventional means of generating stable, legitimate sources of income. Research conducted by Bruce Jacobs and Richard Wright at the University of Missouri examined the motivation and decision-making patterns of 86 active robbers in St. Louis. They found that engaging in a robbery is often associated with the values, beliefs, and behaviors of a street culture.[84]

Robbery can also spring from motives other than money. Jacobs and Wright found the majority of street robbers' activities were characterized by a "quest for excitement and sensory stimulation." Unlike non-drug related street robberies, drug-related ones are sometimes a response to the violation of the informal rules or social norms of a street subculture. Researchers note there are three types of such offenses. *Market offenses* are often related to the drug trade itself, while *status-based offenses* have more to do with a challenge to character or position such as a threat to honor. Robbery is also used as a means for retaliation against *personalistic offenses* such as a sexual assault.[85] Table 14.5 provides a summary of these three types of violations.

With this pattern of offending, robbery becomes a symbol of revenge and retaliation. The intent is to send a message to the perpetrator of the harm in a moralistic attempt to right a wrong. We turn now to a form of interpersonal violence that also represents an emotionally charged attempt to send out a message, hate crime.

HATE CRIMES

The crimes we have discussed so far—murder, assault, rape, and robbery—are acts of interpersonal violence that for the most part target specific individuals without consideration of their race, ethnic background, or other physical

Image 14.7 *What makes this type of expression a form of criminal behavior?*
Alfredo Gonzalez/Demotix/Demotix/Press Association Images

characteristic. Interpersonal violence takes on a different meaning when the crime is motivated by bias. Crimes targeting a specific category of individuals, and motivated by a bias against physical or social characteristics unique this group, are **hate crimes**.

On January 27, 2008, detailed charges were brought against 37-year-old Ivaylo Ivanov for spray-painting swastikas at 23 different locations, including private homes and synagogues, and circulating flyers that read "Kill All Jews." Police had confiscated an array of deadly homemade pipe bombs, rifles, and handguns from Ivanov's Brooklyn Heights apartment when he was arrested on January 20, 2008. Ivanov was indicted on over 100 counts of criminal mischief, including charges of criminal weapons possession and aggravated harassment in connection with a bias crime.

The Southern Poverty Law Center identified and counted 784 active hate groups throughout the United States in 2014, mapping their distribution by state. These groups are identified by their practices and beliefs toward a particular group or class of individuals that are offensive, harmful, and derogatory. They engage in hate activities such as holding rallies and marches and distributing publications that support their ideologies. They also engage in criminal acts. Hate crimes may take several forms and often include physical assault; property damage; arson; vandalism in the form of offensive graffiti; verbal threats, slights, insults, or harassment; and rape and murder. Because they are designed to cause fear and intimidation to an entire social group or class of individuals, hate crimes may have a greater general impact on society than crimes directed at specific individuals.

BOX 14.4: CONNECTING RESEARCH TO PRACTICE

Hate crime laws: criminalizing free speech or protecting human rights?

Since the passage of the federal Violent Crime Control and Law Enforcement Act in 1994, public debates have questioned whether hate crime laws infringe on the constitutional right to free speech. Proponents of hate crime legislation argue that it is necessary to protect minority groups from acts of violence motivated by bias, and that increased sentences protect the rights of the innocent to be free of fear, threat, and intimidation. Moreover, hate crimes affect not only the individual targeted, but the community in which the crime occurred, disturbing its sense of peace and creating fear and panic among those who share the victim's traits.

Opponents argue hate crime laws are unnecessary since the acts they define are already criminal violations punished by law. Adding additional penalties if the offender is also found guilty of bias toward the victim is essentially an attempt to suppress dissension and personal preference and to foster certain views of morality. For example, a minister preaching a sermon on the vices of homosexual marriages can be accused of a crime because the speech discriminates against gays and lesbians. Thus, while claiming to promote tolerance, hate crime laws can become an imminent threat to freedom of thought and speech.

What do criminological studies reveal about the need to both protect freedom of speech and identify crimes motivated by bias? Findings from various research studies show compelling evidence that: 1) bias crime victims of assault experience more severe and prolonged psychological trauma than non-bias assault victims; 2) hateful speech is seen as a form of terrorism that creates fear and panic by inciting violence; 3) minority groups feel hate speech should be more severely punished than some forms of property crimes; 4) The overwhelming majority of adults in the United States support the passage of legislation aimed at curtailing hate crime; and 5) protecting racist speech and hate propaganda are not appropriate signs of our freedom of expression.

Despite these and similar findings, the door remains open for criminologists to explore the true impact of hate crime legislation on freedom of speech, and the benefits it may have in reducing bias-motivated crimes.

Sources

Chakraborti, Neil and Garland, Jon. 2015. *Hate Crime: Impact, Causes, and Responses*. Thousand Oaks, CA: SAGE.

Helms, Janet E, Guerda, Nicolas and Green, Carlton E. 2010. Racism and Ethnoviolence as Trauma: Enhancing Professional Training. *Traumatology* 16(4): 53–62.

Perry, Barbara. 2008. *Hate and Bias Crime*. New York: Routledge.

In 1990, the UCR began collecting data on specific categories of hate crimes, with the passage of the Hate Crime Statistics Act of 1990 (HCSA). The HCSA required the FBI to collect data from law enforcement agencies across the country on crimes motivated by prejudice or bias based on race, religion, sexual orientation, or ethnicity. In 1994, Congress passed the Violent Crime Control and Law Enforcement Act of 1994, which included the collection of data on hate crimes motivated by bias against people with disabilities. Since 1992, the FBI has published an annual report titled *Hate Crime Statistics.*

In 2014, a total of 1,666 law enforcement agencies across the United States reported 5,479 hate crime incidents motivated by bias against a race, religion, disability, ethnicity, or sexual orientation.[86] Of the single-bias incidents, 47 percent were racially motivated, 18.6 percent were motivated by bias against religion, 18.6 percent accounted for bias based on sexual orientation, 11.9 percent were motivated by bias against ethnicity or national origin, and disability-motivated bias accounted for only 1.5 percent. Of the crimes reported in 2014, 63.1 percent were categorized as crimes against persons, 36.1 percent against property, and .8 percent against society or the public order. *Hate Crime Statistics* has played a central role in increasing public awareness and understanding of hate crimes. It has also inspired researchers to study groups often targeted for their personal characteristics, preferences, and lifestyles.

Hate crimes play a unique role in the development of criminal justice policy. This is especially true when debates are evoked about the 1st Amendment protection of free speech versus the control of hateful propaganda embedded in the ideology and teaching of certain groups. Box 14.4 illustrates one perspective on this debate.

SUMMARY

What is criminal homicide?

The category of crimes we call homicide is complex and diverse. Criminal homicide is the unlawful and intentional killing of one human being by another and includes first- and second-degree murder, as well as voluntary and involuntary manslaughter. First-degree murder requires premeditation—the offender has thought out the crime, and malice aforethought—the offender forms the intent to harm. Second-degree murder only requires malice aforethought. Voluntary manslaughter is the unlawful killing of another person while committing a felony without any intention to kill the victim. Involuntary manslaughter is an unlawful death resulting from the negligence or careless acts of the offender.

Why do people kill?

Many homicide offenders are chronic, violent offenders who adhere to a subculture of violence. Other patterns of homicide are situational, unique to a specific relationship or type of interaction between victim and offender. These homicides can be expressive, arising from interpersonal conflict or dispute, or instrumental, serving as a means to an end, such as obtaining money. Homicides can also fall into the categories of serial murder, the killing of three or more individuals in separate events, and mass murder, the killing of three or more individuals in a single event. While serial killers do not fit a particular typology of criminal offender, criminologists have categorized this crime according to motivation, selection of victim, method of killing, and the expected benefit of the crime. Patterns of mass murder are quite distinct from serial murder. Researchers have attempted to differentiate mass murders according to the relationship between victim and offender, the degree of spontaneity, and the motivation.

What constitutes an assault?

In its broadest sense, an assault is an attempt to commit physical harm to another human being. No physical contact has to occur; an individual can commit the crime of assault by simply putting someone in fear of injury, harm, or danger through threats, intimidation, or harassment. When physical contact does occur, the crime is assault with battery. Assaults are also categorized by the degree of injury or harm to the victim, and therefore the law distinguishes between simple and aggravated assault.

Does assault occur more often between strangers or acquaintances?

Assaultive behavior is much more common within the intimate setting of a family and includes intimate partner assault and child maltreatment. Intimate partner assault, also referred to as domestic violence, is abusive behavior including coercion, manipulation, intimidation, and violence upon a spouse or intimate partner. It is a means by which one partner attempts to maintain power and control over the other through some form of physical, emotional, sexual, economic, or psychological abuse.

We defined child maltreatment as any act or failure to act on the part of a parent or caretaker, which results in the emotional harm, physical injury, sexual exploitation, or death of a minor child, or puts the minor child at risk of imminent danger. Most states include physical abuse, neglect, emotional abuse, and sexual abuse in their definitions.

Is rape a sexual act?

In this chapter, we distinguished between forcible rape, defined more recently by the FBI Uniform Crime Report as "penetration, no matter how slight, of the vagina or anus with any body part or object, or oral penetration by a sex organ of another person, without the consent of the victim"; attempted rape, the attempt to commit a rape by force or threat of force; and statutory rape, sexual intercourse with a minor under the age of consent, which varies from state to state. States have developed legal categories that broaden the meaning of rape to include date rape, spousal rape, same sex rape, and gang rape. Contrary to popular beliefs and images about the crime of rape and rape victims, the majority of rapes occur between victims and offenders who know one another, hence the term acquaintance rape.

Despite its many different motives, characteristics, and meaning, criminologists agree rape is a violent form of coercive behavior, not an expression of sexual desire. Offenders fall into various categories centering on their need to express power, anger, retaliation, and sadistic desires. Other studies have developed typologies based on motivation, victim selection, style of attack, and degree of violence.

Why is robbery a violent crime?

Robbery is considered a violent crime because it is a face-to-face confrontation in which the offender uses force or the threat of force to take something of value from the immediate possession or control of the victim. For this reason, the legal consequences of committing robbery are related to the amount of force used during the crime, rather than to the value of what was taken.

What is the motive behind stealing by force?

Economic gain is the main motivation behind most robberies. Stealing by force from a vulnerable target is often seen by offenders as a quick and easy way to get money to meet some immediate financial need, whether it is to buy food, pay rent, or purchase drugs. Studies have also found robbery to be associated with other motives such as retaliation within the street subculture.

What are hate crimes?

Hate crimes can take on several forms such as murder, rape, and assault but also destruction of property and arson. They are unique however, in being motivated by a bias against physical or social characteristics unique to a group or individual. Often, hate crimes are an attempt to create fear and intimidate an entire social group or category of individuals.

CRITICAL THINKING QUESTIONS

1. What categories of criminal homicide elicit the most public and media attention? Are certain types easier to understand than others? Which are the most difficult to comprehend? What makes them so difficult? How does our understanding of the different types of criminal homicide guide policies directed at the social control of this form of interpersonal violence?

2. How is an assault between strangers different from an assault between acquaintances? If you were the victim of an assault, would you be more likely to report it to the police if the perpetrator were a stranger or an acquaintance? If it makes a difference, why does it? How can the field of criminology increase public awareness of domestic violence?

3.   If your neighbor were raped by your best friend, what would you do? Would you gather more information about the victim, her behavior, and her past, rather than question your best friend's integrity? Why or why not? Why is it hard for us to believe that ordinary individuals can commit rape? Why don't we worry about who the victim was, her past, or her reputation in a case of robbery? Why don't we wonder what the victim was wearing when the crime is murder?

4.   When does a theft constitute a robbery? What specific elements make robbery a form of interpersonal violence? Does the victim have to be afraid or intimidated in order for a robbery to occur? Can you think of any interactions between a victim and offender that include a theft but do not constitute a robbery?

5.   How does the tension between individual rights and public order (see chapter 1) influence the adoption of policies forbidding certain types of speech? When does freedom of expression fall under constitutional protection, and when is it subject to control as hate crime?

E-RESOURCES

The role of crime typologies in criminological research is discussed in greater detail at http://law.jrank.org/pages/2217/Typologies-Criminal-Behavior.html.

Additional resources for victims of sexual assault can be found at the National Center for Victims of Crime website at http://victimsofcrime.org/.

For more information about the date-rape drug rohypnol, visit https://www.verywell.com/rohypnol-the-date-rape-drug-3520408.

The U.S. Department of Justice Office on Violence against Women provides a variety of resources on the incidence, cost, impact, and prevention of domestic violence. You can access this information by visiting https://www.justice.gov/ovw.

More details about the Child Abuse Prevention and Treatment Act and programs to prevent and treat child abuse can be found at http://laws.adoption.com/statutes/child-abuse-prevention-and-treatment-act-capta-of-1974.html.

A detailed description of the Hate Crime Statistics Act (28 U.S.C. § 534) can be found at https://www.fbi.gov/about-us/cjis/ucr/hate-crime/2012/resource-pages/hate-crime-statistics-act/hatecrimestatisticsact_final.

The Southern Poverty Law Center's map indicating the distribution of hate groups can be found at https://www.splcenter.org/hate-map.

NOTES

1   Vigdor, Neil. 2013. Husband Arrested in Baseball Bat Attack, Wife in Critical Condition. *ctPost,* Sept. 11. Retrieved from www.ctpost.com/local/article/Greenwich-cops-probe-attempted-murder-4804524.php#photo-5170354.

2 How Widespread is Intimate Partner Violence? 2007. U.S. Department of Justice, Office of Justice Programs, National Institute of Justice. Retrieved from http://www.nij.gov/topics/crime/intimate-partner-violence/pages/extent.aspx.

3 Tjaden, Patricia and Thoennes, Nancy. Full Report of the Prevalence, Incidence and Consequences of Violence Against Women. U.S. Department of Justice, Office of Justice Programs, National Institute of Justice. Retrieved from http://www.cdc.gov/ViolencePrevention/intimatepartnerviolence/datasources.html.

4 Devries, K., Child, J., Bacchus, L., Mak, J., Falder, G., Graham, K., Watts, C. and Heise, L. 2014. Intimate Partner Violence Victimization and Alcohol Consumption in Women: A Systematic Review and Meta-analysis. *Addiction* 109(3).

5 Campbell, Jacquelyn C., Webster, Daniel, Koziol-McLain, Jane, Block, Carolyn R., Campbell, Doris, Curry, Mary Ann, Gary, Faye, McFarlane, Judith, Sachs, Carolyn, Sharps, Phyllis, Ulrich, Yvonne and Wilt, Susan A. 2003. *Assessing Risk Factors for Intimate Partner Homicide.* U.S. Department of Justice, Office of Justice Programs, National Criminal Justice Reference Service.

6 Chuck, Elizabeth. 2015. Charleston Church Shooter Dylann Roof 'Caught Us With Our Eyes Closed'. *NBC News, Sept 10.* Retrieved from http://www.nbcnews.com/storyline/charleston-church-shooting/charleston-church-survivors-shooter-caught-us-our-eyes-closed-n424331.

7 Denise Amber Lee Missing Since January 17, 2008 from North Port Florida ... Abducted by Michael Lee King. 2008. *Scared Monkeys Missing Persons Site.* Retrieved from http://missingexploited.com/2008/01/19/denise-amber-lee-missing-since-january-17–2008-from-north-port-fl-abducted-by-michael-lee-king/.

8 Van Derbeken, Jaxon. 2008. Murder Verdict in Case That 'Shook Up' S.F. Retrieved from http://www.sfgate.com/cgi-bin/article.cgi?f=/c/a/2008/10/01/BAAA138OQS.DTL.

9 Hannon, Lance. 2004. Race, Victim Precipitated Homicide, and the Subculture of Violence Thesis. *The Social Science Journal* 41(1): 115–121. Wolfgang, Marvin and Ferracuti, Franco. 1982. *The Subculture of Violence: Towards an Integrated Theory in Criminology.* Beverly Hills, CA: SAGE.

10 Schmall, Emily. 2015. Memo: Violence Long Simmered Between Rival Texas Biker Gangs. *Associated Press*, May 10. Retrieved from http://lasvegassun.com/news/2015/may/19/memo-violence-long-simmered-between-rival-texas-bi/.

11 Cohen, Albert K. 1955. *Delinquent Boys: The Culture of the Gang.* Glencoe, IL: Free Press. Anderson, Elijah. 1999. *Code of the Street: Decency, Violence and the Moral Life of the Inner City.* New York: W.W. Norton. Jankowski, Martin Sanchez. 1991. *Islands in the Streets.* Berkeley and Los Angeles: University of California Press.

12 Anderson, Elijah. 1999. Code of the Street: Decency, Violence and the Moral Life of the Inner City. New York: W.W. Norton. Jankowski, Martin Sanchez. 1991. *Islands in the Streets.* Berkeley and Los Angeles: University of California Press.

13 Gabbidon, Shaun L. 2015. *Perspectives on Race and Crime,* 3rd ed. London and New York: Routledge. Athens, Lonnie. 2005. Violent Encounters, Violent Engagements, Skirmishes and Tiffs. *Journal of Contemporary Ethnography* 34(6): 631–678.

14 Smith, Dwayne and Parker. Robert Nash. 1980. Types of Homicide and Variation in Regional Rates. *Social Forces* 59: 136–147.

15 Talbot, K. F. and Allen, T. 2014. Examining the Instrumental-Expressive Continuum of Homicides. *Homicide Studies* 18(3): 298–317. Miethe, Terance D. and Drass, Kriss A. 1999. Exploring the Social Context of Instrumental and Expressive Homicides: An Application of Qualitative Comparative Analysis. *Journal of Quantitative Criminology* 15: 3.

16 Hanlon, R., Brook, M., Stratton, J., Jensen, M. and Rubin, L. 2013. Neuropsychological and Intellectual Differences Between Types of Murderers: Affective/Impulsive Versus Predatory/Instrumental (Premeditated) Homicide. *Criminal Justice and Behavior.* doi 10.1177/0093854813479779.

17   NCADV. 2015. Domestic Violence National Statistics. Retrieved from http://ncadv.
      org/files/National%20Statistics%20Domestic%20Violence%20NCADV.pdf.

18   Anglemyer, Andrew, Horvath, Tara and Rutherford, George. 2014. The Accessibility
      of Firearms and Risk for Suicide and Homicide Victimization Among Household
      Members: A Systematic Review and Meta-analysis. *Annals of Internal Medicine*
      160(2): 101–110.

19   Fox, James A. and Levin, Jack. 2014. *Extreme Killing: Understanding Serial and Mass
      Murder: Understanding Serial and Mass Murder.* Los Angeles, CA: SAGE.

20   Bonn, S. 2014. 5 Myths about Serial Killers and Why They Persist. In *Why We Love
      Serial Killers: The Curious Appeal of the World's Most Savage Murderers.* New York:
      Skyhorse Publishing.

21   Miller, Laurence. 2014. Serial Killers: Subtypes, Patterns, and Motives. *Aggression
      and Violent Behavior* 19(1): 1–11.

22   Hickey, E. 2013. *Serial Murderers and their Victims.* Boston, MA: Cengage Learning.

23   Fleming, T. 1996. *Serial and Mass Murder: Theory, Research and Policy.* Toronto:
      Canadian Scholars Press.

24   Fox, James Alan and Levin, Jack. 1996. *Overkill: Mass Murder and Serial Killing
      Exposed.* New York, NY: Plenum.

25   Fox, J. and DeLateur, M. 2013. Mass Shootings in America: Moving Beyond Newtown.
      Homicide Studies, December 18. doi 1088767913510297.

26   Garbarino, James. 1999. *Lost Boys: Why Our Sons Turn Violent and How We Can
      Save Them.* New York: Free Press.

27   Harries, Keith. 1989. Homicide and Assault: A Comparative Analysis of Attributes
      in Dallas Neighborhoods, 1981–1985. *Professional Geographer* 41: 29–38.

28   Miethe, Terance D. and Regoeczi, Wendy C. 2016. Its Prevalence, Correlates, and
      Situational Contexts. In Carlos A. Cuevas (ed.), *The Wiley Handbook on the Psychology
      of Violence.* Wiley-Blackwell, p. 123.

29   Ibid.

30   Logan, T. K. and Walker, R. 2015. Stalking: A Multidimensional Framework for
      Assessment and Safety Planning. In *Trauma Violence and Abuse.*

31   Riedel, Marc and Przybylski, Roger K. 1993. Stranger Murders and Assault: A Study
      of a Neglected Form of Stranger Violence. In Anna Victoria Wilson (ed.), 1993.
      Homicide: The Victim/Offender Connection. Cincinnati: Anderson.

32   Straus, Murray A. 1990. The National Family Violence Surveys. In Murray A. Straus
      and Richard K. Gelles (eds.), *Physical Violence in American Families: Risk Factors
      and Adaptations to Violence in 8,145 Families.* New Brunswick, NJ: Transaction.

33   Straus, Murry A. and Richard J. Gells. 1988. How Violent Are American Families?
      Estimates from the National Family Violence Research and Other Studies. In
      G. Hotaling (ed.), *New Directions in Family Violence Research.* Newbury Park, CA:
      SAGE.

34   United States Department of Justice, Office on Violence Against Women, 2015.

35   Daigle, L. E., and Muftic, L. R. 2015. *Victimology.* Los Angeles, CA: SAGE.

36   Hanmer, J., and Itzin, C. 2013. *Home Truths About Domestic Violence: Feminist
      Influences on Policy and Practice.* London: Routledge.

37   Knapton, S. 2014. Educated and Well Paid Women 'More Likely to Suffer Domestic
      Abuse'. *The Telegraph.* Retrieved from http://www.telegraph.co.uk/journalists/sarah-
      knapton/10679238/Educated-and-well-paid-women-more-likely-to-suffer-domestic-
      abuse.html.

38   Walker, Lenore E. 1979. *The Battered Woman.* New York: Harper & Row.

39   Department of Health and Human Services, Centers for Disease Control and
      Prevention. *Child Maltreatment, Prevention, Definition.* Retrieved from http://www.
      cdc.gov/ncipc/dvp/cmp/CMP-def.html.

40   Child Welfare Information Gateway. Retrieved from https://www.childwelfare.gov/.

41 Nagi, Saad Zaghloul. 2013. *Child Maltreatment in the United States: A Challenge to Social Institutions*. Columbia University Press.

42 Negriff, S., Schneiderman, J., Smith, C., Schreyer, J. and Trickett, P. 2014. Characterizing the Sexual Abuse Experiences of Young Adolescents. *Child Abuse & Neglect* 38(2).

43 Srivastava, Anubha and Jain, Sunitha Abhay. 2015. Child Emotional Abuse: Causes, Effects and Remedies. *IUP Law Review* 5(1).

44 Finkelhor, D., Vanderminden, J., Turner, H., Hamby, S. and Shattuck, A. 2014. Child Maltreatment Rates Assessed in a National Household Survey of Caregivers and Youth. *Child Abuse & Neglect* 38(9).

45 Fleishmann, S. 2015. Toward a Fact-Based Analysis of Statutory Rape under the United States Sentencing Guidelines. *University of Chicago Legal Forum* 17(1).

46 Emanuel, S. and Friedman, J. 2010. *Evidence Elo*. Netherlands: Aspen Publishers Online.

47 Daigneault, I., Hebert, M., McDuff, P., Michaud, F., Vezina-Gagnon, P. and Henry, A., Porter-Vignola, E. 2015. Effectiveness of a Sexual Assault Awareness and Prevention Workshop for Youth: A 3-month Follow-up Pragmatic Cluster Randomization Study. *The Canadian Journal of Human Sexuality* 24(1).

48 Spohn, C. and Horney, J. 2013. *Rape Law Reform: A Grassroots Revolution and Its Impact*. Berlin, Germany: Springer Science & Business Media. Spohn, Cassia and Horney, Julie. 1992. *Rape Law Reform: A Grassroots Revolution and Its Impact*. New York: Plenum.

49 Chun, H. and Love, L. 2013. Fourteenth Annual Gender and Sexuality Law: Annual Review Article: Rape, Sexual Assault, & Evidentiary Matters. *The Georgetown Journal of Gender and the Law* 14: 585–749.

50 Raphael, J. 2013. *Rape is Rape: How Denial, Distortion, and Victim Blaming Are Fueling a Hidden Acquaintance Rape Crisis*. Chicago: Chicago Review Press.

51 Koss, Mary P., Gidycz, C.J. and Wisniewski, N. 1987. The Scope of Rape: Sexual Aggression and Victimization in a National Sample of Students in Higher Education. *Journal of Consulting and Clinical Psychology* 55: 162–170.

52 Fisher, Bonnie S., Cullen, Francis T. and Turner, Michael G. 2000. *The Sexual Victimization of College Women*. Washington, D.C.: National Institute of Justice and Bureau of Justice Statistics, U.S. Department of Justice.

53 Ningard, H. 2014. Going Viral: Exploring the Social Construction of Rape in Steubenville, OH. Doctoral dissertation, Ohio University.

54 Kilmartin, C. and Berkowitz, A. 2014. *Sexual Assault in Context: Teaching College Men About Gender*. Abingdon, England: Psychology Press.

55 Fedina, L. and Holmes, J.L., Backes, B. 2016. Campus Sexual Assault: A Systematic Review of Prevalence Research from 2000 to 2015. *Trauma, Violence, & Abuse*.

56 Schwartz, M. and DeKeseredy, W. 1997. *Sexual Assault on the College Campus: The Role of Male Peer Support*. Thousand Oaks, CA: SAGE.

57 Falk, P. 2014. *Not Logic, but Experience: Drawing on Lessons from the Real World in Thinking About the Riddle of Rape-by-Fraud*. Cleveland, OH: Cleveland State University.

58 Hayes, R., Lorenz, K. and Bell, K. 2013. Victim Blaming Others: Rape Myth Acceptance and the Just World Belief. *Feminist Criminology*. doi 10.1177/1557085113484788.

59 Trickett, L. 2016. Birds and Sluts: Views on Young Women From Boys in the Gang. *International Review of Victimology*.

60 Salter, M. 2012. *Organised Sexual Abuse*. Abingdon, England: Routledge.

61 Vetten, Lisa and Haffajee, Sadiyya. 2005. Gang Rape: A Study in Inner-City Johannesburg. *SA Crime Quarterly* 12.

62 Turchik, J., Hebenstreit, C. and Judson, S. 2015. An Examination of the Gender Inclusiveness of Current Theories of Sexual Violence in Adulthood: Recognizing

Male Victims, Female Perpetrators, and Same-Sex Violence. In *Truama, Violence, and Abuse.*

63 Plummer, L., Levy-Peck, J. and Easteal, P. 2013. *Intimate Partner Sexual Violence: A Multidisciplinary Guide to Improving Services and Support for Survivors of Rape and Abuse.* London: Jessica Kingsley Publishers.

64 Ibid.

65 Groth, Nicholas. 1979. *Men Who Rape: The Psychology of the Offender.* New York, NY: Plenum.

66 Hazelwood, R.R. and A.N. Burgess. 1995. *Practical Aspects of Rape Investigation: A Multidisciplinary Approach.* New York: CRC Press.

67 Stevens, Dennis J. 1999. *Inside the Mind of a Serial Rapist.* San Francisco, CA: Austin and Winfield.

68 Deming, Michelle E., Covan, Eleanor Krassen, Swan, Suzanne C. and Billings, Deborah L. 2013. Exploring Rape Myths, Gendered Norms, Group Processing, and the Social Context of Rape Among College Women A Qualitative Analysis. *Violence Against Women* 19(4): 465–485.

69 Deming, M., Covan, E., Swan, S. and Billings, D. 2013. Exploring Rape Myths, Gendered Norms, Group Processing, and the Social Context of Rape Among College Women: A Qualitative Analysis. In *Violence Against Women.* Thousand Oaks, CA: Sage.

70 Ibid., see 28.

71 Federal Bureau of Investigation. 2015. *Crime in the United States.* Retrieved from https://www.fbi.gov/about-us/cjis/ucr/crime-in-the-u.s/2015/preliminary-semiannual-uniform-crime-report-januaryjune-2015.

72 Federal Bureau of Investigation. 2014. *Uniform Crime Reports.* Retrieved from https://www.fbi.gov/about-us/cjis/ucr/crime-in-the-u.s/2014/crime-in-the-u.s.-2014.

73 Bureau of Justice Statistics. 2014. *National Crime Victimization Survey.* Retrieved from http://www.bjs.gov/content/pub/pdf/cv14.pdf.

74 Morewitz, S. and Goldstein, M. 2013. *Handbook of Forensic Sociology and Psychology.* Berlin, Germany: Springer Science & Business Media.

75 Fuller, G. 2014. Where and When: A Profile of Armed Robbery by Location. *Trends and Issues in Crime and Criminal Justice* 479.

76 John, K. 2013. Special Problems in Criminology (A Case Study of Armed Robbery). *Social Science Research Network.* Retrieved from http://papers.ssrn.com/sol3/papers.cfm?abstract_id=2692960.

77 Cuevas, C. and Rennison, C. 2016. *The Wiley Handbook on the Psychology of Violence.* Hoboken, NJ: John Wiley & Sons.

78 Matthews, R. 2013. *Armed Robbery.* Abingdon, England: Routledge.

79 Wright, Richard T. and Scott H. Decker. 1997. *Armed Robbers in Action: Stickups and Street Culture.* Boston: Northeastern University Press.

80 Miller, Jody. 1998. Up It Up: Gender and the Accomplishment of Street Robbery. *Criminology* 1: 37–66.

81 Dougherty, R. 2015. *Social Disorganization, Extra-Curricular Activities, and Delinquency.* Johnson City: East Tennessee State University.

82 Wright, R. and Decker, S. 2011. *Armed Robbers in Action: Stickups and Street Culture.* Lebanon, NH: UPNE.

83 Feeney, Floyd. 1986. Robbers as Decision-Makers. In Derek B. Cornish and Ronald V. Clarke (eds.). *The Reasoning Criminal: Rational Choice Perspectives in Offending.* New York: Springer-Verlag, pp. 53–71.

84 Ross, Jeffrey I. 2013. *Encyclopedia of Street Crime in America.* Thousand Oaks, CA: SAGE.

85 Miller, L. 2012. *Criminal Psychology: Nature, Nurture, Culture—A Textbook and Practical Reference Guide for Students and Working Professionals in the Fields of Law*

Enforcement, Criminal Justice, Mental Health, and Forensic Psychology. Springfield, IL: Charles C. Thomas Publisher.

86 Federal Bureau of Investigation. 2014. *Hate Crime Statistics.* Retrieved from https://www.fbi.gov/news/stories/2015/november/latest-hate-crime-statistics-available/latest-hate-crime-statistics-available.

CHAPTER OUTLINE

Crimes against property

In this chapter we will explore the following questions

- How do we categorize larceny theft?
- Why do people steal?
- In what ways is burglary different from robbery?
- What are the characteristics of burglary?
- Who steals cars and why do they do it?
- Are all fire setters the same?

KEY TERMS

larceny-theft

constructive
  possession

grand larceny

petit larceny

expressive gain

instrumental gain

shoplifting

kleptomania

snitches

boosters

check duplication

counterfeiting

forgery

embezzlement

false pretense

confidence game

phishing

extortion

professional
  fence

burglary

trespassing

offense
  specialization

motor vehicle
  thefts

carjacking

joy riding

arson

Have you ever thought about taking something that does not belong to you? Could it have been something little such as a stick of gum or something big like an expensive watch? Were you at your friend's house, at the grocery store, or in a building where you didn't belong? Crimes against property take on a variety of forms. They range from the professional practices of career thieves to the opportunistic or careless behavior of first-time offenders. They can make history or go relatively unnoticed. For research purposes, criminologists categorize the property crimes of larceny, burglary, motor vehicle theft, and arson by their success or failure, as well as by the offender's level of skill, degree of planning, and method of execution.[1]

On the evening of March 18, 1990, a group of professional thieves made history when they broke into the Isabella Steward Gardner Museum in Boston, Massachusetts, and stole 13 paintings estimated at $300 million, the largest art theft ever to be committed in the United States. The perpetrators, wearing police uniforms, identified themselves to on-duty museum security officers as Boston police who were responding to a call about a disturbance on the museum grounds. Once they gained access to the museum, the thieves abducted the security personnel, restrained them with duct tape and handcuffs and kept them secure in the basement area of the museum. Video surveillance was removed and taken by the offenders before leaving the museum. To this day, none of the paintings have been recovered. These thieves were no amateurs; they were professionals who made a living out of stealing. How common is

Image 15.1 *This Rembrandt,* A Lady and a Gentleman, *was one of the paintings stolen by professional thieves from the Gardner Museum in Boston, a heist that totaled nearly $300 million in stolen artwork.*

Isabella Stewart Gardner Museum, Boston, MA, USA/Bridgeman Images

this pattern of theft, and how do professional thieves differ from amateurs?

One classic study of the career paths of professional thieves examined the lives and perspectives of over 50 habitual property offenders.[2] Professional thieves identify with a criminal lifestyle and are committed to crime as a way of earning a living. Theirs is a calculated decision made in the context of desperation for money, the need to support a drug habit, or the desire to live a lavish lifestyle. They know the possible consequences—arrest, jail time—and accept them as part of the job. More often than not, professionals specialize in particular forms of theft such as confidence tricks, safecracking, burglary, shoplifting, check forgery, or fraud.[3] They identify with their own subculture, which has a social hierarchy, shared unique language, and ethical code.[4] Professional thieves view their work with pride and see theft as a legitimate enterprise. They compartmentalize their profession according to the degree of specialization, complexity, and training necessary to carry it out and typically begin early in life, learning how to steal and apprenticing with an older, more experienced thief to learn the trade.[5]

Studies indicate professional theft is rare compared to other types of property crime. While we cannot estimate the incidence rate with any accuracy, only a handful of inmates in federal and state penitentiaries at any given time are professional thieves. You may suspect this is a testament to their ability to stay out of prison, and perhaps it is. However, reports of professional theft in cities throughout the United States and Europe, and the only occasional discovery of professional thieves, all suggest the incidence is small. Most arrests for crime are of people between 16 and 25, who will likely not have developed the skills and experience to qualify as a professional thief, further support for the conclusion that professional theft does not account for large amounts of crime.

In this chapter, we explore the unlawful taking and the unlawful destruction of property. Despite the diversity of crimes against property, one common theme cuts across all categories: there is no direct contact between the offender and the victim and therefore no use or threat of force. Let us turn now to a discussion of larceny.

LARCENY

Larceny theft is "the unlawful taking, carrying, leading, or riding away of property from the possession or constructive possession of another."[6] The "immediate possession" part of this definition comes from the common law definition of theft created by English judges to describe the taking of someone else's property for use without the owner's permission.[7] This type of illegal possession implied trespassing upon another's land with the intent to steal. In later years, however, the courts needed also to account for theft by deception or trickery. Thus we use the term **constructive possession** to describe "the condition in which a person does not have physical custody or possession, but is in a position to exercise dominion or control over a thing."[8] As long as the money deposited in the bank is in the possession of its employees, for example, any mishandling of it construes theft, because it is reasonable to assume the money is still the property of the persons who made the deposit and entrusted it to the bank.

States distinguish between **grand larceny**, the theft of an item or merchandise of significant value, and **petit (petty) larceny**, the theft of property of little value. The line is drawn differently according to each state's criminal codes and can vary widely. In New York, grand larceny is the theft of goods valued in excess of $1,000. In Virginia, theft of an item with a value of only $200 or more is grand larceny.

Grand larceny is a felony crime meriting a high monetary fine and imprisonment of more than one year. Petty larceny, more common than grand, is a misdemeanor offense usually handled more leniently, with a lower monetary fine and/or less than one year in jail. As a matter of fact, the overwhelming majority of property theft (over 80%) is of property worth less than $250.[9]

According to data gathered by the National Crime Victims Survey (NCVS), larceny is the most frequent property offense. In the sections to come, we will take a closer look at specific forms of larceny theft in greater detail, in an effort

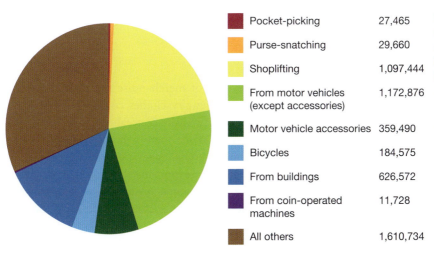

Pocket-picking	27,465
Purse-snatching	29,660
Shoplifting	1,097,444
From motor vehicles (except accessories)	1,172,876
Motor vehicle accessories	359,490
Bicycles	184,575
From buildings	626,572
From coin-operated machines	11,728
All others	1,610,734

Figure 15.1
How do people steal? Reported larceny offenses by type

Source: FBI, Crime in the United States. 2014. Retrieved from www.fbi.gov/about-us/cjis/ucr/crime-in-the-u.s/2014/crime-in-the-u.s.-2014.

to understand the different categories of theft, the various methods by which individuals steal, and the motives behind their crimes. Figure 15.1 shows the breakdown of different larceny types reported to police.

Describing larceny

Why do people steal? How can individuals justify taking something that does not belong to them, cheating the rightful owner? Larceny is one of the few categories of criminal behavior to which criminologists try to attach a rational motive, perhaps because people readily understand that everyone needs material goods so there must be a reason for taking them.[10] However, it seems that thieves apply reasoning to the specific decisions they make about the crime, rather than to the decision to commit it in the first place. For example, a thief may evaluate a store's security system or note its hours of operation. But we must also understand the crime of larceny within the social context of the offender's character and experiences, in order to grasp whether the goal is expressive gain, such as thrill or peer approval, or instrumental gain, to meet a need or support a lavish lifestyle. Contrast for example the thefts committed by Lucy, a successful Detroit businesswoman and mother of three who admittedly stole for the thrill and high that it gave her, with the thefts of the millionaire shoplifter who stole goods from various stores and returned the items for cash with fake receipts, accumulating enough money over the years to wear designer clothes, stay at luxury hotels, and dine in the top restaurants.[11]

The crime of larceny is largely motivated by individual traits such as intelligence and personality; situational factors such as financial need, peer pressure, and drug dependency; and contextual variables such as opportunity and the availability of a vulnerable victim.[12] These variables also affect the specific type of larceny that an offender commits.

Understanding the different types of larceny

We explore the dynamics behind larceny further by taking a closer look at the specific categories, beginning with shoplifting.

Shoplifting

The term shoplifting describes the theft of merchandise from a retail store. Shoplifters commonly steal items such as jewelry, clothes, cosmetics, accessories, electronics, and small appliances they can easily conceal on their bodies—in pockets, under clothing, or in a purse. While there is no typical profile of a shoplifter, a University of Florida study challenges popular stereotypes of shoplifters being females, arguing that men are more likely to steal than women.[13] Moreover, people who steal from stores come from diverse backgrounds and can be of any age, ethnic group, race, and socioeconomic background.[14] The popular idea that shoplifters suffer from some type of mental disorder—kleptomania—that gives them a compulsive urge to steal is a myth. It is also

Image 15.2 *If some people steal out of need and some for the rush, how might the presence of this video surveillance equipment affect a shoplifter's decision to steal depending on their motive?*

iStock/stnazkul

untrue that shoplifters steal out of desperation or a need to survive. Most can actually afford to pay for the items they are stealing.

One ground-breaking study found the overwhelming majority of shoplifters were amateur or casual thieves who simply steal items for their own personal use. This category of shoplifters, commonly referred to as **snitches** by thieves, are generally law-abiding citizens who are not associated with a criminal lifestyle. A small minority of shoplifters are professional thieves or **boosters**, who make part of their living by stealing merchandise they can easily resell to pawnshops or fences.[15]

Shoplifting appears to be pervasive among juvenile offenders. Research findings indicate that two-thirds of juveniles admit to have shoplifted at some point in their life.[16] Some young people view shoplifting as an expected part of adolescence. A Finnish study concluded that shoplifting is a form of deviant behavior among teens who give in to temptation under the effects of weakened ties to social control.[17] They are usually motivated by peer pressure, lack of money, defiance or challenge to authority, and the excitement of getting away with it.

Regardless of the offender's characteristics and motive, shoplifting is a serious crime that costs retailers billions of dollars a year. According to the 2015 Annual Retail Theft Survey conducted by Hayes International Consulting Firm on 25 major retail stores, 1,192,194 shoplifters were apprehended for stealing nearly $159,526,231 in goods. Table 15.1 provides a summary of the findings.

Credit card fraud

Another form of larceny is credit card fraud, which occurs when someone illegally accesses data associated with someone else's credit card, either by physically stealing the card from a wallet or purse, or accessing the credit card number

Table 15.1 Shoplifting trends in 2014: incident and cost at 25 major retailers

Time frame	Dollars	Incidents
Annually	13.26–17.68 billion	265–353 million
Daily (365 days)	36,328,000–48,438,000	726,575–968,767
Hourly (24)	1,513,698–2,018,264	30,274–40,365
Per minute (60)	25,228–33,637	504–672

Source: Information from Jack L. Hayes International. 2015. *Theft Surveys*. Retrieved from http://hayes international.com/news/annual-retail-theft-survey/.

during a legitimate transaction between a customer and merchant. The growth of online shopping has also contributed to security breaches in credit card databases, allowing thieves to illegally access customer accounts and use information to make unauthorized purchases.[18] Between November 27, 2013 and December 15, 2013, during the peak holiday shopping season, a major hack of Target shopping retail stores resulted in the theft of credit and debit card data, including names, numbers, expiration dates, and CVV codes, from over 40 million consumer accounts.[19] This form of credit card fraud is more costly because of the large amount of information compromised. It can also be more difficult to detect, because a perpetrator might hold a compromised account for several weeks before using it. Physical theft of a credit card holds greater risk for the thief, because the victim is likely to quickly discover the theft and immediately report and cancel the missing card.

Check fraud

One of the biggest challenges to businesses and financial institutions is a category of larceny that includes the fraudulent use of checks. Individuals and gangs often carry out **check duplication**, also called **counterfeiting**, by creating bogus financial documents with sophisticated desktop publishing software, or by altering a real check using solvents such as bleach or acetone to remove or change some of its information.[20]

Forgery usually follows a purse-snatching or pick-pocketing in which the thief steals a check, alters it, and presents it for cash or payment at a retail store using false identification. The crime of check forgery includes altering the payee, increasing the value of the check, altering the account number, and forging the signature of the legitimate check holder.[21] The majority of check forgers are amateur criminals who respond to an immediate cash flow crisis by taking the risk of committing a criminal act. The law usually requires that the person presenting the check know it is forged, proving intent to defraud or steal through deception, and that the forgery results in or has the possibility of resulting in loss to someone else.

Embezzlement

Embezzlement is a unique form of larceny that violates the trust of an employer when the property stolen is in the rightful possession of the perpetrator, who has the permission or consent of the owner.[22] A bank teller is entrusted with money that belongs to the bank's customers, for instance; any violation of that trust in order to commit theft is embezzlement. The crime can be a sophisticated theft of a large sum planned for months or years, or it can be repeated thefts of small amounts over time.

Embezzlement can be perpetrated in various contexts, but the primary indicator of this type of theft is a violation of trust on the part of the individual who steals. For example, in 2014, Carmen Batts-Porter, and employee of Marion County, Indiana's Center Township, was charged with embezzlement of more than $66,000 in Social Security benefits from elderly and disabled Hoosiers. She was in charge of overseeing their benefits and used that position to her advantage to steal money to pay off credit card debts. U.S. Attorney Josh Minkler commented on her actions by saying, "If you do not uphold the public trust, our Public Integrity Working Group will find you, investigate you and the U.S. Attorney's Office will prosecute you to the fullest extent of the law."[23]

Embezzlement schemes are often uncovered through financial audits. Table 15.2 provides a summary of personal and organizational indicators businesses use to detect the fraudulent activities of employees. We will take another look at this crime in chapter 17.

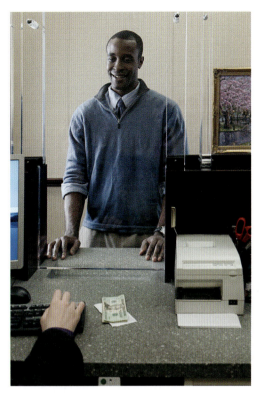

Image 15.3 *If this bank teller kept some of the money from the cash drawers, why would that type of stealing be considered embezzlement?*

iStock/IS_ImageSource

False pretenses/fraud

In a larceny perpetrated by **false pretenses**, the perpetrator uses lies and deception to trick the victim out of his or her money or property, usually by misrepresenting the nature, value, or characteristics of merchandise.[24] The offender must know the information is false and intend to defraud. Suppose a baseball card trader offers an original autographed Babe Ruth card to a collector who later discovers the signature is not authentic. The merchant who sold the card must be shown to know it was a fake and to have sold it with intent to deceive in order for a charge of fraud to be valid.

Non-disclosure of information can also constitute false pretense. A land owner selling a property as commercially zoned who has prior knowledge that it will be converted to agricultural purposes, significantly decreasing its value, is guilty of false pretense. Concealing facts that should be disclosed is a form of fraudulent misrepresentation, because the information could have been an important factor in the buyer's decision.

Table 15.2 Possible indicators of embezzlement

Individual	• Financial troubles, loss of income
	• Sudden change in financial situations/unexplained wealth
	• Declining trend in performance of job
	• Change in mood or personality
	• Deviation from work related policies and procedures
	• Interests in outside or competing businesses
	• Variations in work attendance/hours/vacation time
Organizational	• Poor internal management
	• High rate of employee turnover
	• Out of balance accounts
	• Missing/out of sequence documents
	• Inconsistent billing practices
	• Customer complaints about monetary discrepancies

Source: Pedneault, Stephen. 2010. *Preventing and Detecting Employee Theft and Embezzlement: A Practical Guide.* Wiley Online Library.

Confidence games

Confidence games, also known as cons, scams, and swindles, are schemes devised to trick or cheat unsuspecting victims out of their money by gaining their trust. Anybody can fall prey to an experienced con artist. The essential component of a con game is to gain the confidence of the "mark" or target in order to get him or her to buy into the scheme, which is often built around the victim's particular vulnerability.

Some schemes such as the one perpetrated by televangelists Jim and Tammy Faye Bakker (featured in Image 15.4) are designed to prey upon the weak, naïve, trusting, and compassionate (see Box 15.1). Other types take advantage of individuals who are themselves greedy and dishonest. Nigerian letter scams work this way. Blinded by their own greed, victims are sucked in by the promise of millions of dollars from a supposedly wealthy Nigerian official trying to move large sums of money from his homeland. All the victim has to do is pay several thousand dollars in bribes up front and millions will later be transferred into his or her account, of which the victim will get to keep a large percentage. After paying his or her portion up front, however, the victim never hears from the wealthy foreigner again.[25]

Modern technology has allowed confidence games to take on new power, as widespread use of the internet and telemarketing enterprises have led to the growth of high-tech frauds that are costly and difficult to detect. One common technique is known as **phishing**, wherein identity thieves posing as legitimate financial institutions, government agencies, or retail stores solicit personal information such as social security numbers or bank account numbers from unsuspecting customers via the telephone or through e-mail.

Different types of common confidence games have developed over the years. Here are some examples:

Image 15.4 *Televangelist Jim Bakker and his wife Tammy Faye operated a non-profit religious organization called Praise the Lord (PTL) that eventually became its own television network in the late 1970s, with over 12 million viewers. Contributions solicited from dedicated supporters and compassionate viewers to advance the mission and activities of the PTL organization were estimated to exceed one million dollars a week. The couple lived a lavish and extravagant lifestyle. In 1988, Jim Bakker was indicted on 24 counts of conspiracy and fraud for personal gain. How is this case an example of a confidence game?*

AP/Press Association Images

1. **Romance fraud**: In this type of scheme, the perpetrator takes advantage of a widow or other lonely victim and enters his or her life as a friend and lover with the goal of cultivating a romantic relationship. Having gained the victim's absolute trust, perhaps with the promise of commitment and marriage in return for help meeting some financial hardship, the con artist then drains the victim financially, often leaving him or her penniless. Romance fraud has spread to internet dating as well.

    A group of convicts and complicit prison guards of the Louisiana State Penitentiary in Angola, Louisiana, perpetrated their own version of romance fraud when they found a way to bilk lonely men and women out of thousands of dollars through a phony personals ad scam. When single people responded to the personals ads, letters would immediately be sent back that included a photo and requested money. The FBI got wise to the setup, and eventually investigators found the scheme originated with convicted murderer and Angola inmate Kirksey McCord Nix Jr.[26]

2. **Get-rich-quick schemes**: Get-rich-quick schemes are quite diverse and often rely on selling fake franchises or real estate, soliciting funds for bogus inventions, selling shares of hopeless business ventures, investing in useless or faulty merchandise, and participating in phony insider gambling or stock

BOX 15.1: CONSIDER THIS . . .

Religion or confidence game?

The successful execution of a confidence game depends almost exclusively on the con artist's ability to deceive a vulnerable victim or victims, often by invoking their own moral values and beliefs to spur them to action. Having gained the victim's commitment to the specific cause, the criminal must ensure it continues, no matter how much money and resources he or she demands in exchange for promised benefits and rewards.

Religious confidence games that rely on the promise of divine intervention and supernatural powers for driving a supposedly charitable cause are thus an ideal scheme. The con artist is established as a moral leader who has some type of unique and special connection to a sainted being or to God, who directly charges followers with supporting the leader in order to sustain the mission. Failure to comply is seen as defiance or sin.

To be successful, however, the confidence game must also have some payoff to sustain followers over the long run, which makes religious confidence games even more ideal. Many such schemes solicit money from unsuspecting victims with the promise to use it for some charitable cause such as feeding the hungry, treating disease, or spreading the "good news" to impoverished communities around the world. Very often, these funds are difficult to track, especially by followers convinced of their leader's moral integrity, and can easily be diverted to the pockets of those running the scam.

Victims are convinced of the intrinsic rewards of being the chosen followers and will seek no other material benefit. Often these intrinsic rewards include the leader's personal intervention on behalf of dedicated members to communicate their own personal needs to God and to carry out divine healing, deliverance from sin, and release from financial hardship or addiction. Is it possible for individuals to be that gullible? Are religious confidence games the ideal scam? *What do you think?*

Source

Money Transfer and Business Scams: Scammers Using Religious, God, Jesus to Con You. *Consumer FraudReporting.org*. Retrieved from www.consumerfraudreporting.org/AFFreligion.php

Religious Confidence Games. Retrieved from www.sullivan-county.com/nf0/nov_2000/rel_games.htm

market trades. The perpetrator hopes any victim who uncovers the swindle will be too embarrassed or too fearful of being implicated to report the loss.

This was the case in 1921 when Charles Ponzi dreamed up a scheme to cash in on foreign-to-U.S. currency exchange rates. He told investors he would purchase and trade in international mail coupons and reap them a 40 percent return in just 90 days. Ponzi received over one million dollars from interested investors in less than three hours! He used the money from later investors to pay off earlier ones in order to make the scheme appear legitimate. This is where we get the common term "Ponzi scheme," still used today to describe similar get rich quick schemes that rely on eager investors, such as the infamous fraud scheme operated by financier Bernard Madoff, exposed in 2009.[27]

3. **Charity swindles**: Some swindles rely on the sympathies of the public to solicit money for some type of good cause. They can be as simple as a peddler who displays a sign about being hungry or unemployed, or as sophisticated as the operations of television evangelists who set up non-profit organizations and plead to viewers to help support their ministry, supposedly dedicated to hunger and disaster relief across the world.

    In 2014, Largo Police Department uncovered a scam perpetrated by Shirley Ann Lawyer, founder and president of the Down Syndrome Network of Tampa Bay. Lawyer mismanaged funds raised through charitable donations and was charged with theft of more than $100,000 in goods and payments.[28]

4. **Extortion**: Extortion is the use of threats or blackmail to obtain money or something of value from someone. This often happens, for example, when a married man or woman (usually a man) is seduced into a sexual encounter with the intent of photographing the victim in a compromising situation and threatening him or her with exposure unless a specified amount of money is paid.

    Extortion is also often perpetrated on the rich and famous, often because they have the financial capability to pay for information they do not want to be made public. Such was the case that led actress and singer Jennifer Lopez to file a $20 million lawsuit in 2012 against her former chauffeur Hakob Manoukain, who allegedly demanded $2.8 million from Lopez for staying quiet about secrets he overheard in the car while they were driving.[29]

5. **Purposeful accidents**: A purposeful accident occurs when the perpetrator deliberately sets up the victim to have a car accident, especially to hit the perpetrator from behind, and then fakes injuries in order to collect money from the victim's insurance company. Purposeful accident schemes often require the collaboration and cooperation of a physician or chiropractor who can verify the injuries claimed and document treatment in exchange for payment.

    Purposeful accident schemes usually involve the collaboration or assistance of various individuals who can corroborate the story or use their expertise to verify an accident or injury. This was seen in the case of tow truck driver Jerry Blassengale Jr., who submitted approximately two dozen fake accident and vandalism claims to eleven different insurance companies over the course of almost 5 years. Using phony accident reports he paid for and obtained from ex-Philadelphia highway patrolman Drexel Reid Jr., in addition to dishonest drivers he recruited to report the accidents, Blassengale was able to fraudulently receive over half a million dollars from insurers.[30]

Receiving and fencing stolen property

Purchasing items and thinking you "got a steal" is very different from buying property you know is stolen. Receiving and fencing property acquired through theft or extortion by someone else is a separate crime from actually stealing the property in question. To be convicted of a crime, the receiver must know the goods exchanged were stolen at the time they are received. The fact that the buyer paid for the property is not a valid defense. Moreover, the court assumes an element of premeditation to aid the thief in disposing of the stolen items by selling them to someone else.

Individuals are often well aware the goods they purchase are stolen. These items, often sold on the street, out of car trunks, or at flea markets, are often grossly discounted, in second-hand condition or obviously used, unavailable for purchase through legitimate avenues, on the market, or for legal purchase, such as weapons.

The **professional fence** earns a living by purchasing and reselling stolen merchandise to merchants who turn around and market these items to legitimate customers.[31] The public also play an important role in the perpetuation of this form of theft. The emphasis on material goods and the rising cost of merchandise from retail stores turn individuals in the direction of always looking for a bargain. This is also facilitated by the buying and selling of goods over the convenient and anonymous avenue of the internet. Researcher Darrell Steffensmeier conducted an in-depth study of a professional fence who purchased a variety of stolen goods from different suppliers, including burglars, shoplifters, robbers, and other criminal offenders.[32] Steffensmeier identifies several characteristics of a successful fence:

- An adequate and steady supply of available cash for all transactions.
- Familiarity with the rules, norms, and procedures governing the buying and selling of stolen property.
- Long-term relationships with well-known, trustworthy, and reliable suppliers.
- Access to merchants such as pawn shops who are continuous customers.
- Relationships with local law enforcement in order to avoid detection, perhaps by acting as an informant in particularly important cases or paying cash or merchandise bribes.

The diverse forms of theft we've discussed so far all share one common factor—the legitimate presence of the perpetrator at the place of theft. Whether at a grocery store, in the mall, at work, or in the basement, an alley, or a friend's house, they have a legal right to be there. We turn now to a form of theft that includes unlawful access to the place of theft, the crime of burglary.

BURGLARY

Image 15.5 *What specific elements of this crime makes it a burglary?*
iStock/Ricardo Reitmeyer

The crime of **burglary** is any unlawful entry into a structure for the purpose of committing a theft or felony. The structure can be a home, office, retail store, or some other type of building.[33] The entry can either be forced, such as kicking down a door or breaking a lock, or it can involve no force at all, such as jumping through an open window or fraudulently obtaining a key or security code. The majority of burglary is residential and occurs during the daytime hours (see Figure 15.2).

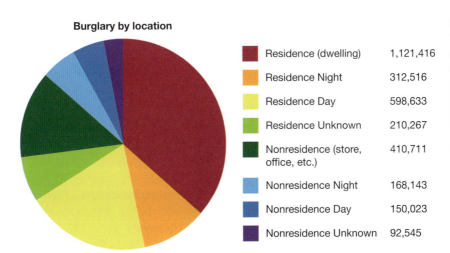

Burglary by location

Residence (dwelling)	1,121,416
Residence Night	312,516
Residence Day	598,633
Residence Unknown	210,267
Nonresidence (store, office, etc.)	410,711
Nonresidence Night	168,143
Nonresidence Day	150,023
Nonresidence Unknown	92,545

Figure 15.2
When and where are burglaries accomplished?

Source: FBI, Crime in the United States. 2014. Retrieved from www.fbi.gov/about-us/cjis/ucr/crime-in-the-u.s/2014/crime-in-the-u.s.-2014.

An individual can be charged with the crime of burglary based solely on intent to commit the crime, without actually completing it. For example, if Fred breaks into a restaurant to steal cash from a safe but discovers it is empty and leaves, Fred can be charged with a burglary. Burglary can also include unlawful entry for the purpose of committing a felony, such as breaking into someone's apartment to commit an assault or rape. This is what distinguishes burglary from **trespassing**, in which the offender does not necessarily possess criminal intent. Jan may come home drunk one evening, for example, and accidentally wander into the neighbor's house without any intent to commit a theft or felony. Jan has committed trespass, not burglary.

Describing burglary

Burglary is very different from larceny in the characteristics of offenders and situational elements of the crime. The main difference is that burglary includes illegal access to the location of the theft, whereas larceny is committed while the offender has lawful access to the place where the crime is committed. If Ray steals from a retail store during regular business hours, he is committing a larceny. If he comes back after closing and forces entry into the store for the purpose of theft, he has committed a burglary. Moreover, burglary is predominantly perpetrated by male offenders.[34] This trend is largely influenced by the availability of potential targets for male offenders through jobs they tend to fill, such as carpenters, television cable installers, and gardeners. Studies also show that women who commit this type of property crime do so under the

BOX 15.2: CRIME IN GLOBAL PERSPECTIVE

Burglary trends in the United States and the United Kingdom

The property crime rate in the United States has been on a steady decline since 1990. According to the FBI's Uniform Crime Reports, arrests for burglary, larceny-theft, motor vehicle theft, and arson have all decreased to the lowest number in two decades. This trend is mirrored by the Department of Justice's National Crime Victimization Survey (NCVS), which has collected crime data from U.S. households since 1973. While some property crime trends, such as motor vehicle theft, have gone down considerably—there were 546,332 fewer such thefts in 2014 than in 2004, for about a 44 percent decrease—other property crimes such as burglary have only inched downward. Still, the overall decline in property crimes in the United States has been on a steady and continuous trend. How do these rates compare with other countries?

The United Kingdom uses similar statistical gathering methods, including the official crime data gathered by the police, as well as victim surveys such as the British Crime Survey. According to their figures, property crimes are on a similar decreasing trend; however, the United Kingdom has a much higher rate of property crimes overall. For example, the U.S. burglary rate was 542.5 per 100,000 inhabitants for 2014; the UK rate was roughly 700 per 100,000 that year.

Some experts note that the difference in burglary rate between the UK and the U.S. is attributed to the difference in sentencing practices between the two countries for that specific crime. Suspects accused of burglary are more likely to be convicted of this crime in the U.S. than in the UK. Moreover, offenders convicted for the crime of burglary in England face fewer sanctions than their U.S. counterparts, such as having their prison term suspended in exchange for a period of community supervision.

Another possibility is the vastly different crime-fighting strategies employed by police in the United Kingdom as opposed to the United States. The U.S. has various well-established community oriented policing strategies and programs, such as Neighborhood Watch and Crime Stoppers. While these programs differ from police department to police department, city to city, and state to state, their central focus is to provide a foundation upon which citizens can become involved to collaborate with local law enforcement to help stop crime in their neighborhoods by making people more aware of crime and crime suspects, providing police with tips to assist with investigation and apprehension and getting citizens involved in crime control to avoid reluctance and apathy. The UK by contrast has a national crime fighting force that addresses criminal activity from a national perspective. This includes the *Home Office Crime Strategy*, the *National Community Safety Plan,* and the *Prolific and Other Priority Offenders Strategy*. Collectively, these strategies approach crime control from the perspective of targeting the small group of offenders committing the greatest and most serious amount of crime.

Sources

Community Safety. 2015. UK Home Office. Retrieved from http://www.local.gov.uk/community-safety.

Crime Survey for England and Wales. 2014/2015. Office for National Statistics. London, England. Retrieved from http://www.crimesurvey.co.uk/.

Crime in the United States. 2014. Federal Bureau of Investigation, U.S. Department of Justice, Washington, D.C. Retrieved from https://www.fbi.gov/about-us/cjis/ucr/crime-in-the-u.s/2014/crime-in-the-u.s.-2014.

The Prolific and Other Priority Offenders Strategy. UK Home Office Crime Reduction. Retrieved from https://view.officeapps.live.com/op/view.aspx?src=https%3A%2F%2Fwww.justice.gov.uk%2Fdownloads%2Foffenders%2Fpsipso%2Fpso%2FPSO_4615_prolific_and_other_priority_offenders_strategy.doc.

coercive effects of a boyfriend or other male. Sometimes, they are unaware of what is going on until it is too late.[35]

Burglary is also distinct from robbery in being inherently evasive and non-confrontational. The majority of burglaries occur with the foreknowledge that residents will be away, buildings empty, or retail stores closed. However, the consequences of burglary on victims can be just as devastating. Their loss goes beyond the monetary value of the stolen items, since the invasive nature of burglary often leaves them with a sense of being personally violated, fearful, and apprehensive. Sometimes stolen items have sentimental value that represents an additional loss.

Figure 15.3
Burglary trends in
the United States:
1988–2014

Source: FBI, Crime in
the United States.
2014. Retrieved from
www.fbi.gov/about-us/
cjis/ucr/crime-in-the-u.s/
2014/crime-in-the-u.s.-
2014/tables/table-1

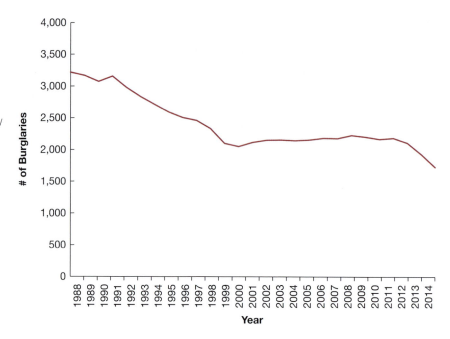

Table 15.3 Four categories of burglary

Location	Time of day	
	Daytime	**Nighttime**
Residential	Daytime residential	Nighttime residential
Commercial	Daytime commercial	Nighttime commercial

Source: Miethe, Terance, D., McCorkle, Richard C. and Listwan, Shelley J. 2016. *Crime Profiles: The Anatomy of Dangerous Persons, Places and Situations*, 3rd ed. New York: Oxford University Press.

Even though the property crime rate in the United States is lower than in most industrialized countries, theft by burglary is a fairly prevalent crime (see Box 15.2). The number of burglaries reported to the police has been steadily declining over the past decade, however (see Figure 15.3). The national burglary rate of 722.5 burglaries per 100,000 inhabitants in 2007 represents one of the lowest rates since the mid-1960s. Despite the shortcomings of UCR data discussed in chapter 3, this trend is consistent with data gathered by victimization surveys.[36]

Police reports allow us to classify burglaries according to their location and time of day. Table 15.3 describes the four distinct categories that emerge when we do so; note how the rates for these categories differ. Nighttime residential and daytime commercial burglaries are considered the most serious categories, because offenders are more likely to run into residents at home at night, and customers or workers in commercial settings during the day. Let's take a closer look at the crime of burglary, in order to better understand the various situational dynamics and patterns of offending that make up the four categories.

Understanding the crime of burglary

Image 15.6 *In* Thick as Thieves, *the 2009 film about a jewel heist, Morgan Freeman plays the role of veteran crook Keith Ripley who describes himself to the novice thief Gabriel Martin (Antonio Banderas) as "born to steal." Are most burglars professional thieves?*
Revelations Entertainment/The Kobal Collection

We can best understand burglary as a combination of three components: offense specialization, offender motivation, and routine activities. Let us begin by examining offense specialization.

Offense specialization

Studies focusing on **offense specialization** examine the degree to which burglars are highly skilled professional thieves or spontaneous, low-level criminal offenders. One study examined the criminal records of 2,000 convicted burglars and found the majority followed a pattern of repeat offending over a wide range of criminal activities, including burglary, robbery, assault, drug-related offenses, and other forms of larceny theft.[37] Thus, their burglary did not follow a pattern of specialization but rather was connected to a more general pattern of predatory behavior.

Researcher Mike Maguire offers three typologies of burglars based on the level of sophistication and planning behind the crime.[38] *Low-level* burglars are often younger offenders who commit burglary in a spontaneous, opportunistic manner. They perpetrate residential and commercial thefts by taking advantage of certain situations such as an open window, an unlocked door, or easy accessibility and are generally deterred by the presence of locks, alarms, and other security devices. They usually get away with a minimal amount of goods, since they have few connections to organized groups that can manage large quantities of stolen items. *Middle-range* burglars are a bit more sophisticated and often engage in other illegitimate pursuits such as drug use. They employ a greater degree of planning, selecting a target by weighing the risk and potential payoff, but still lack the type and level of criminal connections necessary to pull off the major, large-scale operations of high-level burglars.

High-level burglars are professional thieves who commit their crimes as a way of life. They are highly skilled in their planning, techniques, and methods of evading detection. They earn a reasonable amount of income as professional thieves, sometimes engaging in large-scale thefts at retail stores and other sellers of expensive goods such as jewelry, art, and other collectibles. On August 7, 2008, an organized gang of five was convicted in the United Kingdom after stealing $160 million worth of art and antiquities from homes in several counties. One of their raids had netted 300 museum-quality artworks, including a 17th-century painting worth an estimated $133 million.[39] High-level burglars often work in organized groups, with inside information about targets, surveillance, and police activity that facilitates planning.

Offender motivation

The motivations of criminal offenders who commit burglary include a variety of instrumental and expressive rationales that have become the subject of much criminological research.[40] In the rational choice perspective, the primary goal of burglary is economic gain.[41] Studies in fact show that the most prevalent reason for residential burglary is the immediate need for cash.[42] Rather than meeting basic needs for food and shelter, however, the cash allows a certain criminal status, level of comfort, or lavish lifestyle, or it supports a gambling habit or drug addiction.[43]

Commercial burglaries often seem even more deeply driven by instrumental, rational decision processes than residential burglaries, as evidenced by professional burglars who go to great lengths in planning, strategizing, and evaluating potential risks and economic gains when selecting their targets. Criminals often choose burglary as an easier and safer means to obtain money than selling drugs or committing a robbery, both of which can result in greater penalties and more confrontation with the victim.[44]

These calculating and carefully weighed decisions seem to be the primary motivations for the majority of offenders.[45] However, a small portion of burglars identify excitement and thrill as their motivators.[46] For them, burglary provides a level of stimulation above the ordinary activities of everyday life. The crime therefore fulfills an expressive need beyond economic gain. Some burglaries are also motivated by other expressive goals such as revenge, intoxication, and peer pressure.[47] Here, the crime takes on a new meaning associated with a riskier, more opportunistic pattern of offending.

The environment and routine activities

Routine activities theory emphasizes the effects of environmental and lifestyle variables.[48] According to this approach, a burglary is made possible by three interacting components: (1) a motivated offender who wants something; (2) a suitable victim who has what the offender wants and is at the right place at the right time; and (3) the lack of a capable individual or appropriate measure to protect the targeted victim. These dynamics help us to better understand the increase in burglaries on college campuses throughout the United States. On the afternoon of March 26, 2015, Lower Merion police responded to reports of a suspicious woman on the campus of Bryn Mawr College. Police found 24-year-old Philadelphia resident Amaryllis Boger stopped by campus security. At the time of the stop, she was carrying a bag in which police later found a MacBook computer and iPad that were taken earlier that day from unlocked dorm rooms. Boger was charged with burglary and was responsible for several thefts across campus where she entered unlocked dorm rooms on the college grounds and took several items.[49]

We've seen that offenders can have a variety of motivations to commit a burglary, from instrumental goals such as material gain to expressive goals such as revenge and thrill. Moreover, they can be planners or opportunistic actors and will thus select a suitable victim for different reasons that take into consideration the following variables:

(1) *Knowledge and convenience*—does the target minimize the time and effort needed to accomplish the burglary? Is the target close by and the offender possessed of the familiarity and techniques needed?

(2) *Barriers and obstacles*—does the target present potential barriers such as the presence of occupants, security guards, elaborate gates and fences, and alarms? Routine activities theory argues that the lifestyle and daily activities of individuals contribute significantly to their level of vulnerability. One study found that the majority of burglaries in apartment complexes occupied predominantly by college students occurred when the students were attending class, shopping, or participating in recreational activities.[50]

(3) *Expected gains*—do the potential rewards of the burglary outweigh the risks? Burglars assess the possibility that the selected target will have items of value such as computers, television sets, jewelry, and money that are easy to remove, have a high resale value, and can readily be fenced. Burglary has become a more lucrative enterprise for potential offenders as advances in technology have produced attractive, expensive, easily carried electronic items and gadgets.

Finally, the last element that increases the opportunity for burglary is the absence of a law enforcement officer or security guard, an alert neighbor, a neighborhood watch group, or a guard dog. Even having lights on at night is a deterrent. Routine activities theory provides us with a theoretical foundation upon which to build crime prevention strategies geared at altering the structure of opportunity within which burglaries occur. Box 15.3 discusses the policy implications of routine activity theory.

BOX 15.3: CONNECTING THEORY TO PRACTICE

Burglary prevention . . . Lessons learned from routine activities theory

The role of criminology in understanding crime goes beyond trying to discover why some individuals commit crime while others do not. We have learned that an array of psychological, social, and cultural variables in the environment and context drive offenders' constraints and opportunities, giving us a broader insight into why some individuals and some places are more likely to experience crime than others.

Insights from routine activities theory allow us to predict the effect when motivated offenders and criminal opportunities exist within certain contexts. Thus we can develop strategies to reduce specific types of crime. One major effort to reduce burglary relies on "target hardening" or crime prevention through environmental design (CPTED), to strengthen the ability of a neighborhood or community to reduce its risk as a target for burglars. Steps include organizing neighborhood watch groups, educating citizens about behavior patterns that can increase the likelihood of victimization, creating barriers such as security alarms and fences, ensuring doors and windows are locked during appropriate times, and removing trees and bushes that can serve as hiding places for potential burglars.

Strategies like these, which take into consideration situational factors, the routine activities of both potential victims and offenders, and the vulnerability of potential targets, will undoubtedly have a significant impact.

Sources

CPTED Perspective. 2015. Retrieved from http://www.cpted.net/resources/Documents/ICA%20Resources/Newsletters/Perspectives_V12_I1_January%20September%202015.pdf.

Newton, Andrew and Rogerson, Michelle. 2008. Relating Target Hardening to Burglary Risk. *The British Society of Criminology* 8: 153–174. Retrieved from www.britsoccrim.org/volume8/10Newton08.pdf.

Roberts, R.J. *R.A.T. Catcher: Crime Prevention and the Routine Activity Theory*. Retrieved from http://www.jrrobertssecurity.com/articles/rat-catcher-crime-prevention.htm.

MOTOR VEHICLE THEFT

The FBI defines motor vehicle theft as the theft or attempted theft of a motor vehicle, which includes cars, trucks, buses, motorcycles, snowmobiles, and some other methods of transportation.[51] The theft of a boat, an airplane, and a construction or farming vehicle is excluded, as is taking a motor vehicle for temporary use by someone with lawful access to it. Theft of equipment or items *inside* a motor vehicle is considered larceny, not motor vehicle theft. Stealing someone's car by using force or the threat of force is also not considered motor vehicle theft but rather is a specific form of robbery known as carjacking.

Describing motor vehicle theft

The seriousness of motor vehicle theft goes beyond the loss of property. While there is no immediate threat of danger or harm to an individual, there are long-term effects and hardships in losing such a valuable possession and going through the steps of replacing it.

The rate of motor vehicle theft has been steadily declining over the past decade; there were nearly 430,000 motor vehicle thefts in the United States in 2014.[52] Nearly 60 percent of motor vehicle thefts occur at or near the victim's home, and the most commonly stolen motor vehicle is, of course, a car. It is thus understandable, considering the value of the loss, that the rate of reporting motor vehicle theft to police is pretty high compared to other types of property crimes (see Table 15.4). As compared to other offense categories, the reporting percentage is higher for completed thefts than for attempted ones. While the rate of victimization is fairly similar across household income, the rate of reporting increases with the level of household income.

Table 15.4 Reporting crime victimization to the police: how does motor vehicle theft compare?

Type of crime	Number of victimizations	Percent distribution of victimizations reported to police
Household burglary	2,166,890	60.0
Larceny	8,297,290	29.0
Motor vehicle theft	429,840	83.3

Source: Criminal Victimization in the United States. 2014. National Crime Victimization Survey, Bureau of Justice Statistics, Office of Justice Programs, U.S. Department of Justice, Washington, D.C. Retrieved from http://www.bjs.gov/index.cfm?ty=pbdetail&iid=5366.

Understanding the occurrence of motor vehicle theft

The majority of stolen vehicles are recovered by the police or the owner, which makes it a bit puzzling to understand why the theft occurred in the first place.[53] Why do people steal motor vehicles? Who are these offenders and what is their motivation? We turn now to a closer look at the crime of motor vehicle theft, with a specific focus on four patterns of offending: joyriding, commercial theft, transportation, and the commission of other crimes.

Joyriding

Joyriding is considered an expressive act committed by teenagers, mostly boys, as a means of fulfilling a desire for fun or thrills by temporarily stealing a car.[54] Typically youth who engage in this type of crime are seeking excitement and peer approval. They lack the skill and sophistication of professional car thieves, and therefore their motivation has little to do with financial rewards or gains

Image 15.7 *Why do you suppose the majority of joyriding is perpetrated by younger offenders?*

iStock/Joel Carillet

from the theft. Joyriding tends to be impulsive and spontaneous, often committed by groups, with each individual sharing in the excitement and validating the careless, risky behavior of the others.[55]

Criminologists Gottfredson and Hirschi note that joyriding is an opportunistic crime. The typical theft is unplanned and unstructured, taking place on the spur of the moment when a juvenile or group of teens stumbles upon a car in a public street or parking lot, unlocked or with its keys easily accessible.[56] Since they do not intend to keep the car, or use it for other purposes such as stealing parts, the youths usually abandon it somewhere when it runs out of gas, breaks down, or is crashed, or when the thrill and excitement of the moment are gone.

Commercial theft for profit

The vehicle least likely to be recovered is the one taken in a commercial theft and usually either resold or stripped down for parts. Selling parts separately can be a much more lucrative transaction than selling a car whole, as parts are less easy to identify as stolen, and there is a greater underworld market where organized theft rings can traffic stolen stereo systems, tires, batteries, alarms, and other parts.[57] Commercial motor vehicle thieves must therefore develop a working relationship with criminal organizations, often called "chop shops," that can break the vehicle into parts for resale to unscrupulous auto-body shops, salvage yards, and other manufacturers of motor vehicle parts.[58]

A growing trend is the trafficking of stolen vehicles, especially to overseas export rings that operate sophisticated markets and recruit highly skilled professional thieves to steal for them. Most of these groups operate in foreign countries that do not have strict standards and guidelines for verifying VIN numbers, owner titles, and car registration.[59]

Transportation

Occasionally, a motor vehicle thief will steal a car, often a luxury car, as a means of personal transportation for a short period of time or a specific event or occasion. Typically, these individuals will use the car to serve their own purposes or until it becomes too risky to keep it, at which time they will abandon it, unharmed or missing whatever they can remove with ease such as a radio or GPS system. These offenders are usually novice criminals and often leave a trail of fingerprints and other items that can make it easy for law enforcement to trace back the theft to them. As theft prevention equipment and devices have become more advanced, however, offenders in need of a quick method of transportation have often turned to carjacking instead.

Commission of other crimes

Some offenders who steal cars do so to obtain a quick method of transportation when committing more serious crimes such as robberies, drive-by shootings, and burglaries. A stolen car reduces the chances the crime will be traced to them through identification of the vehicle they used to flee the scene.

With the exception of joyriding, most motor vehicle thefts include some degree of planning and reasoning. Reducing theft thus begins with preventive measures that deter by making it more difficult, such as locking cars, taking the keys, and not leaving valuables in plain sight.[60] Alarms, wheel clamps, and electronic tracking systems also reduce accessibility and enhance security. Although they do not address the root causes of the behavior, these measures make sense as prevention strategies. We turn now to a form of property crime that is less easy to understand, and even more difficult to solve, the crime of arson.

ARSON

Arson is the willful or malicious burning or attempted burning of a home, building, motor vehicle or airplane, or other personal property. According to the UCR, 15,324 law enforcement agencies reported 42,934 arsons in 2014, a 4 percent decrease from arson data reported in 2013.[61]

Describing arson

Arson is a very serious crime punished severely all over the world because it puts lives at risk and causes great damage to property.[62] In 2014, the overall average dollar loss per incident due to arson in the United States was $16,055; arsons of industrial/manufacturing structures resulted in the greatest losses,

Image 15.8 *Arsonists enjoy the thrill and attention that such havoc and devastation bring. They like the feeling that they are responsible for the destruction the fire brings, along with all the excitement.*

Richard Wainwright/AAP/PA Images

Table 15.5 Distribution of arsons in 2014: type of structure and how much damage

Property classification	Number of arson offenses	Percent distribution[1]	Average damage
Total	39,174	100.0	$16,055
Total structure:	17,854	45.6	$29,779
Single occupancy residential	8,630	22.0	$27,742
Other residential	3,071	7.8	$26,786
Storage	1,113	2.8	$11,341
Industrial/manufacturing	141	0.4	$167,545
Other commercial	1,594	4.1	$56,592
Community/public	1,513	3.9	$15,948
Other structure	1,792	4.6	$33,161
Total mobile:	9,154	23.4	$7,716
Motor vehicles	8,608	22.0	$7,416
Other mobile	546	1.4	$12,458
Other	12,166	31.1	$2,189

Source: *Crime in the United States.* 2014. U.S. Department of Justice, Federal Bureau of Investigation, Washington, D.C. Retrieved from https://www.fbi.gov/about-us/cjis/ucr/crime-in-the-u.s/2014/crime-in-the-u.s.-2014/tables/arson/arson_table_2_arson_by_type_of_property_2014.xls.

BOX 15.4: CONNECTING RESEARCH TO PRACTICE

Evidence based arson prevention

According to the Technical Working Group on Fire/Arson Scene Investigation, "the United States is one of the few countries where public authorities have statutory responsibility to investigate all fires and determine their origins and causes" (p. 3). Research on arson indicates prevention requires three crucial steps: carefully investigating fires, observing conditions conducive to arson, and taking the profit out of a set fire. These principles have led to breakthroughs in arson prevention.

Investigating

Arson is usually suspected only after all accidental possibilities have been ruled out, which means investigations may take longer. In 2000, the National Institute of Justice (NIJ) and the National Center for Forensic Justice (NCFJ) created "Fire and Arson Scene Evidence: A Guide for Public Safety Personnel," to clarify investigation procedures at arson scenes. It is currently being used as a training document across the country.

Observing

Many security companies have installed surveillance equipment outside businesses where arson is likely to occur and have caught a number of arsonists on camera. In 2008, firefighter Michael Murphy was caught on tape lurking outside a Maryland restaurant minutes before smoke began pouring out; he was arrested on suspicion of arson. Video makes for compelling evidence in a court of law and has proven to be a major factor in preventing arson-related crimes.

Taking the Profit Out

Much arson is committed to cover up other crimes or to profit illegally, such as by insurance fraud. Many insurance companies have programs to help stop arson committed by people trying to defraud them. Safeco Insurance, for example, has a hotline number for reporting suspected arson and will pay up to $25,000 for information leading to arson convictions in connection with fire loss to Safeco-insured property. These measures are in response to a practice known as "fire brokering," in which an arsonist will seek out a dilapidated property, purchase it at low cost, then plan and commit the arson to collect an insurance payment. The most effective method for deterring arson-for-profit is to be aware of these schemes and refuse to provide policies under suspicious circumstances. Further research and improved surveillance technology will make us better prepared to prevent and deter future damage.

Sources

Arson: Behavioral and Economic Aspects—Offender types. *Net Industries*. Retrieved from http://law.jrank.org/pages/529/Arson-Behavioral-Economic-Aspects-Offender-types.html.

Fire and Arson Investigator: Journal of the International Association of Arson Investigators, Inc. 66(3).

Fire and Arson Scene Evidence: A Guide for Public Safety Personnel. 2000. Technical Working Group on Fire/Arson Scene Investigation. U.S. Department of Justice, Office of Justice Programs, Washington, D.C.

Morgan, Charles S. 1953. Preventing Arson. *The Journal of Criminal Law, Criminology, and Police Science* 44(2): 258–261.

Safeco Insurance. 2016. *Fighting Insurance Fraud.* Retrieved from www.safeco.com/insurance-101/consumer-tips/fighting-insurance-fraud.

averaging $167,545 each.[63] Arsons of structures account for the majority of offenses, with vehicle fires following (see Table 15.5).

Understanding different types of arsonists

Motives for arson can range from the very calculated rational decision making of profit-motivated offenders to the irrational fantasies of thrill-seeking offenders. The varied patterns of arson often make prevention strategies challenging (see Box 15.4). We turn now to a discussion of the various categories of arson, in order to better understand the motivation behind this crime and the situational context within which it takes place.

Delinquent fire setters

Delinquent fire setters are typically younger adolescents exhibiting poor judgment and a lack of self-control.[64] They often set fires to schools or abandoned buildings and other hidden locations. Their primary motivation is mischief; their methods are fairly unsophisticated and marked by a desire to maliciously harm and rebel against authority.[65]

Pathological fire setters

Pathological fire setters have a long history of fire-setting behavior that includes a highly sophisticated method of operation with a distinct, often ritualistic approach that leaves a path of destruction the arsonist becomes extremely proud of.[66] Unlike most delinquent arsonists, pathological arsonists often suffer psychiatric difficulties and emotional conflicts that contribute to their fire setting behavior. These individuals generally do not feel any remorse for their behavior or the destruction it has caused. Their crime is a symptom of a generalized pattern of anti-social behavior and inability to identify with the feelings of others.[67]

Excitement-seeking fire setters

Fire-setting to get a rush or thrill from its destructive power, to draw attention, or even to find sexual gratification is called excitement-seeking arson.[68] It is rarely intended to harm people or even create large-scale damage but rather serves an expressive purpose. A typical excitement-seeking fire setter may start a fire then call for help or put it out, appearing as a hero to those around and often basking in the glory of the reaction to his or her accomplishment.

Revenge fire setters

Some arsonists are motivated by a desire for revenge, or to right a wrong.[69] For example, a girl breaks up with her boyfriend. He gets angry and sets her apartment on fire to get back at her. Or, a contractor does some remodeling work in a customer's home and does not feel sufficiently reimbursed as agreed. He sets fire to the home to get even. This type of crime is usually carefully planned, with a very specific target. It can be a one-time event against a specific individual, or a series of fires over time to avenge a grievance or make a political statement to some type of organization such as a church or clinic, the government or military, or society in general.[70]

Instrumental fire setters

Fire-setting is often a secondary pattern of behavior to achieve the primary goals of material profit or personal gain. Personal gain is often the motive when arson is used to cover up a crime that has already taken place, such as burglary, motor vehicle theft, or homicide, in which the fire is an attempt to conceal fingerprints, blood stains, and other forensic evidence that can identify the offender.[71] The desire for material gain can also be a primary motive in the destruction of a property for the purpose of fraud or to collect insurance, conceal loss, or destroy documents. In both cases, instrumental arsons are very carefully planned to create a significant amount of destruction in order to achieve the intended purpose. This category of fire-setters is not likely to re-offend—once they have achieved their goal, the motive to set a fire no longer exists.

The diversity of motives behind each category of arson is indeed a testimony to the diverse nature of crimes against property. In each case however, there is a distinct victim who suffers some form of emotional and financial loss or devastation. In the next chapter, we will turn to a category of criminal behavior where there is no such distinct victim and no clearly defined loss, the category of crimes against public order.

SUMMARY

What are the different categories of larceny theft?

We divide larceny—the unlawful taking of property that belongs to someone else—into two categories, grand and petit (petty), based on the monetary value of the stolen goods. Each state draws the line between the two at a different value. Larceny crimes include purse snatching, pick-pocketing, shoplifting, stealing from motor vehicles, and embezzlement and fraud.

Why do people steal?

Larceny theft is driven by a variety of motives, ranging from the rationally calculated decision of offenders motivated by financial gain, to the impulsive choices made by offenders driven by expressive goals such as peer approval or thrill. Regardless of the motive, the nature and outcome of larceny are also linked to the offender's character, situational factors, and opportunity.

What are the characteristics of burglary?

In larceny the offender has lawful access to the place where the crime is committed, while burglary includes unlawful entry into a structure, with or without the use of force, for the purpose of committing a theft or felony. Patterns of offending include daytime residential burglary, nighttime residential burglary, daytime commercial burglary, and nighttime commercial burglary. We can best understand the elements of burglary as a combination of three variables: offense specialization, offender motivation, and routine activities.

Are there different motives behind motor vehicle theft?

Offenders steal motor vehicles for a variety of reasons: joyriding, commercial theft, transportation, and the commission of other crimes. Joyriding is the temporary theft of a car, usually by younger offenders motivated by a desire for thrill and mischievous adventure. Stealing a motor vehicle for the fun of it is very different from committing commercial theft and either reselling the car or stripping it down into parts to be sold in the black market. Some offenders steal luxury cars as a means of transportation to some special event or occasion, while others use stolen vehicles as a quick means of transportation while committing a more serious crime.

Why do people set fires?

The crime of arson, the willful or malicious burning or attempted burning of property, includes delinquent fire-setting perpetrated by rebellious and mischievous youth, pathological fire-setting where the arson represents a method of coping with some type of emotional stress or mental disorder, fires set for excitement and revenge, and fires set for profit or to cover up other crimes.

CRITICAL THINKING QUESTIONS

1. What characteristics differentiate the occasional from the professional thief? Can someone start as a petty thief and then turn to a career of theft? What variables may influence the likelihood of this outcome? Which deterrents would best prevent it?

2. Let's say you go into an antique store and pay top dollar for a rare item the merchant certifies as authentic. Weeks later, you discover it is merely a replica. When you go back, the merchant swears the store had no

knowledge this item was not authentic. How do you resolve this dilemma? What type of theft is taking place here? Who might be implicated? Is the merchant responsible for your loss?

3. Which type of burglary should we treat more seriously, residential or commercial? Does one do more harm than the other? Should we measure the harm by the financial loss caused by the theft or by the effect on the victim? Does it matter for your answer whether entry was forced or not?

4. What are the primary differences between arsonists motivated by instrumental goals and those motivated by expressive goals? Which theoretical perspectives best explain these two patterns of fire-setting? What type of criminal justice response is most appropriate for different categories of arsonists?

E-RESOURCES

See the U.S. Department of Justice Fraud Section for more information on telemarketing fraud at https://www.justice.gov/criminal-fraud.

Learn more about identity theft by visiting the *Identity Theft Resource Center* website at http://www.idtheftcenter.org/.

Read more about the stolen property market as a function of supply and demand by visiting http://www.popcenter.org/problems/stolen_goods/.

For more information on automobile theft, contact the online auto-theft information clearinghouse at http://www.auto-theft.info/.

Visit the U.S. Fire Administration website at https://www.usfa.fema.gov/index.html for additional reading on arson and other fire related information and statistics.

NOTES

1   Miethe, Terance, McCorkle, Richard C. and Listwan, Shelley J. 2016. *Crime Profiles: The Anatomy of Dangerous Persons, Places, and Situations.* Los Angeles, CA: Roxbury Publishing Company.
2   Shover, Neal. 1996. *Great Pretenders: Pursuits and Careers of Persistent Thieves.* Boulder, CO: Westview Press.
3   King, Harry and Chambliss, William J. 2004. *Harry King: A Professional Thief's Journey.* Bloomington, IN: iUniverse.
4   Clinard, M., Quinney, R. and Wildeman, J. 2014. *Criminal Behavior Systems: A Typology.* London: Routledge.
5   King, Harry and Chambliss, William J. 2004. *Harry King: A Professional Thief's Journey.* Bloomington, IN: iUniverse.
6   Chanbonpin, K. 2014. Larceny (Theft). In *The Encyclopedia of Criminology and Criminal Justice.* Hoboken, NJ: Blackwell.
7   Cuevas, C. and Rennison, C. 2016. *The Wiley Handbook on the Psychology of Violence.* Hoboken, NJ: John Wiley & Sons. LaFave, Wayne R. and Scott, Austin W. 1972. *Handbook on Criminal Law.* St. Paul, MN: West Pub. Co.

8   Tritt, L. 2014. Dispatches from the Trenches of America's Great Gun Trust Wars. *Northwestern University Law Review* 108(2): 743–65.

9   Criminal Victimization in the United States, 2014. National Crime Victimization Survey. Bureau of Justice Statistics, Office of Justice Programs, U.S. Department of Justice, Washington, D.C. Retrieved from www.bjs.gov/index.cfm?ty=pbdetail&iid=5366.

10 Kochel, T., Parks, R. and Mastrofski, S. 2011. Examining Police Effectiveness as a Precursor to Legitimacy and Cooperation with Police. *Justice Quarterly* 30(5); Cornish, D. and Clarke, R.V. (eds.). 1986. *The Reasoning Criminal*. New York, NY: Springer-Verlag.

11 McKay, Mary Jayne. 2002. Addicted: Shoplifting for Thrills. *CBS News.com, 48 Hours Mystery,* Nov. 7. Retrieved from www.cbsnews.com/news/addicted-shoplifting-for-thrills/.

12 Hill, B. and Paynich, R. 2013. *Fundamentals of Crime Mapping*. Burlington, MA: Jones & Bartlett. Shover, Neal and Honaker, David. 1992. The Socially Bounded Decision Making of Persistent Property Offenders. *Howard Journal* 31(4).

13 Hirtenlehner, H., Blackwell, B., Leitgoeb, H. and Bacher, J. 2014. Explaining the Gender Gap in Juvenile Shoplifting: A Power-Control Theoretical Analysis. In *Deviant Behavior* 35(1).

14 Leonard, E. 2015. *Crime, Inequality and Power*. Abingdon, England: Routledge. Klemke, Lloyd W. and Egger, Steven A. 1992. *The Sociology of Shoplifting: Boosters and Snitches Today*. Westport, CT: Praeger.

15 Burke, R. 2013. *Hard Cop, Soft Cop*. London: Routledge. Cameron, Mary O. 1964. *The Booster and the Snitch: Department Store Shoplifting*. Glencoe, NY: Free Press.

16 Shoplifting Statistics. 2016. National Association for Shoplifting Prevention. Why do Shoplifters Steal? Retrieved from www.shopliftingprevention.org/what-we-do/learning-resource-center/statistics/.

17 Kivivouri, Janne. 1998. Delinquent Phases: The Case of Temporally Intensified Shoplifting Behavior. *The British Journal of Criminology* 38: 663–680.

18 Hartono, E., Kim, K., Na, K., Simpson, J. and Berkowitz, D. 2013. *Perceived Site Security as a Second Order Construct and Its Relationship to e-Commerce Site Usage*. New York: Springer.

19 Wallace, Gregory. 2013. Target Credit Card Hack: What You Need to Know. *CNN Money,* Dec 23. Retrieved from http://money.cnn.com/2013/12/22/news/companies/target-credit-card-hack/?iid=EL.

20 Rebovich, D., Allen, K. and Platt, J. 2015. *The New Face of Identity Theft: An Analysis of Federal Case Data for the Years 2008 through 2013*. Utica, NY: Center for Identity Management and Information Protection, Utica College.

21 Check Fraud Prevention. 2016. *National Check Fraud Center*. Retrieved from http://ckfraud.org/index.html.

22 Cornell University Law School. 2016. *Embezzlement*. Retrieved from www.law.cornell.edu/wex/embezzlement.

23 Fischer, Jordan. 2015. Center Township Employee Accused of Embezzlement. Retrieved from http://www.theindychannel.com/news/local-news/center-township-official-accused-of-embezzlement.

24 Davis, J. 2015. Consumer Protection Via the Larceny by Trick Statute. *Akron Law Review* 6(2).

25 Mancl, H. 2012. New Era Bankruptcy. In *Bankruptcy Case Studies*. Knoxville, TN: University of Tennessee.

26 Caldwell, Don. 2011. The Meanest Scam Ever. *Motherboard,* April 6. Retrieved from http://motherboard.vice.com/blog/the-meanest-scam-ever.

27 U.S. Securities and Exchange Commission. What is a Ponzi Scheme? Retrieved from www.sec.gov/answers/ponzi.htm.

28   Charity President Arrested for Fraud. 2015. *10 News,* Feb. 6. Retrieved from www. wtsp.com/story/news/local/2015/02/06/president-of-down-syndrome-charity-charged-in-fraud-case/22999011/.

29   Jennifer Lopez Files $20 Million Extortion Suit. 2012. *TMZ,* Aug. 7. Retrieved from www.tmz.com/2012/08/07/jennifer-lopez-20-million-dollar-extortion-lawsuit/.

30   Former Philadelphia Police Officer Sentenced for Insurance Scam. 2011. Federal Bureau of Investigation, Philadelphia Division. Retrieved from www.fbi.gov/philadelphia/press-releases/2011/former-philadelphia-police-officer-sentenced-for-insurance-scam.

31   Burke, R. 2013. *Hard Cop, Soft Cop.* London: Routledge.

32   Bazley, T. 2010. *Crimes of the Art World.* Santa Barbara, CA: ABC-CLIO.

33   Crime in the United States. 2014. Federal Bureau of Investigation, U.S. Department of Justice, Washington, D.C. Retrieved from www.fbi.gov/about-us/cjis/ucr/crime-in-the-u.s/2014/crime-in-the-u.s.-2014/offenses-known-to-law-enforcement/burglary.

34   Vandeviver, C., Van Daele, S. and Vander Beken, T. 2014. What Makes Long Crime Trips Worth Undertaking? Balancing Costs and Benefits in Burglars' Journey to Crime. *The British Journal of Criminology* 55(2): 399–420. doi: 10.1093/bjc/azu078.

35   Warner, J. 2012. *Women and Crime: A Reference Handbook.* Santa Barbara, CA: ABC-CLIO.

36   National Crime Victimization Survey Property Crime Trends, 1973–2014. Bureau of Justice Statistics, U.S. Department of Justice, Washington, D.C. Retrieved from www.bjs.gov/index.cfm?ty=dcdetail&iid=245.

37   Fox, B. and Farrington, D. 2014. Behavioral Consistency Among Serial Burglars: Evaluating Offense Style Specialization Using Three Analytical Approaches. *Crime & Delinquency.* doi 10.1177/0011128714540275.

38   Maguire, Mark. 1982. *Burglary in a Dwelling.* London: Heinemann.

39   *Artinfo.* 2008. U.K. Crime Family Convicted and Sentenced for £82.5 Million Art Burglaries. Retrieved from www.artinfo.com/news/story/28262/uk-crime-family-convicted-and-sentenced-for-825-million-art-burglaries/.

40   Sanders, A. 2015. Offense Planning in Burglary: A Comparison of Deliberate and Impulsive Burglars. Charlotte, NC: University of North Carolina at Charlotte.

41   Weatherburn, D. and Schnepel, K. 2015. Economic adversity and crime: old theories and new evidence. *Australian Journal of Social Issues* 50(1). Tunnell, Kenneth D. 1992. *Choosing Crime: The Criminal Calculus of Property Offenders.* Chicago: Nelson-Hall.

42   Cullen, F. and Wilcox, P. 2013. Choosing Street Crime. In *The Oxford Handbook of Criminological Theory.* Cary, NC: OUP USA. Cromwell, Paul, Olson, James N. and Wester Avary, D'Aunn. 1992. *Breaking and Entering: An Ethnographic Analysis of Burglary.* Newbury Park, CA: SAGE.

43   Brandl, S. 2014. The Investigation of Burglary, Vehicle Theft, Arson, and Other Property Crimes. In *Criminal Investigation.* Thousand Oaks, CA: SAGE. Wright, Richard and Decker, Scott. 1996. *Burglars on the Job: Street Life and Residential Break-Ins.* Northeastern University Press.

44   Cromwell, Paul and Olson, James N. 2004. *Breaking and Entering: Burglars on Burglary.* Belmont, CA: Wadsworth.

45   Helfgott, J. *Criminal Behavior: Theories, Typologies and Criminal Justice.* Thousand Oaks, CA: SAGE.

46   Ioannou, M., Canter, D., Youngs, D. and Synnott, J. 2015. Offenders' Crime Narratives Across Different Types of Crimes. *Journal of Forensic Psychology Practice* 15(5).

47   Taylor, E. 2014. Honour Among Thieves? How Morality and Rationality Influence the Decision-making Processes of Convicted Domestic Burglars. *Criminology & Criminal Justice* 14(4): 487–502.

48 Branic, N. 2014. *The Encyclopedia of Crime & Punishment.* Hoboken, NJ: Wiley Journals; Clarke, Ronald V. and Felson, Marcus. 1993. *Routine Activity and Rational Choice, Advances in Criminological Theory* Vol. 5. New Brunswick, NJ: Transaction Press.

49 Lower Merion Police Reports: Woman Charged in Alleged Burglaries of Bryn Mawr College Dorm Rooms. 2015. *Mainline Media News,* April 5. Retrieved from www.main linemedianews.com/articles/2015/04/03/main_line_times/news/doc551d66ec727bb58 8124369.txt.

50 Robinson, Matthew B. and Robinson, Christine E. 1997. Environmental Characteristics Associated with Residential Burglaries of Student Apartment Complexes. *Environment and Behavior* 29(5), 657–675.

51 Crime in the United States, 2014. Federal Bureau of Investigation, U.S. Department of Justice, Washington, D.C. Retrieved from www.fbi.gov/about-us/cjis/ucr/crime-in-the-u.s/2014/crime-in-the-u.s.-2014/offenses-known-to-law-enforcement/motor-vehicle-theft.

52 Criminal Victimization in the United States, 2014. National Crime Victimization Survey, Bureau of Justice Statistics, Office of Justice Programs, U.S. Department of Justice, Washington, D.C. Retrieved from www.bjs.gov/index.cfm?ty=pbdetail &iid=5366.

53 Roberts, A. 2012. Motor Vehicle Recovery: A Multilevel Event History Analysis of NIBRS Data. *Journal of Research in Crime and Delinquency,* 49(3): 444–467; Harlow, Caroline W. 1988. *Motor Vehicle Theft.* Bureau of Justice Statistics, Washington, D.C.

54 Miethe, Terance, McCorkle, Richard C. and Listwan, Shelley J. 2016. *Crime Profiles: The Anatomy of Dangerous Persons, Places, and Situations.* Los Angeles, CA: Roxbury Publishing Company.

55 Kellett, Sue, and Gross, Harriet. 2006. Addicted to Joyriding? An Exploration of Young Offenders' Accounts of Their Car Crime. *Psychology, Crime and Law* 12(1): 39–60.

56 Gottfredson, Michael and Hirschi, Travis. 1990. *A General Theory of Crime.* Stanford, CA: Stanford University Press.

57 Copes, H. and Cherbonneau, M. 2013. The Risks and Rewards of Motor Vehicle Theft. In B. Leclerc, and R. Wortley, *Cognition and Crime: Offender Decision Making and Script Analyses.* Abingdon, England: Routledge.

58 Miethe, Terance, McCorkle, Richard C., and Listwan, Shelley J. 2016. *Crime Profiles: The Anatomy of Dangerous Persons, Places, and Situations.* Los Angeles, CA: Roxbury Publishing.

59 Hess, K., Orthmann, C. and Cho, H. 2016. *Criminal Investigation.* Boston, MA: Cengage Learning. Blake, Kevin. 1995. What You Should Know About Car Theft. *Consumer's Research* October, pp. 23–27.

60 Miethe, Terance, McCorkle, Richard C. and Listwan, Shelley J. 2016. *Crime Profiles: The Anatomy of Dangerous Persons, Places, and Situations.* Los Angeles, CA: Roxbury Publishing.

61 Crime in the United States, 2014. Federal Bureau of Investigation, U.S. Department of Justice, Washington, D.C. Retrieved from www.fbi.gov/about-us/cjis/ucr/crime-in-the-u.s/2014/crime-in-the-u.s.-2014/offenses-known-to-law-enforcement/arson.

62 Brownlee, Ken. 2000. Ignoring Juvenile Arson Is Like Playing with Fire. *Claims* 48(3).

63 Crime in the United States, 2014. Federal Bureau of Investigation, U.S. Department of Justice, Washington, D.C. Retrieved from www.fbi.gov/about-us/cjis/ucr/crime-in-the-u.s/2014/crime-in-the-u.s.-2014/offenses-known-to-law-enforcement/arson.

64 MacKay, S., Feldberg, A., Ward, A. and Marton, P. 2012. Research and Practice in Adolescent Firesetting. In *Criminal Justice and Behavior* 39(6).

65 Juvenile Fire Setter Intervention Program. 2016. Retrieved from www.ifsa.org/jfsip.

66 Berkey, M. and Wooden, W. 2012. *Children and Arson: America's Middle Class Nightmare.* Berlin, Germany: Springer Science & Business Media.

67 Gannon, T., Ciardha, C., Barnoux, M., Tyler, N., Mozoca, K. and Alleyne, E. 2013. Male Imprisoned Firesetters Have Different Characteristics Than Other Imprisoned Offenders and Require Specialist Treatment. *Psychiatry: Interpersonal and Biological Processes* 76(4).

68 Van Hasselt, V. and Hersen, M. 2013. *Handbook of Psychological Approaches with Violent Offenders: Contemporary Strategies and Issues.* Berlin, Germany: Springer Science and Business Media.

69 Barnoux, M. and Gannon, T. 2014. A New Conceptual Framework for Revenge Firesetting. *Psychology, Crime & Law* 20(5).

70 Martinez, Brett. 2002. *Multiple Fire Setters: The Process of Tracking and Identification.* Tulsa, OK: PennWell Books.

71 Doley, R., Dickens, G. and Gannon, T. 2015. *The Psychology of Arson: A Practical Guide to Understanding and Managing Deliberate Firesetters.* Abingdon, England: Routledge.

CHAPTER OUTLINE

Public order crimes

- Where and why do we draw the line between what's immoral and what's illegal?
- What types of drugs are illegal and why?
- Are we winning the war on drugs?
- What sexual acts do we define as prostitution?
- Why do some individuals exchange sex for money or drugs?
- When does pornography become a crime?

KEY TERMS

public order crimes

victimless crimes

moral entrepreneurs

social order

drug

drug abuse

addiction

tolerance

Harrison Act of 1914

Marijuana Tax Act of 1937

Boggs Act

narcotics

depressants

stimulants

hallucinogens

cannabis

prostitution

sex tourism

brothels

pornography

child pornography

obscenity

On March 9, 2014, Mexican authorities gunned down Nazario Moreno, Mexican drug cartel leader and founder of La Familia Michoacana, a notorious drug cartel and organized crime syndicate in the Mexican state of Michoacan. Moreno was one of the Mexican government's most wanted criminals. Referred to as "the craziest one" for his dangerous acts of criminal violence, he was reported to have tossed five decapitated heads onto a dance floor.[1]

On December 2, 1993, billionaire Colombian drug lord Pablo Emilio Escobar was gunned down by police in his home. Assisted by communication technology provided by the U.S. government, the Colombian police had found Escobar hiding in a middle-class neighborhood in Medellin. It was estimated that he controlled about 80 percent of the world's cocaine market. He was considered an enemy of both the Colombian and the U.S. governments.[2]

What makes a person an enemy to an entire country? Is it possible to declare war on a specific habit, lifestyle, or commodity? The U.S. government did in the early 1970s. The "war on drugs" is a political campaign begun during the Nixon administration to combat illegal drug trafficking by creating laws and policy initiatives that prohibit the production, distribution, and use of certain substances. Nixon referred to narcotics as "public enemy number one" and equated their use with a culture of crime, lawlessness, and radical anti-government sentiments.

Image 16.1 *Colombian anti-narcotics police officers keep watch in a poppy field near El Silencio in the former rebel safe haven in Colombia. This picture really captures a "war." Who is the enemy here? How does the drug addict get caught up in this alleged "war"?*

William Fernando Martinez/AP/Press Association Images

The war on drugs took on new meaning during the early 1990s, when George H.W. Bush appointed William Bennett his drug czar, doubling annual spending on the war to $12 billion. Much of this money went to military jets designed to combat the Colombian trafficking cartels, Navy submarines to monitor the smuggling of drugs in ships from the Caribbean, and operatives trained to air raid drug fields, ambush suspected drug lords, and capture known traffickers.[3] In the meantime, Congress adopted mandatory minimum sentencing laws that enacted severe penalties on drug users.

The effect of the war on drugs, however, has been decades of costly spending and unprecedented growth in the number of people locked up for drug offenses, while the problems of drug trafficking, abuse, and addiction continue without resolution. What went wrong?

The biggest flaw in the war on drugs was policy makers' failure to rely on scientific studies that could accurately measure the effectiveness of programs and policies in reducing drug use. Studies conducted by the Drug Policy Research Center indicate that illegal drugs represent a $60 billion a year industry affecting about 16 million people in the United States, or 7 percent of the population over the age of 12. Response to the drug problem has generally been directed at law enforcement efforts to make it more difficult to buy, sell, use, and traffic illegal drugs. Researchers note, however, that these measures have not led to a significant reduction in the severity of the U.S. drug problem and may actually have contributed to our reluctance to focus on the treatment of drug addiction and its related social problems.[4]

Unfortunately, the overwhelming evidence of the failure of "get tough" policies runs up against public sentiment that drug use is morally wrong and harmful and should be controlled through strict enforcement of punitive practices. Thus, we continue to impose harsh sentences on drug users and dealers, chase down drug lords, and combat drugs abroad, despite evidence that these efforts are ineffective in reducing the supply of drugs bought and sold on the streets. Somehow, in the debate on public order and morality, the evidence loses its effect. In this chapter, we will take a closer look at this debate and its influence on our understanding of public order crimes, acts considered illegal because they violate the moral standards behind society's values and norms. We then look specifically at drug abuse, prostitution, and pornography.

CRIME V. MORALITY: WHAT IS SOCIAL ORDER?

While criminal law is designed to protect society from harm and preserve peace and order, pursuing this goal becomes a questionable aim when people consent to engage in acts that have no apparent victim. For this reason, crimes against the public order have often been referred to as victimless crimes. Scholars note, however, that this terminology is misleading, because all criminal acts, even when the parties are in agreement, have harmful consequences on innocent people.[5]

Even if we assume crimes against the public order are not as obviously harmful as murder, rape, and robbery, society has traditionally accepted the notion that certain acts should be prohibited and punished by law because they are contrary to the public's collective notion of decent and moral behavior.[6] Legal scholars note that one of the functions of criminal law is to express a collective sentiment that society disapproves of certain acts, even when these acts are not necessarily dangerous or obviously harmful to an apparent victim.[7]

Thus, certain behaviors are outlawed because they are in direct conflict with social policy, prevailing moral standards, and current public opinion. The question, however, is by whose standards are we measuring moral behavior? Is there an objective standard of social harm we apply to certain acts and therefore deem them contrary to the public order? Is marrying an individual of your choice, regardless of sex, threatening to moral order? Does helping a terminally ill loved one to end his or her life harmful to society? How about smoking marijuana to ease the pain of certain types of cancer? (See Box 16.1). While opinions vary, these acts have generally been prohibited by law. Yet we continue to allow the distribution and consumption of alcohol and tobacco, despite our knowledge of their detrimental effects on health. Who decides?

Sociologist Howard Becker calls them moral entrepreneurs. These are individuals who try to persuade the rest of society that their definition of a social problem and its policy resolution represents a shared consensus about what is best or the most right for the social order.[8] The social order consists of the various components of society—institutions, structures, customs, traditions—that preserve and maintain the normative ways of human interactions and relationships.[9] According to Becker, successful moral entrepreneurs

BOX 16.1: CONNECTING RESEARCH TO PRACTICE

Marijuana as medicine . . . The debate continues

Irvin Rosenfeld, 61, is an investment consultant for a brokerage firm in Ft. Lauderdale, Florida. He suffers chronic pain from muscle spasms caused by a bone disorder known as multiple congenital cartilaginous exostosis. For the past 32 years, Rosenfeld has smoked 10 to 12 marijuana cigarettes a day to relieve his pain. He gets his canister filled with 300 marijuana cigarettes from the National Institute of Drug Abuse as a medicine approved by the U.S. Food and Drug Administration. He is the longest surviving federal medical marijuana patient in the United States. How can this be?

Since 1996, 23 states and Washington, D.C. have passed laws which currently make provisions for the medicinal use of marijuana to alleviate and manage chronic pain, musculoskeletal disorders, and nausea from chemotherapy, among other health-related uses. Several other states are currently debating legislation on the use of marijuana for medical treatment. Until recently, the federal government did not recognize state laws permitting the use of marijuana as a prescription drug, arguing that the prescriptive use of marijuana is against the public interest. Federal drug laws continue to prohibit the sale and distribution of marijuana under any circumstances and federal agents continue to pursue drug raids on "legitimate" distributors. In February 2009, however, President Obama brought about a significant change when he pledged that the federal government would cease to prosecute individuals following state laws governing the sale and distribution of marijuana. Nevertheless, marijuana continues to be an offense under Federal law. What does the science of criminology tell us about this apparent paradox in approach to marijuana use?

The political battle over legalizing marijuana for medicinal purposes has been raging. Those opposing legalization argue that adequate treatments for pain and other ailments are already available that don't have marijuana's detrimental effects on lung function. Political propaganda on both sides has made empirical research difficult to develop. Nevertheless, over the years, numerous clinical studies have repeatedly found marijuana to be an effective tool in pain management, with significantly better results than traditionally prescribed treatments.

A recent study of patients with painful diabetic neuropathy found that most participants reported that medicinal cannabis significantly improved their pain. In another study examining the effects of oral cannabis in alleviating symptoms of epilepsy, researchers found that about one third of children suffering from epilepsy experienced over 50 percent reduction of seizures by using oral cannabis extracts. Moreover, a randomized double-blind controlled study on the use of marijuana in the treatment of PTSD found that patients who used an oral medicinal form of cannabis experienced significant reductions in PTSD-related nightmares.

These and many other findings, while quite convincing, continue to be very controversial, and further research is needed to fully guide policies pertaining to the legitimate sale and distribution of marijuana. This research needs to inform State and Federal legislatures on the safety, efficacy of marijuana laws, as well as the necessary and relevant criteria for their implementation and regulation.

Sources:

Bohan, Andrew. 2016. Irvin Rosenfeld HB 5470 Michigan Medical Marijuana Testimony. *MedicalMarijuana 411.com.* Retrieved from https://medicalmarijuana411.com/irvin-rosenfeld-hb-5470-michigan-medical-marijuana-testimony/.

Jetly, Rakesh, Heber, Alexandra, Fraser, George and Boisvert, Denis. 2015. The Efficacy of Nabilone, a Synthetic Cannabinoid, in the Treatment of PTSD-associated Nightmares: A Preliminary Randomized, Double-blind, Placebo-controlled Cross-over Design Study. *Psychoneuroendocrinology* 51: 585–588.

Marijuana Resource Center: State Laws Related to Marijuana. Office of National Drug Control Policy. Retrieved from https://www.whitehouse.gov/ondcp/state-laws-related-to-marijuana.

Press, Craig A., Knupp, Kelly G. and Chap, Kevin E. 2015. Parental Reporting of Response to Oral Cannabis Extracts for Treatment of Refractory Epilepsy. *Epilepsy & Behavior* 45: 49–52.

Gouaux, Ben and Atkinson, Joseph H. 2015. Efficacy of Inhaled Cannabis on Painful Diabetic Neuropathy. *The Journal of Pain* 16(7): 616–627.

Image 16.2 *On June 26, 2015, the U.S. Supreme Court ruled that same-sex couples have the right to marry in all 50 states. How does the definition of social order become redefined in this picture?*

Manuel Balce Ceneta/AP/Press Association Images

are predominantly from the upper class and are able to effectively compete for political voice and power, generate awareness of the issue through their financial resources, and gain public support. That is why their views of morality get represented in decisions about which acts are deemed crimes against the social order and which are not.

Moral entrepreneurs include gun lobbyists, MADD (Mothers Against Drunk Drivers), pro-life/pro-choice groups, medical marijuana advocates, and gay

Image 16.3
*Definitions of crime
are influenced by
moral entrepreneurs.
Prior to the women's
suffrage movement
during the 1800s,
women were banned
from voting in
political elections.
What gave this
relatively powerless
group a voice?*

Library of
Congress/American Press
Association

and lesbian rights advocates. All share the same goals: to influence law makers in the direction of policies that favor their cause or moral sentiment, and to control or limit certain types of behavior they consider a detriment to society, such as minors drinking alcohol. Even the women's suffrage movement during the 1800s that called for voting rights for women was a group of moral entrepreneurs.

What becomes defined as public order is therefore the outcome of a successful moral campaign favoring certain definitions and ideals of right, wrong, and what's best for the social good. We turn our attention now to a discussion of this definition, beginning with a discussion of drug use and addiction.

DRUG USE AND ADDICTION

Why do people use drugs? What makes drug taking deviant? Is it the type of drug, the way it was purchased, or the reason it is consumed? These questions have various medical, legal, and social answers that we look at below.

Drug taking as deviance

In 2014, an estimated 16.7 percent of people in the United States aged 12 and older reported having used illicit drugs in the past month.[10] In fiscal year 2015, the national budget for drug abuse research, prevention, treatment, and enforcement totaled roughly $26 billion.[11] Moreover, the impact of substance

Image 16.4
What type of feelings does screaming on a roller coaster create in the mind? How is this effect similar to that of drugs? Why are these activities not considered deviant behaviors, or are they by some?

iStock/bukharova

abuse in terms of health care, criminal justice, and loss of productivity is estimated to cost about $600 billion annually.[12] The scope of the drug problem cuts across socio-economic class, gender, age, and race. It goes beyond our national borders and includes international traffickers, smugglers, and "public enemies." It is complex, with various intricate operations related to manufacturing, distributing, and dealing that create a variety of illegal activities by individuals, crime rings, and very often corrupt law enforcement officials. Thus, there are various forms of deviance associated with drugs. Here, however, we discuss only the crime of drug abuse.

What is a drug?

A **drug** is a chemical substance that affects the body's physical and psychological functioning by altering the way in which the brain sends, receives, and processes information. Because of this broad definition, many chemical substances are considered drugs, including legal substances such as aspirin and nicotine, and illegal substances such as cocaine and marijuana. **Drug abuse** is the use of any chemical substance, whether legal or illegal, to result in the physical, mental, emotional, or behavioral impairment of an individual.[13] An abused drug can affect the brain by either over- or under-stimulating it. However, the direct or indirect effect of nearly all abused drugs is to alter the functioning of the brain's reward system by disturbing the structure of emotions, motivation, drive, and pleasure.[14]

The brain's reaction to drugs is thus marked by a feeling of euphoria or a "high," which we otherwise derive from experiences such as scoring a touchdown, getting a good grade, being in love, riding a roller coaster, or indulging in our favorite foods. The euphoria, although short-lived, reinforces the effect of the drug, resulting in a desire to repeat the drug use in order to repeat the euphoria.[15] This cycle is what we commonly refer to as addiction.

What is addiction?

Addiction is a chronic condition that causes a physical or psychological compulsion to seek the use of a drug, despite its harmful physical or social consequences.[16] The addict comes to depend on the chemical substance in order to function properly. This strong dependency is what makes drug addiction so challenging to overcome.

Addiction to drugs is complicated by a physiological phenomenon known as tolerance. Tolerance builds over time when the brain adapts to the chemical substance and it produces less of a high. The drug abuser begins to need more and more of the substance in order to enjoy the same pleasurable effects.[17]

The effects of drugs are powerful, creating changes in regions of the brain responsible for reasoning, judgment, cognition, and behavior control.[18] Thus, drugs can have a profound effect on the life of an individual in terms of health, daily functioning, interaction with others, and connection to the social world. For this reason, drug abuse falls under the category of public order crime.

Why are some drugs illegal?

The *deviant* nature of drug taking is seldom related to the chemical composition of any specific drug (meaning any drug can be abused), while debates over the *legal* status of drugs have centered upon fundamental distinctions like the type of drug, and public perception of how it is used and characteristics of users.[19] For example, morphine is commonly given to patients after major surgery to help them tolerate post-operative pain. Yet it is a controlled substance whose use is illegal if not under the control of a physician. Alcohol, on the other hand, is not now a controlled substance and can be consumed by adults in any quantity, despite its addictive qualities and harmful effects on the body when abused.[20] During the Prohibition era of 1919–1933, however, social reaction to alcohol consumption made the manufacture, sale, and use of alcohol criminal. Moreover, even when a drug is legal, the manner in which it is obtained and used can give it a criminal status. Such is the case when individuals abuse prescription pain killers. According to the Centers for Disease Control and Prevention (CDC), teenage abuse of prescription drugs is on the rise, with over 20 percent of teenagers reporting to have taken a prescription drug without a legitimate doctor's prescription.[21] Whether a particular drug is criminal is therefore socially created; it varies from time to time and place to place, as public perception and moral sentiment dictate the course of social control policies.

The use of chemical substances for medicinal or religious purposes has been associated with a wide variety of cultures throughout history.[22] Opium is regarded as one of the earliest drugs to be discovered, and its use has been dated back to the Stone Age, several thousand years BC. Derivatives of opium such as morphine and heroin were introduced later by merchants and traders and became widespread throughout Europe, Asia, and the United States in the 1800s. In 1858, cocaine was extracted from *coca leaves* and was thought to be a cure for certain ailments.[23] By the turn of the century, medicine peddlers were providing highly addictive chemical substances to millions in the United

States, many of them middle-class women, and creating a new social problem that needed immediate attention.

Concern over the increase in addiction and growing public perception of a link between cocaine and crime led to the passage of the federal **Harrison Act of 1914**, designed to regulate and control the manufacture, production, and distribution of cocaine and opiate drugs. Similar concerns drew public attention in the mid-1930s when marijuana use became associated with certain types of deviant subcultures, leading to the passage of the **Marijuana Tax Act of 1937**, which placed a $100-an-ounce tax on the drug, and the **Boggs Act** in 1951, which brought about criminal sanctions for its possession and distribution.

The cumulative effect of these and subsequent laws aimed at controlling drugs was to create a social class of deviants that were now defined as criminal instead of addicted, and to pave the way for the underground drug market to expand and flourish through organized criminal networks of distributors and traffickers.

Categories of drugs

Researchers have traditionally classified drugs into categories according to their chemical composition and how they alter the structure and function of the brain. Of course, certain drugs are more popular than others, according to their accessibility and frequency of use. We can see from Figure 16.1 that marijuana is the most widely used illicit drug among teenagers who report to be drug users. Moreover, according to the 2015 *Monitoring the Future Survey* of high school teen drug use, despite the recent rise in opioid overdose in 2015,

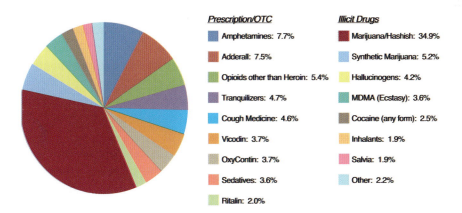

Figure 16.1 Percentage of 12 graders who have used these drugs in the past year

Source: Johnston, Lloyd D., O'Malley, Patrick M., Miech, Richard A., Bachman, Jerald G. and Schulenberg, John E. 2015. Monitoring the Future National Survey Results on Drug Use 1975–2015. The National Institute on Drug Abuse at The National Institutes of Health Key Findings on Adolescent Drug Use. Retrieved from http://monitoringthefuture.org/pubs/monographs/mtf-overview2015.pdf

other than heroin, opioid use amongst teens has decreased significantly over the past five years.[24]

We can divide illegal drugs into five broad categories: narcotics, depressants, stimulants, hallucinogens, and cannabis. **Narcotics** are highly addictive drugs that can be smoked, injected, sniffed, or taken orally. They are often used to relieve pain and produce relaxation and include morphine, codeine, heroin, and opium. **Depressant** drugs are taken orally to relieve tension and anxiety. They produce a state of calmness and relaxation but can also impair judgment and interfere with motor coordination. They have a high potential for addiction because they build tolerance. Examples of depressants include barbiturates and tranquilizers. **Stimulants** can be sniffed, smoked, injected, or taken orally to heighten alertness and reduce fatigue. They include amphetamines, cocaine, crack, and methamphetamines or "ice." They have a high degree of psychological dependence and often produce physiological changes in the body such as elevated blood pressure, blurry vision, and irregular heartbeat. **Hallucinogens** include PCP, LSD, and the drug "ecstasy." They have no known medical use and create profound mind-altering changes and distortions in feelings and perception, often producing a state of confusion and hallucination that can lead to violence and aggression. **Cannabis** is derived from the hemp plant, which yields marijuana and hashish. These drugs are generally ingested by smoking and produce feelings of euphoria and relaxation. Some studies show that prolonged use can damage the lungs and respiratory system, as can cigarette smoking.[25] The degree of physiological dependence is generally unknown. Table 16.1 provides a summary of these five major drug categories.

Trends and patterns in drug use

According to the National Survey on Drug Use and Health (NSDUH), an estimated 27 million individuals age 12 and above report to be current illicit drug users. This represents about 10 percent of the population that is age 12 and older, which means that about 1 in every 10 individuals age 12 and above in the United States report to have used illicit drugs in the past month.[26] Moreover, the percentage of illicit drugs used by people age 12 and up increased from 2002 to 2014 (see Figure 16.2). This trend reflects an increase in illicit drug use by adults aged 26 or older, rather than a rise in use by young adults between 18 and 25 years old.

One variable that continues to concern policy makers and researchers is the connection between drug abuse and crime. There are three possibilities: (1) individuals who abuse drugs and alcohol are more likely to commit crime; (2) individuals commit crime in order to obtain illegal drugs or support a drug habit; and (3) the distribution and trafficking of drugs is a source of criminal activity.

The research literature abounds with studies that persistently find a link between substance abuse and violent crime, with individuals who use drugs

Table 16.1 Categories of drugs

	Drug	Dependence: physical/ psychological	How it is used	Duration (hours)
Narcotics	Opium	High/high	Oral, smoked	3–6
	Morphine	High/high	Oral, smoked, injected	3–6
	Codeine	Moderate/moderate	Oral, injected	3–6
	Heroin	High/high	Smoked, injected, sniffed	3–6
	Hydromorphone	High/high	Oral, injected	3–6
	Meperidine	High/high	Oral, injected	3–6
	Methadone	High/high	Oral, injected	12–24
Depressants	Barbiturates	High/moderate	Oral	1–16
	Methaqualone	High/high	Oral	4–8
	Tranquilizers	High/high	Oral	4–8
	Chloral Hydrate	Moderate/moderate	Oral	5–8
	Glutethimide	High/moderate	Oral	4–8
Stimulants	Cocaine	Possible/high	Sniffed, smoked, injected	1–2
	Amphetamines	Possible/high	Oral, injected	2–4
	Methamphetamine	Possible/high	Oral, injected	2–4
	Phenmetrazine	Possible/high	Oral, injected	2–4
	Methylphenidate	Possible/moderate	Oral, injected	2–4
	Other Stimulants	Possible/high	Oral, injected	2–4
	Ice	High/high	Smoked, oral, injected, inhaled	4–14
Hallucinogens	PCP	Unknown/high	Smoked, oral, injected	Up to days
	LSD (Acid)	None/unknown	Oral	8–12
	Mescaline, Peyote	None/unknown	Oral, injected	8–12
	Psilocybin	None/unknown	Oral, injected, smoked, sniffed	Variable
	Designer drugs (Ecstasy)	Unknown/unknown	Oral, injected, smoked	Variable
Cannabis	Marijuana, pot, grass	Unknown/moderate	Smoked, oral	2–4
	Tetrahydrocannabinol	Unknown/moderate	Smoked, oral	2–4
	Hashish	Unknown/moderate	Smoked, oral	2–4
	Hashish oil	Unknown/moderate	Smoked, oral	2–4

Source: *Drug Categories for Substances of Abuse*. U.S. Department of Health and Human Services, Substance Abuse and Mental Health Services Administration. Retrieved from http://store.samhsa.gov/home.

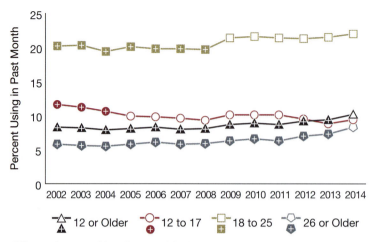

+Difference between this estimate and the 2014 estimate is statistically significant at the .05 level.

Figure 16.2 Trends in drug use by age group: percentages, 2002–2014

Source: Hedden, Sarra L., Kennet, Joel, Lipari, Rachel, Medley, Grace, Tice, Peter, Copello, Elizabeth A. P., and Kroutil, Larry A. 2015. Behavioral Health Trends in the United States: Results from the 2014 National Survey on Drug Use and Health. Retrieved from www.samhsa.gov/data/sites/default/files/NSDUH-FRR1-2014/NSDUH-FRR1-2014.pdf.

being more likely to engage in violent behavior.[27] According to the Department of Health and Human Services, adolescents who use at least one illicit drug are twice as likely to engage in violent behavior as adolescents who do not use drugs at all.[28] Studies have also found that a significant number of individuals arrested for domestic assault, homicide, and other violent crimes test positive for at least one illegal drug.[29] The Arrestee Drug Abuse Monitoring (ADAM II) program is a unique Federal data collection report that shows patterns in drug use among arrestees in five participating U.S. counties. Data collected on male adult arrestees through voluntary interviews and drug tests within 48 hours of their arrest persistently show that an overwhelming percentage test positive for some type of illicit drug, including marijuana, cocaine, opiates, amphetamines/methamphetamine, oxycodone, buprenorphine, PCP, benzo-diazepines, methadone, and barbiturates (see Table 16.2).

Moreover, surveys indicate that an overwhelming majority of prisoners have a history of substance abuse.[30] According to a nationally representative survey of state correctional agencies, nearly 8 million adult offenders are involved in drugs.[31] The substance abuse or dependence rates of offenders are more than four times those of the general population, with about half of all state and federal prisoners meeting the diagnostic criteria.[32]

With the growing number of drug varieties and markets and innovations in the manufacture and distribution of illegal substances, the criminal drug network has become more violent, aggressive, and complex.[33] Drug trafficking has become a divided industry that has found its way into street gangs, started turf battles, and sanctioned the settling of differences through violence and bloodshed. International drug trafficking has also become embedded in

Table 16.2 Percent of offenders testing positive for drugs at time of arrest

	Percent positive for drugs												
	Total testing positive (%)		Testing positive by drug and age (%)						Testing positive by drug and race (%)				
		Std error	<21	21–25	26–30	31–35	36+	Unk.	White	Black	His-panic	Other	Unk.
Any drug	27.0	1.1	9.4	13.8	30.1	31.7	35.8	—	25.5	28.0	16.3	5.4	0.0
Cocaine	14.7	0.9	1.0	4.2	9.8	19.2	23.6	—	15.3	14.9	11.2	5.4	0.0
Opiates	6.9	0.6	1.0	3.6	5.7	3.5	11.5	—	10.2	6.7	5.1	0.0	0.0
Methamphet-amine	0.9	0.2	0.9	1.1	1.6	0.8	0.6	—	0.6	1.0	0.0	0.0	0.0
PCP	9.7	0.7	7.0	6.9	18.0	14.1	7.7	—	4.5	10.7	2.3	0.0	0.0
Multiple drug	4.6	0.5	0.6	1.9	5.0	5.6	6.5	—	5.1	4.7	2.3	0.0	0.0

governments across the globe, including political corruption among high-level officials and assassinations of those who refuse to comply.[34] Indeed, trends and patterns in drug use and violence are a global phenomenon. However, the phenomenon exits because there is an apparent demand. We return to the question: why do people use drugs?

Understanding drug abuse

Our individual traits and experiences do not only affect the many variables associated with drug abuse and addiction Very often they also both affect and reflect the drug of choice, the particular life of the drug user, and the outcome of his or her involvement in criminal activity.

Individual variables include genetic factors that predispose some individuals toward substance abuse. Studies have shown that children of alcoholic parents are more likely to develop substance-abuse problems than children of non-alcoholic parents, even after controlling for environmental variables that influence the relationship between parent and child.[35] Other studies suggest that substance abuse may be linked to psychological disorders such as anti-social personality, and psychotic disorders such as schizophrenia.[36] In many cases, drugs are a means of dealing with traumatic emotional experiences that lead to anxiety and depression. Researchers caution, however, that these studies do not diminish the role of socialization in the abuse of alcohol and drugs.

Studies of environmental influences in the onset of alcohol and drug abuse look at whether drug use is part of a lifestyle or subculture within the inner city. (See chapter 8 on social structure theories) Evidence suggests it tends to be higher in neighborhoods where deteriorated living conditions, high crime rates, and limited legitimate opportunities force youth to turn to the drug subculture for peer approval, as a method of coping with feelings of alienation and rejection, and as a way to earn a living.[37]

Image 16.5 *What individual and environmental variables contribute to drug abuse and addiction?*

iStock/Rebecca Ellis

Patterns of drug use among inner-city residents are most visible to law enforcement, a fact reflected in higher arrest trends for drug-related offenses there than on college campuses across the country.[38] It is also the inner city in which most drug enforcement policies and practices emerge, and where the debate on treatment versus social control continues.

What do we do about drug abuse?

Central to the discussion of what to do about drug abuse and addiction is the question whether certain types of drugs should be legalized or decriminalized, particularly marijuana. A substantial body of literature shows that marijuana use is no more dangerous to health than cigarettes or alcohol.[39] The most widely used illicit drug, marijuana is also not generally perceived by the public as deviant, nor is it associated with a criminal lifestyle as is crack cocaine, for example.[40]

Drug policy experts note that removing the criminal component of drug use will dismantle the underground drug economy, which is a significant source of violence and organized criminal activity[41] (discussed in chapter 17). Moreover, the legalization of restricted drugs would allow for government control of sale and distribution, therefore reducing the high price, which often leads to a variety of criminal activities to support the expensive habit.

Critics note, however, that restricted substances, whether marijuana or crack, are mind altering drugs that have a significant impact on the physical and psychological functioning of individuals and that pose serious risks to health.

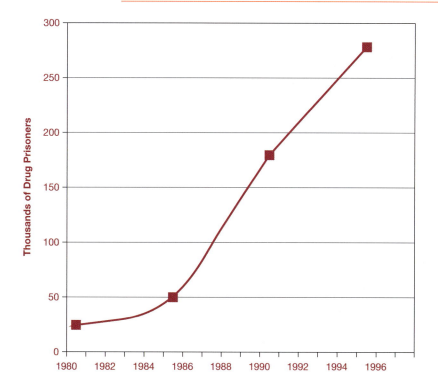

Figure 16.3
Consequences of a war: incarceration for drug arrests, 1980–1996

Source: Correctional Populations in the United States. 1997. Bureau of Justice Statistics, Office of Justice Programs, U.S. Department of Justice, Washington, D.C.

Moreover, the legalization of drugs will only escalate the problems of abuse and addiction, making drugs more readily accessible to a greater number of people. This has been the case throughout history and in different societies when the availability of drugs such as narcotics preceded epidemics of drug use and addiction.

For many years, drug control policies and practices focused primarily on expanding law enforcement efforts to control drug traffickers and punish drug users. The war on drugs launched during the 1980s succeeded in arresting and incarcerating an unprecedented number of drug offenders, with drug-related convictions accounting for nearly 85 percent of the increase in federal prison inmates from 1985 to 1995 (see Figure 16.3).

Despite massive local, national, and international efforts and spending on patrolling borders, eradicating crops, and setting up sting operations to arrest drug smugglers and dealers, drugs continued to be readily available and widely used by youth and adults throughout the country, with the associated problems of overdose, addiction, drug-related crimes, and the spread of disease.[42] Critics of the war on drugs note that U.S. drug policy has been misguided in its emphasis on the arrest and incarceration of anyone associated with illegal drugs, and that this strategy is too idealistic and subject to political rhetoric and manipulation.[43] Moreover, it is simplistic, failing to recognize the social and public health issues related to drug abuse and addiction. Box 16.2 discusses a theoretical flaw in the "get tough on drugs" approach to drug control policies. So, if the war on drugs is a losing battle, what could be the alternative?

An alternative drug control strategy introduced in the mid-1990s by President Bill Clinton accepted that criminal laws and sanctions alone could not solve the complicated issues and problems related to drug abuse and addiction. A national effort began to advance a model of drug control that focused on drug education programs as well as treatment interventions. This model recognizes the underlying economic and social variables associated with drug use and relies on research findings to support intervention strategies.

BOX 16.2: CONNECTING THEORY TO PRACTICE

"Get tough" doesn't always get it right!

The goal of drug control policy and legislation is to eliminate the trafficking, sale, distribution, and abuse of all illegal drugs. How to accomplish this overwhelming task, however, has been the subject of much debate. Proponents of drug prohibition call for a strict ban and punitive enforcement. Advocates of decriminalization favor legislation that either regulates or reduces penalties for the use or possession of certain drugs such as marijuana. Legalization is the outright removal of any form of legal restriction on the use or possession of drugs.

Regardless of these divisions, drug control policies must be based on an approach that accounts for the fact that strict laws enacting harsh penalties for drug offenders have largely failed to reduce the market for drugs. The idea behind strict laws and harsh sentencing is that offenders will be less likely to make the *choice* to use or sell drugs if the punishment is so great it is "not worth the risk." The problem with using this theory to guide drug policy is that it assumes drug abuse is a rational decision, based on hedonistic calculations of pros and cons (See chapter 8 which discusses rational choice theory). It fails to recognize the emotional, psychological, and physiological components of drug use and addiction, and the social and psychological variables that can influence the onset of abuse. "Get tough" policies do not have the intended effect of decreasing drug abuse because they ignore the irrational nature of drug use as a form of thrill-seeking, often self-destructive behavior pattern.

A more practical approach to drug control should integrate law enforcement with education, especially for at-risk youth, about the devastating effects of drugs. Moreover, preventive measures must recognize the role of psychology and social variables in the onset of drug abuse, and holistic treatment programs should be available as an alternative to punitive measures for drug offenders.

Sources

Kreek, Mary Jeanne, Nielsen, David A., Butelman, Eduardo R. and LaForge, K. Steven. 2005. Genetic Influences on Impulsivity, Risk Taking, Stress Responsivity, and Vulnerability to Drug Abuse and Addiction. *Neurobiology of Addiction* 8(11).

National Drug Control Policy. 2015. Office of National Drug Control Policy, Washington D.C. Retrieved from https://www.whitehouse.gov/ondcp/national-drug-control-strategy.

Volkow, Nora D. *Drugs, Brains, and Behavior: The Science of Addiction*. July 2014. National Institute on Drug Abuse, National Institute of Health, Washington, D.C. Retrieved from www.drugabuse.gov/publications/drugs-brains-behavior-science-addiction/preface.

Since 1996, drug use among teens has been declining, with the period between 2002 and 2008 showing a significant drop of 25 percent.[44] In 2010 the Obama Administration published its first *National Drug Control Strategy*, redefining drug use and its effects as a disorder, a "disease of the brain" that can be cured with proper treatment and intervention.[45] Since then, drug control efforts have been based on a combination of evidence-based public health and safety initiatives. In 2015, this strategy focused on seven main areas:[46]

- Preventing drug use in our communities.
- Seeking early intervention opportunities in health care.
- Integrating treatment for substance use disorders into health care and supporting recovery.
- Breaking the cycle of drug use, crime, and incarceration.
- Disrupting domestic drug trafficking and production.
- Strengthening international partnerships.
- Improving information systems to better address drug use and its consequences.

Moreover, a new emphasis emerged that focused on the need to combat the misuse of prescription drugs, as well as the growth in heroin abuse and addiction, with Obama's 2016 budget including $133 million in funds aimed at expanding state-level prescription drug overdose prevention strategies, medication-assisted treatment programs, and access to the overdose-reversal drug naloxone.[47] Today, nationwide drug control strategies focus on combining law enforcement efforts, treatment programs, and prevention to achieve three major goals: stop initiation, reduce drug abuse and addiction, and disrupt the market for illegal drugs. The goal of stopping initiation is achieved through national drug prevention efforts designed to deter drug use, especially by youth. These efforts include such initiatives as the National Youth Anti-Drug Media Campaign, state-level prescription drug monitoring programs, and community-based coalitions that implement random drug testing programs in schools and workplaces to promote safe, drug-free environments.

Treatment is prioritized as part of the goal to reduce drug abuse and addiction. It begins with the early identification of substance abuse problems through such programs as Screening and Brief Intervention and Access to Recovery. These encourage individuals to recognize their substance abuse issues through screening in a healthcare setting, in order to stop the behavior pattern before it becomes even more problematic. An outgrowth of the treatment priority has been the emergence of drug courts, which allow drug abusers who have come into contact with the criminal justice system the opportunity to participate in a drug treatment program while remaining under community supervision.

The third goal, to disrupt the market for illegal drugs, focuses on reducing the supply of drugs by enhancing law enforcement efforts at the federal, state, and local level. Moreover, international cooperative agreements have been set up with governments such as Colombia and Mexico to protect shared borders from drug traffickers. The long-term success of these and other social control measures to reduce drug abuse will require a continued investment in policies and programs that combine prevention, treatment, and law enforcement efforts both globally and at home, until social reaction re-defines what it is we are trying to control. We turn now to an examination of prostitution, another area in which the question of public order has been the subject of debate.

PROSTITUTION

Prostitution can most broadly be defined as the non-marital consensual exchange of sexual acts for material gain. The sexual acts can range from sexual intercourse to any other behavior from which the client derives sexual gratification. We traditionally think of prostitutes as women whose clients are men. However, individuals engaging in acts of prostitution can be male or female, and their clients can be same or opposite sex. Although the research literature on male prostitution is very limited, studies suggest that the social dynamics of male prostitution are not significantly different from those of female prostitution.

Suppose a man and a woman meet at a bar, and they agree to go out to dinner and then have sex. If the man pays for dinner, is the woman engaging in prostitution? What distinguishes prostitution from consensual sexual acts is an accompanying economic transaction. Something of economic value is gained by providing the sexual act, such as money, drugs, or material goods. If the stipulation for having sex was that the man would pay for dinner, then this *could* be considered a prostitution transaction. Some may be shocked by this conclusion. However, it is this example that represents the gray area when it comes to defining sexually deviant behavior. It also illustrates the difficulty of determining the incidence of prostitution.

How common is prostitution?

Experts estimate approximately 1 million prostitutes operate in the United States in any given year.[48] According to the Uniform Crime Report, there were 47,598 arrests for prostitution in 2014.[49] Arrest rates for prostitution have declined over the years. Some argue that this drop is largely due to the fact that the crime has become less visible to law enforcement. The widespread use of technology has allowed prostitution to go "cyber," with sexual exchanges being made via the use of web cameras. Moreover, the use of the internet has made setting up prostitution transactions more easily hidden.[50] This does not mean the actual incidence of prostitution has gone down, just arrest data. As we noted in chapter 3, this is one of the pitfalls of relying on official data sources on crime. We only know who gets caught, not everyone who commits the crime. And who gets caught, whether prostitute or customer, may sometimes surprise us (see Box 16.3).

BOX 16.3: CONSIDER THIS . . .

Prostitution's "unlikely clients"

Jimmy Swaggart was one of the most popular television evangelists in history. His ministry and weekly telecast programs which began in 1975 were broadcast throughout the United States and in over 100 other countries worldwide. In the late 1980s, Jimmy Swaggart resigned from his ministry after being exposed for a sexual scandal that led to his confession to "moral failure" in front of a congregation of 7,000 in Baton Rouge, Louisiana. Confronted by photos of himself and a prostitute taken by a private investigator acting on the behalf of a pastor from a rival church in New Orleans, Swaggart admitted to church elders that he had paid a prostitute to perform pornographic acts.

Eliot Spitzer was a graduate of Harvard Law School who worked for the Manhattan District Attorney's Office and was elected New York Attorney General in 1998, successfully prosecuting organized crime and launching the investigation that brought the downfall of the infamous Gambino crime family. In 2006, he was elected as the 54th Governor of New York, and began serving his term in 2007. On February 13, 2008, New York Governor Spitzer ordered a prostitute from the Emperors Club, unaware that the service was being monitored by federal agents as part of a sting operation. His solicitation quickly became front-page news.

The Emperors Club V.I.P. was an international prostitution ring that provided expensive prostitutes to wealthy clients in New York, Washington, Los Angeles, Miami, London, and Paris. Women could be "ordered" online by the hour (for prices reaching $5,500 per hour) or the day (over $31,000).

Spitzer, who was 48 and had been governor for only a year and a half, had been elected in part for his reputation of being tough on corruption. Often referred to as "Mr. Clean," he was active in prosecuting 18 people on charges of promoting prostitution. Now he was forced to apologize to his family and the public and soon after to resign from office. Likewise, decades earlier, televangelist Jimmy Swaggart, known for his stance against sexual immorality, stepped down in shame. Publicly humiliated, he faced his wife, son, and daughter-in-law, looking directly at them and confessing on national television, "I have sinned against you."

Why would a respectable, law-abiding governor, husband, and father of three teenage daughters pay for sex with a high-priced call girl; what would prompt a religious leader of millions to cross moral and ethical boundaries and seek the paid services of a prostitute?

What do you think?

Sources

Eliot Spitzer Biography (U.S. Governor, 1959–). 2016. *A & E Biography*. Retrieved from http://www.biography.com/people/eliot-spitzer-279076.

Kaufman, Joanne. The Fall of Jimmy Swaggart. *People.com*. Retrieved from http://www.people.com/people/archive/article/0,,20098413,00.html

Other argue that the actual *incidence* of prostitution has gone down, because fewer clients are willing to engage in sexual acts with a prostitute given the widely known risks of sexually transmitted diseases and AIDS.[51] Moreover, as expressions of sexuality have become more liberal and legal opportunities for sex more readily available over the past couple of decades, individuals have become less inclined to seek the services of a prostitute.

Notwithstanding declining arrest rates for prostitution in the United States, the sex tourism industry has grown.[52] In **sex tourism**, clients, usually men from wealthier countries, travel abroad to where young girls are readily available, either through need or by force, and where the sex industry is legalized or not well regulated. Locations considered hot spots for this type of activity include Bangkok, Amsterdam, Jamaica, and Kenya.

Types of prostitutes

Individuals who engage in prostitution come from a variety of backgrounds, have a variety of reasons for entering this pattern of behavior, and operate by different methods. While each category of prostitute that we describe below seems to be unique, they are not in fact mutually exclusive.

Skeezers

Skeezers are women who engage in prostitution in exchange for drugs, most commonly crack cocaine. Research suggests a significant association with age; women 25 or younger are more likely to exchange sex for crack than women older than 25.[53] Moreover, skeezers tend to be poor minority women from inner cities, who have been socially and economically marginalized by poverty and addiction.[54] Most use sex as a means of supporting their addiction.

Streetwalkers

Streetwalkers are prostitutes who walk the street soliciting sexual activity from customers. Often easily identifiable by their flashy, revealing clothes, high heels, and elaborate makeup, they may be independent entrepreneurs, or they may be controlled by a pimp for whom they work.[55] Many times streetwalkers congregate in particular areas known as "red light districts."

Often homeless, impoverished runaways or addicts, streetwalkers are described in the literature as the lowest form of prostitution.[56] They are also much more likely to be arrested and are at greater risk of suffering violence.[57] Streetwalkers are the lowest paid prostitutes in the profession and few ever climb out of this category of prostitution into other types.

Bar girls and dancers

Women who work at a bar under the guise of being a hostess or dancer but are also expected to provide sexual entertainment to customers are bar girls and dancers. Patterns of prostitution vary among them.[58] Some provide short-term individual entertainment, such as "lap-dancing," to many different

Image 16.6 *How do visibility and bias play a role in arrests for prostitution? Does the frequency of arrest for this type of prostitute affect our interpretation of prostitution as a threat to the public order?*

iStock/piranka

customers on a given night. Others may have long-term or returning clients, with whom they spend an entire evening or whom they accompany home. Many young women enter into this type of prostitution believing they are being hired for a legitimate job as a dancer, singer, or entertainer and find out later that sexual activity is an expectation.

In a growing trend, bar girls at "juicy bars" (commonly found near military bases)[59] entice male customers into buying them expensive drinks, usually watered-down alcoholic fruit beverages, with the promise of an exciting evening of sexual pleasure that does not always materialize. These bar girls often get a commission on the drinks they sell and may be pushed by the bar owner to engage in further sexual acts with the customer depending on how much money they generate.

Call girls and escorts

Call girls and escorts are the usually middle-class females living a fairly lavish lifestyle and charging wealthy clients hundreds or thousands of dollars per night. In this more organized and professional form of prostitution, they often work for private companies that claim to provide escort services for both male and female clients. Clients are often checked out to make sure they are legitimate "upstanding" customers willing and able to pay top dollar. They can call and "order" a girl to come to a home or hotel room and provide a private strip tease or provocative dancing and fulfill sexual fantasies. Some call girls establish a clientele and entertain them in their own homes.

Indentured sex slaves

Sexual slavery occurs when an individual must prostitute herself to pay off some type of debt, often to a drug dealer or a pimp from whom she is trying to get away. Sexual slavery operations are sometimes controlled by organized crime rings or gangs.[60] Thousands of young women and teenagers are smuggled into the United States and other countries every year, predominantly from Southeast Asia and Eastern Europe.[61] Often from poor families, they are promised a better life and a job good enough to send money to their families back home. In reality, they find themselves forced into prostitution to pay for their own home and food.

Factors related to becoming a prostitute

Some individuals engage in prostitution voluntarily, having weighed the pros and cons and made a choice of their own free will. Others work out of necessity to support an addiction or pay a debt, or just to survive in particular circumstances.[62] In any case, a question still remains; why would an individual engage in sexual activity for economic gain?

Studies identify several pathways and factors that can attract, precipitate, or predispose a person to prostitution.[63] *Attracting variables* lead an individual to consider prostitution as a form of financial support. One such variable can be a false image, like the one portrayed by Julia Roberts in the film *Pretty Woman,* where prostitution is associated with glamour and excitement and the possibility of meeting the man of your dreams who will take you away from it all and spoil you with gifts and an expensive lifestyle.

Precipitating factors are circumstances or experiences that can place certain vulnerable men and women at risk of turning to prostitution. These are often sudden changes such as running away from home or being kicked out of the house by a boyfriend. Research shows that a majority of young girls turn to prostitution after running away from abusive or dysfunctional families and relationships.[64] Turning to the streets, they are often recruited into prostitution by a pimp or other men and women already in the business.

Finally, *predisposing factors* increase the chances or likelihood of an individual turning to prostitution.[65] These include economic hardship, low education, drug abuse, and homelessness. Many prostitutes enter the sex trade at an early age, with a history of sexual exploitation and abuse.[66] They are also the most likely to experience similar patterns of abuse as adults, often by pimps and customers, finding themselves caught up in a cycle of alcohol and drug abuse, violence, and risk of disease.[67]

While these variables paint a picture of prostitution as predominantly occupied by individuals from dysfunctional backgrounds—runaway teens, victims of sexual abuse, and homeless drug addicts—researchers note that it often reflects studies of street walkers and not the other categories of prostitutes, which can be occupied by middle-class men and women who turn to the sex-for-profit industry as a lucrative means of economic gain. In the more liberal attitude towards sexuality that has emerged over the years, the exchange of money for sex is seen as an acceptable form of instant gratification in a controlled environment, without the commitment and expectations of a long-term relationship.[68] Despite these changing mores, the U.S. government continues to challenge the notion of prostitution as a socially acceptable behavior, and it continues to be illegal everywhere except in brothels—houses run by a madam who recruits and "trains" young women as prostitution—in various counties of Nevada.

What do we do about prostitution?

The debate over the illegal status of prostitution presents conflicting views on the governments' ability to regulate sexual activity that occurs in private between two consenting adults.[69] At the core of these arguments is whether or not prostitution presents a threat to the public order. Some feminist theorists argue that prostitution is degrading to women and a further example of the exploitation of women by men. Prostitution promotes the view of women as objects, which facilitates violence against women, and renders women powerless against the conditions of poverty, drugs, and abuse that may have led to their entry into prostitution. Moreover, prostitution is linked to other forms of criminal activity such as the abduction and trafficking of young women, sex slavery, and organized crime.[70] The social control of prostitution is therefore necessary for the public good. This social control should also extend to the pursuit of criminal charges against the clients of prostitution. Studies show that prostitution is emotionally and physically harmful to women, and therefore, the individual who buys sex should also be charged with a crime.[71]

Some scholars note, however, that the criminalization of prostitution is a violation of an individual's right to privacy and actually represents the subjugation of women by the imposition of primarily male-created laws governing their behavior.[72] According to this perspective, whether an individual chooses to engage in consensual sexual activity for pleasure or for a monetary exchange is a matter of personal choice not to be regulated by government interference. In addition, making prostitution illegal exacerbates the problems associated with it, imposing legal sanctions on women who are already suffering from abuse and addiction. Researchers note that prostitutes who work in areas where it is legal actually feel more safe and protected and are less vulnerable to disease and exploitation.[73]

Despite arguments supporting the decriminalization of prostitution, there seems to be a general consensus, at least among law makers, that the public order crime of prostitution, in its various types and forms, will continue to be prohibited by the law. A more difficult task is the definition and control of pornography, which directly challenges constitutional rights.

PORNOGRAPHY

A judge once said, "I can't define pornography . . . but I know it when I see it."[74] What is pornography and how do we describe it? It is subject to interpretation that may vary from individual to individual and culture to culture.

What is pornography?

Pornography can be defined as any material, either depicted or in words, that contains sexually explicit material and is *primarily* designed to incite sexual arousal in those who seek it out. Including books, magazines, films, and computer images, pornography is a billion-dollar industry that spans the international market. The widespread use of pornography has been facilitated by the development of new technologies that have allowed nude and provocative pictures to be quickly transmitted through internet social networking sites or via cell phones, now known as "sexting."[75] Of course, what is considered sexually explicit varies by cultural context. In some countries in the Middle East, the sight of a woman's ankles is considered sexually explicit and even forbidden in public. In some African villages, it is common for females to wear clothing that exposes their breasts due to the hot climate. These differences may affect the ways in which people judge what is and what is not sexually explicit.

One type of sexually explicit material portrays men or women either posing nude or engaging in voluntary sexual acts such as oral or anal sex. Another portrays sexual acts that are violent or coercive in nature, such as people being

Images 16.7 and 16.8 *How do cultural norms about dress influence the definition of pornography?*

iStock/wundervisuals, iStock/AG-ChapelHil

tied up, tortured, penetrated vaginally or anally by objects, or being humiliated or raped. Implicit in the definition of pornography is the idea that it is objectionable material. Is all pornography considered bad or harmful? Or only a certain type or category? Without engaging in a moral debate, it would be very difficult to answer these questions. We can however, gain a better understanding of the debate by looking more closely at the context within which pornography takes place.

Is pornography illegal?

Certain types of pornographic material have been deemed harmful, morally reprehensible, and detrimental to the well-being of society. One of these is **child pornography**, which depicts children in sexually explicit positions or engaging in sexual acts. Child pornography is widely regarded as harmful and exploitive; studies show long-term emotional damage to child victims.[76] Referred to as "kiddie porn," this type of pornography has also become an international phenomenon (see Box 16.4).

Some types of pornography are considered forms of **obscenity** and are also forbidden by the law. In *Miller v. California* (1973) the courts ruled that materials deemed obscene include those that appeal to the "prurient interest in sex, depicts sexual conduct in a patently offensive manner, and lacks serious literary, artistic, political, or scientific value" and therefore are not protected by the 1st Amendment.[77] The Supreme Court also ruled that the 1st Amendment does not protect obscenity, because it completely lacks any social importance.[78] Here the Court not only attempted to define obscenity but also set forth standards

BOX 16.4: CRIME IN GLOBAL PERSPECTIVE

Protecting children worldwide: INHOPE

Over the past decade, child pornography has become more accessible than ever. Studies show that every second, 28,258 users are watching some type of pornographic material on the internet, with an average of 40 million American people regularly visiting porn sites. Moreover, an estimated $3,075.64 is being spent every minute on internet pornography, with search engines getting about 116,000 queries each day related to child pornography. In 2013, the National Center for Missing and Exploited Children (NCMEC) reviewed 22 million images and videos of suspected child sexual abuse, representing a 5000 percent increase from 2007. Since the creation of the Child Victim Identification Program (CVIP) in 2002, the NCMEC has reviewed more than 138 million child sexual abuse images and videos at the request of law enforcement.

Statistics show that the number of images forwarded to CVIP for review continues to increase dramatically. In 2014, over 4,612 requests comprising more than 28 million images and videos were submitted by law enforcement agencies for review, an 18 percent increase in files reviewed by CVIP between 2013 and 2014. A significant factor contributing to this rapid increase is that child pornography has become a global epidemic, with an international proliferation of child sexual abuse images and videos being sent between offenders worldwide.

Child pornography is often distributed through the operation of pedophile rings, consisting of individuals from different countries who communicate to collect and disseminate sexually explicit images of children for personal gratification. Advances in media and internet technology have facilitated this type of communication and made it even more difficult to detect the source, causing serious concern among international agencies in the business of protecting children from this type of abuse.

In response, almost every country has created a taskforce to focus solely on combating this problem on the internet. The United States Department of Justice is responsible for monitoring child pornography both on the national and international levels. A number of other countries are also fighting this particular crime on a global level, and a number of organizations have been created to coordinate and facilitate the reporting of websites that contain child pornography.

In 1999, the International Association of Internet Hotlines (INHOPE) was founded. INHOPE represents internet hotlines around the world, providing support and assistance in responding to tips and reports about illegal or questionable content found on the internet. INHOPE also maintains a worldwide network of hotlines to increase awareness, provide technical support and expertise in quick and effective methods of responding to reports of illegal content, and educate policy makers on best practices for combating child pornography at the international level.

Sources

Child Pornography Statistics. 2016. *Thorn*. Retrieved from https://www.wearethorn.org/child-pornography-and-abuse-statistics/.

INHOPE Annual Report 2014. *INHOPE Public Reports*. Retrieved from http://www.inhope.org/tns/resources/statistics-and-infographics/statistics-and-infographics-2014.aspx.

Internet Pornography Statictics. 2016. Top Ten Reviews. Retrieved from http://internet-filter-review.topten reviews.com/internet-pornography-statistics.html.

National Center for Missing and Exploited Children. 2016. Retrieved from http://www.missingkids.com/About.

by which material can be judged obscene, by (1) determining whether the average person applying contemporary community standards would find that the material generally appeals to the prurient interest; (2) deciding whether the work depicts or describes in a patently offensive way sexual conduct that is specifically defined by the state's laws; and (3) determining whether the work, taken as a whole, lacks serious literary, artistic, political, or scientific value.[79] Moreover, in *Pope v. Illinois,* in order to ensure uniformity in the interpretation of obscenity, the Supreme Court ruled that material should be considered obscene by using "objective national standards."[80]

The definition of obscenity is therefore the central issue in the enforcement of laws prohibiting certain pornographic materials.

Is pornography harmful?

Feminist theorists have extensively researched the harmful effects of pornography on women,[81] with some arguing that pornography in any form is degrading and exploitive, picturing women in a sexually subordinate status.[82] Researchers also note that some of the acts depicted in pornographic materials such as the double penetration of women, or the penetration of women by large objects, are both physically and psychologically harmful.[83] Moreover, the widespread dissemination of pornographic material objectifies the human body and allows men to justify the treatment of women as objects.[84] Does this mean that there could be a relationship between pornography and sexual violence against women?

A growing body of literature examines the effects of viewing pornography, especially violent pornography, on perpetuating and reinforcing sexual assault.[85] While studies have not been able to establish a direct cause-effect relationship between viewing pornography and sexual assault, research suggests that pornography contributes to attitudes and patterns of behavior that are exploitive and abusive to women.[86] Pornography very often portrays individuals as either willing participants who enjoy being dominated and subordinated, or forced participants engaging in brutal acts of violence and degradation. Pornography may serve to reinforce coercive behavior in individuals inclined toward violence and sexual aggression because of their individual traits or sociocultural upbringing.[87] Moreover, researchers note that pornography plays a factor in the misperception among men that women like, enjoy, and fantasize about violent sexual acts.[88]

What do we do about pornography?

If studies confirm pornography as at least contributing to attitudes and behaviors that foster the degradation and mistreatment of women, then why is there not a general ban on the production and distribution of sexually explicit magazines, books, movies, and websites? The answer lies in the 1st Amendment's protection of free speech and expression. This becomes an even more complex matter when we consider the vast use of the Internet as a medium for the distribution of pornographic materials. However, one area where there is no question with regard to constitutional protection is child pornography, which is clearly forbidden and illegal,[89] as is obscenity. However, other forms of pornography are not as easily prohibited. The restriction on pornographic materials is thus limited to what is considered obscene.

Despite past court rulings, the debate about pornography will continue to put those advocating freedom of speech against those favoring stricter control of sexually explicit material, with advances in technology raising ever more complicated issues related to computer-generated images. The question about how much the government can influence the definition of public order will therefore continue to be in the forefront of criminological discourse.

SUMMARY

Where do we draw the line between what's immoral and what's illegal?

Society favors the formal social control of certain acts contrary to the public's collective sentiment about what decent and moral behavior is. These acts are called public order crimes and are often the outcome of collective campaigning by moral entrepreneurs who have certain ideas of what is for the social good.

What sexual acts do we define as prostitution?

Prostitution is a behavior pattern that is quite diverse, with prostitutes coming from a variety of backgrounds, with different reasons and means of entering prostitution, methods of engaging in prostitution, and interpreting their behavior. Prostitution has one common, legal variable: it involves sexual acts that are exchanged for monetary gain.

Why do some individuals exchange sex for money or drugs?

Some do it as a financially lucrative exchange. Others do it out of necessity to support an addiction or pay off a debt, or just to survive particular circumstances. Some prostitutes are forced or coerced into the behavior.

When does pornography become a crime?

Forms of sexually explicit materials that are forbidden by law include child pornography and those deemed to be obscene.

What types of drugs are illegal and why?

The deviant nature of drug taking is not specifically related to the chemical composition of the drug itself, but rather has more to do with the public's perception of who uses the drug and the need for its social control, which very often defines the drug's illicit status. Whether a particular drug is deviant, criminal, or both, is therefore socially created and varies according to moral sentiment.

Are we winning the war on drugs?

Scholars note that efforts to reduce drug abuse and addiction that focus exclusively on the arrest and incarceration of drug users and dealers are misguided and destined to fail because they do not recognize the social and public health issues related to drug abuse and addiction. Successful strategies must integrate components of law enforcement, treatment, and prevention.

CRITICAL THINKING QUESTIONS

1. Why is prostitution legal in parts of Nevada and not at all legal in other states? How far should the government go in legislating moral behavior? Are there any behaviors currently considered to be illegal that you feel should not be subject to control by the law? What are these behaviors and who's keeping them on the books?

2. What guidelines should be used to define what constitutes obscenity? Given the empirical evidence in support of the correlation between pornography and violence against women, should all forms of pornography be considered illegal? Why or why not?

3. Do you think the moral climate is changing in the direction of legalizing certain drugs? How do you feel about this issue? What are the pros and cons in the debate on the legal regulation of certain types of drugs such as marijuana?

E-RESOURCES

You can learn more about international efforts at tracking the trafficking of women and children by visiting the United Nations Educational, Scientific and Cultural Organization (UNESCO) website at http://en.unesco.org/.

Research on pornography as a catalyst to violence against women can be found at http://socialcostsofpornography.com/Layden_Pornography_and_Violence.pdf.

Find more facts, figures and trends on drug use and drug control policies at http://www.whitehousedrugpolicy.gov/publications/policy/ndcs09/2009ndcs.pdf.

Read more about drug courts and other problem solving oriented efforts by referring to *Painting the Current Picture: A National Report Card on Drug Courts and Other Problem-Solving Court Programs in the United States* at http://www.ndci.org/sites/default/files/nadcp/PCP%20Report%20FINAL.PDF.

NOTES

1   Shoichet, Catherine. 2014. Notorious Mexican Cartel Leader Nazaro Moreno Dead. *CNN.com,* March 11. Retrieved from www.cnn.com/2014/03/09/world/americas/mexico-drug-lord-nazario-moreno-killed/index.html.
2   Rockefeller, J. 2016. *Cocaine King Pablo Escobar: Crimes and Drug Dealings.* Self-published.
3   A Brief History of the War on Drugs. *Drug Policy Alliance.* Retrieved from www.drugpolicy.org/new-solutions-drug-policy/brief-history-drug-war.
4   Caulkins, Jonathan P., Reuter, Peter, Iguchi, Martin Y. and Chiesa, James. 2005. *How Goes the War on Drugs? An Assessment of U.S. Drug Problems and Policy.* Drug Policy Research Center, RAND Corporation.

5   Bergelson, V. 2013. Victimless Crimes. In *The International Encyclopedia of Ethics.* Hoboken, NJ: Blackwell.

6   Mograbi, G. and Batista de Sousa, C. 2015. *Decision-Making Experiments under a Philosophical Analysis: Human Choice as a Challenge for Neuroscience.* Lausanne, Switzerland: Frontiers Media SA.

7   Cohen, Morris R. and Cohen, Felix S. 2008. *Readings in Jurisprudence and Legal Philosophy*, Volume 2. Washington, D.C.: Beard Books-Law Classic.

8   Becker, Howard. 1963. *Outsiders: Studies in the Sociology of Deviance.* New York: Macmillan.

9   Garland, D. 2012. *The Culture of Control: Crime and Social Order in Contemporary Society.* Chicago, IL: University of Chicago Press.

10 *National Survey on Drug Use and Health: National Findings.* 2014. National Institute of Health, Washington, D.C.

11 Drug Policy Alliance. February 2015. *The Federal Drug Control Budget: New Rhetoric, Same Failed War.* Retrieved from www.drugpolicy.org/sites/default/files/DPA_Fact_sheet_Drug_War_Budget_Feb2015.pdf

12 Ibid., see 11.

13 Verster, J., Brady. K., Galanter, M. and Conrod, P. 2012. *Drug Abuse and Addiction in Medical Illness: Causes, Consequences, and Treatment.* Berlin, Germany: Springer Science and Business Media.

14 Feng, J. and Nestler, E. 2013. Epigenetic Mechanisms of Drug Addiction. *Current Opinion in Neurobiology* 23(4): 521–528.

15 Miller, P. 2013. *Biological Research on Addiction: Comprehensive Addictive Behaviors and Disorders*, Volume 2. Cambridge, MA: Academic Press.

16 Goldberg, R. 2009. *Drugs Across the Spectrum.* Boston, MA: Cengage Learning.

17 Powell, J. and Samanich, J. 2008. *Alcohol and Drug Abuse.* New York: Gareth Stevens.

18 Brick, J. and Erickson, C. 2013. *Drugs, the Brain, and Behavior: The Pharmacology of Drug Use Disorders.* New York: Routledge.

19 Abadinsky, H. 2013. *Drug Use and Abuse: A Comprehensive Introduction.* Boston, MA: Cengage Learning.

20 Segal, E. 2015. Health Care Policy. In *Empowerment Series: Social Welfare Policy and Social Programs.* Boston, MA: Cengage Learning.

21 *Centers for Disease Control and Prevention.* 2010. CDC Survey Finds 1 in 5 High School Students Abuse Prescription Drugs. Retrieved from www.cdc.gov/media/pressrel/2010/r100603.htm.

22 Hagan, Frank E. 2010. Drugs and History. *Crime Types and Criminals.* Thousand Oaks, CA: Sage.

23 Agnew, J. 2010. *Medicine in the Old West: A History, 1850–1900.* Jefferson, NC: McFarland.

24 Monitoring the Future 2015 Survey Results. National Institute on Drug Abuse. National Institute of Health, Washington, D.C. Retrieved from www.drugabuse.gov/related-topics/trends-statistics/infographics/monitoring-future-2015-survey-results.

25 Lee, M. and Hancox, R. 2014. Effects of smoking cannabis on lung function. *Expert Review of Respiratory Medicine* 5(4): 537–546.

26 Behavioral Health Trends in the United States: Results from the 2014 National Survey on Drug Use and Health. 2015. Retrieved from http://www.samhsa.gov/data/sites/default/files/NSDUH-FRR1–2014/NSDUH-FRR1–2014.pdf.

27 Shafii, M. and Shafii, S. 2008. *School Violence: Assessment, Management, Prevention.* American Psychiatric Publishers.

28 Department of Health and Human Services. September 2014. National Survey on Drug Use and Health, National Survey on Youth Violence and Illicit Drug Use. Retrieved from http://www.samhsa.gov/data/sites/default/files/NSDUHresultsPDFWHTML2013/Web/NSDUHresults2013.pdf.

29   Ibid.

30   Steele, V., Fink, B., Maurer, M., Arbabshirani, M., Wilber, C., Jaffe, A., Sidz, A., Pearlson, G., Calhoun, V., Clark, V. and Kiehl, K. 2014. Brain Potentials Measured During a Go/NoGo Task Predict Completion of Substance Abuse Treatment. In *Biological Psychiatry* 76(1).

31   Prisons, Jails, and People Arrested for Drugs. 2016. *DrugWarFacts.org*. Retrieved from www.drugwarfacts.org/cms/Prisons_and_Drugs#sthash.M9scRWet.dpbs.

32   Taxman, F. and Pattavina, A. 2013. *Simulation Strategies to Reduce Recidivism: Risk Need Responsivity (RNR) Modeling for the Criminal Justice System*. Berlin, Germany: Springer Science & Business Media.

33   Gaines, L. and Kappeler, V. 2014. Policing the Drug Problem. In *Policing in America*. Abingdon, England: Routledge.

34   Jordan, D. 2016. *Drug Politics: Dirty Money and Democracies*. Norman: University of Oklahoma Press.

35   Kaminer, Y. 2013. Prevention of High-Risk Behaviors: Adolescent Substance Use, Adolescent Psychoactive Substance Use Disorders, and Suicide. In *Adolescent Substance Abuse: A Comprehensive Guide to Theory and Practice*. Berlin, Germany: Springer Science and Business Media.

36   Hollandsworth, J. Jr. 2013. *The Physiology of Psychological Disorders: Schizophrenia, Depression, Anxiety, and Substance Abuse*. Berlin, Germany: Springer Science and Business Media.

37   Miller-Day, M., Alberts, J., Hecht, M., Trost, M. and Krizek, R. 2014. *Adolescent Relationships and Drug Use*. Abingdon, England: Psychology Press.

38   Bucerious, S. and Tonry, M. 2014. *The Oxford Handbook of Ethnicity, Crime, and Immigration*. Oxford, U.K.: Oxford University Press.

39   Volkow, N., Baler, R., Compton, W. and Weiss, S. 2014. Adverse Health Effects of Marijuana Use. In *The New England Journal of Medicine* 370(23): 2219–2227.

40   Goode, E. 2015. *The Handbook of Deviance*. Hoboken, NJ: John Wiley & Sons.

41   Drug Policy Alliance. 2015. Drug Prohibition and Violence. Retrieved from www.drugpolicy.org/drug-prohibition-and-violence.

42   Granfield, R. and Reinarman, C. 2014. *Expanding Addiction: Critical Essays*. Abingdon, England: Routledge.

43   Bertram, Eva, Blackman, Morris, Sharpe, Kenneth and Andreas, Peter. 1996. *Drug War Politics: The Price of Denial*. Oakland: University of California Press.

44   Bush, G.W. 2010. *National Drug Control Strategy*. Collingdale, PA: DIANE Publishing.

45   National Drug Control Strategy. 2015. Office of National Drug Control Policy. Washington, D.C. Retrieved from https://www.whitehouse.gov/ondcp/national-drug-control-strategy.

46   Ibid.

47   Lubin, Gus. 2012. There Are Approximately 42 Million Prostitutes in the World, and Here's Where They Live. *Business Insider*. Retrieved from http://www.businessinsider.com/there-are-42-million-prostitutes-in-the-world-and-heres-where-they-live-2012–1.

48   Ibid.

49   *Crime in the United States, 2014*. Federal Bureau of Investigation, U.S. Department of Justice, Washington, D.C.

50   Persak, N. and Vermeulen, G. 2014. *Reframing Prostitution: From Discourse to Description, From Moralisation to Normalisation?* Belgium: Maklu.

51   Sterk, Claire E. 2000. *Tricking and Tripping: Prostitution in the Era of AIDS*. New York, NY: Social Change Press.

52   Sex-Tourism Operation Nets Three. 2009. *CNN.com*, Sept. 1. Retrieved from http://www.cnn.com/2009/CRIME/08/31/cambodia.sex.tourism/.

53   Stark, Claire E. 2000. Female Crack Users and Their Sexual Relationships: The Role of Sex-For-Crack Exchanges. *The Journal of Sex Research* 37(4).

54   Edwards, Jessica M., Halpern, Carolyn T. and Wechsberg, Wendee M. 2006. Correlates Of Exchanging Sex For Drugs Or Money Among Women Who Use Crack Cocaine. *AIDS Education And Prevention* 18: 420–429.

55   Flowers, R. 2011. *Prostitution in the Digital Age: Selling Sex from the Suite to the Street*. Santa Barbara, CA: ABC-CLIO.

56   Flowers, Barri. 2001. *Runaway Kids and Teenage Prostitution*. Westport, CT: Praeger Publishers.

57   Barkan, S. and Bryjak, G. 2011. *Fundamentals of Criminal Justice: A Sociological View*. Burlington, MA: Jones & Bartlett Learning. Flowers, R. 2011. *Prostitution in the Digital Age: Selling Sex from the Suite to the Street*. Santa Barbara, CA: ABC-CLIO.

58   Agnes, Flavia. 2008. The Bar Dancer and the Trafficked Migrant. In Letherby, Gail, et. al., *Sex As Crime*. Willan Publishing.

59   Vine, D. 2015. *Base Nation: How U.S. Military Bases Abroad Harm American and the World*. New York: Metropolitan Books.

60   Walker-Rodriguez, A. and Hill, R. 2011. *Human Sex Trafficking*. Washington, D.C.: Federal Bureau of Investigations.

61   Vijeyarasa, R. 2016. *Sex, Slavery and the Trafficked Woman: Myths and Misconceptions about Trafficking and Its Victims*. Abingdon, England: Routledge.

62   Hwang, Shu-Ling and Bedford, Olwen. 2003. Precursors and Pathways to Adolescent Prostitution in Taiwan. *Journal of Sex Research* 40(2).

63   Servin, A., Brouwer, K., Gordon, L., Rocha-Jimenez, T., Staines, H., Vera-Monroy, R., Strathdee, S. and Silverman, J. 2015. Vulnerability Factors and Pathways Leading to Underage Entry into Sex Work in Two Mexican-U.S. Border Cities. *The Journal of Applied Research on Children: Informing Policy for Children at Risk* 6(1).

64   Ross, J. 2013. *Encyclopedia of Street Crime in America*. Thousand Oaks, CA: Sage.

65   Dodsworth, J. 2015. Routes into Sex Work: Who, Why and How? In *Pathways into Sexual Exploitation and Sex Work*. London: Palgrave Macmillan UK.

66   Roe-Sepowitz, D. 2012. Juvenile Entry into Prostitution: The Role of Emotional Abuse. In *Violence Against Women,* 18(5).

67   Hayes, S., Carpenter, B. and Dwyer, A. 2012. *Sex, Crime and Morality*. Abingdon, England: Routledge.

68   Sex for Sale: Confessions of a Client. 2008. *Today.com*. Retrieved from http://www.today.com/id/27651436/ns/today-today_news/t/sex-sale-confessions-client/#.Vw0eEY-cGP8.

69   Mishra, V. 2013. *Human Trafficking: The Stakeholders' Perspective*. India: SAGE India.

70   Arrigo, B. 2014. *Encyclopedia of Criminal Justice Ethics*. Thousand Oaks, CA: SAGE.

71   Jones, S. 2016. *Sex Work and Female Self-Empowerment*. Abingdon, England: Routledge.

72   Altemimei, D. 2013. Prostitution and the Right to Privacy: A Comparative Analysis of Current Law in the United States and Canada. *Illinois Law Review* 625.

73   Albert, Alexa. 2002. *Brothel: Mustang Ranch and Its Women*. Ballentine Books.

74   Justice Stewart in *Jacobellis v. Ohio* 378 US 184 (1964).

75   Davies, Shaun. 2009. Kids Face Porn Charges Over 'Sexting'. *NineMSN,* Jan. 17. Retrieved from http://www.ninemsn.com.au/article.aspx?id=719928.

76   Hughes, Donna Rice. 2001. How Pornography Harms Children. *ProtectKids.com*. Retrieved from http://www.protectkids.com/effects/harms.htm.

77   *Miller v. California*, 413 U.S. 15 (1973).

78   *Roth v. United States*, 354 U.S. 476 (1957).

79   *Miller v. California*, 413 U.S. 15 (1973)

80   *Pope v. Illinois*, 481 US 497 (1987).

81   Whittier, N. 2014. Rethinking Coalitions: Anti-Pornography Feminists, Conservatives, and Relationships between Collaborative Adversarial Movements. *Social Problems* 61(2).

82   Boyle, Karen. 2000. The Pornography Debates: Beyond Cause and Effect. *Women's Studies International Forum* 23(2): 187–195.

83   Cooper, K. and Short, E. 2012. T*he Female Figure in Contemporary Historical Fiction.* Basingstoke, UK: Palgrave Macmillan.

84   Burns, Ryan J. 2002. *Male Internet Pornography Consumers' Perception of Women and Endorsement of Traditional Female Gender Roles*. Austin: University of Texas, Department of Communication Studies.

85   Braithwaite, S.R., Coulson, G., Keddington, K. and Fincham, F.D. 2015. The Influence of Pornography on Sexual Scripts and Hooking Up Among Emerging Adults in College. *Archives of Sexual Behavior* 44(1): 111–123.

86   Cornell, D. 2016. *The Imaginary Domain: Abortion, Pornography and Sexual Harrassment.* London: Routledge.

87   Wright, P.J., Tokunaga, R.S. and Kraus, A. 2015. A Meta-Analysis of Pornography Consumption and Actual Acts of Sexual Aggression in General Population Studies. *Journal of Communication* 66(1): 183–205; Seto, Michael C., Maric, Alexandra and Barbaree, Howard E. 2001. The Role of Pornography in the Etiology of Sexual Aggression. *Aggression and Violent Behavior* 6: 35–53

88   Hald, Gert Martin and Malamuth, Neil N. 2015. Experimental Effects of Exposure to Pornography: The Moderating Effect of Personality and Mediating Effect of Sexual Arousal. *Archives of Sexual Behavior* 44(1): 99–109.

89   *New York v. Ferber*, 458 U.S. 747 (1982).

CHAPTER OUTLINE

Crimes of the powerful

In this chapter we will explore the following questions	KEY TERMS

- What are the key features of crimes of the powerful?
- In what context does white-collar crime occur?
- What is state-corporate crime?
- What is the relationship between organized crime, government, and business?
- Why should we care about the crimes of the powerful?

In May 2015, the Federal Bureau of Investigation indicted 14 high-ranking officials from the Federation Internationale de Football, better known as FIFA, the governing body that coordinates and promotes international professional soccer. According to the FBI, those officials, and the entire FIFA organization, had been engaging in "rampant, systemic and deep-rooted corruption"[1] for perhaps as long as 24 years. Among the criminal charges levied against this group were racketeering, wire fraud, money laundering, and conspiracy.[2]

By December 2015, the total number of FIFA officials implicated in various bribery and corruption scandals had risen to 30.[3] Among the corrupt activities engaged in by members of FIFA and governments of FIFA member nations were game selling and taking bribes to allow Russia and Qatar to host upcoming world cup soccer tournaments. These allegations are quite serious, as the World Cup soccer matches draw more viewers—in person and on television—than any other sporting event in the world. As a result, those countries that host the games stand to make hundreds of millions of dollars in revenue as fans flood their country and buy hotel rooms, food, gifts, and more.

The FIFA corruption scandal is a prime example of the type of criminal event we examine in this chapter on the "crimes of the powerful." In the following pages, you'll learn more about the nature, seriousness, and varieties of crimes that the powerful, including individuals and organizations, commit.

Image 17.1 *Clockwise from top left: FIFA officials Jeffrey Webb, Jose Maria Marin, Nicolas Leoz, Eugenio Figueredo, Jack Warner, and Eduardo Li, all of whom were implicated in a massive FIFA soccer corruption scandal.*

AP/Press Association Images

CRITICAL CRIMINOLOGY AND THE CRIMES OF THE POWERFUL

state-initiated corporate crime

state-facilitated corporate crime

genocide

1948 United Nations Convention on the Prevention and Punishment of the Crime of Genocide

The sociological study of crime has experienced a paradigm revolution[4] since the 1960s that has impacted how crime is defined and studied. Prior to the 1960s, most criminological research was guided by the idea that we should take a legalistic perspective and only study acts and events defined within the law as criminal. Today, to the benefit of the academic study of crime and society, crime scholars adopt a host of legalistic, socio-legal, and cultural understandings of "crime."

The seeds for this development were already being sown in the early works of Karl Marx, Edwin Sutherland, and others. However, it took until the late 1960s for the necessity of expanding the criminological portfolio to gain a large following. This movement among a diverse group of people arose in response to a variety of conflicts occurring in societies across the globe, including the Vietnam War, the American civil rights struggle, and various social conflicts and protests in Britain.

These conflicts focused attention on issues of power, inequality, and justice. They also raised some important "critical" questions:

- Who wins and who loses if we only associate the label "crime" with those acts prohibited under the criminal law?
- How can we trust that the political process of law creation will produce categories that capture the full range of criminal behavior?
- If our basic conception of crime and criminality is flawed, how do we understand who society's criminals really are?
- Finally, how do we understand the relationship between power, justice, and crime once we start examining actions and events that have escaped sanction under the criminal law?

The questions above, and the criminological paradigm shift that gained momentum in the 1960s, are now associated with an orientation known as critical criminology. **Critical criminology** is a popular umbrella perspective that draws on ideas from many viewpoints to examine "crimes" as defined in the law and acts that are not legally criminal, but which cause significant harm to society. As you already know, harm is a key element in defining any crime, but not all harmful acts are legally criminal. Thus, a critical criminological perspective looks at many types of harmful behavior, especially those acts committed by the powerful. Thus, when we explore the "crimes of the powerful"—white-collar crime, corporate crime, state crimes, and organized crime—we do so from a critical criminological viewpoint.

Image 17.2 *The 1960s were a turbulent time in the U.S. and around the world. Many social movements began, each seeking to advance the rights or interests of certain groups, and society as a whole. Out of this dynamic milieu arose critical perspectives, which have been hugely influential in shaping the study of social topics like crime and justice ever since.*

Wikimedia Commons/Lyndon B. Johnson Library/Frank Wolfe

Who are the powerful and what crimes do they commit?

The topic of this chapter—crimes of the powerful—is as important as any in the criminological field. But, before we explain why this topic is so meaningful and worthy of our attention, let us broadly explore who the powerful are and what crimes they commit.

When we say "crimes of the powerful" we have a specific type of offender in mind. We're not talking about the "average" criminal—the person of low-income and low educational attainment who is, statistically speaking, most likely to end up arrested and incarcerated.

genocidal
   mentality
organized crime
Omerta
Racketeer
   Influenced and
   Corrupt
   Organization
   Act (RICO)
racketeering

Images 17.3 and 17.4
The "average offender" and the atypical "crimes of the powerful offender."

iStock/shironosov;
iStock/poba

Our interest is in a group of unique offenders, comprised of both individuals and organizations, who possess power, money, high status, and significant social connections. In other words, the offenders we study under the title "crimes of the powerful" are often those who we *least* expect to commit crimes. After all, why would someone with lots of money commit theft or fraud? Why would an organization with an international reputation knowingly sell a dangerous, lethal, product to consumers?

Crimes of the powerful shock us because we don't understand why people or organizations would risk so much by engaging in criminal activity.

Indeed, powerful individuals and organizations, including state governments, commit incredibly harmful crimes far more often than you probably realize. Their criminal acts fall broadly under three categories: (1) white-collar crime, (2) state crime, and (3) organized crime. We deal with each of these categories in detail in the sections that follow, but it is worth pointing out that the range of crimes committed within these categories is incredibly diverse and includes murder, genocide, fraud, narcotics trafficking, embezzlement, theft, insider trading, manufacture of harmful products, bribery, conspiracy, and more.

Simply put, crimes of the powerful cause more physical, economic, and psychological harm than all property and violent crimes combined. Crimes committed by the powerful are far more harmful than the crimes we are preoccupied with in our modern culture: the "street crimes" that attract so much media, political, and public attention and which divert so many criminal justice system resources.

Key features of crimes of the powerful

Crimes of the powerful are important to study because they are committed by entities we wouldn't expect to commit crimes. This fact raises interesting questions about why powerful people and organizations engage in criminal behavior. The crimes of the powerful can serve as an important motivation for criminologists to develop better theories of crime. As you read through the various forms of crime committed by the powerful, think about which criminological theories work best to explain those behaviors and which are least useful. Try to identify holes in existing theories or areas that need better theoretical explanation.

Beyond pushing our criminological thinking, crimes of the powerful have several other key features. Most important, the crimes of the powerful often go: (1) unnoticed, and (2) under-punished. That is, we (the public) don't hear about crimes of the powerful nearly as much as hear about street crimes, drug crimes, and the like. This is because the media chooses not to focus its gaze on these crimes. Likewise, despite their harmfulness, crimes of the powerful are not the primary focus of our law enforcement agencies. That is, their investigation and control is not where most of our law enforcement resources are spent.

Even when we do hear about, investigate, and prosecute a powerful individual or organization for a criminal act, it is more likely than not that they will receive a comparatively more lenient sentence than the average street criminal, if they are even found guilty (more on this below). Why is this the case? Because power, money, and high status provide access to the best legal counsel money can buy, which translates into a greater likelihood of victory in the courtroom. Moreover, the limited and highly coveted resources possessed by the powerful allow them to practically buy their way out of trouble or criminal sanction, create media campaigns to sway public opinion and insulate themselves from the repercussions of their harmful acts.

The "unseen" crimes of the powerful

Chances are you've at least heard the name Bernie Madoff, even if you aren't completely sure who he is or what he did. As a reminder, Madoff orchestrated one of the largest investor fraud schemes in recent history, stealing nearly $20 billion in funds entrusted to him. His ponzi scheme—one of this century's most significant examples of a crime committed by a powerful person— unraveled at the height of the recent "great recession" and was widely publicized. Bernie Madoff's case, however, is the exception rather than the rule. For each Madoff-like case that gains national and international publicity, countless more crimes of the powerful occur with hardly any attention paid to them by the press, politicians, or the public.[5]

For example, have you heard about the criminal escapades of Royal Caribbean Cruise lines? What about the recent trouble Apple Computer company got into? Or HSBC Bank?

Our guess is that you probably know something about these large corporations, maybe you've used their services or own their products. But, it's likely you know very little about the very serious, harmful, criminal activities they, and many like them, have been engaged in.

However, what if we asked you who Bundy, Dahmer and Gacy are? If you're like most students, you'd probably recognize that those names belong to three infamous American serial killers. Our guess is you'd also be able to tell us quite a lot about what they did, where, and when.

Why is that? Remember that being a good criminologist and sociologist requires that you think critically about what you know and what you are learning about. Why is it that we know so much about people who rape, rob, and murder, but so little about the powerful who poison, defraud, and debilitate?

If you haven't heard about the crimes committed by Royal Caribbean, Apple, and HSBC there is a reason for that. Criminologist Greg Barak[6] explained that

> our lack of knowledge of the crimes of the powerful—compared to our knowledge of the crimes of the powerless—persists in part . . . because the crimes and victims of the powerful remain relatively invisible thanks to the concerted efforts of lawyers, governments, and corporations to censor or suppress these disreputable pursuits from going viral when they succeed. This absence of knowledge also continues, in part, because the discipline of criminology spends only five percent of its time researching, teaching, and writing about "white-collar" crime while devoting ninety-five percent of its time to "blue-collar" crime.
>
> (McGurrin et al. 2013)

In short, the phrase "too big to fail,"[7] coined during the federal bailout of corporations responsible for sending the American and world economy into a tailspin, is an apt summarization for why we hear so little about the crimes of the powerful and why their harmful exploits fall so quickly out of the spotlight. When a criminal offender has power, money, and status on their side, it is very easy for them to engage in all manner of awful behavior without anyone paying attention to it. Even professional crime researchers like us contribute to this problem on occasion.

Failing to punish crimes of the powerful

The Ford Motor Company manufactured and sold the compact Ford Pinto in the 1970s. While designing the Pinto, Ford engineers and corporate executives became aware of a major defect in the engineering and placement of the Pinto's gas tank. Specifically, prior to selling the Pinto, Ford Motor Company knew that the Pinto gas tanks could easily rupture during rear-end collisions, resulting in fires which could cause serious injuries and deaths to the vehicle's occupants. With this knowledge in hand, Ford Motor Company engaged in a common accounting practice known as **risk-benefit analysis**. The results of this analysis told Ford Motor Company several things.

If they chose to fix the faulty gas tank design in the Pinto prior to selling the vehicles, that choice would cost Ford $11 per vehicle to implement (it would also require halting production momentarily). The total estimated cost of fixing the Ford Pinto before the public could buy them was $137 million.

From their risk-benefit analysis Ford also learned that if they made no changes to the Pinto's gas tank design, they could expect roughly 180 burn deaths and over 1,200 burn-related injuries to occur. However, the economic

Image 17.5 *Patty Ramge, posing with her 1975 Ford Pinto, had little trouble with motorists tailgating since she decked her car with a sign warning of its' explosive nature if hit from the rear. Mrs. Ramge posted the warning after weeks of trying to convince Ford Motor Co., and its dealers to modify the fuel tank so it would not pose a fire hazard in a rear-end crash.*

JCH/AP/Press Association Images

cost of doing nothing—meaning taking no action to fix the faulty gas tanks—would total only $49.5 million. In other words, Ford Motor Company calculated the cost of a human life and what they would be likely to pay out in lawsuits.

Ford executives reviewed the results of their risk-benefit analysis.

What decision do you think they made? Conversely, what decision would you have made?

Ford, perhaps unsurprisingly, chose to continue producing the Pinto without fixing the gas tank issue. In other words, at a definite moral fork in the road, Ford Motor Company made a decision to sell a potentially lethal product and place human lives at risk because it was cheaper to do that than spend $11 per car to make the Ford Pinto safer.

The result of Ford's decision was predictable. According to Ford itself *only* 23 people were killed in fires resulting from ruptured Pinto gas tanks. However, other estimates place the number of deaths closer to 500 people!

In 1980, Ford became the first corporation in America to be brought to trial on the criminal charge of reckless homicide. However, they were found not guilty by an Indiana jury. Importantly, no Ford executives were ever imprisoned for the Pinto case. Ford Motor Company was not shut down and, as you know, continues to function as a profitable, well-known corporation to this day.

Pause for a moment and consider this. What if a lone individual tampered with the fuel tanks in other people's vehicles so that when those people got into an accident the fuel tanks would rupture easily and kill them? Do you think the person who intentionally tampered with the fuel tanks would avoid criminal sanctions? Not likely. They would probably be charged with first degree, pre-meditated, or at least second degree murder.

Again, ask yourself whether there is any significant difference between the actions of the hypothetical individual mentioned above and the actions of Ford's executives who knew they were selling cars with faulty gas tank designs that could—and most certainly would—hurt and kill innocent people.

The courtroom battle to hold Ford Motor Company and its executives criminally responsible for the deaths their defective vehicles caused has since been described as a "David v. Goliath" encounter,[8] referring to the Christian bible's Old Testament story. Unlike the bible's rendering of David v. Goliath however, in the case of the Ford Pinto trial, Goliath, not David, won.

David v. Goliath is an apt phrase to characterize most cases where an extremely powerful entity, either individual or corporation, commits a crime.

Rarely, like in the 1985 Film Recovery Systems[9] case in Illinois, corporate executives are held criminally responsible for their actions. A jury in the Film Recovery Systems case actually found three executives guilty of murder after one of their factory workers died from cyanide poisoning.[10,11] This outcome, however, is uncommon.

Most often, fines and civil sanctions (i.e., damages) are used to penalize the powerful, in particular corporations, for the crimes they commit. This is because it is often difficult to prove the element of criminal intent (i.e. "the guilty mind", chapter 10) when a corporation's actions or products ultimately do cause injury or death. It's far easier to demonstrate negligence or a simple regulatory violation. Even still, when penalties are handed out to powerful corporations, they amount to a small fraction of the company's gross revenue and, ultimately, the company and its executives are allowed to continue on as if nothing even happened.

Take, for example, Royal Caribbean Cruise Lines. Royal Caribbean is considered a repeat, or recidivist, criminal corporation because they, like many others, repeatedly violate regulatory statutes and criminal laws. In the mid- and late 1990s, the popular cruise line was charged not once, but twice, for dumping toxic chemicals, including dry cleaning fluid and film developer, into the ocean and at ports of call, including Miami, Florida.

Not only did Royal Caribbean lie about their actions, they also actively tried to cover them up. The first time they were charged and ultimately fined just $9 million dollars. The company promised not to offend again. However, just two years later the cruise line was back in court facing similar charges of illegal dumping and obstruction of justice. This time they were forced to pay $18 million in fines. Royal Caribbean regularly posts revenue of over $7 billion per year.

The Royal Caribbean case is not just an example of powerful criminal offenders skating with light penalties. It is also a terrific illustration of how powerful corporations truly represent Goliath's in the courtroom. For their

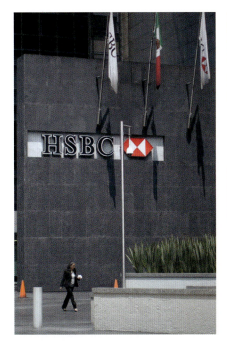

Image 17.7 *Royal Caribbean Cruise Lines has twice been accused and found guilty of criminal fraud, illegal dumping, and other crimes, yet the massive company remains in operation.*

Lynne Sladky/AP/Press Association Images

Image 17.6 *A woman walks in front of the HSBC bank headquarters in Mexico City. An investigation found that lax controls at the international bank allowed Mexican drug cartels to launder billions of dollars through it. It is highly likely bank officials were aware of these transactions but did not act to stop them.*

Alexandre Meneghini/AP/Press Association Images

second trial on illegal dumping charges, Royal Caribbean hired a defense team consisting of two former directors of the Justice Department's Environmental Crimes section, two former United States Attorney Generals, two former federal prosecutors, and two former State Department officials. They also retained the services of four retired Navy admirals and initiated a huge, multi-million-dollar marketing and public relations campaign, including taking out ads during the Super Bowl, all in an effort to escape serious sanctions. Opposing Royal Caribbean in the federal court were just two federal prosecutors.

More recently, in 2013, the multi-national HSBC Bank admitted that several of its bank branches in Mexico and South America willfully allowed Mexican and Colombian drug cartels to launder more than $881 million in illegal drug profits through their banks. The money laundering operation was so blatant, some of the HSBC bank branches retrofitted their deposit windows to accept large boxes full of cash.[12]

Even though HSBC managers and executives knew the sums of cash being deposited were highly suspicious, they did nothing to report them. Instead, the bank willingly accepted the deposits, which, like all other funds entrusted to the bank, could be used to support various financial and investment activities. For its crimes, HSBC was fined $1.92 billion—a record amount—but no executives were charged with crimes. Again, HSBC was not shut down. Indeed, HSBC is only one in a long list of major banks that still continue to operate that have been caught engaging in illegal money laundering on behalf of criminal organizations and governments. Other banks implicated and found complicit in criminal money laundering schemes include Credit Suisse, Barclays, and ING, among others.

Even the golden child of corporations, Apple, which manufactures products like the iPad, iPhone, and Apple Watch, was convicted of a serious criminal offense. In 2013, Apple was charged with several criminal counts, most notably conspiring with book publishing companies like Simon & Schuster to "fix"— that is, illegally and artificially raise—the price of e-books (electronic versions of books and textbooks). The conspiracy, which began just before Apple released its iPad in 2010 was intended to raise the price of e-books in order to help Apple's iBook store compete with Amazon, the top seller of e-books. Ultimately, however, had Apple's plan gone through, the real victims would have been consumers like you and me who would have unfairly had to pay more for e-book purchases and rentals. For its actions, Apple, which lost its most recent appeal in 2015, must pay $450 million dollars.[13] To the ordinary person $450 million is a lot of money. For Apple, however, a $450 million fine is a drop in the bucket. In just one-quarter of the fiscal year 2015, Apple earned a profit of $8.5 billion![14]

In sum, the odds are stacked against the successful identification and prosecution of crimes of the powerful. Powerful individuals and organizations can, essentially, buy their way out of trouble—the American legal system is not blind to the elements of social class, including income, wealth, and status. As we explore the main categories of crimes of the powerful in the sections below, consider how often you hear or read about these forms of criminality as well as the impacts they produce in society.

WHITE-COLLAR CRIME

What is white-collar crime?

White-collar crime is one of the broadest categories of crime committed by powerful entities. Criminologist **Edwin Sutherland** (chapter 12) referred to **white-collar crime** as the illegal acts of high-status, respectable individuals in the course of their occupation.[15] Sutherland noted that individuals used their positions in business enterprise for personal gain, disregarding the rule of law. Contemporary criminologists use the term white-collar crime to encapsulate both the criminal acts of individuals occupying positions of power to benefit themselves as well as the criminal acts of individuals working to benefit a larger organization.

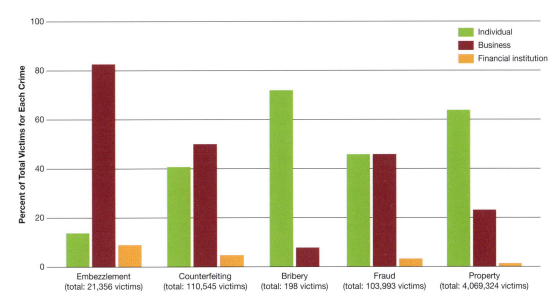

Figure 17.1 Victims of white-collar crime by offense type

Source: U.S. Department of Justice, Federal Bureau of Investigation, Criminal Justice Information Services Division. Barnett, Cynthia. The Measurement of White-Collar Crime Using Uniform Crime Reporting (UCR) Data. Retrieved from www.fbi.gov/ucr/whitecollarforweb.pdf. National Criminal Justice Reference Service (NCJRS) Library.

Characteristics of white-collar crimes

White-collar crime is business or work-related crime that can be perpetrated by a single individual or a group of individuals. White-collar crimes mostly involve deception, concealment, and breach of trust.[16] Often, the motivation for committing white-collar crime is to obtain money and gain privilege, status or respect or to avoid the loss of money and privilege, status, and respect.[17] White-collar crimes are usually non-violent, but their impacts on society and harms to victims are still quite serious. Victims can be individuals, corporations, or the general public (see Figure 17.1). For the sake of organization, we will divide white-collar crime into three sub-categories: individual, occupational, and corporate/organizational crime.[18]

Varieties of white-collar crime

Occupational crime

Occupational crime involves the illegal acts of individuals to promote their *own* self-interests, rather than the interest of the organization.[19] Occupational crime is the category of white-collar crime Edwin Sutherland was most interested in when he began exploring the topic many years ago. Occupational crime is interesting because, while it is certainly crime, a form of criminal behavior committed by powerful people, it is simultaneously crime committed against powerful organizations.

For example, the trusted senior accountant who embezzles millions from their employer is certainly exploiting their position of power. Yet, their actions are also harming the powerful organization of which they are a part. Here, we limit our examination of occupational crime to only two particular forms of fraud: embezzlement and chiseling.

Embezzlement

Very often, perpetrators of occupational crime use their positions of employment to steal company property or funds entrusted to their care. This is a form of occupational crime known as **embezzlement**. The major difference between larceny, discussed in chapter 15, and embezzlement is the manner in which the property is stolen: when a larceny is committed, the perpetrator did not have legal possession of the stolen money or goods; when embezzlement takes place, the perpetrator *does* have legal possession of the money or item but misappropriates it for his or her own benefit.

For example, if Billy who walks into a convenience store, sees the cash register open, and takes a $20 bill he has committed larceny theft. However, if Rita, an employee of the convenience store who works the cash register takes a $20 bill at the end of the day, she has embezzled company property. Notice the key difference: Billy had no legal right to the register or its contents; Rita, the employee, had the legal possession over the register and its contents, but still lacked the legal right to take the money for her own benefit. Embezzlement can, and usually is, a great deal more complicated than taking $20 from a cash register. It often includes elaborate schemes to alter records, interfere with bookkeeping, or manipulate accounts (see Box 17.1).

Embezzlement often produces significant financial losses for an organization. However, an even more pernicious, likely more common form of low-level

---

BOX 17.1: GETTING RICH IN PASADENA

Three residents of Pasadena, CA, including two former Department of Public Works employees—Danny Wooten, Tyrone Collins, and Melody Jenkins—were arrested in 2014 and charged with embezzling more than $6 million from the city of Pasadena over an eleven-year period.

The trio exploited various flaws and loopholes in the city's accounting and oversight procedures to siphon the money from a special public works account that collected a $30 per year surcharge from Pasadena city residents. The ringleader, Wooten, utilized his position as a senior management analyst in the Department of Public works to access the special account. He, Collins, and Jenkins then engaged in an elaborate scheme of faked invoices complete with forged signatures and other tactics, including laundering much of the money through Collins' electrical contracting business. The Pasadena trio have yet to go to trial; all have been charged with both criminal and civil violations.

embezzlement is called pilferage. **Pilferage** is the systematic theft of fairly small amounts of company property over an extended period of time. The property stolen could be anything from money to supplies to products, including food. Pilferage is very common and can cost companies hundreds of thousands of dollars a year. Nevertheless, employees continue to steal from their employers, justifying their actions with a variety of rationales. Some believe they are being mistreated with regard to compensation and promotion, so they are entitled to compensation by stealing or "taking what is owed to them." Others do it because of the easy accessibility of the funds. Still others are motivated by financial reasons, either out of personal greed or due to economic hardship.

Chiseling

Another type of occupational crime that consists of the regular cheating of a company or organization, its consumers, or both is called **chiseling**. Chiseling can be very difficult to detect and prove, because victims have often put their trust in someone they know nothing about.

Consider what happens if your car breaks down. You go to an auto mechanic who tells you several parts need to be replaced. Without detailed knowledge of the problem or your vehicle's working components, you have to trust that what the mechanic is telling you is correct. But what if it is not? What if you only needed one $10 part replaced, but the mechanic sells you on a $1,500 repair? This form of fraud is illegal and it happens all the time.

However, let's not just single out auto mechanics or other blue-collar workers. Medical professionals are some of the worst, most prevalent chiselers around. In the medical field, chiseling occurs when a doctor or treatment specialist recommends treatments and procedures that are not a medical necessity. For example, a dentist sells you on a new filling when the old one was fine or a

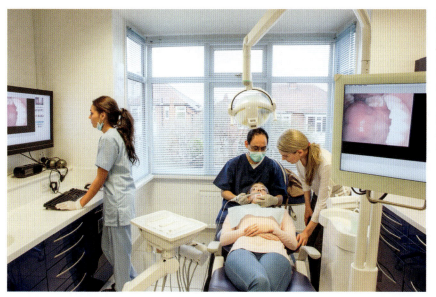

Image 17.8
In the medical field, chiseling occurs when a doctor or treatment specialist recommends treatments and procedures that are not a medical necessity.

iStock/SolStock

Image 17.9
Chiseling is an all too common form of fraud, which includes the manufacture of fake merchandise. New York City's canal street is known for its backroom shops where knock-off designer goods can be had at bargain prices. At first glance harmless, this type of fraud not only violates the intellectual property of the original designers/owners of the merchandise, it also reduces the profits of these legitimate businesses and negatively impacts their employees.

iStock/ferrantraite

doctor orders lab and blood tests that you don't need. Often, chiseling in the medical field is also linked to insurance fraud, since the victim is not just you but your insurance company who has to pay for the unnecessary services.

Chiselers are individuals who cheat their customers to increase the profits of their business or practice. They can also be employees who are cheating their customers and their own employers by pocketing the profits for themselves, such as would be the case if the mechanic in the example above created bogus repairs without the shop owner's knowledge and then kept the profits.

Other examples of chiseling include retailers who advertise and sell expensive fake and/or replica merchandise as "genuine": sports memorabilia, handbags, shoes, watches, etc. The Internet has made this type of transaction more widespread and created the need for a more aggressive approach to control. Several websites have been created to monitor such sales and increase consumer awareness of fraudulent merchants.[20]

Organizational and corporate crime

Corporate or **organizational crime** describes the illegal acts of people who occupy positions of power within institutions and willfully, knowingly break the law to advance their interests and the interests of their institution.[21] For many years, the acts of these individuals remained relatively unnoticed and were not considered as obviously harmful to society as murder, rape, and robbery. However, a surge in corporate and organizational crimes during the 1990s turned the tide of criminal prosecution, which began to crack down on the actions of corporations that violate criminal codes.[22]

Acts within this category of white-collar crime are quite diverse (see Table 17.1). Linking them, however, is that they are all committed by individuals

Table 17.1 Various types of corporate and organizational crimes

Non-delivery of services	Securities fraud
Confidence fraud	Auction fraud
False claims	Price-fixing
Money laundering	Overbilling
Market-rigging	Insurance overcharging
Corporate espionage	Mortgage fraud

within corporations or organizations acting in the interest of their organization. The acts are socially harmful and include crimes against employees, crimes against the general public, and crimes against the environment (chapter 18).

CRIMES AGAINST EMPLOYEES

The **Occupational Safety and Health Act of 1970** was designed to create and enforce federal standards to ensure that companies are providing their employees with safe and healthy working conditions.[23]

Standards developed under the act are set forth by the *Occupational Safety and Health Administration* (OSHA), which makes guidelines and provisions regarding the proper use of hazardous chemicals, the maintenance of equipment and machinery, the inspection of vehicles, sanitation standards, and a variety of other codes ensuring safe and healthy work environments. According to OSHA, there were 3.4 million cases reported of workplace injuries and illnesses among private-industry employers in 2014, representing a slight decline from 4 million cases reported in prior years.[24] Over 4,000 people were killed on the job in 2014—nearly 13 people per day.[25]

To keep costs down and increase their profits, corporations often cut corners and ignore or fail to correct safety and health violations. Table 17.2 presents the most commonly violated OSHA workplace safety standards when injuries or deaths take place. Notice that most of the standards violated refer to very basic issues, like failing to provide proper respiratory equipment to workers.

Employers who willingly put their employees at risk do so because they are willing to incur a fine, which is often less costly than correcting a violation in the first place. Moreover, there is only one OSHA compliance officer for every 59,000 workers in the U.S. who are spread across 8 million different worksites.[26] The odds of being caught for violating an OSHA standard are, thus, quite low. However, employers that engage in workplace safety violations can be held criminally responsible for injuries and deaths especially if

Table 17.2 Most common causes of American workplace injury and death

1.	Inadequate fall protection
2.	Failing to communicate information about hazards
3.	Inadequate or improper scaffolding
4.	Inadequate or improper respiratory equipment
5.	Injury caused by contact with improperly controlled energy storing machines/devices (i.e., electrical conductors)

it is determined that they purposefully neglected or subverted OSHA safety standards as occurred in the Film Recovery Systems case mentioned earlier in the chapter.

CRIMES AGAINST THE PUBLIC

Corporations commit a variety of crimes that involve deceiving the public in order to increase their own profits by providing misleading information about a product or service. This is known as **false claims advertising**. Sometimes a fine line exits between the aggressive marketing of a product and the fraudulent and purposeful deception of consumers to increase sales and meet stockholders' expectations (see Box 17.2).

Drug manufacturing companies have also been accused by the *Food and Drug Administration* (FDA) of making false claims about the effects of certain medicines in their efforts to promote them to the pharmaceutical industry.[27] This is an especially prevalent problem in the multi-million-dollar sport and diet supplement industry, where products typically do not need to be reviewed by the FDA prior to being marketed.[28]

Corporations also often manipulate free market competition by conspiring with their own competitors to maintain high prices for a particular commodity,

---

BOX 17.2: MARBLES IN THE SOUP?

You probably don't think of the soup industry as a cut-throat business landscape. But, as with any industry where millions of consumers and their dollars are up for grabs, competition is the rule of the day. And, where there is competition, there are often attempts made to bend, if not completely break, the rules of fair play.

In the late 1960s, Campbell's Soup Company partnered with an advertising firm from New York City to launch a new ad campaign. The creative minds at the ad firm had a dilemma, however. When they poured the soup into bowls to photograph it, the heavier contents, like vegetables, sank to the bottom meaning the only thing to photograph was the liquid. Understandably, the ad team was concerned that photos of bowls of liquid, no matter how tasty, would fail to capture the hearts and minds of the consuming public. Their solution: fill the bottom of the bowls with marbles; the liquid would seep down around the marbles but the vegetables would stay on top. Thus, the soup would appear in the photos to be chunkier and more "full" of delicious tidbits.

In 1968, one member of the ad team was testifying before the Federal Trade Commission (FTC), which regulates false advertising. Unaware that putting marbles in the soup was a violation, the ad team member volunteered that information while explaining the goal is to "make the food look as good as possible." Quickly, Campbell's came under intense fire, and got sued by the FTC to boot, for creating "false impressions" about its soups. Many argued, convincingly, that people seeing the ads where the veggies were so prominent in the soup would expect their bowls to look similar.

a practice known as price fixing. We discussed earlier how Apple and several major book publishers recently conspired to "fix" the price of e-books. This practice is strictly forbidden by law and can result in criminal sanctions that include both a fine and a prison sentence. While it is a common practice for businesses to adjust prices to meet supply and demand, it is illegal for them to conspire to set and control those prices in order to stifle competition. Distinguishing between the two purposes, however, can be an arduous task for investigators.[29] A better understanding of the dynamics in each industry may help control widespread shifting of prices in high-demand commodities such as gasoline.

State crime

What is state crime?

The crimes that occupy our imaginations and nightly news programs are those of the street: murders, rapes, muggings, assaults, arsons. We typically don't think of government or "state" officials as dangerous or criminal. The study of state crime, however, shows that government officials can, and do, commit heinous criminal acts, including acts of violence, on a regular basis.

When we study state crime we are studying crimes committed by state governments in carrying out their functions. Our focus is not on the crimes of individuals committed against state governments (i.e., treason, espionage, terrorism). Rather it is on the criminal or non-criminal, but analogously harmful, actions perpetrated by the state as it pursues its goals and interests. That is, we are looking at how the states themselves become criminals, not how individuals commit crimes against states.

States can engage in criminal conduct by breaking existing criminal laws. However, because states wield so much power and influence, it is necessary to examine their "criminality" in terms of harm not just legality. The reason for this is simple: a state, if it so chooses, can write, revise, interpret, and enforce the law in whatever way it needs to in order to avoid "breaking" it.

Thus, many examples of awful state crimes exist, like the Nazi holocaust, where no state laws were broken. Indeed, in the case of the holocaust, the extermination of "undesirable" people was carried out *legally*. As a result, we must use a critical perspective to evaluate the actions of states and we must not be afraid to call attention to both violations of the law as well as actions that, while not violating the law, are just as harmful, if not more so, than most crimes. Thus, nearly all state crime researchers utilize a very broad definition of "crime," where crime includes violations of laws, human rights, and a diverse range of harms to people, the environment, and even other species.

Characteristics of state crime

State crimes can occur through commission (i.e., actually doing something) and omission (i.e., failing to do something). An example of a state crime of commission would be engaging in genocide. Conversely, a state crime of omission could involve state officials willfully failing to act to prevent an outbreak of disease, resulting in the injuries and deaths of many people.

State actors possess immense power. Even in the most democratic of countries, like the United States or nations of western Europe, the influence and control of the state extends to all spheres of social life: polity, economy, culture, and media, etc. In totalitarian, dictatorial, or despotic government regimes, control is even more complete and intense. State crimes thus represent a terrible abuse of government power. Likewise, state crimes violate and exploit the trust vested in the government of a particular place. Some people don't trust the government, but many do and are taught to. Just like police corruption and abuse of force (discussed in chapter 5) state crimes violate the immense public trust that the state has.

As a result, state crimes inflict far greater social and economic costs upon the world's populations than do crimes like treason, property crimes like burglary, violent crimes like assault and murder, and public order crimes like prostitution, drug use, etc.[30] (see Box 17.3).

The hidden consequences of state crimes—the psychological, emotional, and cultural scars they leave behind—cannot be justly equated with the effects stemming from other forms of crime or criminality.[31]

Varieties of state crime

Abuse of power and corruption

Government and elected officials must use their positions of power and institutional privilege for the public good. Often, however, in the struggle to reach office and to maintain power, officials cross ethical lines and, even worse, engage in criminal behaviors like corruption, bribery, and extortion. As criminologist Nubia Evertsson noted in her study of political corruption in western Europe, "electoral donations are cloaked with legality," but may "facilitate corruption."[32]

We broadly define **political corruption** as the misuse of entrusted power by political or elected officials to maintain privilege and reap personal gain.[33] For example, former Nigerian national security advisor Sambo Dasuki engaged in serious political corruption when he abused his power and position by "awarding phantom" military contracts "for supplies . . . like fighter jets, bombs, and ammunition" in order to pocket over $2 billion.[34] Likewise for the prime minister of Malaysia Najb Razak, who has allegedly accrued over $700 million worth of government funds in his personal bank account.[35]

Influence peddling is a specific sub-type of corruption that occurs when government or elected officials exploit their influence in exchange for favors, financial gain, or material advantages. Accepting large campaign contributions in exchange for the awarding of government contracts to specific contributors is one example of influence peddling. Using a public office to hire relatives, giving preferential treatment to certain interest groups, misdirecting state

BOX 17.3: CRIME IN GLOBAL PERSPECTIVE

State crime, the Bennett Freeze, and Native American reservations

Contributed by **Lynda Marie Robyn, Associate Professor, Northern Arizona University**

Nowhere in the United States are government crimes more evident than on the Navajo Nation in northeastern Arizona. The Hopi people first occupied land where Arizona, Utah, Colorado, and New Mexico meet, an area known today as the Four Corners. In 1934, Congress decided to set aside a large portion of land in Arizona for the Navajo and "other such Indians as may already be located thereon." In effect, the U.S. government created a situation that would cause conflict over land between the Navajo and the Hopi village of Moenkopi, which was already in this area.

To prevent one tribe from taking unfair advantage of the other during land negotiations, Robert Bennett, commissioner of Indian Affairs, instituted a ban on any type of development in the area. The ban took effect in 1966 and left thousands of Navajos living in third world conditions for over 40 years, because under it they could not build or repair their homes (even to fix leaking roofs or broken windows), take care of the roads, or ensure adequate schools or health facilities. Even though the Navajo Nation produces most of the energy for the Southwest, the ban also meant no electric lines could reach homes in the so-called Bennett Freeze area. There were no gas lines for heat, and no water lines for indoor plumbing or any type of sanitation. People have either hauled in water fit for human consumption or drunk from the same wells as their livestock. But these wells have been contaminated by companies that have mined and processed uranium ore, leaving huge toxic tailings in piles polluting streams and underground aquifers, with no obligation to clean up the devastation left behind.[36]

People living on the reservation also used sand and crushed rock from old uranium mines to make concrete slabs for floors in hogans and ovens, not knowing these materials were radioactive. Exposure to uranium is lethal, and new evidence shows gastric cancer rates rose 50 percent during the 1990s among Navajo in two New Mexico counties with uranium sites. Uranium has also been linked to reproductive cancers, and a sharp increase in breast, ovarian, and other cancers has been recorded among teenage girls. Cancer rates 17 times the national average were found in the entire Navajo Nation.[37]

The creation of reservations forced the Navajo off their ancestral lands to live in abysmal conditions on the reservation, while the Bennett Freeze, by preventing the construction of any life-saving infrastructure, contributed to hundreds of cancer deaths. Who will pay for this needless suffering?

President Obama lifted the Bennett Freeze in May 2009.[38] Though it will take time and work to make infrastructure repairs, thousands of tribal members are now eligible for federal compensation for health problems caused by past uranium exposure. Recently, with renewed interest in uranium on the reservation, mining companies have filed mining claims and promised jobs, safe working conditions, and environmental prudence. We can hope past mistakes will never be repeated.

resources, and making expensive and lavish trips and purchases on government accounts are also all examples of this kind of political corruption.

Sometimes the abuse of power and institutional privilege can include the more serious illegal financial exchange called **bribery**. Bribery occurs when a government official accepts a direct payment in exchange for official government action, such as gaining votes, sponsoring legislation, and appropriating government funds to private contractors.[39] A recent case in the African nation of Ghana illustrates both influence peddling and bribery in action, as 32 Ghanaian judges were caught on hidden cameras accepting bribes in exchange for shorter prison sentences.

State representatives and government officials often abuse their positions of power to force or coerce individuals into providing them with some type of financial reward or material gain. This type of abuse is known as **extortion**. Withholding legislation, failing to renew a contract or issue a permit, and threatening to close down a business due to lack of compliance with financial demands are all examples of extortion. A recent high-profile case also illustrates extortion in action.

In April 2015, two former New Jersey state government officials who were close associates of Governor Chris Christie, were indicted by the U.S. Department of Justice for engaging in a conspiracy to arbitrarily close down traffic lanes leading from New Jersey to the George Washington Bridge and into Manhattan. The purpose of the traffic jam was to "exact political vengeance against a mayor" of a town where the traffic backups would be felt the most. The mayor's sin? He didn't support Governor Christie during his reelection campaign.[40]

Table 17.3 illustrates that government corruption occurs not just in other countries, but all over America, even at the lowest levels of state and local government.

State-corporate crime

There are times when the criminal conduct of governments aligns with the criminal conduct of other organizations, like businesses. The sub-field of state-corporate crime is the study of "how the actions of corporations and governments intersect to produce social harm."[41] A **state-corporate crime** is defined as a criminal act that results when one or more government institutions pursue a goal in direct cooperation with one or more corporations or businesses.

State-corporate crimes occur in two general forms. **State-initiated corporate crimes** occur when "corporations, employed by the government, engage in criminal or deviant conduct, at the direction or with the approval of the government."[42] An example of this type of state-corporate crime is the 1986 NASA space shuttle challenger disaster which resulted in the deaths of NASA astronauts, including New Hampshire school teacher Christa McAuliffe. Research has shown that this preventable tragedy resulted from the manufacture and use of a defective O-ring seal in the space shuttle; despite warnings being raised over this issue, NASA officials pushed forward with the launch of the

Table 17.3 Corruption in government by state 2001–2010

State	Public corruption convictions 2001–2010	Corruption rate: convictions per 100,000 citizens in 2010	State	Public corruption convictions 2001–2010	Corruption rate: convictions per 100,000 citizens in 2010
Alabama	226	2.3	Montana	59	6
Alaska	–	–	Nebraska	26	1.4
Arizona	175	2.7	Nevada	35	1.3
Arkansas	87	3	New Hampshire	16	1.2
California	679	1.8	New Jersey	429	4.9
Colorado	95	1.9	New Mexico	45	2.2
Connecticut	100	2.8	New York	589	3
Delaware	46	5.1	North Carolina	184	1.9
DC	337	5.6	North Dakota	55	8.2
Florida	674	3.6	Ohio	495	4.3
Georgia	226	2.3	Oklahoma	133	3.5
Hawaii	–	–	Oregon	37	1
Idaho	23	1.5	Pennsylvania	542	4.3
Illinois	482	3.8	Rhode Island	23	2.2
Indiana	140	2.2	South Carolina	53	1.1
Iowa	53	1.7	South Dakota	59	7.2
Kansas	35	1.2	Tennessee	258	4.1
Kentucky	281	6.5	Texas	697	2.8
Louisiana	384	8.5	Utah	38	1.4
Maine	34	2.6	Vermont	15	2.4
Maryland	220	3.8	Virginia	413	5.2
Massachusetts	208	3.2	Washington	84	1.2
Michigan	245	2.5	West Virginia	72	3.9
Minnesota	66	1.2	Wisconsin	117	2.1
Mississippi	178	6	Wyoming	16	2.8
Missouri	184	3.1			

Source: Public Corruption Convictions: State Totals, 2001–2010. Retrieved from http://www.governing.com/gov-data/politics/public-corruption-case-convictions-state-data.html.

Challenger.[43] The other form of state-corporate crime is called **state-facilitated corporate crime** and it occurs when "government regulatory institutions fail to restrain deviant or criminal business activities."[44] An example of this type of state-corporate crime is the fire at the Imperial Food Products processing plant in Hamlet, North Carolina in September 1991 that killed 25 plant workers and injured over 50 more. The fire caused such significant injuries because Imperial

Food Products locked several fire doors; federal inspectors from OSHA and the U.S. Department of Agriculture knew about this illegal practice, but did nothing to fix the issue prior to the fire, thus playing a key role through their omission to act, in the deaths of the workers.[45]

Crimes against humanity

One of the most challenging topics in criminological study is the large-scale, organized acts of violence and other criminal conduct committed by governments at the domestic and international level. These crimes flout the rule of law and threaten the very peace and stability of the land as well as the fundamental human rights to which we are all entitled. Often, however, these events occur under the guise of legality or within the fog of war and revolution.

Throughout history, **genocide**, the systematic destruction of a particular national, religious, ethnic, racial or political group, has been practiced by many societies around the world. It was a point of pride among ancient rulers to eliminate an entire enemy, including civilians and children in addition to soldiers.

The practice of genocide was not considered a crime until after World War II. Once the atrocities of the holocaust perpetrated by the Nazi regime in Europe (and to a lesser extent, the Japanese in Asia) came to light, there was a push to monitor and prevent genocide, as well as bring to justice its perpetrators. The **1948 United Nations Convention on the Prevention and Punishment of the Crime of Genocide**, officially made it a crime to "commit genocide, plan or conspire to commit genocide, incite or cause other people to commit genocide, or be complicit or involved in any act of genocide."[46] This agreement among UN members created a potentially powerful new political reality by declaring that "States would no longer have the right to be left alone" to pursue internal conflicts as they saw fit. In other words, State sovereignty would no longer shield a country from the consequences of committing genocide within its borders.

Genocide has devastating and destructive consequences. Acts of genocide include torturing members of a targeted group, eliminating them through mass killing, imposing harsh conditions intended to bring about physical deterioration and eventual death, forcing sterilization to prevent future births, and removing the group by forced transfer or migration. Examples of genocides include the 1915 Armenian genocide, which killed more than 1 million people, the Nazi Holocaust, the Cambodian holocaust in the 1970s, the Rwandan and Bosnian genocides in the early 1990s, and the genocide in the Darfur region of Africa which began in the early 2000s. Genocidal acts are not relegated only to far off or distant lands, however. Both the colonial and later the United States federal governments, engaged in the aggressive, systematic elimination of Native American tribal peoples, reducing the population of indigenous Americans from over 10 million in the 15th century to fewer than 300,000 by 1900.[47]

Criminologists and researchers seeking to understand this form of collective, state sponsored violence against a particular group of people have identified

Image 17.10 *Human skulls from victims of the Rwandan genocide, which killed over 1 million people, provide a glimpse into the extent of human pain and suffering that genocides produce. These often state-sanctioned or condoned mass killings produce far more death, destruction, and trauma than all the violent street crimes combined.*

Getty

different political climates and social environments that increase the likelihood of genocide occurring, such as when governments are authoritarian, when countries are plagued by civil war, and when political leaders are heavily engaged in vice and corruption. Under these conditions, government officials may use genocide as a mechanism of achieving social control, eliminate threats to their rule, spread fear among enemies and dissenters, acquire wealth, maintain status, or implement a particular belief or ideology.

Genocide cannot be carried out by one or even a dozen people, however. Many people, sometimes entire armies or ethnic groups, must be involved. People often engage in genocidal actions after a "genocidal mentality" has

BOX 17.4: CONNECTING THEORY TO PRACTICE

The role of dehumanization in mass killing

Ethnic conflict between Hutu crop growers and Tutsi herdsmen was a fact of life in the Rwandan villages in the tropical heart of the African continent. Although the Hutu vastly outnumbered the Tutsi, the Tutsi occupied the more prestigious, privileged, and advantaged positions in government and society. As the Hutu population became more alienated socially and politically, a revolution ensued, and by the late 1950s the Hutu gained control, exiling many Tutsi and taking away their land and property. Civil war broke out and lasted for decades. After a brief ceasefire in 1993, conflict broke out again when a plane carrying Rwandan's Hutu President was shot down on April 6, 1994—an act the Tutsi's were accused of plotting. Anti-Tutsi sentiment grew and spread among Hutu civilians. Getting even became a national agenda, and Hutu citizens began to believe it was their duty to avenge the death of their leader by wiping out the Tutsi. From April to June 1994, an estimated 800,000 Rwandans were slaughtered, most of them Tutsis.

How could such a large scale act of genocide happen in such a short time? How could neighbors and community members justify killing men, women, and children they knew?

Researchers note that participants in genocide are manipulated into accepting a dehumanized image of their victims by the widespread dissemination of hate propaganda.[48] In the years before the genocide in Rwanda, for example, political debates, demonstrations and rallies, speeches by government officials and broadcasts on radical radio stations filled the air with what official reports describe as "vicious, pornographic, inflammatory rhetoric designed to demonize and dehumanize the Tutsi." The Tutsi became the enemy, a threat to the very existence of Hutus and not to be spared, and the motivation of every good Hutu was to eradicate them all. Thus, Tutsi men, women, and children alike became objects, not humans, making it easier to commit unthinkable acts of torture, rape, and murder.

Many scholars would agree that when it comes to genocide, perpetrators are socially constructed, made to hate, and made to kill.

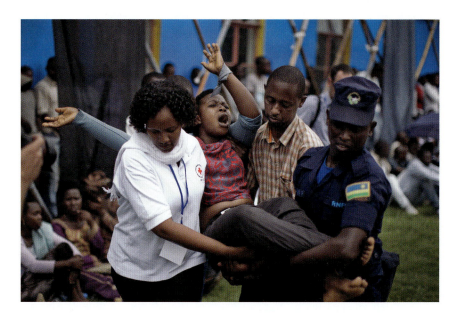

Image 17.11 *A wailing and distraught Rwandan woman, one of dozens overcome by grief at recalling the horror of the genocide, is carried away to receive help during a public ceremony to mark the 20th anniversary of the Rwandan genocide, held at Amahoro stadium in Kigali, Rwanda, Monday, April 7, 2014. Sorrowful wails and uncontrollable sobs resounded as thousands of Rwandans packed the country's main sports stadium to mark the 20th anniversary of the beginning of a devastating 100-day genocide.*

Ben Curtis/AP/Press Association Images

been created. This mindset dehumanizes potential victims. The Nazi's labeled Jews, homosexuals, and others "inferior" and concocted stories about how they were disrupting society and harming innocent people. Rwanda's Hutus called their Tutsi targets "cockroaches." Radio broadcasts imploring Hutus to "kill cockroaches" fostered mass killings (see Box 17.4). In modern society, media have made the process of disseminating the propaganda of dehumanization even easier. The establishment of institutions and organizations that justify and carry out the atrocities is a key component of the spread of genocide. From academia to the government to the military, the leadership mobilizes organizations in its power to destroy those defined as "others."

Predictably, governments are reluctant to label genocides as such because under United Nations rules, a genocide requires intervention. It was partly a fear of incurring such an obligation, as well as a desire to carefully guard its sovereign decision-making powers, that caused the United States to delay ratifying the U.N. convention against genocide for decades. Governments thus resort to labeling genocides as civil wars or ethnic conflicts—none of which carry any obligation to intervene.

In this section, we have seen how the collective actions of governments and their representative organizations can lead to violent crimes against citizens. These actions are the result of conscious decisions by powerful and influential political figures, using their legitimate authority to coerce compliance in destructive acts. We turn now to a different form of coercion based on *illegitimate* authority derived from a reputation for brutality, crime, and violence.

Organized crime

What is organized crime?

In the history of crime, everything from sheep to people, wool, wine, gold, drugs, military weapons, books, and even ideas have been prohibited at some time. The paradox of prohibition, however, is that the commodity made illegal will continue to be in great demand by certain segments of the public. This demand will inevitably create the desire on the part of some group to distribute the prohibited goods. The control, organization, and distribution of illegal goods and services on a national and transnational (i.e., international) scale is what we refer to as **organized crime**.[49] Our best estimates indicate that organized crime groups generate revenues totaling $870 billion or more per year.[50]

The organization of organized crime

At the heart of our study of organized criminal behavior is an understanding of its connection to the larger social structure. Organized crime relies on the cooperation of a network of individuals who have a mutually beneficial relationship. Corrupt politicians, dishonest judges, deceitful bankers, crooked law enforcement officers, and a breakdown of the legal system protect, sustain, and facilitate organized criminal activities.[51]

Knowing who belongs to criminal networks and how they differ from one another helps criminologists better understand organized crime and guides law enforcement strategies and policies to combat it. The public also needs to grasp the reality of organized crime and the diverse activities it encompasses, beyond the glamorized images generated by popular films.

Researchers have developed various typologies of organized criminal networks based on their structural organization. Five different types of networks have been identified[52] (see Table 17.4).

Table 17.4 Organized crime networks

Type of network	Operational structure
Standard hierarchy	• Clearly defined with a single leader • A specific name is often linked to a social or ethnic identity • Strong system of internal discipline • Operates within and controls a clearly defined territory • Violence is embedded in most activities
Regional hierarchy	• Operates under a single central leader, but its regional organizations have a degree of autonomy • Often share an ethnic and social identity • Operate under the control of the central group to engage in multiple activities and help spread their influence • Internal discipline is high and violence is a part of most dealings
Clustered hierarchy	• Consists of a set of criminal groups with an established system of coordinating and controlling illicit activities • A core group acts as the central or oversight body, with clusters branching off into relatively autonomous groups, each with an identity of its own • Clusters often control divided markets • The potential for competition between groups and disruption of activity is high, making clustered hierarchies somewhat rare
Core group	• A small, tight, structured group of individuals conduct a criminal enterprise • The distribution of power is flat, with activities divided evenly among core group members • Internal discipline is maintained by virtue of the small number of members and limited number of criminal activities • Core groups usually have very little social or ethnic identity
Criminal network	• Loosely connected networks of individuals • Engage in ongoing criminal transactions • Are often built around individuals with particular characteristics, skills, or connections • Criminal networks are characterized by shifting alliances, with members providing their services to different components and "middlemen" serving as the connecting link between them and the central figures through which most connections operate

Source: Results of a Pilot Survey of Forty Selected Organized Criminal Groups in Sixteen Countries. Sept. 2002. Global Program Against Transnational Organized Crime, United Nations Office on Drugs and Crime.

In addition to differing in structure, criminal groups may change their characteristics and operations over time and according to supply and demand. This variability in turn influences the nature and characteristics of organized crime.

Characteristics of organized crime

Organized crime and organized criminal groups exist in every country in the world. While it is true that the Italian mafia (*La Cosa Nostra)* was once a very powerful organized criminal group in the United States, today there are dozens of organized crime groups operating in the country. In fact, the FBI now organizes its investigations of organized crime by world region and nationality/ethnicity,[53] noting in bold letters on its organized crime website: "it's not just the mafia anymore." Currently operating in the U.S. are powerful, dangerous and very wealthy organized crime groups from the Baltics (Russian Mafia), Asia (Japanese Yakuza, Chinese Triads), Central and South America (Mexico's Sinaloa Cartel) and more all operating at the same time (see Table 17.5). Increasingly, organized criminal groups including those mentioned above are going transnational, meaning they are extending, expanding, and diversifying their operations to multiple countries around the globe.

Organized crime requires the secret, often rapid, movement of goods, money, people, drugs, weapons, and information. Transnational organized criminal groups are becoming more involved every day in the commission of cybercrimes, particularly identity theft (see more in chapter 19). A common characteristic of organized crime groups is strict adherence to codes of conduct. These codes, for example the Italian Mafia's code of silence called **Omerta**, hardly differ from other subcultural codes of conduct. In fact, the Omerta code is almost exactly similar to the Blue Wall of Silence that governs the actions of police officers (see chapter 5). In short, organized crime groups utilize formal and informal codes that dictate rules for members and also help settle disputes, divide territories and establish control of markets.[54] How exactly one becomes a member of organized crime differs with the group. Some people are born into organized crime and enter the "family business" as part of their socialization. Others are recruited to participate. And, some people are forced or coerced into participation with, or supporting, organized crime often due to their role

Table 17.5 The world's most profitable organized crime groups[55]

Organized crime group	Nationality/ethnicity	Annual revenue ($ billion)
Solntsevskaya Bratva	Russia / Russian	8.5
Yamaguchi Gumi (Yakuza)	Japan /Japanese	6.6
Camorra	Naples, Italy / Italian	4.9
'Ndrangheta	Calabria Region of Italy /Italian	4.5
Sinaloa Cartel	Mexico /Mexican	3

Image 17.12 *In this courtroom sketch, James "Whitey" Bulger, left, and his girlfriend, Catherine Greig, are shown during their arraignment in a federal courtroom in downtown Los Angeles, Thursday, June 23, 2011.*

Bill Robles/AP/Press Association Images

in some type of legitimate business or government that organized crime hopes to gain control or influence over. Such was the case in the 1950s when many American labor unions were infiltrated by major organized crime networks.[56] Regardless of how participants enter the illegal service industry, the price of refusal or betrayal is violence and murder.

In a 2002 study, the *United Nations Office on Drugs and Crime* surveyed forty organized crime groups in sixteen different countries. The following were identified as key characteristics of organized crime:

- Organized crime is the sustained and systematic coordination of illegal activities.
- Criminal activities revolve around the organization and provision of illegal goods and services for economic gain, such as drugs, gambling, pornography, prostitution, loan sharking (lending money to pay debts at illegal interest rates), human trafficking, and weapons trafficking.
- Most organized crime groups engage in one particular type of criminal activity.
- The majority of organized crime groups have a classical hierarchical structure with twenty to fifty members and participants.
- Violence, intimidation, corruption, and fraud are key elements in sustaining organized crime activities.
- The majority of crime groups operate in multiple countries.
- Organized crime activities penetrate the legitimate economy in order to launder illegal profits through legal businesses.

From this overview, we see that what makes organized crime a unique category of criminal behavior is the ability of ethnically diverse groups of individuals to both cooperate and compete for the control and distribution of goods and services in various geographic locations. It sounds like the operation of global corporations in the business industry. The only difference, however, is that the goods and services in demand are illegal, and the illegitimate operation often involves the use of violence and coercion to negotiate transactions.

Criminologists recognize the difficulty in monitoring and controlling organized crime because of the secretive and protective manner by which it is conducted, and the interconnection between the legitimate world of business, government, and politics and the illegitimate world of vice and corruption.

BOX 17.5: CONSIDER THIS . . .

The making of organized crime

Because organized crime is embedded within the social structure, institutional factors such as political unrest, civil struggle, and the decline of authoritarian government can compromise the rule of law, making a society particularly vulnerable and paving the way for widespread corruption. A case study in Afghanistan illustrates the making of organized crime.

The war in Afghanistan began in 2001 when, in response to the September 11th terrorist attacks, the United States and allies such as Great Britain launched a military offensive to disband and overthrow the Taliban and al-Qaeda terrorist groups. This offensive marked the beginning of an ongoing counterinsurgency by Taliban forces to survive and rebuild. In the struggle between allied forces and the Taliban, several changes within the social, political, and economic structure took place. A decline in authoritarian rule, the transition to democracy, and a shift toward a market based economy led to a power vacuum that shook the foundation of key government institutions. Moreover, in the aftermath of the conflict, the capacity of police to enforce the rule of law became severely compromised, as resources were hampered by civil struggle and attacks by Taliban forces.

As society adjusts to rapid change, organized criminal groups—including drug lords, terrorists, and corrupt government officials—take advantage of weak legal and political institutions, and their organized criminal activity flourishes. Researchers have identified six trends that demonstrate the escalation of organized crime.[57]

- A decline in the number of smaller criminal operators (individuals, loose networks, or small groups) and the appearance of a limited number of larger and more powerful ones.
- The identification by law enforcement officials of clear organized criminal groups as opposed to just the naming of individual "smugglers" or "traffickers."
- Evidence of close and mutually beneficial associations among government, business, and criminal enterprises, including elements of the state or business being held in criminal hands.
- The exclusion from criminal markets of new operators or groups and the forced exit of others.
- The emergence of responses to increasingly vigorous law enforcement, such as higher levels of secrecy in the operation of criminal markets.
- The development of well-organized mechanisms of criminal protection that is well understood and coordinated by key players in the criminal markets.

The weakened state institutions in post-conflict Afghanistan has made it fertile ground for the rapid growth of organized criminal networks, with their strong connections to corruption in law enforcement and government.[58] How does this connection influence the reliability of data on the nature and extent of the organized crime problem in Afghanistan? *What do you think?*

The RICO Act and organized crime

Until the 1970s, federal and state governments did very little in terms of developing strategies to combat organized crime. In 1970, however, Congress passed the *Organized Crime Control Act* which created the Racketeer Influenced and Corrupt Organization Act (RICO). The intention of the RICO Act was to limit and control organized criminal activities by creating new categories of offenses in racketeering, the organized operation of an illegal business by a structured group for the purpose of making a profit. Under RICO, being engaged in two or more activities prohibited by 24 federal statutes and 8 state statutes—including such crimes as murder, kidnapping, arson, robbery, extortion, bribery, prostitution, and fraud—constitutes racketeering. The goal of RICO was to disband the core of organized criminal enterprise by making it illegal to:

- Use income derived from racketeering activity or the illegal collection of debt.
- Acquire interest in a business or enterprise through a pattern of racketeering activity.
- Conduct the affairs of an enterprise through a pattern of racketeering activity.
- Conspire to commit any of the offenses listed above.

An individual convicted of racketeering could be fined up to $25,000 and serve 20 years in prison. The accused could also forfeit to the federal government any and all property related to the racketeering violations. RICO paved the way for the investigation of organized crime by focusing attention on aggregate acts of criminal enterprise rather than individual or isolated incidents of crime.[59] However, RICO laws have also been a great source of controversy.

The application of RICO laws continues to stir up legal debates decades after their passage. Ambiguity lies in the application of the terms "enterprise" and "pattern of racketeering". The original intention behind RICO was to target organized crime. However, a broad interpretation of the law would argue that it can be applied to all forms of white-collar crime, and can also define an enterprise by reference to patterns of racketeering. This ambiguity has been the source of controversy in cases where legitimate businesses have been subject to forfeiture because of patterns of illegal activities by the owner in the course of its operation.[60]

WHY CARE ABOUT THE CRIMES OF THE POWERFUL?

At the beginning of this chapter, we noted that the crimes of the powerful often go (1) unnoticed, and (2) under-punished. Those two characteristics ensure that we, the public, pay less attention to the crimes of the powerful than to "street crimes" and that the powerful will continue to engage in criminal conduct since it is fairly easy to get away with.

In closing our discussion of the crimes of the powerful it is worth noting several other key reasons why we should care about the crimes of the powerful. For example, we must look at the (3) extent, and (4) types of harm the crimes of the powerful cause.

Whenever a powerful individual or organization engages in criminal behavior, that action violates the immense trust placed in them. That violation of trust, particularly when committed by government officials, is itself a serious harm. Crimes of the powerful also produce immense financial losses in society, cause deaths and result in many serious environmental harms. Importantly, the people most vulnerable to victimization and most likely to be harmed by the crimes of the powerful are the powerless—the ordinary, every-day folks like you and I.

Let's consider the extent of the harm caused by the crimes of the powerful as well. Earlier, we mentioned that the crimes of the powerful cause more harm to society than all the drug, street and property crimes—which we are taught to fear—combined.

Just one event, the 2008 economic recession, which resulted from the criminal activities of big corporations and banks and inadequate government oversight, cost Americans over $12.8 trillion.[61] The last major national economic crisis, produced by the 1980s savings and loan fraud scandal, cost Americans between $300–500 billion. In both cases, the people most harmed were those who could least afford to be harmed; middle- and lower-class Americans can't afford to lose their homes, jobs, or retirement savings, but they did. Yet again, the big banks and financial corporations that caused these forms of trouble were not disbanded. No one was sent to prison for 25 to life. Instead, innocent people were left on the hook to pay for the cost of their own victimization.

Researchers estimate that the annual financial cost of all street crimes combined to be $3.8 billion.[62] Now compare that sum to the estimated financial costs[63] of just some of the various crimes of the powerful:

- Health care fraud = $100 to $400 billion per year.
- Auto repair fraud = $40 billion per year.
- Securities fraud = $15 billion per year.

Finally, let us compare the toll exacted on human life by the crimes of the powerful. In the Armenian genocide, 1915–1923, 1.5 million people were killed.[64] The Nazi holocaust killed over 11 million innocent people.[65] Close to 2 million died in the Rwandan genocide between Hutu and Tutsi.[66] That is, in just three genocides perpetrated by powerful state actors, nearly 15 million people's lives were snuffed out. Each year, more than 50,000 Americans die from preventable workplace hazards and illnesses linked to their occupations.[67]

Now, there are dozens of violent crime TV shows and movies made and aired each year. Many focus on homicides, especially serial murders. Yet, our yearly statistics show that despite living in a country whose population is north of 320 million, only around 12–14,000 people are murdered in any given year in the United States; serial homicides account for less than 1 percent of that already small total. Moreover, rates for all violent crimes including homicide have been decreasing since the 1990s.

There is literally no comparison between the harms the result from the crimes of the powerful with those that accrue from street crimes. The crimes of the powerful cause more economic, physical, psychological, and emotional harm per year, and throughout history, than all of those violent and property crimes we are so concerned with combined. For this reason, and the others noted above, we must care about, study, and discuss the crimes of the powerful.

SUMMARY

In this chapter we introduced the important topic of the crimes of the powerful, beginning our discussion by situating the study of the crimes of the powerful within the perspective known as critical criminology. That perspective draws attention to the fact that we can define crime in two ways, as the violation of criminal law (the traditional way), or more broadly as any act, even those legal ones, that generate significant harms.

Crimes of the powerful have several distinct features. First, they are often committed by the least likely offenders—people or organizations with money, status, power, and prestige. Additionally, crimes of the powerful are important to study because they often go unnoticed and under-punished. This means that many crimes committed by the powerful do not get reported and even if they do, the media tends not to focus on them as intensely as street crimes. Additionally, even when crimes of the powerful come to the attention of law enforcement, prosecutors, and the courts, the punishments handed out tend to be, on average, far less severe than would be given to an individual committing a violent or property crime.

We discussed three broad types of crimes committed by the powerful: white-collar crime, state crime, and organized crime. Each of those broad forms of crime are united by the fact that they rely on power, money, status, and influence to occur. White-collar crime, for example, occurs in the context of one's occupation and may involve embezzlement, fraud, or some other illegal, harmful act. State crime is crime committed by governments in pursuit of their interests and sometimes involves state actors conspiring within corporate actors to create state-corporate crimes. Organized crime is committed by sophisticated groups, many of whom operate across borders and online. Importantly, in order for organized crime to occur and persist, there is almost always collusion between members of the organized criminal group, corporate, and government actors. In other words, organized crime typically could not occur without the corruption of legitimate organizations and their employees or staff.

Lastly, a key takeaway point from this chapter is this: we must care about the crimes of the powerful, because this category of crime generates more physical death and injury, economic, psychological, and emotional harm than all the so-called "street" crimes combined. Despite the very serious harms that result from the crimes of the powerful, our public and political attention and fascination remains focused on low-level street and drug crimes. Only by continuing to educate people about the true costs of the crimes of the powerful can that pattern change.

NOTES

1   O'Grady, S. 2015. The Worst Corruption Scandals of 2015. *Foreign Policy,* Dec. 29.
2   FIFA Corruption Timeline: The Events That Led up to the Resignation of President Sepp Blatter. 2015. *The Independent,* June 3.
3   Ibid.
4   Kuhn, T.S. 1962. *The Structure of Scientific Revolutions.* Chicago, IL: University of Chicago Press.
5   Barak, G. 2015. Introduction: On the Invisibility and Neutralization of the Crimes of the Powerful and their Victims. In *Routledge International Handbook of the Crimes of the Powerful.*
6   Ibid.
7   Bernanke, B.S. 2010. Causes of Recent Financial and Economic Crisis. Testimony before the Financial Crisis Inquiry Commission, Washington, D.C.
8   Dole, C.E. 1980. Pinto Verdict Lets Jury off the Hook. *The Christian Science Monitor,* March 14.
9   Grogin, J.P. 1986. Corporations Can Kill Too: After Film Recovery, Are Individuals Accountable for Corporate Crimes? *Loyola of Los Angeles Law Review* 19(1411).
10 Dold, R.B. 1985. The Charge: Murder By Executive Decision. *The Chicago Tribune,* April 16.
11 Maakestad, W. 1987. Redefining Corporate Crime. *Multinational Monitor* (8)5.
12 Burnett, J. 2014. Awash In Cash, Drug Cartels Rely On Big Banks To Launder Profits. NPR. Retrieved from http://www.npr.org/sections/parallels/2014/03/20/291934724/awash-in-cash-drug-cartels-rely-on-big-banks-to-launder-profits.
13 Roberts, J.J. 2015. Apple Conspired with Book Publishers, Appeals Court Confirms. *Fortune Magazine,* June 30.
14 Apple Investor Relations. 2016. Retrieved from http://investor.apple.com.
15 Sutherland, Edwin Hardin. 1949. *White Collar Crime.* New York: Dryden Press.
16 Shover, Neal and Hochstetler, Andy. 2006. *Choosing White Collar Crime.* New York: Cambridge University Press.
17 Ibid.
18 Miethe, Terance D., McCorkle, Richard C. and Listwan, Shelley J. 2006. *Crime Profiles: The Anatomy of Dangerous Persons, Places, and Situations,* 3rd ed. New York: Roxbury Publishing Company.
19 Friedrichs, David O. 2002. Occupational Crime, Occupational Deviance, and Workplace Crime: Sorting Out the Difference. *Criminal Justice* 2: 243–256.
20 *Internet Security.* 2009. Bank of New York Mellon Corporation. Retrieved from https://www.bnymellon.com/it/it/widgets/security.jsp.
21 Clinard, Marshall B. and Yeager, Peter Cleary. 2005. *Corporate Crime.* Somerset, NJ: Transaction Publishers.
22 Crackdown on Corporate Crime. 2003. *Citizen Works,* March 16. Retrieved from http://www.citizenworks.org/12reforms-full.pdf.
23 OSH Act, 1970. 2004. Occupational Safety and Health Administration, U.S. Department of Labor, Washington, D.C. Retrieved from Retrieved from http://www.osha.gov/pls/oshaweb/owadisp.show_document?p_table=OSHACT&p_id=2743.

24   *Workplace Injuries And Illnesses—2014.* Bureau of Labor Statistics, U.S. Department of Labor, Washington, D.C.

25   Ibid.

26   OSHA. 2015. Commonly cited statistics. U.S. Department of Labor. Retrieved from https://www.osha.gov/oshstats/commonstats.html.

27   FDA Issues Warning for Plavix, Prilosec Users. 2009. *wibw.com,* Nov. 18. Retrieved from http://www.wibw.com/home/nationalnews/headlines/70429472.html.

28   Public Health and Safety Organization. 2016. Guide to Understanding Dietary Supplement Regulations. Retrieved from http://www.nsf.org/consumer-resources/health-and-safety-tips/dietary-sports-supplements-tips/understanding-regulations/.

29   Gobert, James and Punch, Maurice. 2003. *Rethinking Corporate Crime.* New York: Cambridge University Press.

30   Chambliss, William J. 2000. *Power, Politics and Crime.* Boulder, CO: Westview Press.

31   Chambliss, W.J. and Moloney, C.J. 2014. *State Crime: Critical Concepts in Criminology.* London: Routledge.

32   Evertsson, N. 2013. Political Corruption as a form of State Crime. In W.J. Chambliss and C.J. Moloney (eds.), *State Crime.* London: Routledge.

33   Green, Penny and Ward, Tony. 2004. *State Crime: Governments, Violence and Corruption.* London: Pluto Press.

34   O'Grady, S. 2015. The Worst Corruption Scandals of 2015. *Foreign Policy,* Dec. 29.

35   Ibid.

36   Cole, C. 2010. Closing Coal Plant a Numbers Game. *Arizona Daily Sun,* March 8.

37   Pasternak, J. 2006. Navajos' Desert Cleanup no More Than Mirage. *Los Angeles Times,* Nov. 21.

38   President Obama Repeals 'Bennett Freeze' Law. 2009. *Nhonews.com.* Retrieved from http://nhonews.com/main.asp?SectionID=1&subsectionID=1&articleID=11493.

39   Wrage, Alexandra Addison. Bribery and Extortion: Undermining Business, Governments, and Security. Praeger Security International.

40   Zernike, K. Santora, M. 2015. 2 Indicted in George Washington Bridge Case; Ally of Christie Pleads Guilty. *The New York Times,* May 1.

41   Kramer, R.C., Michalowski, R.J., Kauzlarich, D. 2002. The Origins and Development of the Concept and Theory of State-corporate Crime. *Crime & Delinquency* 48(2): 263–82.

42   Ibid., p. 419

43   Kramer, R.C. 1992. The Space Shuttle Challenger Explosion: A Case Study of State-corporate Crime. In K. Schlegel & D. Weisburd (eds.), *White Collar Crime Reconsidered.* Boston: Northeastern University Press, pp. 212–241.

44   Kramer, R.C., Michalowski, R.J. and Kauzlarich, D. 2002. The Origins and Development of the Concept and Theory of State-corporate Crime. *Crime & Delinquency* 48(2): 263–82.

45   Aulette, J.R. and Michalowski, R. 1993. Fire in Hamlet: A Case Study of a State Corporate Crime. In K.D. Tunnell (ed.), *Political Crime in Contemporary America: A Critical Approach.* New York: Garland, p. 171–206.

46   Convention on the Punishment and Prevention of the Crime of Genocide, United Nations General Assembly, 1948. Articles I–IV, p. 281.

47   United to End Genocide. 2015. Atrocities Against Native Americans. Retrieved from http://endgenocide.org/learn/past-genocides/native-americans/.

48   *Rwanda: The Preventable Genocide.* 2000. Council on Foreign Relations. Retrieved from www.cfr.org/rwanda/rwanda-preventable-genocide/p15629.

49   Siegel, Dina, von de Bunt, Henk and Zaitch, Damian (eds.) *Global Organized Crime: Trends and Developments.* Boston: Kluwer Academic.

50 Global Research Center, 20 July 2012. Turnover of Global Organized Crime: $870 Billion . . . a Year. Retrieved from http://www.globalresearch.ca/turnover-of-global-organized-crime-870-billion-a-year/31995.

51 Glenny, Misha. 2008. *McMafia: A Journey Through the Global Criminal Underworld.* Knopf Publishers.

52 *Results of a Pilot Survey of Forty Selected Organized Criminal Groups in Sixteen Countries.* 2002. Global Program Against Transnational Organized Crime, United Nations Office on Drugs and Crime.

53 Federal Bureau of Investigation. 2016. Organized Crime. Retrieved from https://www.fbi.gov/about-us/investigate/organizedcrime.

54 Lyman, Michael D. and Potter, Gary W. 2004. *Organized Crime.* Upper Saddle River, NJ: Pearson Prentice Hall.

55 Matthews, C. 2014. Fortune 5: The Biggest Organized Crime Groups in the World. *Fortune Magazine*, Sept. 14.

56 Witwer, David. 2008. *Corruption and Reform in the Teamsters Union.* Champaign: University of Illinois Press.

57 Shaw, M. 2005. Drug Trafficking and the Development of Organized Crime in Post-Taliban Afghanistan. Retrieved from http://siteresources.worldbank.org/SOUTHASIA EXT/Resources/Publications/448813–1164651372704/UNDC_Ch7.pdf.

58 Rubin, B. 2004. *Road to Ruin: Afghanistan's Booming Opium Industry.* Center for American Progress and Center on International Cooperation, New York University.

59 McFeeley, Richard. 2001. Enterprise Theory of Investigation. *FBI Law Enforcement Bulletin* 70(5): 19–26.

60 Lambert, Kent A. 2009. RICO Class Action Controversy Continues. *Litigation News,* Oct. 8 Retrieved from http://www.abanet.org/litigation/litigationnews/top_stories/class-action-rico-williams.html.

61 Puzzanghera, J. 2012. Financial Crisis, Recession Cost U.S. $12.8 Trillion, Report Says. *The Los Angeles Times,* Sept. 12.

62 Mohkiber, R. 2000. Top 100 Corporate Criminals of the Decade. *Corporate Crime Reporter.* Retrieved from http://www.corporatecrimereporter.com/top100.html.

63 Ibid.

64 Fidanakis, I. 2014. 15 Worst Genocides in History. Retrieved from http://www.rantpolitical.com/2014/12/06/15-worst-genocides-in-history/.

65 Ibid.

66 Ibid.

67 Ibid., see 55.

CHAPTER OUTLINE

Green crimes and harms

| In this chapter we will explore the following questions | KEY TERMS |

- What are green crimes and harms?
- What is the connection between the environmental movement and green criminology?
- How does the study of green crimes and harms overlap with the study of the crimes of the powerful?

KEY TERMS

green criminology
green crime
green harm
environmentalism
air pollution
Great Smog of 1952
Air Quality Index (AQI)
photosynthesis
ocean-carbon uptake
water pollution
e-waste
Great Pacific Garbage Patch
hazardous waste
fracking
e-waste
environmental justice movement
environmental racism
poaching
global illegal wildlife trade
wildlife trafficking
greenwashing
prosecution gap

BHOPAL

Methyl isocyanate (MIC). Chances are you have never heard of it. That's probably a good thing, because methyl isocyanate is a very lethal gas. It is one of the dangerous byproducts of manufacturing pesticides—lethal chemical cocktails whose sole purpose is to kill.

Union Carbide, an American chemical corporation, began operating a chemical production plant in Bhopal, India, in the 1960s. Bhopal was a small city by Indian standards and the huge plant employed over 1,000 residents in stable, decent-paying, blue-collar jobs.

On the night of December 2, 1984, a methyl isocyanate storage tank at the plant began leaking after water entered the tank and began a chemical reaction that forced open a pressure release valve. The leaking MIC gas—30 to 45 tons in all—could not be contained. A gas cloud spread quickly from the plant into surrounding areas, where, over several decades, thousands of poor Indian citizens had built up shanty towns.

The gas cloud hung low to the ground and, as it slowly drifted through streets, through doorways, and open windows, it killed indiscriminately: men, women, children, animals, young and old alike, some 3,800 in the first few hours.[1] The lucky ones—those not killed immediately—suffered chemical burns to their eyes, noses, throats, and skin. Over the next days and weeks thousands more died from their injuries—nearly 15,000 killed in all.[2] Many others were left permanently scarred, disabled, and blinded from their exposure to the gas.

The world watched in horror as pictures and reports on the Bhopal tragedy emerged. The dead, including thousands of cattle and other important livestock, were hastily buried in mass graves or burned for fear that their corpses would spread other lethal diseases. In all, nearly 600,000 people are believed to have been exposed to the MIC gas cloud released from the Bhopal plant. Decades later, repercussions in the form of physical birth defects, mental disabilities, higher rates of illness, disease, and death persist.

Union Carbide was immediately blamed for the tragedy, accused by many of running a shoddy operation without concern for health and safety issues that were well known and reported prior to the gas leak. The company shifted responsibility for the tragedy to its Indian subsidiary, which it claimed had complete and sole responsibility for the design, maintenance, and operation of the Bhopal plant. Court actions dragged out for years. Union Carbide eventually claimed that the only way water could have entered the mix tank was through a direct act of industrial sabotage, citing the results of its own and the Indian government's investigation.[3] However, others dispute that claim, arguing that the water could easily have entered the tank through faulty seals or other means given the poor condition of the plant at the time of the leak.

Eventually, Union Carbide, which was purchased by the Dow Chemical Corporation in 2001, settled various lawsuits related to the gas leak in 1989. In all, Union Carbide paid $470 million to the victims of the tragedy, amounting

Image 18.1 *A worker cleans the dust off a panel of photos of victims of the 1984 Bhopal gas disaster at the forensic department of Gandhi Medical College in Bhopal, India. Thousands of men, women, and children were killed in this single, preventable, man-made environmental disaster.*

Prakash Hatvalne/AP/Press Association Images

to just over $500 per person.[4] Union also agreed to clean up the many acres of land and the plant area itself; however, that clean-up has yet to occur in any meaningful sense. For its part, the Indian government charged various Union Carbide officials, including then-CEO Warren Anderson, with various crimes, including homicide and assault. In 1992, the Indian government issued an arrest warrant for Anderson, though that symbolic gesture was never expected to result in any actual arrest.

Today, the Bhopal tragedy remains the "world's worst, man-made, preventable, industrial disaster."[5] Bhopal is the type of event that qualifies as both a green crime and green harm, the topic of this chapter.

INTRODUCING GREEN CRIMINOLOGY

It is difficult today to turn on the TV, pick up a magazine or go online and not find some story related to the health of the natural environment, its ecosystems or non-human species. It feels as if those topics are more widely and enthusiastically dissected and discussed now than ever before, and they probably should be given what we know about the negative repercussions of global climate change and declining biodiversity on our planet.

As the natural environment and environmental problems have garnered more attention, so to have environmental, or "green," crimes and harms. Several decades ago, criminologists led by Michael J. Lynch began carving out an intellectual space within the field of criminology to study both crimes and harms that affect the environment, humans, and other species.[6] The result has been the creation of **green criminology**, an umbrella category under which scholars with different backgrounds, interests, and perspectives unite to study "harms against humanity . . . the environment . . . and non-human animals committed by both powerful institutions and ordinary people."[7] Most green criminological research begins where crime, harm, law, justice, victimization, and the environment meet.[8] A key assumption unifying most research within the field of green criminology is that most ecological problems produce social problems (i.e., desertification leading to food insecurity) and many social problems produce ecological ones (i.e., poverty leading to wildlife trafficking or illegal poaching). Thus, green criminology, as a discipline, is actively engaged in debunking the myth that ecological and social problems can be understood independent of one another.[9,10,11]

As you have likely noticed, the definition of green criminology we offered here overlaps with our earlier discussion about the crimes of the powerful. Indeed, the study of the crimes of the powerful would be incomplete without examining their role in producing significant environmental harms and crimes. Likewise, there is no way to study environmental harm and crime without examining the actions of organizations, like corporations, and governments.

Image 18.2 *Rachel Carson's book* Silent Spring *played a key role in advancing the American Environmental movement.*

Bob Schutz/AP/Press Association Images

Additionally, studying the crimes of the powerful and environmental crimes and harms requires that we adopt a critical perspective and broad definition of crime to include "harms" that, while not illegal, cause significant economic, social, cultural, and environmental damage.

Lastly, it is worth noting that the increasing attention paid to green crimes and harm, both by criminologists as well as the media, politicians and the public, is linked to the rise of the environmental movement in the 1960s. That movement owed its existence to early efforts to preserve the majestic American whooping crane in the 1930s, which was headed toward extinction due to habitat destruction and pollution.

By the time the 1960s rolled around, people in America were primed for social change on a number of fronts. Social movements grew up around civil rights, women's rights, prisoner's rights, and environmental rights and protection. With regard to the environment, people began to see and understand that the quality of their and their children's lives could not be divorced from the quality of the environment in which they lived. Rachel Carson's influential book *Silent Spring*, which described in detail the awful effects pesticides were having on song bird populations, helped draw more attention to environmentalism—the belief in protecting and improving the environment for its own benefit and for the benefit of human life.

Throughout the 1960s and 1970s, Congress responded by passing many influential laws and regulations (see Table 18.1). These policy changes,

Image 18.3 *In this photo, steam seeps up through the ground in Centralia, PA. The steam is caused by a fire that began in 1962 at the town dump and ignited an exposed coal vein in the local coal mine, eventually forcing an exodus of the town's entire 1,000+ population.*

Carolyn Kaster/AP/Press Association Images

in conjunction with high profile environmental disasters like the Centralia, PA, coal mine fire, Santa Barbara oil spill, Cuyahoga River fire, led to the formation of the Environmental Protection Agency (EPA) in 1970. Thanks to the environmental movement we now have an entire field devoted to the ongoing study of green crimes and harms; we also live in a much safer, healthier place than we once did.

Table 18.1 Environmental legislation, 1960s and 1970s

Policy or regulation name	Year
Clean Water Act	1962
Solid Waste Disposal Act	1965
Clean Air Act	1967
National Environmental Policy Act	1969
Environmental Protection Agency	1970
Toxic Substance Control Act	1972

WHAT ARE GREEN CRIMES AND HARMS?

You might be wondering why we have named the study of crimes and harms that effect the natural environment green criminology and not simply environmental crime. The answer is that the name "environmental crime" had already been used by the 1990s to identify a field of criminological research that looks at the spatial nature of criminal events. Thus, in criminology, most people know environmental crime refers to where, when, and under what conditions crime events happen (i.e., day/night, specific location etc.) *not* to

Table 18.2 Examples of green crimes and harms

Illegal dumping	Air pollution
Poaching	Illegal logging
Hazardous waste disposal	Electronic (E) waste disposal
Resource extraction: oil, methane, fracking	Overfishing
Deforestation	Ecoterrorism
Animal abuse	Ecological disasters
Global warming	Wildlife trafficking and sale
Water pollution	Mining (strip, open pit, etc.)

crimes *against* the environment. Thus, to solve this problem, we came up with the name green criminology! This means that we will refer to crimes against nature, ecosystems, and other species as "green" crimes and harms, not environmental ones.

What are green crimes and harms? Pretty much anything so long as there is a significant connection to the natural world, its ecosystems, other species, and people! **Green crimes** include acts that violate environmental laws or regulations. So, for example, poaching, illegal dumping, violating air pollution regulations, and so on. **Green harms** include anything that is not criminalized, but which causes significant measurable damage or injury to the environment, ecosystems, non-human species, and people. Things like overfishing, logging, strip mining, and more might qualify as green harms. Table 18.2 presents just a small sampling of issues and topics that are considered green crimes or harms suitable for study. As you can see, there are a lot of green crimes that occur around the world.

VARIETIES OF GREEN CRIMES AND HARMS

Air pollution and water pollution

You are probably most familiar with the green crimes and harms that pollute and befoul our air and water. In order to be healthy, we need clean air and clean water. Yet these forms of ecological destruction have completely altered the planet we inhabit and continue to negatively impact people in the U.S. and around the world. Imagine what it must have been like to breathe truly fresh air prior, or drink from wells or cold running streams without fear of being poisoned by heavy metals or contracting a water-borne, human initiated illness like cholera.

Air pollution

The industrial revolution changed our planet as well the experience of everyone living on it. **Air pollution** is primarily caused by burning fossil fuels, things like coal, oil, and natural gas[12] (see Box 18.1). As industry and manufacturing ramped up in the 19th century, factories relied on cheap and very dirty coal as energy to power smelters, looms, and other machines that would sometimes run 24 hours per day to meet product demands. With the invention of the automobile and airplane, we began burning copious amounts of gasoline. As the world's population continues to grow, we rely on home heat derived from burning fuel oil and natural gas. The combustion of all these dirty fossil fuels

BOX 18.1: THE ALISO CANYON GAS LEAK

Box 18.1 Image 1 *Protestors carry a photo of Gov. Jerry Brown and demand a shutdown of the Southern California Gas Company's Aliso Canyon Storage Facility near Porter Ranch in Los Angeles. A 12-week-old gas leak had plagued Los Angeles residents and driven thousands from their homes.*

Richard Vogel/AP/Press Association Images

About midway between the surfing mecca of Dana Point, California, and Lake Elsinore, near the Interstate 15 freeway, is a Los Angeles County neighborhood called Porter Ranch. Nearby to Porter Ranch, which is located in the Santa Susana Mountains, is Aliso Canyon. The Southern California Gas Company stores and pumps over 80 billion cubic feet of natural gas from underground storage wells near Aliso Canyon. On October 23, 2015, one of those wells began to leak, spewing natural gas into the air.[13] At first, officials from SoCalGas thought the leak was easily fixable and would last, at most, a few days. Nearly five months later the leak remained active.

Described as a "mega-leak"[14] and potentially the largest natural gas leak in history,[15] the Aliso Canyon leak was dumping an estimated 44,000 kilograms of methane, benzene, and other noxious toxic and carcinogenic compounds into the air per hour.[16] This is the equivalent of the emissions from over 200,000 vehicles.[17] The gas is not visible to the naked eye but can be seen with infrared cameras and led to the forced relocation of over 11,000 people. Frighteningly, officials said the leak may have also released radioactive material into the surrounding air.[18]

Image 18.5 *This combination of photos taken Sunday, November 1, 2015, top, and Tuesday, December 1, 2015, bottom, show pedestrians walking through a shopping and office complex in Beijing amid widely differing levels of air pollution. Schools in Beijing were ordered to keep students indoors after record-breaking air pollution in the Chinese capital soared to up to 35 times safe levels.*

Mark Schiefelbein/AP/Press Association Images

is unsustainable and releases huge quantities of carbon dioxide (CO_2) into the air (see Box 18.2). This creates "smog" and is the key contributor to our world's greatest ecological and social problem: global climate change.

Serious crimes and harms result from air pollution that are of significant interest to green criminologists.[19] The air quality in London, England, was so bad from the 1850s through the 1950s, that days of heavy, lingering smog were nicknamed "pea-soupers."[20] So much coal was burnt in London that buildings were left covered in black coal soot.[21] London's **Great Smog of 1952** is directly responsible for killing between 4,000 and 12,000 citizens and injuring over 100,000 more.[22] Of course, there was nothing illegal about the Great Smog; it was the result of perfectly legal actions. Still, the magnitude of the harm caused is worthy of note: in just this one event, nearly as many people died as are killed each year in homicides in the U.S.

China is now the world's leader in air pollution. In fact, some have coined the term "airpocalypse" to describe especially bad air pollution events in China's major cities like Beijing, Shanghai, and Chengdu.[23] The causes of air pollution in China are the same as they were in places like London and the U.S. a hundred years ago: the burning of fossil fuels in automobiles and factories.

Today, we measure and track air quality for public health purposes using the **Air Quality Index (AQI)**. The AQI measures and reports levels for "five major pollutants: ground-level ozone, particle pollution (also known as particulate matter), carbon monoxide, sulfur dioxide, and nitrogen dioxide"[24] and reports air quality levels that range from 0 to 500. The higher the score, the worse the air quality.

Air pollution levels in developing countries and countries burning dirty fossil fuels can be incredibly bad. According to air quality index (AQI) readings (see Table 18.3), many Chinese cities like Beijing and Chengdu regularly experience unhealthy to very unhealthy air quality measurements, meaning people should stay indoors, avoid exertion, and wear masks or even respirators. Record AQI readings have been taken in Beijing, including what many consider the worst-ever recorded AQI reading of 755 in 2013.[25] Conversely, across the United States AQI levels average between 25 and 35.

BOX 18.2: THE CRIME OF CLIMATE CHANGE

Climate change is an emerging issue being studied intensely by green criminologists and others.[26] With all the discussion over global climate change, you've undoubtedly heard much about the role of carbon dioxide emissions in warming the earth. You've probably also heard phrases like "carbon sequestration," "ocean carbon uptake," and "carbon tax." What do these phrases mean and how exactly does carbon relate to the study of green crimes and harms? Let's find out.

Carbon is the sixth element in the periodic table; as such, it is considered a frequently occurring or common element. For example, diamonds and graphite are formed from carbon, and so are things like coal and charcoal. When carbon is burned, it combines with oxygen to form carbon dioxide (CO_2); however, carbon dioxide also results from respiration (i.e., breathing) and fermentation. Carbon dioxide is naturally occurring—whenever a volcano erupts or a forest fire occurs, carbon dioxide is produced. It is also naturally absorbed by plants, trees, and oceans—carbon "sinks"—through processes called **ocean-carbon uptake**[27] and **photosynthesis**.

The natural occurrence of carbon dioxide is not a serious concern and the natural absorption of CO_2 is a good thing. However, the man-made production of CO_2, from homes, automobile exhausts and factory emissions, is a huge issue since it disrupts the natural balance of CO_2 in the atmosphere and overwhelms the ability of plants, trees, and oceans to filter and store it. Data show that the atmospheric CO_2 levels remained steady—between 260–280 ppm (parts per million)—for thousands of years.[28] However, following the Industrial Revolution the amount of CO_2 in the air shot up, increasing 36 percent since the 19th century.[29] Indeed, most of that increase has occurred just since 1973. The amount of CO_2 in the atmosphere is now 373 ppm and growing.[30]

All that CO_2 makes the earth warmer. A warming earth means different and sometimes bizarre climate and weather patterns—abnormally wet, dry, hot, cold—with more severe storms. Keep in mind, this climate change impacts everything else in a trickle-down effect: agriculture and crops, biodiversity, housing, tourism, and so on. So, CO_2 is a really big deal.

Thus, a lot of effort has gone into figuring out how to slow down the rate of CO_2 emissions. Understandably, developing alternative fuel and energy sources is a solution, but one that takes time, money, and effort, which are sometimes in short supply. Other stop-gap options include **carbon sequestration**, capturing CO_2 before it is released into the atmosphere and storing it underground.[31] Another option is a **carbon tax** that will raise the costs of relying on carbon-based fuels so that it becomes more cost effective to invest in alternative energy measures.[32]

All of the discussion about what to do about CO_2 is being followed by green criminologists who see many opportunities for both research and civic engagement in the topic. Important questions to consider include: should high CO_2 producing industries or corporations be considered "criminal" entities? Is global climate change one the most significant state-corporate crime ever perpetrated? Who is most harmed by the effects of rising CO_2 levels and related consequences—the rich or the poor? How will climate change effect the types, extent and frequency of criminal offending?

These questions and more highlight the relevance of green criminology to some of today's most pressing social, ecological, economic, and cultural issues.

Table 18.3 Guide to AQI levels

AQI value	Meaning
0–50	Air quality good; little or no risk to human health from air pollution.
51–100	Air quality acceptable; moderate health risk from air pollution for people who are very sensitive.
101–150	Air quality unhealthy for sensitive people; at-risk people, including elderly, ill and those with compromised respiratory systems are at greater risk of complications.
151–200	Air quality unhealthy; risk is of ill-health effects higher for all people; at-risk groups likely to experience health problems.
201–300	Air quality very unhealthy; every person is at risk; health alters and warnings issued; outdoor exertion should be avoided.
301–500	Air quality hazardous; all people at significant risk of health issues; emergency conditions and avoidance of outdoors is necessary.
Beyond index	Air quality so bad it's off the charts; major health effects for all living things.

Water pollution

Water pollution is a major concern for green criminologists since 70 percent of the earth is covered in water and it is absolutely critical to the healthy functioning of life on Earth. Unfortunately, human beings, and in particular powerful governments and corporations, have a long history of polluting and poisoning the world's water resources, be they salt water oceans or fresh water rivers, streams, and aquifers. The net effect, as with air pollution, has been commission of serious crimes and harms that have killed and seriously injured millions of people.

American citizens are fortunate that, in comparison to millions of people living in other places around the world, they don't need to worry about the quality of the water they drink or bathe in. That has not always been the case however and, depending on where you live today, water quality in the U.S. is still a serious concern (see Box 18.3). One of the key catalysts for the modern environmental movement was when Ohio's Cuyahoga river became so polluted with chemicals that it actually caught on fire.

Water pollution is caused by the intentional and unintentional, direct and indirect, release of substances that negatively modify the water. Sewage, waste in the form of trash or debris, and agricultural and industrial chemicals are also substances that can negatively modify the health of a water body or system.

The direct release of pollutants into water bodies would involve, for example, pumping wastewater straight into a river or draining old chemicals right into the ocean (see Box 18.4). Because of stronger laws, regulations, and oversight, this form of pollution is less common in the United States today than it was in the past, when people utilized rivers and streams like open sewers. However, in many still industrializing and developing nations, direct water pollution is very common.

BOX 18.3: UNSAFE TO DRINK

Between 1965 and 1980, 19 children in the small town of Woburn, Massachusetts, were diagnosed with childhood leukemia, a type of cancer that is often deadly.[33] Six of the children lived next door to each other.[34] The rate of childhood leukemia in quaint Woburn was three times the national average.[35] Other individuals in the town reported developing strange skin rashes and other ailments.[36]

Concerned citizens initiated a campaign and subsequent investigation into the quality and chemical content of the drinking water in Woburn. That investigation revealed that 184 barrels containing toxic chemicals and chemical "sludge" had been illegally buried near where the City of Woburn had subsequently drilled two drinking water wells from which the effected children and residents got their water.[37] The EPA found high levels of the carcinogen TCE, trichloroethylene, in the drinking well's water supply, but was unable to determine whether the TCE came directly from the barrels or who was responsible for burying them.

Town residents filed a civil lawsuit against two companies, W.R. Grace and Beatrice Foods, who each had industrial factories and utilized potent chemicals within close proximity to the contaminated drinking water wells, which were closed in 1979. After a lengthy civil trial, detailed in the book *A Civil Action* by Jonathan Harr, a jury found insufficient evidence against Beatrice Foods and returned a contradictory verdict against W.R. Grace. Eventually, W.R. Grace settled their case for $8 million in 1986.[38]

Almost thirty years after the Woburn case was settled, another large scandal arose in the city of Flint, Michigan, over the issue of contaminated drinking water. In this case the party responsible is the City of Flint, not a corporation.

In April 2014, in order to cut costs, city officials began drawing drinking water from the Flint River rather than the City of Detroit's system. Despite many complaints about the water's taste and reports of rashes, the city issued a statement saying "Flint water is safe to drink."[39] Over the ensuing months, residents were advised to boil their water to kill harmful bacteria, and an automotive plant stopped using it because it "corroded car parts."[40] Nevertheless, in early February 2015, the City of Flint continued to dismiss concerns over the city's drinking water and refused an offer to reconnect to Detroit's system for free.[41]

A few weeks later, testing revealed excessive amounts of lead in the tap water of many Flint residents. One test showed 104 parts per billion of lead in the water; the EPA limit for "safe" consumption is 15 parts per billion. A follow up test at the same home showed lead levels in excess of 395 parts per billion! Lead exposure and poisoning can cause serious health effects such a brain and nervous system damage, kidney damage, and even death, especially in children.[42] Despite results showing high levels of lead in the city's water, officials continue to downplay the issue in July 2015.

Outside pressure from groups, researchers, and health officials revealed that drawing corrosive water from the Flint river had eaten away at the interior of the city's old water pipes, allowing lead and other heavy metals to enter the city's water supply. By January 2016, city officials could no longer deny that a serious emergency was taking place in Flint.[43] All residents, many of whom are low-income African Americans, were advised to stop using the city's water.[44] The federal government declared a state of emergency in Flint. Many of the residents are too poor to pack up and leave.

For example, some Chinese rivers run indigo blue when dyes from denim factories are discharged into them. In many African nations, the release of human waste into rivers used for bathing, cooking and drinking continues to cause lethal outbreaks of disease. The Great Pacific Garbage Patch (GPGP)—a floating miasma of junk from around the world that coagulates into an island of trash twice the size of Texas—famously attracts tourists from around the world each year, despite being only one of several such floating trash islands in our oceans. Thanks to the abundance and longevity of plastics, sites like the GPGP will only continue to grow.

The indirect release of pollutants into water remains a serious concern anywhere that industrial, mining or manufacturing activities occur. This form of pollution is harder to detect and control than more direct forms since the substances may seep or leech into aquifers, wells, municipal water supplies, rivers, and streams over many years and great distances.

Disposal of hazardous waste and e-waste

Ever since people stopped living nomadic lives and began congregating into more permanent settlements, the issue of what to do with all the waste we generate has been an issue.[45] Unfortunately, despite stronger national and international laws and regulations, municipal dumps, recycling programs and more, waste disposal remains a significant issue in the United States and around the world. It is also an important public health and criminological issue.

Green criminologists are most focused on the illegal or harmful disposal of hazardous and electronic waste (e-waste). Hazardous waste is any liquid, solid, gas, or sludge harmful or dangerous to the environment and/or human health.[46] Examples of hazardous wastes include household cleaning fluids, pesticides, paints, batteries, radioactive materials, and many byproducts from industrial

---

BOX 18.4: FRACKING

Fracking—a controversial method for extracting natural gas from deep inside the Earth by using high pressure water—is raising new legal and public health concerns. For example, in 2013, California officials required oil companies to test the waste water from fracking operations for chemical and toxic compounds. The results confirmed some people's worst fears. Levels of benzene, a lethal cancer-causing chemical, were on average 700 times higher than state and federal regulations permitted or considered safe.[47] Worse still, California officials allowed this "flow back fluid" to be re-injected into groundwater, meaning it could have ended up in drinking water, given to livestock, or sprayed onto agricultural crops. This, of course, represents a serious violation of state regulations, which the EPA called "shocking." This issues remains a dynamic one of great interest to those who study or research green crimes and harms.

and manufacturing processes. "E-waste" is a newer, but rapidly growing problem. **E-waste** is used to describe any electronic product that is "nearing the end of its useful life" or no longer utilized and includes televisions, computers, cell phones, stereos, and more.[48] E-waste often contains hazardous materials and components (see Box 18.5). Over 400 million tons of hazardous waste[49] is produced each year around the world along with enough e-waste to fill 1.15 million tractor trailer trucks full (41 million metric tons of e-waste)![50]

Image 18.6 *Groups of workers in Dhaka, Bangladesh dye clothes in the river around their factory. The water is severely polluted by factories along the river, which release dyes and chemicals into the publicly used river.*

mohammad asad/Demotix/Press Association Images

Researchers have long noted that the location of waste producing industrial and manufacturing facilities, along with waste disposal sites, is not evenly distributed.[51] Indeed, these facilities are often constructed in the poorest, most disorganized communities, with large minority populations.[52] These communities lack the political, economic, and social capital to organize to resist or oppose the construction of these facilities moving in their neighborhoods and, often, they come to rely on these places as vital sites of employment. This means that exposure to the risks from hazardous and toxic wastes is heightened among particular groups of people living in specific places, both in the U.S. and around the world.[53] The term attached to this phenomenon is **environmental racism** and is a key issue in the larger **environmental justice movement**, which seeks to promote fairness and justice in terms of exposure to environmental risks as well as the investigation, prosecution, and punishment of criminal and civil offenders.[54]

A significant issue in the illegal and/or harmful disposal of hazardous and e-waste is the role played by organized criminal groups. In 1985, two sociologists, Alan Block and Frank Scarpitti, published a book exposing the role of organized criminal groups in the disposal of toxic waste.[55] *Poisoning for Profit* revealed how organized crime had infiltrated many "legitimate" waste disposal companies in order to gain access to the lucrative contracts awarded to those hauling away corporate and industrial America's unwanted waste.

The problem with organized criminal involvement in hazardous waste disposal is that they have no incentive to follow regulations or abide by waste disposal laws—their interest is solely in making a profit. Moreover, the presence of organized crime in the waste disposal industry undoubtedly results in the corruption of the waste disposal oversight system, as regulators and police are bribed or coerced to "look the other way."

For example, just a few years prior to the publication of *Poisoning for Profit,* an exposé in the *New York Times* described how organized criminal groups in New York were "illegally dumping vast quantities of dangerous chemicals" by "flushing them into sewer systems, pouring them into garbage landfills, dumping

BOX 18.5: CRIME IN GLOBAL PERSPECTIVE

E-waste

In 2014, Americans purchased over $211 billion dollars of consumer electronics.[56] The worldwide figure is much, much higher. Growth in the sale of electronics is fueled by constantly changing and improving technologies as well as the planned obsolescence of existing machines and devices (i.e., intentionally designing them to ensure they won't function or be "up to date" for long).[57] Our "throw-away culture" also feeds the growing mountain of e-waste, which now totals more than 65 million metric tons.[58] Just consider how many cell phones, TVs, or computers you, your friends, and family have owned. If you are like the authors of this text, the answer is probably a lot.

You probably have not thought much about where all your old devices, computers, TVs, stereos, and more, go after you are done with them. While some e-waste ends up discarded into the trash and in our landfills, most is "recycled."[59] Indeed, most municipalities in the U.S. now require that electronic items be sorted from trash and recycled.

What this often means in practice, however, is that our American e-waste, is recycled by being legally exported overseas to places like China, India, Nigeria, or Ghana.[60] Worse still is that the United Nations Environment Program estimates that as much as 90 percent of the world's e-waste is illegally traded or dumped each year.[61]

Once it arrives in one of those foreign destinations, it becomes the job of the poorest, least educated, and least protected workers to sort through it. Many engage in dangerous practices to extract the gold, silver, platinum, palladium, copper, and coltan from the devices. For example, it is common for workers to burn the electronics or use cyanide or some other agent to retrieve the metals, which can release mercury, lead, and cadmium into the air, ground, and their bodies.[62,63] While each device yields incremental amounts of these precious metals, when you consider the volume of e-waste generated, it becomes more obvious why workers would risk their lives mining these metals.

Today, much of the burden posed by toxic and hazardous wastes, including the e-waste from all of our old, broken or unwanted electronics, is falling on the shoulders of the poor and disenfranchised in countries far removed from where we live in the United States. This represents a significant green crime and harm, as well as a form of environmental racism and injustice. Thankfully, green criminologists, along with regulators and prosecutors, are taking on the task of publicizing this form of ecologically and socially harmful criminality.[64]

them into waterways, mixing them into heating oil, stacking them in warehouses, and burying them in unmarked pits."[65]

As recently as July 2013, the FBI indicted 32 organized crime figures from three New York area crime families with plotting to "control the commercial waste disposal industry"[66] in the city. The pervasiveness of organized crime's illegal control and disposal of hazardous and toxic wastes and law enforcement's efforts to combat it was aptly summarized by the Manhattan U.S. Attorney in a press release: "organized crime still wraps its tentacles around industries it has fed off for decades, but law enforcement continues to pry loose its grip."[67]

Poaching and illegal wildlife trafficking

Zimbabwe's Hwange Game Reserve is a popular destination for tourists hoping to glimpse Africa's most notable, and endangered, animals: lions, elephants, rhinoceros and more. On the night of July 1, 2015, American dentist Walter Palmer lay in the brush on private land abutting Hwange Game Reserve. Nearby was Theo Bronkhorst, a safari guide who Palmer, a self-proclaimed big-game trophy hunter, paid $50,000 to help him "bag" an African lion.[68] Using a dead elephant carcass as bait, the duo created a scent trail to lure a lion off the game reserve.[69] They succeeded in drawing Cecil, a 13-year-old black-maned male lion outside of Hwange's park boundaries. In the darkness, Cecil approached the dead elephant when Palmer and Bronkhorst illuminated him with a high-powered spotlight, temporarily blinding him. Palmer then fired an arrow which seriously injured, but did not immediately kill Cecil, who then fled. Early the next day, July 2, Palmer and Bronkhorst tracked the badly bleeding and weakened Cecil and killed him. They then posed for pictures with his body before cutting off his head and skinning him.

The killing of Cecil the lion is unique in that Cecil's murder immediately became an international news and social media sensation. Cecil, it turned out, was one of the park's most popular, well-loved and highly photographed animals. He was also part of a long running Oxford University lion research project and, as such, was outfitted with a GPS tracking collar, which eventually led research team members to his remains outside of Hwange. Once Cecil was discovered dead, an investigation by park authorities and the Zimbabwean government commenced, and it was determined that Cecil was killed illegally. Palmer and Bronkhorst lacked the required hunting permits and, even if they had them, luring a lion from the park was not a legal practice.

Bronkhorst and the private landowner were arrested and charged with criminal poaching and other counts.[70] **Poaching** is the illegal killing, or attempted taking, of any game—including fish, reptiles, birds, or animals.[71] Palmer, who had already arrived back in the U.S., received a significant amount of negative publicity,

Image 18.7 *American dentist Walter Palmer killed Cecil the lion during an illegal hunt in Zimbabwe. Palmer allegedly paid park guides $50,000 (£32,000) to hunt and kill Cecil at the Hwange National Park, not realizing that the animal was a local favorite and part of an ongoing scientific study. Cecil was lured away from the safety of the park before being shot with a bow. He was then tracked for 40 hours and shot with a rifle. Palmer posed for a 'trophy' photo with his corpse before it was decapitated and skinned.*

REX/Shutterstock

including death threats, but was not criminally charged.[72] He rationalized his actions by saying "I had no idea that the lion I took was a known, local favorite, was collared and part of a study until the end of the hunt ... I relied on the expertise of my local professional guides to ensure a legal hunt."[73]

Cecil the Lion's illegal killing shed light on the lucrative trophy hunting industry, where hunting guides and companies charge anywhere from $10,000 to $150,000 per hunt.[74] Importantly, trophy hunting is often perfectly legal, despite outcry from wildlife researchers, animal rights activists, and ordinary citizens that it is morally reprehensible and ecologically harmful. Indeed, one of the key reasons trophy hunting exists is because it supports local economies

Map 18.1
Illegal animal trade in the world: Main routes of animal smuggling and prices.

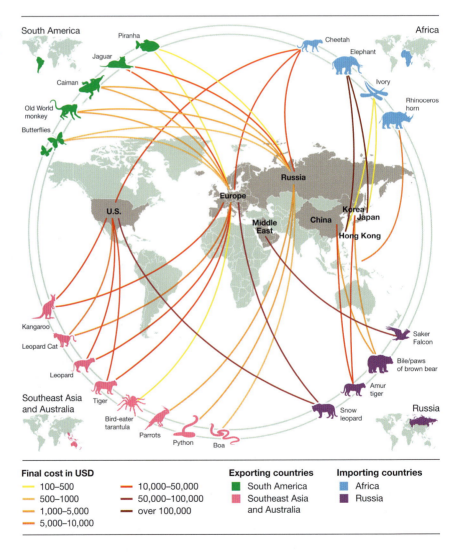

in places and countries where financial resources are minimal, especially struggling nations in Africa.

Illegal poaching, however, is a serious crime that contributes to global biodiversity loss, wildlife endangerment, and extinction and the destabilization of communities and nation-states. Illegal poaching is also a significant component that feeds the **global illegal wildlife trade**. That trade is massive, involving more than 30,000 distinct plant and animal species—many of which are rare, threatened, endangered, or on the verge of extinction—and the movement of hundreds of millions of species or products derived from them each year,[75] including things like ivory, shark fins, exotic hardwoods,[76] and more.

Wildlife trafficking is the term applied to the "entire journey of an endangered and/or protected animal, plant, or derivative thereof, from being taken in the wild to arrival at their final destination."[77] Trafficking in wildlife is conservatively estimated to generate more than $10 billion in revenue each year, making it the third most lucrative illegal market and industry in the world, trailing only the illegal trades in drugs and weapons.[78] As a result, the global trade in wild plant and animal species is increasingly run by sophisticated transnational organized criminal networks, who also traffic in drugs, weapons, and people.[82]

BOX 18.6: CONNECTING THEORY TO PRACTICE

The treadmill of production

The treadmill of production theory (ToP)[79] has been called "the single most important sociological concept and theory to have emerged within North American environmental sociology."[80] Recently, it has been adopted by green criminologists to help understand a host of green crimes and harms. The theory argues that capitalism is an inherently ecologically destructive economic system; that is, there is a fundamental conflict and contradiction between capitalism's goals of low-cost economic growth and expansion with environmental protection and sustainability.

ToP focuses on ecological withdrawals and additions that occur within a capitalist economic system.[81] Ecological withdrawals are the ways that capitalists extract natural resources to fuel growth (i.e., mining for gold, platinum, or coal; fracking for gas; drilling for oil). Since World War II, the rate and intensity of ecological withdrawals has greatly increased. Ecological additions are the emissions and pollutants which the capitalist mode of production adds back into the natural environment.

From a green criminological perspective, green crimes and harms occur during both ecological withdrawals and additions. In fact, many of the varieties of green crimes and harms we've discussed in this chapter can be placed under one or the other of these categories. In short, ToP can help us understand the driving force behind most forms of ecological crime and harm within the world's most dominant economic system.

Within the illegal wildlife trade corporate, organized, and state criminal actors converge, making it one of the most dynamic and interesting areas of study within the green criminology field.

Many trafficked animal and reptile species up-sold to zoos, wildlife shows, or into the pet industry. The transport and introduction of non-native species into new ecosystems and habitats may result in them being labeled "invasive species"—organisms capable of causing significant ecological, economic, and human health related harms.[83] Byproducts or derivatives from illegally acquired, traded, or harvested species are often sought after for use in traditional medicines,[84] foods and in the manufacturing of consumer products, including souvenirs, and musical instruments.[85]

The global wildlife trade is a major political, social, ecological, and economic problem, particularly because the trade threatens national security and because the illegal proceeds from the trade support organized criminal and terrorist groups. As a result, 179 countries have ratified the **Convention on International Trade in Endangered Species (CITES)**, an international treaty designed to reduce and control the global trade in all wildlife and plants. Recent data indicate that CITES is playing an effective role in limiting the scale of the global wildlife trade.[86]

THE CONTROL AND PROSECUTION OF GREEN CRIMES AND HARMS

We have highlighted some green crimes and harms that have attracted the attention of the media, politicians, and law enforcement. However, the vast majority of green crimes and harms escape public, media, political, and law enforcement attention. Green crimes and harms often go unnoticed and under punished, much like the crimes of the powerful discussed in chapter 17. One reason for this is because of their close association with the actions of the powerful—corporations, governments, and organized crime. When powerful entities, from organizations to individuals, engage in ecologically and socially harmful behavior they can leverage their resources (money, status, political, and media connections) to obscure their conduct or deflect public and law enforcement attention from it.

One term used to describe this process is greenwashing. **Greenwashing** occurs when an organization uses its power and influence to create an environmentally friendly or responsible public image of itself, despite engaging in environmentally criminal or harmful practices. Many times, greenwashing campaigns thwart the control and prosecution of green crimes and harms. For example, Professor Melissa Jarrell has detailed the criminal actions of CITGO Petroleum in Corpus Christi, Texas. Despite clear evidence that CITGO knowingly and willfully failed to regulate the amount of cancer causing benzene being released into the air from its East Plant Refinery in the mid-2000s, the company avoided significant

Image 18.8
These homes in the Hillcrest, Texas neighborhood are contrasted by stacks of refineries.

Rachel Denny
Clow/AP/Press
Association Images

negative publicity.[87] One key reason: their ability to manipulate the media and create an image of themselves as a positive force in the local communities impacted by their malfeasance.[88]

Efforts to formally combat and control green crimes in the U.S. fall to local, state, and federal law enforcement and administrative agencies, while at the international level organizations like the U.N., Interpol, and Europol. At the national level, the responsibility for controlling green crimes falls primarily to the Environmental Protection Agency's Criminal Investigation Division, Department of Justice Environmental Crimes Section, and the U.S. Fish and Wildlife Service (USFWS). Collectively, these agencies are responsible for enforcing a myriad of environmental laws and regulations (i.e., the Clean Air Act, Clean Water Act, CITES, etc.), investigating offenses, filing charges, and prosecuting cases. But, how successful have they been?

Data from the Department of Justice show that environmental crime prosecutions between 1998 and 2014 resulted in 774 years of incarceration and $825 million in fines.[89] However, it is rare for those committing green crimes to see their cases end in a jury verdict. Most often offenders, especially corporations, reach a plea deal. This was the case following the massive BP oil spill in the Gulf of Mexico. In 2012, two years after eleven people were killed and millions of gallons of oil poisoned the Gulf, BP agreed to pay a fine of $4.5 billion; four company officials also pled guilty to reduced criminal charges.[90] According to data maintained by the Environmental Protection Agency (EPA), over 64,000 companies or facilities are in violation of one or more environmental regulations in any given year, yet less than one-half of one percent are criminally investigated; even fewer are prosecuted or held

BOX 18.7: CONNECTING RESEARCH TO PRACTICE

Dealing with pollution

The 1990s ushered in a new era of concern over the Earth's natural resources. Nations worldwide began to reevaluate their exploitation of metals and fossil fuels, excessive production of waste, and depletion of land, air, and water resources. A growing body of literature demonstrated the impact of environmental degradation on the quality of life and health, especially among the poor.[91]

National policies emerged to promote the use of abundant resources over scarce ones, to reduce or eliminate waste resources such as forests, and to increase recycling of materials such as glass and aluminum. Researchers focused on strategies to reduce the harmful effects of pollution and sustain natural resources.[92] In the late 1990s, the office of research and development (ORD) of the U.S. Environmental Protection agency provided a long-term strategic plan to expand the scientific study of the environment.[93] The plan included providing research data and technical support to government agencies, organizational entities, corporations, and the general public; increasing awareness of wasteful practices; managing ecological resources, and understanding the health hazards of pollution. The research on risk assessment and risk management identified four areas of priority:

- Contaminated sites—groundwater.
- Contaminated sites—soil or vadose, the unsaturated zones of the Earth.
- Emissions from waste combustion facilities.
- Active waste management facilities.

The process made by the ORD represents the first research driven policies and practices to systematically identify and manage risks to the environment.

accountable for their actions.[94] Indeed, even as many environmental issues and crimes have grown in importance and scale, criminal investigations by the EPA have declined.

What explains this criminal "**prosecution gap**"[95] in the United States?

One explanation is a lack of political will to prioritize holding the powerful accountable for their green crimes. It took until 1988 for the United States government to even vest the Environmental Protection Agency (EPA) with the authority to prosecute violations of environmental statutes resulting in harm to our nation's air, water, public land, and wildlife.[96] As a result, most green crimes are punished using the civil and administrative court systems, which at best can dole out fines and restitution. Those systems, however, are ineffective at sending strong messages to green crime offenders, many of which continue on with business as usual, becoming green crime recidivists.

Another explanation for the criminal prosecution gap is a lack of both personnel and financial resources to adequately combat and control green

BOX 18.8: THE ANNIHILATION OF NORTH AMERICAN BISON[97]

Between 1865 and 1890, America's population of bison declined from approximately 15 million to fewer than 1,000 animals. The primary cause of this rapid population reduction was the rise of a market for bison hides and bison leather and an influx of thousands of commercial hunters to the American mid-west. The bison slaughter commenced with amazing speed and efficiency, covering the Plains with rotting carcasses and piles of bones and overflowing train cars bound for the East coast with hides.

Certainly, this event would qualify as a significant green harm. It also serves as a prime example of how capitalism drives ecological withdrawals and how important regulation is to prevent ecological harm. However, the case of the North American bison is much more complicated than it first appears.

During the same time period that the bison population declined, the federal government was engaged in conflict with dozens of American Indian tribal groups that depended on the bison as their primary food source. For those tribes, the bison were also an important cultural symbol. News reports from the time indicate that the media and public supported the massacre of the bison as a means for subduing those tribal groups. Legal and congressional records further show that while some efforts were made to control and mitigate the bison slaughter, none of those efforts was ever successful. In fact, military officials, law makers and even the president of the United States, Ulysses S. Grant, voiced support for the bison slaughter because it would weaken American Indian tribes and make it easier to coerce them away from their lands and onto federal reservations. As a result, the bison were wastefully and wantonly slaughtered in a rampage of excessive brutality. Only too late did the voices of a minority of concerned citizens and politicians begin to speak out and demand an end to the bison killing, but it was too late. The bison as a species were reduced to such an extent that they have never recovered and the American Indian tribes so dependent upon them had been conquered.

Box 18.8 Image 1 *Photograph from the mid-1870s of a pile of American bison skulls waiting to be ground for fertilizer.*

crimes when they occur. Collectively, the EPA Criminal Investigation Division, DOJ Environmental Crimes Section, and U.S. Fish and Wildlife Service employee only about 540 criminal investigators and attorneys. These individuals are further limited by budgetary constraints, which may sometimes be impacted by the political orientations and priorities of the president and members of Congress.

As a result, some of the most effective methods of controlling green crimes and non-criminal, but very harmful actions, may be informal. Many non-profit organizations work tirelessly to raise awareness and publicity of green crimes and harms. These groups, including Green Peace, the World Wildlife Fund, Sierra Club, and Environmental Investigation Agency, therefore play key roles in helping to combat and control green crimes when and where they occur. Lastly, ordinary citizens who find the courage to raise their voice and demand justice are pivotal in ensuring that green crimes and harms, especially those the mass media is unlikely to devote their attention to, are known about. However, as the case of the American bison indicates (see Box 18.8), sometimes the efforts to raise awareness about a serious green crime come too late.

SUMMARY

In this chapter, we introduced the sub-field of green criminology, where researchers from many backgrounds come together to study and raise public awareness about green crimes (i.e., illegal acts) and acts that are very harmful, but not criminal, and which negatively impact the natural world and human life.

Green criminology is a diverse area of study whose origins lie in the U.S. environmental movement of the 1960s and 1970s and the European "green" political movement that began generating attention in the late 1970s, 1980s, and 1990s. Importantly, these social movements created a legitimate public space within which discussions about the relationship between people and the natural world, including other species, could occur. Absent the rise of the Environmental and Green movements, it's very unlikely we would be discussing green criminology or any harmful conduct toward the environment.

A key point to remember is that our discussion of crimes of the powerful from chapter 17 overlaps and intersects with our discussion in this chapter of green crimes and harms. Many green crimes and harms, especially the most significant ones, occur as a result of the actions of powerful corporations and governments. Indeed, an ongoing debate within green criminology is whether "climate change" can be considered a criminal event? Some say yes, and, in doing so, they point to the willful conduct of corporations that have polluted our natural environment for decades and intentionally subverted environmental laws and regulations in order to make or increase profits. Some argue governments are equally responsible for the crime of climate change, by failing to enact strict environmental regulations or vigorously pursue and punish environmental criminals and wrongdoers. In the eyes of some of those who regard climate change as the single greatest, and gravest, criminal act in human history, climate change is the result of a criminal collusion among government and the corporate world.

Unsurprisingly then, there does exist a green crime prosecution gap. This "gap" refers to the difference between the number of known green crimes and the number of prosecutions that take place. The pattern tends to be that prosecutions fall far short of the actual number of green crimes known to law enforcement and prosecutors.

What was covered in this chapter is just the tip of the iceberg in terms of the research and activism being carried out by green criminologists.

If you are concerned about environmental issues and also like the idea of studying crime, harm, and the law, then green criminology might be a great fit for you. We hope you continue to explore the subject and pay attention to the coverage and control (or lack thereof) that green crimes and harms receive in our modern world.

CRITICAL THINKING QUESTIONS

1. In your opinion, how important is the study of green crimes and harms within the scope of the entire criminological enterprise? Are green crimes and harms more important to study than street crimes? Should they be given equal priority and resources? If not, why? What makes green crimes and harms less worthy of our attention both as criminologists and criminal justice practitioners?

2. Envision a world where green crimes and harms are treated as *the* most important criminal acts and are afforded resources to match that categorization. What would that world look and feel like? Would you want to live there? What obstacles obstruct such a world from taking shape?

3. One reason given for the lack of interest and attention paid to green crimes and harms is that it's hard for people to imagine becoming a victim of such a crime, while its easier to imagine being raped, robbed, or murdered. Do you think this is true? Or is this actually the result of public perception being manipulated over time by corporate and government actors who stand to benefit from this misconception via the exploitation of the natural environment? Imagine your relatives were living in Bhopal, India or Aliso Canyon when those gas leaks occurred; consider how you would feel if your family had been drinking and bathing in poisonous, toxic water, as happened to people in Flint, Michigan, and Woburn, Massachusetts. Is it really that hard to imagine becoming a victim of these crimes? Or, have people consistently been fed the message that these crimes and harms, which occur quite frequently, are not very common or dangerous? What role does environmental racism play in this issue of perception?

4. What can be done to reduce the green crime prosecution gap? Develop a list of strategies—don't limit yourself creatively. What do you think are real obstacles in the path of prosecuting green crimes on the same level with street crimes? Is it lack of resources, manpower, political will, public interest, or some combination of all these factors?

NOTES

1   Taylor, A. 2014. Bhopal: The World's Worst Industrial Disaster, 30 Years Later. *The Atlantic,* Dec. 2.

2   Ibid.

3   Union Carbide Corporation, 2016. Cause of the Bhopal Tragedy. Retrieved from http://www.bhopal.com/Cause-of-Bhopal-Tragedy.

4   The New Scientist. 2002. Fresh Evidence on Bhopal Disaster. Retrieved from www.newscientist.com/article/dn3140-fresh-evidence-on-bhopal-disaster/.

5   Ibid.

6   Lynch, M.J. 1990. The Greening of Criminology: A Perspective on the 1990s. *The Critical Criminologist* 2(3): 1–4, 11–12.

7   Beirne, P. and South, N. (eds.), 2007. *Issues in Green Criminology: Confronting Harms Against Environments, Humanity, and Other Animals.* Portland, OR: Willan Publishing.

8   Brisman, A. and South, N. 2013. Horizons, Issues, and Relationships in Green Criminology. In Nigel South and Avi Brisman (eds.), *Routledge International Handbook of Green Criminology.* London and New York: Routledge.

9   Dillard-Wright, D.B. 2009. Thinking Across Species Boundaries: General Sociality and Embodied Meaning. *Society and Animals* 17(1): 53–71.

10 Goedeke, T.L. 2004. In the Eye of the Beholder: Changing Social Perceptions of the Florida Manatee. *Society and Animals* 12(2): 99–116.

11 Jerolmack, C. 2008. How Pigeons Became Rats: The Cultural-Spatial Logic of Problem Animals. *Social Problems* 55: 72–94.

12 National Geographic. 2015. Air Pollution. Retrieved from http://environment.nationalgeographic.com/environment/global-warming/pollution-overview/.

13 South Coast Air Quality Management District. 2016. Aliso Canyon Update. http://www.aqmd.gov/home/regulations/compliance/aliso-canyon-update.

14 Environmental Defense Fund. 2016. Aliso Canyon Leak Sheds Light on National Problem. https://www.edf.org/climate/aliso-canyon-leak-sheds-light-national-problem

15 WND. 2016. Huge natural disaster gets little media attention. http://www.wnd.com/2016/02/lethal-levels-radioactive-fears-at-l-a-gas-leak/.

16 Ibid.

17 Ibid.

18 Ibid.

19 Walters, R. 2013. Air Crimes and Atmospheric Justice. In N. South and A. Brisman (eds.), *Routledge International Handbook of Green Criminology.* London: Routledge, pp. 134–149.

20 Cleaner Air for London. 2015. History of Air Pollution in London. Retrieved from http://www.cleanerairforlondon.org.uk/londons-air/air-quality-data/trends-london/history-air-pollution-london.

21 Ibid.

22 Ibid.

23 London and Beijing: A Polluted Tale of Two Cities. 2013. *The Globalist,* Nov. 12.

24 Air Now. 2015. Air Quality Index (AQI) Basics. Retrieved from http://airnow.gov/index.cfm?action=aqibasics.aqi.

25 Wong, E. 2013. On Scale of 0 to 500, Beijing's Air Quality Tops 'Crazy Bad' at 755. *The New York Times,* Jan. 12.

26 Hall, M. Farrall, S. 2013. The Criminogenic Consequences of Climate Change: Blurring the Boundaries between Offenders and Victims. In N. South and A. Brisman (eds.), *Routledge International Handbook of Green Criminology* London: Routledge, pp. 120–133.

27 National Oceanic and Atmospheric Administration. 2016. Ocean Carbon Uptake. PMEL Carbon Program. Retrieved from http://www.pmel.noaa.gov/co2/story/Ocean+Carbon+Uptake.

28 Midwest Geological Sequestration Consortium. 2016. The Ins and Outs of Carbon Sequestration. Retrieved from http://sequestration.org/science/carbondioxide.html.

29 Ibid.

30 Ibid.

31 Ibid.

32 Carbon Tax Center. 2016. Retrieved from http://www.carbontax.org.

33 Cutler, J.J., Parker, G.S., Rosen, S., Prenney, B., Healey, R. and Caldwell, G.G. 1986. Childhood Leukemia in Woburn, Massachusetts. *Public Health Reports* 10(2): 201–205.

34 Ibid.

35 Ibid.

36 Seattle University School of Law. 2015. *Anderson v. W.R. Grace.* Retrieved from http://www.law.seattleu.edu/centers-and-institutes/films-for-justice-institute/lessons-from-woburn/about-the-case.

37 Ibid.

38 Ibid.

39 Lin, Jeremy C.F., Rutter, Jean, and Park, Haeyoun. 2016. Events That Led to Flint's Water Crisis. *The New York Times.* Retrieved from http://www.nytimes.com/interactive/2016/01/21/us/flint-lead-water-timeline.html?_r=0.

40 Ibid.

41 Ibid.

42 World Health Organization. 2015. Lead Poisoning and Health. Retrieved from http://www.who.int/mediacentre/factsheets/fs379/en/.

43 Ibid.

44 Bernstein, L. 2016. Hope, and Clean Water, Remains Elusive for the People of Flint. Retrieved from https://www.washingtonpost.com/national/health-science/for-the-people-of-flint-hope—and-clean-water—remains-elusive/2016/02/06/1a6013c0-caa0–11e5–88ff-e2d1b4289c2f_story.html.

45 Cart, J. 2015. High Levels of Benzene Found in Fracking Waste Water. *The Los Angeles Times,* Feb. 11.

46 Oklahoma Department of Environmental Quality. 2015. A Brief History of Waste Regulation in the United States. Retrieved from http://www.deq.state.ok.us/lpdnew/wastehistory/wastehistory.htm.

47 Environmental Protection Agency. 2016. Wastes—Hazardous Waste. Retrieved from https://www.epa.gov/hw.

48 CalRecycle. 2015. What is E-Waste? Retrieved from http://www.calrecycle.ca.gov/electronics/whatisewaste/.

49 The World Counts. 2016. Hazardous Waste Statistics. Retrieved from http://www.theworldcounts.com/counters/waste_pollution_facts/hazardous_waste_statistics.

50 Causes International. 2016. E-Waste Facts. Retrieved from https://www.causesinternational.com/ewaste/e-waste-facts.

51 Mata, R. 1994. Hazardous Waste Facilities and Environmental Equity: A Proposed Siting Model. *Virginia Environmental Law Journal* 13(3): 375.

52   Lynch, M.J. and Stretesky, P.B. 2014. *Exploring Green Criminology: Toward a Green Criminological Revolution*. Farnham, UK: Ashgate Publishing.

53   Massey, R. 2004. *Environmental Justice: Income, Race and Health*. Global Development and Environment Institute. Medford, MA: Tufts University.

54   Bullard, D. Robert. 1990. *Dumping in Dixie: Race, Class and Environmental Quality*. Westview Press.

55   Consumer Technology Association. 2014. Consumer Electronics Industry Revenues to Reach All-Time High in 2014, Projects CEA's Semi-Annual Sales and Forecasts Report. https://www.cta.tech/News/News-Releases/Press-Releases/2014/Consumer-Electronics-Industry-Revenues-to-Reach-Al.aspx.

56   Doyon, J.A. 2014. Corporate Environmental Crime in the Electronic Waste Industry: The Case of Executive Recycling, Inc. Special edition of *Internet Journal of Criminology*. Retrieved from http://www.internetjournalofcriminology.com/Critical_Perspectives_On_Green_Criminology_June_2014.pdf.

57   Bidwell, A. 2013. U.N. Seeks to Solve Growing Global E-Waste Problem. *U.S. News and World Report,* Dec. 16.

58   Bradley, L. 2014. E-Waste in Developing Countries Endangers Environment, Locals. *U.S. News and World Report*, Aug. 1.

59   Beivik, K., Armitage, J.M., Wania, F. and Jones, K.C. 2014. Tracking the Global Generation and Exports of E-Waste. *Environmental Science and Technology* 48(15): 8735–8743.

60   United Nations Environment Program. 2016. Global Partnership on Waste Management: E-Waste Management. http://www.unep.org/gpwm/FocalAreas/E-Waste Management/tabid/56458/.

61   Ibid.

62   Bidwell, A. 2013. U.N. Seeks to Solve Growing Global E-Waste Problem. *U.S. News and World Report,* Dec. 16.

63   Doyon, J.A. 2014. Corporate Environmental Crime in the Electronic Waste Industry: The Case of Executive Recycling, Inc. Special edition of *Internet Journal of Criminology*, online. Retrieved from http://www.internetjournalofcriminology.com/Critical_Perspectives_On_Green_Criminology_June_2014.pdf.

64   Block, Alan A. Scarpitti, Frank R. 1985. *Poisoning for Profit: The Mafia and Toxic Waste in America*. New York: William and Morrow Company Inc.

65   Blumenthal, R. Franklin, B.A. 1983. Illegal Dumping of Toxins Laid to Organized Crime. *The New York Times,* June 5.

66   Federal Bureau of Investigation, New York Field Office. 2013.

67   Ibid.

68   Dorian, M. Putrino, L. Rakowski, C. and Valiente, A. 2015. What Happened in the Harrowing Hours Before Cecil the Lion was Killed. *ABC News*, Aug. 13.

69   Ibid.

70   Ibid.

71   Hurteau, D. 2011. So, Just What Is Poaching? *Field and Stream,* May 26.

72   McLaughlin, Eliot C. 2015. Zimbabwe Won't Press Charges Against Cecil the Lion's Killer. *CNN*, Oct. 12.

73   Ibid.

74   Dobson, J. 2015. Cecil the Lion Killing Highlights Flourishing Trophy Hunter Market for the Elite. *Forbes.com*, July 29. Retrieved from http://www.forbes.com/sites/jimdobson/2015/07/29/cecil-the-lion-killing-highlights-flourishing-big-game-hunter-market-for-the-elite/#5bede4d772e9.

75   Wyatt, T. 2013. Uncovering the Significance of and Motivation for Wildlife Trafficking. In N. South and A. Brisman (eds.), *The International Handbook of Green Criminology*. London: Routledge, pp. 303–316.

76   Corporate Crime Reporter. 2016. Lumber Liquidators to Pay More than $13 Million for Felony Environmental Crimes. Retrieved from http://www.corporatecrime reporter.com/news/200/lumber-liquidators-to-pay-more-than-13-million-for-felony-environmental-crimes/#sthash.N1ffybn7.dpuf.

77   Wyatt, T. 2013. Uncovering the Significance of and Motivation for Wildlife Trafficking. In N. South and A. Brisman (eds.), *The International Handbook of Green Criminology*. London, U.K.: Routledge, pp. 303–316.

78   Ibid., p. 304

79   World Wildlife Fund. 2015. Illegal Wildlife Trade: Overview. Retrieved from http://www.worldwildlife.org/threats/illegal-wildlife-trade.

80   Moloney, C.J. and Unnithan, P. [unpublished]. Reacting to Invasive Species: Moral Panic, Deviance and the Social Construction of Nature.

81   Traffic. 2015. Chinese TCM Industry Says No to Illegal Wildlife Trade. Retrieved from http://www.traffic.org/home/2015/10/15/chinese-tcm-industry-says-no-to-illegal-wildlife-trade.html.

82   Sheppard, K. 2012. Gibson Guitars and Feds Settle in Illegal Wood Case. *Mother Jones,* Aug. 7. Retrieved from http://www.motherjones.com/blue-marble/2012/08/gibson-and-feds-settle-illegal-wood-case.

83   Convention on International Trade in Endangered Species in Wild Flora and Fauna. 2016. Retrieved from https://www.cites.org/eng/disc/what.php.

84   Schnaiberg, A. 1980. *The Environment: From Surplus to Scarcity*. London, UK: Oxford University Press.

85   Buttel, F.H. 2004. The Treadmill of Production An Appreciation, Assessment, and Agenda for Research. *Organization & Environment* 17(3): 323–336.

86   Lynch, M.J. 2014. Treadmill of Production Theory. *The Green Criminology Monthly Blog*, Sept. 6. Retrieved from http://greencriminology.org/glossary/treadmill-of-production-theory/.

87   Jarrell, M.L. 2009. Environmental Crime and Injustice: Media Coverage of a Landmark Environmental Crime Case. *Southwestern Journal of Criminal Justice* 6(1): 25–44.

88   Ibid., p. 25

89   Natural Resource Management. 2009. Retreived from www.pactworld.org/cs/natural_resource_management http://www.pactworld.org/our-approach/nrm.

90   Social Science in Natural Resource Management. (n.d.) U.S. Geological Survey, U.S. Department of the Interior. Retrieved from http://www.nrs.fs.fed.us/units/socialscience/.

91   *Waste Research Strategy*. 1999. Washington, D.C. U.S. Environmental Protection Agency, Office of Research and Development.

92   U.S. Department of Justice, Environmental Crimes Section. 2016.

93   Environmental Crime: The Prosecution Gap. 2015. The Crime Reporter.

94   Ibid.

95   Ibid.

96   Kennedy, Robert F. Jr. 2004. *Crimes Against Nature*. New York: HarperCollins.

97   Summarized from: Moloney, C.J. and Chambliss, W.J. 2013. Slaughtering the Bison, Controlling Native Americans: A State Crime and Green Criminology Synthesis. *Critical Criminology* 22(3): 319–338.

CHAPTER OUTLINE

Technology and cybercrime

- What are the three primary ways that technology impacts modern crime?
- How is cybercrime defined?
- What are the major types of cybercrime that occur today?
- How are law enforcement agencies responding to and controlling cyber-crime?

KEY TERMS

cyberspace

hacktivism

cybercrime

computer crime

hackers

cyber deviance

networked
  devices

Internet

DARPA

ARPANET

intranets

computer
  intrusions

cyber vandalism

cybertheft

ransomware

identity theft

phishing

smishing

vishing

cyberbullying

online child
  pornography

sexploitation

National Center
  for Missing and
  Exploited
  Children

History professor Christopher Haas, 60, had achieved much in his academic life: full tenure at prestigious Villanova University, many publications, and strong ratings from students that had taken his courses. Thus, it came as quite a shock to Hass's colleagues and students when he was arrested on March 25, 2016, and charged with 415 counts of accessing online child pornography from a University computer.[1]

However, even more shocking was the revelation that the Department of Homeland Security had been investigating Dr. Haas since at least 2012, when they first learned of his involvement in online child porn and found over 400 explicit sexual images of children on his home computer. Unfortunately, online child pornography is not a rare cybercrime, nor is it the only form of serious criminal conduct that occurs in the virtual world of cyberspace. The purpose of this chapter is to introduce you to the topic of cybercrime and give you a general sense for its origins, characteristics, types and impacts as well as the efforts being taken to combat and control it.

TECHNOLOGY, CRIME, AND CRIME CONTROL

Technology is remaking what is possible for individuals and institutions and for the international order.

President Barack Obama, January 17, 2014

In 1878, Thomas Edison invented the aerophone—a new device capable of recording and playing back sounds at an amplified volume. Not long after Mr. Edison's invention, the following appeared in the *New York Times:*[2]

> Something ought to be done to Mr. Edison, and there is a growing conviction that it had better be done with a hemp rope. Mr. Edison has invented too many things, and almost without exception they are things of the most deleterious character ... The result will be the complete disorganization of society. Men and women will flee from civilization and seek in the silence of the forest relief from the roar of countless aerophones. Business, marriage, and all social amusements will be thrown aside, except by totally deaf men, and America will retrograde to the Stone Age with frightful rapidity ...

Whether the above opinion was authored in seriousness or in jest is hard to determine now, but it does hit upon a common theme: almost always when people have developed new technologies, there has been at least some segment of society that has feared their impact. Often, those fears have been voiced in reference to greater societal disorganization and increases in deviant and criminal behavior.

This is as true today as it has ever been. Just consider the societal response to video games or the Internet—both of which have been condemned as contributing to increases in deviant and violent criminal behavior, particularly among children.[3] While these fears may be overinflated, there is a factual basis for being concerned about the role technologies play in deviance, crime, and the crime control realm.

Technologies, including the Internet, are rapidly changing the landscape of crime and crime control (see Box 19.1 on the San Bernardino Mass Shooting). The technological and cyber realms are truly the new frontier of crime commission and control. Now, more than ever before in human history, advanced technologies, including those capable of connecting and communicating in cyberspace—the virtual realm where online interactions, transactions and communications occur—are pushing the boundaries of criminal behavior and our responses to it.

There are four primary ways that technology intersects with crime in today's world (see Figure 19.1).

First, today's technologies, particularly the internet, make it easier than ever before to commit criminal acts, including many new types of criminal behavior that never occurred before. As Marc Goodman, a terrorism and cyber-security

BOX 19.1: THE TENSION BETWEEN SECURITY AND PRIVACY

A small, state-run developmental disabilities service center in San Bernardino, California, seems an unlikely target for a terrorist attack.

Nevertheless, on December 2, 2015, during an annual training day and holiday party for the center's employees, Syed Rizwan Farook, a center employee, and his wife, Tashfeen Malik, arrived at the center and began shooting those in attendance, ultimately killing 14 people and injuring 17 more.[4] Farook and Malik fled in their SUV, only to be cornered later by San Bernardino police officers and SWAT team members. After a brief shoot out, both Farook and Malik were killed.

The story of the San Bernardino mass shooting did not end with the deaths of Farook and Malik, however, whom police and federal law enforcement officials learned were radicalized Islamic terrorists. During their search of the couple's belongings, police also recovered a county-issued iPhone used by Syed Farook. That iPhone has since become the subject of intense scrutiny and debate.

The FBI claimed it could not access the data contained on the iPhone without assistance from the phone's manufacturer, Apple,[5] because Apple installs hard-to-break encryption

Box 19.1 Image 1 *Police respond to the scene of an active shooting at the Inland Regional Center in San Bernardino, CA where 14 people were killed and 17 wounded. Two shooters, husband and wife, went on a calculated rampage using military style semi-automatic rifles and tactical vests. They were later killed in a shootout with police.*

Steven K. Doi/Zuma Press/PA Images

technology on its devices. Law enforcement officials filed a federal lawsuit to force Apple to provide them access to the encrypted phone. From the FBI's perspective, the iPhone might contain evidence of their crimes and, possibly, communications between the couple and other terrorists. Additionally, police believed the couple may have used the iPhone to upload a "lying dormant cyber pathogen" into the San Bernardino County computer system,[6] which could be used to access sensitive government information at a later date. Apple, Microsoft, Google, Facebook, and various civil liberties groups, strongly opposed the FBI's request, seeing it as a manipulative trick that would help the government commit its own cybercrimes, like spying on citizens. They also feared that providing government agencies with the "secret" to hacking the protected information on the San Bernardino iPhone would set a dangerous precedent for the future. A federal district court judge sided with the FBI, ordering Apple to assist in cracking the iPhone's encryption; however, before Apple complied, a mysterious "third party" came forward at the end of March 2016 to assist the FBI in breaking into the locked phone.[7] After successfully hacking the protected phone, the FBI dropped its current lawsuit against Apple. The issue is now about exactly *who* this third party is and *how* they managed to crack what most believed was a nearly unbreakable encryption technology.

At its core, the standoff between Apple and the United States government, which will surely continue to unfold into the future, is about finding a balance between the abstract concepts of national security and personal privacy. The San Bernardino/Apple case is a perfect example of the tension that exists all throughout our modern society between technology, freedom, crime, and crime control.

expert rhetorically asked, "When in human history has it ever been possible to steal from 100 million people at once?" The answer is, of course, never, until the Internet came along and made it possible for a single individual to hack private bank and personal accounts while sitting in the comfort of their own living room.

Second, new technologies are making it easier for law enforcement agencies to investigate and solve crimes as well as control criminal behavior. This dualism—where technology makes it easier to commit crime as well as control it—is critical for any student of criminology and criminal justice to understand. A few examples may help illustrate how technology is aiding the goal of crime control.

Washington, D.C., and several other major cities across America have purchased and installed high-powered microphones that can detect and pinpoint the location of gunfire to within several feet of its origin. In 2009, Washington, D.C., police learned of more than 9,000 gunfire incidents that were not officially reported.[8] These "shot-spotter" microphones have helped police respond more quickly to shooting situations and more efficiently direct their resources to areas prone to gun violence.

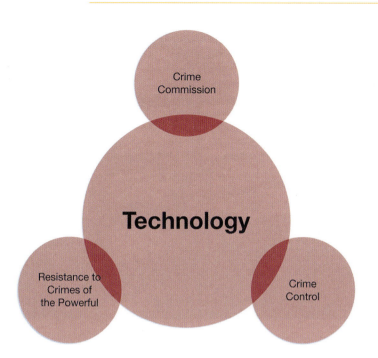

Figure 19.1
Three ways
technology impacts
crime in the 21st
century

Still other developments include the use by law enforcement of high-resolution CCTV cameras. Britain, for instance, employs about one CCTV camera for every 11 people, virtually covering every major intersection and public gathering place.[9] Surveillance drones[10] (see Box 19.2), mobile surveillance platforms, and real-time tactical operations centers similar to those found on modern battlefields in Iraq and Afghanistan are also gaining in popularity and use. Camden, New Jersey, invested in these technologies, as well as forward and backward scanning license plate readers, and witnessed a rapid reduction in drug-related and violent crime in the city.[11]

Lastly, a host of advanced technologies have made it easier to investigate crimes and crime scenes, making it harder than ever before for criminals to avoid detection and capture. These almost futuristic technologies include magnetic fingerprinting; 3D forensic facial reconstruction; retinal (i.e., eyeball) and thermal (i.e., body-heat) imaging scanners; and photographic systems that can reproduce 3D images of crime scenes, capture high-speed ballistics information, and even detect physical trauma like "bruising" before it is visible to the naked eye; advanced DNA testing equipment; and more.[12]

Finally, a third way technology intersects with crime in our modern society is by making it easier for ordinary citizens to resist the crimes of the powerful and police the police.

Groups like Anonymous and individuals like Edward Snowden have demonstrated that the power of technology can be leveraged to uncover what types of activities, including criminal ones, powerful organizations, including governments are engaged in (see Box 19.3). Technology has long been pivotal

Image 19.1
*Inside the real-time
Tactical Operations
Center of the
Camden County
Metro police in
Camden, N.J. The
New Jersey city near
Philadelphia relies on
high-tech gear to
police its dangerous,
crime prone streets
where drug sales and
use are rampant.
Many other cities
around the world are
adopting the types of
technologies used in
Camden.*

Mel Evans/AP/Press
Association Images

Image 19.2 *Video tape shot by George Holliday from
his apartment in a suburb of Los Angeles captured a
group of white LAPD and LA Sherriff's department
officers beating and kicking Rodney King following a
traffic stop on March 3, 1991. Black residents saw the
video as confirmation of the bias and abuse they had
long suffered at the hands of the mostly white police
officers patrolling Los Angeles. The subsequent
acquittal of the officers involved in the beating led to
the Los Angeles Riots of 1992. Increasingly, video
surveillance is playing a key role in uncovering the
crimes and abuses of those in power.*

George Holliday/AP/Press Association Images

in uncovering injustices committed by those in
power, particularly law enforcement positions,
against those they are entrusted with protecting.

For example, if not for the amateur video tape
that captured the beating of African American
Rodney King by four white LAPD and LA County
Sherriff's Department officers on March 3, 1991,
it is likely that the oppressive dynamic between
those law enforcement agencies and the minority
citizens of Los Angeles County would have
continued with little change. Thanks to the video,
however, national and international attention was
focused on the issue of police misconduct and
the excessive use of force. While the Rodney King
beating did not fix these problems, it helped
motivate discussion about them and instigate
policy reform.

More recently, Anthony Abbate Jr., a 265-
pound off-duty Chicago police officer, would
have escaped serious criminal prosecution for
viciously beating a 115-pound-female bartender
after she told him she could no longer serve him
drinks. However, a CCTV video that captured
Abbate's actions went public, and both Abbate

BOX 19.2: CONNECTING RESEARCH TO PRACTICE

The eye in the sky

In 2004, one of the biggest issues facing the United States was how to gain control over a chaotic and violent environment in Iraq. Suicide, car, and roadside bombs were detonating with increasing frequency, killing both civilians and U.S. troops. Researchers and engineers employed by the United States Air Force began thinking about how to address this problem.

Their solution: an airborne photographic camera system capable of taking high resolution images of an entire city, even one as large as 30 square miles or more. The camera system, dubbed "Project Angel Fire" was so powerful, in fact, that it could take one photograph per second, every second, for an entire day. Those digital images, which an analyst could zoom in on far enough to pick out a single car or motorcycle, would then be transmitted to and downloaded at a command center.

If a hidden roadside bomb exploded at 9:30 a.m. at the intersection of Alpha and Charlie streets in the city of Fallujah, Iraq, the camera system would capture the exact moment of the explosion. More importantly, because the system was taking one photo per second, a trained analyst could, figuratively, engage in time travel. They could begin at the exact moment of the explosion and work backward—one second and one image at a time—to see who was last at the scene where the bomb exploded, what vehicle did they arrive in, where did the vehicle come from and, importantly, where did the vehicle go afterward? This information could be sent to U.S. troops, who could use it to track down and capture the suspect bombers and others involved. Project Angel Fire significantly reduced the number of bombings and bombing casualties in Iraq and helped U.S. troops control the country.

Fast forward six years. Project Angel Fire has moved from the military realm to the civilian world. Persistent Surveillance Systems (PSS), based in Ohio, now manufactures and markets even more powerful 190+ megapixel airborne camera surveillance systems based on the original Angel Fire design and can track vehicles and people. The hope of PSS is that their technology will be adopted by law enforcement agencies; they tout its crime fighting effectiveness and ability to assist investigators.

The PSS system was effectively used in Dayton, Ohio, and Juarez, Mexico, to fight crime. In Juarez, a city just across the border from the U.S. riddled with drug crime and violence, PSS employed their "hawk-eye" camera to locate and capture Mexican drug cartel members who assassinated a local female police officer.

The "eye in the sky"[13] technology isn't without critics, however. Who decides what information is recorded? Can the technology be used to track anyone, like a cheating spouse? Who decides and who monitors this powerful tool? Ultimately, these questions are just a few of many that must be resolved before this sort of powerful crime-fighting surveillance technology can be put into wide practice in the United States.

BOX 19.3: CRIME IN GLOBAL PERSPECTIVE

Anonymous, Edward Snowden, and technological transparency

Hacktivism, using computer hacking capabilities and the platform of the Internet to engage in activism about economic, social, and political issues, is a new 21st-century phenomenon; in fact, dictionaries pre-2001 wouldn't even have contained the word. Hacktivism, however, is quickly becoming a powerful tool and method for raising awareness about certain events and issues; it is a modern method of leveraging cyber technology to produce greater transparency in the world.

Groups like Anonymous, for example, an online collective of computer-savvy hackers, takes pride in engaging in hacktivism, often targeting governments and individuals they view as corrupt or disingenuous. Anonymous has focused its efforts against the Motion Picture Association of America; the local prosecutors and law enforcement in Steubenville, Ohio; Facebook; the NSA; the KKK; and more.

Individuals have also gotten into the hacktivism game. The most notable case is that of Edward Snowden. Snowden formerly worked for the CIA. Later he became a private computer professional, contracted to work for Dell and Booz Allen Hamilton, both of which had contracts with the National Security Agency. It was while working on behalf of the National Security Agency that Snowden learned of that agency's covert domestic surveillance and spying program. He secretly copied tens of thousands of sensitive and classified files and then fled the United States. He divulged many of the files to journalists, who subsequently brought the issues of NSA domestic spying on American citizens to the public's attention. It should be noted that the NSA domestic spying program was both unconstitutional and illegal.

At first glance, hacktivism might not seem like such a negative thing. Clearly, it is important for powerful organizations and governments to be kept in check. Committing crimes against your own citizens and exploiting your power to oppress or exploit people are bad things. At the same time, hacktivism is, by definition, illegal. The members of Anonymous and people like Edward Snowden have all violated multiple criminal laws—from online theft to espionage—in carrying out their hacktivism agendas. The question is: should we view them as criminals?

The broader issue here is who gets to define what is criminal? Policing and prosecuting hacktivism may be in the best interests of governments and corporations, but is it in the best interests of the people? There are no clear or black-and-white answers to these questions. Each person has to decide for themselves where they stand with regard to hacktivism and its illegality.

What do you think?

and the City of Chicago were held accountable, with Abbate being fired and criminally prosecuted. Most notable in the Abbate case is the fact that Chicago police officers initially tried to cover up for Abbate, by ignoring the existence of the video tape and refusing to mention that Abbate was a police officer in their crime incident report.

Lastly, another case that strikes close to home for college students involves former University of Maryland undergraduate John McKenna. Along with thousands of other students, McKenna spilled onto U.S. Route 1 to celebrate following a UMD upset victory over Duke in men's basketball. CCTV footage shows the moment when McKenna approached several officers on horseback and was then rushed and beaten by five uniformed Prince George's County police officers. Before video of his unprovoked beating surfaced, McKenna was charged with resisting arrest, assaulting a police officer, and more.

Image 19.3 CCTV video was vital in proving that off-duty Chicago police officer Anthony Abbate Jr. beat and injured a female bartender after she refused to serve him with more drinks in 2007. Without the video, the police cover-up of the crime would likely have been successful.

AP Photo/Ekl Williams PLLC via Fox News Chicago

WHAT IS CYBERCRIME?

> *We are building our lives around our wired and wireless networks. The question is, are we ready to work together to defend them?*
> FBI Cyber crime web page,
> 2016

Within the fields of criminology and criminal justice, the study, investigation, and prosecution of cybercrime represents the cutting edge. A **cybercrime**, also sometimes called a cyber-enabled,[14] high-tech, or network crime,[15] occurs when an individual utilizes the Internet to engage in any behavior or activity that violates a local, state, federal, or international criminal law. Often, a person committing a cybercrime does so by using a computer, thus committing a **computer crime** as well. However today it's fairly easy to access the Internet through cell phones and even electronic gaming systems.

Image 19.4 University of Maryland student John McKenna was initially charged with several crimes, including assaulting a police officer and resisting arrest, until video surfaced showing that police committed an unprovoked attack against him.
In the video, McKenna is seen being thrown against a concrete wall, before being beaten and kicked by police. Had the video not surfaced, it is likely that he would have been convicted of his alleged crimes and the officers would have escaped any penalties.

Roberts and Wood, *The Washington Post*

As a result, the concept of computer crime, with its limited meaning, is fading in use. While not always true, many cybercrimes—especially theft and vandalism—are committed by hackers, individuals who secretly and without authorization access computer systems or networks.

Cybercrime is a more specific category than cyber deviance, which entails using the Internet or a networked device to engage in behavior or activities that, while not criminal, might be considered offensive, abnormal, or strange. Pretty much any behavior or activity could be considered deviant to someone or some group, thus the category of cyber deviance is very large. Examples of things that might commonly fall under the heading of cyber deviance include many sexual behaviors like using online pornography, "sexting," and advertising sexual services for sale, joining a subculture like NAMBLA (the North American Man Boy Love Association), and more. It is important to remember the basic rule that applies to any discussion of crime v. deviance: most crime is considered deviant, but not all deviance is considered criminal.

THE EVOLUTION OF CYBERCRIME

Modern cybercrime owes its origins to the creation of two technologies: computers and the Internet.

Early computers, like the University of Pennsylvania's Electrical Numerical Integrator and Calculator (ENIAC) machine, were cumbersome, had limited functionality, and were difficult to use by anyone except the most patient, highly trained, and intelligent individuals. The ENIAC machine, for example, took up 1,800 square feet of space and generated just as much heat per hour as would result from cramming 1,200 people into a room! However, despite its size, ENIAC could only perform very simple mathematical calculations and its primary role was to calculate ranges and trajectories for artillery shells.[16] By the 1960s, computers had grown smaller, more powerful, easier to use, and more commonplace in industrial, government, and corporate settings, but not within the home. It wasn't until the late 1970s that "personal computers." which we all know and enjoy using today, hit the market with the introduction of the Apple II personal computer.

Today, computers and computer technology are ubiquitous and vital to the functioning of everything from business and industry to government, healthcare, education, and personal life. Our lives revolve around computers. Just consider how many things you use or depend upon each day that require computing technology to function: cellphones, tablets, laptops, desktops, and gaming systems, not to mention calculators, vehicles, traffic lights, industrial equipment, and more. Indeed, it isn't just that we depend upon computer devices, but also that we depend on the fact that these devices will be able to communicate with each.

A **networked device** is one that is connected to other devices and able to communicate with them (i.e., share information back and forth). This communication is made possible by the Internet.

In 1995, the Federal Networking Council officially defined the "**Internet**" as a "global information system . . . that is logically linked together by a unique Internet Protocol (IP) address . . . and able to support communications and provide, use or make accessible . . . high level services."[17] With the rise of the modern Internet in the 1990s, our lives changed forever, and so too did the nature of crime.

However, the Internet has a history that goes back well before the 1990s to the late 1950s and early 1960s, when scientists, including J.C.R. Licklider, Ivan Sutherland, Bob Taylor, Lawrence G. Roberts, and Leonard Kleinrock, began conceptualizing a "globally interconnected set of computers" capable of communicating with each other. Many of these scientists worked for the United States military technology research and development organization known as **DARPA**— Defense Advanced Research Projects Agency, as well as universities like MIT and UCLA, and the RAND group. Together, researchers from these agencies and institutions succeeded in building what many consider the earliest version of the modern Internet in 1969, which they called the **ARPANET** (Advanced Research Projects Agency Network).

Like computers, the Internet has come a long way since its first incarnation in the 1960s.

U.S. Army Photo, http://ftp.arl.army.mil/~mike/comphist/

Mary Evans/Interfoto

Image 19.5 The invention and evolution of computers, from huge, simple machines to highly portable, incredibly powerful devices, has altered the criminological landscape in multiple ways. Computers, particularly networked ones, now allow new crimes to be committed without regard to physical proximity of victim and offender. They also provide a powerful tool for combatting crimes and maintaining crime statistics which can be used to strategically utilize law enforcement resources.

iStock/gece33

Table 19.1 Timeline of major events in cybercrime history 1971–2001

Year	Event
1971	"Captain Crunch" phone phreaker John Draper uses a cereal box whistle to make free calls in an act of wire fraud.
1973	Bank teller at New York Dime Savings Bank uses a business computer to embezzle $2 million.
1978	The first electronic bulletin board (BBS) is created allowing for virtual communication, especially among hackers.
1981	Ian Murphy, also known as "Captain Zap" becomes the first person convicted of a felony for "computer crime" after he unlawfully hacks into AT&T's computer system.
1982	One of the first intentionally created computer viruses, "Elk Cloner," is written and targets the Apple II computer system.
1983	Hollywood creates its first big-budget movie focusing on computers, the Internet, and crime, "War Games." The film also presents much of the American public with its first introduction to the phenomena known as "hacking."
1986	The U.S. Congress passes the Computer Fraud and Abuse Act after numerous hacks and break-ins into government computers. It criminalizes the actions of adults only, however.
1987	The first Computer Emergency Response Team, CERT, is created at Carnegie Mellon University. Its job is to help deal with computer security incidents, especially the creation of viruses and malware.
1988	High profile investigations and prosecutions of computer and cybercrimes begin. Three individuals, Kevin Mitnick, Kevin Poulsen, and Robert T. Morris, Jr. are indicted in separate computer/cybercrime events. Morris Jr. is the most high-profile case. As a Cornell University grad student, Morris Jr. launches the "Morris Worm," a self-replicating virus into ARPA-NEt that spreads to over 6,000 networked computers. Also, the 1st National Bank of Chicago has over $70 million in funds stolen electronically.
1989	First computer extortion case investigated.
1993	1st ever hacker conference held in Las Vegas, NV.
1994	Hacker's and hacker groups (i.e., "collectives") begin communicating extensively via the "world wide web" and not electronic bulletin boards (BBSs).
1995	Hollywood releases the movies "The Net" and "Hackers," both of which focus on cybercrime.
1996	U.S. Government Accounting Office reports that hackers attempted to break into Defense Dept. computer files 250,000 times in 1995 and were successful 65% of the time. CIA Director John Deutsh testifies before Congress that foreign organized crime groups are leading cyber attacks and intrusions against American government agencies and businesses.
1997	Amidst rising levels of computer hacking, fraud and theft, the FBI issues a report from its newly formed Computer Crimes Squad noting that 85% of American companies are "hacked" but do not know it.
1999	"Melissa" virus is written and released by David Smith. This virus is the most costly ever. Smith's subsequent prosecution marks the first time someone is prosecuted for creating and releasing a computer virus.
2000	Major companies like Yahoo, Amazon, Ebay, and more are hit by DoS (denial of service) cyber attacks.
2001	Popular music and video file sharing site NAPSTER shuts down after lawsuits are filed by musical acts like Metallica. The September 11th terror attacks in the U.S. result in creation of the U.S.A. PATRIOT Act, which allows law enforcement to target computer hackers and cyber criminals more harshly and reframe some as cyber "terrorists."

Source: Adapted from Wave-front Consulting Group, A Brief History of Cybercrime.

It is faster and easier to access than ever before. All but the most isolated communities are now, to some degree, dependent on the Internet for everything from engaging in global finance, managing traffic, and distributing electrical power, to personal banking, entertainment, travel, news, and even carrying out basic tasks like purchasing groceries, talking to friends, and receiving healthcare. Most businesses and organizations make use of both the public Internet to carry out their affairs as well as non-public networks called "intranets" where internal communications and other information is stored.

The rise of computers and the Internet has significantly impacted our lives in many positive ways. (Who doesn't like relaxing and watching your favorite show on Netflix or ordering take out online?) However, with the good also comes the bad—cybercrime is a natural outgrowth of our increasing reliance and use of computers and the Internet.

CHARACTERISTICS OF CYBERCRIME

The FBI's Internet Crime Complaint Center (IC3) was started in May 2000, with the goal of collecting better data on cybercrimes. The IC3 depends upon cybercrime victims to self-report their victimization. In 2014, over 269,000 such complaints were filed,[18] and the IC3 has collected more than 3.1 million internet related crime complaints from U.S. citizens since 2001.[19] However, the FBI estimates that only 15 percent of all Internet crime victims ever report their victimization to law enforcement and that less than 10 percent report anything to the Internet Crime Complaint Center.[20] Thus, IC3 data on cybercrime provide us only a glimpse of a very small fraction of all cybercrime that occurs in the U.S. Just as our official data on violent and property crimes is limited (see chapter 3), so too is our data on cybercrime. As a result, the "dark figure" of cybercrime—how much actually occurs—is unknown.

Given that the United Nations has reported that as many as 14 adults become cybercrime victims every second—about 1 million per day,[21] we can conclude that cybercrime is a massive global problem occurring with a frequency that is hard to fathom! Thus, one of the most important characteristics of modern cybercrime (see Figure 19.2) is this: traditional violent and property crime rates in the U.S. are consistently decreasing, but cybercrime rates are rapidly increasing as more and more criminal conduct shifts to the cyber realm.

Another defining characteristic of cybercrime is that cybercrimes produce a huge amount of financial harm. Estimates of the financial losses resulting from the commission of cybercrimes are staggering. In the U.S. alone, the cost of cybercrime in 2014 is estimated to have exceeded $800 million,[22] while the global cost of cybercrime is likely in excess of $1 trillion per year.[23,24]

Cybercrimes, like traditional street and property crimes, also occur along a wide, diverse spectrum of sophistication and harm. Just as there are significant differences between liquor store robbers and high-end jewel thieves, so too are there differences between cyber criminals. Hacking into government servers or financial institutions, for example, requires a significant degree of sophistication and technological savvy. Posting a false ad on Craigslist or engaging in cyberbullying, however, require only technological competence and an Internet connection. Likewise, while crimes on the streets produce many types of harms, those harms are not all equivalent: theft of a slice of pizza is far less harmful than aggravated rape. This logic holds true in cyberspace as well. The harm from Internet-facilitated murder is far more notable than the harm from planting a malware program inside a single computer.

Cybercrime today is expanding and diversifying so fast that law enforcement is struggling to combat and control it. Laws, which form the foundations of law enforcement activities, lag behind cybercrimes and new types of cybercrime arise more quickly than new laws that can criminalize and control them. Consider also that traditional crimes possess a real physical component (e.g., a specific neighborhood, type of business, address, etc.). They are fairly easy for police to respond to and we have become pretty good at creating strategies to control them.

For example, shootings or robberies may yield actual physical evidence that can be easily collected at a pace that suits law enforcement and then used as the basis for a subsequent prosecution. Likewise, if you're worried about someone driving a car bomb up to a sensitive government facility, you can install concrete barriers, divert traffic, utilize bomb detection equipment, and specially trained explosive detecting dogs and deter that form of criminal behavior pretty well. But, the connection between cybercrimes and the physical world are tenuous; they occur in a virtual world, which seriously alters how law enforcement agents can respond to and investigate them, how and what types of evidence we can collect, and even alters the characteristics of the offenders who commit them. All of these factors give cybercrime and cyber criminals the advantage over legal systems and law enforcement officers whose mission is to combat and control them.

Lastly, one of the most important characteristics of cybercrime is that it is increasingly international. In fact, it is so easy for someone in, say, Ukraine, to commit a cybercrime against a business based in Argentina that this pattern of offending has become the rule, rather than the exception to it. According to a United Nations Office of Drugs and Crime Report, more than half of all cybercrime incidents today have an "international dimension"[25] to them, a trend first predicted in 1979 by Interpol, the international police agency based in France.[26] This trend has serious implications for how we respond to cybercrime and negatively impacts our abilities to control it.

As cybercrime is becoming an offense that knows no borders, it is also increasingly being committed by transnational organized crime groups and collectives of cybercriminals.[27] The United Nations estimates that 80 percent or more of cybercrimes originate from an "organized activity" among a group of offenders.[28] These organized cybercrime groups are capable of committing crimes on a massive scale. Over a two year period (2013–2015) an organized group of cybercriminals drawn from around the world—Russia, Eastern Europe,

Figure 19.2
Primary characteristics of cybercrime

China—stole approximately $1 billion from more than 100 banks located in 30 countries, including Japan, Switzerland, and the United States.[29] Organized cybercrime groups see great opportunities for profit by engaging in cybercrimes and they are leveraging their resources to commit crimes within the virtual space of the Internet. They may commit these offenses for profit or to generate profits that can be used to fund more traditional criminal activities that have a real physical dimension, like drug or weapons trafficking. Other cybercriminals and crime groups may engage in offending as a form of "resistance," or political protest, against the policies or practices of a government or organization.

VARIETIES OF CYBERCRIME

Computer intrusions

The Federal Bureau of Investigations has characterized computer intrusions— which entail the unauthorized access to a computer or network for any purpose—as the "21st-century form of burglary" and has listed this cybercrime as one of their top law enforcement priorities. In 2014, the FBI issued a statement that read in part:

> Every day, criminals are invading countless homes and offices across the nation—not by breaking down windows and doors, but by breaking into laptops, personal computers, and wireless devices via hacks and bits of malicious code.

Those entities committing computer intrusions, "hackers," are diverse, as are their motivations for doing so. Certainly, individuals access information stored on computers and networks all the time without permission. These are the "hackers" we think of so often and see depicted in TV shows and movies. However, increasingly businesses, organized crime rings, governments, and terrorist organizations are unlawfully entering computers and computer networks for unlawful purposes. They may want to steal patent information, a secret recipe, sensitive government information or secrets, or personal information that can be sold on the black market.

In response, the FBI has formed 54 Cyber Crime Divisions along with smaller Cyber Crime Squads and rapid response "Action Teams" to deal with computer intrusions as they occur. Likewise, agencies like the NSA, CIA and international organizations like Interpol and Europol have begun working together, forming large cybercrime taskforces as policing computer intrusions has become a bigger and bigger global law enforcement priority.

One reason for the high level of attention paid to computer intrusions is national security. Governments fear that criminals and criminal networks exploit the Internet and computer technologies to gain access to sensitive and secret government information. Another reason computer intrusions attract so much attention is because many hackers commit cyber vandalism. **Cyber vandalism** takes many forms, but could include defacing a website or altering its content or planting a computer virus, worm, bot, spyware, or malware into a computer system[30] (see Box 19.4).

According to an official Bureau of Justice Statistics survey of over 7,000 businesses, more than two-thirds reported a cyber intrusion incident in a one-year period; many were not aware of the intrusion until well after the fact, even when money or information was stolen.[31] It is likely that the number of known computer intrusions underestimates the actual extent of the problem and the financial losses from these acts, which total well into the billions of dollars each year.[32]

Identity and cybertheft

In February 2016, an unknown hacker or group of hackers secretly broke into the Central Bank of Bangladesh and electronically stole $81 million dollars.[33] The sophisticated **cybertheft**—unlawfully obtaining personal or financial information, goods or services via the Internet or a networked device—took

BOX 19.4: RANSOMWARE

Imagine that you open your laptop to send an email, but the screen stays black. Then, a cryptic message appears: "pay us if you ever want to see your files again." What would you do? Where would you turn for help?

One of newest forms of cybercrime, and an increasingly prevalent one, is called "ransomware."[34] It is the cyber equivalent of kidnapping a person and demanding a ransom, except that instead of a person, the thing taken is your computer hard drive and all your files, documents, and photos. This awful form of online criminal conduct is impacting individuals and, especially, institutions and organizations, and it has grown in frequency in recent years.

How does it work? First, hackers illegally gain access to a computer or a computer network; they then implant a malicious code that paralyzes the system and locks out everyone accept for them—this means anything on the computer is inaccessible. After taking control, the hackers will demand a ransom, often in an untraceable online currency like Bitcoin, and they will deliver an ultimatum: either pay us what we ask or we will destroy your files and you will never see them again.

School districts, hospitals, companies, and individuals have been targeted and, generally speaking, they have been left with no alternative but to give in to the hacker's demands. For example, Hollywood Presbyterian Hospital in Los Angeles paid $17,000 in ransom to gain back control of their computer system, which contained important patient and doctor records; Horry School District in South Carolina paid $10,000 to free its computers, and so on. In 2015, the FBI got over 2,000 ransomware complaints, which cost victims nearly $25 million.

Worse still, this form of cybercrime is proving incredibly difficult for law enforcement to police or control. There is simply no effective way for police or the FBI to provide assistance if a system is taken over and ransomed; with a few commands the hackers can destroy thousands of important files, far more quickly than law enforcement could act to apprehend them. Basically, the role of law enforcement is entirely reactive, with investigators relegated to chasing down criminals within a vast virtual world *after* such criminals have received payments from their victims.

place despite multiple safeguards to prevent such an occurrence. In the modern age of cybercrime, cyberthefts like that against Bangladesh's Central Bank are growing more and more common, even as advances are made to protect financial and other sensitive information. For example, SONY Pictures Studios, Target, Anthem Health Insurance, and many more corporations and organizations have been the victims of large scale cyberthefts in just the last few years (see Table 19.2).

Particularly common targets of cyberthefts are financial institutions, including banks, credit card companies, and market trading houses. However, any institution or organization with funds stored in bank accounts accessible through networks or the Internet are susceptible to theft. This includes trucking

Table 19.2 Recent high profile cyberthefts

Anthem Health Insurance	In February 2015, hackers breached the Anthem Health Insurance firewall. Sensitive identifying information (social security numbers, birth dates, medical ID numbers, etc.) for over 80 million Anthem health insurance subscribers was illegally accessed and likely sold on the online black marketplace.
Central Bank of Bangladesh	An unknown hacker or group of hackers operating from the Philippines stole more than $80 million in funds in 2016.
Target Corporation	Hackers breached superstore chain Target's credit and debit card transaction information in December 2013. The credit and debit card information for 40 million consumers was stolen; this stolen information was sold for around $27 per card on the black market.
SONY Motion Pictures Studios	SONY made a film called *The Interview*, about North Korean leader Kim Jong Il. Not long after, a group hacked the studio's private email accounts, obtaining private information about upcoming projects, and sensitive information about employees, contracts, and more.
SONY Playstation Network	The SONY Playstation Network (PSN) allows users of Sony devices to play games online against others and access other online content including movies, television, and more. In April 2011, 56 million SONY PSN subscribers had their sensitive account and credit card information stolen in a cybertheft that likely netted the thieves more than $53 million.

companies, corporations big and small, and towns and cities. Even school districts are victims, such as in New York, where one school district had $3 million stolen from its account by a cyber thief.[35] FBI Cyber Division Assistant Director Gordon M. Snow explains the basic process whereby cybercriminals steal millions of dollars each year from unsuspecting victims:

> The attack vector is usually an e-mail that contains either an infected file or a link to an infected website. The e-mail recipient is generally a person within a targeted company who can initiate fund transfers on behalf of the business or another valid online banking credential account holder. Once the recipient opens the attachment or navigates to the website, malware is installed on the user's computer, which often includes a keylogging program that harvests the user's online banking credentials. The criminal then either creates another account or directly initiates a funds transfer masquerading as the legitimate user. The stolen funds are often then transferred overseas.

Identity theft is a sub-type of cybertheft and occurs when someone unlawfully obtains another's personal information and uses it to commit theft or fraud.[36] Personal information could be anything from birthdates and social security numbers, to account numbers, PINs, addresses, passport numbers, death certificates, and even fingerprints. Today, many identity theft crimes originate in cyberspace. Hackers may breach e-mail accounts, computer hard drives, credit card agencies, or any number of other networked deviances or services to steal someone's identifying information.

Additionally, today's cyber criminals frequently utilize phishing, smishing, or vishing[37] scams to steal personal information. The difference between the three is that phishing scams generally target computers, while smishing and vishing scams target mobile phones. In all three instances, cyber criminals send out deceptive messages, via e-mails, phone calls, voicemails, and text messages. Regardless of how they arrive, these messages often claim that your bank account has experienced some suspicious activity. They then direct you to respond by writing or calling back or visiting a website, where you'll be asked to provide sensitive personal information, which is used to steal your money or identity.

The extent of cyber and identity theft is hard to measure accurately because many people may not even be aware their information has been stolen in the first place. Indeed, one of the authors of this textbook received a letter from the United States government informing them that their sensitive information, contained in a job application they filled out eight years earlier, might have been breached by hackers. What data we do have indicate that identity theft is a rapidly growing problem as more and more people store sensitive information on vulnerable public and private networks. In 2014, more than 17 million people were victims of identity theft in the U.S. alone, according to data from the National Crime Victimization Survey.

One the gravest concerns of law enforcement, especially national and international law enforcement agencies like the FBI and Interpol, is that stolen personal information may be used to provide false identities and a "powerful cloak of anonymity"[38] to terrorists intent on causing harm to large numbers of people. While the FBI has successfully prosecuted more than 1,600 cyber and identity theft cases since 2008,[39] their efforts have hardly made a dent in the problem, since many people and businesses never know, or only realize too late, that they have become a victim of this type of cybercrime.

Cyberbullying, harassment, stalking, and exploitation

When 18-year-old Rutgers University freshman Tyler Clementi leapt to his death from the George Washington Bridge connecting New Jersey and New York, his family, friends, and classmates were shocked. What could have caused a vibrant young man with no history of significant mental health issues to commit suicide?

An investigation by police eventually revealed that Tyler Clementi's death was the tragic result of the bullying and harassment he encountered at Rutgers University. However, Tyler's case was not of the typical "face-to-face" bullying that often occurs at school; in fact, Tyler's victimization was made possible thanks to computer technologies and the Internet.

As a freshman at Rutgers, Tyler shared a room with another boy named Dharun Ravi. One night, Tyler asked to have the room to himself in order to have a date come over and Dharun agreed to give him some privacy.[40] What Tyler did not know is that Dharun Ravi made plans to secretly record Tyler's activities using his computer's webcam.[41] That camera recorded Tyler having

Image 19.6 Former Rutgers University student Dharun Ravi was found guilty of hate crimes for using a webcam to spy on his roommate Tyler Clementi, who was gay, during the latter's date with another man in their shared dorm room. Ravi sent this video to other students on campus. Clementi later committed suicide as a result. Technology has changed how people interact, for good and bad, and it is now the role of law enforcement and the legal profession to invasions of privacy, cyberbullying, harassment, and stalking that occur via computers and the Internet.

John Munson/AP/Press Association Images

a sexual encounter with another man. Ravi invited other Rutgers students to view the video of Tyler.[42] Soon, Tyler had become the subject of mean jokes, ridicule, and more on social media sites like Twitter and Facebook.[43]

Tyler's homosexuality was not widely known; his personal sexual and romantic preferences were his to share at his discretion and he certainly never intended to have his personal life broadcast for everyone to see. Worse still, after learning that his sexual encounter had been captured on video and shared on the web, Tyler learned that Ravi and another Rutgers student, Molly Wei, had made plans to record him a second time when his date was going to come over. Feeling alienated from his classmates, without friends he could turn to, embarrassed, and in despair, Tyler made the decision to end his own life.

The Tyler Clementi case is used by many educators and law enforcement professionals as an example of just how serious **cyberbullying**, stalking, harassment, and exploitation can be. While Ravi and Wei were both prosecuted criminally for their actions, this hardly lessened the pain experienced by Tyler's family and friends, and, of course, it could not undo his death.

From a research standpoint, the cybercrimes of bullying, stalking, harassment, and exploitation exemplify how traditional forms of criminal behavior have made the transition to the cyber realm.[44,45,46] In the case of cyberbullying and online harassment, research indicates that people who are bullied face-to-face are likely to be the same people bullied online. Likewise, the impacts of cyberbullying are equal to, if not worse than, those associated with traditional bullying—anger, frustration, depression, self-harm, and suicide. What often makes cyberbullying and harassment worse is the fact that so much of our social lives take place online and public comments, videos, and photos all become permanent fixtures of cyberspace.

The internet and computer technologies make it easier to stalk, harass, and exploit people because so much personal information—from social media accounts to phone numbers and addresses are stored online, not to mention photographs. Celebrities and famous people are often the targets of criminal hackers, as the hack of thousands of Apple iCloud accounts in 2014 demonstrated. In that "Celeb-gate" case, personal photos, including nude and intimate ones, of many celebrities were stolen and shared via the Internet.[47]

In some cases, the Internet is used to facilitate even more heinous crimes, especially those involving the sexual exploitation of men, women, and children. **Online child pornography** and "**sexploitation**"—the sexual exploitation of children and adults—are serious state and federal crimes that are, unfortunately, far too common today.

Since first becoming aware of the role that computers and the Internet play in the enabling the sexual exploitation of children in 1993, the FBI, along with state and local law enforcement agencies, have become particularly concerned with this issue. Since beginning the task in 2002, the National Center for Missing and Exploited Children's Child Victim Identification Program has analyzed more than 139 million online images and videos depicting children and minors in illegal sexual activities[48] in an effort to identify them and any suspects. Child pornography is traded among child porn users like trading cards and the Internet is key to this process of file-sharing and exploitation. Unfortunately, the more law enforcement focuses its efforts on combating this form of crime, the more we learn about just how significant a problem it is.

For example, between 2004–08, state and local law enforcement reported a 230 percent increase in complaints about people trying to entice or lure children into meetings or sexual activities online and a more than 1,000 percent increase in the number of complaints about child sex trafficking—a form of modern day sexual slavery. As Table 19.3 shows, this form of cybercrime is truly global in its scope.

Table 19.3 Recent examples of major internet child pornography cases

Case or suspect (individual or organization)	Case description
Papal Ambassador and Archbishop Josef Wesolowski—Vatican City, Rome[49]	In 2015, Josef Wesolowski, a high-ranking member of the Catholic Church, was found in possession of over 100,000 images of child pornography. The images were stored on his laptop. He was also implicated with child sex pornography and sex offenses in the Dominican Republic, where he spent much time working on behalf of the Roman Catholic Church. He died, aged 66, in Rome before he could be prosecuted. Also charged and awaiting trial is Wesolowski's assistant, Deacon Javier Occi Reyes, who found children and participated in their sexploitation on behalf of Wesolowski.
Jared Fogle—"Subway Jared"[50]	Jared Fogle, the TV personality and pitch-man for fast-food sandwich chain Subway, was arrested and charged with receiving child pornography and traveling to engage in sexual conduct with a minor. He plead guilty in November 2015 and received a fifteen year prison sentence.
Patricia and Matthew Ayers[51]	This husband and wife criminal team were sentenced to 2,340 years in prison for producing and trading pornographic images of a child in their care.
Operation Cross Country[52]	A June 2014 U.S. child porn investigation involving Federal, state, and local law enforcement agencies that targeted the pimps and suspects involved in child sex trafficking and online child pornography. Over 168 children were rescued and 281 pimps arrested.
Operation Rescue[53]	A 2011 EUROPOL (European Police Agency) investigation into online child pornography and sex trafficking rings yielded more than 670 arrests in 13 countries and resulted in the rescue of 230 children. The global sex trafficking ring was believed to have more than 70,000 members. Those arrested included teachers, police officers, youth camp employees, and more.

Illicit goods and black markets

In the early 1990s, U.S. government researchers were posed with a problem: how could they help spies, foreign dissidents, and others communicate safely and secretly with their government handlers at the FBI, CIA, NSA, and other agencies? Their eventual solution to this problem was a device called **TOR—The Onion Router**—which made it possible in the early 2000s for users to cloak their identity and location and communicate through the Internet in secret. Essentially, the TOR device adds layers of anonymity and secrecy to a user's identity and location (i.e., the layers of an "onion") by disguising their unique Internet address and bouncing their location around to various places in the globe. This makes it virtually impossible to uncover the true location or identity of a person using the TOR device.

TOR quickly became a public technology by the early 2000s. Today anyone can download a TOR browser and use it to cloak their Internet usage. Most importantly, the TOR technology also allows access to what is called the "Deep Web" or darknet.

The **Deep Web** or **darknet** has been described as the "vast ocean of hidden websites."[54] That is, what most of us consider the "Internet" or world wide web—Google, Yahoo, Facebook, news, business, and shopping websites—actually represents just a tiny fraction of the actual Internet universe, perhaps 1 percent or less. The other 98 or 99 percent of Internet content and websites—tens of trillions of them—lie beyond our grasp in the Deep Web. Unless, of course, you have TOR (see Figure 19.3).

Many of the hidden websites in the Deep Web are business, University, or organizational intranets of little interest to anyone other than a hacker. However, also contained within the Deep Web are thousands of websites, internet message boards, and forums where illegal goods and services are bought, sold, and traded, and where illegally obtained or produced content, like child pornography, is stored and shared. In essence, thanks to TOR, the Deep Web has gone from being a place where secret government communications can occur, to a sprawling, diverse, virtual, illegal marketplace—quite possibly the modern world's largest criminal black market.

From a research, and even a law enforcement, perspective, we know very little about the Deep Web or the illegal and criminal activities that occur within it. However, what we do know is disturbing.

In 2013, FBI agents arrested a 29-year-old man named Ross Ulbricht after a lengthy and complicated criminal investigation. Federal prosecutors charged Mr. Ulbricht with running the "most sophisticated and extensive criminal marketplace on the Internet."[55] That marketplace was named the **Silk Road**.

The Silk Road has been described as a massive illegal version of commerce websites like Amazon, e-Bay, and Craigslist.[56] Users accessing the Silk Road through their TOR devices could purchase drugs, including cocaine, MDMA (ecstasy), heroin, marijuana, and more from sellers around the world.[57] They could buy fake IDs, including driver's licenses, passports, and social security

Figure 19.3 Most people are only familiar with the surface web—the common news, social media, commerce, and shopping websites that are easily accessible and frequently used. However, like an iceberg, the bulk of content on the Internet is invisible, lying hidden just below the surface in what is called the deep, dark web. It takes a special internet browser called TOR to access the deep, dark web which contains, among other things, illicit message and file sharing boards, and more.

Image 19.7 In this courtroom drawing, defendant Ross William Ulbricht, center foreground, is seated at the defense table along with his attorneys during opening arguments at his criminal trial in New York in 2015. The 30-year-old was found guilty on numerous charges including narcotics trafficking, computer hacking, and money laundering in connection with the online marketplace he created on the Deep Web.

Elizabeth Williams/AP/Press Association Images

Image 19.8 A 28-gram portion of speed is shown on sale on the screenshot of the illegal internet retail platform "SilkRoad 2.0" during a press conference at the Hesse Office of Criminal Investigations in Wiesbaden, Germany in November 2014. German investigators have closed four similiar retail platforms as part of "Operation Onymos."

Boris Roessler/DPA/PA Images

cards. They could search for weapons and explosives, hacking tools, malicious software, and tutorials for committing cybercrimes like theft or hacking into an ATM. And they could even allegedly hire hit-men to kill on their behalf.[58] All of this illegal commerce occurred within an environment modeled after legitimate e-commerce websites. Users could leave ratings and reviews of the sellers they did business with.

In just two years, the FBI estimated that Ulbricht's Silk Road black marketplace generated over $1.2 billion in illegal revenue; likely a conservative estimate.[59] Even though the FBI arrested Ulbricht and saw him convicted and sentenced to life in prison for his crimes in 2015, this has not altered the role of the Deep Web in serving as a site for illegal transactions. There are dozens of similar darknet markets in operation at this moment and more being created each day, even as the FBI and other law enforcement agencies take them down.

Thus, although the original Silk Road site might have "represented the new frontier of crime, a digital-era Wild West"[60] the speed at which cybercrime is evolving and growing has quickly made it a relic of the past.

Murder and cyber-terrorism

The Internet and computer technologies also facilitate the commission of serious violent crimes like robbery, murder, and terrorism. While statistics on Internet facilitated violent crimes are virtually non-existent, we can say that the Internet provides potential offenders with easier access to a wider population of victims than would be possible otherwise. That is, thanks to the Internet, killers and robbers can post ads to lure victims into bad situations and engage in pre-violence stalking behaviors.

For example, Phillip Markoff has been dubbed the "Craigslist killer"[61] after he used that online classified posting service to commit several armed robberies. One of those robberies ended in the murder of a young woman in 2010 after she met Markoff at a hotel after advertising sexual services on Craigslist.

More recently, Ronnie Towns was arrested and charged with the double murder of an elderly Georgia couple, Jude Runion and Bud Runion. Towns, who was unemployed when the murders occurred, used the website Craigslist to lure the couple to a secluded area. The couple arrived thinking they were meeting a person interested in selling a 1966 Ford Mustang, but instead they met Towns, who shot the couple and stole their money.[62]

In an even more disturbing case, an eight-months-pregnant woman named Michelle Wilkins was brutally stabbed and left for dead at the home of a woman she'd gone to visit after seeing an ad the woman placed on Craigslist to sell baby clothes. In fact, the woman, Dynel Lane, had no intention to sell such clothes. She lured Wilkins to her home with the intention of stealing her baby. Once at the home, Lane attacked the expectant mother, stabbing her and cutting her unborn child from her womb using a knife and broken glass. Lane brought the unborn child to a hospital, claiming she had had a miscarriage.[63] The child died and Lane was charged with murder, attempted murder, and many other felonies.

In addition to interpersonal violent crimes like robbery and murder, the Internet is also increasingly being used by organized terror groups to facilitate their recruitment efforts, disseminate propaganda, and organize attacks (as the discussion of San Bernardino in Box 19.1 at the beginning of this chapter indicated). In 2008, the terrorists that attacked foreign hotels in Mumbai, India, received real-time updates from a terrorist command center via text messages on their mobile phones. Today, the terrorist group ISIS utilizes the Internet and social media sites like Twitter and YouTube to post messages and videos and recruit followers to its ranks.

Other organized terrorist groups, including those working on behalf of governments, are leveraging the power of the internet to engage in **cyber-terrorism**. The goals of cyber-terrorists are much like those of any terrorist group—to influence the policies and/or actions of a government, organization, or group of people through threat or fear.

However, rather than effect this influence via outright violence, cyber-terrorists work behind the scenes to access and steal sensitive and protected information in the forms of "government and trade secrets, ideas and technologies,"[64] which they can leverage to achieve their goals. Additionally, cyber-terror groups may attempt to access networked technologies critical to the functioning and safety of a nation. For instance, many critical infrastructure technologies, from traffic lights to power plants, utilize networks. Any network can be hacked by an individual or group with the skill and time. Thus, a terrorist group could potentially access and hack a city's traffic control system, or an electric plant, or any number of other important systems. They could thus cause even more disruptions and, potentially, deaths, through these sorts of actions than traditional bombings or shootings.

COMBATING, CONTROLLING, AND PREVENTING CYBERCRIME

In our modern world, we are increasingly hyper-connected:[65] more than a third of the global population has access to the Internet,[66] nearly 70 percent of people have broadband Internet service through their smartphones,[67] and networked devices—computers, phones, printers, databases, and more—outnumber human beings six to one.[68] In short, we now live in a "multi-mediated"[69] social world. Looking toward the future, this means that cybercrime is not going away. If anything, as technology improves and we spend more time doing more things in cyberspace, cybercrime will increase. Thus, combating, controlling, and preventing cybercrime is a top priority for governments, lawmakers, and law enforcement as well as private organizations, corporations, and citizens. In this section, we will briefly survey what is being done in both the government and private sectors to combat, control, and prevent cybercrime.

Cybercrime: government responses

What makes cybercrime especially difficult to combat, control and prevent is that it occurs within a virtual space. As a result, entities in the public sector—governments, lawmakers, law enforcement agencies—must rethink how best to respond to the cybercrime problem. After all, it is the responsibility of government and its agencies to protect citizens from harm and victimization. As if this weren't motivation enough, the public sector also has a strong incentive to protect itself from the predations of cybercriminals and terrorists.

U.S. context

Cybercrime is a serious issue in the United States. The battle between cyber criminals and law enforcement agencies is a continuous one. Lawmakers and law enforcement agencies at the local, state, and federal level are working to combat, control, and prevent it. Primary responsibility for investigating and combating cybercrime in the U.S. falls on the Federal Bureau of Investigation (FBI), which has formed a cybercrime division employing thousands of investigative analysts, computer techs, and agents. The FBI coordinates, facilitates, and assists with cybercrime investigations at the local, state, national, and international scales, and also works closely with other Federal law enforcement agencies—like the National Security Agency, Drug Enforcement Agency, and more—to combat and control cybercrime via the **Comprehensive National Cyber Security Initiative (CNCI)** and **National Cyber Investigative Joint Task Force (NCIJTF)**. In fulfilling its obligation to police cybercrimes, the FBI also established the **Internet Crime Complaint Center (IC3)**, which serves as a clearinghouse for cybercrime data.

Unfortunately, while traditional street level law enforcement agencies have adopted the proactive problem oriented policing (POP) approach (see chapter 5) to combat, control, and prevent crime, the principles of this approach are much harder to implement in cyberspace. Thus, much of the time the law enforcement response to cybercrime is reactive, rather than proactive. At the same time, the nature and characteristics of cybercrime makes it very hard for police and federal agents to identify crime incidents, victims, offenders and collect evidence of wrongdoing. Further impeding our abilities to control, combat, and prevent cybercrime domestically is the fact that, historically and today, cybercrime and criminals have been a step or two ahead of the law (see Box 19.5).

Generally speaking, law makers and law enforcement agencies were slow to realize the criminal potential of computers and the Internet; this is much less true for the many creative hackers and criminal entrepreneurs who realized early on the potential for exploiting computers and the Internet for harmful,

BOX 19.5: CONNECTING THEORY TO PRACTICE

Routine activities theory and cybercrime

The **routine activities theory** helps explain why individuals become victims of crime. The theory was originally developed to explain criminal victimization and changes in crime rates over time. It does so by referencing how changes in the "routine activities of daily life" can lead to greater chances of becoming a crime victim, or conversely, more opportunities to commit crime. For example, when both women and men began working outside the home in the middle of the 20th century, opportunities for residential burglaries rose, as did opportunities for committing robberies and rapes or sexual assaults against women, who were now "easier victims."

Can routine activities theory help us understand victimization and criminal offending in cyberspace as well? Many researchers argue that it can.

For example, the principles of routine activities theory can help us understand how young kids become victims of cyberbullying or online child sexual exploitation. Essentially the changing "routines" of kids provide them greater access to online spaces where they may get bullied or be preyed upon by adults looking to sexually exploit them[70]. Likewise, routine activites theory can provide a way for us to understand how other forms of internet crime victimization occur, for example identity theft, phishing, and other forms of cyber-fraud.[71]

In turn, by recognizing that changes in how we live our lives open up new avenues for us to become crime victims, and that changes our social world may open up new opportunities for criminal behavior, we can develop policies, ranging from laws to public education campaigns, to address these issues.

For example, if cyberbullying and online sexploitation of kids are concerns, parents can supervise kid's computer time or set parental controls and monitoring features on computers to ensure that their risk of victimization is lowered. Likewise, if online frauds and scams are targeting people via email or targeting specific classes of people (e.g., the elderly), law enforcement can create public awareness campaigns and other initiatives to deal directly with these crime problems.

illicit, and criminal ends. For example, it took Congress until 1984 to institute the first basic federal cybercrime legislation, which was included in the Comprehensive Crime Control Act of 1984. Specifically, only three computer/network based activities were made illegal at that time: (1) accessing any classified information on a computer without permission (a felony), (2) obtaining financial or credit card information without authorization (a misdemeanor), and (3) trespassing into any government computer (a misdemeanor). In 1986, the Federal government raised the stakes for engaging in cybercrime with passage of the **Federal Computer Fraud and Abuse Act (CFAA)**, which made "hacking" offenses and computer tampering felony offenses, punishable by prison time and heavy fines. Unfortunately, this legislation was itself reactionary, arising only after a serious case of computer espionage occurred at the Lawrence Berkeley National Laboratory and after **the Morris Worm** was released, infecting and damaging over 6,000 private, corporate, and government computers causing nearly $100 million in damage.[72] Illustrating the speed at which cybercrime has evolved and the fact that cybercrime law is constantly playing catch up, since 1986 the CFAA has been amended no fewer than eight times. Among the more notable alterations to the CFAA are criminalization of "threats" to publicly disclose stolen data, engaging in conspiracy to commit computer hacking, and trafficking in stolen passwords. The penalties for violating elements of the CFAA are now quite significant (see Table 19.4).

Since the 1980s the United States Federal Criminal Code, along with state level criminal codes, have grown significantly with respect to cybercrime. Section 18 of the United States Code, which contains information on acts criminalized at the Federal level, now has more than fifteen statutes specifically designed to control and punish cybercrimes, ranging from identity theft to the sexual exploitation of children (see Table 19.5).

Since September 11, 2001, terror attacks on the United States, the issues of cybercrime and terrorism have merged, while drawing significant attention from law makers and law enforcement agencies at all levels of government. Originally, signed into law in 2001 and then amended in 2005, the **USA PATRIOT Act** (2001, 2005) has been utilized to combat certain cybercrimes—in particular hacking and cyber trespass—and punish them more severely. The PATRIOT Act has also made it easier for law enforcement to characterize some forms of cybercrime as cyberterrorism, thus expanding the arsenal of tools and penalties that can be leveraged against them. Additional laws passed in recent years have expanded cybercrime research funding and information sharing, increased cybersecurity employment and enhanced cybersecurity agency

Table 19.4 Federal penalties for violations of the CFAA

Offense	Penalty
Obtaining national security information	10 to 20 years
Extortion involving computers	5 to 10 years
Accessing a computer and obtaining Information	1 to 10 years
Trespassing in a government computer	1 to 10 years
Intentionally damaging by knowing transmission (i.e., virus, worm, etc.)	1 to 20 years

Source: Adapted from United States Department of Justice, Prosecuting Computer Crimes Manual, p. 3. Retrieved from https://www.justice.gov/sites/default/files/criminal-ccips/legacy/2015/01/14/ccmanual.pdf.

organization.[73] Currently, two new Congressional cybercrime bills have been proposed, while nineteen more are under review. If successfully passed and signed into law, these new efforts would strengthen the ability of U.S. law enforcement agencies to combat, control, and prevent cybercrimes.

International context

Cybercrime is, of course, a global, trans-national problem. It is common for cybercrime victims to be located in one country and offenders in another—sometimes cybercrime victims and offenders are separated by thousands of miles of physical space. This fact has serious implications for the control and prevention of cybercrime.

Table 19.5 Federal criminal statutes related to cybercrimes

Statute(s)	Focus
18 U.S.C. 1029, 1030, 1037, 1343	Computer fraud
18 U.S.C. 1028, 1028A	Identity theft
18 U.S.C. 2251	Sexual exploitation of children
18 U.S.C. 1462	Importation or transportation of obscene matters
18 U.S.C. 2319	Criminal infringement of copyright

First, countries have different legal systems. This means different laws, rules of criminal procedure, investigatory tactics, and so on. From a legal and law enforcement perspective, these differences make effectively combating cyber crimes that have an international dimension a real complicated mess.

Second, when cybercrimes cross international borders, the issues of jurisdiction and extradition become important. Who will investigate the crime? Who will prosecute the offender? Will a country where a person or organization has been victimized even be able to bring a cybercriminal to trial in their territory? None of these questions has simple answers.

Generally speaking, if a cybercrime does cross national boundaries, multiple law enforcement agencies will be involved in the investigation. Globally, two agencies, the **European Union Police Organization (Europol)** and the **International Police Organization (Interpol)** carry much responsibility for combating, controlling, and preventing cybercrimes. Europol's focus is limited to serving member countries of the European Union, while Interpol boasts a membership of 190 nations worldwide. If the cybercrime involves the United States, then investigators from these international agencies will work closely with their partners at the FBI and other federal law enforcement organizations.

Over the last decade there has been a strong push to develop better cooperation among nations in terms of addressing crime issues of global significance, such as terrorism, drug trafficking, human smuggling, and cyber crime. Some progress has been made. For example, 82 countries signed binding agreements about how to respond to cybercrime and provide assistance to other countries in combatting this problem and apprehending criminals.[74] Still, there remains a lack of harmony among laws and policies between countries as well as major differences in resources and expertise needed to sufficiently address the cybercrime problem.

Cybercrime: private sector responses

Criminal laws are only as effective as the mechanisms in place to enforce them. In the current cybercrime arms race, the criminals have the advantage, while lawmakers and law enforcement agencies struggle to keep up. This means that the private sector—corporations, organizations, individuals—shoulder much more responsibility for combating, controling, and preventing cybercrimes than they do in thwarting traditional violent and property crimes.

To aid the private sector in dealing with cybercrime, there are increasingly strong partnerships developing between federal and international police agencies and private entities. In the U.S., for example, there is the **National Cyber-Forensics and Training Alliance (NCFTA)**, sponsored by the FBI. The goal of the NCFTA is to "develop responses to evolving threats to the nation's critical infrastructure by participating in cyber-forensic analysis, tactical response development, technology vulnerability analysis, and the development of advanced training."[75] Similarly, the FBI and Department of Homeland Security have sponsored the **Domestic Security Alliance Council (DSAC)**, with the aim of improving inform-ation sharing about cybercrime threats between law enforcement and private businesses.

Beyond those assistance programs, corporations and organizations can do much to control and prevent cybercrimes. Strategies currently in use by many private sector entities include hiring highly skilled information security professionals and teams of IT security professionals as well as creating internal information security divisions to handle and mitigate cybercrime threats.[76] Other initiatives include data loss prevention training, in which employees are taught to avoid making mistakes that might open up vulnerabilities within computer networks or systems that criminals could exploit and limiting access to sensitive electronic information to only a select group of individuals, not an entire employee group (for other options see Table 19.6).

Table 19.6 Private sector cybersecurity initiatives

Hiring Information Technology Security professionals and teams
Better data loss prevention training and enforcement
Proactive cybercrime detection strategies
Limiting access to sensitive electronic information
Creating better, stronger information firewalls
More training on how individuals can protect their privacy and information in cyberspace (e.g., blocking cookies, filtering email, using a VPN, etc.)
Adoption of Security Intelligence Systems which provide advanced cybersecurity threat detection and monitoring for suspicious activity

SUMMARY

In this chapter we explored the new frontier of criminology and criminal justice: cybercrime—a criminal act that results when an individual or organization utilizes the Internet to engage in criminal behavior. This topic is of great interest and importance to the fields of criminal law, criminal justice, criminology, and public policy.

Our discussion began with looking at three ways modern technology impacts crime. To summarize, technology now makes it easier for crimes to be committed, such as "cybercrime"; it makes it easier for law enforcement to control crime, for example via CCTV and other technologies; and it makes it easier for the public to observe and resist the crimes of the powerful.

We then embarked on a wide-ranging discussion of various types of cyber crime that occur today. These include computer intrusions, which are burglaries that occur via the Internet; identity and cybertheft; cyberbullying, harassment, stalking, and exploitation; illicit goods and black markets; and murder and cyber-terrorism. All of these forms of cybercrime are changing and expanding on a daily, weekly, and monthly basis.

Finally, we concluded our discussion of technology and cybercrime by examining government responses. These can be divided by responses that occur within the U.S. and at the international level. A host of agencies take cyber-crime seriously, particularly the FBI, the agency with primary jurisdiction for policing this category of criminality. Numerous laws have been created to control cybercrime, but, importantly, these laws continue to fall behind the pace at which cybercrimes are developing and occurring. Regardless of context, it is important to remember that efforts to combat and control cybercrimes are severely limited by the nature of the crime itself. Cybercrime breaks the traditional mold: it can occur anywhere anytime; there is no need for victims and offenders to be in physical proximity. Likewise, cybercrimes are far easier to obscure; evidence can be difficult to collect and jurisdictional issues presented by the fact that cybercrimes are often transnational make policing cybercrime very difficult.

While we could only provide an overview of the topic in this chapter, you should now understand how cybercrime came into existence and how tech-nology impacts modern crime. You now have a basic understanding of the major characteristics and types of cybercrime as well as the massive scale that cybercrime occurs on.

There is truly no form of criminal conduct capable of impacting so many lives as quickly as cybercrime can. The future of criminal justice and criminology will undoubtedly intersect more and more with this important topic, which means creative energy must be expended by those in research, policy, law, and law enforcement to figure out how best to control it and protect people from becoming victims.

CRITICAL THINKING QUESTIONS

1. Where do you stand with respect to debate between privacy and security? Do you favor more government control and access to personal data and records? If so, where do you draw the line?

2. Does the use of modern surveillance technologies seem like a positive or negative development to you? What are the pros and cons of CCTV, drone surveillance, and other forms of technological surveillance? Could this be a real solution to crime or not?

3. What is your opinion about hacktivist's like Edward Snowden and the group Anonymous? Regardless of what the law says about their behavior, do you consider them criminals? Why or why not?

4. Now that you know the brief history of computer and cybercrime, what do you think the future holds? Try to imagine what the landscape of crime will look like in 25, 50, and 100 years. What will the major criminal issues and subjects be then? How will technology advance and how will the criminal exploitation keep up with or even outpace it?

5. Do you feel like cybercrime is a serious issue? What varieties of cyber-crime seem most troubling or significant to you? What can be done to mitigate or reduce these forms of crime?

NOTES

1   Fulgiheri, C.E. 2016. 415 Counts of Child Porn for Villanova Professor. *The Daily Pennsylvanian,* April 5.
2   *The New York Times,* March 25, 1878.
3   Technology Liberation Front, Moral Panics-Techno Panics. Retrieved from https://techliberation.com/ongoing-series/ongoing-series-moral-panics-techno-panics/.
4   Ortiz, E. 2015. San Bernardino Shooting: Timeline of How the Rampage Unfolded. *NBC News,* Dec. 3.
5   Lichtblau, E. and Benner, K. 2016. Apple Fights Order to Unlock San Bernardino Gunman's iPhone. *The New York Times,* Feb. 17.
6   Prosecutor: iPhone Could ID Unknown Shooter. 2016. *CBS/AP News,* March 4. Retrieved from http://www.cbsnews.com/news/san-bernardino-shooting-prosecutor-iphone-could-id-unknown-attacker/.
7   Barrett, D. 2016. FBI Analyzing Data From San Bernardino iPhone for Leads. *The Wall Street Journal,* April 5.
8   Pethos, A., Fallis, D. and Keating, D. 2013. Shot-Spotter Detection System Documents 39,000 Shooting Incidents in the District. *Washington Post,* Nov. 2.
9   Barrett, D. 2013. One Surveillance Camera for Every 11 People in Britain, Says CCTV Survey. *The Telegraph,* July 10.
10 ACLU. 2014. Domestic Drones. Retrieved from https://www.aclu.org/blog/tag/domestic-drones.
11 Taibbi, M. 2013. Apocalypse, New Jersey: A Dispatch from America's Most Desperate Town. *Rolling Stone.*

12   Forensic Colleges, 2015. 10 Modern Forensic Science Technologies. Retrieved from http://www.forensicscolleges.com/blog/resources/10-modern-forensic-science-technologies.

13   Radio Lab, 2015. The Eye in the Sky, WNYC, June 18. Transcript retrieved from http://www.radiolab.org/story/eye-sky/.

14   INTERPOL. 2016. Cyber crime. Retrieved from http://www.interpol.int/Crime-areas/Cyber crime/Cyber crime.

15   Department of Justice. 2006. *Manual for the Prosecution of Computer Crimes.* Computer Crime and Intellectual Property Section, Criminal Division. United States Department of Justice.

16   Swaine, M.R. 2016. ENIAC. *Encyclopedia Britannica.*

17   Internet Society. 2015. Brief History of the Internet. Retrieved from http://www.internetsociety.org/internet/what-internet/history-internet/brief-history-internet.

18   Internet Crime Complaint Center. 2014. 2014 Internet Crime Report. Federal Bureau of investigation, United States Department of Justice.

19   Ibid.

20   Ibid.

21   United Nations Department of Economics and Social Affairs. 2011. Cybersecurity: A Global Issue Demanding a Global Approach. Retrieved from http://www.un.org/en/development/desa/news/ecosoc/cybersecurity-demands-global-approach.html.

22   Internet Crime Complaint Center. 2014. 2014 Internet Crime Report. Federal Bureau of Investigation, United States Department of Justice.

23   Ibid.

24   Wiederhold, B.K. 2014. The Role of Psychology in Enhancing Cybersecurity. *Cyber-Psychology, Behavior and Social Networking* 17(3): 131–132.

25   United Nations Office on Drugs and Crime. 2013. Comprehensive Study on Cyber crime. Retrieved from https://www.unodc.org/documents/organized-crime/UNODC_CCPCJ_EG.4_2013/CYBER CRIME_STUDY_210213.pdf.

26   Interpol. 2016. Cyber Crime. Retrieved from http://www.interpol.int/Crime-areas/Cyber crime/Cyber crime.

27   Ibid.

28   United Nations Office on Drugs and Crime. 2013. Comprehensive Study on Cyber crime. Retrieved from https://www.unodc.org/documents/organized-crime/UNODC_CCPCJ_EG.4_2013/CYBER CRIME_STUDY_210213.pdf.

29   Lennon, M. 2015. Hackers Hit 100 Banks in 'Unprecedented' $1 Billion Cyber Heist: Kaspersky Lab. *Cyber Security Week*, Feb. 15.

30   Federal Bureau of Investigation. 2016. Computer Intrusions. Retrieved from www.fbi.gov/about-us/investigate/cyber/computer-intrusions.

31   Fitzpatrick, D. and Griffin, D. 2016. 'Ransomware' Crime Wave Growing. *CNN.* Retrieved from http://money.cnn.com/2016/04/04/technology/ransomware-cyber crime/.

32   U.S. Bureau of Justice Statistics. 2008. Special Report: Cyber Crimes Against Businesses. U.S. Department of Justice, Office of Justice Programs.

33   Federal Bureau of Investigation. 2016. Computer Intrusions. Retrieved from https://www.fbi.gov/about-us/investigate/cyber/computer-intrusions.

34   Gladstone, R. 2016. Bangladesh Bank Chief Resigns After Cyber Theft of $81 Million. *The New York Times*, March 15.

35   Snow, G. 2011. Testimony of Assistant Director Gordon M. Snow, Cyber Division, Federal Bureau of Investigation before the House Financial Services Committee, Subcommittee on Financial Institutions and Consumer Credit, Washington, D.C. Sept. 14.

36   Federal Bureau of Investigation. 2016. Identity Theft Overview. Retrieved from https://www.fbi.gov/about-us/investigate/cyber/identity_theft/identity-theft-overview.

37   Federal Bureau of Investigation. 2016. Smishing and Vishing Scams to Beware of this Holiday Season. Retrieved from https://www.fbi.gov/news/stories/2010/november/cyber_112410.

38   Ibid.

39   Federal Bureau of Investigation. 2016. Identity Theft. Retrieved from https://www.fbi.gov/about-us/investigate/cyber/identity_theft.

40   The Tyler Clementi Foundation. 2016. Tyler's Story. Retrieved from http://www.tylerclementi.org/tylers-story.

41   Ibid.

42   Ibid.

43   Ibid.

44   Grabosky, P.N. 2001. Virtual Criminality: Old Wine in New Bottles? *Social and Legal Studies* 10: 243–249.

45   Beran, T. and Li, Q. 2005. Cyber-Harassment: A Study of a New Method for an old Behavior. *Journal of Educational Computing Research* 32: 265–277; Beran, T. and Li, Q. 2007. The Relationship Between Cyberbullying and School Bullying. *Journal of Student Wellbeing* 1: 15–33.

46   Bocij, P. 2004. *Cyberstalking: Harassment in the Internet Age and How to Protect Your Family*. Westport, CT: Praeger.

47   Khandelwal, S. 2016. FBI Has Named Hacker Allegedly Responsible for The Fappening Leaks. *The Hacker News*. Retrieved from http://thehackernews.com/2016/01/fappening-celebrity-hacking.html.

48   National Center for Missing and Exploited Children. 2016. Child Victim Identification Program. Retrieved from http://www.missingkids.org/CVIP.

49   Payne, E., Messia, H. and Greene, R. 2015. Vatican Official Accused of Child Porn, Pedophilia Dies. http://www.cnn.com/2015/08/28/europe/vatican-sex-abuse-trial-death/

50   Ortiz, E. Bogert, N. 2015. Jared Fogle, Ex-Subway Pitchman, Gets 15 Years in Prison for Child Porn Charges. Retrieved from http://www.nbcnews.com/news/us-news/jared-fogle-ex-subway-pitchman-pleads-guilty-child-porn-sex-n466256.

51   Federal Bureau of Investigation, 2014. National Press Release, Child Pornography Case Results in Lengthy Prison Sentences. Retrieved from https://www.fbi.gov/news/stories/2014/november/child-pornography-case-results-in-lengthy-prison-sentences/child-pornography-case-results-in-lengthy-prison-sentences.

52   Federal Bureau of Investigation, 2014. National Press Release, 168 Juveniles Recovered in Nationwide Operation Targeting Commercial Child Sex Trafficking. Retrieved from https://www.fbi.gov/news/pressrel/press-releases/168-juveniles-recovered-in-nationwide-operation-targeting-commercial-child-sex-trafficking.

53   McVeigh, K. 2011. Police Shut Down Global Pedophile Network in Operation Rescue. *The Guardian,* March 11.

54   Kushner, D. 2014. Dead End on Silk Road: Internet Crime Kingpin Ross Ulbricht's Big Fall. *Rolling Stone Magazine.*

55   Ibid.

56   Ibid.

57   Ibid.

58   Ibid.

59   Ibid.

60   Bearman, J. 2016. The Rise and Fall of Silk Road, Part I. Retrieved from http://www.wired.com/2015/04/silk-road-1/.

61   Biography.com Editors. 2016. Phillip Markoff Biography. *Biography.com.* Retrieved from http://www.biography.com/people/philip-markoff-438836.

62   Kovac, J., Jr. 2015. Prosecutor: Alleged Craigslist Killer Tried to Prey on Others. *The Macon Telegraph*, April 10. Retrieved from http://www.macon.com/news/local/article30225942.html.

63   Chan, M. 2015. Colorado Woman Who Had Baby Cut From Womb Details Attack, Describes Moment she Held Lifeless Daughter: 'She was Perfect'. *The New York Daily News*, Sept. 10. Retrieved from http://www.nydailynews.com/news/national/colorado-woman-baby-cut-womb-details-attack-article-1.2355647.

64   Federal Bureau of Investigation. 2014. Testimony of Robert Anderson Jr. before the Senate Committee on Homeland Security and Governmental Affairs.

65   United Nations Office on Drugs and Crime (UNDOC). 2013.

66   Ibid.

67   Ibid.

68   Internet World Stats. 2013. Usage and Population Statistics. Retrieved from http://www.internetworldstats.com/stats.htm.

69   McRobbie, A. and Thornton, S. 1995. Rethinking Moral Panic for Multi-Mediated Social Worlds. *British Journal of Sociology* 46(4): 559–574.

70   Navarro, J.N. Jasinski, J.L. 2012. Going Cyber: Using Routine Activities Theory to Predict Cyberbullying Experiences. *Sociological Spectrum* 32(1): 81–94.

71   Pratt, T.C., Holtfreter, K. Reisig, M.D. 2010. Routine Online Activity and Internet Fraud Targeting: Extending the Generality of Routine Activity Theory. *Journal of Research in Crime and Delinquency* 47(3): 267–296.

72   Lee, T.B. 2013. How a Grad Student Trying to Build the First Botnet Brought the Internet to its Knees. *Washington Post,* Nov. 1.

73   The Cyber Security Enhancement Act of 2014 provides a voluntary private-public partnership primarily to further research and development into cyber security as well as education and public awareness of ongoing threats; the National Cyber Security Protection Act of 2014 organizes current task force centers for cyber security analysis; the Cyber Security Workforce Assessment Act of 2014 directs the Secretary of Homeland Security to annually evaluate the cyber security workforce within the Department of Homeland Security (DHS).

74   United Nations Office on Drugs and Crime. 2013, February. Comprehensive Study on Cyber Crime. Retrieved from https://www.unodc.org/documents/organized-crime/UNODC_CCPCJ_EG.4_2013/CYBER CRIME_STUDY_210213.pdf.

75   FBI, 2016. Cyber Crime. Retrieved from https://www.fbi.gov/about-us/investigate/cyber.

76   Westervelt, R. 2013. Crime Doesn't Pay: 10 Ways to Control and Reduce Cybercrime Costs. *CRN*. Retrieved from http://www.crn.com/slide-shows/security/240162631/crime-doesnt-pay-10-ways-to-control-and-reduce-cybercrime-costs.htm/pgno/0/1?itc=refresh.

A look ahead

PART V

CHAPTER OUTLINE

Crime today, crime tomorrow: the future of criminological theory

In this chapter we will explore the following questions

- How can we benefit from the study of crime in different parts of the world?
- What types of criminal activities violate the rules of more than one country?
- In what ways has technology contributed to crime?
- Is the science of criminology effectively dealing with crime in modern society?
- How do we arrive at a comprehensive definition of crime?
- What will be the role of criminological theory in solving crime today and in the future?
- Should crime control strategies today be driven by theory, reality, or both?
- In what ways has criminological research impacted social policy?

KEY TERMS

intellectual property laws

globalization

comparative criminology

International Criminal Police Organization (INTERPOL)

United Nations Surveys on Crime Trends and the Operations of Criminal Justice Systems (CTS)

International Crime Victims Survey

meta level research studies

parallel research studies

single case research studies

transnational crime

terrorism

international crime

On December 2, 2015, coworkers at the San Bernardino County Public Health Department were gathered for a training event and holiday party. Amongst those attending was Syed Rizwan Farook, a 28-year-old American-born citizen of Pakistani descent and a city health inspector. During that event, Farook left his coworkers and returned later on with his wife, Tashfeen Malik. The couple opened fire on dozens of individuals in the banquet hall, killing 14 people and seriously injuring several others. According to his coworkers, Farook was a well-liked devout Muslim who rarely discussed religion at work. They said he had recently traveled to Saudi Arabia to marry a woman he had met online. The couple had a baby and by all accounts appeared to be living the "American Dream." FBI Director James B. Comey referred to the couple as "homegrown violent extremists" who were influenced by overseas terrorist groups.[1]

In March 2009, the International Criminal Court (ICC) issued a warrant for the arrest of the president of Sudan, Omar Hassan al-Bashir, on criminal charges of war crimes and crimes against humanity. The warrant was based on evidence that al-Bashir was responsible for intentional and strategic attacks on segments of the civilian population of Darfur, in the Sudan, including acts

Image 20.1 *Syed Rizwan Farook and his wife Tashfeen Malik are what we call "homegrown terrorists." Here, family, friends, and supporters remember the victims who were killed in the terrorist attack by the couple. What makes such a crime particularly disturbing to people all over the world?*

Ringo Chiu/Zuma Press/PA Images

Rome Treaty

international criminal court

risk factor analysis paradigm

developmental pathways

of pillage, torture, rape, and genocide. This historic event marked the first warrant of arrest issued to a President or Head of State currently in office. It also marked the beginning of international jurisdiction in the prosecution and control of war crimes.[2]

Do certain types of criminal activities transcend the borders of nations? The warrant for al-Bashir's arrest says yes, and that faced with such crimes, different societies will unite in their prevention and control. These are generally criminal acts that jeopardize the interests of all humankind by threatening the peace and security of citizens.

The National Intellectual Property Law Enforcement Coordination Council (NIPLECC), for instance, consists of a group of seven officials: the Under Secretary of Commerce for Intellectual Property and Director of the United States Patent and Trademark Office; the Assistant Attorney General, Criminal Division; the Under Secretary of State for Economic, Business, and Agricultural Affairs; a Deputy United States Trade Representative; the Commissioner of Customs; the Under Secretary of Commerce for International Trade; and in a consulting capacity, the Register of Copyrights, that coordinate both domestic and international activities in the enforcement of intellectual property laws, or laws designed to protect the patents or copyrights applied to products, ideas, inventions, and artistic creations.[3] A NIPLECC report highlights the importance of cross border enforcement of intellectual property laws noting the profound impact on public health, safety, and the international economy that results when intellectual property rights are compromised.[4] Moreover, cross-border cooperation will prove the most effective way to combat the manufacture and distribution of counterfeit and pirated products in the global illicit trade that compete with genuine products.

A comprehensive understanding of modern criminal justice policy and practice warrants an exploration of criminological issues of global concern, as well as international strategies for the prevention of crime. By relying on cross-cultural research on various crime control policies and programs, the international criminal justice community can collaborate to combat common concerns about protecting the public order without jeopardizing the rights of individuals. After all, we have seen in chapter 1 that striking a balance between these two goals is not an easy task within the boundaries of our own society. It is much more difficult when crossing over to other societies, with their own definitions of individuals' rights and public order! This is the task of comparative criminology, to which we now turn.

COMPARATIVE CRIMINOLOGY

The 21st century has brought vast changes in the way people communicate and exchange goods and services. These changes were brought about by **globalization**, a process that eases interaction and integration among the people, corporations, and political systems of different countries. Globalization is driven by international trade and investment made possible through advances in communication technology, especially the Internet. It has profound effects on culture, the environment, and politics, as well as on the daily lives of individuals around the world.[5]

One effect of globalization on the field of criminology is the emergence of globalized crime networks that operate across national borders.[6] This trend has led to a renaissance in the study of comparative criminology.

Image 20.2 *Globalization affects many aspects of social interaction. It enables people around the world to connect faster and allows money, goods, and information to flow much more easily than ever before. What impact does globalization have on crime and crime control efforts within our own borders?*

iStock/Maxiphoto

What is comparative criminology?

Comparative criminology is the systematic study of crime and crime control policies and practices in different cultures and societies around the world.[7] The benefit of this approach is that with it we can identify common variables within criminological theory, better understand cross-national patterns of criminal behavior, and integrate new aspects of social control policies and practices that may be unfamiliar to us.[8]

The idea that sharing information between countries and cultures can help us both understand criminal behavior and develop crime control policies is not new. Criminologists have long recognized the need for comparative data in the evolution of criminological thought and practice. With globalization this need became more urgent. Testing our own theories and ideas in multiple socio-cultural environments was only made possible, however, with the evolution of criminology as a reliable scientific discipline. And comparative research and analysis came into existence only when international crime data and statistics on a variety of criminal justice topics appeared during the latter half of the 20th century. With the ease of access to international trends in criminal justice information, criminologists today are in a better position to pursue comparative criminological research.

How do we conduct comparative criminology?

The task of comparative research is to find trends and patterns in criminal behavior and crime control practices at a cross-national level, as well as to examine criminological theories in diverse cultural contexts. To accomplish this task, comparative criminological researchers must have comprehensive knowledge of the social, political, and economic structure of the country or countries they are studying, including the cultural norms, value systems, and legal codes that comprise the social order and guide daily interactions. Research data they gather from other countries must be of the highest quality and integrity, and it must be compatible with other statistical reports in terms of data-gathering techniques, legal definitions, and crime measurement.[9]

Much comparative criminological research relies on data sources that compile crime statistics at an international level. One such data source is prepared by the **International Criminal Police Organization**, or **INTERPOL**, an international police organization that publishes crime data from 188 participating countries.[10] Another data source is the **United Nations Surveys on Crime Trends and the Operations of Criminal Justice Systems (CTS)** which provides statistics on crime, crime trends, and criminal justice operations at the international level.[11] These are considered official crime data sources and must be approached with the same cautions as apply to our own official national crime data sources, discussed in chapter 3. Another valuable data source for comparative research is the **International Crime Victims Survey (ICVS)** (also discussed in chapter 3). The ICVS surveys households in different countries on their experiences with crime and police response, as well as matters related to crime prevention and safety.[12] When we compare official data sources with the ICVS, trends in victimization are fairly similar, although the ICVS shows slightly higher rates over time.

Comparative criminologists focus on three different types of research studies.[13] **Meta-level studies** rely on the comparison of criminological issues in various countries. This type of research analyzes certain variables that may represent common trends in different societies, for example, the relationship of poverty to property crime trends in several countries, or the relationship between modernization and domestic violence trends in different societies. In a comparative study of American and Canadian crime rates, for example, researchers studied the effects of residential segregation of the poor in large metropolitan cities and the availability of firearms on patterns of homicide, robbery, burglary, and car theft. Their findings challenge the notion that differences in values, culture, and political views between the two countries are responsible for the gap in crime rates.[14] **Parallel research studies** usually focus on a comparison and contrast analysis of criminal justice components in two different countries. They may shed light on criminal justice policies and practices dealing with common crime and criminal justice problems such as drug trafficking, terrorism, racial profiling, and prison overcrowding. A 2006 comparative analysis examined the issue of prosecutorial discretion by comparing criminal court proceedings in Italy, the Netherlands, and the United States. The study highlights the importance of developing uniform criteria in the decision to initiate criminal action against an offender.[15] Finally, a third research approach within comparative criminology is the use of **single-case studies** that describe and analyze diverse criminal justice issues within a single country, often from a historical standpoint and as they relate to social, economic, and political changes over time. In a study of violence and abuse of women in Nigeria, researchers attribute the ineffective enforcement of laws preventing rape and torture to the decentralized nature of the Nigerian legal system as well as the embedded nature of rape in the culture of institutions designed to maintain peace and social control.[16] With increased availability of reliable and valid cross-national crime data sources, all three methods of comparative research are becoming more popular ways to produce groundbreaking studies in crime and delinquency.

What do we learn from comparative criminology?

We can learn a lot from the study of crime on a global level. One tremendous benefit is the ability it gives us to validate criminological theories in different social environments. For example, how does social disorganization affect human interaction in the urban communities of Copenhagen? What structural correlates affect juvenile delinquency in the different cultures of Southeast Asia? What role do routine activities play in victimization in Canada? Testing hypotheses in different cultural and national contexts allows criminologists to further refine theories and make them more informative and generalizable. It also makes them more reliable for informing criminal justice policy and research (see Box 20.1).

Comparative criminology sheds light on what other nations have tried in dealing with issues such as human trafficking, insider-trading, child abuse, and the legalization of drugs.[17] Comparative criminologists analyze the policies and practices implemented by law enforcement agencies, the courts, and corrections. Comparative research on the methods and approaches different communities use in responding to crime is a valuable tool in developing the most effective crime control mechanisms. We can learn for example about how the city of Sao Paulo, Brazil experienced an 80 percent decline in homicides by establishing a 10 point action plan that included the creation of a municipal security department that mapped criminal activity, the development and integration of police forces in the city, the mandated closure of bars between 11 p.m. and 6 a.m., and the institution of an array of social, educational, and environmental

BOX 20.1: CONNECTING THEORY TO PRACTICE

Crime control via shaming . . . An application of labeling theory

Though cultures vary around the world, each has developed a consistent set of ideals or norms of expected member behavior. When an individual acts against societal norms, the punishment represents the collective majority's moral reaction. That reaction often includes assigning deviant status to the individual, or labeling. Social reaction to crime is an integral component of labeling theory as we have seen in chapter 12.

While U.S. society goes to extreme measures to avoid labeling juveniles, the Chinese have embraced labeling theory as a means to prevent and reduce juvenile delinquency and rehabilitate youthful offenders. Because in Chinese culture violating societal norms is seen as undesirable and disgraceful, the Chinese believe juveniles will resist delinquent behavior to avoid being shamed. The two cultures differ most in the personal reaction to the deviant label. In U.S. society, individuals labeled deviant come to internalize the label and see deviant status as part of their identity. They often start reoffending in a self-fulfilling prophecy.

Chinese culture is very dependent on social groups and bonds with family, friends, peers, and neighbors as the primary basis for interaction, and even for the basic necessities of life. Moreover, social conformity is a key element of Chinese culture. Those who act selfishly by seeking personal satisfaction through criminal acts are scorned, labeled, and eventually cast out of their original social group. Mass public trials and mass public announcements of judicial rulings are a significant threat to social bonds. Individuals labeled deviant in the Chinese culture will do everything in their power to shed the status of "criminal" in order to remain accepted members of society. Social control measures for preventing delinquency among Chinese youth therefore begin with shaming methods of punishment. Shaming becomes more effective, however, when combined with efforts at reintegrating offenders back into the community so as not to create a permanent and terminal sense of alienation.

Sources

Chen, Xiaoming. 2002. Social Control in China: Applications of the Labeling Theory and the Reintegrative Shaming Theory. *International Journal of Offender Therapy and Comparative Criminology* 46(1): 45–63.

Jiang, Shanhe and Lambert, Eric. 2009. Views of Formal and Informal Crime Control and Their Correlates in China. *International Criminal Justice Review* 19(1): 5–24

Li, Enshen. 2016. China's urban underclass population and penal policy. *Criminology and Criminal Justice* 16(1): 80–98.

policies aimed at mentoring youth, reducing violence, and increasing support to schools.[18]

Finally, comparative criminology helps us identify common issues in criminal justice such as urban violence and disorder, drug abuse, gangs, terrorist threats, child pornography, stock market fraud, and piracy, a necessary step to developing collaborative efforts to control criminal activities that transcend physical barriers, legal definitions, and cultural norms. It increases our universal understanding of criminal justice by exploring the connections between crimes in different societies. In 2015, the International Center for the Prevention of Crime published their fourth *International Report on Crime Prevention and Community Safety: Trends and Perspectives,* accompanied by the *International Compendium of Crime Prevention Practices to Inspire Action across the World.* Through collaborative research endeavors between university researchers, experts, and law enforcement organizations from various countries across the globe, the report provides an international overview of the main problems and concerns linked to crime, safety and victimization, as well as the criminal justice prevention measures that are undertaken to address them. Topics such as the impact of organized crime and substance on community safety, and safety in public spaces are highlighted as matters of global concern. Strategies for program evaluation as well as social and education approaches to crime prevention within vulnerable and at risk populations are also discussed. An emphasis on integrated, participative initiatives that target prevention and safety at local, national, and international levels as well as a focus on the evaluation of programs and strategies as effective frameworks for crime control are key components.[19]

CRIMES REACHING BEYOND NATIONAL BORDERS

Comparative research in criminology has increased our awareness that the challenge of crime control is not unique to our own society but rather is a common dilemma across the globe. It only makes sense that countries collaborate to share information and development of programs to combat crime, especially transnational and international criminal activities. We look at these two crime categories next.

Transnational crime

The National Institute of Justice (NIJ) has defined transnational crime as the criminal activities of individuals and groups who commit illegal activities that cross national borders. Transnational crimes are typically perpetrated by organized criminal groups that use violence, bribery, and corruption to carry out their illegal enterprises. Studies show these groups thrive most in countries characterized by weak political structure and civil unrest, often undermining government leadership and adding to the disruption in peace.[20] Advances in information technology and the ease of travel have facilitated the expansion

Image 20.3 *In April 2015, Interpol, an international police organization that facilitates cross-border police collaboration, sponsored a two-day conference that brought together law enforcement officials from around the world to discuss innovative security solutions for global challenges such as cyber safety, border management, and creating safe environments in center cities. This international forum allowed police officers to compare data, learn new investigative techniques, and become informed on best practices in handling crime.*

Roslan Rahman/AFP/Getty Images

and scope of transnational criminal activities, too, making this a problem in various countries around the world, including the United States. We will discuss four major categories of transnational crimes: intellectual property crimes, money laundering, illegal trafficking, and terrorism.

Intellectual property crime

Intellectual property crimes include the theft of trade secrets and trademarks and the violation of copyrights and patents, very often by selling counterfeit or illegally manufactured computer software, movies, music, books, and other commodities. Illegally manufactured products are mostly circulated in foreign markets and compete with the products of the rightful business owners, disrupting their industries and undermining legitimate commerce. East and southeast Asia and Latin America are major markets for the manufacture and distribution of counterfeit merchandise.

In 2000, an *Intellectual Property Crime Unit* was added to Interpol and mandated to collaborate with international government units, cross-border private sector industries, and patent protection entities to monitor and enforce intellectual property laws. One of their strategies has been the creation of an *International Intellectual Property Database* that serves as a depository for information about transnational intellectual property crime within the private sector industry.[21]

Money laundering

International banks and financial institutions are often used to conceal the origins of money from illegal enterprises such as gambling, drug trafficking, and fraud. After all, an individual who owns a small, run-down grocery store in downtown Manhattan that also operates as a front for a methamphetamine lab will have a hard time explaining a yearly profit of $100,000 beyond the sales of the grocery store. Organized crime groups thus "launder" money to hide their illegal enterprises behind legitimate businesses, making it very difficult for law enforcement to identify and trace their activities. In a typical money laundering scheme, the perpetrator will transfer money obtained from illegal activities through several financial institutions in order to obscure its origin. The money will eventually be funneled into a legitimate business in order to disguise its illegal origins and make it more difficult to detect. The extent of global money-laundering is estimated at about $3 trillion annually, a large portion of which represents illegal proceeds from drug trafficking.[22]

Illegal trafficking

The illegal trafficking of drugs, humans, and weapons creates a substantial threat to the social, political, and economic stability of countries around the world. According to the United Nations, international criminal organizations are the source of most illicit drugs smuggled into the United States, providing a global black market for the manufacture and distribution of substances such as cocaine, heroin, and methamphetamine.[23] The illegal trafficking of drugs presents a great challenge to crime control efforts, because some primary countries of origin are riddled with corruption at all levels of government (see Box 20.2).

Human trafficking (also discussed in chapter 16) is the movement of people from one place to another using force, fraud, or deception, with the

Image 20.4 *Children in India participate in a rally protesting the international trafficking of children. While child trafficking is a crime under international law, there is no comprehensive law against it in India, making these children more vulnerable to being preyed upon by human trafficking crime networks.*

Aijaz Rahi/AP/Press Association Images

goal of exploiting them for material or financial benefit.[24] Approximately 700,000 women and children are moved across international borders by trafficking rings each year.[25] The victims are usually poor, vulnerable, and desperate individuals from developing countries who are looking for a better life and are promised legitimate work in a rich society. Instead, they find forced servitude, slave-like labor, prostitution, sexual exploitation, and the removal of their organs for transplant.[26] The *United Nations Convention Against Transnational Organized Crime*, adopted in November 2000, is the primary mechanism for the global monitoring, control, and punishment of human trafficking operations.[27] The goal of the convention is to recognize the seriousness and global nature of the illegal trafficking of persons, and to enhance the collaboration of law enforcement agencies around the world in the development of policies and practices to combat this form of transnational crime.

The *United Nations Protocol against the Illicit Manufacturing of and Trafficking in Firearms, their Parts and Components and Ammunition* was adopted in May 2001. The primary goal of this resolution is "to promote, facilitate and strengthen cooperation among States Parties in order to prevent, combat and eradicate the illicit manufacturing of and trafficking in firearms, their parts and components and ammunition."[28] The black market transfer of arms has been a growing global concern since the early 1990s; it includes the trafficking of nuclear materials, assault rifles, spare parts for large weapons, ammunition, and anti-air/tank weapons, usually to countries under United Nations restrictions or sanctions. The implications for international security and foreign policy of illegal traffic in arms are profound; these weapons and the money made from their sale support the activities and operatives of paramilitary groups, combatants, insurgents, and terrorist organizations around the world.

BOX 20.2: CRIME IN GLOBAL PERSPECTIVE

The war in Afghanistan . . . A war on terror or a war on drugs?

In the aftermath of the 9/11 attack on the United States, drug-trafficking warlords in Afghanistan had taken advantage of the disruption in power resulting from global efforts to infiltrate the government and seize power. As a result, the illegal drug industry became intertwined with military power and government leadership. In late 2003, President Bush began to initiate measures for the removal of warlords from powerful government positions in Afghanistan, measures collectively referred to by the Bush administration as its "warlord strategy."

In 2006, the U.S. Government estimated that 94 percent of the world's opium came from the Southeast Asian poppy—specifically from Afghanistan and Pakistan. Most of the heroin produced in these regions is distributed in the European and Asian drug markets. Today, U.S. Officials note that poppy fields have spread over thousands of acres in remote Afghan countryside, making the nation one of the largest sources of opium and heroin in the world, and making the production of poppy one of the most dangerous weapons in the war against terrorism. Why is the production of a plant considered a dangerous weapon?

Since the onset of the U.S. invasion into Afghanistan in 2001, the aim to dismantle al-Qaeda by removing the Taliban from power has been a central mission supported by the United States and key allies, including the United Kingdom, and joined in 2003 by the National Atlantic Treaty Organization (NATO). Over time, it became apparent to military officials and government personnel in Washington that the new war on terror was intertwined with the old global war on drugs, as taxes on poppy farmers and opium dealers helped finance the Taliban's operatives, and the drug market became a means of laundering money and funding terrorist attacks.

As the war continued over the years to become the longest U.S. war since Vietnam, American policy makers recognized that the key to stabilizing and rebuilding Afghanistan and control the Taliban threat was to cut off the lucrative drug trade that was sustaining terrorist efforts. Although there was disagreement over how to strategize coordinated efforts to disrupt the drug trade, the threat to national and international security from terrorist organizations became linked to the aggressive pursuit of their major source of revenue.

Sources

Drug Trafficking in Afghanistan. *The New York Times*. Retrieved from http://topics.nytimes.com/top/news/international/countriesandterritories/afghanistan/drug_trafficking/index.html.

Munir, Allesandro Scotti. 2012. Corruption in Afghanistan: Trends and Patterns. United Nations Office on Drugs and Crime. Retrieved from http://www.unodc.org/documents/frontpage/Corruption_in_Afghanistan_FINAL.pdf.

Terrorism

No single crime garners a larger share of news coverage around the world today than terrorism. While there are different ways of defining the term, terrorism means premeditated, politically motivated violence designed to spread fear and perpetrated against civilians by sub-national groups or clandestine agents.[29]

Terrorist acts include threats made by vigilante groups and extremists who are either seeking to maintain the status quo or trying to bring about radical social and political change. We have seen many of these acts in the past, ranging from the arson and vandalism of abortion clinics that began in the early 1970s, to the 1995 attack on a Federal building in Oklahoma City. While terrorism is not a new phenomenon, transnational terrorism, where radical groups from one or more nations organize acts of violence against the citizens of another country has in recent years become a matter of global concern.

The most widely recognized terrorist groups in the recent past have been al-Qaeda—who, under the leadership of Osama Bin Laden, orchestrated the September 11, 2001 attack on the World Trade Center in New York City and the attack on the Pentagon—as well as the Taliban, the religious and political faction who fought the Soviets in Afghanistan; the Palestinian Islamic Jihad;

Image 20.5 *Over a million people joined more than 40 world leaders, including presidents and prime ministers from around the globe, in one of the most profound shows of solidarity against the threat of Islamic extremism in November 2015. The series of terrorist tactics and suicide bombings, perpetrated by ISIS attackers, took place in Paris, France on November 13, 2015, killing 130 people and wounded several hundred more. This act of terrorism received worldwide attention and people of all races, ages, religions, and political affiliations all around the world united in support against the violence.*

Kvin Niglaut/Newzulu/PA Images

Lebanon's Hezbollah; the Palestinian Hamas; and Egypt's al-Gama'a al-Islamiyya. Today, the most significant presence of a terrorist threat is posed by the Islamic State of Iraq and Syria, also known as ISIS. During testimony at a House Armed Services Committee hearing on the threat of Islamic extremism, retired Lieutenant General Michael Flynn, former Defense Intelligence Agency director, referred to ISIS by saying, "We are at war with violent extreme Islamists."[30]

Currently under U.S. federal law, the State Department is required to compile information on the number of individuals killed, injured, or kidnapped by each identified terrorist group within a given year. In 2012, the National Consortium for the Study of Terrorism and Responses to Terrorism (START) contracted with the US Department of State to provide a statistical report to include in the State Department's annual *Country Reports on Terrorism*. A few of their most recent findings:[31]

- In 2012, a total of 6,771 terrorist attacks occurred worldwide, resulting in more than 11,000 deaths and more than 21,600 injuries.
- On average, there were 564.25 attacks, 924.83 deaths, and 1,804.33 injuries per month in 2012. There were 1.64 fatalities and 3.20 injuries per attack, including perpetrator casualties.
- The high number of fatalities in January (1,378) was due in large part to terrorist violence in Iraq (425 deaths) and Nigeria (348 deaths).
- The increase in terrorist violence from February through June includes the onset of spring "fighting season" in Afghanistan, where there was a 153 percent increase in attacks and a 158 percent increase in fatalities.
- Although terrorist attacks occurred in 85 different countries in 2012, they were heavily concentrated geographically. Over half of all attacks (55 percent), fatalities (62 percent), and injuries (65 percent) occurred in just three countries: Pakistan, Iraq, and Afghanistan.
- The highest number of fatalities occurred in Afghanistan (2,632); however the country with the most injuries due to terrorist attacks was Iraq (6,641).
- The average lethality of terrorist attacks in Nigeria (2.54 deaths per attack) is more than 50 percent higher than the global average of 1.64. The average lethality of terrorist attacks in Syria (4.94 deaths per attack) is more than 200 percent higher than the global average.
- The average number of people wounded per terrorist attack was especially high in Syria, where 1,787 people were reportedly wounded in 133 attacks, including four attacks that caused 670 injuries.
- In contrast, the rates of lethality for India (0.42 deaths per attack), the Philippines (0.77 deaths per attack), and Thailand (0.78 deaths per attack) were relatively low among the countries with the most attacks.

The global rage over transnational terrorism took on new meaning after September 11, 2001, when terrorists hijacked four airplanes and crashed two of them into the World Trade Center in New York and another into the Pentagon outside Washington, D.C. A fourth plane, apparently intended for the White House, crashed in a field in Pennsylvania after passengers fought with the hijackers. Today more than ever, through international satellite television networks and Internet videos, millions of people are now able to watch hijackings, torture, missile firings, executions, and suicide bombings. This global threat to security will continue to be at the forefront of law enforcement and strategic military planning worldwide in the ongoing assessment of threat and the development of counterterrorist operatives. Our success in this endeavor will largely depend on the ability of international organizations, regional institutions, and local governments to implement coordinated strategies that rely on a collaborative understanding of this type of criminal activity.

International crime

While terrorism receives global attention as one of the most challenging transnational crimes, certain other criminal offenses designated as gross violations of human interests are governed by international laws. These offenses are collectively referred to as **international crime**. The *International Law Commission* describes the following "crimes against the peace and security of mankind":[32]

- *Crime of aggression*—An individual who, as leader or organizer, actively participates in or orders the planning, preparation, initiation, or waging of aggression committed by a State shall be responsible for a crime of aggression.
- *Crimes against humanity*—A crime against humanity involves particularly repulsive offences in that they constitute a serious attack on human dignity or grave humiliation or a degradation of one or more human beings. They are not isolated or sporadic events, but are a part of either a government policy or of a wide systematic practice of atrocities tolerated or condoned by a government, including genocide, murder, torture, rape, and political, racial, or religious persecution and human rights violations.
- *Crimes against United Nations and associated personnel*—These are crimes committed intentionally and in a systematic manner or on a large scale against United Nations and associated personnel involved in a United Nations operation with a view to preventing or impeding that operation from fulfilling its mandate, including murder, kidnapping, and attack upon the official premises.
- *War crimes*—A war crime is a systematic or large scale violation of international humanitarian law, including willful killing, torture, or inhuman treatment, willfully causing great suffering or serious injury to body or health, extensive destruction and appropriation of property, not justified by military necessity, compelling a prisoner of war or other protected person to serve in the forces of a hostile power, willfully depriving a prisoner of war or other protected person of the rights of fair and regular trial,

unlawful deportation, transfer or confinement of protected persons, taking of hostages, making the civilian population or individual civilians the object of attack, and using methods or means of warfare not justified by military necessity with the intent to cause widespread, long-term, and severe damage to the natural environment and thereby gravely prejudice the health or survival of the population and such damage occurs.

Recognizing the need to hold accountable the most serious perpetrators of international crime, leaders from around the world convened a diplomatic conference in Rome in the summer of 1998. The outcome of that meeting came to be known as the **Rome Treaty**, which established the first **International Criminal Court (ICC)**. It was not until July 2002, however, that the court took full force when the number of states required to ratify the treaty reached sixty. As of January 2015, 123 countries have ratified the Rome Statute of the International Criminal Court.

The magnitude and scope of international crime has increasingly become the subject of criminological research.[33] At the heart of this dialog is a discussion of the complex role of technology.

THE ROLE OF TECHNOLOGY IN FACILITATING CRIME

Not a year goes by when we are not flooded with new opportunities to partake in new technology. Whatever the latest hi-tech innovation is, whether it tickles our musical fancy or connects us to the world around us, its cumulative effect is always the same, allowing us to process, access, and store information faster, more easily, more efficiently, and in less space. While technology is designed to make life more convenient, bringing the three-dimensional world right to our fingertips, it can also create an array of complications for law enforcement and criminology.

Image 20.6 *Technology has dramatically facilitated the theft of information. In an age where storing paper documents is a thing of the past, confidential files containing personal data, financial records, and sensitive materials are now available to hackers at the touch of a button.*

Tek Image/Science Photo Library

The expansion of technology also enables criminals to better organize, profit from, and conceal illegal drug trafficking, prostitution, pornography, and other criminal enterprises at the national and international level, using on-line financial transactions to hide and launder illicit gains. Over the years, criminologists have attempted to shed some light on the growing trend in crimes facilitated through the use of technology.[34] Studies note that the rise in crimes using technology coincides with the age of the computer and the expanded use of the internet.[35]

Advances in technology have indeed expanded the scope and magnitude of criminal behavior, transforming crime into a global phenomenon. This has made the detection of criminal activities difficult and the apprehension of suspects a daunting task, as organized crime groups use technology to create databases that facilitate the trafficking and distribution of drugs, weapons, and other transactions in support of their criminal enterprises.

Box 20.3 illustrates the use of technology such as chat rooms as a resource for disseminating pornography, soliciting sex from children, gambling, and inciting hate, violence, and terrorism (see Box 20.3).

BOX 20.3: CONSIDER THIS . . .

"Calling all haters" . . . Using the internet to solicit terrorism

On February 18, 2016, a southwest Missouri woman was charged with using Internet social media sites to convey threats of violence based on pro-Islamic statements and group messages. The 38-year-old resident of Buffalo was charged on allegations that she posted the names, addresses, and phone numbers of two FBI agents under the heading "Wanted to Kill."

On July 16, 2013, American Muslim Emerson Winfield Begolly received a sentence of 102 months in prison for solicitation to commit a crime of violence. The 24-year-old native of New Bethlehem, Pennsylvania, used an Internet website in 2011 to urge Muslim radicals living throughout the United States to engage in a wide variety of terrorist acts, including sabotaging train tracks, destroying telephone and power lines, starting forest fires, and engaging in attacks against American civilians, military officers, and police.

On June 22, 2012, Jesse Curtis Morton, aka Younus Abdullah Muhammed, was sentenced to 138 months in prison in a federal court in New York. The 33-year-old leader of the "Revolution Muslim" organization's Internet sites was found guilty of conspiring to solicit murder and make threatening communications through use of the Internet. According to U.S. Attorney Neil H. MacBride, Morton "sought to inspire Muslims to engage in terrorism by providing doctrinal justification for violence against civilians in the name of Islam."

Exploitation of the Internet is all but inevitable thanks to the huge number of unmonitored sites and transactions and numerous opportunities for hacking, identity theft, and the spread of viruses. One of the most recent criminal applications of the Internet is the use of websites and chat rooms to plan and coordinate terrorist attacks across national borders. More than ever, extreme terrorist organizations are turning to the Internet to recruit, train, and indoctrinate members and solicit funds to carry out attacks, all with little threat of detection.

One of the most notorious terrorist organizations of modern times is the Islamic extremist militant group known as al-Qaida. Although this group is known to be a decentralized network of affiliates with no structure, hierarchy, or chain of command, it had been an international threat for years through its global alliance of independent groups connected through one central component of organization: the Internet. Intelligence sources note that al-Qaida continues to survive despite being heavily targeted by the 2001 War on Terrorism due to its significant reliance on forming a worldwide network of alliances via Internet communication. For al-Qaida, the Internet has been a major source of group solidarity and social cohesion, providing a platform and instrument to spread their ideologies and propaganda, as well as creating a database for recruitment and networking. It is estimated that al-Qaida operates 5,600 websites including jihadist websites, forums, chat rooms, electronic message boards, and blogs.

In 2006, civil rights activists were outraged by the United Kingdom's passage of the Terrorism Act of 2006. The Act strictly prohibits the publication or dissemination of even so much as language that instigates, induces, or provokes terrorist acts and prohibits the publication of any work that may be interpreted as encouragement, training, and preparation of terrorism. British civil rights activists claimed this was a violation of citizens' right to freedom of speech; in the end, however, the threat to human life and safety proved more important. Besides creating new offenses relating to the sale, distribution, and transmission of terrorist publications, the Terrorism Act of 2006 also extends the authority of law enforcement by allowing the police to hold terrorist suspects from 14 days to 28 days without filing formal charges. Moreover, the Act grants the home secretary greater powers to ban groups that glorify terrorism and to prevent restricted groups from using other organizations as "fronts" for their continued operation.

Society as a whole is racing to pass enforceable anti-terrorism legislation before another human life is lost or threatened. The Terrorism Act is an example of a step in that direction. Nevertheless, monitoring all forms of online communication will continue to be a challenge, never mind screening the content of all Internet sites, social media, and email. *What do you think?*

Sources

Leader of Revolution Muslim Sentenced to 138 Months for Using Internet to Solicit Murder, Encourage Violent Extremism. 2012. Office of Public Affairs, Federal Bureau of Investigation, U.S. Department of Justice, Washington, D.C.

Missouri Woman Accused of Threatening FBI Agents on Twitter. 2016. *Associated Press,* Feb. 18. Retrieved from http://www.ksdk.com/news/crime/missouri-woman-accused-of-threatening-fbi-agents-on-twitter/48069816.

Pennsylvania Man Sentenced for Terrorism Solicitation and Firearms Offense. 2013. Office of Public Affairs, Federal Bureau of Investigation, U.S. Department of Justice, Washington, D.C.

The Terrorism Act 2006. 2006. UK Home Office. Retrieved from https://www.gov.uk/government/publications/the-terrorism-act-2006.

The growth of technology has also guided the direction of law enforcement and crime control in investigating crimes and improving public safety.[36] Scientific advances in imaging systems, for example, have increased the speed and accuracy of the detection of concealed weapons at security checkpoints.[37] Enhanced recordkeeping and identification systems, advances in information sharing, crime-solving innovations, and the speed of data transmission are all by-products of the age of technology that have improved crime control policies and practices worldwide.

MODERN RESPONSES TO MODERN PROBLEMS

With the expansion of technology and an increase in globalization, the prevalence of international and transnational criminal activity has posed a threat to the national and international security and stability of countries across the world. The widespread smuggling of contraband, the illegal traffic of humans, the host of fraudulent schemes and the intricate development of organized crime networks has changed the scope and meaning of criminal justice enforcement. Box 20.4 elaborates on the connection between technology, research, and law enforcement.

In 1995, in response to the urgent threat posed by the globalization of crime, President Bill Clinton issued a directive ordering agencies of the executive branch of government to prioritize resources devoted to combating this threat, improve internal coordination, collaborate with other governments to develop a global response, and aggressively and creatively use all legal means available to combat international crime.[38] During a speech at the United Nations, President Clinton described the threat as follows:

> The nation's critical infrastructure systems—such as energy, banking, and telecommunications—are increasingly based on commercial information technologies, and, for economic and operational reasons, are increasingly interconnected. As a result, these systems are vulnerable to increasingly varied threats and are at a heightened risk of catastrophic failure. The range of potential adversaries that may seek to attack U.S. infrastructure systems is broad and growing. Disgruntled employees, disaffected individuals or groups, organized crime groups, domestic and international terrorists, and hostile nations are all potential sources of attack. [International criminals] jeopardize the global trend toward peace and freedom, undermine fragile new democracies, sap the strength from developing countries, [and] threaten our efforts to build a safer, more prosperous world.[39]

Since the 1995 presidential directive, various initiatives have focused crime control on comprehensive strategies dealing with the threat of transnational and international criminal activities. One outcome was the development and implementation of the **International Crime Control Strategy (ICCS)**, an action plan describing a far-reaching strategy with broadly defined goals and objectives that serves as an outline for a coordinated, forceful, and enduring federal response to global crime threats. Table 20.1 lists the goals and objectives of the ICCS.

The worldwide expansion of criminal networks has created a critical need for law enforcement agencies around the globe to enhance crime control measures to create a coordinated effort in the attack on transnational and international crime threats. Leading agencies in the United States, including the Departments of Justice, State, Treasury, Homeland Security, Defense, and

BOX 20.4: CONNECTING RESEARCH TO PRACTICE

Criminals beware! Fighting crime with "cybergenetics"

Technology research has played a significant role in the development of criminal justice policies and practices. Modern Geographic Information Systems (GIS) mapping, for example, has allowed researchers to analyze and interpret the impact of sex offender residency laws within the area being mapped by comparing exclusions zones to the available housing in a community. Policy makers can then use this data to determine whether or not affordable housing is available for sex offenders within approved areas and to evaluate their suitability in terms of access to transportation to and from treatment facilities.

Today more than ever, technology has become a crime fighting tool and research has produced new mechanisms by which the apprehension of criminal suspects is better, faster, and more reliable. One area where research has made significant strides is DNA analysis. According to the National Institute of Justice, DNA technology programs have been a leading resource in solving 'cold' homicide and sexual assault cases, with advances in biotechnology research increasing the successful analysis of compromised evidence at crime scenes, evidence that was once deemed unusable due to age, corruption, or decomposition.

In the United States, the most well-known DNA database system is the FBI's Combined DNA Index System, or CODIS. Blending computer software and forensic science, researchers have produced a multi-level technology platform where DNA profiles can be searched and stored at the local, state, and national levels. This allows crime scene analysts to interface databases in order to match profiles from across jurisdictions. So, for example, DNA evidence obtained from a crime scene can be searched and matched with profiles from other crime scenes and also from convicted or arrested offenders to see if a match can be generated. As of December 2015, CODIS contained over 12,113,810 offender profiles, 2,201,763 arrestee profiles, and 674,150 forensic profiles, producing over 315,410 matches and assisting in more than 303,201 investigations.

Technology research in criminal justice continues today and advances in crime fighting will continue to make it difficult for suspects to hide. The newest research in the fighting of crime is emerging, and recent developments have been made in what is now being referred to as Rapid DNA Analysis. According to a recent FBI factsheet, this new technology is a "Fully automated (hands free) process of developing a CODIS Core STR profile from a reference sample buccal swab. The swab in—profile out process consists of automated extraction, amplification, separation, detection, and allele calling without human intervention."

Sources

Frequently Asked Questions (FAQs) on the CODIS Program and the National DNA Index System. Retrieved from https://www.fbi.gov/about-us/lab/biometric-analysis/codis/codis-and-ndis-fact-sheet.

National Institute of Justice. What is CODIS? 2010. *National Institute of Justice Journal* 266. Retrieved from http://nij.gov/journals/266/Pages/backlogs-codis.aspx.

Table 20.1 Global crime concern ... What are we doing about it?

International crime control strategy goals	How will these goals be achieved?
Goal 1: Extend the first line of defense beyond U.S. borders	• prevent acts of international crime planned abroad, including terrorist acts, before they occur • use all available laws to prosecute select criminal acts committed abroad • intensify activities of law enforcement, diplomatic, and consular personnel abroad
Goal 2: Protect U.S. borders by attacking smuggling and smuggling-related crimes	• enhance our land border inspection, detection, and monitoring capabilities through a greater resource commitment, further coordination of federal agency efforts, and increased cooperation with the private sector • improve the effectiveness of maritime and air smuggling interdiction efforts in the transit zone • seek new, stiffer criminal penalties for smuggling activities • target enforcement and prosecutorial resources more effectively against smuggling crimes and organizations
Goal 3: Deny safe haven to international criminals	• negotiate new international agreements to create a seamless web for the prompt location, arrest, and extradition of international fugitives • implement strengthened immigration laws that prevent international criminals from entering the United States and provide for their prompt expulsion when appropriate • promote increased cooperation with foreign law enforcement authorities to provide rapid, mutual access to witnesses, records, and other evidence
Goal 4: Counter international financial crime	• combat money laundering by denying criminals access to financial institutions and by strengthening enforcement efforts to reduce inbound and outbound movement of criminal proceeds • seize the assets of international criminals through aggressive use of forfeiture laws • enhance bilateral and multilateral cooperation against all financial crime by working with foreign governments to establish or update enforcement tools and implement multilateral anti-money laundering standards • target offshore centers of international fraud, counterfeiting, electronic access device schemes, and other financial crimes
Goal 5: Prevent criminal exploitation of international trade	• interdict illegal technology exports through improved detection, increased cooperation with the private sector, and heightened sanctions • prevent unfair and predatory trade practices in violation of U.S. criminal law • protect intellectual property rights by enhancing foreign and domestic law enforcement efforts to curtail the flow of counterfeit and pirated goods, and by educating consumers • counter industrial theft and economic espionage of U.S. trade secrets through increased prosecution of offenders • enforce import restrictions on certain harmful substances, dangerous organisms, and protected species
Goal 6: Respond to emerging international crime threats	• disrupt new activities of international organized crime groups • enhance intelligence efforts against criminal enterprises to provide timely warning of changes in their organizations and methods • reduce trafficking in human beings and crimes against children • increase enforcement efforts against high tech and computer-related crime

continued

Table 20.1 *continued*

International crime control strategy goals	How will these goals be achieved?
	• continue identifying and countering the vulnerabilities of critical infrastructures and new technologies in telecommunications, financial transactions, and other high tech areas
Goal 7: Foster international cooperation and the rule of law	• establish international standards, goals and objectives to combat international crime by using bilateral, multilateral, regional, and global mechanisms, and by actively encouraging compliance • improve bilateral cooperation with foreign governments and law enforcement authorities through increased collaboration, training, and technical assistance • strengthen the rule of law as the foundation for democratic government and free markets in order to reduce societies' vulnerability to criminal exploitation
Goal 8: Optimize the full range of U.S. efforts	• enhance executive branch policy and operational coordination mechanisms to assess the risks of criminal threats and to integrate strategies, goals, and objectives to combat those threats • mobilize and incorporate the private sector into U.S. government efforts • develop measures of effectiveness to assess progress over time

Source: International Crime Control Strategy. Retrieved from http://fas.org/irp/offdocs/iccs/iccstoc.html.

Commerce are building programs and initiatives that are built upon the foundation of cooperation from foreign governments. It is up to criminologists to integrate this trend into the theoretical understanding of criminal behavior, as well as assess its implication for criminal justice research, policy and practice within our own borders and beyond. We turn now to a discussion of the future of criminological theory.

TOWARD A "NEW" CRIMINOLOGY

Within society, one variable has remained a constant feature of social interaction: the entanglement of individual traits with environmental circumstances. A toddler with poor impulse control pulls her classmate's hair to get back a toy; a college athlete with low ethical standards cheats on an exam in order to maintain his scholarship; an urban mother with limited financial means and no social support network shoplifts to make ends meet; a corporate executive is swayed by board members to fix prices in order to maintain profits. Examples of flawed human interactions are diverse and endless. Some are common occurrences that have become embedded in the way people handle conflict and strife. Others shock us and leave us with unanswered questions.

Such was the case when Dr. Amy Bishop methodically opened fire on her university colleagues during a faculty meeting in February 2010, killing three and stopping only after her gun jammed. The Harvard-trained biology professor at the University of Alabama at Huntsville had been upset at being denied tenure, which would force her to look for work elsewhere. Records indicate she had episodes of violence in her past, including an incident, officially labeled an accident, in which she shot and killed her brother in 1986. Bishop was also questioned in regard to a pipe bomb that was sent to one of her colleagues at Children's Hospital in Boston.[40]

The attack by Dr. Bishop is riddled with questions. What individual characteristics define her mental and emotional state? What social correlates contributed to the strain and frustration leading up to the shooting? Why were measures not taken to investigate Dr. Bishop's questionable past? How did the structural dynamics of the tenure process affect the hostile interaction that took place between her and her colleagues? In this section, we look back and reflect on the various paradigms in theoretical criminology that have guided our discussions of crime causation, criminological research, and policy development.

Defining crime: a practical synthesis

The task of criminology has traditionally revolved around answering the question why some people commit crime while others do not. This question was sufficient for an understanding of crime until the 1960s ushered in an era of civil disobedience, anti-war demonstrations, marijuana and cocaine use by the middle class, corruption among political leaders, and criminal violations by leading corporations. At that point, criminologists became more concerned with the changing definition of certain behaviors as criminal, patterns and trends in arrest statistics, and the distribution of different types of crimes among women and men, ethnic and racial groups, as well as social classes.

We began this text at the heart of criminology, with a study of the law-making process, and discovered that many acts come to be defined as criminal because of the interplay between power, politics, and economic conditions.

Image 20.7 *The many faces of deviance in mainstream society, as seen at this Mardi Gras parade, are constantly defining the nature and meaning of crime and crime causation. Acts of deviance and crime committed by college students in different contexts don't always fit the molds of differential associations or violent subcultures.*

Gerald Herbert/AP/Press Association Images

We also learned that because certain acts were defined as crimes, those arrested, prosecuted, sentenced, and confined were not necessarily the ones posing the greatest threat to society but instead were those whom society *defined* as the greatest threat. They were also usually the poorest and most vulnerable. For a long time, our definition of crime ignored the acts of white-collar offenders, government officials, and organized criminals.

The definition of crime as behavior unique to certain individuals and their personal experiences led to a plethora of theoretical frameworks that searched for the origin of criminal behavior within the individual. Such individual level analyses led to biological theories which searched for abnormalities within the structure and function of the brain, as well as psychological theories that explored the human mind, and identified weaknesses and pathological traits within the personality. Some sociological theories found the origin of crime within the conflicts and strains that make up the daily lives of individuals, while others proposed that criminality was a normal response for some people because they learned crime from their peers, parents, or subculture or had differential opportunities to achieve status, wealth, and power. Labeling theory argued that everyone committed initial acts of crime or primary deviance, but some were labeled deviant by their peers, community, or selves and their self-image changed to reflect the labels attached to them. This collective level of analysis forced us to explore the role of social reaction in the perpetuation of crime and deviance. With this understanding, conflict theories directed our attention to different forms of inequality within the social structure, which helped us understand why some people are labeled criminal while others are not. Through this revelation, we were able to see that a comprehensive understanding of the nature and meaning of crime had to go beyond the definition of individual acts of deviant behavior.

In order to effectively guide criminal justice policy and practice, criminological theory must therefore approach the study of crime through the shining light of cultural, political, and economic influences on the development of criminal laws, the distortion of the crime problem, and the prediction of criminal behavior. The challenge for criminology is to link the study of crime with political and economic forces shaping our institutions and our social relations. The most promising leads today employ the methodology of the dialectic and an integrated theoretical approach.

Integrating theories

We have seen throughout our journey in this text that, in order to understand the dynamics of criminal behavior and crime causation, criminology must be driven by a desire to study, explain, and solve the crime problem, and not be misguided by political rhetoric, media distortion, and unfounded public fear over escalating crime rates. We must also acknowledge the cultural and structural characteristics of society that shape social interactions and define the nature of our communities. Moreover, a scientific criminology, whether Marxist or behaviorist, must commit itself to understanding the full range of criminality by explaining the entire range of phenomena called crime, as well as the political, economic, and social forces leading to differences in crime rates across different historical periods and between different countries in the same period.

The study of crime causation from the separate perspectives of biology, psychology, and sociology has for years created a divide between what we think people are like and how we think they behave. Increasingly, criminologists are recognizing the need to integrate a variety of views, acknowledge that each is at least partially correct, and recognize that they offer greater insight when taken together.[41] Contemporary criminological theory is thus marked by an interdisciplinary approach. It goes beyond the effort to change individuals and instead seeks to understand the underlying components of social structure that shape human behavior.[42] Criminologists are abandoning the schisms that have traditionally divided theoretical development in favor of a more pragmatic approach that integrates the various paradigms. In doing this, we are putting human behavior within a context, recognizing not only that people are different and unique in their ways of thinking, processing information, and reacting, but that their circumstances, conditions, and experiences are also diverse.

We have seen that comparative criminological research has taught us a valuable lesson, namely, that human behavior is not tied to any particular society, group, or individual. Through the study of crime in various parts of the world, criminology has evolved to study crime as a product of interactions between people, in which individual motivations are intertwined in social organization and structural relationships. In order to better understand crime today and in the future, we need multi-dimensional models of crime causation that combine, link, and synthesize various theoretical constructs.[43]

By integrating components of various theories, we can make sense of the different types of crimes that span the interpersonal, organizational, and structural levels of society, advancing away from cause-effect relationships that focus on narrow explanations of particular types of crime. Just because events happen at the same time, we cannot assume the relationship between them will be constant every time or even over time. We can see, for example, that anomie and strain can be primary sources of frustration leading to white-collar crime, but more so within corporate subcultures that neutralize moral obligation and thereby threaten social bonds.[44] Moreover, when we consider why some people conform to societal norms and expectations while others do not, we also need to consider that social conformity is a bigger motivation for self-control in cultures where non-conformity is shameful.[45]

Theoretical criminology has laid the foundation for the study of crime for the past several centuries. From the founders of the discipline, we have discerned various ideas about the nature of crime, the origins of legal definition, and the pursuit of social control. The different perspectives on crime have traditionally proposed diverse, often conflicting sets of underlying assumptions about the definition of crime and the origin of criminal behavior. As we move forward toward an integrated, solutions-oriented approach to combating the social problems leading to crime, we will continue to rely on theoretical foundations that rest on the shoulders of scientifically based research methods.

CRIMINOLOGY'S IMPACT ON SOCIAL POLICY: AN INTEGRATED APPROACH TO CRIME PREVENTION

Our search for reliable knowledge about the origins of crime must be embedded in the social realities that surround us. The fact is, street crimes such as robbery and assault are more common in poor, urban communities; white-collar crime reflects a value system in which cooperation and community are stifled by competition and power; political corruption is embedded in the structure of government; and globalization has redefined the nature of organized crime. We must therefore pursue crime-reducing solutions that are rooted in these and other realities revealed to us through criminological research.

Undoubtedly, criminal behavior is a matter of public concern. It is a social harm committed against an individual, a community, and society as a whole. We even build our criminal court cases based on that premise when we say "People v. John Doe" or "State v. Jane Doe." Indeed, reacting to crime is an age-old phenomenon, from ancient witch hunts and public hangings, to neighborhood watches, and community action groups of today. What has changed over the years is that due process and civil liberties have affected our reaction to crime and criminals, and the manner in which we implement different techniques of fighting crime, as we discussed in chapter 5.

Crime-control strategies must go beyond funneling more lawbreakers into the criminal justice system, since this has proven the costliest and least effective method of reducing crime over the years.[46] We must address the question of crime prevention at its cultural and structural roots. Crime prevention occurs through two major models of intervention. At the primary level, crime control strategies focus on conditions within the social environment that are known to be associated with high rates of crime. At the secondary level, crime control strategies identify behavior patterns, relationships and situations that increase the likelihood of criminal behavior. Let's look at some major new developments at each level.

Primary prevention: targeting risk

A hallmark contribution of criminological theories over the past several decades is the development of scientifically based methods of identifying individuals at risk of delinquency and crime and intervening in their lives at the earliest possible stage.[47] This is often referred to as **risk factor analysis** in the prevention of crime and delinquency.[48] The analysis of risk approaches the study of crime with an understanding of the socio-demographic distribution of criminal behavior. The defining and measuring of risk factors is grounded in research-based evidence on the distribution of crime among different segments of the

Image 20.8 *The Wilmington, North Carolina, police department sponsors an annual "Santa Cop" program that matches children in need with a police officer for a day of shopping during Christmas. The children are of different ages, up to the seventh grade, and have experienced some type of physical or emotional trauma or personal struggle. The program is a partnership with several area business and individual donors. It is an example of how agents of criminal justice can reach out to the community and contribute in a way that builds partnership, trust, and mutual respect.*

Borut Zivulovic/FA Bobo/PIXSELL/Pixsell/PA Images

population. Risk factor analysis recognizes that delinquency is high among youth from dysfunctional families, that street crime is more common in densely populated urban communities, and that sexual violence is fairly high on college campuses throughout the country.

Criminology has served as a cornerstone for risk factor analysis research and the implementation of policies shaping crime prevention. Individual- and community-level solutions can now be based on an understanding of the multiple risk factors associated with child development, social relationships, and structural disadvantage.[49] Initiatives for early intervention, for example, have been based on five principle components that have direct theoretical relevance to various biological, psychological, and social structure theories of criminal behavior:

(1) Expanding pre- and post-natal healthcare to identify early any neurological impairments associated with behavioral problems.
(2) Providing a comprehensive array of services to high-risk children and their families, including preschool enrichment programs, parenting classes, and in-home counseling.
(3) Allowing parents to be gainfully employed by providing quality, affordable childcare and flexible work schedules.

(4) Improving the quality of education within school systems plagued by the dysfunctions of urban deterioration.

(5) Establishing social support networks for victims of crime in order to break the cycle of violence and abuse.

Risk factor analysis has indeed paved the way for understanding the social context within which crime takes place. However, there is still some disconnect between the variables identified and targeted within risk reduction programs, and the broader social structure. In order to bridge this gap, criminological theory has to provide crime control policy makers with some guidance on the connection between social problems and risk assessment, where risk is an identified variable but does not alone drive programs and initiatives. Changes in individual behavior must be connected to changes within the larger social-structural context of organizations and institutions. Who we are and the different experiences that we encounter span the life-course as we transition through different phases of maturity that bring us into contact with different social, cognitive, emotional, and physical experiences. Targeting risk factors related to offending must take into account these variations.

Secondary prevention: targeting development

Researchers have identified a model of prevention based on the concept that interventions aimed at multiple risk factors and over a long period of time are more likely to have positive results.[50] This model is known as **developmental pathways**. By analyzing the way in which different life experiences contribute to change at the individual level, as well as change within the social environment around the individual, the developmental pathways model invests in strategies and programs that target multiple risk factors at various crucial points of transition throughout life, from birth, to preschool, throughout the school years and adolescence, and into the adult experiences of higher education and employment. This approach is guided by six major principles:[51]

(1) Interventions in one context (such as the home) interact with, complement, and support interventions in other contexts (such as school).

(2) Relationships, trust, and cooperation between staff and clients are valued equally with evidence about what works.

(3) Better individual outcomes are achieved through the enrichment of all relevant developmental settings. Child-oriented programs are best integrated with family support initiatives and programs introduced through appropriate systems such as schools, childcare and family health centers, or community groups.

(4) Intervention effects are more effective if they coincide with life transitions (such as birth and starting school or high school), when people are both vulnerable and receptive to help.

(5) A continuum of age-appropriate programs and resources can enhance developmental pathways over time.

(6) Well-integrated programs and practices are best achieved by building partnerships between organizations, institutions, and agencies relevant to child and family wellbeing.

The developmental pathways model focuses our attention on the cultural and structural roots of crime as they contribute to individual risk. Under this approach, we acknowledge that risk is a symptom of the failure of social structures to initiate and support an individual's proper social development.[52] Through our understanding of criminological theory, we are able to identify key elements that contribute to this failure:

- The lack of employment or underemployment that leaves people bound to poverty and its associated social conditions.
- Segregated, densely populated public housing that contributes to deteriorated neighborhoods, weak social institutions, and high crime rates.
- The inherent suspicion and distrust in urban communities where social bonds are weak, community ties are fragile, and individuals are alienated.
- Socialization into roles in which the virtues of cooperation and respect are secondary to advancement, greed, and economic success.
- Structural inequalities that are embedded in the traditional roles of men and women, contributing to social subordination.

Crime prevention measures must therefore go beyond the assessment of individual risk factors to helping communities create a structure within which we can combine individual intervention strategies with the right resources, opportunities, and social processes. Would we ask a child to go get a drink of water without giving that child directions for turning on the water source, providing that child with a cup, and making sure the water source is actually working?

Criminal justice policies and practices must rely on mutually beneficial relationships within the community to address social concerns, as well as to raise public trust in law enforcement. The role of criminology is to guide criminal justice to make a long-term commitment to programs and services embedded in the structure of local communities. Researchers have identified the most successful initiatives as those that incorporate the following elements:[53]

- Create a network of support that links home, school, and community agencies.
- Encourage community members to take a stake in the wellbeing of their neighborhoods and streets, incorporating principles of situational crime prevention such as increasing lighting in streets, cleaning up parks, maintaining properties well, creating neighborhood watch groups, reporting suspicious activity, and collaborating with law enforcement.

- Invest in community resources and diversion programs that aim at reintegrating offenders into society as opposed to incarceration.
- Expand upon the paradigm of community oriented policing and direct police activities to crime "hot spots." Studies show that concentrating police activities in areas that are at greater risk of crime and disorder can reduce criminal activities.
- Undertake to increase public trust in law enforcement by removing elements of discrimination and profiling.
- Recognize the role of structural disadvantage, inequalities, and contradictions in the development of criminal behavior.

Criminologists around the world are engaging in groundbreaking research every day to guide criminal justice policy toward an effective solution to criminal behavior. Will they ever solve the problem of crime in society? Probably not. We can only hope that their research is guided by evidence-based criminological theories that analyze and explain crime as it relates to the social structure, as a phenomenon that encompasses people in all social classes, races, historical time periods, and personal circumstances. It is this message we hope we have conveyed to you as a student of criminology. It is this message we hope you can carry to criminal justice administrators, policy makers, and legislators.

SUMMARY

How can we benefit from the study of crime in different parts of the world?

By studying crime in different parts of the world, criminologists are better able to identify common variables within criminological theory and test concepts and ideas under multiple socio-cultural environments. Moreover, using comparative data to understand cross-national patterns of criminal behavior can effectively direct law enforcement policies and practices.

What types of criminal activities violate the rules of more than one country?

Criminal activities that violate the laws of multiple countries and cross national borders are known as transnational crimes. Criminal groups use violence, bribery, and corruption to engage in criminal activities involving the theft of intellectual property, cyber crimes, money laundering, illegal trafficking, and terrorism. Gross violations of human interest are considered crimes against the peace and security of humankind and are therefore governed by international laws. These acts are collectively referred to as international crime and include genocide, war crimes, and crimes against humanity.

In what ways has technology contributed to crime?

Advances in technology, especially the use of computers and the Internet, have made quick and easy access to information almost universal and transformed crime into a global phenomenon. Crimes like malicious hacking, online pornography, and identity theft can now compromise the integrity of computer networks and use technology itself as a resource in the commission of crime.

Is the science of criminology effectively dealing with crime in modern society?

With the globalization of crime and the expansion of criminal networks around the world, the science of criminology must continue to engage in research endeavors that represent a collaborative and cooperative effort between governments and law enforcement agencies around the world in the attack on transnational and international crime threats.

How do we arrive at a comprehensive definition of crime?

Any comprehensive definition of crime must capture the various acts of criminal behavior in light of the various cultural, political, and economic influences on the development of criminal laws, the distortion of the crime problem, and the prediction of criminal behavior.

What will be the role of criminological theory in solving crime today and in the future?

The role of criminological theory in crime control is to pursue and communicate an understanding of crime through research driven policies and practices that are embedded in the social and cultural realities of criminal behavior.

Should crime control strategies today be driven by theory, reality, or both?

The reality of crime control is that people want to feel safer at home and on the street, and this is what tends to drive policies in the direction of funneling more law breakers through the criminal justice system. However, this reality does not address what we know about crime and its relationship to the larger social structure. It is the role of criminology to bridge the gap between theory and reality by guiding crime control policy in a holistic direction of understanding social problems.

In what ways will criminological research have an impact on social policy?

Criminological research will continue to search for integrated crime prevention solutions that are embedded in the structure of local communities, and that rely on mutually beneficial relationships within the community to address social concerns as well as raise public trust in law enforcement.

CRITICAL THINKING QUESTIONS

1. What particular transnational crime do you think is the most urgent threat to the United States? Why? What makes this crime a global problem? What aspects of it could we better understand by using comparative data from other countries?

2. What role has technology played in providing more criminal opportunities? In what ways has technology affected traditional crimes such as theft, burglary and child abuse? How can advances in surveillance and detection technologies be used to control these and other types of crimes?

3. In what ways does the use of technology in crime control challenge the balance between individual rights and public order? In what circumstances, if any, can the use of technology to fight crime justify the compromising of personal freedoms?

4. How do violations of international laws present a direct threat to our own national security here in the U.S.? What role does the science of criminology play in guiding the effective understanding of this threat and in bringing to justice perpetrators of international crimes?

E-RESOURCES

Learn more about the field of comparative criminology by visiting the *International Center For Comparative Criminological Research (ICCCR)* website at http://www.open.ac.uk/icccr/index.php.

For more information on the structure and organization of INTERPOL, visit http://www.interpol.int/.

Visit the United Nations Surveys on Crime Trends and the Operations of Criminal Justice Systems (CTS) website at http://www.unodc.org/unodc/en/data-and-analysis/United-Nations-Surveys-on-Crime-Trends-and-the-Operations-of-Criminal-Justice-Systems.html for more information on the compiling and comparing of international crime statistics.

Read more on financing terrorism through drug trafficking enterprises at the *United Nations Office On Drugs And Crime* website at http://www.unodc.org/.

NOTES

1   Botelho, Greg and Ellis, Ralph. 2015. San Bernardino Shooting Investigated as 'Act of Terrorism'. *CNN.com,* Dec. 5. Retrieved from http://www.cnn.com/2015/12/04/us/san-bernardino-shooting/index.html

2   South Africa Court Bid to Arrest Sudan's Omar al-Bashir. 2015. *BBC News,* June 14. Retrieved from http://www.bbc.com/news/world-africa-33125728.

3   United States National Intellectual Property Law Enforcement Coordination Council. January 2008. *Report to the President and Congress on Coordination of Intellectual Property Enforcement and Protection.* Retrieved from http://2001–2009.commerce.gov/s/groups/public/@doc/@os/@opa/documents/content/prod01_005189.pdf.

4   Ibid.

5   Turner, Bryan S. and Holton, Robert J. (eds.). 2015. *The Routledge International Handbook of Globalization Studies.* London: Routledge.

6   Bertrand, O. and Lumineau, F. 2015. Partners in Crime: The Effects of Diversity on the Longevity of Cartels. *Academy of Management Journal* 59(3): 983–1008.

7   Sheptycki, James and Wardek, Ali. (eds.). 2005. *Transnational and Comparative Criminology.* London: GlassHouse Press.

8   Dammer, Harry R. and Albanase, Jay. 2013. *Comparative Criminal Justice Systems.* Boston, MA: Wadsworth.

9   Myamba, Flora. 2009. Cross-National Comparative Criminological/Victimological Research: Methodological Barriers and Future Directions. Paper presented at the annual meeting of the *American Society of Criminology.* Royal York, Toronto, October 26. Retrieved from http://www.allacademic.com/meta/p34851_index.html.

10   About Interpol. 2016. Retrieved from http://www.interpol.int/public/icpo/default.asp.

11   United Nations Surveys on Crime Trends and the Operations of Criminal Justice Systems (CTS). 2016. United Nations Office on Drugs and Crime, Vienna, Austria. Retrieved from http://www.unodc.org/unodc/en/data-and-analysis/United-Nations-Surveys-on-Crime-Trends-and-the-Operations-of-Criminal-Justice-Systems.html.

12   International Crime Victims Survey. United Nations Interregional Crime and Justice Institute. 2016. Retrieved from http://www.unicri.it/services/library_documentation/publications/icvs/.

13   Thompson, R. Bankole, Fields, Charles B. and Barker, Thomas. 2009. *Comparative and International Criminal Justice.* Upper Saddle, NJ: Prentice-Hall.

14   Ouimet, Marac. 1999. Crime in Canada and in the United States: A Comparative Analysis. *The Canadian Review of Sociology and Anthropology* 36.

15   Belli, Roberta. 2006. *To Prosecute or Not To Prosecute? A Comparative Study of Prosecutorial Discretion at the National and International Level.* Paper presented at the annual meeting of the American Society of Criminology (ASC), Los Angeles Convention Center, Los Angeles, CA, November 1, 2006.

16   Uchendu, O. J. and Igbe, A. P. 2015. Sexual Assault in Benin City, Nigeria, a Silent Epidemic. *Indian Journal of Forensic Medicine & Toxicology* 9(1), 28–32.

17   Farrington, David. P. 2015. Cross-national Comparative Research on Criminal Careers, Risk Factors, Crime and Punishment. *European Journal of Criminology* 12(4): 386–399.

18   Shaw, Margaret. 2007. *Comparative Approaches to Urban Crime Prevention Focusing on Youth.* London: International Center for the Prevention of Crime.

19   International Report on Crime Prevention and Community Safety: Trends and Perspectives. 2015. International Center for the Prevention of Crime. Montreal, Quebec.

20   Kalyvas, Stathis. N. 2015. How Civil Wars Help Explain Organized Crime—and How They Do Not. *Journal of Conflict Resolution* 59(8): 1517–1540. Roslycky, Lada L. 2009. Organized Transnational Crime in The Black Sea Region: A Geopolitical Dilemma? *Trends in Organized Crime* 12(1): 21–29. Piazza, James A. 2008. Incubators of Terror: Do Failed and Failing States Promote Transnational Terrorism? *International Studies Quarterly* 52 (3): 469–488.

21   *Database on International Intellectual Property.* 2016. *World Intellectual Property Organization.* Retrieved from http://www.wipo.int/reference/en/.

22   Money Laundering and Globalization. 2016. *United Nations Office on Drugs and Crime.* Retrieved from https://www.unodc.org/unodc/en/money-laundering/globalization.html.

23   Ibid.

24   *What is human trafficking?* 2016. United Nations Office on Drugs and Crime. Retrieved from http://www.unodc.org/unodc/en/human-trafficking/what-is-human-trafficking.html.

25   *Trafficking In Persons Report.* 2015. U.S. Department of State, Washington, D.C. Retrieved from http://www.state.gov/documents/organization/245365.pdf.

26   Ibid.

27   *United Nations Convention against Transnational Organized Crime and its Protocols.* 2016. United Nations Office on Drugs and Crime, Vienna, Austria. Retrieved from http://www.unodc.org/unodc/en/treaties/CTOC/index.html.

28   Ibid.

29   Ruby, Charles L. 2002. The Definition of Terrorism. *Analyses of Social Issues and Public Policy*: 9–14.

30   Islamic Extremism Threat. 2015. Testimony before U.S. House Armed Services Committee. Retrieved from http://www.c-span.org/video/?324256–1/hearing-islamic-extremism.

31   *National Consortium for the Study of Terrorism and Responses to Terrorism Statistical Annex.* 2013. Office of the Coordinator for Counterterrorism, U.S. Department of State, Washington, D.C.

32   Draft Code of Crimes against the Peace and Security of Mankind. United Nations. *Yearbook of the International Law Commission, 1996*, Vol. II (Part Two). Retrieved from http://legal.un.org/ilc/texts/instruments/english/commentaries/7_4_1996.pdf.

33   King, Elizabeth. B. L. 2015. Big Fish, Small Ponds: International Crimes in National Courts. *Ind. LJ* 90: 829.

34   Dawson, Maurice, ed. 2015. New Threats and Countermeasures in Digital Crime and Cyber Terrorism. IGI Global. Byrne, James Michael and Donald J. Rebovich. 2007. *The New Technology of Crime, Law and Social Control.* The Criminal Justice Press.

35   Sharma, Vatsla. 2015. Information Technology and Cyber Crime. *IITM Journal of Information Technology* 1: 75.

36   Stroshine, Meghan S. 2015. Technological Innovations in Policing. *Critical Issues in Policing: Contemporary Readings* 911: 229. *Law Enforcement Analytic Standards.* 2004. International Association of Law Enforcement Intelligence Analysts. Global Justice Information Sharing Initiative, U.S. Department of Justice, Washington, D.C.

37   Korneev, D.O., L.Yu. Bogdanov and A.V. Nalivkin. 2004. *Passive Millimeter Wave Imaging System With White Noise Illumination For Concealed Weapons Detection.* Infrared and Millimeter Waves, 2004 and 12th International Conference on Terahertz Electronics, 2004. Conference Digest of the 2004 Joint 29th International Conference on Terahertz Electronics.

38   Presidential Decision Directive 42 (PDD-42). *International Crime Control Strategy, June 1998*. Retrieved from www.fas.org/irp/offdocs/iccs/iccsi.html.

39   President Bill Clinton, Speech at the United Nations, October 22, 1995.

40   Gates, Verna. 2012. Alabama Professor Gets Life in Prison for Killing Co-Workers. *Reuters,* Sept. 24. Retrieved from www.reuters.com/article/us-usa-crime-professor-id USBRE88N11C20120924.

41   Krohn, Marv and Jeffrey T. Ward. 2015. Integrating Criminological Theories. *The Handbook of Criminological Theory*, pp. 318–335.

42   Henry, Stuart. 2009. School Violence Beyond Columbine: A Complex Problem in Need of an Interdisciplinary Analysis. *American Behavioral Scientist* 52(9): 1246–1265.

43   Brown, Sheila. 2006. The Criminology of Hybrids: Rethinking Crime and Law in Technosocial Networks. *Theoretical Criminology* 10(2): 223–244.

44   Colvin, Mark. 2000. *Crime and Coercion: An Integrated Theory of Chronic Criminality.* New York: St. Martin's Press.

45 Chen, Xiaoming. 2002. Social Control in China: Applications of the Labeling Theory and the Reintegrative Shaming Theory. *International Journal of Offender Therapy and Comparative Criminology* 46(1): 45–63.

46 Reiman, Jeffrey and Leighton, Paul. 2015. The Rich Get Richer and the Poor Get Prison: Ideology, Class, and Criminal Justice. New York and London: Routledge.

47 France, Alan and Crow, Iain. 2005. Using The 'Risk Factor Paradigm' In Prevention: Lessons From The Evaluation Of Communities That Care. *Children and Society* 19(2): 172–184.

48 Dubow, Eric F., Huesmann, L. Rowell, Boxer, Paul and Smith, Cathy. 2016. Childhood and Adolescent Risk and Protective Factors for Violence in Adulthood. *Journal of Criminal Justice.*

49 Braga, Anthony A. and Weisburd, David L. 2015. Focused Deterrence and the Prevention of Violent Gun Injuries: Practice, Theoretical Principles, and Scientific Evidence. *Annual Review of Public Health* 36: 55–68. Hawkins, David, Brown, Eric, Oesterle, Sabrina, Arthur, Michael W., Abbot, Robert D. and Catalano, Richard F. 2008. Early Effects of Communities that Care on Targeted Risks and Initiation of Delinquent Behavior and Substance Abuse. *Journal of Adolescent Health* 43: 15–22.

50 Turanovic, Jillian J., Reisig, Michael D., and Pratt, Travis C. 2015. Risky Lifestyles, Low Self-control, and Violent Victimization Across Gendered Pathways to Crime. *Journal of Quantitative Criminology* 31(2): 183–206.

51 France, Alan, Freiberg, Kate and Homel, Ross. 2010. Beyond Risk Factors: Towards a Holistic Prevention Paradigm for Children and Young People. *British Journal of Social Work.* doi:10.1093/bjsw/bcq010.

52 Haines, Kevin and Case, Stephen. 2008. The Rhetoric and Reality of the 'Risk Factor Prevention Paradigm' Approach to Preventing and Reducing Youth Offending. *Youth Justice* 8(1): 5–20.

53 Bjorgo, Tore. 2016. *Preventing Crime: A Holistic Approach.* United Kingdom: Palgrave Macmillan.

Image Acknowledgments

Every effort has been made to locate the copyright owners of the material in this book, but if any have been inadvertently overlooked, the publishers will be pleased to make the necessary arrangements at the earliest opportunity.

1. Crime, deviance, and criminology: a brief overview

Image 1.1 (p. 4): In this June 9, 2015 file photo, former U.S. House Speaker Dennis Hastert arrives at the federal courthouse in Chicago for his arraignment on federal charges in his hush-money case. A filing in Hastert's hush-money case confirms prosecutors intend to call at least one witness at the former U.S. House speaker's sentencing, though the order posted on Wednesday, March 23, 2016, by the presiding judge doesn't identify that witness. Hastert pleaded guilty to violating bank laws in seeking to pay $3.5 million in hush money to some referred to in the indictment only as "Individual A." Prosecutors have spoken before about giving victims closure but never identified any.
Charles Rex Arbogast/AP/Press Association Images

Image 1.2 (p. 6): In this artist's sketch, figures in the Robert Blake civil trial are shown in court as verdicts are read at a Burbank, Calif., courthouse Friday, Nov. 18, 2005. Before Judge David M. Schacter are, from top left, Blake, his attorneys Nancy Lucas and Peter Ezell, attorney Gary Austin and his client Earle Caldwell, and plaintiff's attorney Eric Dubin. Eight months after Blake was acquitted at a criminal trial of murdering his wife, the civil jury decided the tough-guy actor was responsible for her slaying. After eight days of deliberations, the jury determined by a vote of 10–2 that Blake "intentionally caused the death" of Bonny Lee Bakley and ordered the former "Baretta" star to pay Bakley's children $30 million in damages.
Mona Shafer Edwards/AP/Press Association Images

Image 1.3 (p. 7): Thousands of anti-war protesters assemble in York before marching through the City to a rally at York Minster.
John Giles/PA Archive/Press Association Images

Image 1.4 (p. 10): iStock/Slavaleks

Image 1.5a (p. 11): 3rd Annual Brent Shapiro Foundation Sober Day Party, Beverly Hills, America—17 May 2008
Stewart Cook/REX/Shutterstock

Image 1.5b (p. 11): NBCUniversal "I Am Cait" Winter TCA Tour—Day 10, Pasadena, America—14 Jan 2016
David Buchan/Variety/REX/Shutterstock

Image 1.6a (p. 18): iStock/Yuri

Image 1.6b (p. 18): In this June 13, 1990 file photo, New York hotel queen Leona Helmsley arrives at New York State court with attorney Alan Dershowitz for another round in her battle against state tax fraud charges. The papers of Dershowitz are now available to researchers at his alma mater, Brooklyn College. Dershowitz donated his papers to Brooklyn College rather than Harvard, where he is a professor.
Richard Drew/AP/Press Association Images

Box 1.2 Image 1 (p. 19): In this Aug. 1, 2013 file photo, Ariel Castro pauses as he makes a statement in the courtroom during his sentencing phase in Cleveland. As authorities launched two probes to try to determine how Cleveland kidnapper Ariel Castro managed to commit suicide while in prison, his family was scheduled to claim his body two days after he hanged himself with a bedsheet in his cell.
Tony Dejak/AP/Press Association Images

2. Criminal law

Image 2.1 (p. 42): Three women are hanged as witches. Woodcut from an English pamphlet, 1569
Mary Evans Picture Library/Interfoto Agentur

Image 2.2 (p. 43): Signing of the Declaration of Independence by Thomas Jefferson, John Adams, Benjamin Franklin, and James Madison amongst others. Painting by John Trumbull, 1787. Interfoto.
Mary Evans/Interfoto

Image 2.3 (p. 47): Attempted assassination of President Ronald Reagan by John Hinckley Jnr outside Hilton Hotel, Washington DC, America—30 Mar 1981
ZUMA/REX/Shuttestock

Image 2.4 (p. 47): John W. Hinckley, Jr. is shown arriving in chains at the Quantico Marine Base, Tuesday, August 18, 1981, after arriving by helicopter from the Federal Correctional Institution in Butner, NC. Hinckley, accused of shooting President Reagan on March 30, has been undergoing psychiatric tests at the institution in North Carolina since his arrest. The label on Hinckley's chest identifies a bulletproof vest he is wearing.
Bob Daugherty/AP/Press Association Images

Image 2.5 (p. 59): French socialist philosopher and professor Emile Durkheim (1858–1917) sits for a portrait.
Bettmann/Contributor

Image 2.6 (p. 61): Depression: Unemployed, destitute man leaning against vacant store: photo by Dorothea Lange
Franklin D. Roosevelt Library

Image 2.7 (p. 62): Karl Marx, German radical political thinker
Mary Evans Picture Library

Image 2.8 (p. 62): Max Weber (1864–1920), German political economist and sociologist, one of the fathers of modern sociology. His best known work is *The Protestant Ethic and the Spirit of Capitalism*. Ca. 1910.
Mary Evans/Everett Collection

Image 2.9 (p. 64): Women demonstrators march down 5th Ave., at 52nd street in New York City on Aug. 26, 1970. Their demonstration is in support of women's liberation.
AP/Press Association Images

Image 2.10 (p. 66): A cafe near the tobacco market, Durham, North Carolina. Signs: Separate doors for "White" and for "Colored."
Library of Congress Prints and Photographs Division

Image 2.11 (p. 67): Operation Arkansas: A Different Kind of Deployment Photo by Courtesy of the National Archives September 20, 2007 Soldiers from the 101st Airborne Division escort the Little Rock Nine students into the all-white Central High School in Little Rock, Ark.
US Army/National Archives

3. How much crime is there?

Image 3.1 (p. 76): Convicted serial killer Dennis Rader walks into the El Dorado Correctional Facility with two Sedgwick County sheriff's officers Friday,

Aug. 19, 2005 in El Dorado, Kan. Rader, the self styled BTK killer, admitted killing 10 people in a 30 year span and sentenced to 10 consecutive life terms.
Jeff Tuttle/AP/Press Association Images

Image 3.2 (p. 85): iStock/Joseph C. Justice Jr.

Image 3.3 (p. 88): iStock/Kivilcim Pinar

Image 3.4 (p. 93): iStock/monkeybusinessimages

Image 3.5 (p. 96): iStock/PeopleImages

Image 3.6 (p. 100): In this 1993 file photo, 12-year-old Polly Klaas of Petaluma, Calif., is shown. More than 15 years after Richard Allen Davis confessed to kidnapping and killing Klaas, the state's high court will hear his appeal on Tuesday, March 3, 2009.
AP/Press Association Images

Image 3.7 (p. 100): Richard Allen Davis, who is targeted as the prime suspect in the Polly Klaas abduction, sits in Mendocino County Court in Ukiah, Calif., on Thursday, December 2, 1993, during his arraignment on drunken driving charges.
Ben Margot/AP/Press Association Images

4. Doing criminology: research and theory

Image 4.1 (p. 118): The U.S. led War on Drugs has been costly, both in terms of dollars spent fighting it and human lives lost or damaged as a result of it. The reach of the War on Drugs now extends well-beyond America's borders, to the poppy fields of Afghanistan and coca groves of Colombia.
Getty

Image 4.2 (p. 123): Washington, DC—October 26: Rashad Robinson, Executive Director, ColorOfChange speaks at a press conference for coalition's Ban The Box Petition Delivery to The White House on October 26, 2015 in Washington, DC.
Larry French/Stringer

Image 4.3 (p. 131): Scene still from *The Ninth Gate*, dir. Roman Polanski, 1999
Artisan Pics/The Kobal Collection/Mountain, Peter

Image 4.4 (p. 133): Testing a laboratory rat (*Rattus norvegicus*). Rat being used in a maze in order to test the effects of administered medications. Mazes reveal abnormalities in orientation and spatial memory. Photographed at the Zentralen Tierlaboratorien (ZTL, Central Animal Laboratory) in Berlin, Germany.
Patrick Landmann/Science Photo Library

Image 4.5 (p. 139): Philip G. Zimbardo, Inc.

5. Law enforcement in America

Image 5.1 (p. 150): In this Sept. 23, 1997 file photo, former New York City Detective Frank Serpico testifies

at a City Council hearing in New York. Things haven't changed much since Serpico broke the NYPD's code of silence more than 40 years ago. Police officers are still encouraged to turn a blind eye to wrongdoing within their ranks and never question authority, or else face harassment by peers and punishment by superiors.
Kathy Willens/AP/Press Association Images

Image 5.2 (p. 151): Glendale, CA, USA—August 5, 2014: A mother and two children discuss neighborhood crime prevention with a member of the Los Angeles County Sheriff's Department at a National Night Out against crime community fair in Glendale, California on August 5, 2014.
iStock/DnHolm

Image 5.3 (p. 154): Santiago, Chile—May 28, 2013: Chilean Carabineros—the national police—clash with protestors on the streets of Santiago. The civilians tried to pass a police road block while protesting for reform of the Chilean education system.
iStock/Evan_Lang

Image 5.4 (p. 156): Within every culture are thousands of subcultures, which each have their own values, language, and practices. Members of the law enforcement share many subcultural similarities with people who serve in the military, like those engaging in Navy Seal Hell Week training in the image above. Both law enforcement and military personnel emphasize trust among one another and often abide by a strict code of silence.
Getty

Image 5.5 (p. 160): Peel, Robert, 1788–1850, British politician, Prime Minister 1834–1835 and 1841–1845, portrait, engraving, 19th century, later coloured, Great Britain.
Mary Evans/Interfoto/Sammlung Rauch

Image 5.6 (p. 161): *Texas Rangers*, lithograph of a wash drawing by Frederic Remington, 1896.
Mary Evans/Everett Collection

Image 5.7 (p. 161): A man is arrested in New York and led through the streets by a policeman to the station.
Mary Evans Picture Library

Image 5.8 (p. 162): August Vollmer, "father of modern law enforcement."
Library of Congress Prints and Photographs Division

Image 5.9 (p. 162): Alice Stebbins Wells, originally her LAPD photo.
Wikimedia Commons

Image 5.10 (p. 173): A poster featuring fugitives James "Whitey" Bulger and Catherine Greig is seen at the FBI field office in Boston, in this June 20, 2011 file photo. FBI agents on the trail of Bulger are turning to TV ads aimed at women as they try to bring the fugitive Boston mob boss to justice after 16 years on the run. The 30-second ad is scheduled to start running Tuesday in 14 television markets. The FBI finally caught the 81-year-old Bulger Wednesday June 22, 2011 at a residence in Santa Monica along with his longtime girlfriend Catherine Greig, just days after the government launched the new publicity campaign to locate the fugitive mobster, said Steven Martinez, FBI's assistant director in charge in Los Angeles.
Michael Dwyer/AP/Press Association Images

Image 5.11 (p. 178): iStock/Sean Boggs

Image 5.12 (p. 180): Minneapolis police guard the entrance to the Fourth Precinct as Black Lives Matter supporters continued their protest, Wednesday, Nov. 18, 2015, in Minneapolis. It was the fourth day of protests of the killing of 24-year-old Jamar Clark, an unarmed black man, by a Minneapolis police officer.
Jim Mone/AP/Press Association Images

Image 5.13 (p. 182): In this image from video, Walter Scott is shot by police officer Michael Thomas Slager in Charleston, S.C., on April 4, 2015.
Feidin Santana/AP/Press Association Images

Image 5.14 (p. 186): U.S. President Barack Obama speaks as Commissioner of the Philadelphia Police Department Charles Ramsey (seated next to him on the right) and others listen during a meeting of his Task Force on 21st Century Policing. President Obama met with the task force "to discuss their recommendations on how to strengthen community policing and strengthen trust among law enforcement officers and the communities they serve."
Getty

6. Courts

Image 6.1 (p. 196): Supreme Court of the United States Building, Washington, DC, as seen from the west side of 1st St NE.
Wikimedia Commons/350z33/Pine

Image 6.2 (p. 200): United States—Circa 1910: The original Juvenile Court Building and Detention Home near the corner of Halsted and Des Plaines streets. Chicago was the first city in the United States to establish a separate court to cater to the specific needs of juvenile offenders, Chicago.
Chicago History Museum/Getty Images

Box 6.6 Image 1 (p. 210): Michael Dunn returns to his seat after reading his statement, which included an apology to the Davis family, during his sentencing

hearing Friday, Oct. 17, 2014 at the Duval County Courthouse in Jacksonville, Fla. Dunn, convicted of first-degree murder in a retrial in September for fatally shooting 17-year-old Jordan Davis in November 2012 in an argument over loud music outside a Florida convenience store was sentenced to life in prison without parole.
Bruce Lipsky/AP/Press Association Images

Image 6.3 (p. 212): In this July 23, 2012 file photo, Colorado movie theater shooting suspect James Holmes, whose trial is to begin with lengthy jury selection on Jan. 20, 2015, sits in Arapahoe County District Court in Centennial, Colo. Psychiatrists and attorneys interviewed by The Associated Press say that it would be unlikely that Holmes would be released from a state mental institution should a jury find him not guilty by reason of insanity.
RJ Sangosti/AP/Press Association Images

Image 6.4 (p. 221): An undated portrait of Emmett Louis Till, a black 14-year-old Chicago boy, whose weighted down body was found in the Tallahatchie River near the Delta community of Money, Mississippi, August 31, 1955. Local residents Roy Bryant, 24, and J.W. Milam, 35, were accused of kidnapping, torturing and murdering Till for allegedly whistling at Bryant's wife.
AP/Press Association Images

Image 6.5 (p. 221): In this 1955 file photo, Mamie Mobley, mother of Emmett Till, pauses at her son's casket at a Chicago funeral home. The 14-year-old Chicagoan was killed in 1955 after reportedly whistling at a white woman during a visit to his uncle's house in Mississippi. Nearly 100,000 people visited his glass-topped casket during a four-day public viewing in Chicago. Images of his battered body helped spark the civil rights movement. On Thursday, July 9, 2009, the original casket was found at Burr Oak Cemetery in Alsip, Ill., by authorities investigating where four workers are accused of digging up bodies to resell plots. Till's grave site was not disturbed. When Till was exhumed in 2005 during an investigation of his death, he was reburied in a new casket. The original casket was supposed to be kept for a planned memorial to Till.
AP/Press Association Images

Image 6.6 (p. 222): Luzerne County Judges Mark A. Ciavarella, center, and Judge Michael T. Conahan, far left, leave the William J. Nealon Federal Building and United States Courthouse in Scranton, PA., Thursday, Feb. 12, 2009, after pleading guilty to corruption charges.Pamela Suchy/AP/Press Association Images

7. American corrections

Image 7.1 (p. 233): Laws of code of Hammurabi, from Code of the Hammurabi, black basalt, 18th century BC Mesopotamian, from Susa, Iran (detail)
The Art Archive/Musée du Louvre Paris/Gianni Dagli Orti

Image 7.2 (p. 234): Mamertine Prison, Rome, Italy
Wikimedia Commons/Bgabel

Image 7.3 (p. 235): Tengler, Ulrich, 1447–1511, German jurist, works, Laienspiegel, 1509, coloured woodcut, three defendants in the stocks at the town square, Strassbourg, 1512, private collection
Mary Evans/Interfoto/Bildarchiv Hansmann

Image 7.4 (p. 236): Charles Louis De Secondat, baron de Montesquieu, French philosopher.
Mary Evans Picture Library

Image 7.5 (p. 236): Francois-Marie Arouet (Voltaire) the French writer and philosopher
Mary Evans Picture Library

Image 7.6 (p. 236): Kant, Immanuel, 1724–1804, German philosopher, portrait, wood engraving.
Mary Evans/Interfoto/Sammlung Rauch

Image 7.7 (p. 236): Denis Diderot, French encyclopaedist and philosopher.
Mary Evans Picture Library

Image 7.8 (p. 236): Howard, John, 1726–1790, Brit. jurist and reformer of the English prisons, portrait, side face, engraving.
Interfoto/Sammlung Rauch/Mary Evans

Image 7.9 (p. 237): Cesare Bonesana, Marchese Di Beccaria, Italian economist and jurist.
Mary Evans Picture Library

Image 7.10 (p. 237): Jeremy Bentham (1748–1832), Philosopher and economist
Mary Evans Picture Library

Image 7.11 (p. 238): England, 18th century, private collection, justice, penitentiary system, ducking, cucking
Interfoto/Bildarchiv Hansmann/Mary Evans

Image 7.12 (p. 239): The Old Jail in Barnstable, MA was built in 1690. National Register of Historic Places.
Wikimedia Commons/Kenneth C. Zirkel

Image 7.13 (p. 240): William Penn, 1644–1718, English Quaker and founder of Pennsylvania, receiving the Charter of Philadelphia from Charles II, engraving
The Art Archive/Culver Pictures

Image 7.14 (p. 247): Hallway of the Eastern State Penitentiary
Wikimedia Commons/Seeminglee

Image 7.15 (p. 248): Aerial view of the Sing Sing prison at Ossining, New York (USA), in 1920.
Library of Congress/George Grantham Bain Collection

Image 7.16 (p. 250): Convicts Leased to Harvest Timber, around 1915, Florida
Library of Congress/State Library and Archives of Florida

Image 7.17 (p. 251): This Dec. 10, 2008 file photo shows the entrance of the Corrections Corporation of America (CCA) detention center in Elizabeth, N.J., which is run for the government by CCA, a private prison contractor. Daniel Guadron, a straight A high school student from Trenton who emigrated from Guatemala at age 13, was detained at this center for nearly seven months in 2008.
Mel Evans/AP/Press Association Images

Image 7.18 (p. 253): Prisonization is the process of adopting the prison/inmate subculture. This often contributes to the formation and persistence of prison gangs. Often, prison gangs congeal along racial or ethnic lines, like the white supremacist gang members from a Texas prison pictured above.
Getty

Image 7.19 (p. 259): Dorothea Dix (1802–1887) began her lifelong campaign for humane treatment of the mentally ill in the 1840s. At that time, the insane were often incarcerated with violent criminals, who preyed upon them in jails. She successfully advocated the building.
Mary Evans/Everett Collection

Image 7.20 (p. 266): A Jan. 28, 2016, photo shows a solitary confinement cell known all as "the bing," at New York's Rikers Island jail. It is similar to a cell Candie Hailey was sent to after her arrival for arguing about cleaning a jailhouse shower. During more than three years in jail waiting on a trial, she spent two-thirds in solitary. When she finally went to trial, jurors took two days to come back with their verdict: not guilty.
Bebeto Matthews/AP/Press Association Images

Image 7.21 (p. 269): Surrounded by family and supporters, three of five men exonerated in the Central Park jogger rape case stand before microphones, Raymond Santana, second from left front, Yusef Salaam, center, and Kevin Richardson, second from right front, at a news conference in front of City Hall, Friday June 27, 2014 in New York. The New York City comptroller said Thursday that he has approved a tentative $40 million settlement with the five men, wrongly convicted in the 1989 Central Park jogger attack.
Bebeto Matthews/AP/Press Association Images

Box 7.4 Image 1 (p. 273): George Stinney mugshot, 1944.
Wikimedia Commons/State of South Carolina

8. Crime as rational behavior: classical and rational choice theory

Image 8.1 (p. 288): iStock/ReeseImages

Image 8.2 (p. 289): A noble Spanish lady is exorcised by a priest in her own home, while her family register their concern in various ways and even the servants show interest. Painting by D. Serafin Martinez del Rincion, reproduced in *Ilustracion Espanola y Americana*, 15.4.1878, page 233.
Mary Evans Picture Library

Image 8.3 (p. 290): Locke, John, 1632–1704, British philosopher, portrait.
Interfoto/Sammlung Rauch/Mary Evans

Image 8.4 (p. 290): Portrait of Voltaire. Anonymous copy of the original portrait by Quentin Latour. Oil on canvas. France. Versailles. National Museum of Versailles.
Mary Evans/Iberfoto

Image 8.5 (p. 290): Rousseau, Jean-Jacques, 1712–1778, French philosopher, portrait, pastel by Maurice Quentin de La Tour, 1753
Interfoto/Sammlung Rauch/Mary Evans

Image 8.6 (p. 291): Scene still from *Ocean's Thirteen*, dir. Steven Soderbergh, 2007
Warner Bros./The Kobal Collection/Gordon, Melinda Sue

Image 8.7 (p. 295): Police stand over David Sweat after he was shot and captured near the Canadian border Sunday, June 28, 2015, in Constable, N.Y. Sweat is the second of two convicted murderers who staged a brazen escape three weeks ago from a maximum-security prison in northern New York. His capture came two days after his escape partner, Richard Matt, was shot and killed by authorities.
AP/Press Association Images

Image 8.8 (p. 295): This Friday, June 12, 2015 photo provided by the New York State Police shows Joyce Mitchell. Mitchell is accused of helping inmates David Sweat and Richard Matt escape from the Clinton Correctional Facility in Dannemora, N.Y. on June 6, 2015. Authorities say that Mitchell, a tailor shop instructor at the prison provided some of the tools that the men used in their escape. They are still at large.
AP/Press Association Images

Image 8.9 (p. 297): People scatter as police officers fire tear gas on West Florissant Rd on Monday, August 11, 2014, in Ferguson, MO, USA.
St Louis Post-Dispatch/ABACA/PA Images

Image 8.10 (p. 301): Los Angeles, California, USA—January 28th 2015: Gas station, 76 brand, at night. Sidewalk and palm trees and bushes in the foreground, a man wiping his car's windshield in the background, left side of the image.
iStock/Stele10

Image 8.11 (p. 305): American Michael Fay, 19, accompanied by his father George, behind, leaves the Queenstown Prison in Singapore following his release Tuesday, June 21, 1994. Fay, who was convicted for spray-painting cars, became the focus of an international uproar when he was flogged for vandalism.
Tan Ah Soon/AP/Press Association Images

Image 8.12 (p. 306): iStock/Tzido

Image 8.13 (p. 307): A group of "Tent City" jail inmates clean an empty field as part of the chain gang made up of undocumented immigrants. Maricopa County Sheriff Joe Arpaio rolled out a new Driving Under the Influence chain gang the day after the All-Star Game. The chain gang is made up of undocumented immigrants convicted of drunken driving. USA. 13th July 2011 Men guilty of DUI wear pink and pick up trash in Arizona—Tempe.
Eduardo Barraza/Demotix/Press Association Images

9. Biological theories: crime is in the brain

Image 9.1 (p. 318): Adrien Raine

Image 9.2 (p. 320): Franz Joseph Gall (1758–1828) was a neuroanatomist, physiologist, and pioneer in the study of the localization of mental functions in the brain. Gall developed "cranioscopy," a method to determine the personality and development of mental and moral faculties on the basis of the external shape of the skull. Cranioscopy was later renamed to phrenology by his follower Johann Spurzheim.
Photo Researchers/Mary Evans Picture Library

Image 9.3 (p. 321): Stages in human evolution, illustration. At left, Proconsul (23–15 million years ago) is shown as an African ape with both primitive and advanced features. From it Australopithecus afarensis (>4– 2.5 mya) evolved and displayed a bipedal, upright gait walking on two legs. Homo habilis (2.5 mya) resembled Australopithecus but also used stone tools. At centre is Homo naledi (discovered 2013). About 1.5 mya Homo erectus appeared in Africa, used fire, wooden tools, and migrated into Eurasia. Homo neanderthalensis (200,000 years ago;

Europe and the Middle East) was closely related to modern humans (Homo sapiens, right).
David Gifford/Science Photo Library

Image 9.4 (p. 327): In this Thursday, Feb. 23, 2006 photo, contractors Luis Benitez, foreground, and Jose Diaz, background, clean up lead paint in a contaminated building in Providence, R.I. For the first time in 20 years, U.S. health officials have lowered the threshold for lead poisoning in young children. The new standard announced Wednesday, May 16, 2012 means that hundreds of thousands more youngsters could be diagnosed with high levels of lead. Too much lead is harmful to developing brains and can mean a lower IQ.
Chitose Suzuki/AP/Press Association Images

Image 9.5 (p. 329): Brain scan image of normal brain v. murderer's brain.
Public domain

Image 9.6 (p. 331): iStock/guvendemir

Image 9.7 (p. 331): iStock/shironosov

Image 9.8 (p. 332): iStock/BraunS

Image 9.9 (p. 336): iStock/praetorianphoto

Image 9.10 (p. 336): iStock/DragonImages

10. Psychological theories: crime is in the mind

Image 10.1 (p. 352): Goidsargi Estibaliz Carranza Zabala (C) is flanked by her lawyers Rudolf Mayer (R) and Werner Tomanek (L) at the beginning of her trial at the regional court in Vienna on November 19, 2012. The woman, who has joint Spanish-Mexican citizenship and who is described as "singularly cold-blooded," is accused of murdering two men and setting their sawn-up body parts in concrete in the cellar of her ice cream parlour.
Dieter Nagl/AFP/Getty Images

Image 10.2 (p. 354): Charles Manson is escorted on his way back to jail after court arraignment in Los Angeles, Ca., Dec. 22, 1969.
AP/Press Association Images

Image 10.3 (p. 355): iStock/Pamela Moore

Image 10.4 (p. 356): iStock/deimagine

Box 10.1 Image 1 (p. 358): A photo taken by a forensic team and released by the Austrian police with permission of Austria's prosecution office on Monday, April 28, 2008 shows a view into a hidden room in a house in Amstetten, Austria, in which a woman is believed to have been held captive for 24 years. Austria's police on Monday, April 28, 2008 questioned a man identified in a police statement as Josef F., they say held his daughter captive for 24 years and sexually

abused her in what stunned Austrians dubbed a "house of horrors" in Amstetten, a high-tech, windowless cell where she allegedly gave birth to at least six children. Two police forensics teams arrived on the scene Monday morning and technicians in white suits entered the apartment block in Amstetten, a blue-collar town about 120 kilometers (75 miles) west of Vienna.
Anonymous/AP/Press Association Images

Image 10.5 (p. 364): iStock/Jaimie D. Travis

Image 10.6 (p. 364): Italian and Canadian team members fight during the group B match between Canada and Italy at the Ice hockey World championships in Mannheim, Germany, on Saturday, May 8, 2010. Canada won the match with 5–1.
Jens Meyer/AP/Press Association Images

Image 10.7 (p. 368): iStock/PhotoTalk

Image 10.8 (p. 370): Security personnel guard the main entrance to the Walton Crossing apartments after law enforcement personnel discovered multiple bodies in one of the apartments Tuesday, Jan. 27, 2015, in Austell, Ga. Cobb County Police said in a statement that 35-year-old Kisha S. Holmes of Austell was found dead Tuesday morning along with her 9-month-old daughter, her 4-year-old son and her 10-year-old son. The children's identities have not been released.
David Tulis/AP/Press Association Images

11. Sociological theory: crime is in the structure of society

Image 11.1 (p. 384): In this May 17, 2015 file photo, authorities investigate a shooting in the parking lot of Twin Peaks restaurant in Waco, Texas. A Texas grand jury indicted 48 more bikers Wednesday, March 23, 2016, in connection with a May 2015 shootout outside a Twin Peaks restaurant that left nine dead, bringing the total number of people facing felony charges to 154.
Jerry Larson/AP/Press Association Images

Image 11.2 (p. 385): Job seekers stand in line during U.S. Rep. Jaime Herrera Beutler's "Getting Southwest Washington Back to Work Job Fair," Wednesday, Sept. 28, 2011, in Vancouver, Wash. The number of people seeking unemployment benefits fell to the lowest level in 5 months.
Rick Bowmer/AP/Press Association Images

Image 11.3 (p. 388): Manaus, Amazonas, Brazil— October 18, 2015: Manaus, once a very wealthy city, today has many heavily deteriorated buildings and almost totally abandoned neighborhoods.
iStock/shakzu

Image 11.4 (p. 389): iStock/Kali Nine LLC

Image 11.5 (p. 394): Beverly Hills, California, USA— August 11, 2012: Rodeo Drive with shoppers visible, in Beverly Hills on Aug. 11, 2012. Rodeo Drive is an affluent shopping district known for designer label and haute couture fashion.
iStock/littleny

Image 11.6 (p. 397): Martha Stewart testifies at the New York State Supreme Court Tuesday, March 5, 2013 in New York. Stewart, 71, is at the center of a bitter legal battle between two of the nation's largest retailers, Macy's Inc. and J.C. Penney Co. Macy's sued the media and merchandising company Stewart founded for breaching an exclusive contract when she signed a deal with Penney in December 2011 to open shops at most of its stores this spring. Macy's, which has sold Martha Stewart products including towels and pots since 2007, is trying to block Penney from selling those products.
David Handschuh/AP/Press Association Images

Image 11.7 (p. 398): London, UK—September 6, 2015: Crowd of people walking along the bankside district of the Thames, Tower Bridge in the background.
iStock/Nikada

Image 11.8 (p. 402): Canada's Jocelyne Larocque, left, fights for the puck with Kendall Coyne of USA during the 2015 IIHF Ice Hockey Women's World Championship group. A match between USA and Canada at Malmo Isstadion in Malmo, southern Sweden, on March 28, 2015.
Claudio Bresciani/TT News Agency/Press Association Images

Image 11.9 (p. 405): iStock/hoozone

12. Sociological theory: crime is socialized behavior

Image 12.1 (p. 420): Authorities carry a shooting victim away from the scene after a gunman opened fire at Umpqua Community College in Roseburg, Ore., Thursday, Oct. 1, 2015.
Mike Sullivan/AP/Press Association Images

Image 12.2 (p. 422): iStock/Steve Debenport

Image 12.3 (p. 425): iStock/wundervisuals

Image 12.4 (p. 432): Volkswagen AG executive Herbert Diess (C) is surrounded by reporters at the venue of the Tokyo Motor Show, which opened to the press on Oct. 28, 2015. Diess apologized for the emissions scandal (Kyodo).
AP/Press Association Images

Box 12.1 Image 1 (p. 433): United States—January 17: Probe of Enron Corporation Collapse—Staff for the House Energy and Commerce Committee sift

through Enron Corporation documents at the Ford House Office Building.
Scott J. Ferrell/Congressional Quarterly/Getty Images

Image 12.5 (p. 442): Teacher Marcus Tate, left, does sit-ups during an exercise session with his class at the Z.L. Madden Learning Center in Spartanburg, Wednesday morning, May 15, 2013. Tate has been named the Head Start Teacher of the Year for the state. He was selected from a field of 21 nominees representing Head Start and Early Head Start programs statewide and is the first man to win.
Tim Kimzey/AP/Press Association Images

13. Sociological theory: crime is from conflict inherent to society

Image 13.1 (p. 454): Thousands gather outside a community pool during a protest Monday, June 8, 2015, in response to an incident at the pool involving McKinney police officers in McKinney, Texas.
Ron Jenkins/AP/Press Association Images

Image 13.2 (p. 458): Black Americans being hosed by police and firemen, Birmingham, AL, 5/3/63
Mary Evans/Everett Collection

Image 13.3 (p. 459): A pro-choice and a pro-life activists confront each other during the March For Life in front of the US Supreme Court in Washington, DC, January 22, 2015. Tens of thousands of Americans who oppose abortion are in Washington for the annual March for Life, marking the 42nd anniversary of the Supreme Court's Roe v. Wade decision.
Olivier Douliery/Abaca USA/PA Images

Image 13.4 (p. 461): Karl Marx, German political theorist, working on *Das Kapital* with Engels. Drawing by Shukow.
Mary Evans Picture Library

Image 13.5 (p. 463): El Segundo, California, USA—November 25th, 2011: Hundreds of hoppers form a line before entering a Best Buy store in El Segundo, California on Black Friday. The day after Thanksgiving is often considered the busiest shopping event in America.
iStock/P_Wei

Image 13.6 (p. 466): iStock/shaunl

Image 13.7 (p. 470): iStock/Piotr Adamowicz

Image 13.8 (p. 472): iStock/mediaphotos

Image 13.9 (p. 475): iStock/Susan Chiang

Image 13.10 (p. 479): Junior doctors from Guy's and St Thomas's hospital in London are outside on a picket line near the Houses of Parliament on 10 February 2016. Junior doctors across the UK are on strike in a

dispute over the terms of a new contract (photo by Jay Shaw Baker/NurPhoto).
Xinhua/SIPA USA/PA Images

14. Interpersonal crimes of violence

Image 14.1 (p. 492): iStock/John Gomez

Image 14.2 (p. 493): Rev. Jacqueline J. Lewis, left, of the Middle Collegiate Church in New York City and Muhiyidin D'Baha, right, of Black Lives Matter Charleston leads those in attendance in a song at the memorial in front of the Emanuel AME Church, Friday, June 19, 2015 in Charleston, S.C.
Stephen B. Morton/AP/Press Association Images

Image 14.3 (p. 499): Accused murderer Theodore Bundy smiles during the second day of jury selection in his murder trial in a Dade County courtroom in Miami, Fla., on June 27, 1979. Bundy is being tried for the murders of two women in Tallahassee on Jan. 15, 1978.
AP/Press Association Images

Image 14.4 (p. 509): U.S. pop star Michael Jackson dangles an unidentified child, its head hidden by a towel, over a balcony of the Adlon Hotel in Berlin, Tuesday Nov. 19, 2002, in this image made from television. Jackson, in Germany to attend an awards ceremony, had been waving to German fans, when he brought the baby onto the balcony.
AP/Press Association Images

Image 14.5 (p. 511): Dublin, Ireland. 26th January 2013—Protesters stand outside Leinster House, holding a banner from the Rape Crisis Center and black balloons. People protest outside Leinster House in support of rape victim Fiona Doyle and sexual abuse victims everywhere. The protest comes in the wake of the release of her father on bail, even though he was convicted of her rape. Bail was later revoked. Protest march in support of rape victims.
Michael Debets/Demotix/Press Association Images

Image 14.6 (p. 518): Düsseldorf, Germany—December 14, 2014: A few people are standing at ATMs in Altstadt of Düsseldorf in winter and Christmas season. In center are two men.
iStock/Michael Luhrenberg

Image 14.7 (p. 521): Phoenix, United States. 21st August 2015—Pro-Life protesters hold graphic images to make their point, in the Phoenix protest at Planned Parenthood office. Women's health facilities protested around the United States in a national "Day of Action" against Planned Parenthood, and its alleged selling of aborted fetal tissue, that is a violation of Federal law. Pro-Life activist rally at Planned Parenthood in Phoenix.

Alfredo Gonzalez/Demotix/Demotix/Press Association Images

15. Crimes against property

Image 15.1 (p. 534): *Portrait of a Man and Woman in Black*, 1633 (oil on canvas), Rembrandt Harmensz. van Rijn (1606–1669).
Isabella Stewart Gardner Museum, Boston, MA, USA/Bridgeman Images

Image 15.2 (p. 537): iStock/stnazkul

Image 15.3 (p. 539): iStock/IS_ImageSource

Image 15.4 (p. 541): Television evangelists Jim Bakker and wife Tammy Faye Bakker talk to a television audience in this Aug. 20, 1986, file photo. Messner, who as Tammy Faye Bakker helped her husband, Jim, build a multimillion-dollar evangelism empire and then saw it collapse in disgrace, died Friday, July 20, 2007, said her booking agent, Joe Spotts. She was 65.
AP/Press Association Images

Image 15.5 (p. 545): iStock/Ricardo Reitmeyer

Image 15.6 (p. 549): Scene still from *Thick as Thieves*, dir. Mimi Leder 2009.
Revelations Entertainment/The Kobal Collection

Image 15.7 (p. 554): iStock/Joel Carillet

Image 15.8 (p. 556): Trees smoulder after a major bush fire close to the town of Waroona in Western Australia, on Friday, Jan. 08, 2016. The town of Waroona, 100 km south of Perth and the surrounding area have been experiencing severe bush fire conditions.
Richard Wainwright/AAP/PA Images

16. Public order crimes

Image 16.1 (p. 568): Colombian narcotic police officers stand guard in an opium poppy field in Tuquerres, 330 miles from Pasto, southwest of Bogota, Colombia, Sunday, Nov. 19, 2006.
William Fernando Martinez/AP/Press Association Images

Image 16.2 (p. 571): Sasha Altschuler of San Diego, Calif., joins the celebrations outside the Supreme Court in Washington, Friday, June 26, 2015 after the court declared that same-sex couples have a right to marry anywhere in the US.
Manuel Balce Ceneta/AP/Press Association Images

Image 16.3 (p. 572): Suffrage parade, New York City, May 4, 1912
Library of Congress/American Press Association

Image 16.4 (p. 573): Vaughan, Ontario, Canada—July 26, 2014: People riding the Leviathan rollercoaster at Canada's Wonderland amusement park
iStock/bukharova

Image 16.5 (p. 580): iStock/Rebecca Ellis

Image 16.6 (p. 587): iStock/piranka

Image 16.7 (p. 590): iStock/wundervisuals

Image 16.8 (p. 590): iStock/AG-ChapelHil

17. Crimes of the powerful

Image 17.1 (p. 602): This is a combo of six file photos of the soccer officials involved in the US Justice Department of investigation into corruption at FIFA. From top left clockwise a Jeffrey Webb: Current FIFA vice-president and executive committee member, Concacaf president, Jose Maria Marin Current member of the FIFA organising committee for the Olympic football tournaments, Nicolas Leoz former FIFA executive committee member and Conmebol president, Eugenio Figueredo current FIFA vice-president and executive committee member, Jack Warner, former FIFA vice-president and executive committee member, Concacaf president, and Eduardo Li, current FIFA executive committee member-elect, Concacaf executive committee member.
AP/Press Association Images

Image 17.2 (p. 603): Vietnam War protestors march at the Pentagon in Washington, D.C. on October 21, 1967.
Wikimedia Commons/Lyndon B. Johnson Library/Frank Wolfe

Image 17.3 (p. 604): iStock/shironosov

Image 17.4 (p. 604): iStock/poba

Image 17.5 (p. 607): Patty Ramge, posing Sept. 1, 1978 with her 1975 Ford Pinto, has little trouble with motorists tailgating since she decked her car with a sign warning of its explosive nature if hit from the rear. Mrs. Ramge posted the warning after weeks of trying to convince Ford Motor Co. and its dealers to modify the fuel tank so it would not pose a fire hazard in a rear-end crash.
JCH/AP/Press Association Images

Image 17.6 (p. 609): A woman walks in front of the HSBC bank headquarters in Mexico City, Tuesday, July 17, 2012. The chief compliance officer of Britain's HSBC Tuesday said he was stepping down from that position after an investigation found that lax controls at the international bank allowed Mexican drug cartels to launder billions of dollars through its U.S. operation and other illicit transactions.
Alexandre Meneghini/AP/Press Association Images

Image 17.7 (p. 609): The Royal Caribbean Freedom of the Seas heads out to sea from the Port of Miami, Sunday, Dec. 7, 2008. Vacations are among the first things to go when money gets tight, but the cruise ship industry has insulated itself somewhat by offering shorter trips.
Lynne Sladky/AP/Press Association Images

Image 17.8 (p. 613): iStock/SolStock

Image 17.9 (p. 614): New York City, United States—December 21, 2015: Chinese woman walks past a souvenir shop in China Town's Canal Street in New York City.
iStock/ferrantraite

Image 17.10 (p. 623): Human skulls from victims of the Rwandan genocide, which killed over 1 million people, provide a glimpse into the extent of human pain and suffering that genocides produce. These often state-sanctioned or condoned mass killings produce far more death, destruction, and trauma than all the violent street crimes combined.
Getty

Image 17.11 (p. 624): A wailing and distraught Rwandan woman, one of dozens overcome by grief at recalling the horror of the genocide, is carried away to receive help during a public ceremony to mark the 20th anniversary of the Rwandan genocide, held at Amahoro stadium in Kigali, Rwanda Monday, April 7, 2014. Sorrowful wails and uncontrollable sobs resounded Monday as thousands of Rwandans packed the country's main sports stadium to mark the 20th anniversary of the beginning of a devastating 100-day genocide.
Ben Curtis/AP/Press Association Images

Image 17.12 (p. 628): In this courtroom sketch, James "Whitey" Bulger, left, and his girlfriend, Catherine Greig, are shown during their arraignment in a federal courtroom in downtown Los Angeles, Thursday, June 23, 2011.
Bill Robles/AP/Press Association Images

18. Green crimes and harms

Image 18.1 (p. 638): This June 8, 2010 file photo, a worker cleans the dust as he displays a panel of photos of people who died in the 1984 Bhopal gas disaster at the forensic department of Gandhi Medical College in Bhopal, India. India's Supreme Court issued notices Monday, Feb. 28, 2011 to Dow Chemicals and Union Carbide Corp. seeking payment of $1.7 billion in enhanced compensation for survivors of the world's worst industrial disaster that occurred more than 26 years ago.
Prakash Hatvalne/AP/Press Association Images

Image 18.2 (p. 640): Rachel Carson, author of "Silent Spring," poses at her Washington home, March 14, 1963.
Bob Schutz/AP/Press Association Images

Image 18.3 (p. 640): In this photo, steam seeps up through the ground in Centralia, PA. The steam is caused by a fire that began in 1962 at the town dump and ignited an exposed coal vein, eventually forcing an exodus of more than 1,000 people, nearly the entire population of this mountain town. Almost every house was demolished. After years of delay, state officials are trying to finish their demolition work in Centralia, a borough in the mountains of north eastern Pennsylvania that all but ceased to exist in the 1980s after a mine fire spread beneath homes and businesses.
Carolyn Kaster/AP/Press Association Images

Image 18.4 (p. 641): In this June 25, 1952 file photo, a fire tug fights flames on the Cuyahoga River near downtown Cleveland, Ohio, where oil and other industrial wastes caught fire.
Anonymous/AP/Press Association Images

Box 18.1 Image 1 (p. 643): Protestors carry a photo of Gov. Jerry Brown and demand a shutdown of the Southern California Gas Company's Aliso Canyon Storage Facility near Porter Ranch in Los Angeles on Saturday, Jan. 16, 2016. A 12-week-old gas leak has plagued Los Angeles residents and driven thousands from their homes.
Richard Vogel/AP/Press Association Images

Image 18.5 (p. 644): This combination of photos taken Sunday, Nov. 1, 2015, top, and Tuesday, Dec. 1, 2015, bottom, show pedestrians walking through a shopping and office complex in Beijing amid widely differing levels of air pollution. Schools in Beijing were ordered to keep students indoors Tuesday, Dec. 1, 2015 after record-breaking air pollution in the Chinese capital soared to up to 35 times safe levels.
Mark Schiefelbein/AP/Press Association Images

Image 18.6 (p. 649): Dhaka, Bangladesh. 20th June 2013—Groups of workers dye clothes in the river around the factory. Most of the area is under water during the monsoon rains. The water is polluted by factories along the river as they release most dyes and chemicals into the publicly used river.
mohammad asad/Demotix/Press Association Images

Image 18.7 (p. 651): Walter Palmer (L) poses with a lion he killed (not Cecil). An American dentist who killed Cecil the lion with a bow and arrow during an illegal hunt in Zimbabwe has said that he "deeply regrets" his actions. Walter Palmer, 55, from Minnesota, allegedly paid park guides $50,000 (£32,000) to hunt

and kill Cecil at the Hwange National Park, not realising that the animal was a local favourite. According to reports Cecil was lured away from the safety of the park before being shot with a crossbow. He was then tracked for 40 hours and shot with a rifle. Palmer then posed for a "trophy" photo with his corpse before it was decapitated and skinned. Palmer has insisted that he believed the hunting trip was legal. The two local guides are due to appear in court today and if convicted face up to 15 years in prison.
REX/Shutterstock

Image 18.8 (p. 655): These homes in the Hillcrest neighborhood are contrasted by stacks of refineries, Thursday, May 17, 2012 in the Hillcrest neighborhood in Corpus Christi, Texas.
Rachel Denny Clow/AP/Press Association Images

Box 18.8 Image 1 (p. 657): Photograph from the mid-1870s of a pile of American bison skulls waiting to be ground for fertilizer.
Wikimedia Commons/Unknown

19. Technology and cybercrime

Box 19.1 Image 1 (p. 667): Police respond to the scene of an active shooting at Inland Regional Center where at least 14 people were killed and 17 wounded. Three shooters went on a shooting rampage with rifles wearing ski masks and vests. A man and a woman connected to the shooting were killed in a firefight with police officers after a car chase.
Steven K. Doi/Zuma Press/PA Images

Image 19.1 (p. 670): In this Tuesday, April 22, 2014 photograph, employees look closely at a live video in the command center of the Camden County Metro police in Camden, N.J. The New Jersey city near Philadelphia officially disbanded its police department on May 1 and handed patrols over to the new Camden County-run department that promised more officers for the same cost, largely because it could shed provisions of a union contract that officials saw as onerous. The Camden County Metro police patrol only in Camden, not its suburbs. Clerical, analytical and crime-scene processing jobs once done by gun-carrying sworn officers were given to civilians, and most of the cops were put on beats on the street.
Mel Evans/AP/Press Association Images

Image 19.2 (p. 670): Video tape shot by George Holliday earlier this month from his apartment in a suburb of Los Angeles shows what appears to be a group of police officers beating a man with nightsticks and kicking his as other officers look on, March 3, 1991. A copy of the video tape was turned over to the police department's Internal Affairs Division for

investigation, said Deputy Police Chief William Booth.
George Holliday/AP/Press Association Images

Image 19.3 (p. 673): This image from video released by Attorneys Ekl Williams PLLC, shows an alleged altercation between a Chicago police officer, center, and a female bartender, center on floor, at a Chicago bar on Feb. 19, 2007. The officer, identified as Anthony Abbate, 38, was expected to be fired after the investigation into the attack on the bartender, allegedly after she refused to continue to serve alcohol to the 12-year police veteran, Chicago Police Department spokeswoman Monique Bond said. The man at left is an unidentified bystander.
AP Photo/Ekl Williams PLLC via Fox News Chicago

Image 19.4 (p. 670): The Prince George's County police have dropped charges against a University of Maryland student they claimed struck mounted Park Police officers and their horses after a basketball game in March. This video, shot by another student, shows police beating the student without apparent provocation (broadcast April 12, 2010).
Roberts and Wood, *The Washington Post*

Image 19.5, top image (p. 675): Two women wiring the right side of the ENIAC with a new program, in the "pre-von Neumann" days. "U.S. Army Photo" from the archives of the ARL Technical Library. Standing: Marlyn Wescoff Crouching: Ruth Lichterman.
U.S. Army Photo, http://ftp.arl.army.mil/~mike/comphist/

Image 19.5, center image (p. 675): 1980s personal computer—robotron CM1910, manufactured by VEB Kombinat Robotron Dresden, 1989.
Mary Evans/Interfoto

Image 19.5, bottom image (p. 675): iStock/gece33

Image 19.6 (p. 684): In a March 9, 2012 file photo, Dharun Ravi, the former Rutgers University student who was found guilty of hate crimes for using a webcam to view his roommate at Rutgers University kissing another man, waits before court proceedings in New Brunswick, N.J. In a legal filing Tuesday, May 1, 2012, Ravi's lawyers asked a judge to overturn the jury's conviction. They said the jury convicted Ravi in March despite evidence that he was not guilty of invading the privacy or intimidating roommate Tyler Clementi, who killed himself days after the webcam was used.
John Munson/AP/Press Association Images

Image 19.7 (p. 688): In this courtroom drawing, defendant Ross William Ulbricht, center foreground, is seated at the defense table along with his attorneys during opening arguments at his criminal trial in New

York, Tuesday, Jan. 13, 2015. The 30-year-old has pleaded not guilty to charges of narcotics trafficking, computer hacking and money laundering in connection with charges he launched an underground website where buyers and sellers of illegal drugs to do business online.

Elizabeth Williams/AP/Press Association Images

Image 19.8 (p. 688): A 28 gram portion of speed is shown on sale on the screenshot of the illegal internet retail platform "SilkRoad 2.0" during a press conference at the Hesse Office of Criminal Investigations in Wiesbaden, Germany, 11 November 2014. German investigators have closed four retail platforms as part of "Operation Onymos."

Boris Roessler/DPA/PA Images

20. Crime today, crime tomorrow: the future of criminological theory

Image 20.1 (p. 704): Thousands of people gather to pray for the victims of San Bernardino Mass Shooting during a Candlelight Vigil at San Manuel Stadium.

Ringo Chiu/Zuma Press/PA Images

Image 20.2 (p. 705): iStock/Maxiphoto

Image 20.3 (p. 710): Mireille Ballestrazzi (L), president of Interpol, S Iswaran (C), Singapore's second minister for home affairs and Jurgen Stock (R), secretary general of Interpol officiate at the official opening of Interpol World 2015 conference and exhibition in Singapore on April 14, 2015. The three day inaugural Interpol World Congress conference on global security threats and mainly talking about cyber-security is being held from April 14 to 16 in Singapore

Roslan Rahman/AFP/Getty Images

Image 20.4 (p. 711): Children hold hands during a protest, organized by Campaign Against Child Trafficking (CACT) in, Bangalore, India, Tuesday, Dec. 12, 2006. Child trafficking is one of the worst forms of child labour affecting 1.2 million children worldwide. It is the movement of children from place to place through force, coercion or deception into situations involving their economic and sexual exploitation.

Aijaz Rahi/AP/Press Association Images

Image 20.5 (p. 713): France, Rennes: People gather for a unity rally (Marche Republicaine) on January 11, 2015 in Rennes where some 115,000 people took part in tribute to the 17 victims of the three-day killing spree in Paris. The killings began on January 7 with an assault on the satirical magazine *Charlie Hebdo* in Paris that saw two brothers massacre 12 people, including some of the country's best-known cartoonists, and the hostage-taking of a Jewish supermarket on the eastern fringes of the capital, which killed four people.

Kvin Niglaut/Newzulu/PA Images

Image 20.6 (p. 716): Typing on a laptop computer.

Tek Image/Science Photo Library

Image 20.7 (p. 723): Parade-goers vie for beads and trinkets as the Krewe of Endymion Mardi Gras parade rolls through New Orleans, Saturday, Feb. 6, 2016.

Gerald Herbert/AP/Press Association Images

Image 20.8 (p. 727): Borut Zivulovic/FA Bobo/PIXSELL/Pixsell/PA Images

Index

Note: Page numbers in **bold** type refer to **figures**. Page numbers in *italic* type refer to *tables*.